D0844203

THE ELGAR COMPANION TO RADICAL POLITICAL ECONOMY

The Elgar Companion to Radical Political Economy

Edited by
Philip Arestis
University of East London

and

Malcolm Sawyer
University of Leeds

Edward Elgar

Published by
Edward Elgar Publishing Limited
Gower House
Croft Road
Aldershot
Hants GU11 3HR
England

Edward Elgar Publishing Company
Old Post Road
Brookfield
Vermont 05036
USA

British Library Cataloguing in Publication Data
Elgar Companion to Radical Political Economy
I. Arestis, P. II. Sawyer, Malcolm C.
335

Library of Congress Cataloguing in Publication Data
The Elgar companion to radical political economy/edited by Philip Arestis and Malcolm Sawyer.
p. cm.
1. Radical economics—Encyclopedias. I. Arestis, Philip, 1941– II. Sawyer, Malcolm C.
HB97.7.E37 1994
330'.03—dc20 93-29063
CIP

ISBN 1 85278 460 1

Printed and bound in Great Britain by
Hartnolls Limited, Bodmin, Cornwall

Contents

List of contributors viii
Introduction xii

Accumulation *Claudio Sardoni* 1
Aggregate demand *John Hillard* 5
Aggregate supply *Johan Deprez* 10
Animal spirits *Bill Gerrard* 15
Banks and financial institutions *Jan Toporowski* 20
Business cycles *Marc Jarsulic* 24
Capital theory controversies *G.C. Harcourt* 29
Class and social relations *Geoff Kay* 34
Competition, antitrust and beyond *Mark Glick* 38
Consumer behaviour *Dean Baker* 43
Corporatism *Richard Wright* 47
Costs of production *Mario Morroni* 52
Crisis *David Green* 57
Cumulative causation *A.P. Thirlwall* 62
Decision making *Frank Skuse* 66
De-industrialization *John R. Wells* 70
Dependency theories *Gabriel Palma* 75
Development *Ron Ayres* 81
Dialectics *Ali Shamsavari* 86
Discrimination *Patrick L. Mason* 91
Distribution: class and functional *Mauro Baranzini* 97
Division of labour *John Grahl* 101
Dual labour markets (in Third World countries) *Edward J. Amadeo* 106
Econometrics *Ron Smith* 110
Effective demand *J.A. Kregel* 114
Efficiency *Francis Green* 119
Employment relations and contracts *Geoffrey M. Hodgson* 123
Equilibrium analysis *Christof Rühl* 127
Expectations *Jochen Runde* 133
Exploitation *P.N. Junankar* 138
Female employment and unemployment *Jean Gardiner* 143
Finance capital *Jerry Coakley* 148
Financial instability hypothesis *Hyman P. Minsky* 153

Firms and corporations *Paul Marginson* 158
Fordism and post-Fordism *Peter Nolan* 162
Gender and political economy *Eleni Paliginis* 167
Global political economy *James A. Caporaso* 171
Growth poles *Joseph Halevi* 174
Growth theories (Keynesian growth) *Peter Skott* 180
Growth theories (neo-Marxian growth) *Peter Skott* 185
Human motivation *Shaun Hargreaves Heap* 191
Hysteresis *Alan G. Isaac* 195
Industrial policy *Peter Mottershead* 199
Inequality *Rima Horton* 203
Inflation *Nicholas Sarantis* 208
Input–output analysis *E. Ray Canterbery* 212
Interest rates *Colin Rogers* 216
International finance *E.V.K. FitzGerald* 221
International trade *Lynn Mainwaring* 226
Investment theory and radical perspectives *Ciaran Driver* 231
Labour process debate *Colin Haslam* 236
Labour theory of value *Jonathan Michie* 240
Liquidity *L. Randall Wray* 244
Long period *Man-Seop Park* 249
Long waves *L.A.V. Catão and S.N. Solomou* 255
Markets *Paul Auerbach* 260
Methodology in Economics *Tony Lawson* 263
Modes of production *George Catephores* 269
Monetary circuits *Augusto Graziani* 274
Money and credit *Marc Lavoie* 278
Monopoly capitalism *Tracy Mott* 282
Multinational/transnational corporations *Christos N. Pitelis* 286
Peripheral Fordism in Europe *Philip Arestis and Eleni Paliginis* 292
Planning *Martin Cave* 296
Power in economic theory *Samuel Bowles and Herbert Gintis* 300
Prices and pricing *Peter J. Reynolds* 305
Productive–unproductive labour in Marxist economics *John Ure* 310
Profits *M.C. Howard* 315
Public expenditure *George Hadjimatheou* 319
Rate of profit *Michael Syron Lawlor* 324
Regulation theory *Bob Jessop* 328
Rent *Gary Mongiovi* 333
Savings *Michael Bleaney* 338
Sectoral balance *Amitava Krishna Dutt* 342
Segmented labour market theory *Ben Fine* 346

Short period *Fernando J. Cardim de Carvalho* 350
Social contracts *Marino Regini* 353
Social conventions *Robin Naylor* 357
Social policy *M.G. Marshall* 362
Social structure of accumulation *Michele Naples* 366
Socialism *Ferdinando Targetti* 371
Socialization of investment *Mario Seccareccia* 375
Speculation *Victoria Chick* 380
Structuralism *Gabriel Palma and Jonathan Pincus* 384
Surplus approach *Roberto Ciccone* 389
Surplus labour *John E. King* 393
Tax incidence *Douglas Mair* 398
Taxation *Anthony J. Laramie* 401
Technological change *Norman Clark* 406
Technological unemployment *Harald Hagemann* 410
Technology gap *William S. Milberg* 415
Theory of the state *Thanos Skouras* 419
Time *O.F. Hamouda and B.B. Price* 424
Trade unions *William Brown* 429
Uncertainty *Sheila C. Dow* 434
Underconsumption *Howard J. Sherman* 438
Underdevelopment *J. Mohan Rao* 443
Unemployment, The social pathology of *Terry Moreton* 448
Unequal exchange *Bill Gibson* 453
Utility *Paul Anand* 458
Value *Heinz D. Kurz* 462
Wage-earner funds *Hans-Michael Trautwein* 468
Wages, money and real *Philip Arestis and Malcolm Sawyer* 473

Index 479

List of Contributors

Amadeo, Edward J.: Pontíficia Universidade Católica do Rio de Janeiro, Brazil

Anand, Paul: University of Oxford, UK

Arestis, Philip: University of East London, UK

Auerbach, Paul: Kingston University, UK

Ayres, Ron: University of Greenwich, UK

Baker, Dean: Economic Policy Institute, US

Baranzini, Mauro: Catholic University of Milan, Italy

Bleaney, Michael: University of Nottingham, UK

Bowles, Samuel: University of Massachusetts at Amherst, US

Brown, William: University of Cambridge, UK

Canterbery, E. Ray: Florida State University, US

Caporaso, James A.: University of Washington, US

Carvalho, Fernando J. Cardim de: Universidade Federal do Rio de Janeiro, Brazil

Catão, L.A.V.: School of Oriental and African Studies, University of London, UK

Catephores, George: University College London, University of London, UK

Cave, Martin: Brunel University of West London, UK

Chick, Victoria: University College London, University of London, UK

Ciccone, Roberto: Terza Universita' di Roma, Italy

Clark, Norman: University of Sussex, UK

Coakley, Jerry: London Guildhall University, UK

Deprez, Johan: Alabama State University, US

Dow, Sheila C.: University of Stirling, UK

Driver, Ciaran: Imperial College, University of London, UK

Dutt, Amitava Krishna: University of Notre Dame, US

Fine, Ben: School of Oriental and African Studies, University of London, UK

FitzGerald, E.V.K.: University of Oxford, UK

Gardiner, Jean: University of Leeds, UK

Gerrard, Bill: University of York, UK

Gibson, Bill: University of Vermont, US

Gintis, Herbert: University of Massachusetts at Amherst, US

Glick, Mark: University of Utah, US

Grahl, John: Queen Mary and Westfield College, University of London, UK

Graziani, Augusto: University of Rome, La Sapienza, Italy

Green, David: South Bank University, UK

Green, Francis: University of Leicester, UK

Hadjimatheou, George: London Guildhall University, UK

Hagemann, Harald: University of Hohenheim, Germany

Halevi, Joseph: Sydney University, Australia and University of Grenoble 2, France

Hamouda, O.F.: York University, Canada

Harcourt, G.C.: University of Cambridge, UK

Hargreaves Heap, Shaun: University of East Anglia, UK

Haslam, Colin: University of East London, UK

Hillard, John: University of Leeds, UK

Hodgson, Geoffrey M.: University of Cambridge, UK

Horton, Rima: Kingston University, UK

Howard, M.C.: University of Waterloo, Canada

Isaac, Alan G.: The American University, US

Jarsulic, Marc: University of Notre Dame, US

Jessop, Bob: University of Lancaster, UK

Junankar, P.N.: Australian National University, Australia

Kay, Geoff: City University, UK

King, John E.: La Trobe University, Australia

Kregel, J.A.: University of Bologna, Italy

Kurz, Heinz D.: University of Graz, Austria

Laramie, Anthony J.: Merrimack College, US

Lavoie, Marc: University of Ottawa, Canada

Lawlor, Michael Syron: Wake Forest University, US

Lawson, Tony: University of Cambridge, UK

Mainwaring, Lynn: University College of Swansea, UK

Mair, Douglas: Heriot-Watt University, UK

Marginson, Paul: University of Warwick, UK

Marshall, M.G.: University of East London, UK

Mason, Patrick L.: University of California at Riverside, US

Michie, Jonathan: University of Cambridge, UK

Milberg, William S.: New School for Social Research, US

Minsky, Hyman P.: Jerome Levy Economics Institute of Bard College, US

Mongiovi, Gary: St John's University, US

Moreton, Terry: University of Leeds, UK

Morroni, Mario: University of Pisa, Italy

Mott, Tracy: University of Denver, US

Mottershead, Peter: University of East London, UK

Naples, Michele: Trenton State College, US

Naylor, Robin: University of Warwick, UK

Nolan, Peter: University of Leeds, UK

Paliginis, Eleni: Middlesex University, UK

Palma, Gabriel: University of Cambridge, UK

Park, Man-Seop: University of Leeds, UK

Pincus, Jonathan: University of Cambridge, UK

Pitelis, Christos N.: University of Cambridge, UK

Price, B.B.: York University, Canada and MIT, US

Rao, J. Mohan: University of Massachusetts at Amherst, US

Regini, Marino: University of Trento, Italy

Reynolds, Peter J.: University of Staffordshire, UK

Rogers, Colin: University of Adelaide, Australia

Rühl, Christof: University of Hohenheim, Germany and University of California, US

Runde, Jochen: University of Cambridge, UK

Sarantis, Nicholas: Kingston University, UK

Sardoni, Claudio: University of Rome, Italy

Sawyer, Malcolm: University of Leeds, UK

Seccareccia, Mario: University of Ottawa, Canada

Shamsavari, Ali: Kingston University, UK

Sherman, Howard J.: University of California at Riverside, US

Skott, Peter: University of Aarhus, Denmark

Skouras, Thanos: Athens University of Economics and Business, Greece

Skuse, Frank: University of East London, UK

Smith, Ron: Birkbeck College, University of London, UK

Solomou, S.N.: University of Cambridge, UK

Targetti, Ferdinando: University of Trento, Italy

Thirlwall, A.P.: University of Kent, UK

Toporowski, Jan: South Bank University, UK

Trautwein, Hans-Michael: University of Hohenheim, Germany

Ure, John: University of Hong Kong, Hong Kong

Wells, John R.: University of Cambridge, UK

Wray, L. Randall: University of Denver, US

Wright, Richard: University of Cambridge, UK

Introduction

This *Elgar Companion* is designed to provide a comprehensive coverage of radical political economy. Making such a statement raises the inevitable question of what is meant by 'radical political economy'. To some extent our answer would be that the subject matter is set out in this *Companion*. But we can here give some general indications of what we mean by the term.

The term 'political economy' was used prior to the 1870s 'to describe the subject of economic theory' (Rothschild, 1989, p. 1). James Steuart used it in his *Inquiry into the Principles of Political Economy* (1767) and the concept lasted until the emergence of neoclassical economics in the 1870s. The distinction between economics and political economy goes back to the ancient Greeks. Economics referred to the study of the household, political economy to macroeconomic aspects and to the management of the economic affairs of the state as they impinged upon households. Many classical theorists (with some notable exceptions including Marx), emphasized the capacity of markets to regulate themselves, implying that the economy need not be political, so that with the emergence of capitalism the economy was depoliticized. Ever since, the term economics has increasingly replaced that of political economy. Over the last 20 to 30 years or so, however, there has been a resurgence of interest in political economy. The modern usage of 'political economy' is actually 'characterised by a conscious opposition to the ruling neoclassic paradigm and various attempts to develop alternative approaches, methods, and theories' (Rothschild, 1989, p. 3). In this way radical political economy can be defined as a multi-paradigm study of the economy where the paradigm is problematic (unlike orthodox economics where the paradigm remains largely unquestioned). It is radical in the sense that it re-examines the roots of economic analysis.

Capitalist economies are viewed as both dynamic and subject to cycles and crises. A major element of study is the accumulation of capital (broadly conceived to include, for example, intellectual capital) and the generation and usage of the economic surplus. One further characteristic of radical political economy is the premise that there are conflicts of power and interests between groups and classes in society and that the dominant groups exercise determining influences on economic thought as well as on economic activity. The economy is viewed as part of a socio-cultural system; it is formed by this system, but at the same time influences culture and society. Our understanding of economic phenomena can only take place in a transdisciplinary way. When the economy is viewed in this way, a major role is given to institutions in the determination of economic life. Most important of these institutions are large enterprises, which dominate economic activity, and trade unions which can, on occasions, contain the influence of large enterprises. Problems of developing countries and disadvantaged regions within rich countries also engage the interest of political economists. Relevance is valued rather more than formalism.

The radical political economy tradition on which this volume focuses derives from the work of a wide range of economists, who may variously describe themselves as Post Keynesian, Kaleckian, Marxian, radical political economists, institutionalist, Sraffian, classical and post-classical. From that list of schools of thought, it can be seen that radical political economy is not a single coherent approach; there are, of course, disputes within each of the paradigms, while many authors draw on aspects of different paradigms. Indeed, in spite of various sharp differences between the paradigms, some common themes can be picked out as particularly important.

It is possible to identify at least four approaches within radical political economy (Arestis, 1990, 1992; Hamouda and Harcourt, 1988). The first, associated with a particular approach to the work of Keynes, stresses the inherent uncertainty of the world as a key to understanding decision-making processes, the operation of markets and the evolution of money. Further, monetary factors have to be fully integrated with real forces (in contrast to the neoclassical general equilibrium approach). However there is tension within the radical political economy tradition on this point, with many emphasizing the role of real rather than monetary forces. The money-wage is viewed as central to the level of price in this analysis, not just because it is the fundamental determinant of the price level, but because the money-wage is the most widely utilized contract in the entrepreneurial system where money is used (Davidson, 1992).

A second approach, which could be labelled Kaleckian, begins from a social class perspective rather than from an individualistic one, reflecting the Marxian influence on Kalecki. It views economies as inherently cyclical and prone to unemployment and excess capacity. This view suggests that equilibrium analysis may be unfruitful (or at a minimum requires supplementation), and focuses on the explanation of cycles and growth. The relationship between social classes is inherently antagonistic, and market power (broadly conceived) strongly influences the distribution of income between classes. The level of and cycles in economic activity are driven by effective demand, with investment demand playing an important role.

A third approach concentrates on and provides an explanation of long-period levels of prices, income and employment. It encompasses the Sraffian contributions along with Keynes's effective demand in a way that rejects the proposition that supply and demand determine price. Relative prices in long-period analysis arise from the equalization of the rate of profit, with the price of a commodity being based on the costs of production. This equalization of the rate of profit, which may only be a centre of gravity towards which the economy moves, is brought about by the mobility of capital as part of the process of competition. This analysis also undermines the theoretical basis of a negative relationship between factor price and factor demand (see, e.g. Steedman, 1985).

This analysis is based on the notion of the competitive long period with equalized rates of profit. As such it is based on the premise that there are persistent forces which drive the economy towards a long-period position. In some respects, the analysis stands on a methodological par with general equilibrium analysis and, as such, has played an important role as a critique of neoclassical economics. However, the approach stands in some contrast to the Post Keynesian emphasis on uncertainty and nominal contracts and to the Kaleckian stress on non-equilibrium and barriers to capital mobility.

A fourth approach is rooted firmly in the institutionalist tradition of Veblen and others. It is process and evolutionary oriented and thus dynamic, emphasizing the structure of power in an economic system. The economy is not just the atomistic 'market mechanism', but the institutional and organizational structure of the larger economy which is the main mechanism whereby resources are allocated (Tool, 1988a, 1988b). Institutionalism demonstrates that economic performance should be judged according to emerging societal values, in which case the economy becomes a 'valuating mechanism'. An interdisciplinary approach is propounded, along with a detailed and painstaking study of institutions and their evolution.

A theme which runs through all of these approaches is the rejection of the neoclassical analysis of the operation of market economies, with its focus on equilibrium outcomes and with the harmonious coordination of decentralized decision-making. Instead these approaches to radical political economy often view the free market economic processes as involving considerable instability, with forces being generated from within the system that are responsible for such instability and for fluctuations in economic activity. Market forces tend to exacerbate the disparities evident in such a system. There is plenty of evidence to suggest the persistence of economic disparities and that markets perpetuate inequalities (Sawyer, 1989, especially Chapters 3 and 12). Consequently, the capitalist economic system, based on free market principles, is inherently cyclical and unstable. Whether a decentralized market economy has ever operated without some State intervention is open to considerable doubt. But radical political economy analysis would postulate that such an economy would not achieve, let alone maintain, the full use of existing resources nor their equitable distribution: hence appropriate government intervention is required. These features of the capitalist system are due mainly to the behaviour of private investment, which is attributed to volatile expectations and business confidence. Under these circumstances full employment is very difficult to achieve.

As indicated above, the creation of resources and the use of economic surplus comprise a further common theme in radical political economy. Thus it involves much more than the study of the allocation of resources, which has often been described as the key feature of neoclassical economics (Robbins, 1932). Economies generally produce a surplus over their consumption needs, the use to which the surplus is put influencing future growth (both in terms of amount and composition). Control over the surplus depends on the power relations in the economy concerned. A not unrelated theme is a focus on production rather than the neoclassical emphasis on exchange. Exchange is not unimportant, but it must be preceded by production. More importantly, the conditions of production strongly influence the efficiency of an economy and the general well-being of the working population. Conflict at the workplace is an important element of the antagonistic nature of capitalism.

Many within the radical political economy tradition subscribe to the view that, at least for the present stage of development of economic analysis, different techniques are appropriate for different problems, with a range of criteria relevant for evaluating the adequacy of a theory. These techniques would include formal (including mathematical) modelling and historical and institutional analyses, alongside empirical investigations. The criteria would encompass explanation, understanding, as well as accuracy of prediction (though it is widely recognized that the application of all of these criteria is very difficult). Further, it is recognized that economists (as well as scientists and other social scientists) do not closely adhere to their methodological precepts when evaluating a particular theory (see, for example, McCloskey, 1986).

There are certain fundamental methodological premises within the realm of radical political economy. Theories should represent economic reality as accurately as possible and many recent developments in the philosophy of language, which offer relevant criteria for theory adequacy, provide support for the methodological approach advanced here. The most important of these criteria is the ability of the theory to account for and successfully explain economic reality so that 'the success with which that theory as a whole captures reality can be explained in terms of the referential capacity of its key concepts and expressions' (Davis, 1989, pp. 424–5). Consequently, radical political economy theory is context-specific and as such requires continuous and repeated reappraisal of its uses in view of current developments (Dow, 1988, p. 15). To do so, political economy theory begins with observation (Dow, 1985, p. 76) and proceeds to build upon 'realistic abstractions' rather than 'imaginary models' (Rogers, 1989, pp. 189–92). An important implication of this methodology is that explanation is emphasized and rather less attention is given to prediction (especially as compared with the positivist approach to which many economists claim adherence). But it is true to say that political economy theory – with its emphasis on *realism* – utilizes as criteria of theory adequacy both the depth of explanatory power and the ability to elucidate a range of empirical phenomena, rather than predictive accuracy (Lawson, 1989).

When *realism* is important in the methodology of political economy, history and institutions inevitably become an integral part of such methodology. A further integral part is the premise that an organic, rather than atomistic, approach to economic processes is more relevant and appropriate (see, for example, Dow, 1990). In this sense, radical political economy proponents adopt a more complex view of human nature and of individual behaviour insofar as they see individuals as social rather than atomistic beings. These propositions facilitate the introduction into the analysis of the role played by dominant institutions and organizations (including firms). Naturally, political economy theorists do study the causes and consequences of structural change, but with respect to production and distribution and not so much with respect to exchange. The major concern of production analysis is with the causes of the growth of output and resources rather than with the allocation of existing resources. With the existence of the 'reserve army of unemployed' and the possibility of increasing the rate of capacity utilization, the principle of scarcity is de-emphasized within this framework of thought. Indeed, in many theories advanced in radical political economy, excess capacity is predicted, though it may arise from an insufficiency of aggregate demand or through the decisions of individual firms.

The distinction has been drawn between the exchange paradigm (i.e. neoclassical economics) and the production paradigm (i.e. political economy; see Baranzini and Scazzieri, 1986). In a similar vein, neoclassical economics is concerned with the scarcity of resources, whereas political economy is concerned with the creation of resources as well as the use of existing resources. But further important strands of radical political economy emphasize the scarcity of demand; that is, that effective demand often falls short of supply. Both in the short run and the long run, the level of demand can be seen as relevant for the actual level of supply, without any automatic mechanisms to bring demand into line with potential supply. The precise role of demand, especially in the long run, is however a matter of considerable debate, especially as between Kaleckians and neo-Ricardians (Roncaglia, 1992; Garegnani, 1978, 1979; Eatwell, 1983).

The imbalance between demand and supply in the labour sector generates unemployment (open and disguised), with the general balance of economic power lying with employers rather than employees. In the product markets, consumers appear to have choice; however, individual choice is limited, determined by income, class and the technical conditions of production rather than by relative prices. In the sphere of production, monopolies and oligopolies assume socio-political, as well as economic, power in product markets, which gives them the prerogative to set prices in their own interests. This capacity relative to the power over input costs, especially wage costs, determines the surplus which monopolies and oligopolies can capture. This surplus can be translated into investment which provides the engine of growth, though it may flow into conspicuous consumption. But the potential surplus can only be realized if it is spent. Whether, however, spending is forthcoming depends crucially both on long-term expectations about the health of product markets and short-term expectations that relate to the prices of financial assets. These prices are essentially determined by social relations, themselves influenced by the relative power of financial institutions. It is important to stress at this stage that within political economy theory, institutional structure and industrial organization are by no means fixed. Instead, these structures and organizations are continuously evolving and influencing the historical development of economies, while themselves remaining the main objects of analysis. They play a vital role in terms of the determination of income distribution, the level and composition of output, as well as the generation of surplus and its translation into vital investment.

Individuals are not viewed as omniscient (contrary to the usual neoclassical assumptions as exemplified by 'rational' expectations). Individuals are seen as able to acquire information gradually, though it is in the nature of information that what is to be learnt cannot be known before it is learnt. The capacity of the individual to process and use information is seen as limited. Some would adhere to the view that individuals have 'bounded rationality'; that is, they purposefully pursue their goals subject to the information available and their capacity to process it. However, this leaves open a number of issues, such as how is information obtained?, is information codifiable? etc. Further, how are individuals' objectives formulated? In an uncertain and changing world, rationality (bounded or otherwise) is an essentially untestable assumption: a change in observed decisions or behaviour may result from changes in circumstance, in information, in preferences, etc.

Uncertainty (as opposed to risk) refers to the unknowability and unpredictability of the future. It relates to an unsureness about the future in an ever-changing world where the past is not a good guide to the future. A clear and robust reassertion of this view has been provided by Davidson (1988), Roncaglia (1978) who argues that uncertainty is structural in nature, Bharadwaj (1983) who sees uncertainty endemic in the real world, and others. Some authors (notably Shackle, 1949, 1972) view the presence of uncertainty as meaning that human behaviour cannot be modelled, and further that since new ideas and thoughts spring from the human brain, it is impossible to trace their origin. The way in which people respond to pervasive uncertainty may depend on the nature of the decision to be made and the circumstances in which it is made.

In an uncertain world people are not able to make precise calculations concerning the future. As such, when they have found that past decision rules have served them reasonably well, they are likely to continue to use those rules. Major changes in the decision rules or searches for improved outcomes are associated with the perception of failure. Since views about the future can be formed from past events alone, it follows that only 'indirect knowledge' can be held concerning the future. Such knowledge of the future can be ascertained with only a probable degree of certainty. Now, the conditions under which this type of probability can be calculated are rarely met in everyday life. Consequently, in general terms, such probabilities cannot be arrived at. And to quote Keynes (1973), 'By uncertain knowledge … I do not mean merely to distinguish what is known for certain from what is only probable. … About these matters there is no scientific basis to form any calculable probability whatever. We simply do not know' (pp. 113–14).

The notions of irreversible time – that production takes time and that economic agents enter into commitments well before outcomes can be predicted – are closely related to this notion of uncertainty. Economic agents therefore commit themselves to contracts denominated in money, so that money and contracts are intimately and inevitably linked. In this sense, the importance of money is that it is a link between the past and the present and also between the present and the future (Keynes, 1936, p. 294). Thus, much of political economy analysis is crucially concerned with historical time as distinct from logical time. Essentially, the importance of emphasizing historical time in an economic system is that its past is given and cannot be changed, and that the future is totally uncertain and consequently unknown (Robinson, 1974).

Since radical political economy is fundamentally concerned with analyses which emphasize change over time, growth and dynamics are central features. Mathematical models may provide some insights into the processes of cycles and of growth, though we would not wish to associate the mathematical determinism of such models with causality in the explanation of 'unstable' economic processes. In any case, economic processes are generally to be seen as path-dependent; as such, any outcome, whether equilibrium or not, depends on the route followed. It is often (usually implicitly) assumed that economic processes are ergodic, which means that movements of the economy are *not* time- and path-dependent. In contrast, in radical political economy, economic processes are generally viewed as path-dependent. In other words, current developments depend on past events as reflected in expectations, beliefs, institutions, etc. The economy is modelled as a group of dynamic subsystems, so that economics is no longer the study of how scarce resources are allocated between a set of infinite needs. It is rather the study of how economic systems are able to expand their output over time by creating, producing, distributing and using the resulting social surplus.

The term radical political economy is used to encompass a range of different schools of thought which could be said to share the common theme of production, in contrast to the exchange focus of neoclassical and Austrian economics. It is concerned with the generation and use of the surplus, leading to an interest in dynamics, income distribution, growth and development. Underlining this interest – as the fundamental determinant of these aspects – is capital accumulation. These themes are elaborated in the entries which follow.

The entries in this *Elgar Companion to Radical Political Economy* relate to ideas and concepts. It will be noticed that there are no biographical entries since such material has been covered in our *Dictionary of Dissenting Economists* (published by Edward Elgar in 1992). This *Companion* is thus complementary to their *Dictionary*.

We are grateful to the authors of the entries for their enthusiastic involvement in this project. A number of other people have also been particularly helpful to us. June Daniels (Department of Applied Economics, University of East London) and Sue Howard (Edward Elgar Publishing) have provided excellent secretarial and other assistance. Edward Elgar, Julie Leppard and Jo Rix have, as always, been excellent commissioning editor, editor and editorial assistant respectively.

References

Arestis, P. (1990), 'Post-Keynesianism: A New Approach to Economics', *Review of Social Economy*, Fall.

Arestis, P. (1992), *The Post-Keynesian Approach to Economics: An Alternative Analysis of Economic Theory and Policy*, Aldershot: Edward Elgar.

Baranzini, M. and Scazzieri, R. (eds) (1986), *Foundations of Economics: Structure of Inquiry and Economic Theory*, Oxford: Blackwell.

Bharadwaj, K. (1983), 'On Effective Demand: Certain Recent Critiques' in J.A. Kregel (ed.), *Distribution, Effective Demand and International Economic Relations*, London: Macmillan.

Davidson, P. (1988), 'A Technical Definition of Uncertainty and the Long-Run Non-Neutrality of Money', *Cambridge Journal of Economics*, **12**.

Davidson, P. (1992), 'The Asimakopulos View of Keynes's General Theory', Paper read at the conference on Employment, Distribution, and Markets, Levy Institute, Bard College, New York, 24–26 September 1992.

Davis, J.B. (1989), 'Axiomatic General Equilibrium Theory and Referentiality', *Journal of Post Keynesian Economics*, Spring.

Dow, S.C. (1985), *Macroeconomic Thought: A Methodological Approach*, Oxford: Basil Blackwell.

Dow, S.C. (1988), 'Post Keynesian Economics: Conceptual Underpinnings', *British Review of Economic Issues*, Autumn.
Dow, S.C. (1990), 'Beyond Dualism', *Cambridge Journal of Economics*, **14**.
Eatwell, J. (1983), 'Theories of Value, Output and Employment' in J. Eatwell and M. Milgate (eds), *Keynes's Economics and the Theory of Value and Distribution*, London: Duckworth.
Garegnani, P. (1978), 'Notes on Consumption, Investment and Effective Demand: I', *Cambridge Journal of Economics*, **2**.
Garegnani, P. (1979), 'Notes on Consumption, Investment and Effective Demand: II', *Cambridge Journal of Economics*, **3**.
Hamouda, O.F. and Harcourt, G.C. (1988), 'Post-Keynesianism: From Criticism to Coherence?', *Bulletin of Economic Research*, January. Reprinted in J. Pheby (ed.), *New Directions in Post-Keynesian Economics*, Aldershot: Edward Elgar.
Keynes, J.M. (1936), *The General Theory of Employment, Interest and Money*, London: Macmillan.
Keynes, J.M. (1973), *The General Theory and After*, Collected Writings, Vol. XIV, London: Macmillan.
Lawson, T. (1989), 'Realism and Instrumentalism in the Development of Econometrics', *Oxford Economic Papers*, January. Reprinted in N. De Marchi and C. Gilbert (eds), *The History and Methodology of Econometrics*, Oxford: Oxford University Press.
McCloskey, D.N. (1986), *The Rhetoric of Economics*, Brighton: Harvester Wheatsheaf.
Robbins, L. (1932), *An Essay on the Nature and Significance of Economic Science*, London: Macmillan.
Robinson, J. (1974), 'History Versus Equilibrium', *Thames Papers in Political Economy*, Autumn.
Rogers, C. (1989), *Money, Interest and Capital: A Study in the Foundations of Monetary Theory*, Cambridge: Cambridge University Press.
Roncaglia, A. (1978), *Sraffa and the Theory of Prices*, New York: John Wiley.
Roncaglia, A. (1992), 'On the Compatibility Between Keynes's and Sraffa's Viewpoints on Output Levels', Paper given to a conference in memory of A. Asimakopulos at the Levy Institute in Bard College, New York, September.
Rothschild, K.W. (1989), 'Political Economy or Economics?', *European Journal of Political Economy*, **5**.
Sawyer, M.C. (1989), *The Challenge of Radical Political Economy*, Brighton: Harvester Wheatsheaf.
Shackle, G. (1949), *Expectations in Economics*, Cambridge: Cambridge University Press.
Shackle, G. (1972), *Epistemic and Economics*, Cambridge: Cambridge University Press.
Steedman, I. (1985), 'On "Input" Demand Curves', *Cambridge Journal of Economics*, **9**.
Tool, M.R. (1988a), *Evolutionary Economics, Volume I: Foundations of Institutional Thought*, Armonk, New York: M.E. Sharpe.
Tool, M.R. (1988b), *Evolutionary Economics, Volume II: Institutional Theory and Policy*, Armonk, New York: M.E. Sharpe.

Accumulation

Accumulation of capital, the process through which the 'wealth of nations' grows, was at the core of both classical political economists and Marx, who studied it as an important aspect of the more general process of economic, social and political transformation. Post Keynesian economics has drawn on this tradition and on Keynes's revolution to develop its own analysis of accumulation.

Adam Smith provided the basic analytic framework for the study of accumulation. In *The Wealth of Nations* (1776), the rate of accumulation was shown to determine the rate of growth of the national product through its effects on the employment level of productive labour and on its productivity. The number of productive workers employed is directly determined by the amount of revenue that is saved, accumulated and invested. Workers' productivity directly depends on the *division of labour*, which is limited by the *extension of the market*. The higher the rate of accumulation, the higher is the rate of growth of output, and of the extension of the market, the deeper is the division of labour and the higher is productivity. In turn, an increasing productivity favours the process of accumulation.

In Smith there is also the idea of a relationship between income distribution and accumulation. The source of accumulation is saving: what is saved is invested, i.e. devoted to employ productive workers. Profits of the capitalist class are essentially the exclusive source of saving as workers' wages are at a subsistence level that does not allow saving while *rentiers* tend to consume the whole of their income in an unproductive way. Therefore, the higher are profits, the higher are both saving and the rate of accumulation. The process of accumulation and growth must be favoured by eliminating those feudal 'residuals' which prevent the capitalist class from promoting the general progress of the nation both by precluding a full development of the market and by encouraging unproductive consumption rather than saving and accumulation.

Ricardo, in his *Principles* (1817), accepted Smith's analysis and focused his attention on income distribution. Ricardo studied the conditions that, by shrinking profits, are the cause of a slackening in the process of accumulation. The main threat to profits derives, for Ricardo, from decreasing returns in agriculture that bring about an inevitable reduction in profits through an increase in rents and real wages. Ricardo's analysis of accumulation was strictly connected and functional to his political battle against restrictions on the import of corn into England. Importing corn from abroad, where it was produced at lower costs, would have kept its price and land rents lower and so profits higher.

Also for Ricardo, all that is saved is invested and, therefore, there are no limits to the accumulation of capital other than that deriving from decreasing returns in agriculture. Ricardo was so convinced that all savings are necessarily invested and that capitalists' 'natural' tendency is to save and invest that he considered the *motives* for accumulation as obvious, concentrating his attention instead on the *effects* of accumulation, namely the effects on agricultural production and, hence, on wages and profits. Ricardo also provided an innovative analysis of the effects of accumulation on employment by pointing out that the accumulation of capital did not necessarily favour the working class: technical progress, which implied the progressive introduction of machines into productive processes, could cause an increasing level of unemployment.

In *Das Kapital* (1867–83), Marx further developed the analysis of accumulation of Smith and Ricardo. For Marx, the capitalist mode of production, in which accumulation and growth take place at the highest rate, would eventually be replaced by a socialist society which, by benefiting from the wealth produced by the capitalist system, should represent a superior form of human organization no longer dominated by the drive for profit.

In Marx's analysis, accumulation is not simply promoted by the capitalists' drive for profit. Competition forces individual entrepreneurs to accumulate and invest, as this is the only way to survive in the market: the existence of dynamic economies of large scale and increasing returns allows the firms that grow faster to earn higher profits while they expand their market share. The competitive struggle, on the other hand, is the main factor which induces firms to introduce technical innovations in the form of a progressive mechanization of the productive process. For Marx, accumulation of capital is not a smooth and orderly process: whenever expected profits become too low, capitalists stop the process of accumulation and investment; by doing so, they precipitate a general crisis with unsold commodities and higher unemployment. The rise in unemployment, with the consequent fall in real wages and rise in profits, is one of the factors which allows the economy to start a new cycle of accumulation and investment. Wage changes for Marx are no longer regulated by changes in population, as they were for Ricardo, but by changes in the rate of unemployment. Accumulation and growth take the form of a *cyclical process* and, once again, accumulation and income distribution are strictly related. Marx also held that capitalist competition would turn into monopoly, which is characterized by lower dynamism in terms of accumulation and growth.

In the post-classical era, Schumpeter can correctly be regarded as the inheritor of the classical and Marxian vision of the process of accumulation and growth, in spite of his more conservative view concerning capitalism in general. Schumpeter's *Theory of Economic Development* was published, in German, in 1912, when marginalism was the dominant paradigm in economics. Schumpeter held that the static approach of marginalism was of no use in the study and understanding of the dynamic process of growth. For Schumpeter, as for classical economists and Marx, capitalism is essentially characterized by its tendency to grow through accumulation and innovation. In the search for profits, entrepreneurs introduce innovations into the productive process; in doing so, they trigger phases of rapid accumulation and growth, which are followed by recessive phases: it is a cyclical process. Schumpeter, however, did not succeed either in reviving interest in the classical dynamic approach or in acquiring for himself a dominant position in the profession.

A new interest in accumulation and growth followed the Keynesian revolution of the 1930s. Although Keynes's own analysis was essentially focused on the short period, the fact that he gave investment the key role in explaining the working of the economy denotes, on the one hand, an inherent link with the classical and Marxian tradition; on the other hand, it allowed Post Keynesians to develop a theory of accumulation as an almost direct derivation of Keynes's analysis. In this respect, there is no doubt that Harrod was the pioneer. Harrod (1939) set out a dynamic model that was intended to establish a new method of thinking – thinking dynamically. This model is at the origin of the Post Keynesian theory of accumulation and growth. Domar, Joan Robinson, Kahn and Kaldor are other Keynesian economists who set out to develop Keynes's analysis in a long-period dynamic framework. In some cases, these developments were taking place together with the elaboration of *The General Theory*. The Post Keynesian analysis of accumulation has been carried out by paying overriding attention to two issues: (1) the determination of the rate of accumulation which ensures a process of steady growth in full employment, and (2) the relationship between capital accumulation and income distribution. With the renewed interest of Post Keynesians in accumulation and dynamics, technical progress also came to the forefront once again.

Harrod introduced the notion of *warranted* and *natural* rates of growth and the equilibrium condition: $n = g = s/v$ where n is the natural rate of growth (the population growth plus the rate of technical progress;); g is the warranted rate of growth (ensuring the equality of aggregate supply to demand); s is the community's marginal propensity to save; and v is the (constant) capital/output ratio. In order that the economy can grow by ensuring full employment dynamically, n must be equal to g. Any divergence between the two rates triggers a cumulative process that carries the economy away from its equilibrium path with no self-adjusting forces at work. Joan Robinson (1962) further developed the analysis of the relationship between accumulation and employment. She introduced a taxonomy of possible regimes of accumulation which allow both for steady growth with full employment and for situations in which the full employment of labour over time cannot be ensured.

In his model Harrod did not consider the relation between the overall propensity to save and income distribution. Kaldor (1955–56) removed the hypothesis of a unique propensity to save by allowing for different propensities of workers and capitalists. In so doing, he gave rise to the ensuing wide debate on accumulation and income distribution. Kaldor, moreover, offered fundamental contributions concerning accumulation and technical progress. From 1960 onward, he elaborated a number of models in which technical progress is an endogenous variable dependent on the rate of accumulation, an idea that comes from Smith and Marx.

Inspired by Keynes's 'widow's cruse' and by Kalecki's work, Kaldor developed a model in which it is capitalists' expenditure (investment plus consumption) which determines aggregate profits. Kaldor's analysis of income distribution was flawed by his incorrect treatment of workers' savings because he did not take into consideration workers as owners of the wealth accumulated through saving. Pasinetti (1962) amended the model containing this 'slip' and showed that the rate of profits of the economy depends on the rate of accumulation and on capitalists' propensity to save, while workers' propensity to save does not play a relevant role in the distribution process.

Post Keynesian analysis revived the classical idea of a connection between distribution and accumulation and, at the same time, offered an alternative to the neoclassical theory of distribution because no role was left to the marginal productivity of factors in the explanation of distributive shares which, instead, are crucially determined by capitalists' behaviour with respect to investment and saving decisions. Post Keynesian economics was also significantly influenced by Kalecki. Kalecki is the obvious link between the classical-Marxian tradition and the Keynesian tradition. He arrived independently at results which are close to Keynes's but by starting from Marx and Rosa Luxemburg more than from Marshall. In particular, the Marxian influence led Kalecki to develop his analysis by considering an economy in which oligopoly rather than free competition is the dominant market structure.

Following Kalecki's line, Steindl (1952) developed an analysis of contemporary capitalism where the oligopolistic market form is an important factor affecting the overall rate of accumulation. The existence of oligopolistic markets is likely to determine a slackening of the rate of accumulation as firms become less pressured than in free competition to invest and grow at the highest possible rate. Neo-Marxist economists have tried to combine Marx's ideas on the capitalist tendency towards monopoly with Kalecki's theory of effective demand to argue that modern capitalism (the so-called 'monopoly capitalism') inevitably tends to chronic stagnation due to difficulties in absorbing the whole surplus produced. For some (e.g., Baran and Sweezy, 1966), stagnation can be avoided only through growing public spending and social wastes which create effective demand without implying a growing productive capacity.

By drawing primarily on the work of Smith, Schumpeter and Kalecki, Sylos Labini (1962) has further developed a dynamic analysis of oligopoly by giving technical innovations the centre-stage in the explanation of accumulation and growth and by analysing the relationship between the oligopolistic structure of markets and aggregate outcomes.

Goodwin has developed a dynamic analysis of capitalism through formal models which are able to explain the cycle and growth at the same time. In his analysis Goodwin combines Marx's and Schumpeter's vision of the evolutionary process of cyclical growth promoted by technical progress with Keynes's concern for the problems of effective demand and decision making in an uncertain world. Recent developments in chaos theory have been used by Goodwin (1990) to develop a formal model of cyclical growth.

CLAUDIO SARDONI

References

Baran, P. and Sweezy, P. (1966), *Monopoly Capital: An Essay on the American Economic and Social Order*, New York: Monthly Review Press.
Goodwin, R.M. (1990), *Chaotic Economic Dynamics*, Oxford: Clarendon Press.
Harrod, R.F. (1939), 'An Essay in Dynamic Theory', *Economic Journal*, **49**, March, 14–33.
Kaldor, N. (1955–56), 'Alternative Theories of Distribution', *Review of Economic Studies*, **23**, 83–100.
Pasinetti, L.L. (1962), 'Rate of Profit and Income Distribution in Relation to the Rate of Economic Growth', *Review of Economic Studies*, **29**, 267–79.
Robinson, J.V. (1962), *Essays in the Theory of Economic Growth*, London: Macmillan.
Steindl, J. (1952), *Maturity and Stagnation in American Capitalism*, Oxford: Basil Blackwell.
Sylos Labini, P. (1962), *Oligopoly and Technical Progress*, Cambridge, Mass.: Harvard University Press.

Aggregate demand

Whatever its technical connotations, the term 'aggregate demand' encapsulates and symbolizes a vision of the economic process which is at odds with the dominant faith in the absolute virtue of the free market. According to the orthodox equilibrium approach, if the economy is composed of perfectly informed optimizers operating within a system of unhampered markets, then relative price movements guarantee the maintenance of an equality between the demand for and supply of commodities. In the labour market, which is like any other market, the level of employment and the real wage are determined simultaneously by the forces of demand and supply. If market forces are allowed to operate smoothly, the real wage adjusts to the market clearing level where all those seeking work find employment. Unemployment is either voluntary or explicable as a misallocation phenomenon caused by microeconomic imperfections. There is no logical room within the equilibrium system for involuntary unemployment. The policy implication of equilibrium economics is to eradicate the obstacles within the market which prevent the achievement of market clearing prices for labour. In all, by promoting the mutual readjustment of money prices and demands in the various goods markets, an unhindered free market ensures the accomplishment of a full employment equilibrium.

Faced with the facts of experience, some economists have dared to question this orthodox vision of the economy as a perfectly self-correcting automaton. The aggregate demand approach, associated with the work of J.M. Keynes, epitomizes a fundamental misgiving concerning the notion that the economic system, even if it is left to its own devices, behaves in the manner claimed by the self-adjusting school. Underlying 'the whole classical theory, which would collapse without it' (*CW VII*, p.19) is the tacit premise that aggregate demand always accommodates itself to aggregate supply as given by the level of employment determined within the labour market. In his struggle to break away from 'the assumption in some shape or form of Say's Law', Keynes realized that 'the classical theory had given no attention at all to the problem at what point the supply of output as a whole and the demand for it would be in equilibrium' (*CW XXIX*, p. 215). This led him to question the equilibrium chain of causation which proceeds from the labour market to the level of output and then from saving to investment.

The basis of Keynes's critique was methodological and directed at the 'unreal assumption' of equilibrium theory, namely that 'the processes of consumption and production are in no way organic' (*CW IX*, p. 284). Keynes's holistic approach was dictated by the failure of equilibrium theory to provide a *logical* explanation of employment and output as a whole. He attacked the atomistic ontology of equilibrium economics which made aggregate outcomes a mere sum of the individual parts of which the economy is composed (Carabelli, 1988). The problem of organic interdependence confined the relevance of the equilibrium approach to the analysis of 'the rewards and the distribution between different uses of a *given* quantity of resources' (*CW VII*, p. 293; emphasis in original). Only in this special case is it legitimate to postulate an aggregate labour market with a supply and demand curve mediated by a real wage. The transfer of the argument from the individual to the aggregate level also involves the transfer of the assumption that aggregate effective demand is fixed:

> The rewards of the factors of production must, directly or indirectly, create in the aggregate an effective demand exactly equal to the costs of current supply, i.e. *aggregate* effective demand is constant (*CW XXIX*, p. 80).

With this caveat, individual wage bargains do not affect aggregate demand or the aggregate price level. In effect, equilibrium theory describes a market where a given quantity of labour is allocated between alternative employments.

If aggregate price and output levels are not fixed, however, a change in money wages or the price of wage-goods produces an indeterminate effect on the aggregate level of employment:

> there is an interdependence among the factors underlying the conditions of supply and demand which preclude the unique definition of an aggregate labour market by which employment in the aggregate is defined. At any other point than the limiting point of full employment, there is an interdependence among all firms such that, from the perspective of industry as a whole, aggregate effective demand is liable to fluctuate (Rotheim, 1992, p. 36).

The attempt to reason from the micro level to the macro level by simple aggregation is riddled with fallacy. Keynes's theory of aggregate effective demand was a reaction to the indeterminacy of equilibrium analysis at the macro level. It was expressly designed to take into account changes in demand which (for example, by lowering prices with a given money wage) could raise the real wage above its market-clearing level, with no feasible means of its being *voluntarily* reduced within the labour market:

> The aggregate of employment can fluctuate for reasons quite independent of a change in the relation between the marginal utility of a quantity of output and the marginal disutility of the employment required to produce that output (*CW XXIX*, p. 91).

The concept of an aggregate labour market, except at the unique point of full employment, was rendered meaningless. Keynes rejected the real wage as the determinant of the demand for labour, seeing it instead as a residual outcome of the money-wage bargain and firms' pricing decisions.

Similar problems of interdependence plagued the equilibrium notion of an aggregate capital market with a supply of savings and a demand for investment mediated by a real rate of interest. Under Say's Law, there can be no deficiency of *aggregate* demand because, in effect, every act of sale is necessarily an act of purchase. When saving is brought into the picture, however, the link between sale and purchase is broken, making it necessary to match withdrawals from the income-expenditure stream with a corresponding amount of investment. The rate of interest is the adjustment mechanism that ensures the mutual compatibility of decisions to save and decisions to invest. But again this line of argument fails to account for the effect of income changes on the level of saving, and of investment expenditure on the level of income. The amount of saving is not independent of the amount of investment. Keynes argued that investment spending determines the level of saving via changes in national income; 'there is no counterpart to the marginal product of capital' (Brothwell, 1992, p. 196). Keynes rejected the loanable funds theory on the grounds that there is no mechanism to restore the interest rate to its former level following an increase in the demand for money. The interest rate equalized money demand and money supply, not investment and saving at the level of income generated by the supply side of the economy:

> A decrease in spending will tend to lower the rate of interest and an increase in investment spending will tend to raise it. But if what these two quantities determine is, not the rate of interest, but the aggregate volume of employment, then our outlook on the mechanism will be profoundly changed (*CW VII*, p. 185).

Keynes's 'outlook on the mechanism' stressed that the monetary context exerts a profound influence on the behaviour of economic agents. The qualitative difference between Keynes's analysis of a monetary production economy and the equilibrium approach is the characteristic of money as being something more than a numeraire within the economic system. In the equilibrium system money is assumed to have no substantive form, thereby restricting the analysis to a barter economy unless it is assumed (rather heroically) that there is no net hoarding. If the impossibility of overproduction is to be guaranteed, the conditions of a barter economy have to be imposed on the analysis. The theory of liquidity preference takes into account the role of money as a store of wealth and thus a medium of speculation. It follows that changes in the demand for money have important economic effects. In other words, there is an interdependence of monetary and real relations. For Keynes, the levels of output and employment depend primarily on the monetary flow of aggregate demand, which is comprised of two elements: consumption and investment. Consumption (and hence saving) varies with the rate of monetary flow of income. The critical factor for the determination of employment is the investment decision which, through the multiplier, regulates total expenditure. The multiplier process shows how investment demand can materialize without any prior accumulation (in contrast to a Say's Law world where there is no demand without a prior supply). If the amount of investment exceeds the level of saving, there is a net injection of demand which induces firms to increase output and employment, thereby raising income and hence saving until a new equilibrium is achieved where the level of saving equals the level of investment.

Before Keynes, then, it was generally believed that aggregate demand would be coincidental with aggregate supply as given by the level of employment fixed in the labour market. The key question for Keynes was how unemployment can persist despite a freely flexible price of labour. He argued that employment and real wages are not determined simultaneously in the labour market by the forces of demand and supply, but in the product market by the short-term expectations of sale proceeds. The focus of analysis shifts from the supply side of the economy to that of demand because firms set their output and employment levels in relation to their short-term expectations concerning the prospect for product demand. The position of equilibrium is not fixed by the supply side of the economy but is conditional upon the state of expectations affecting demand. The demand side of the economy evokes the level of income and the rate of interest, which creates the possibility of an equilibrium level of income inconsistent with full employment. His emphasis was on the possible emergence of a macro equilibrium with involuntary unemployment, the explanation of which was not dependent on imperfections preventing the price mechanism from achieving a general equilibrium.

The debate over the significance of Keynes's theory of aggregate demand has revolved around the extent to which these insights can be accommodated within the equilibrium structure. The dominant response has been to argue that the price mechanism *is* being constrained in some way by structural and informational imperfections at the micro level from achieving a market clearing outcome at the macro level. This interpretation of Keynes is inevitable given the nature of the equilibrium method. Bryce (*CW XIII*, p. 133) noted 'the fundamental difficulty involved in trying to use orthodox equilibrium theory to explain the amount and causation of unemployment when one of its fundamental postulates denies the possibility of unemployment'. As a result

> classical theory is locked into an allocation/misallocation duality where all observed outcomes fall into one of two mutually exclusive categories of perfect allocative equilibria and non-perfect allocative equilibria, the latter being cases of misallocation (Gerrard, 1989, p. 38).

Beyond the bounds of such dualism (Dow, 1990), however, Keynes's contribution can be seen as arguing that the price mechanism, however flexible, is incapable of affecting *directly* the total level of output and employment. The economy possesses no innate self-adjusting tendency to gravitate towards full employment equilibrium. By stepping out of the equilibrium framework, Keynes (unlike the majority of his successors) saw involuntary unemployment as being independent of supply and demand factors operating in the labour market. The theory of aggregate demand is primarily concerned with the full utilization of the economy's potential resources rather than the efficient allocation of a fixed amount of resources. The economy is viewed as demand-constrained not resource-constrained. Hence involuntary unemployment exists until 'a situation in which aggregate employment is inelastic in response to an increase in the effective demand for its output' (*CW VII*, p. 26).

Far from being the rule, full employment is just as much an exception in the 1990s as it was in the 1930s. If economists wish to take seriously such a tragic waste of potential resources, the first step is to follow Keynes and start from the premise that the market is not capable of achieving a pattern of prices consistent with demands to promote sufficient aggregate demand to support the equilibrium level of aggregate supply. This implies that the reality of persistent mass unemployment is taken as a datum rather than being assumed away from the outset. From this vantage point, the notion of a unique condition of full employment equilibrium determined by supply factors is replaced by the vision of a capitalist economy which 'seems capable of remaining in a chronic condition of sub-normal activity for a considerable period without any marked tendency either towards recovery or towards complete collapse' (*CW VII*, p. 249). Who knows, if present trends continue, some academic scribbler in the mid-1990s may reiterate Keynes's suggestion that 'a somewhat comprehensive socialisation of investment will prove the only means of securing an approximation to full employment' (*CW VII*, p. 378).

JOHN HILLARD

References

Brothwell, J.F. (1992), 'Extending the General Theory into the Medium Run' in W.J. Gerrard and J.V. Hillard (eds), *The Philosophy and Economics of J.M. Keynes*, Cheltenham: Edward Elgar.
Carabelli, A.M. (1988), *On Keynes's Method*, London: Macmillan.
Dow, S.C. (1990), 'Beyond Dualism', *Cambridge Journal of Economics*, **14**, 143–57.
Gerrard, W.J. (1989), *Theory of the Capitalist Economy*, Oxford: Blackwell.
Keynes, J.M., Moggridge, D.E. and Johnston, E. (eds), *The Collected Writings of J.M. Keynes* (*CW*), Cambridge: Macmillan/Cambridge University Press.
Rotheim, R.J. (1992), 'Interdependence and the Cambridge Economic Tradition' in W.J. Gerrard and J.V. Hillard (eds), as above.

Aggregate supply

In *The General Theory* (1964), Keynes developed a model of aggregate supply and aggregate demand in order to explain the equilibrium determination of employment and output. The revolutionary nature of this analysis stems mainly from the specification of aggregate demand as a function that, in a monetary production economy, is not coincident with the aggregate supply function at all levels of employment. Keynes (pp. 25–6) was thereby rejecting Say's Law that held that these two functions are coincident at all levels of employment and can therefore not contribute to explaining the determination of employment and output levels. Keynes's separation of these functions is the foundation that allowed for the conclusion that, in general, aggregate supply and demand equilibrium occurs at levels of employment below full employment (Keynes, p. 254).

The centrality and relative novelty of aggregate demand led Keynes to devote Books III and IV of *The General Theory* to the details of the aggregate demand function (Keynes, p. 89). This emphasis led many neoclassical Keynesian and other orthodox authors to ignore the aggregate supply component of Keynes's theory. As a result, their interpretation of Keynes failed to recognize that his aggregate supply and aggregate demand model is fully capable of providing (1) an analysis of the full range of supply considerations like technology, cost and firm structure; (2) a comprehensive theory of inflation; (3) an explicit theory of income distribution, and (4) the basis for a theory of economic growth. Only a minority of authors persistently highlighted these components of Keynes's analysis (cf. Weintraub, 1958; Davidson, 1962; Davidson and Smolensky, 1964; Casarosa, 1981).

Keynes's *aggregate supply function* is directly derived from competitive Marshallian micro-foundations, 'involving few considerations which are not already familiar' (Keynes, p. 89), but is presented in an unfamiliar fashion and is used for macroeconomic problems. The aggregate supply function, for the firm, industry or economy, is a function between Keynes's two fundamental units of quantity: 'quantities of money-value and quantities of employment' (p. 41). The aggregate supply function for the individual firm is a direct mapping of the short-run Marshallian flow-supply schedule, presented in price-quantity space, into employment-money-value space. Hence, the aggregate supply function presents the minimum value of sales, Z_r, that would lead the firm to employ a certain amount of labour, N_r. The aggregate value of supply of the specific firm, Z_r, is equal to the product of the physical quantity of output produced with a particular amount of employment, $O_r = \psi_r(N_r)$, and the unit supply price associated with that output level, $P_{s,r} = \lambda_r(O_r)$. Formally, following Keynes (pp. 44–5):

$$Z_r = P_{s,r}\, O_r = \lambda_r(O_r)\, \psi_r(N_r) = \phi_r(N_r) \qquad (1)$$

A particular level of output and employment is chosen by the profit-maximizing competitive firm when its expected sales proceeds are equal to the value of aggregate supply (Keynes, p. 25). The equality of the *aggregate (expected) demand function* of the firm and its aggregate supply function is equivalent to the unit expected demand price being equal to the unit supply price (and marginal prime cost) in the more common microeconomic analyses (Casarosa, 1981, pp. 189–90).

The aggregate supply function of an industry is simply the summation of the aggregate supply functions of the individual firms in that industry. This type of aggregation is equivalent to that carried out in deriving the traditional Marshallian supply function of an homogenous output industry.

When trying to aggregate across industries, one encounters the problem of aggregating heterogenous physical goods 'since ΣO_r is not a numerical quantity' (Keynes, p. 45). The same type of problem exists in trying to aggregate unit supply prices. These problems are avoided in Keynes's analysis because (1) quantities of money-value are homogeneous by definition and (2) heterogenous labour is aggregated into a common *labour-unit*, paid the *wage-unit*, by Keynes (p. 41) on the basis of constant relative money wages. The major issue in terms of aggregation to achieve an economy-wide aggregate supply function relates to the composition of output and employment. If one assumes that the aggregate level of employment is distributed between industries in some unique way, this problem is solved (Keynes, pp. 45, 281).

The economy-wide aggregate supply function presents the minimum value of sales for all firms in the economy, *Z*, that is needed for the whole of industry to offer to employ a certain amount of labour, *N*:

$$Z = \phi(N) \tag{2}$$

The economy-wide aggregate supply value is a function of the total employment in the economy in a way that (1) incorporates a function of how the total amount of employment is divided between the different industries; (2) the unit supply prices are a function of the employment levels in each industry; and (3) the quantities of physical output produced are a function of the labour used in each industry.

A particular level of output and employment is chosen by profit-maximizing competitive firms when their expected sales proceeds are equal to the value of aggregate supply (Keynes, p. 25). This equality of the aggregate (expected) demand function of the firm sector as a whole and the economy-wide aggregate supply function is the point of *effective demand* (Keynes, p. 25). At this point the unit expected demand prices in each industry are equal to the unit supply prices (and marginal prime costs) of the respective industries. The aggregate (expected) demand function differs from the *actual aggregate demand function* or *aggregate expenditure function* (Casarosa, 1981, pp. 190–93) in that the latter is derived from the *demand-outlay function* (Weintraub, 1958, pp. 30–39) and determines actual sales and income results and the possible existence of short-period equilibrium.

The key consideration that Keynes brings into the aggregate supply function that is not common to the basic theory of the competitive firm is the notion of user cost (Keynes, pp. 53–9, 66–73). *User cost* is the depreciation of the capital stock that is due to its use. It is directly attributable to production, depends partially on expectations of future sales, and varies with the current level of output and employment. Keynes (p. 53) defines *prime cost* as the sum of factor cost and user cost. Hence, *marginal prime cost* is equal to the sum of marginal factor cost and marginal user cost (Keynes, p. 67). This means that the unit supply price and, consequently, the aggregate supply function depend upon this subjective element related to the depreciation of the fixed capital stock and may take on different values for the same value of the marginal factor cost. While Keynes (p. 24 fn.2) carried out most of his macroeconomic discussion (on both the aggregate supply and the aggregate demand side) net of user cost, this notion is important in the full-blown and dynamic version of Keynes's aggregate supply function.

The aggregate supply function is capable of directly incorporating different degrees of competition (Keynes, p. 245; Weintraub, 1958, pp. 65–75). For example, the aggregate supply function can be specified to include a mark-up over marginal prime cost that depends upon the price elasticity of demand facing the firm. The unit supply price is then a function of the marginal factor cost (MFC), the marginal user cost (MUC) and this mark-up (k):

$$P_{s,r} = \alpha(MFC, MUC, k) \tag{3}$$

The potential exists to extend this type of analysis away from Marshallian firms in general (cf. Weintraub, 1958, pp. 69–71) to incorporate the alternative types of firms that dominate Post Keynesian analyses.

The shape of the aggregate supply function depends upon the relationship between employment and the physical output it produces and how the supply price depends upon output and employment. The shape of the economy-wide aggregate supply function also depends on the relative importance of each industry and the degree of integration between firms. In the most simple presentation that employs a short-run production function or capital-utilization function exhibiting diminishing returns in labour – the only variable input used – it is usually argued that the aggregate supply function is convex to the employment axis (Davidson, 1962). Concavity of the aggregate supply function with respect to the employment axis may arise from (1) particular forms of the production technology; (2) the inclusion of user cost; (3) the inclusion of a degree of monopoly above perfect competition; (4) the variation in industry composition; and (5) the variation in the degree of integration between firms (Davidson, 1962).

The aggregate supply function allows Keynes's model to address comprehensively the full range of inflation issues (Keynes, pp. 292–309; Weintraub, 1958, pp. 102–4; Davidson and Smolensky, 1964, pp. 178–92). Differences in the wage-unit, technology, the degree of competition, marginal user cost, the degree of integration between firms and other mark-up effects mean that the aggregate supply function and the unit supply price will be different. Changes in the composition of employment between industries may have a further effect on the economy-wide aggregate supply function. In addition to these cost-based elements, Keynes's full model allows aggregate (expected) demand to choose the specific supply prices in existence and allows actual aggregate expenditures to determine the market prices of new and used commodities. Consequently, in the short period, an 'increase in effective demand will ... spend itself partly in increasing the quantity of employment and partly in raising the level of prices' (Keynes, p. 296). In the long period, higher levels of effective demand may be associated with lower unit supply prices, depending on the shifts that have occurred in the aggregate supply function.

The aggregate supply function directly presents a theory of income distribution in that the supply value is split between the wage bill and the supply value of gross profits, plus any other divisions of income (Weintraub, 1958, pp. 46–107). Variations in the same elements that affect the unit supply price may also impact on the distribution of income. Keynes (pp. 17–18) pointed out that, under simple conditions, the short-period equilibrium real wage is equal to the marginal product of labour. The diminishing marginal productivity of labour then means that a lower real wage is associated with a higher level of output and employment.

Keynes's *employment function* relates 'the amount of effective demand ... directed to a given firm or industry or to industry as a whole with the amount of employment' (p. 280). In other words, it gives the amounts of employment that would be associated with particular amounts of effective demand. It is therefore the inverse of the aggregate supply function (Keynes, p. 280). Full employment for a firm, industry or the economy as a whole exists when the elasticity of employment with respect to demand is zero (Keynes, p. 306). This also means that Keynes's demand curve for labour is derived from the aggregate supply and demand results and is not equal to the marginal product of labour curve (Weintraub, 1958, pp. 109–17).

Keynes's aggregate supply and demand model is fully capable of dealing with movements over time by the application of his theory of *shifting equilibrium* (Keynes, p. 293). This means that the model can deal with questions of dynamics, including the theory of growth and technical change (Weintraub, 1958, pp. 80–85). The discussion of these questions does not have to be limited to pure production models. The aggregate supply part of Keynes's model allows these elements to be discussed in the context of his complete model.

The recognition of the aggregate supply side in Keynes's model is crucial to appreciating the full range of capabilities of his approach. Not only can Keynes's model be applied to issues of aggregate demand, but it can also incorporate the full range of aggregate supply issues that include questions of technology, cost, user cost, different firm structures and behaviour, as well as issues of income distribution, economic growth and inflation. Keynes's model is, consequently, not susceptible to the critiques made of orthodox Keynesian models that lack the ability to deal with the above issues. Keynes's aggregate supply function is, obviously, also very different from the current orthodox aggregate supply function that is derived from labour-market behaviour.

JOHAN DEPREZ

References

Casarosa, C. (1981), 'The Microfoundations of Keynes's Aggregate Supply and Expected Demand Analysis', *Economic Journal*, **91** (361), March.

Davidson, P. (1962), 'More on the Aggregate Supply Function', *Economic Journal*, **72** (286), June.

Davidson, P. and Smolensky, E. (1964), *Aggregate Supply and Demand Analysis*, New York: Harper & Row.

Keynes, J.M. (1964), *The General Theory of Employment, Interest and Money*, New York and London: Harcourt Brace Jovanovich. Originally published 1936.

Weintraub, S. (1958), *An Approach to the Theory of Income Distribution*, Philadelphia: Chilton.

Animal spirits

The term 'animal spirits' is used three times by Keynes in *The General Theory* (1936) in the penultimate section of Chapter 12 on the state on long-term expectations. Keynes defines animal spirits as a 'spontaneous urge to action rather than inaction' (p. 161) and an 'innate urge to activity' (p. 163). Animal spirits are closely associated with the notion of 'spontaneous optimism'. Unfortunately the subsequent Keynesian literature has tended to use the term 'animal spirits' in an inexact and confusing manner to describe behaviour under uncertainty.

The origin of the term 'animal spirits' in Keynes's thought can be traced back to his undergraduate days. In his handwritten notes on modern philosophy, Keynes quotes the following passage from Descartes: 'The body is moved by animal spirits – the fiery particles of the blood distilled by the heat of the heart. They move the body by penetrating and moving the nerve and muscles; animal spirits are always in motion – the will only directs them.' Keynes added the comment 'unconscious mental action' (Carabelli, 1988, p. 298). O'Donnell (1989, p. 372) also notes the origin of the term in early physiological theory. Fitzgibbons (p. 85) suggests a connection with Plato's *Republic*, specifically Plato's argument that a guardian requires 'high spirits' akin to those of a watchdog. This possible Platonic connection is rather tenuous and lacks supporting textual evidence.

In *The General Theory* Keynes introduces animal spirits into his analysis of the investment decision. This analysis is set out in Chapters 11 and 12. Chapter 11 formulates the concept of the marginal efficiency of capital, the internal rate of return of a capital project calculated on the basis of anticipated revenues and costs. Entrepreneurs rank potential capital projects in terms of their marginal efficiency of capital and undertake those which offer a rate of return above the market rate of interest. Keynes points out in Chapter 12 that the motivation for investment has not always been dominated by a concern with prospective yields. In former times investment activity was a 'way of life'. The change in motivation was associated with the emergence of joint stock companies, with the separation of ownership and management, and the creation of an organized stock market. The latter development meant that investment is no longer purely a matter of enterprise, of forecasting prospective yields of assets over their entire life, but is now affected by speculation, that is, forecasting the psychology of the market. Speculative activity is seen as one potential source of instability in the investment process. For the economy as a whole, the rate of investment is determined at that point on the aggregate investment demand schedule where the marginal efficiency of capital in general is equal to the market rate of interest. Thus, in Keynes's analysis, the two key determinants of the rate of investment are the marginal efficiency of capital and the rate of interest. The marginal efficiency of capital is determined by the state of long-term expectations; the rate of interest is determined by liquidity preference.

The factors affecting the state of long-term expectations are discussed in Chapter 12. A long-term expectation consists of two elements: the most probable forecast and the confidence with which the forecast is made. This mirrors the distinction which Keynes made in *A Treatise on Probability* between probability and weight (O'Donnell, 1989, Ch. 4). Confidence reflects the likelihood of the best forecast turning out to be wrong. Keynes argues that the state of long-term expectations, and hence the rate of investment, is not a matter of strict mathematical calculation because of the uncertainty surrounding the future flows of revenues and costs. The uncertainty surrounding the investment decision is qualitatively different from that involved in the production decision. Keynes highlights this difference by distinguishing between the long-term expectations affecting the investment decision and the short-term expectations determining the production decision. In the case of the latter the best decision depends on current market and production conditions, knowledge of which is, for the most part, available. Uncertainty arises only from the relatively short time lag between the decision to produce and the point of sale. This limited degree of uncertainty allows the production decision to be treated as a matter of strict mathematical calculation. Likewise with speculation, which involves short-term forecasting of stock market movements.

Enterprise, however, is not a matter of strict mathematical calculation. The uncertainty associated with investment decisions based on long-term forecasts shows itself in at least four ways. (1) It may not be possible to quantify the future outcomes and/or their associated probabilities. The importance of non-quantitative probabilities is a key element in *A Treatise on Probability*. (2) Uncertainty about long-term outcomes leads to conventional behaviour, particularly the convention of assuming that the future will resemble the present in the absence of any specific knowledge indicating otherwise. (3) Long-term forecasts are evaluated with respect to the degree of confidence with which they are held. An investment project with an anticipated marginal efficiency of capital above the market rate of interest is unlikely to be undertaken if there is insufficient confidence in the forecast. (4) The decision to invest in many situations is a matter of animal spirits, not calculation:

> Even apart from the instability due to speculation, there is the instability due to the characteristic of human nature that a large proportion of our positive activities depend on spontaneous optimism rather than on mathematical expectations, whether moral or hedonistic or economic. Most, probably, of our decisions to do something positive, the full consequences of which will be drawn out over many days to come, can only be taken as a result of animal spirits – of a spontaneous urge to action rather than inaction, and not as the outcome of a weighted average of quantitative benefits multiplied by quantitative probabilities. Enterprise only pretends to itself to be mainly actuated by the statements in its own prospectus, however candid and sincere. Only a little more than an expedition to the South Pole, is it based on an exact calculation of benefits to come. Thus if the animal spirits are dimmed and the spontaneous optimism falters, leaving us to depend on nothing but a mathematical expectation, enterprise will fade and die; – though fears of loss may have a basis no more reasonable than hopes of profit had before (Keynes, pp. 161–2).

The calculation of an expected profit may be a necessary condition for an investment project to be undertaken, but it is not a sufficient condition; '... individual initiative will only be adequate when reasonable calculation is supplemented and supported by animal spirits' (Keynes, p. 162). The actualization of potentially profitable investment projects requires an 'innate urge to activity'. Investment decisions cannot be understood purely as a matter of logic; there is always, and necessarily, a psychological dimension.

Keynes mentions two consequences of the dependence of investment on animal spirits: (1) 'slump and depressions are exaggerated in degree'; and (2) 'economic prosperity is excessively dependent on the political and social atmosphere which is congenial to the average business man' (Keynes, p. 162). Keynes did not conclude, however, that the economy would be subject to 'waves of irrational psychology'. Rather animal spirits only created the potential for instability, a precariousness that tended paradoxically to result in protracted periods of stability, especially recessions, with relatively few sharp spontaneous shifts in the state of confidence. The main policy implication which Keynes draws is the likely inability of a purely monetary policy of interest rate adjustment to stimulate sufficient investment during a period of recession in which confidence is low and animal spirits are lacking.

The role of animal spirits in Keynes's analysis of investment has received relatively little attention. Mainstream Keynesians adopted a deterministic approach to investment, with particular emphasis on the accelerator theory. It was left to the 'old' Keynesian fundamentalists such as Shackle and Robinson to stress the role of animal spirits as evidence of the essential irrationality of the investment decision, this insight being a key element in Keynes's revolutionary break from orthodox modes of thought. The irrationality interpretation of animal spirits is adopted by Littleboy (1990, pp. 163, 285) in his recent study of Keynes. This is in sharp contrast to most recent contributions on the subject which have tended to interpret animal spirits as rational in some sense. One reason for this change is the desire to repudiate the traditional charge that the old Keynesian fundamentalism is nihilistic with respect to the possibility of economic analysis.

The rationality of animal spirits emerges in the 'new' Keynesian fundamentalism, the attempt to interpret Keynes's later economic and political writings in terms of his early philosophical thought. In particular much attention has been devoted to the links between *A Treatise on Probability* and *The General Theory*. In the former, Keynes developed a logical theory of probability in which probabilities are viewed as the degrees of belief it is rational to hold in some statement given the available evidence. Those who stress the link between Keynes's early philosophical work and *The General Theory*, the so-called 'continuity thesis', seek to interpret Keynes's analysis of economic behaviour in terms of the rationalism of *A Treatise on Probability*. Fitzgibbons (1988, pp. 84–6) argues that animal spirits are the rational response to uncertainty, the loss of animal spirits leading to subjective and irrational behaviour which creates volatility in economic affairs. Carabelli (1988, pp. 214, 298) considers animal spirits not as rational but rather as intuitive, supplying reasons which entrepreneurs are unaware of in a Freudian sense. Hence investment is a reasonable, but non-deliberative, action. However both Fitzgibbons and Carabelli treat investment as a way of life, undertaken for its own sake. Keynes deems this view as applicable only 'in former times'. Thus Fitzgibbons and Carabelli, unlike Keynes, give little attention to the calculating aspect of the investment decision. Indeed Carabelli claims that Keynes did not study investment as a relationship between the marginal efficiency of capital and the rate of interest. Dow and Dow (1985) view animal spirits as an alternative source of guidance for the rational investor in making judgments about future revenues and costs. There is no sensible information in such situations, and present values are undefined. Animal spirits are rational but not in the orthodox sense. Dow and Dow argue that Keynes adopted a wider notion of rationality since the orthodox notion cannot cope with choices made in the context of an unknowable future. O'Donnell (1989) also argues for a wider conception of rationality.

The new Keynesian fundamentalists rightly stress the role of animal spirits in the investment decision, but it seems inappropriate to refer to this as rational or reasonable behaviour. Keynes portrays the entrepreneur as a multi-faceted individual, rational to the extent that calculation can aid in the decision-making process, but often relying on other motives – on animal spirits:

> ... human decisions affecting the future, whether personal or political or economic, cannot depend on strict mathematical expectation, since the basis for making such calculations does not exist; and that it is our innate urge to activity which makes the wheels go round, our rational selves choosing between the alternatives as best we are able, calculating where we can, but often falling back for our motive on whim or sentiment or chance (Keynes, pp. 162–3).

Keynes sought to encompass the orthodox conception of the rational, calculating investor within a more general framework which recognizes the important role of non-rational factors such as animal spirits and spontaneous optimism. This implies, as Dow and Dow highlight, the use of more open, non-deterministic methods of analysis, the 'Babylonian' mode of thought. Thus a Keynesian theory of investment should not deny the role of formal project appraisal methods in determining investment decisions, but rather consider this aspect in the context of a fuller understanding of human motivations, particularly animal spirits.

BILL GERRARD

References

Carabelli, A.M. (1988), *On Keynes's Method*, London: Macmillan.

Dow, A. and Dow, S. (1985), 'Animal Spirits and Rationality' in T. Lawson and H. Pesaran (eds), *Keynes' Economics: Methodological Issues*, London: Croom Helm.

Fitzgibbons, A. (1988), *Keynes's Vision: A New Political Economy*, Oxford: Clarendon Press.

Keynes, J.M. (1936), *The General Theory of Employment, Interest and Money*, London: Macmillan.

Littleboy, B. (1990), *On Interpreting Keynes: A Study in Reconciliation*, London: Routledge.

O'Donnell, R.M. (1989), *Keynes: Philosophy, Economics and Politics*, London: Macmillan.

Banks and financial institutions

Radical political economy questions the stability and efficiency of capitalism: thus it constitutes more than just a set of critiques of economic policy and particular institutions. Capital markets, which lie at the heart of a modern capitalist economy, and banking, which mediates all of its significant transactions, have therefore been accorded a central role in radical political economy.

Radical economic analyses of banking and finance have tended to fall into two traditions corresponding with the two main systems of banking and finance present in the advanced capitalist countries: the general banking system of mainland Europe and Japan, in which capital market functions are performed by banks; and the dual system of separate banking and capital markets, existing in Britain and its former colonies (including the US).

The general banking system owes its inspiration to Claude Henri, the Comte de Saint-Simon. He regarded the aristocracies of Europe as an unproductive class who held back social progress by wasting their wealth, instead of advancing progress by assisting entrepreneurs and workers to create new wealth. He attracted a French banker, Jacques Lafitte who, together with another banker and disciple of Saint-Simon, Prosper Enfantin, propounded the view that the wealth of the idle rich should be put at the disposal of the industrial classes by an entrepreneurial banking system. This led to the creation in 1852 of just such a bank, the first *Crédit Mobilier*, which was then imitated in Germany.

By the turn of the century, the entrepreneurial banking system had evolved into the general banking system that is widespread on the continent of Europe. However, it had also become what it is today – the core of an industrial-financial complex in which a few big banks hold large equity stakes in the biggest industrial and commercial concerns. The possibility and reality of bankers coordinating the investments and activities of apparently competing firms inspired German Marxists (and not a few German anti-Semites in pursuit of Jewish conspiracies) to suggest that this was a new phase of capitalism, in which monopolies were financed and controlled by a smaller number of finance capitals.

For the revisionist Marxists, such as Eduard Bernstein and Rudolf Hilferding, this was a mature capitalism in which market manipulation was a form of planning which enabled capitalist crises, due to disproportions in production, to be limited if not actually eliminated. It would also allow social democratic governments eventually to take control over the economy without large-scale nationalization by the relatively simple expedient of regulating or taking over finance capital. Radical Marxists, such as Rosa Luxemburg and Lenin, saw no evidence that the ascendancy of finance capital was limiting (let alone eliminating) crises in the capitalist economy. Indeed, they saw it as intrinsically linked to militarism and imperialism.

Rosa Luxemburg herself developed a theory of development finance which in many respects anticipated that of Kalecki. According to her *Accumulation of Capital* (1951), the (colonial) developing countries required finance from the capitalist countries for development in order to create markets for those capitalist countries. However, when the repayments and interest on those liabilities grew excessive, the capital accumulation financed by them would cease, until the claims of those capitalist liabilities had been reduced or eliminated in a general financial crisis. In this way, a financial crash enabled capital accumulation to resume until the next crisis.

The nature and significance of bank domination of industry on the continent of Europe remain a central theme in radical approaches to finance and banking in countries with a general banking tradition. In particular, this domination gives a distinct Continental air to European theories of monopoly capitalism.

In the British Empire and Commonwealth, and in North America, the enterprising idle rich preferred to put their money into the stock market, and a different set of financial arrangements gave rise to different theories. These countries are characterized by banking institutions that engage in short-term finance, and separate capital markets which engage in the medium- and long-term finance of commerce and industry. From Ricardo and Marx onwards, conventional theory has supposed that it is the capital markets that bring together savings for capital accumulation, reallocating them around capitalist enterprises so that eventually a uniform rate of profit is obtained throughout the economy.

In the wake of the 1929 Wall Street Crash, Keynes (1936) pointed out that in fact stock markets are inherently unstable (rather than just accident-prone, as their apologists maintained); this instability disrupts the financing of fixed capital investment and exacerbates the trade cycle by discouraging such investment in a recession (pp. 150–64). A particular mechanism is liquidity preference, whereby uncertainty induces financiers to shun the medium- and longer-term financing of companies. Keynes clearly enjoyed ribbing bankers about their innate conservatism and their often suicidal herd instinct. His condemnation of the stock market 'casino' and his soliciting of the 'euthanasia of the rentier' qualify Keynes to be regarded as a radical.

But despite his innovations in monetary theory, Keynes's detailed analysis of the role of banking and finance was essentially conventional, with two major exceptions. He insisted that saving is a residuum in the economy and does not have an active function in it. Furthermore, he placed considerable emphasis on the way in which uncertainty brings expectations to the fore in business and financial decision-making. This radical departure from conventional theory was developed later by George Shackle who showed that the subjective and irrational elements in expectations are an important source of instability in investment.

Keynes's tentative critique of finance was taken up by Minsky (1976) who sought to detail precisely why capital markets disrupt investment. He argued that capital markets tend to encourage companies to over-invest in a boom, creating 'fragile financing structures' in markets, banks, financial institutions and companies, where claims arising out of financial market liabilities drain companies' liquidity. Another Post Keynesian, Jan Kregel, has consistently criticized the claim that capital markets operate as the perfect Walrasian markets of neoclassical theory.

The economic stagnation that set into the economies of North America and the British Commonwealth in the late 1960s, after the end of the long post-Second World War boom, gave rise to numerous critiques of supposed tendencies towards under-investment. Among some radicals it became fashionable to argue that the capital markets were denying finance to companies for investment. Richard Minns argued that industry was now under the direction of a small group of merchant banks who controlled the pension and investment funds which, since the 1970s, have come to dominate the capital markets. In an unconscious echo of Keynes and earlier German Marxists, he argued for direct state control over the capital markets to ensure an adequate supply of finance for investment. In their own unconscious echo of the pre-Keynesian 'crowding-out' view, the British Trades Union Congress and its allies argued that the foreign direct investment of British multinationals was a cause of under-investment in the UK because it transferred investment funds abroad. Others, such as Laurence Harris and Ben Fine, argued that companies themselves preferred not to engage in fixed capital investment because the terms of bank credit encouraged them to keep large liquid reserves.

Three economists stand out as transcending the institutional boundaries of the Anglo-Saxon and the Continental European financial systems. Chick (1992) has used Keynes's notion of liquidity preference to examine how finance changes in a capitalist economy as the banking system evolves from its early basic functions of on-lending deposits. In modern banking the supply of loans determines deposits, and banks can match reserves to the resulting balance sheet structure. A result of this is that finance severs its traditional links with investment; by implication, saving no longer constrains investment as it does in classical economic theory.

Kalecki (*CW*, Vol. I) casts off the notion that saving limits investment. In his view, capital accumulation is effectively limited by companies' reserves; this is affected by the liquidity in the economy and, by implication, the liquidity of those reserves. Most economists, including radical Keynesians such as Joan Robinson, have seen the rate of interest as a direct determinant of investment, because that rate sets the terms on which funds for investment are borrowed and acts as a general indicator of the opportunity cost of particular projects. But in Kalecki, the rate of interest is significant only because it influences liquidity and acts as an indicator of future business conditions (op. cit. p. 308).

Finance is also central to Kalecki's development economics (*CW*, Vol. V). He regards finance as being the main constraint on the growth of developing countries. This is supposedly so because public sector-led development is limited by the narrow fiscal base of governments in those countries, while the indigenous corporate sector lacks accumulated reserves commensurate with the task of development.

Finally, Steindl (1976) devoted a large part of his work to questions of finance. He followed Kalecki in distinguishing between what Steindl calls the 'internal savings' of companies and the 'outside savings' which they obtain through the capital market. Like Kalecki he regarded 'internal savings' as the key to stable accumulation: a rise in the ratio of rentiers' 'outside' savings to investment is reflected in an increase in companies' gearing, and hence the riskiness of their enterprise. Thus, if investment falls and the rate of rentiers' saving does not, then the resulting increase in gearing would further depress investment. Steindl saw the development of the joint stock system of capital ownership, and capital markets in general, as disposing companies further towards monopolistic practices of maintaining high profit margins at the expense of investment. This therefore contributes to the stagnation which he regarded as a feature of mature capitalism.

Banking and finance are central to radical analyses of money, monetary policy and investment. However, most Marxist economists have not differed greatly from conventional economists in the assumptions that they make about banking and finance (Luxemburg, Kalecki and Steindl are exceptions), while neo-Keynesian economists, with such notable exceptions as Kregel, Chick and Minsky, have been preoccupied with monetary policy and investment. They have therefore not examined in particular detail the operations of banking and finance, nor the actual functions that they perform in a capitalist economy. The issue has become more urgent with the declining importance of manufacturing industry in the UK and the US and the singling out, by advocates of *laissez-faire*, of banking and finance as the most dynamic sectors of 'mature' capitalist economies.

JAN TOPOROWSKI

References

Chick, V. (1992), 'The Evolution of the Banking System and the Theory of Saving, Investment and Interest' in P. Arestis and S.C. Dow (eds), *On Money, Method and Keynes: Selected Essays*, London: St Martin's Press.

Kalecki, M. (1990 onwards), *Collected Works* (*CW*), Vols I to VII, Oxford: Oxford University Press.

Keynes, J.M. (1936), *The General Theory of Employment, Interest and Money*, London: Macmillan.

Luxemburg, R. (1951), *The Accumulation of Capital*, London: Routledge and Kegan Paul.

Minsky, H.P. (1976), *John Maynard Keynes*, London: Macmillan.
Steindl, J. (1976), *Maturity and Stagnation in American Capitalism*, New York: Monthly Review Press.

Business cycles

Business cycles are economic phenomena which have appeared in capitalist economies since the early 19th century. The most detailed information about cycles is derived from the reference cycle dating procedure developed by W.C. Mitchell and subsequently elaborated by the National Bureau of Economic Research in the US. Detailed study of many economic time series suggested several kinds of regularities to Mitchell and his collaborators. For example, Burns and Mitchell (1946) defined cycles in the following way:

> Business cycles are a type of fluctuation found in the aggregate economic activity of nations that organize their work mainly in business enterprises: a cycle consists of expansions occurring at about the same time in many economic activities, followed by similarly general recessions, contractions and revivals which merge into the expansion phase of the next cycle; the sequence of change is recurrent but not periodic; in duration business cycles vary from more than one year to ten or twelve years; they are not divisible into shorter cycles of similar character with amplitude approximating their own (p. 1).

Contemporary US business cycle researchers would add the observation that, in the post-war period, the cycle has become markedly asymmetric. Expansions have usually been longer than contractions. Similar cyclical behaviour appears present in all advanced capitalist countries for which reference cycle data have been constructed, although cycle lengths vary.

In practice, business cycle researchers do three things. First, they find economic time series which consistently reflect aggregate economic activity. Series such as real GNP and employment rates are obvious candidates. Many other series, such as bank clearings and number of bond trades, are also included. Second, they locate turning points in aggregate activity. Changes in movement must be widely diffused across the relevant time series for a turning point to be identified. It is frequently the case that some series do not conform to the general trend in movement. Finally, business cycle researchers identify time series which consistently lead or lag these turning points.

There are difficulties with traditional business cycle methods. The criteria for selecting relevant time series seem quite broad, and timing patterns are not always consistent across cycles. Many economists, however, find the observed empirical regularities to be impressive. They think it important to account for the dynamic patterns observed; these include strong co-movement between significant economic variables, aperiodicity and asymmetry.

The dominant tendency in business cycle theory derives from the work of Slutsky. His starting point was simple and his results remarkable. Using random numbers generated by a Russian lottery, he produced a synthesized time series. He then constructed a variety of weighted moving averages of these random numbers. When these moving averages were plotted, they showed a strong similarity to cyclical economic time series. This similarity, perhaps as much as the accompanying analytical results on cyclicality, captured the interest of economists who wanted to explain business fluctuations. Indeed, Slutsky had implicitly created a ready-made analytical framework. If an aggregate economic variable x can be explained by a linear difference equation as simple as $x_t = \alpha x_{t-1} + \varepsilon_t$, where ε_t is a serially uncorrelated random term, then a Slutsky-like process can be produced. Recursive substitution of the equation into itself will produce a moving average of εs, hence a rudimentary cyclical series.

In this one-dimensional example and in linear models of higher dimension, theorists are forced to choose parameter values which correspond to local stability. If they do not, shocks would produce explosive behaviour everywhere around the equilibrium. Linear models can produce oscillations, but the range of parameter values which do so are implausibly narrow. Thus linear cycle models are stable equilibrium systems subject to perturbations.

A successful linear-stochastic account of cycles might reasonably be expected to do several things. First, explain why it is correct to assume that market economies gravitate to some stable economic equilibrium. Second, give a convincing account of the existence of time lags. There needs to be a good reason why x_t is a function of x_{t-1}. If x_t is determinate, with a shock term added on, there will be random behaviour but no serial correlation of the xs, and hence no cyclical behaviour. Third, it is necessary to explain just what the 'exogenous shocks' are meant to represent.

Mainstream cycle theory, which is predominantly linear-stochastic, has some difficulty in dealing with these issues. The continued existence of unemployment and other apparent disequilibria suggest that the equilibrium metaphor is misplaced. Also, the introduction of time lags into mainstream models is often done in a casual fashion. Moreover, the shocks which are so important to dynamics in these models have received scant attention. No one has compiled a convincing list of 'big' events, affecting entire economies at once, which are frequent and large enough to cause cycles. Nor has anyone explained why small shock events, which may well affect individuals and firms, should not wash out in the aggregate, as the law of large numbers suggests they should. Because of these problems, there is continuing interest in alternatives to mainstream theory and techniques.

Endogenous business cycle theory provides an alternative class of explanation for observed dynamics. Stochastic theory describes the capitalist economy as a stable mechanism, frequently perturbed from its centre of gravity by non-economic impulses. Endogenous theory, on the other hand, tried to explain the dynamic behaviour of the economy in terms of the interaction of economic variables themselves. It relies on the techniques of non-linear difference and differential equations. These methods make it possible to analyse dynamic systems which are locally unstable but globally bounded. Such systems make it possible to represent accounts of self-sustained oscillations.

Endogenous cycle theory was pioneered by economists working in the Keynes-Kalecki-Marx tradition. To a first approximation, nonlinear Keynesian-Kaleckian models depict market economies as inherently unstable because of the interaction of investment demand and multiplier effects. However, acknowledging that market economies do not usually explode or collapse, they attempt to describe the economic constraints on market dynamics. Kalecki, who independently formulated the principle of effective demand, consistently used the time lags and the dependence of investment on past profits to introduce cyclical dynamics into a multiplier framework. In an early paper he used a shifting investment decision function, which changes the location of the stable macroeconomic equilibrium, to create an implicitly nonlinear system and an explanation of how business cycles can be self-sustaining. Soon after, Harrod demonstrated that an investment accelerator would destabilize a linear Keynesian growth model. Kaldor (1940) quickly produced a synthesis of Kalecki and Harrod. Like Harrod, he assumed that the accelerator-like effects on investment would produce unstable equilibria at intermediate levels of output. Like Kalecki, he assumed that financial constraints and changes in income distribution would provide a ceiling to the growth of demand, and that autonomous investment would prevent a collapse of demand. The resulting trade cycle model has rich dynamics and has proven to be of lasting influence.

Parallel to the work on aggregate demand, economists interested in the Marxian account of cyclical behaviour have worked to formalize it. A highly influential initial contribution was made by Goodwin (1967). He provided a very concise version of the 'reserve army' theory of the business cycle which Marx develops in *Capital*. Fixed production coefficients and full employment of capital are assumed. Savings, exclusively from profits, determine investment. Labour is treated as 'something of a rent good', commanding a real wage that varies positively with the employment rate. High rates of accumulation raise employment rates, which in turn raises the real wage. This reduces the rate of accumulation, and the real wage is ultimately reduced, stimulating accumulation once again. Model formulation allows for lags in the effect of employment on profitability. Like its Keynesian counterparts, it produces periodic behaviour. The Goodwin-Marx model has produced a substantial literature in which assumptions about technology, utilization and income distribution have varied.

While the endogenous cycle literature offers explanations for self-sustained oscillations, many such models are periodic or asymptotically periodic. Therefore they offer incomplete explanations of observed behaviour. Adding a stochastic component would allow for aperiodicity. However, this would only raise the issue of accounting for the shocks.

Recent discoveries about the mathematics of chaotic dynamical systems offer potentially important extensions of endogenous cycle theory. Mathematicians and applied natural scientists have demonstrated that simple, low-dimension nonlinear difference and differential equations can produce behaviour which is both deterministic and extremely complex. Hence, if an economically plausible nonlinear cycle model can produce chaos, it suggests that the not-quite-periodic behaviour of aggregate economic time series may have deterministic origins.

Chaotic dynamical systems have several defining characteristics. One is sensitive dependence on initial conditions. Formally, this means that given a point on an attractor, there is another arbitrarily close which will separate exponentially over time. It implies that any error about the initial state of the dynamical system will cumulate and frustrate numerical computation of the evolution of a trajectory. Since everyone in the economic world does make measurement errors, sensitive dependence implies unpredictability about dynamical behaviour. Even if the deterministic structure of a chaotic economic system is known with complete certainty, a failure to specify initial conditions perfectly will mean significant errors of forecast.

A second characteristic of chaotic dynamical systems is the existence of orbits of arbitrarily high period. Thus, although there is unpredictability, some of the dynamics involve infinitely complicated regularities. A third characteristic of chaos is 'topological transitivity', which means that dynamical behaviour of the system cannot be confined to any disjoint subsets. Among other things, this implies that the infinite periodic orbits cannot be stable, an additional complication of dynamics. Finally, it is sometimes possible to show that chaotic systems have an infinite number of aperiodic orbits. The operational difference between this and the presence of arbitrary periodic orbits may not be significant.

As might be expected, theorists have re-examined existing endogenous cycle models to see when they might be chaotic. Both aggregate demand models (Lorenz, 1987) and Marxian models (Pohjola 1981) can produce chaotic trajectories. Since the transition to chaos in this sort of model is controlled by parameter values, it becomes possible to account for dynamics in terms of structural or behavioural factors. Simple calibrations of parameters, based on 'stylized facts', allow for easy checks on the prima facie plausibility of outcomes.

Although chaos models do allow for deterministic explanations of irregular time series behaviour, it is not yet widely accepted that business cycles are generated by chaotic systems. One major objection is that, in their present state, the models are too elementary to be useful representations of actual economies. Most are one-dimensional discrete equations, which in chaotic mode produce behaviour too erratic to replicate cycles. Since the mathematics of chaos is still in its early phases, it will take some time for economic models of higher dimension and more believable behaviour to be handled with ease.

Attempts to apply existing empirical tests for chaos to economic time series data have provoked controversy. Using these tests, which measure such markers of chaos as Lyapunov exponents or attractor dimension, some researchers have concluded that the empirical evidence is against the existence of chaos in macroeconomic data. However, it has been shown that, even in cases where strongly chaotic behaviour can be established analytically, this behaviour may be missed by standard empirical tests when time series are of the length commonly available to macroeconomists (Jarsulic, 1993). It seems fair to say that this issue remains unresolved. Again, this area of research is in its infancy and future progress may be expected.

MARC JARSULIC

References

Burns, A. and Mitchell, N. (1946), *Measuring Business Cycles*, New York: National Bureau of Economic Research.

Goodwin, R. (1967), 'A Growth Cycle' in C.H. Feinstein (ed.), *Socialism, Capitalism and Economic Growth*, Cambridge: Cambridge University Press.

Jarsulic, M. (1993), 'A Nonlinear Model of the Pure Growth Cycle', *Journal of Economic Behaviour and Organization*, **22**, 133–51.

Kaldor, N. (1940), 'A Model of the Trade Cycle', *Economic Journal*, **50**, 78–92.

Lorenz, H.-W. (1987), 'Strange Attractors in a Multisectoral Business Cycle Model', *Journal of Economic Behavior and Organization*, **8**, 397–411.

Pohjola, M. (1981), 'Stable and Cyclical Growth: The Dynamics of a Discrete Version of Goodwin's Growth Cycle Model', *Zeitschrift fur Nationalokonomie*, **41**, 27–38.

Capital theory controversies

Looking back with hindsight from the early 1990, we may say that the capital theory controversies of the 1950s to 1970s related not so much to the *measurement* of capital as to its *meaning* (Harcourt, 1976). Related to this perspective is the following question: what is the appropriate method with which to analyse processes occurring in capitalist economies (especially those related to production, distribution and accumulation)? In addition there are queries about the meaning of price and the source of value in two opposing traditions: price as an index of scarcity, and utility as the source of value in the subjective theory of value; or price as an index of the difficulty of reproduction, and labour as the source of value in the labour theory of value. (The last is a portmanteau term which encompasses an explanation of the origin and size of profits in the capitalist mode of production.)

The bulk of the controversies took place within the confines of the theory of value and distribution. In the 1970s the application of the results was extended to a critique of the foundations of mainstream international trade theory (see entry on International trade). Very recently, the results have been applied, principally by Colin Rogers (1989), to a critique of the foundations of mainstream monetary theory (see entry on Interest rates). This *should* lead to a revival of interest in the results of the debate themselves, but it would be optimistic to expect this actually to come about. With the deaths in the 1980s of Joan Robinson, Piero Sraffa, Nicholas Kaldor and Richard Kahn, the bulk of the profession has started to behave as if they and their work never existed. Aggregate production function models and accompanying marginal productivity results, together with the long-period method, are being applied in the work which reflects the new interest in growth theory of the late 1980s and early 1990s associated, for example, with the contributions of Lucas and Romer. The intellectual dishonesty – or, at best, ignorance – which characterizes these developments is breathtaking in its audacity and arrogance, reflecting the ruthless use of power by mainstream economists in dominant positions in the profession.

The first question posed historically in the modern debates was: can we find a unit with which to measure capital which is independent of value and distribution? Why should anyone want such a measure? If we are to use a demand and supply approach in an explanation of distributive variables – the rate of profits (r), the wage rate (w) – and distributive shares; if we are to make explicit the intuition of this approach, that price is an index of scarcity; and if we are to accept that in a competitive situation there is a tendency to uniformity of r in all activities, so that we need a theory to explain the origin and size of the overall economy-wide rate of profits, *then* we need an answer to the question: what do we mean by a quantity of capital? For if the intuition is to be confirmed, *one* of the reasons why *r* is high or low must have to do with whether we have a little or a lot of 'capital' (relative to labour). (Incidentally, with labour there is *not* a similar problem. We may for simplicity assume homogeneous labour measured in terms of hours and so have only one competitive wage rate to be explained. But if we wish to consider different types of labour, we may easily adjust our theory to include a different wage rate for each class, measuring each in terms of hours of work by each class). The measure of 'capital' must exist *before* the analysis starts; i.e. it must be exogenous or a given, a determinant measured in its own technical unit – not endogenous, something to be determined by the analysis itself. So the criticism that people such as Joan Robinson or Piero Sraffa did not understand the nature of mutual determination is beside the point. They did, but they also understood the difference between what is in the list of determinants and what is in the list of what is to be determined.

If it is not possible to find a unit with which to measure 'capital', then it is not possible to say that *r* takes the value it does partly because we have so much 'capital' and also because 'its' marginal product has a particular value. The marginal product of 'capital' becomes an incoherent concept if it is not possible to say what a quantity of 'capital' is and feed the answer into the production function format to help determine the values of *w* and *r* and the respective shares of labour and 'capital' in the national product. So far, the problem has not been solved by the demand and supply theorists. Joan Robinson's 'solution' – measure 'capital' as real capital in terms of labour time – was an attempt to answer a neoclassical question in a neoclassical setting: what limited meaning may be given to 'capital' as a factor of production? She showed that real capital could not be defined until we knew the value of either *r* or *w*, and that the limited meaning that we could give with this construction to the marginal product of 'capital' produced results which have no simple nor obvious relationship to the accompanying return to 'capital'. Champernowne's (1953–54) chain index measure of 'capital' *seemed* to restore the 'good old theory'. However, when his analysis is examined closely, it is seen that the measure is *not* independent of distribution and prices, and that the marginal product of 'capital' which is related in a simple manner to *r* (as is the corresponding marginal product of labour to *w*) is in fact subtly different from the traditional concept. Piero Sraffa's 1960 book (which was over 30 years in the making) is subtitled *Prelude to a Critique of Economic Theory*. The particular criticism which forms the core of his critique is made abundantly clear in his reply (1962) to Roy Harrod's review of the book: '… what is the good of a quantity of capital … which, since it depends on the rate of interest, cannot be used for its traditional purpose … to determine the rate of interest? (p. 479). While the problem of induction means that the door will always be left open for such a measure to be found, at this moment it seems it is still a search for a will-o'-the-wisp, or even for the grin of a black cat in a dark room who is not there anyway.

Two further avenues of discussion arose from this aspect of the debate. The first relates to the distinction between differences and changes; the results of the debate are mostly drawn from comparisons of long-period positions and reflect differences in the initial conditions. They are unable to tell us anything about processes, in particular the process of accumulation. This led on to the methodological critique which Joan Robinson made of the neoclassicals and neo-Ricardians alike, summed up in the phrase 'history *versus* equilibrium' (see Joan Robinson, 1974).

A favourite analogy was the pendulum. Its ultimate resting place is independent of whether it is given a slight nudge or is arbitrarily lifted high and let go – not so for analogous disturbances in a market or an economy. Thus, many years before, Joan Robinson (and Kaldor (1934) even earlier) put what we now call path-dependent equilibria back on the agenda. Ultimately she went even further, arguing that equilibria may not even be out there to be found, thus denying the legitimacy of distinguishing the factors which determine existence from those which determine stability, and of separating those responsible for the trend from those responsible for the cycle.

The second avenue relates to the *nature* of the accumulation process itself. Here we may identify two different visions. The first is the Fisherian, whereby the dominant force is the consumption/saving behaviour of individuals over their lifetimes. All other entities and institutions – firms, stock exchanges and so on – are subservient to the primary purpose of achieving maximum utility over the lifetimes of consumers. Rates of time preference, rates of return over cost and the money rate of interest which clears the market for money loans are crucial here. In the other scenario, which is more associated with Marx, Keynes, Veblen, Kalecki, Robinson, Kaldor (and the later Hicks), accumulation and profit-making are ends in themselves. The ruthless swashbuckling entrepreneurs call the tune and all else must dance to it. Profits and the rate of profits arise from social relationships in production, together with the forces of effective demand associated with the different saving and spending behaviour of the main classes and the animal spirits of business people.

The reaction to the criticism of the aggregate production function approach to distribution associated with the exchanges between Joan Robinson, Swan, Champernowne and Solow was to revert to the Fisherian model, trying to explain r without ever mentioning 'capital' or 'its' marginal product – not always successfully, it has to be said. This was the rationale of Solow's de Vries Lectures, published in 1963: to use the social rate of return on investment as the key concept in capital theory – a concept which provides on the productivity side of the story what the rate of time preference does on the psychological side. Again price as an index of scarcity is the conceptual background.

Parallel with this movement was the attempt by Samuelson (1962) to rationalize the use by Solow of J.B. Clark, J.R. Hicks models in growth theory and econometric work by showing that the rigorously derived results of the simple model were robust, that they were illuminating of the behaviour of the more complex *n* commodity general equilibrium systems with which the high theorists at MIT were more prone and happy to work. Lying behind this was the same conceptual understanding that 'capital' and *r* were related in such a way that the demand curve for capital was well-behaved, i.e. downward sloping. It was this result in particular, as well as the other neoclassical parables – a negative association between *r* and the capital-output ratio, and sustainable levels of consumption per person – together with the marginal productivity theory itself, which were put at risk by the capital-reversing and reswitching results. The capital-reversing result (or Ruth Cohen Curiosum) was that a less productive, less capital-intensive technique could be associated with a lower value of *r*; the reswitching result has it that the same technique which is the most profitable for a particular range of values of *r* or *w*, could also be the most profitable for another range, even though a different technique is more profitable at the range of values of *r* and *w* in between. Both of these results are counter-intuitive in the supply and demand framework and both contradict the rigorous results of the simple model, so destroying its robustness. Pasinetti (1966) was the first to understand and emphasize the significance of these phenomena for the critique of the supply and demand theories. The methodological debate also becomes relevant in that it is not always clear in the discussion whether it is the existence or the stability of an equilibrium, or both, that is being queried.

The outcome of the surrogate production function debate of the 1960s was to show that Samuelson's simplifying assumption of the same capital-labour ratio in each sector for a given technique in effect took seemingly heterogenous models back into the simple one-commodity world where it was known that the intuitively satisfying neoclassical parables and the marginal productivity theory ruled OK. This, together with the Robinsonian critique that short-period equilibria cannot in general be regarded as stations on the way to the long-period equilibrium cross, put paid to the application of the aggregate production function (Lucas and Romer please note); but what was the implication for Fisherian theory as revived and extended by Solow?

In 1969 Pasinetti argued that price as an index of scarcity in Solow's work only survived if an 'unobstructive postulate' (no capital-reversing allowed) were slipped into the analysis. Otherwise a well-behaved demand curve for 'capital' could not be guaranteed and the rate of return over cost did not lead to an intuitively satisfying explanation of *r* within the supply and demand, marginal framework. This was disputed by Solow, while Fisher was defended by Dougherty. Yet those who claimed that proper general equilibrium theory was immune to these criticisms also conceded that general equilibrium theory itself, properly understood, was not descriptive theory anyway. Moreover, its own equilibrium solutions were not necessarily either unique or stable, an admission that supply and demand curves are not necessarily monotonic. So the simple theory did not provide coherent results and the logically immune theory was not applicable. Here the matter rested: Cambridge (UK) won, but who cares, let us assume that they never existed – a good economist's ploy.

In the 1980s the implications of the application of the results came to the fore in another area. Rogers (1989) identified two major traditions leading to the foundations of modern monetary theory, the neo-Wicksellian and the neo-Walrasian. The central concept of the former was the natural rate of interest – a *real* concept that dominated the money rate of interest which ultimately had to conform to it. The capital theory results suggested that the natural rate was not a coherent concept or, at least, only a concept within an analysis where neither existence nor stability could necessarily be proved – an argument which goes back to the exchange between Garegnani and Bliss in 1970. As for the neo-Walrasian tradition, it was argued that this was unaffected by the capital theory results (a view not unanimously accepted – dissenters include Garegnani, Eatwell, Milgate and Panico); but, in any case, the neo-Walrasian foundations support an approach in which, as Hahn in particular has pointed out, it is impossible to introduce money in any meaningful sense. Again, it has to be said that the critique is more successful than the alternatives proposed. This, essentially, is because they lack both the coherence – there are internal disagreements within the Post Keynesian camp concerning both method and theory (see Hamouda and Harcourt, 1988) – and the generality of the system that has been attacked.

Thus the current position is an uneasy state of rest, under the foundations of which a time bomb is ticking away, planted by a small, powerless group of economists who are either ageing or dead.

G.C. Harcourt

References

Bliss, C.J. (1970), 'Comment on Gregnani' *Review of Economic Studies*, **XXXVII**, 437–8.

Champernowne, D.G. (1953–54), 'The Production Function and the Theory of Capital: a Comment', *Review of Economic Studies*, **XXI**, 112–35.

Garegnani, P. (1970), 'Heterogenous Capital, the Production Function and the Theory of Distribution', *Review of Economic Studies*, **XXXVII**, 407–36.

Hamouda, O.F. and G.C. Harcourt (1988), 'Post Keynesianism: From Criticism to Coherence?', *Bulletin of Economic Research*, **40**, 1–33.

Harcourt, G.C. (1976), 'The Cambridge Controversies: Old Ways and New Horizons – or Dead End?', *Oxford Economic Papers*, **28**, 25–65.

Kaldor, N. (1934), 'A Classificatory Note on the Determinateness of Equilibrium', *Review of Economic Studies*, **1**, 122–36,

Pasinetti, L.L. (1966), 'Changes in the Rate of Profit and Switches of Techniques', *Quarterly Journal of Economics*, **LXXX**, 503–17.

Pasinetti, L.L. (1969), 'Switches of Technique and the "Rate of Return" in Capital Theory', *Economic Journal*, **LXXIX**, 508–31.
Robinson, Joan (1953–54), 'The Production Function and the Theory of Capital', *Review of Economic Studies*, **XXI**, 81–106.
Robinson, Joan (1974), *History versus Equilibrium, Thames Papers in Political Economy*, London.
Rogers, Colin (1989), *Money, Interest and Capital. A Study in the Foundations of Monetary Theory*, Cambridge: Cambridge University Press.
Samuelson, P.A. (1962), 'Parable and Realism in Capital Theory: The Surrogate Production Function', *Review of Economic Studies*, **XXIX**, 193–206.
Solow, R.M. (1963), *Capital Theory and the Rate of Return*, Amsterdam: North-Holland.
Sraffa, P. (1960), *Promotion of Commodities by Means of Commodities: Prelude to a Critique of Economic Theory*, Cambridge, Cambridge University Press.
Sraffa, P. (1962), 'Production of Commodities: a Comment', *Economic Journal*, **72**, 477–9.

Class and social relations

Should class be treated as a social factor which affects economic relations at one remove, or should it be considered as a category which affects economic relations directly and, if so, how significant a category is it? Generally speaking, modern economics favours an approach which sets social relations at a distance; to find theories in which class features prominently at the heart of economic analyses, it is necessary to turn to the classical and Marxist traditions of political economy. However, it is also necessary to distinguish between these traditions as they do not interpret the significance of social relations in the same way. In Marxist theories they lie closer to the centre of analysis than they do in classical and classical-inspired theories. One reason for this is the different meanings placed upon the concept of 'surplus'. Although differences between different schools of economic thought cannot be explained completely from this standpoint, as far as class and social relations are concerned, the concept of surplus is the single most important factor to consider.

Despite neglect by neoclassical theory, the concept of surplus, which was present from the very beginning of modern economic thinking in the 17th century, has proved durable. The idea of the product of a society comprising two parts – one necessary to its maintenance and another for which there is no immediate need – proved far too compelling to disappear entirely; social theorists continued to employ it even when economists let it fall into abeyance. One area where it played a central role (significantly far removed from the conditions of the modern economy whose analysis dominated mainstream economics), was economic anthropology, particularly the study of economic change in primitive societies. Thus, for example, to explain why the Hottentots had developed greater specialization than the Bushmen of South Africa, one anthropologist had no doubt – 'the reason is simple: the

Bushmen produce no surplus' (cited by Pearson, p. 322). Perhaps too simple, for while it is obvious that only societies which develop the capacity to produce a surplus can sustain social relations which are not shaped in detail by the material requirements of subsistence production, the influence of social relations upon this capacity also demands attention.

A formal definition of economic surplus presents few difficulties. According to Sraffa, a surplus is present where an 'economy produces more than the minimum necessary for replacement' (1960, p. 6). That part of necessary production which replaces instruments and materials is straightforward, but the other part, covering the needs of producers, is more difficult to specify. At the very time Sraffa was putting the finishing touches to his seminal work, a dispute broke out among anthropologists concerning the definition of necessary consumption in terms of basic needs (Pearson, 1957). Although anthropologists were studying primitive societies, the questions they raised about the extent to which necessary consumption is socially determined have a general significance which did not escape the notice of economists in their attempts to produce a theory of wages. In this context, Ricardo had noted that the 'natural price of labour ... depends on the habits and customs of the people' (1951, pp. 96–7); Marx had argued that 'in contrast ... with the case of other commodities, the determination of the value of labour-power contains a moral and historical element' (p. 275); and Sraffa had observed that 'wages ... besides the ever-present element of subsistence ... may include a share of the surplus product' (1960, p. 9). But their approach, though perfectly adequate for setting in motion a theory of economic surplus, leaves the question open. Can the social factors which determine subsistence be treated as part of the economic environment (like climate), or should they be considered as part of the economic process itself?

By emphasizing the importance of surplus as a social factor, specifically the form of surplus, the studies of the classical historian, Ste. Croix (1981), bring the question into sharp focus. As a result of his work, theories of the relation between class and economic magnitudes can be counterposed more clearly than previously: on the one side, a concept of economic surplus as the basis of social relations; on the other, a concept of social surplus as the basis of economic relations. Are social relations a subset of economic relations defined technically as methods of production? Or are they inseparably connected to economic relations as part of a single complex?

According to Ste. Croix, overall production and consumption, from which the concept of economic surplus is derived, are less important than the way in which the surplus is extracted from its direct producers:

> My point is that the most significant distinguishing feature of each social formation, each 'mode of production', is not so much how the bulk of the labour of

> production is done, as how the dominant propertied classes, controlling the conditions of production, ensure the extraction of the surplus which makes their own leisured existence possible ... (Ste. Croix, 1981, p. 52).

As he found this theory in Marx, Ste. Croix does not pretend that it is new, 'but I have never seen it stated clearly and explicitly'. To support his claim about its provenance, Ste. Croix cites four passages by Marx. This is the crucial part of what 'seems to me one of the most important [passages] which Marx ever wrote':

> The specific economic form in which unpaid labour is pumped out of the direct producers determines the relation of domination and servitude as this grows directly out of production itself and reacts back on it in turn as a determinant. On this is based the entire configuration of the economic community arising from the actual relations of production, and hence also its specific political form (Marx, 1981, p. 927).

'What I think has been often overlooked,' Ste. Croix sums up, 'is that what Marx is concentrating on as the really distinctive feature of society is not the way in which the bulk of the labour of production is done, but how the extraction of surplus from the immediate producer is secured' (Ste. Croix, p. 52).

The existence of a biological minimum level of consumption is not in dispute; in every form of society some consumption is physically necessary. But the coexistence in many types of societies of malnutrition, high rates of infant mortality and low life expectancy with high levels of non-necessary consumption has been cited as evidence that a definition of surplus as what is left after basic needs have been met is far too abstract for social analysis (Pearson, p. 324). Access to means of consumption, it has been argued, has never depended exclusively on the level of production. Invariably it is governed by the social relations and political structures which determine how the product is allocated; in other words, by precisely those relations and structures which, according to Ste. Croix's reading of Marx, are determined by the form of surplus production and extraction. In this view, necessary consumption is what is needed to sustain the producers of surplus as producers of surplus, not the autonomous needs of these producers and certainly not the autonomous needs of society at large. To the extent that command of surplus production carries with it command of society at large, surplus production is the independent variable and necessary consumption is the dependent variable.

In the ancient Greek world the majority of the population were independent producers and slaves were relatively few in number. Yet, according to Ste. Croix, it was slaves who produced the surplus which gave classical society its character. The distinction between the mode of production in general and the form of surplus extraction was particularly clear-cut. By contrast, in capitalist society, where all production is organized through wage-labour, necessary production and surplus production involve identical social relations. But this does not call into question Marx's view, as interpreted by Ste. Croix, that the form of surplus production is decisive. On the contrary, it can be argued that, insofar as the form of surplus production is extended to all spheres of economic activity, its grip on society is that much tighter. It is no longer simply the direct producers of the surplus who are under the sway of the form of surplus extraction, but the whole of society – immediately or at one remove.

One implication of this approach for the interplay of economic magnitudes and social relations is particularly important: that the definition of surplus is itself directly social. Thus, in contrast to the view associated with Sraffa that surplus is an excess of output over necessary consumption, which is then distributed between different classes, we now have a definition of surplus which is already distributional in the sense that it refers exclusively to that part of output which falls into the hands of the appropriators of surplus – slave-owners, seigneurs, capitalists. This does not mean that producers are unable to claim considerably more than they need for survival, but that nothing the class of producers acquires counts as surplus because they do not play the social role of surplus appropriators. Admittedly, where producers treat part of their income from work as surplus (in capitalist societies this entails investing it), the definition of surplus by class is no longer exact. Nevertheless the distinction between the two approaches to surplus – between the economic approach on the one hand and the social approach on the other – remains clear-cut.

Given the importance of the concept of surplus for grounding the notion of class as a category of economic analysis, these two approaches intimate the different ways in which it is possible to consider the connections between economic magnitudes and social relations. Both address the same questions, and in many instances the distinctions they draw are fine. But the majority of disputes among economists derive from just such distinctions. In the nature of things, there are no clearly defined or generally accepted criteria for adjudicating their claims: one approach is mathematically more rigorous; the other draws support from outside economics, from anthropological and historical studies. To introduce class into the core of economic theory inevitably dilutes the mathematical rigour which has played such an important part in the development of analysis; on the other hand, if this rigour requires consigning class and social relations to the margins of analysis, its price may be considered too high. Class is not only an 'unsettled question' of economics, to use Mills' term, but a sign of the unsettled nature of the discipline itself.

GEOFF KAY

References

Marx, Karl (1976), *Capital* Vol. I, and (1981), *Capital* Vol. III, Harmondsworth: Penguin Books.

Pearson, Harry W. (1957), 'The Economy Has No Surplus' in Polanyi, Arensberg and Pearson (eds), *Trade and Market in the Early Empires*, New York: The Free Press.

Ricardo, David (1951), *On the Principles of Political Economy and Taxation*, Cambridge: Cambridge University Press.

Sraffa, Piero (1960), *Production of Commodities by Means of Commodities*, Cambridge: Cambridge University Press.

Ste. Croix, G.E.M. de (1981), *The Class Struggle in the Ancient Greek World*, London: Duckworth.

Competition, antitrust and beyond

One of the great historical discoveries in the field of economics was Adam Smith's initial conceptualization of long-run prices or 'natural prices' as the 'centres of gravity' of actual existing market prices. The notion that a long-run equilibrium price could be delineated from accidental day-to-day market prices opened the possibility for studying the systematic competitive forces that determine such prices, helping to establish economics as a truly scientific endeavour.

According to Smith, and later Ricardo and Marx (the 'classical economists'), the key social force establishing natural prices (Smith, Ricardo) or prices of production (Marx) was competition. According to such classical economists, the competitive process consists of a double mechanism that pushes industry profit rates towards equality in the long run. The first mechanism is initiated by investors who move capital across industries in search of the highest rate of profit. This movement of resources then expands the supply in those industries with above-average profitability. The second mechanism concerns the effect of output on price. When augmented supplies meet demand constraints, both prices and profits are forced downward. The same process also works in reverse as well, as capital exits low-profit-rate sectors. This process thus forces profits towards equality. Complete adjustment is only theoretical, since constant perturbations in the economy transform this convergence process into one of oscillation. Thus, at any particular point in time, unequal rates of profit will be observed. But over a long-run period, industries should tend to exhibit equal average profit rates.

Marx must be credited with distinguishing between firms and industries in this process. According to Marx, competition first establishes a single uniform price for each industry. Given different cost structures, this single industry price must imply that firm profit rates are differentiated by competition. At the same time, the process of the formation of prices of production through capital movements equalizes the average rates of profit between industries. Thus, in Marx's view, a uniform price and differentiated firm profit rates within industries are compatible with an equalized rate of profit across industries. In fact, this is the situation that Marx believed would exist empirically because of the constant process of unequal firm innovation. Thus, one can distinguish between two types of equilibrium states in classical theory. The situation emphasized by Marx is a 'quasi' equilibrium state as opposed to a 'full' equilibrium, the latter being the long-run state where both firms' and industry profit rates are equalized.

Following Marx's death, the classical theory of competition lay dormant for almost a century, while the rise of neoclassical economics at the end of the 19th century led to a wholly different conception of competition. Why did early neoclassical economists choose not to build on classical foundations? George Stigler (1957) provided one explanation when he argued that the classical theory had to be abandoned because it lacked the rigour necessary to derive definite mathematical results. For neoclassicals, the drawback of the classical view of competition was that it was merely descriptive; neither the existence of equilibrium nor the welfare conclusions concerning the efficiency of a free market economy could be clearly derived when the classical conception was taken as a foundation. As a result, neoclassical economists developed the alternative model of 'perfect competition'. Although the model was acknowledged to lack realism and required extreme assumptions (such as an infinite number of price-taking firms but none with any influence in the market), its advantage was that all of the welfare results concerning capitalism could be easily derived. This advantage apparently outweighed any loss of realism.

At the turn of the century, Marxist economists were also moving away from the classical theory of competition. In Marxist circles all theories of competition were felt to lack realism and instead research was focused on developing the notion that capitalism had moved into a new stage called 'monopoly capitalism'. There is no doubt that the Marxists of this period were strongly influenced by the rise of giant trusts during the first great wave of mergers and acquisitions in the 1890s. They concluded from these dramatic events that such centres of corporate power were not only novel because of their size, but were also capable of subverting the competitive process described by Marx. (Readers are referred to the entry on Monopoly capitalism in this volume for an extensive discussion of the rise of the monopoly theory during this period.) It was the embrace of this theory by prominent Marxists at the turn of the century (e.g. Hilferding, Lenin and others) that resulted in the monopoly theory's rise to the status of political gospel among radicals for the next six decades.

The first crack in the monopoly capital edifice was instigated, not by Marxists, but by Sraffa and his followers who came to be called the 'neo-Ricardians'. The first phase of this effort involved a criticism of perfect competition. Sraffa (1926) argued that the equilibrium supposedly rigorously derived in perfect competition was actually logically incoherent. One simple way to view Sraffa's concern is to consider the supply curve, defined in the neoclassical model as the portion of the rising marginal cost curve above the average cost curve. Sraffa posed the following question: if the price of output is given (since all firms are price takers), how can the price of inputs rise as outputs are increased? The result depended on the existence of diminishing returns to a scarce factor of production being used up. But this only seemed to make sense when a large firm or industry was involved – the opposite of the assumption of perfect competition. Although Sraffa himself did not take up the issue again for three decades, others such as Joan Robinson tried to develop an alternative model of imperfect competition that did not depend on price-taking behaviour. Instead, in her theory each firm faced a downward sloping demand curve. Although currently the received wisdom on monopoly market structures, Robinson herself abandoned the project because, in her view, supply and demand curves were not independent in her model. Before one could know how much output a supplier would produce at each price, one had first to know his/her demand curve.

Sraffa (1960) returned to price theory with a model of price formation that he believed was wholly independent of supply and demand and based on constant returns to scale. His work was followed by a series of papers formalizing the static model of classical long-run competitive equilibrium. The key assumption in all of these models was that profit rates between sectors were equalized. But this assumption made sense only if a classical-type competitive process was at work. Sraffa's book thus further inspired followers such as Clifton, Garegnani and Eatwell to develop theories showing how giant corporations were in fact compatible with competition. These new theories postulated that large conglomerate firms would continue to move capital between sectors to equalize profit rates either through internal allocation or through financial markets. Thus, although the mechanisms differed somewhat from the classical description, the competitive process itself, it was argued, was still intact.

By the late 1970s and early 1980s, Marxists themselves began to question the monopoly capital dogma. Anwar Shaikh and Willi Semmler in New York, Jane Wheelock in England, Gerard Dumenil in France, the editorial board of *Against the Current* in California and E.K. Hunt at the University of Utah were all early pioneers. The inspiration for the rebellion came not only from the neo-Ricardians, but again from developments in orthodox economics. Industrial organization economists in the 1950s and 1960s abandoned the earlier case study method that had dominated their field and began to examine empirically the economy-wide relationships between market structure and firm performance. In particular, the relationship between industrial concentration, barriers to entry and industrial profits were the subject of much investigation. Believing that industrial concentration was a prerequisite for a successful cartel and that barriers to entry were pervasive, the early expectation was that concentration and barriers to entry should be strongly related to higher profits. Unfortunately, the results were stubbornly disappointing.

While industrial organization economists such as Bain, Stigler, Mann, Weiss, Fuchs and others did find weak relationships, these studies came under intense scrutiny and criticism by economists at the University of Chicago and UCLA. This group of 'Chicago school' economists argued that even the weak relationships previously found were actually only the result of either disequilibrium or efficiency differences. In their view, the overwhelming weight of empirical evidence actually pointed to confirmation of a real competitive process. The process that they described, however, was not the perfect competition of the neoclassical model, but rather a model of competition very close, if not identical, to the classical conception. This highly influential work, while aimed at supporting conservative antitrust policies, also had the unexpected effect of helping to revive the classical competitive tradition.

A threshold difficulty still plagued the Marxists, however. The neo-Ricardians had only advanced verbal arguments concerning how the competitive process might continue to operate. As yet, no one had provided an adequate reply to the original neoclassical criticism that the classical conception lacked the rigour needed to derive actual results mathematically. Nor had the industrial organization economists demonstrated empirically the existence of an equalized rate of profit. To make matters worse, in the midst of this theoretical vacuum, Nikaido, a Japanese economist, authored a well-circulated paper in 1977 purporting to demonstrate that once the classical process was modelled, it could not actually reach an equilibrium. In addition, a series of papers appeared in France in 1981 on the same topic, again with discouraging results.

The breakthrough came in 1983 in Paris when Gerard Dumenil and Dominique Levy (1987) demonstrated that, under realistic conditions, the classical process could be modelled and equilibrium achieved with local stability. Very soon after, Semmler and Flashel made a similar demonstration. Nikaido's error was that he had modelled only half of the classical process. Although prices are determined by quantities in his model, there was no feedback mechanism by which prices could affect quantities through the profit rate. However, once the full cross-over dynamic was modelled, it became clear that the rigorous achievement of equilibrium (and without the aid of the neoclassical auctioneer) was clearly possible. As reviewed by Dumenil and Levy (1991), an entire new field of 'disequilibrium dynamics' subsequently emerged staffed by a large number of talented individuals. The results of this research continue to grow and include a number of interesting links between classical competitive 'microfoundations' and macroeconomic phenomena such as growth, crises and stagnation.

Although the Chicago school had raised serious doubts concerning the evidence presented in support of pervasive monopoly in the American economy, they failed to demonstrate that the competitive process was actually working. For economists within the classical perspective, the biggest drawback to the industrial organization literature was that profit rate differentials were always studied over very short time periods, using questionable variable definitions and always in relation to other variables. Mark Glick and Hans Ehrbar, in a series of papers beginning in 1986, attempted to study the actual convergence process empirically. They found that a process of competition acting to equalize industrial profit rates did indeed exist. The process operates in the long run, but is repeatedly interrupted by the business cycle. Glick and Ehrbar (1988, 1990) found this to be the case both in the US as well as in all other industrialized capitalist countries. Using modern econometric techniques and data sets that became available only in the 1980s, they showed that little or no evidence appeared to exist to support the monopoly capital thesis and that profit rates between industries do tend nearly to equalize.

Today, radical economists supporting aspects of the classical version of competition are in the ascendancy. This means that a larger group of economists should be expected to expand the current set of theoretical and empirical results. If the past is any guide, the evolution of this area of research will continue to be influenced by events in the neoclassical literature. Because the focus in the industrial organization field in the US has shifted to studies of strategic behaviour and their policy implications for antitrust enforcement, and because of the growing interest in competition policy in Europe as of 1992, we should expect that the next important direction for radical economists will be to develop the concrete policy implications of their work. This task has not yet begun.

MARK GLICK

References

Dumenil, G. and Levy, D. (1987), 'The Dynamics of Competition: A Restoration of the Classical Analysis', *Cambridge Journal of Economics*, **11**(2), June, 133–64.

Dumenil, G. and Levy, D. (1991), 'Convergence to Long-Period Positions, with the Benefit of Hindsight', *CEPREMAP Working Paper*.

Glick, M. and Ehrbar, H. (1988), 'Profit Rate Equalization in the U.S. and Europe: An Econometric Investigation', *European Journal of Political Economy*, Special Issue.

Glick, M. and Ehrbar, H. (1990), 'Long-Run Equilibrium in the Empirical Study of Monopoly and Competition', *Economic Inquiry*, **28**(1), January, 151–62.

Nikaido, H. (1977), 'Refutation of the Dynamic Equalizations of Profit Rates in Marx's Scheme of Reproduction', Modelling Research Group, No. 7722, USC (unpublished).

Sraffa, P. (1926), 'The Laws of Returns Under Competitive Conditions', *Economic Journal*, December.

Sraffa, P. (1960), *Production of Commodities by Means of Commodities*, Cambridge: Cambridge University Press.
Stigler, G.J. (1957), 'Perfect Competition Historically Contemplated', *Journal of Political Economy*, **65**(1).

Consumer behaviour

There is probably no major area of economics where so little agreement exists among radical economists as the treatment of consumption. There are significant schools that adhere to each of three broad perspectives: the classical view inherited from Ricardo and Marx, the neoclassical perspective developed by Walras and Jevons, and an institutionalist approach loosely derived from Veblen. These three perspectives contain sharply conflicting views of the individual and the economy. Radical economists have carried out research that can be placed within each of these frameworks, as well as some work that has attempted to combine these approaches.

The classical view places very little emphasis on consumption behaviour. Standard treatments regard consumption as class based, where capitalists and landlords are assumed to engage in luxury consumption, while workers consume a fixed bundle of subsistence goods. The luxury consumption of the former is usually treated as being extraneous to the analysis, except insofar as it constitutes a drain on the resources available to finance investment. The consumption bundle received by workers is regarded simply as a cost in the production process; differences in consumption patterns among workers are assumed away. Ricardo and Marx referred to this bundle as being workers' 'subsistence'. While this use of subsistence was not intended to mean literally physical subsistence, the biological metaphor does accurately convey the sense of uniformity in consumption that characterizes this perspective. Unlike the neoclassical view, in the classical perspective consumption is not viewed as the motivating purpose for economic activity. The motivating purpose is accumulation, which is pursued by capital as an end in itself.

This view is incorporated into modern neo-Ricardian or neo-Marxist models which, in their attempts to analyse the dynamics of the economy, attribute fixed consumption bundles to workers. In the most common formulation, these models assume constant returns to scale, which means that the actual composition of the workers' consumption bundle has absolutely no effect on relative prices or the rate of profit. Economists working in these frameworks follow Marx in recognizing that 'subsistence', or the actual content of workers' consumption bundles, is socially and historically determined, but they see no importance to either the specific contents of the consumption bundles, or to differences in consumption patterns among workers. In this framework, such considerations have no effect on the major economic phenomena these models attempt to explain (relative prices, the rate of profit and the rate of accumulation); therefore they are generally left out of the analysis altogether. The wage itself is usually taken as being determined exogenously through class struggle or through other social and historical circumstances.

Many Post Keynesian or Kaleckian models similarly ignore distinctions among workers, treating consumption simply as one of the components of aggregate demand. These models typically include a consumption function which defines a fixed relationship between aggregate consumption and disposable income. Some models include different consumption functions for workers and capitalists, usually indicating that a higher proportion of wage income goes to consumption than does income generated through profits. In both types of models, however, there is no importance attached to the actual basket of goods that is consumed, nor to differences among individuals.

The neoclassical perspective reverses the logic of the classical approach and treats consumption rather than accumulation as the end of economic activity. In the framework developed by Walras and Jevons in the 19th century, and refined by Samuelson, Arrow, Debreu and others in this century, individuals are assumed to act in a way that maximizes their utility. The actions assumed to be covered by the individual's utility maximization decisions include not only consumption choices, but also the individual's labour supply decisions, their savings decisions (inter-temporal consumption), and even decisions about having children. In short, the utility maximization framework is intended to provide a comprehensive explanation of all individual behaviour. This in turn becomes the basis for all social phenomena, since from this perspective social phenomena are reducible to the actions of individuals.

Neoclassical economists have continually struggled to minimize the number of assumptions needed to usefully apply the utility maximization framework. Perhaps most importantly, they eliminated any basis for comparisons of utility between individuals by arguing that individuals can simply order the desirability of choices for themselves. This removed the Benthamite notion that utility was some underlying substance that could be added and compared across individuals. However the neoclassical approach still requires some very stringent assumptions. In particular it is necessary that individuals either have fixed utility functions (or preference orderings) or that their utility functions change in a well-defined and predictable way. It is also necessary that individuals' valuations of choices, or preferences, are invariant to changes in society. Both of these assumptions are necessary to use comparative static analysis to evaluate different hypothetical situations. In the absence of these assumptions, individuals' preference orderings could not provide the common yardstick that serves as the basis of comparison. For example, if a change in the tax code caused income to be redistributed in a way that substantially altered people's utility functions, it would be impossible to determine if this increased utility, even if all individuals were able to buy at least as much as they could previously.

Many radical economists have explicitly or implicitly accepted the utility maximization framework in their analysis. Foremost among this group would be the 'rational choice Marxists' such as John Roemer, who are explicitly committed to developing the same sort of individualistic explanations used in neoclassical economics. They argue that the structuralist approaches used by more traditional Marxists (or neo-Ricardians) are insufficiently rigorous, and are either incomplete or wrong. An approach that is less explicitly wedded to the neoclassical framework is the 'contested exchange' model developed by Bowles and Gintis (1990). This approach seeks to derive Marxist conclusions by applying the utility maximization framework to workers' behaviour at the work place. The contested exchange approach, along with the larger social structures of accumulation framework with which it is associated, can be distinguished from rational choice Marxism in that it explicitly recognizes that individuals' preferences are determined by the social environment around them, although it also assumes that they can be treated as fixed for most types of analysis. Also, the contested exchange approach explicitly incorporates non-individualistic factors, such as norms of solidarity at the work place, that are generally excluded from neoclassical analysis.

The most important work discussing consumption from an institutionalist perspective is *The Theory of the Leisure Class* (Veblen, 1899). Here Veblen presents an account of consumption behaviour that is explicitly and completely social. He argues that it is impossible for individuals to evaluate an object apart from the social context in which it appears, and that even individuals' notions of the bare necessities of life are socially determined. Furthermore, he argues that the ends served by consumption are primarily social in nature, rather than individual. Individuals perform acts of consumption primarily to establish their place within a social hierarchy, instead of maximizing their utility. Veblen saw little meaning in the notion of utility maximization, since he believed that preferences would constantly change in accordance with fashions and trends within society.

Veblen's view of consumption has the advantage of being consistent with work being carried out in related fields such as sociology, social psychology and marketing. Research in all three disciplines has pointed towards a view of individuals as being very responsive to changing social attitudes and norms. It is very difficult to reconcile the stable preference orderings of the neoclassical approach with such evidence. In addition, Veblen's approach is more consistent with recent writings in epistemology, which increasingly have accepted the notion that knowledge is socially constructed. If individuals' knowledge of the world, and therefore the choices available to them, is mediated by society, it is difficult to then maintain that the choices themselves can be seen as primarily individual in nature. In other words, it is seemingly inconsistent to argue that individuals' knowledge is shaped by their social environment, but that their tastes and desires can be treated as fixed and impervious to changes in this environment.

The disadvantage of an institutionalist approach modelled on Veblen is that his work does not readily lend itself to formalization. Since the claim of economics to scientific status has often rested on the extent to which it has been able to construct formal models of the economy in a manner analogous to physics (Mirowski, 1989), an approach that is not amenable to formalization is quite problematic. Nonetheless, a small but increasing number of economists in both mainstream and radical circles seem willing to adopt an institutionalist perspective (e.g. Hodgson, 1988).

Levine (1981) has perhaps gone furthest in this direction, where he has attempted to incorporate a more social view of consumption into a dynamic model of the economy loosely following Steindl and Keynes. In this work, the rate at which the economy grows depends on investment, which will in turn depend in part on the rate at which new products can be introduced into the consumption patterns of different economic strata. The rate of product diffusion of course has a quantitative element, in that growth in income is necessary to allow for increased consumption, but it also has a qualitative element in that consumption entails actually using an object, and not simply its purchase. The use of an object, for example using a car in place of a bicycle, involves altering an individual's lifestyle. There is a limited rate at which individuals can adopt and fully familiarize themselves with these changes in lifestyle. This will limit both the rate at which individuals can incorporate new items in their patterns of consumption and also the rate at which firms can develop new products to meet needs that evolve out of these new lifestyles. Levine's framework allows for a far more extensive treatment of the qualitative aspects of economic development, but it lacks the sort of mathematical elegance that characterizes work coming out of the neoclassical framework.

It is unlikely that these distinct approaches to consumption will be reconciled in the foreseeable future. Each is firmly grounded in a broader paradigm that excludes the claims made by the competing approaches. For example, the classical view treats the class division of society as being the central feature of economic life. Distinctions between individual workers, and the choices workers are able to make, are seen as inconsequential. Similarly, the neoclassical paradigm takes individual preference orderings as the foundation of all economic and social analysis. From this perspective, any explanation is incomplete until it can be grounded in the actions of rational individuals attempting to maximize their utility. There is comparatively little in the way of a common conceptual framework that could provide the grounds for deciding between these views. Nor are there any obvious empirical tests which could be a basis for rejecting one or more of these perspectives. In short, it is likely that radical economists will continue to perform research that is based on each of these three approaches to consumption.

DEAN BAKER

References

Bowles, S. and Gintis, H. (1990), 'Contested Exchange: New Microfoundations for the Political Economy of Capitalism', *Politics and Society*, **18**(2), June.

Hodgson, G.M. (1988), *Economics and Institutions*, Philadelphia: University of Pennsylvania Press.

Levine, D.P. (1981), *Economic Theory*, Vol. II, London: Routledge and Kegan Paul.

Mirowski, P. (1989), *More Heat Than Light*, Cambridge: Cambridge University Press.

Veblen, T. (1899), *The Theory of the Leisure Class*, Boston: Houghton Mifflin Company: reprinted 1973.

Corporatism

The idea of a progressive social order subject to the influence of human action evolved simultaneously with the rise of capitalism. Subsequent theories of capitalism have offered competing explanations of this order and its consequences for individual and social well-being. Among the competing explanations, economic theories of capitalism have gained preeminence, in part from the legitimacy derived by conforming to the methodological strictures of mathematics and physics, but also because they have provided compelling explanations of how *homo oeconomicus* can produce social cohesion even when pursuing his or her own narrow interest simply by responding to competitive market pressures and the rule of law embodied in private property rights.

Economic theories have not altogether disregarded social ties other than those established through the market. However, their inclusion has been to correct market coordination failures rather than as integral to the reproduction of the capitalist order itself; moreover, they have been almost exclusively identified with political ties established through the state. Even so, the collective expression of state action has coexisted uneasily with the independent and selfish maximizing individual, and the opportunity to influence economic choices through political ties has remained at odds with the allocative efficiency of perfectly competitive markets. The resulting state-market dichotomy has provided fertile ground for policy debate amongst economists.

Dissatisfaction with this economic vision of the capitalist order has given rise to two recurring questions. First, if the effectiveness of competitive pressures cannot be isolated from political and social ties, can a uniform set of coordinating mechanisms adequately explain different national economic experiences? Second, if uncertainty and conflict are endemic to the social landscape, can order be expected to emerge spontaneously in response simply to price incentives? These challenges to *homo oeconomicus* have been felt with particular force on the labour market where social ties and political expression have been inseparable from purely economic forces.

Corporatism epitomizes the challenge to an exclusively economic coordination of the labour market. As such it is a concept which implies that the organizational consensus between the two sides of industry required to achieve socioeconomic stability can only be reached through appropriate political structures which integrate economic interests at the national level, thereby providing a framework for managing the conflict associated with the employment contract. That said, corporatism is a far from transparent concept and has itself undergone considerable mutation and transformation in the course of its intellectual life.

Although corporatist sentiments can be found in the ideas of many 19th-century thinkers, it was only in the latter part of the century and in reaction to the rise of industrial capitalism and the fledgling voices of organized labour that the Catholic church found an opportunity to propagate alternative organizational structures, resembling the feudal system of guilds, to foster social harmony between employer and worker. Later, following the carnage of the First World War and the subsequent collapse of existing economic and social ties, the Italian fascist state was able to introduce a corporate legal order aimed at suppressing the conflictual relations of the market, particularly those emanating from the labour market. Despite its brief moment of triumph, Italian fascism faced a deep-seated contradiction between its belief in a *natural* consensus of the nation and the need to *impose* this consensus on conflicting interest groups.

Corporatism as an alternative to the market order, at least in the more developed capitalist world, disappeared with the defeat of the authoritarian state. Rather, an agenda for the modern state was better expressed by more technocratic responses to the new economic realities of the period. In light of the economic and political experiences of the 1930s, the new macroeconomic agenda for the state, closely identified with Keynes's *General Theory*, offered a timely response to the imbalances and inequities emanating from the labour market that was also consistent with democratic practices. However, despite its association with the interests of organized labour in the fight against mass unemployment, Keynesianism largely failed to include a satisfactory explanation of trade union behaviour in its analysis of macroeconomic disequilibrium. This was already apparent in Keynes's own ambiguous explanation of wage determination and was reflected more generally in the institutional assumptions made by the new macroeconomics. On the one hand, Keynesians assumed that trade unions would acquiesce to a reduction in real wages following a general price increase, but not to a cut in money wages. This provided the opportunity for fiscal and monetary policy instruments to forge a convergent interest between macroeconomic and microeconomic outcomes. On the other hand, their instrumental solution to economic problems assumed that the state – and more specifically those responsible for economic policy – could restore equilibrium in abstraction from the collective expression of powerful interest groups. These assumptions were symbolized by the Phillips curve which provided empirical support for active demand management to steer the economy between the twin dangers of mass unemployment and accelerating inflation, but did little to provide a more convincing institutional rationale for such a policy.

The triumph of Keynesianism fostered a reassessment and revival of corporatism among political scientists who observed a growing interaction between political and economic coordination in the post-war economy. Their critique of the instrumental notion of state action and their concern to explain the growing politicization of economic policy were much indebted to Michal Kalecki's (1971) political business cycle theory. However, in contrast to Kalecki's own pessimistic expectation that the fusion of political and economic forces would prefigure a return to fascism, political corporatists perceived a new form of regulated capitalism in which the appropriate political representation of economic interests and their inclusion in policy making had become a necessary condition for the formation and implementation of measures to guarantee macroeconomic stability.

A burgeoning literature identified emergent corporatist institutions, detailed a new policy agenda and situated political alliances behind the new regime. The analysis quickly converged on the idea that an effective macroeconomic policy regime which could guarantee full employment, low inflation and growth required a political consensus or a social contract incorporating labour in the process of policy formation. The resulting political exchange between major economic interest groups implied trading Keynesian expansionary policy for wage restraint and a managerial prerogative on the shop floor. Although political corporatists argued over whether this was an equal exchange (cf. Lehmbruch, 1979), the successful outcome of corporatist management of labour market conflict was generally recognized to hinge on a viable incomes policy which could generate consent from the national centres of industrial bargaining to the enterprise level. Beginning with the Dutch experience in the 1950s, the consolidation of the Swedish model in the 1960s, concerted agreements in Germany from the late 1960s and the British experience with social contracts during the 1970s, political corporatists have found support for their argument of a widespread and structural convergence in modern capitalist societies towards labour market consensus.

Despite its plausible analysis of state policy, the life of political corporatism was brief, cut short by two striking challenges to its core analysis. On the one hand, further research on particular episodes of incomes policy revealed very different institutional foundations. In particular, the organization of trade unions and corresponding patterns of wage bargaining did not seem to warrant a uniform corporatist label. On the other hand and perhaps more significantly, the notion of a convergent response to common economic problems seemed inconsistent with the divergent policies introduced by ostensibly similar political structures after the oil shock of the early 1970s (Scharpf, 1985).

These findings have been absorbed by macroeconomists, who have revised the notion of corporatism to fill the vacuum left by the breakdown of the Phillips curve and to rebuff critics who insisted that, by impeding labour market flexibility, active macroeconomic policy had increased the equilibrium rate of unemployment and prevented an efficient response to supply shocks compatible with the expectations of labour market agents.

Bruno and Sachs (1985) were the first to extend corporatism in this direction, explaining the different speeds at which economies closed the gap between real wages and the marginal productivity of labour, following the price shocks of the early 1970s, by their different patterns of wage bargaining. In particular, they suggested that the informational asymmetries which produce inflexible wages could be corrected by centralized organizations of workers and employers more certain of each other's actions and less likely to engage in opportunistic behaviour. Their analysis has been refined by subsequent research into a corporatist hypothesis which purports to find a U-shaped relation between labour market performance and the scope of labour market bargaining institutions. Nominal wage stability is a public good whereby the benefits, in terms of higher employment or lower inflation, are not exclusively captured by those making the required sacrifice in response to unexpected shocks. Under these circumstances, prisoner's dilemma problems and free-riding are likely to produce sub-optimal outcomes. Consequently, the labour market response to external shocks depends upon the level of bargaining between employees and management and the extent to which trade unions bear the costs of their actions. In enterprise-level wage bargaining, trade union demands for higher wages are immediately translated into a fall in employment, reducing the likelihood that workers will price themselves out of a job and ensuring that pressure is quickly exerted on nominal wages to restore labour market equilibrium following a price shock. Under central bargaining, although unions are in a stronger position to impose their demands on labour market outcomes, they are also in a position to assess the wider impact of their own actions on others and subsequently back on themselves; any benefits from wage moderation, following a price shock, could thereby be internalized and opportunistic behaviour by any group of workers rapidly punished by the central authority. Between these extremes, unions are strong enough to impose disequilibrating outcomes on the labour market but not encompassing enough to bear a large enough fraction of the cost to ameliorate their actions.

The corporatist hypothesis has subsequently been tested against various indicators of economic performance: inflationary pressure, investment and growth rates, levels of income inequality and the skill profile of the labour force have all been measured in relation to the degree of centralization, with varying success. However, at least on theoretical grounds, the greater the presence of externalities, the more likely centralized structures can steer towards a satisfactory outcome (Pohjola, 1991).

The identification of corporatism with centralized labour market institutions has clarified the mechanics of wage bargaining, but has largely ignored the concerns raised by political scientists. Recent attempts towards integration have tried to locate different patterns of wage bargaining in their broader institutional context by addressing the balance of power within centralized bodies and their resulting priorities (see Pekarinnen *et al.*, 1991). Additionally, the one-sided attention previously paid to trade union organization in determining labour market performance has been corrected by considering the organization and scope of employer organizations (Soskice, 1990). In both cases, the important role of longer-term ties between potentially hostile parties has been emphasized and the diversity of coordinating structures in determining the performance of capitalist societies has been confirmed.

The concept of corporatism has evolved from a broadly conceived alternative to the market order, through a concept of state regulation to a more benign theory of centralized wage bargaining. The unifying thread is the idea that competitive market pressures do not guarantee an orderly or acceptable economic outcome at the national level and that bargaining and other social ties are required for reaching some degree of consensus between conflicting parties on the labour market. Missing from this discussion, however, has been the integration of coordination problems with the processes of economic development which, under capitalist relations, have reflected a delicate balance between creative and destructive forces. Consequently, dynamic issues of technological change and innovation, as well as how the burdens and benefits of economic growth are distributed, have eluded the corporatist discussion of labour market coordination.

RICHARD WRIGHT

References

Bruno, M. and Sachs, J. (1985), *The Economics of Worldwide Stagflation*, Oxford: Basil Blackwell.

Kalecki, M. (1971), *Selected Essays on the Dynamics of the Capitalist Economy, 1933–70*, Cambridge: Cambridge University Press.

Lehmbruch, G. (1979), 'Liberal Corporatism and Party Government' in G. Lehmbruch and P. Schmitter (eds), *Trends towards Corporatist Intermediation*, London: Sage Publications.

Pekarinnen, J. *et al.* (eds) (1991), *Coping with the Crisis: Some Lessons from the Corporatist Experience*, Oxford: Oxford University Press.

Pohjola, M. (1991), 'Corporatism and Wage Bargaining' in Pekarinnen, op. cit.

Scharpf, F. (1985), 'Economic and Institutional Constraints of Full Employment Strategies: Sweden, Austria and West Germany, 1973–1982' in J. Goldthorpe (ed.), *Order and Conflict in Contemporary Capitalism*, Oxford: Clarendon Press.

Soskice, D. (1990), 'Wage Determination: The Changing Role of Institutions in Advanced Industrial Countries', *Oxford Economic Policy Review*, No. 4, 36–61.

Costs of production

This entry focuses on the definition of cost and on the problem of changes in costs in relation to the quantity produced. Cost is defined as the value of the resources needed for an economic operation.

In Marx the value of goods is given by the quantity of socially necessary labour, that is, the 'average' quantity of labour needed for producing in normal conditions. The quantity of socially necessary labour is considered the 'real cost' and is regarded as both the substance and measure of exchange value. 'Capitalist cost' corresponds only to the anticipated capital, obtained by adding up the costs for the raw materials and equipment wear and tear (constant capital), and the costs for wages (variable capital).

The definition of 'real cost' is abandoned by Sraffa (1960) even though, in his rigorous theory of relative prices he does take up the classical concepts of reproducibility, surplus, circularity of production and free competition (assumption of freedom of movement of financial capital and uniform rate of profits). In Sraffa's model, input and output prices are determined by a simultaneous equations system. Consequently, there is a reciprocal interdependence between cost and price for all commodities which enter (directly or indirectly) into the production of all commodities. Sraffa prefers to avoid the term 'cost of production' because this term has come to be 'inseparably linked with the supposition' that it stands for quantities that can be measured 'independently of, and prior to, the determination of the prices of the products' (Sraffa, 1960, pp. 8–9).

The problem of variations in costs in relation to changes in the quantity produced is analysed by the classics. Decreasing costs are discussed in relation to technical change and the division of labour (Adam Smith's dynamic increasing returns), while increasing costs are tied to the scarcity of fertile land and are considered within the theory of income distribution (Malthus, Torrens and Ricardo's theory of rent).

Marx shares Ricardo's belief that 'if all circumstances remained unchanged', the increased quantity produced of a good would make for constant average production costs. But in the capitalist system, the social and technical conditions of the labour process are continuously being revolutionized in order to get higher profit by raising the productivity of labour. Dynamic increasing returns are obtained by improving equipment and by augmenting, at the same time, the dimension of scale.

It is self-evident that productivity increases, resulting from variations in the size of *a single firm*, are incompatible with a static theory of perfect competitive equilibrium. If an individual firm can decrease its average costs by increasing production, 'it will obtain a monopoly of the whole business of its trade' (Marshall, 1890, p. 380; Sraffa, 1925, pp. 41–2). Therefore, in perfect competition there may be increasing returns internal to industry, but they have to be external to the firm. It *must* be assumed that the individual firm operates with diminishing returns to scale beyond a certain point (U-shaped long-period cost curves).

As far as the collective supply curve is concerned, Sraffa showed that neither rising nor decreasing long-period industry supply curves are compatible with the static partial equilibrium analysis in perfect competition. In fact, the collective long-period supply curve may increase or decrease only if input prices rise or fall with a change in the total quantity supplied. But in a partial equilibrium analysis, input price variations cannot be considered because input prices are given as parameters. In short, as the hypothesis of *ceteris paribus* imposes, the supply curve of a commodity must be independent of demand and supply conditions of all other commodities, inputs included. If the price of inputs is assumed as a parameter and each firm produces the optimal quantity, the long-period collective supply curve will be horizontal, because the quantity supplied can only be increased with the entry of new firms operating with optimal plant. With a horizontal long-period collective supply curve, cost determines price, while demand determines quantity (Sraffa, 1925, pp. 56ff; 1926, p. 541].

Sraffa notices some contradictions between these *logical conclusions* (U-shaped individual firm long-period average cost curve in perfect competition and horizontal collective long-period supply curve in partial analysis) and the *empirical evidence*.

Firstly, increasing returns external to the firm and internal to the industry are quite rare phenomena in modern industry, where industrial firms usually operate with diminishing internal total unit costs. Consequently, the limit of firm expansion does not arise from costs, but from the difficulty of selling a larger quantity of goods without reducing their price.

Secondly, Sraffa observes that an industry may turn out to be characterized by an increasing or decreasing supply curve according to the definition of 'industry' adopted:

> the wider the definition which we assume for 'an industry' – that is, the more nearly it includes all the undertakings which employ a given *factor* of production, as, for example, agriculture or iron industry – the more probable will it be that the forces which make for diminishing returns will play an important part in it; the more restrictive this definition – the more nearly it includes, therefore, only those undertakings which produce a given type of consumable *commodity*, as, for example, fruit or nails – the greater will be the probability that the forces which make for increasing returns will predominate in it (Sraffa, 1926, p. 538).

In conclusion, 'it is very difficult to classify the various industries' according to whether they belong to one or the other category (ibid.).

Sraffa's critique led him to formulate his theory of relative prices independent of the partial equilibrium method, of the concepts of 'supply and demand curves' and, more generally, of the marginalist analysis itself. In his theory no hypothesis on returns to scale is required because Sraffa leaves the volume of production unchanged (Sraffa, 1960, p. v). The assumption of given quantities produced enables the formulation of a consistent theory of relative prices based on production conditions and on income distribution. It excludes the possibility of studying, *within the same theory*, (i) the variation of costs in relation to the quantity produced, (ii) the behaviour of the firm and (iii) the changes in techniques and in demand for the final goods. This entails a distinction between the theory of relative prices on the one hand, and theories of the behaviour of the firm and innovative processes on the other. This analytical separation does not necessarily imply incompatibility between the various non-neoclassical lines of research which focus on different analytical issues (Roncaglia, 1991, pp. 205–6).

From the 1930s on many scholars started analysing the costs of the firm in a non-neoclassical context. Empirical investigations have confirmed the idea, suggested by Sraffa and taken up by Kalecki, that industrial firms operate, at least as a first approximation, in conditions of constant average variable costs if the fixed input is divisible. In the short period, decreasing total average costs are due to a variation in proportions between inputs, permitting a more efficient use of the plant, increasing its degree of utilization and reducing idle periods. Beyond the point of optimal utilization, increases in output bring about a rise in total average costs. However, industrial firms generally design their plants to run at 70–80 per cent of maximum productive capacity, thereby ensuring themselves reserve capacity to handle temporary increases in demand or unexpected plant breakdowns.

Production processes are often characterized by the presence of 'limitational inputs'. For instance, measuring marginal productivity of labour in a textile firm means varying the quantity of labour while keeping constant other inputs such as yarn, energy, water, machines hours, etc. But if the quantity of yarn is kept constant, no increase in output will be obtained and marginal productivity will appear to be zero. A similar difficulty occurs with team production, because each team member's marginal productivity is impossible to determine. In both these cases, the concepts of marginal productivity and thus marginal costs appear analytically weak and with no practical relevance.

In long-period static analysis, increasing returns are obtained when a larger scale leads to reduced input requirements per unit of product. Increasing returns to scale are linked to the possibility of increasing the quantity of all inputs. This usually allows a reorganization of production as well as changes in the combination of inputs. Decreasing returns to scale occur when there is some restriction that prevents some elements of production from increasing in optimal proportion.

Organizational capacity is often considered as a limit to the expansion of increasing returns. But there are no reasons why this capacity might not in the long period be increased by adopting more efficient control systems and allocating many administrative and organizational tasks to specialist staff. Organizational capacity ought to be considered as a limit on the growth rate of a firm at any moment in time, rather than on size *per se* (Kalecki, 1937, p. 105).

Returns of scale are technical in nature because they are independent of any assumptions about the prices of inputs. The notion of economies of scale is used to refer to a situation where the prices of inputs may vary in relation to the quantities acquired. Economies of scale occur when a larger dimension of scale leads to a lower total average cost. The scale dimension is generally expressed by productive capacity, i.e. the optimal producible quantity in relation to given organizational and institutional conditions.

In spite of methodological differences, numerous empirical studies seem to agree on the presence of significant economies of scale in most of the industries examined (cf. Pratten, 1988). Four groups of factors which combine to produce economies of scale can be identified:

1. Technical factors related to the three-dimensionality of space, heat dissipation and the indivisibility of some production elements.
2. Statistical factors arising from the possibility of reducing all types of stocks or reserves (e.g. raw materials, machine spare parts, working capital) by increasing the overall quantities involved in production.
3. Organizational and administrative factors linked to the growth of coordination capacity as the company expands.

4. Economies by controlling input and output markets (pecuniary economies in buying inputs, advantages in raising capital, more discretion in fixing the output price).

Economies of scale determine a decrease in total average costs to the point of minimum optimum scale (MOS) or minimum efficient scale (MES). If the firm wants to increase its productive capacity further, the number of plants may be multiplied (Kalecki, 1937, p. 105). Beyond this limit, the average cost becomes constant and we are faced, not with a curve, but with a series of discrete corresponding points and different technologies available at any given moment. Moreover, if discontinuities exist in the sizes of available plants, there will be no continuous curve even in that part preceding the limit corresponding to the maximum plant, as it is impossible to move from one plant to another by small increases (Sylos Labini, 1956, ch. 1).

With multi-plant firms, a scale increase in one plant may lead to reductions in unit costs in other plants, due to a better balance of processes which cuts the waste of productive capacity. The need to combine the productive capacities of single machines, plants or single stages of the production process, according to specific relations of complementarity, means that an increase in scale takes place in discrete jumps.

Efficiency is not only linked with size. It also depends on many other factors: capital endowment and the conditions of the financial markets; the characteristics of entrepreneurship; accumulated output over time and the time profile of production processes; technical training; the number of different outputs produced by an individual firm; transaction costs and market characteristics; regulations affecting employment; tax legislation and mechanisms of innovation diffusion. All these factors change from firm to firm and in relation to how its specific institutional environment evolves. Hence the problem of the optimum size of a firm is not unequivocally predetermined, since it 'is not a technical problem like that of the optimum size of a plant. The optimum size of an organization involves comparisons of quality and efficiency, and therefore belongs to the qualitative residual of the analysis of a productive process' (Georgescu-Roegen, 1964, p. 296).

Efficiency is also linked to technical change. There is a close interdependence between technical change and economies of scale, because an increase in dimensions may favour the adoption of new techniques, just as the introduction of new techniques may allow an increase in the scale of production. If a new technique is associated with an increase in the dimension of scale, we have dynamic economies of scale. Dynamic economies of scale are also due to an increase in specialization and to learning processes.

New technologies may require high investment in fixed capital and often cause the importance of service activities – such as planning, design, organization, marketing, advertising, administration – to increase significantly. This entails a reduction in the share of direct cost (in particular labour cost) in relation to total cost. The introduction of computer-based technology may bring about shorter production processes and a lower cost of production flexibility. The cost reduction in producing differentiated goods in a flexible way with the same equipment is mainly due to decreased set-up times. A shorter set-up time allows the production of a wide range of outputs in small batches without the need for large inventories. Computer-based technology may thus provide the opportunity to enjoy both economies of scale and economies of scope at the same time.

MARIO MORRONI

References

Georgescu-Roegen, N. (1964), 'Measure, Quality and Optimum Scale' in C.R. Rao (ed.), *Essays in Econometric and Planning*, Oxford: Pergamon Press; reprinted in *Energy and Economic Myths*, New York: Pergamon Press (1976), 271–96.

Kalecki, M. (1937), 'Entrepreneurial Capital and Investment', *Economica*; new version in *Theory of Economic Dynamics*, London: George Allen and Unwin (1954); reprinted in *Selected Essays on the Dynamics of the Capitalist Economy*, Cambridge: Cambridge University Press (1971).

Marshall, A. (1890), *Principles of Economics*, London: Macmillan; 8th ed. 1920; reprinted 1982.

Pratten, C.F. (1988), *A Survey of the Economies of Scale*, Economic Papers, Brussels: Commission of the European Communities.

Roncaglia, A. (1991), 'The Sraffian Schools', *Review of Political Economy*, **3**(2), 187–219.

Sraffa, P. (1925), 'Sulle relazioni tra costo e quantità prodotta', *Annali di Economia*, reprinted in *Saggi*, Bologna: Il Mulino (1986), 15–65.

Sraffa, P. (1926), 'The Laws of Returns under Competitive Conditions', *The Economic Journal*, **36**, 535–50.

Sraffa, P. (1960), *Production of Commodities by Means of Commodities*, Cambridge: Cambridge University Press.

Sylos Labini, P. (1962), *Oligopoly and Technical Progress*, Cambridge Mass.: Harvard University Press (revised ed. 1969); original edition in Italian (1956), *Oligopolio e progresso tecnico*, Torino: Einaudi.

Crisis

Crisis is a critical, if over-used, term in the lexicon of radical political economy. The term appears in many and various radical writings but with rather different meanings.

The more classical uses of the term in radical political economy accord with its definitions in the *Oxford English Dictionary* (On Historical Principles, 1933 edition), namely: 'The point in the progress of a disease when a change takes place which is decisive of recovery or death ... or ... A turning point in the progress of anything; also a state of affairs in which a decisive change for better or worse is imminent' (p. 124).

Both these meanings feature in *The Communist Manifesto* and other classical Marxist works. The notion of crisis as a turning point is central to Marxist economics. Crises are endemic in capitalism, with continual, temporary epidemics of overproduction which form part of the trade cycle. The sequence identified runs as follows. The first phase is growth. Increasing production leads to increasing employment, which in turn leads to greater demand, which in turn causes asset and commodity prices to rise, increases profits and investment and leads to further increases in production. This expansion takes place in a competitive, unplanned way. In the later periods of this phase, growth becomes chaotic and unsustainably fast. Expectations of ever-growing markets lead firms to increase supply rapidly. Eventually supply exceeds demand. There is a crisis of overproduction. This crisis must be resolved by a phase of recession during which prices and profit rates fall. The weakest firms go bankrupt. Companies remaining in production engage in every possible form of cost minimization and rationalization. This leads to increasing unemployment and a fall in demand which in turn leads to more bankruptcies. This process has a cumulative nature but does not continue forever. Eventually, the combination of the improved productivity of the firms still in business with exogenous factors such as the development of new markets, significant technological innovation or government action lead to recovery. Once the firms who weathered the recession have disposed of their surplus stocks, prices and profits start to rise. Production is increased. This then leads to a new phase in which growth becomes self-sustaining and cumulative. Eventually, supply exceeds demand. There is a new crisis of overproduction.

Such crises are wholly integral to the development of capitalism, playing an important functional role in creating a new, albeit temporary, equilibrium. The development of capitalism does not proceed smoothly, but rather in fits and starts, with two steps forward being followed by one step back. Analysing these crises in *The Communist Manifesto*, Marx and Engels (1848) said, 'And how does the bourgeoisie get over these crises? On the one hand by enforced destruction of a mass of productive forces; on the other, by the conquest of new markets, and by the more thorough exploitation of the old ones. That is to say, by paving the way for more extensive and more destructive crises, and by diminishing the means whereby crises are prevented' (p. 86).

This analysis lays the foundation for discussing the second type of capitalist crisis identified by Marxist economics. This is where the crisis is structural, where it becomes more than a turning point in the progress of capitalism and instead marks a decisive turning point between the recovery or death of the capitalist system as a whole. Lives have been inspired by, dedicated to and lost in the conviction that the final crisis of capitalism has arrived. In fact, the capitalist economic system has shown remarkable powers of development and mutation which have kept it relatively healthy and vigorous while many socialist economic systems (which were to have supplanted capitalism) faced their own structural crises in the 1980s and died, to be replaced by new capitalist forms. Despite the failure of the more millenarian Marxist vision of the capitalist crisis to materialize, the less dramatic form certainly remains a modern phenomenon. In fact, it has gained in importance since the mid-1970s after the long boom of the post-World War II years fizzled out.

More recent writers influenced by Marx have also used the term crisis to represent a turning point, although its time span sometimes shifts from a brief period to decades. In an essay on 'The Forward March of Labour Halted?', Hobsbawm (1981) argued that '... the forward march of labour and the labour movement, which Marx predicted, appears to have come to a halt in this century about twenty-five to thirty years ago. Both the working class and the labour movement since then have been passing through a period of crisis ...' (p. 1). Later on in the same piece, Hobsbawm used crisis in the more dramatic, decisive life-and-death sense when he argued, '...we are today in a period of world crisis for capitalism, and more specifically, of the crisis – one might almost say the breakdown – of the British capitalist society' (p. 18).

When Hobsbawm talked of the crisis, 'almost the breakdown' of capitalism, he also moved towards using the term in the same way as many other recent writers of radical political economy have done. I will define this as using crisis to represent deep-seated, fundamental economic and social problems. To such writers a situation of crisis is one in which profound economic and social ills indicate that the system which has given rise to them is sick and must be changed. Whether the system is inherently terminally ill or not is usually left undiscussed, often for pragmatic political reasons. Examples of this are to be found across the political spectrum of the left. The opening sentence of the *Brandt Report* (1985) reads: 'It is widely recognised that the prevailing economic crisis is the worst since the 1930s, when mass unemployment spawned nationalism, fascism and the seeds of global war' (p. 13).

This conception of crisis, in more or less dramatic forms, has been a central component of the thinking of Socialist and Communist parties for many years. For example, the Communist party of Great Britain's 1978 programme, 'The British Road to Socialism', opened with the statement: 'Britain is in deep economic, political and social crisis. It is not the result of natural catastrophes, of forces beyond our control, but of the capitalist system under which we live, and of the world crisis of capitalism' (p. 5).

Greens as well as Socialists and Communists have shared this notion of crisis. Germany's best known Green activist of the 1980s and then member of the Bundestag, Petra Kelly, began *Fighting for Hope* (1984) by speaking of 'a period of crisis ... [in which] a third to a half of the 2,000 million people in the developing world are either starving or suffering from malnutrition' (pp. 11–12).

The notion of crisis as a set of serious problems produced by failures of the system has also found favour in a host of publications dealing with particular local and regional economic problems.

The rediscovery of Gramsci by the English-speaking left in the 1970s gave a further twist to the analysis of crisis. When Gramsci (1971) employed the concept of 'organic' crisis, he suggested that a 'crisis occurs, sometimes lasting for decades. This exceptional duration means that uncurable structural contradictions have revealed themselves ...' (p. 178). This concept of organic crisis has subsequently been widely employed in discussing numerous political, institutional and cultural questions.

The analysis of crisis and the desire for 'solutions' were also critical features of Keynes's *General Theory* (1936). Keynes used crisis in the sense of a major turning point: 'There is, however, another characteristic of what we call the Trade Cycle which our explanation must cover if it is to be adequate; namely, the phenomenon of the crisis – the fact that the substitution of a downward for an upward tendency often takes place suddenly and violently ...' (p. 314).

Crisis was of major concern to both Marx and Keynes and to the traditions which subsequently flowered in their names. A fair, first approximation is that Marxists saw crisis as an inherent characteristic of capitalism which could only be finally cured by the overthrow of the system which produced it. For Keynes, crisis was a treatable illness which would only become fatal if left untended. This difference lead to major antagonisms. But during the 1980s it became clear that both traditions were outside the mainstream of the then prevailing orthodoxy in economics, which defines away crisis altogether in the endless pursuit of equilibrium. As Galbraith (1987) argues: 'In the United States ... economics divides today as between classicists (the overwhelming number) and institutionalists, between those committed to the inevitable and constant equilibrium and those who, with much less claim to scientific precision, accept a world of evolution and continuing change' (p. 129).

There are a number of problems with the popular, widespread use of the term crisis to represent deep-seated, fundamental economic and social ills which indicate that the system which has given rise to them is sick and must be changed. There is a tendency to overestimate the instability of the situation. This frequently leads to the belief that because there are deep-seated problems, the situation is bound to change dramatically, either by a decisive move towards the left or by a shift to a new period of extreme authoritarianism or even fascism. Of course, in the advanced industrialized, capitalist countries, neither course has occurred since the end of the Second World War. However this does not mean that the notion of crisis is entirely redundant. Disequilibrium and unceasing change are characteristic of modern societies, not cold mechanical equilibrium. At the very least, there are market and coordination failures.

Radical economists are used to fighting a battle in which even the possibility of structural disequilibrium, let alone crisis, is denied. In neoclassical economics, crisis and serious social problems are simply defined away or attributed to the effects of bad government. Of course, the relative inability of radical economists to analyse the economic problems and profound crises of the former Soviet Union and similar societies has weakened the appeal of any radical analysis of crisis in advanced industrial societies. But the recurrence of recession in many industrial countries in the early 1980s and then again in the early 1990s, the international debt crisis, big fluctuations in asset prices and the persistence of widespread unemployment in most industrial states have brought ideas of disequilibria and even crisis back on stage.

In truth, both mainstream and radical economics themselves are in a period of crisis. Trusted prescriptions no longer work. Old explanations no longer serve. A turning point is being reached. The outcome is unclear. Perhaps a useful way of interpreting this crisis is as a drama. Nobel prize-winner Myrdal's analysis in Asian Drama (1968) has a modern resonance:

> Behind all the complexities and dissimilarities we sense a rather clear-cut set of conflicts and a common theme as in a drama. The action in this drama is speeding toward a climax. Tension is mounting: economically, socially, and politically. … In the classic conception of drama – as in the theoretical phase of a scientific study – the will of the actors was confined to the shackles of determinism. … In life, while the drama is still unfolding – as in the practical phase of a study, when policy inferences are drawn from value premises as well as from premises based on empirical evidence – the will is instead assumed to be free, within limits, to choose between alternative courses of action. History, then, is not taken to be predetermined, but within the power of man to shape. And the drama thus conceived is not necessarily tragedy (p. 35).

DAVID GREEN

References

Brandt, W. and Manley, M. (1985), *Global Challenge, From Crisis to Cooperation: Breaking the North-South Stalemate (The Brandt Report)*, London: Pan.

Galbraith, J.K. (1987), *A History of Economics*, London: Penguin.

Gramsci, A. (1971), *Selections from Prison Notebooks* (edited and translated into English by Quintin Hoare and Geoffrey Nowell Smith), London: Lawrence and Wishart.

Hobsbawm E. (1981), 'The Forward March of Labour Halted', London: Verso Editions and NLB.

Kelly, P. (1984), *Fighting for Hope*, London: Chatto and Windus.
Keynes, J.M. (1936), *The General Theory of Employment, Interest and Money*, London: Macmillan.
Marx, K. and Engels, F. (1848), *The Communist Manifesto* (translated into English by S. Moore, 1888), Harmondsworth: Penguin Books. (Quotation from 1967 edition.)
Myrdal, G. (1968), *Asian Drama*, Harmondsworth: Allen Lane.

Cumulative causation

The term 'cumulative causation' was first used by the Swedish economist, Gunnar Myrdal, in his classic book *Economic Theory and Underdeveloped Regions* (1957), and is designed to convey the reinforcing processes by which the patterns of uneven development between regions, between countries and between many economic and social phenomena may be perpetuated and even accentuated. The concept of cumulative causation is thus a direct challenge to static equilibrium theory which teaches that, if divergences in economic phenomena exist, forces will come into play which narrow those differences and ultimately eliminate them. Static equilibrium theory relies on the functioning of free-market forces but, in Myrdal's model of cumulative causation, the free play of market forces works towards inequality. The literature on trade and development abounds with equilibrium theorems. Take the case of regional inequalities in wages and unemployment rates. Assume one high wage/low unemployment region (A) and another low wage/high unemployment region (B). According to static neoclassical equilibrium theory, the process of factor migration between the regions should in time eliminate the regional divergence. According to the neoclassical story, labour should migrate from B to A where the wage is higher, and capital should 'flow' from A to B where the rate of profit is higher (because the wage is lower), thus equalizing wages, the rate of profit and the rate of unemployment. What the story forgets, however, is that migration is a dynamic process, and that movements in factor supplies also affect demand. Labour migrating from depressed to prosperous regions brings its own demand which makes region A a more attractive region to invest in than B, perpetuating the divergences between A and B.

Trade is supposed to be a substitute for factor mobility which will equalize returns to factors of production across regions or countries, but trade is another mechanism in the Myrdal model which in practice is likely to perpetuate or exacerbate inequalities. Trade benefits the strong at the expense of the weak, particularly if some regions are forced by comparative advantage to specialize in diminishing returns activities, while other regions specialize in increasing returns activities. Diminishing returns depresses the growth of productivity and per capita incomes and makes regions less competitive, while increasing returns does the opposite. Increasing returns provides the basis of a cumulative process of economic growth based on trade, whereby increasing returns leads to greater competitiveness which leads to faster export growth. This in turn leads to faster output growth and faster productivity growth through the stimulus that faster output growth gives to capital accumulation and technical progress (including scale economies and learning by doing).

The American economist, Allyn Young (1928), was the first to incorporate increasing returns into a macro model of growth and development. He derived inspiration from Adam Smith's discussion in *The Wealth of Nations* of the process whereby the division of labour depends on the size of the market, but where the size of the market depends on the division of labour. The ability to specialize and to acquire learning and human capital is one of the fundamental bases of increasing returns, as many of the new breed of American growth theorists are rediscovering (see, for instance, Romer, 1991). As Young observed, 'Adam Smith's famous theorem amounts to saying that the division of labour depends in large part on the division of labour. [But] this is more than mere tautology. It means that the counterforces which are continually defeating the forces which make for equilibrium are more pervasive and more deep rooted than we commonly realise – *change becomes progressive and propagates itself in a cumulative way*' (1928, p. 533; my emphasis). The more demand is focused on commodities with a large supply response and the larger the demand response (direct and indirect) induced by increases in production, the greater the expansionary process is likely to be. For there to be cumulative expansion in Young's model, two conditions must hold: the demand for commodities must be price elastic, and production must be subject to scale economies. These are the characteristics of industrial output and not, in general, those of primary products or many service activities. Hence, regional (and country) differences in economic welfare are likely to be associated with different productive structures, as indeed we witness across the world economy. There is a strong association across countries between the share of resources devoted to industry and the level of per capita income.

The idea of cumulative causation based on increasing returns and the characteristics of different productive activities form the basis of centre-periphery models of growth and development which are the antithesis of equilibrium models. Myrdal's model is a classic centre-periphery model which highlights the deleterious backwash effects that stronger regions can have on weaker regions by denuding them of resources and out-competing them in trade. Hirschman (1957) has a similar model in which he refers to the polarization effects that buoyant regions have on other regions which are depressed.

Nicholas Kaldor, in his wide-ranging attacks on neoclassical equilibrium theory (see the various essays in Targetti and Thirlwall, 1989), builds on the ideas of Adam Smith and Allyn Young in identifying exports of manufactured goods as the engine of regional growth, with increasing returns as the mechanism by which success breeds success in a cumulative way. This accounts for the concentration of manufacturing production in certain selected parts of the world. Kaldor also derives inspiration from the work of Verdoorn (1949) who found a strong association across countries between the growth of output and the growth of labour productivity, with the former assumed as causal. This finding has come to be known as Verdoorn's Law and has been replicated by many other investigators across regions, countries and industries. Verdoorn derived his theoretical relation from an ordinary static Cobb-Douglas production function where the Verdoorn 'effect' depends on the degree of homogeneity of the production function and on the rate at which capital is growing relative to labour. But the Verdoorn 'effect' can also be thought of as a much more dynamic relation depending variously on the degree to which capital accumulation is induced by growth (through the accelerator), the degree to which technical progress is embodied in capital, and learning by doing. Whatever the basis for the link, it provides a vital linchpin in models of cumulative causation and represents a decisive nail in the coffin of equilibrium models in which, by definition, there are no positive (reinforcing) feedback loops. Dixon and Thirlwall (1975), who formalize the Kaldor model, show that differences in regional growth rates may persist if differences in the income elasticity of demand for exports persist between regions; also that growth rates will diverge through time if the product of the price elasticity of demand for exports and the Verdoorn coefficient (i.e. the elasticity of productivity growth with respect to output growth) exceeds unity. Differences in the income elasticities of demand for exports are closely related to industrial structure – sophisticated manufactured goods having high income elasticities, and primary products and standard manufactured goods having lower income elasticities.

Within a development context, the idea that poor people accommodate to poverty (to use Galbraith's phrase), and models of unequal exchange, both have a close affinity with the idea of circular and cumulative causation. Indeed, it may be noted that Myrdal first developed the concept in his pioneering study of the conditions of the American negro and of the difficulties faced by depressed social groups of breaking out of vicious circles of poverty (Myrdal, 1944). Poor people 'respond' to poverty, for example, by having large families, partly as an insurance policy, which makes them poorer. Poor people also tend to be more risk averse, because to take risks which might raise incomes in the long run is to threaten survival if things go wrong. Unequal exchange arises from the fact that cheap labour turns the terms of trade against poor regions *vis-à-vis* what would be the case if labour were scarce and the wage rate higher (see Emmanuel, 1967).

In conclusion, it can be seen that there are many forces operating within economic and social systems which work towards disequilibrium rather than equilibrium once initial differences in economic and social phenomena arise. They are all part and parcel of Myrdal's pioneering notion of circular and cumulative causation – a process, as he puts it himself, by which 'a change does not call forth countervailing changes but, instead, supporting changes, which move the system in the same direction as the first change but much further. Because of such circular causation a social process tends to become cumulative and often to gather speed at an accelerating rate' (1957, p. 13).

A.P. THIRLWALL

References

Dixon, R.J. and Thirlwall, A.P. (1975), 'A Model of Regional Growth Rate Differences on Kaldorian Lines', *Oxford Economic Papers*, **27**, July.

Emmanuel, A. (1967), *Unequal Exchange: A Study of the Imperialism of Trade*, New York: Monthly Review Press.

Hirschman, A. (1957), *Strategy of Economic Development*, New Haven: Yale University Press.

Myrdal, G. (1944), *An American Dilemma: The Negro Problem and Modern Democracy*, New York: Harper's.

Myrdal, G. (1957), *Economic Theory and Underdeveloped Regions*, London: Duckworth.

Romer, P. (1991), 'Increasing Returns and New Developments in the Theory of Growth' in W. Barnett (ed.), *Equilibrium Theory and Applications*, Cambridge: Cambridge University Press.

Targetti, F. and Thirlwall, A.P. (1989), *The Essential Kaldor*, London: Duckworth.

Verdoorn, P.J. (1949), Fattori che Regalano lo Sviluppo della Produttivita del Lavoro, *L'Industria*, translated by A.P. Thirlwall in D. Ironmonger, J. Perkins and T. Hoa (eds) (1988), *National Income and Economic Progress: Essays in Honour of Colin Clark*, London: Macmillan.

Young, Allyn (1928), 'Increasing Returns and Economic Progress', *Economic Journal*, **38**, December.

Decision making

Mainstream economics treats decision making as an entirely rational process, the decision maker being modelled as pursuing a clearly defined goal, single-mindedly sifting between alternative courses of action to find that one which maximizes attainment of the goal. It is usually assumed that he/she is possessed of perfect information, or at least adequate levels to be able systematically to evaluate all alternatives.

Radical political economy is not concerned with establishing rules for optimum behaviour, but with providing a realistic account of the decision-making process. Any tenable view of this process must accept that most decisions are taken against a background of imperfect information and uncertainty. Bounded rationality – the ability to take into account only some of the alternatives, or only some of the information required to evaluate an alternative – is more likely than complete rationality. Both information and decision-making processes will inevitably depart in a significant way from the model of complete rationality. Rules of thumb, habit and existing practice will play a role in many decisions. In addition it must be recognized that many decision processes involve not any single individual, but a group (the household, corporate management) and to assume a single goal in such circumstances is also unrealistic. Decision making will of necessity involve a degree of compromise as the constituencies involved in the process seek to ensure not only that their own goals are achieved, but that the extent of encroachment of other goal pursuits is kept within reasonable bounds.

Bounded rationality implies that economic agents do not evaluate all available alternatives when faced with a decision, but rather consider a subset of them. This is for two reasons: it accommodates the information deficiency, and it economizes on decision-making ability. Agents do not possess adequate information for a complete evaluation of all possible alternatives, and may not even know what some alternatives are. Choice will be between a restricted set of alternatives and will usually involve an incomplete evaluation of those that are known. The target is threshold levels of attainment with respect to desired goals, rather than an attempt to maximize any one objective. For example, in price setting decisions, management may have insufficient information to evaluate the consequences of each pricing strategy completely and will choose that which is likely to produce an adequate return in terms of profits, sales level or market share. Rules of thumb are thus used as an aid to decisions. Taking the example of advertising budget decisions, the Dorfman-Steiner theorem may indicate the conditions for optimum expenditure, but in the absence of adequate information on appropriate elasticities, management will fall back on administrative rules, such as percentage of sales revenue, which have no rational basis in terms of a calculus of maximization. Screening devices as a proxy for full evaluation in labour hire decisions constitute another example. In the case of household consumption decisions, search, experience and credence goods are distinguished on the basis of the degree of information possessed by the consumer decision maker. In the case of the latter, the decision maker is argued to be poorly informed about a good's attributes both at the point of purchase and even subsequent to the act of consumption, meaning that the consumption decision in such cases depends on surrogate information from advertising, brand loyalty developed from knowledge or other products, etc. Producers may attempt to control the effects of information deficiency by engaging in advertising to limit post-purchase dissonance and reinforce the household's decision. To argue that the decision was originally taken on the basis of an informed evaluation is scarcely tenable in such circumstances and is only likely to be credible in the case of search goods.

Even where a high level of information may be available, inability to deal with it may still imply bounded rationality. In the case of the household, partial or irregular evaluation may underlie purchase decisions. The political economy view of consumption decisions based on a lexicographical ordering, with choice between alternatives being exercised only within sub-categories of this ordering, is a formalization of such a decision process. Although it does not always receive attention in economics, marketing literature – concerned as it is with *how* the household reaches a particular decision – considers different purchase decisions in terms of the degree of buyer involvement. For many purchases, this will be low, implying an important role for habit and established patterns of behaviour, rather than a careful evaluation of all alternatives at each decision point. As Eichner (1991) indicates, the importance of habit in a significant proportion of household decisions is 'designed to prevent the household's decision-making capability from being overtaxed' (p. 638). Similarly, many management decisions will involve a degree of inertia and the formulation of decisions along routine lines since, even in large organizations, decision-making ability is a scarce resource. The organizational structure of the firm and the extent of divisionalization in large firms reflect this scarcity; indeed, one of the benefits of division into quasi-autonomous units is the reduction in demands on decision-making capacity. In the case of both households and firms, a major piece of new information with potentially important consequences will be required to trigger a reformulation rather than continuing with established practices. For households, this may be a significant change in discretionary income or the emergence of a new product. For management, examples will include technological change and significant shifts in competitive conditions.

The result is that a calculus of maximization will not explain the process of decision making in these circumstances. Whilst it could be argued that evaluation is pushed to the point where the benefits of further evaluation match the costs, this again implies a demand on the decision-making process in determining where this point is and avoids the central import of bounded rationality: that inherent in any decision-making process is the ability to deal with only a limited range of information, and that decision makers often choose from only a subset of that information in order to simplify the process. In the case of incomplete information, arguing that search will similarly be taken to an optimum point (in terms of the costs and benefits of that search) simply pushes the information problem back one stage. It will not be possible to know in advance whether further search is warranted and so the decision maker has no operational guide as to the optimum extent of search; the problem of lack of information cannot be made to disappear in this way.

Incomplete information and the associated possibility of search both imply that, in principle, the required information is knowable, though not currently known. Radical political economy, however, emphasizes the problems created by the widespread existence of uncertainty. The distinction between risk (with a range of possible outcomes to each of which a probability can be attached) and uncertainty (where even the range of outcomes, let alone the probability attaching to any one of them, is unknown) is well established. Mainstream economics has concentrated attention on the former, developing approaches in terms of expected values, certainty equivalents and game theory to deal with it. Such approaches ignore the fundamental problem of many decisions – that they are taken against a background of uncertainty in the strict sense, involving potential future outcomes which are not only unknown but also, in principle, unknowable. Keynes made this distinction clear and emphasized that many economic decisions involve consequences not only which we do not know, but which it is in principle impossible to know. We cannot reduce such situations to calculations in terms of probability, nor can game theory strategies help if outcomes are unknown. In such situations, rules of thumb are almost inevitable, and Keynes himself suggested the use of the idea that, in the absence of alternative information, decision makers will assume that the future will reflect the past. Thus a common assumption in share price valuation models is that dividend growth will occur at a constant rate, determined to a significant extent on historical grounds. Even where this is not the assumption, the best we are likely to be able to do is to place greater weight on the immediate past where this breaks a longer-term trend and is believed to be a better indicator of the future. We cannot escape the fact that the future is inherently unknowable and that belief is an important element of any judgment about it.

In such circumstances, systematic maximization is simply impossible. For example a strict theory of profit maximization, either short term or based upon the discounted value of a future stream of earnings, becomes difficult to justify. As Kalecki (1971) made clear, 'In view of the uncertainties faced in the process of price fixing, it will not be assumed that the firm attempts to maximise its profits in any precise sort of manner' (p. 44). Again we have opened the door for the use of administrative rules and allowed that the decision will be influenced by targeting a satisfactory outcome rather than by the systematic pursuit of some optimum. According to Çapoĝlu (1991), 'Profit-targeting behaviour reflects firms' response to uncertainty' (p. 85), indicating that decisions are made, not on the basis of maximizing, but on achieving a satisfactory outcome, in this case generating adequate investment funds.

As indicated above, there is a final consideration for a realistic understanding of economic decision making, namely that most decisions are not taken by individual economic agents, but by organizations of various kinds. Even consumption decisions are, for the most part, taken within the context of the household. Corporate decisions are even more obviously taken by groups of individuals. In either case this introduces the possibility of goal conflict amongst group participants and renders nugatory the notion of the ultra-rational pursuit of a single well-specified objective. Decision making will have to accommodate the conflicting demands of the constituencies represented in the process' and only by reducing the objective to a non-operational notion of group utility can a maximizing approach be considered. The result is that decision making will involve elements of bargaining and damage limitation in that each interest group will wish to ensure a decision that preserves at least acceptable outcomes in terms of its objective. Targeting of satisfactory achievement with regard to each constituency's aim, rather than maximization of a single clearly-defined objective, is inevitable.

Radical political economy thus emphasizes the difficulties inherent in decision making and the context in which it takes place, taking issue with the more mechanistic, rule-oriented approach of mainstream theory. Consequently it is more realistic and more accurately reflects the difficulties of real world decision-making processes. It is suggested that the apparently greater precision of the mainstream view is in fact a chimera as the conditions necessary for its operationalization are lacking. Decision making is fraught with problems of information deficiencies, limits on decision-making powers and the intractable problem of uncertainty in the Keynesian sense. It also takes place in the context of organizational structures rather than single rational agents. We cannot understand the problems if we pretend otherwise.

FRANK SKUSE

References

Çapoĝlu, G. (1991), *Prices, Profits and Financial Structures: A Post-Keynesian Approach to Competition*, Aldershot: Edward Elgar.

Eichner, A.S. (1991), *The Macrodynamics of Advanced Market Economies*, Armonk: M.E. Sharpe.

Kalecki, M. (1971), *Selected Essays on the Dynamics of the Capitalist Economy*, Cambridge: Cambridge University Press.

De-industrialization

De-industrialization refers, first and foremost, to an aspect of economic structural change. Early and intermediate stages of development in successful economies appear to be characterized by a process of 'industrialization', involving rising shares of industry in total output and employment and, possibly, improved net exports of industrial products. But in advanced industrial countries, beyond a certain high level of per capita income, industrialization appears to give way to a process of de-industrialization, involving a shift in the pattern of resource use away from industry towards services. Industry is defined broadly so as to include, in addition to manufacturing, mining, public utilities and construction, whilst services, also defined broadly, include: transport and communication; wholesale and retail distribution; banking, insurance and business services; and social, community and personal services, including health and education.

Despite the use of the term 'de-industrialization', concern has focused mainly on a possible shift in resource use away from manufacturing because of that sector's crucial contribution to successful economic development. Manufacturing not only accounts for most of total industrial output and employment, but it exhibits rates of productivity growth above the economy-wide average, displays strong forward and backward linkages, possesses huge scope for the development of new products and processes – and hence for forging national technological autonomy and exploiting high income-elasticities of demand in international trade. Given the high income-elasticity for manufactures in domestic markets and the sector's high tradeability and hence exposure to international competition, manufacturing (by way of both exports and import-competing production) makes a vital contribution to reconciling internal and external balance. It is for these reasons that de-industrialization has been a source of concern.

The existence of de-industrialization in output terms is frequently identified via the use of time-series data for individual advanced industrial countries on the share of industrial value added in total GDP measured at *current* prices; it is also established from international cross-section data from countries at different levels of development, incorporating each country's *own* relative price structure. However, such data are extremely misleading as evidence of fundamental structural change since the decline in industry's value added share in GDP as a function of rising per capita income mainly reflects the decline which has occurred in the relative price of industrial products compared to the general price level; this in turn reflects industry's above (the economy-wide) average rate of productivity growth and the scope this affords for relative price reductions.

Evidence for de-industrialization as fundamental structural change is much clearer in the case of employment. Thus, for the OECD as a whole, industry's share in total employment declined from 37.1 per cent in 1969 to 29.9 per cent in 1989. Moreover, all OECD countries now appear to have passed their peak in terms of industry's employment share. This includes both early-industrializers, whose industrial employment share was at its maximum in the 1950s and 1960s (UK (1955: 47.9 per cent); Belgium (1964: 45.6 per cent); France (1964: 40.0 per cent); US (1966: 36.1 per cent); Germany (1970: 48.5 per cent)), as well as late-industrializing countries, whose industrial employment share peaked slightly later and at somewhat lower levels (Japan (1973: 37.2 per cent); Italy (1971: 39.7 per cent); Spain (1975: 38.4 per cent); Portugal (1982: 37.5 per cent)). The lower trajectory of the industrial employment share in late-industrializing nations mainly reflects super-high relative industrial productivity levels achieved through importing capital equipment from already-industrialized countries with a more capital-abundant, labour-scarce endowment composition.

In terms of absolute numbers, industrial employment in the OECD as a whole is now 1.0m below its 1973 peak, with an apparent trend decline recorded in all Western European nations except for late-industrializers, such as Portugal and Turkey. However, in the US, Japan and Canada, the trend in industrial employment (cyclical fluctuations apart) still appears to be upwards.

The services have been the great beneficiaries of industry's employment decline, though the increase in (non-domestic) service employment in advanced countries, far from being a recent phenomenon, has probably been underway since the early stages of the industrial revolution.

The most controversial issue regarding de-industrialization and economic structural change concerns the stylized facts relating to industry's value added share in total GDP, measured either from time-series data for individual countries at *constant* prices, or from international cross-section data incorporating a *single* relative price structure applied to all countries. Here, attention focuses on the possible existence of a curvilinear, inverse U-shaped relationship between industry's *constant* price share and real per capita income. OECD-wide data suggest a slight (2 per cent) fall in industry's value added share at *constant* prices since peaking in the early 1970s, though short-run factors impinging adversely on the demand for industrial output (such as the mid-1970's global recession and the widespread adoption of restrictive monetary and fiscal policies in the early 1980s) make it difficult to identify this fall necessarily as a long-run trend. An additional factor has been the decline in industry's *constant* price GDP share in Japan and Germany from early 1970's peaks, coinciding with a deceleration in output growth and an associated reduction in the tempo of capital accumulation (especially intensive in industrial products).

The stylized facts on both employment and output, described above, can be accounted for quite easily *analytically* as the product of the interaction between technological developments (in particular, differential productivity growth between sectors) and changes in patterns of demand (as reflected in domestic expenditure and in net exports between sectors), as follows.

1. Technological factors: industry's above-average productivity growth rate accounts for the decline in the relative price of industrial products and hence for the fall in industry's value added share in GDP, measured at *current* prices. Rapid industrial productivity growth also ensures that the ever-growing demand for labour emanating from the services (where, in the case of many personal and social services, there exist certain intrinsic constraints to easy productivity improvements) could be accommodated, once the reserve army of agricultural labour had been exhausted, at the expense of industry's employment share.
2. Demand factors: the income-elasticity of demand for industrial products probably reaches its maximum during the intermediate stages of development, due to the super-rapid rate of capital accumulation linked to major structural changes, such as the redistribution of population from rural to urban areas and the associated requirements for urban and industrial infrastructure. However, even so, at advanced levels of development, there is little evidence (contrary to conventional wisdom) of any significant shift in the pattern of domestic expenditure away from industrial products towards services, at least from individual country time-series data at *constant* prices or from international cross-section data incorporating a single set of relative prices. Thus, the overall income-elasticity of demand for industrial products (incorporating the effects of both relative price and income changes) appears to be at least as great as that for services. It is this which mainly explains why industry's value added share in GDP, measured at *constant* prices, remains relatively invariant with respect to real per capital income.
3. Foreign trade structure: the pattern of net exports between different sectors differs markedly amongst the highly-developed OECD countries, ranging from highly-specialist net manufacturing exporters (such as Germany and Japan) to specialist net primary producers (such as Canada and Australia, which have traditionally depended on substantial net imports of manufactures to meet their domestic industrial requirements). Such differences in foreign trade structure, reflecting different patterns of com-

> parative advantage, are the most important factor accounting for variations in the inter-sectoral composition of output and employment amongst countries at a similar level of per capita income.

When de-industrialization is the result of the interaction between technological developments and changing patterns of demand, both domestic and foreign, in an otherwise healthy economy (i.e. one that is able to reconcile internal with external balance, whilst achieving a satisfactory rate of growth), then it must be rated a perfectly normal and healthy phenomenon.

There is, nevertheless, still widespread concern regarding the shift in employment composition towards services. It is maintained that many service jobs are inferior to those generated by industry, with poorer conditions of employment (including lower wages, less security, reduced right to benefits such as holiday pay and unemployment compensation) and less amenable to trade union organization. Against these very genuinely-held concerns, it must be noted that the services are an extremely heterogeneous sector in terms of conditions of employment, skill requirements, scope for creativity, etc. On these grounds, therefore, there is no reason why the shift from 'blue' to 'white' collar employment should necessarily be a cause for concern.

In addition to such structural change processes, 'de-industrialization' has also been used to refer to weak national industrial performance in the open and internationally integrated markets for manufactures which have resulted from the post-war drive to create a global, liberal trading and financial order. Intense competition in such open markets inevitably gives rise to uneven development, as a result of which relatively unsuccessful countries, such as the UK and US, appear to have undergone a process of 'negative' de-industrialization: slow industrial output growth, due to competitive weakness, combined with continued rapid technological progress resulting in labour-shedding from manufacturing which, if not fully offset by compensating improvements in performance and employment creation in non-industrial activities (services), results in a gradual inability to reconcile internal and external balance.

The UK, for example, has experienced the largest decline in industrial employment of all OECD countries both in terms of industry's share in total employment (1955: 47.9 per cent; 1992: 26.5 per cent) and in absolute numbers (1966: 11.6m; 1992: 6.7m). Simultaneously, while most other OECD competitor countries have experienced strongly-rising trend increases in output, the UK has flirted with industrial stagnation, taking the period 1973–92 as a whole. Finally, the UK has ceased to be a specialist net manufacturing exporter and now incurs a substantial deficit in manufacturing trade – even at levels of domestic expenditure far below that required to attain full employment. The reasons for the international competitive failure of UK-based manufacturing are complex and inadequately researched, but include government policy errors as well as aspects of the country's culture, class system, financial sector, education and training shortcomings, etc. However, the consequences of poor manufacturing performance are only too clear: a chronic inability to be able to reconcile internal and external balance, with the prospect of at least 3m unemployed (10 per cent of the labour force) for most of the 1990s.

Concern about economic performance amongst the OECD countries is not limited only to the UK and the US. During the 1980s, the OECD countries exhibited much higher unemployment levels, together with massive imbalances on trade and current account. Poor OECD economic performance has highlighted the competitive challenge arising from LDC manufacturers. In earlier decades, such threats could easily be dismissed since, although the labour-intensity of OECD production displaced by LDC manufactured imports exceeded that of OECD manufactured exports to LDC markets, the OECD had a healthy export surplus in two-way trade in manufactures with LDCs. However, the Third World debt crisis, involving a sharp reduction in new capital flows to LDCs, imposed deflation, causing many Third World countries to undergo de-industrialization, and prematurely too, given their stage of development. It also caused external adjustment, as LDCs sought to improve their trade balances in order to maintain debt service: this squeezed export opportunities for OECD exporters to the Third World and accentuated competitive pressures in their domestic markets. These spillovers from the debt crisis are a foretaste of the adjustment challenges facing the OECD countries if the industrialization drives of the Third World are to be accommodated successfully. However, the strong human capital base of the OECD countries holds out the prospect of developing wholly new areas of comparative advantage – in the services, broadly-defined – which can offer equivalent scope to manufacturing for economic dynamism. Nevertheless, it should be recognized that any shift to the services probably implies a reduction in the potential rate of economic growth in the OECD countries, given that services on average exhibit a lower rate of productivity growth compared to industry; this may, however, be one of the few factors making for greater economic convergence between nations.

JOHN R. WELLS

References

Rowthorn, R.E. and Wells, J.R. (1987), *De-Industrialization and Foreign Trade*, Cambridge: Cambridge University Press.

Singh, A. (1987), 'Manufacturing and De-industrialization' in J. Eatwell *et al.* (eds), *The New Palgrave: A Dictionary of Economics*, London: Macmillan, Vol. 3.

Summers, R. and Heston, A. (1988), 'A New Set of International Comparisons of Real Product and Price Levels: Estimates for 130 countries, 1950–85', *Review of Income and Wealth*, Series 34, 1–25.

Wells, J.R. (1989), 'Uneven Development and De-industrialization in the UK since 1979' in F. Green (ed.), *The Restructuring of the UK Economy*, Brighton: Harvester Wheatsheaf.

Dependency theories

Dependency theories emerged in Latin America in the early 1960s as attempts radically to transform both Marxist and structuralist thinking about the obstacles facing capitalist development in the periphery.

There can be little doubt that the Cuban Revolution was a turning point in Marxist analysis of capitalist development in the periphery. The events in Cuba gave rise to a new approach – of which most of dependency analysis forms part – which argued against the need (and feasibility) of a 'bourgeois-democratic' revolution in the underdeveloped regions of the capitalist world. Consequently, this approach also argued against the politics of popular fronts and in favour of a policy of immediate transition towards socialism.

The pre-Cuban Revolution approach saw capitalism as historically progressive in the periphery, although the necessary 'bourgeois-democratic' revolution was being impeded by a new alliance between imperialism and the traditional elites. Therefore, this approach identified imperialism as the main enemy. The allied camp, including everyone except those internal groups in collusion with imperialism, was also clear. Thus, the anti-imperialist struggle was at the same time a struggle for capitalist development and industrialization. The local state and the 'national' bourgeoisie appeared as the potential leading agents for capitalist development, which in turn was viewed as a necessary stage.

The Cuban Revolution questioned the very essence of this approach, insisting that the local bourgeoisies in the periphery no longer functioned as an active social force, but had become 'lumpen', incapable of rational accumulation or rational political activity, ravaged by consumerism and blind to their own best interests. It is within this framework, and with the explicit motive of developing (theoretically) and documenting (historically) this new form of 'dependency' analysis of the Latin American revolution, that Frank (1967) appeared on the scene. At the same time, both inside and outside the Economic Commission for Latin America (ECLA), two other major approaches to 'dependency' began to develop.

With the necessary degree of simplification which every classification of intellectual tendencies entails, I shall distinguish between three major approaches in 'dependency' analysis which are not mutually exclusive from the point of view of intellectual history. First is the approach begun by Frank which essentially attempted to construct a comprehensive theory to prove that capitalist development in the periphery is impossible. In such theories, the 'dependent' character of these economies is the hub on which the whole analysis of underdevelopment turns; that is, dependency is seen as *causally* linked to permanent capitalist underdevelopment. The second approach is associated with one branch of the ECLA structuralist school, including especially Furtado, Pinto and Sunkel. These writers sought to reformulate the classical Prebisch-ECLA (1969) analysis of Latin American development in terms of a critique of the obstacles to 'national' development. The final approach (Cardoso and Faletto, 1967), deliberately avoided the formulation of a mechanico-formal theory of dependency – and especially a mechanico-formal theory of the inevitability of underdevelopment in the capitalist periphery based on its dependent character. Instead it concentrated on what has been called the study of 'concrete situations of dependency'; that is to say, the study of the precise forms in which the different economies and polities of the periphery have been articulated with those of the advanced nations at different times, and how their specific dynamics have thus been generated.

There is no doubt that the 'father' of the first approach to 'dependency' was Baran (1957). He took up the position of the Sixth Congress of the COMINTERN regarding the supposedly *irresoluble nature* of the contradictions between the economic and political needs of imperialism and of those on the process of industrialization and economic development of the periphery.

To defend its interests, international monopoly capital would not only form alliances with pre-capitalist domestic elites intended to block progressive capitalist transformations in the periphery, but its activities would also have the effect of *distorting* the process of capitalist development in these countries. As a result, international monopoly capital would have easy access to peripheral resources, and the traditional elites in the periphery would be able to maintain traditional modes of surplus extraction and enjoy a continued monopoly of power. The possibilities for economic growth in dependent countries were thus extremely limited, the surplus generated being either expropriated in large proportion by foreign capital or otherwise squandered by traditional elites. This process would necessarily lead to economic stagnation and underdevelopment in the periphery. The only way out was political. Very prematurely, capitalism had become a fetter on the development of the productive forces in the periphery; therefore its historical role had already come to an end.

In developing his ideas, Baran was influenced both by the Frankfurt school's general pessimism regarding the nature of capitalist development and by Sweezy's proposition that the rise of monopolies imparts to capitalism an intrinsic tendency towards stagnation and decay. He also followed the main growth paradigm of his time, the Harrod-Domar theory, which held that the size of the investable surplus was the crucial determinant of growth (together with the efficiency with which it was used: the incremental capital output ratio).

Starting out with Baran's analysis, Frank (1967) attempted to prove the thesis that the only political and economic solution to capitalist underdevelopment was a revolution of an immediately socialist character.

One may identify three levels of analysis in Frank's model of the 'development of underdevelopment'. In the first (arguing against 'dualistic' analyses), he attempts to demonstrate that the periphery had been incorporated and *totally integrated* into the world capitalist economy from the very early stages of colonial rule. In the second, he attempts to show that such incorporation into the world capitalist economy had transformed the countries in question immediately and necessarily into *fully capitalist* economies. Finally, in the third level, Frank tries to prove that the integration of these supposedly capitalist economies into the world capitalist system was achieved through an interminable *metropolis-satellite chain*, through which the surplus generated at each stage was successfully drawn off towards the centre.

However, Frank never defines what he means by capitalism; he simply affirms that, since the periphery was never 'feudal' and has always been fully incorporated into the world capitalist system, it must have been capitalist from the beginning of colonial times. For Frank it is capitalism – with its metropolis-satellite relations of exploitation – which alone has produced underdevelopment. The choice is clear: socialist revolution or continuing endless underdevelopment within capitalism.

The central concerns of Frank's theory of the 'development of underdevelopment' are addressed from a critical point of view by dos Santos, Marini, Caputo, Pizarro and Hinkelammert and continued later by Amin (1972) and many non-Latin American social scientists. The most thoroughgoing critiques of these theories of underdevelopment have come from Laclau, Cardoso, Lall, Warren, Brenner and Palma (1978).

The theories of dependency examined in this context are mistaken not only because they do not 'fit the facts', but also – and more importantly – because their mechanico-formal nature renders them both *static and unhistorical*. Their analytical focus has not been directed to the understanding of how new forms of capitalist development have been marked by a series of *specific* economic, political and social contradictions, but only to assert that capitalism had lost, or never had, an historically progressive role in the periphery. Now, if the argument is that the progressiveness of capitalism has manifested itself differently in the periphery than in advanced capitalist countries, or in diverse ways in different branches of the peripheral economies; or that it has generated inequality at regional levels and in the distribution of income, and has been accompanied by such phenomena as underemployment and unemployment, and has benefited the elite almost exclusively; or again that it has taken on a cyclical nature – then this argument does no more than affirm that the development of capitalism in the periphery (as in any other area and at all times) has been characterized by its contradictory and exploitative nature. The *specificity* of capitalist development in the Third World stems precisely from the particular ways in which these contradictions have been manifested, the different ways in which many of these countries have faced and temporarily overcome them, the ways in which this process has created further contradictions, and so on. It is through this process that the *specific dynamic* of capitalist development in different peripheral countries has been generated.

Reading these political analyses of dependency, one is left with the impression that the whole question of what course the revolution should take in the periphery revolves solely around the problem of whether or not capitalist development is *viable*. In other words, their conclusion seems to be that if one accepts that capitalist development is feasible *on its own terms*, one is automatically bound to adopt the political strategy of waiting and/or facilitating such development until its full productive powers have been exhausted, and only then to seek to move towards socialism.

Towards the middle of the 1960s the ECLA approach to Latin American development suffered a gradual decline, mainly due to growing pessimism regarding the viability of capitalist development in the periphery. This pessimism led 'structuralist' thinkers to change their basic paradigm in the same way that the Cuban Revolution had affected the traditional Marxist left.

The process of import-substituting industrialization which ECLA recommended seemed to have aggravated rather than alleviated balance-of-payments problems. Foreign investment was partly responsible as, after a certain period of time, there was a tendency for a net flow of capital away from Latin America; it also did not seem to bring with it the other positive effects that ECLA had expected. In several countries income distribution was also worsening significantly. The problem of unemployment was also growing more acute, in particular as a result of rural-urban migration. Industrial production was becoming increasingly concentrated on products typically consumed by the elites, and was not generating 'ripple effects' upon other productive sectors of the economy, particularly on the agricultural sector.

This apparently gloomy panorama of capitalist development in Latin America in the 1960s led to substantial ideological changes in many influential ECLA thinkers, and also strengthened the convictions of the Marxist 'dependency' writers reviewed earlier. The former were faced with the problem of trying to explain some of the unexpected consequences of their policies, particularly concerning industrialization. The latter were led to deny with the greatest possible vehemence any possibility of dependent capitalist development.

Furthermore, by making a basically ethical distinction between 'economic growth' and 'economic development', their research followed two separate lines, one concerned with the obstacles to economic growth (and in particular to industrial and agricultural growth), and the other concerned with the perverse character taken by local 'development'. The fragility of this formulation lies in its inability to distinguish between *a socialist critique* of capitalism and the analysis of the *obstacles* to capitalism in the periphery.

The third approach to the analysis of dependency can be summarized as follows: in common with the two other approaches, it sees the Latin American economies as an integral part of the world capitalist system, in the context of the *increasing internationalization* of the system as a whole. It also argues that the central dynamic of that system lies outside the peripheral economies, and that therefore the options open to them are *limited* (but not determined) by the development of the system at the centre. In this way the 'particular' is *in some way* conditioned by the 'general'. Therefore, a basic element for the analysis of these societies rests on an understanding of the 'general determinants' of the world capitalist system, which itself is changing rapidly. The 'dependency' analysis therefore requires an understanding of the contemporary characteristics of the world capitalist system. However, the theory of imperialism, which was originally developed to explain the dynamics of that system, has had enormous difficulty in keeping up with the significant and decisive changes in capitalism since the death of Lenin. This approach to dependency has in fact been able to incorporate these transformations more successfully. For example, this approach was quick to grasp that the rise of multinational corporations progressively transformed centre-periphery as well as centre-centre relationships. As foreign capital became increasingly directed towards manufacturing industry in the periphery, the struggle for industrialization, previously seen as anti-imperialist, in some cases increasingly became the goal of foreign capital. Thus dependency and industrialization ceased to be necessarily contradictory processes, and a path of 'dependent development' became possible for important parts of the periphery.

This approach has also accepted and enriched the analysis of how developing societies are structured through unequal and antagonistic patterns of social organization, identifying social asymmetries, the exploitative character of social organization and its relationship with the socio-economic base. This approach has also given considerable importance to elements like the effect on each economy of the diversity of natural resources, geographic location and so on, thus also extending the analysis of the 'internal determinants' of the development of the Latin American economies.

The most significant feature of this approach, however, is that it attempts to go beyond these elements, insisting that, from the premises so far outlined, one arrives only *at a partial, abstract and indeterminate* characterization of the Latin American historical process. This can only be overcome by understanding how the general and specific determinants *interact* in particular and concrete situations. It is only by appreciating the specificity of 'movement' in peripheral societies as a dialectical unity of both – as a synthesis of these 'internal' and 'external' factors – that one can explain the particularity of their social, political and economic processes.

The study of the dynamic of dependent societies *as a dialectical unity of internal and external factors* implies that the conditioning effect of each on the development of these societies can be separated only by undertaking a static analysis. Equally, if the internal dynamic of the dependent society is a particular aspect of the general dynamic of the capitalist system, this does not imply that the latter produces concrete effects in the former, but only that *it finds concrete expression* in that internal dynamic.

The system of 'external domination' reappears as an 'internal phenomenon' through the social practices of local groups and classes who share the interests and values of external forces. Other internal groups and forces oppose this domination; it is in the concrete development of these contradictions that the specific dynamic of the society is generated. It is not a case of seeing one part of the world capitalist system as 'developing' and another as 'underdeveloping', or of seeing imperialism and dependency as two sides of the same coin, with the underdeveloped or dependent world reduced to a passive role determined by the other. Instead, in the words of Cardoso and Faletto,

> We conceive the relationship between external and internal forces as forming a complex whole whose structural links are not based on mere external forms of exploitation and coercion, but are rooted in coincidences of interest between local dominant classes and international ones, and, on the other hand, are challenged by local dominated groups and classes. In some circumstances, the networks of coincident or reconciliated interests might expand to include segments of the middle class, if not even of alienated parts of working classes. In other circumstances, segments of dominant classes might seek internal alliance with middle classes, working classes, and even peasants, aiming to protect themselves from foreign penetration that contradicts their interests (1978, pp. 10–11).

There are, of course, elements within the capitalist system which affect all developing economies, but it is precisely *the diversity within this unity* which characterizes their historical processes. Thus the analytical focus should be oriented towards the elaboration of concepts capable of explaining how the general trends in capitalist expansion are transformed into specific relationships between individuals, classes and states; how these specific relations in turn react upon the general trends of the capitalist system; how internal and external processes of political domination reflect one another, both in their compatibilities and their contradictions; how the economies and polities of the periphery are articulated with those of the centre, and how their specific dynamics are thus generated.

GABRIEL PALMA

References

Amin, S. (1972), 'Underdevelopment and Dependence in Black Africa: Origins and Contemporary Forms', *Journal of Modern African Studies*, **10**(4).

Baran, P. (1957), *The Political Economy of Growth*, New York: Monthly Review Press.

Cardoso, F.H. and Faletto, E. (1967), *Dependencia y Desarrollo en America Latina*, Mexico, Siglo XXI Editores, 1969. English edition (with a new Preface), Berkeley: University of California Press, 1978.

ECLA (1969), *El Pensamiento de la CEPAL*, Santiago: Editorial Universitaria.

Frank, A.G. (1967), *Capitalism and Underdevelopment in Latin America: Historical Studies of Chile and Brazil*, New York: Monthly Review Press.

Palma, J.G. (1978), 'Dependency, a Formal Theory of Underdevelopment or a Methodology for the Analysis of Concrete Situations of Underdevelopment?', *World Development*, **6**(7/8).

Development

Development economics has its roots in classical political economy (Smith, Ricardo and Mill) and the writings of Marx, but did not emerge in its modern forms until after the Second World War. In the post-war period there was renewed concern to understand and theorize about the process of transformation and growth taking place in a reconstructed world. Moreover, the rapid and widespread break-up of colonial empires in Asia and Africa left many former colonies in a state of low productivity and economic backwardness, while at the same time the emergence of new nation-states changed the balance of world forces and precipitated a motivation and push for development in the periphery.

The neoclassical approach to development, a minority view until the 1970s, put emphasis on economic growth, capital accumulation, free trade policies, open markets and individual decision making; there was also a notion that modernity could be achieved by following a linear path through a series of stages.

In the early years most contributions to the development debate were based on the assumption that the state had a central role to play in the transformation of both advanced and backward economies. The case for state intervention was partly founded on the contrasting experiences of the Soviet Union and the developed and developing countries during the capitalist crisis of the 1930s, but it was also justified on clear theoretical grounds, namely that the conditions necessary for competitive efficiency were not met.

Radical development economics, which rejected the orthodox theory of free trade and the prevailing international division of labour, can be split into four broad, albeit arbitrary and overlapping, theoretical approaches:

1. the structuralist/institutionalist school, which emphasizes the existence of rigidities, bottlenecks and lags in the economic structure, requiring government intervention and specific economic and other policies;
2. the post Keynesian school, which is concerned with problems of growth and distribution;
3. the Marxist/neo-Marxist/dependency schools, which analyse development and 'underdevelopment' in terms of the historical process through which capitalism was exported and imposed upon the less-developed countries; and
4. the Regulation school, which analyses capitalist change in terms of 'modes of development' that are characterized by a distinct 'mode of regulation' and 'regime of accumulation'.

The 1950s was a rich period for structuralist analysis which explained many of the economic problems facing the LDCs in terms of the failure of the price system. In Latin America, Raul Presbisch theorized the long-run deterioration in the terms of trade for primary producers as a function of technical economic factors and/or monopolization of factor and commodity markets in centre countries, using this to argue for inward-looking development based on state protected and directed import-substituting industrialization (ISI).

Subsequent disillusionment with ISI led Prebisch (1950) and others to explain its failures in terms of social obstacles and of inequalities in income distribution limiting the market for mass consumption goods. More recently, with the rise in oil prices in the late 1970s and the growth of international debt in the 1980s, many structuralists have become concerned with analysing short-run adjustment problems in the context of long-run structural change.

The Post Keynesian school has its roots in the work of Ricardo and Marx and, more recently, Keynes and Kalecki. Keynesian theory and policies were recognized as being inadequate for the type of unemployment to be found in LDCs, but the Post Keynesian analysis of growth, capital accumulation and distribution was relevant to both backward and developed economies.

The development of two-gap models, which linked external transactions with domestic savings, represented an important extension to the Harrod-Domar equation ($g_w = s/v$). However, Kalecki (1976) and other Post Keynesians emphasized that investment and growth had to be analysed together with employment and income distribution. Moreover, the orthodox assumption that the benefits of growth would trickle down or be redistributed to the poor proved to be unduly optimistic in the less developed world.

Kalecki's pioneering work emphasized that there are fundamental differences between developed and less developed countries. Firstly, there is the importance of investment for the supply side, that is, as a means of increasing the capacity to produce in addition to creating effective demand. Secondly, that sufficient private investment may not be forthcoming or that resource constraints might limit the scope for producing investment goods. Thirdly, that even if other constraints could be overcome, there are structural rigidities which result in an inelastic supply of wage-goods which becomes more pronounced as employment expands and consumer demand increases.

The notion of balanced (as opposed to unbalanced) growth, which is central to the models of Nurkse (1953) and Rosenstein-Rodan (1943), takes on a wider meaning in the work of Kalecki. He stresses the need for rises and changes in the pattern of demand to be matched by the expansion of output. But unlike dual-sector theorists and many of the structuralists who emphasize ISI, Kalecki gives special attention to the problems of expanding agricultural production. This is not just a technical economic problem, but one also requiring institutional and land reform to change the pattern of land ownership and the structure of property rights and tenancy arrangements in order to provide the necessary security and incentives for agricultural production to increase. For Kalecki the notion of a 'big push' takes on a more complex meaning which includes institutional change.

With the assumption of an inelastic supply of wage-goods, Kalecki's model explains how a rise in output in the capital goods sector will cause a rise in the price of consumer goods. By further assuming a fixed real wage and monopoly elements in production with fixed mark-ups or profit margins, the model shows how the rise in prices becomes generalized. Workers force up wages to restore real wage levels, which in turn leads to further price rises in a continuous inflationary spiral.

The structuralists have also been concerned with inflation and reach similar conclusions to Kalecki, but early theorizations, as exemplified in the work of V. Rao (1952), took the relevant structural rigidity to be in the supply of capital goods. Furthermore, whereas Rao predicted that inflation would peter out, for Kalecki there is no such inevitability. Later structuralist analysis of inflation incorporates a propagation mechanism which is heavily influenced by Kalecki.

The link between growth and distribution continues to be central to the Post Keynesian analysis. The basic model assumes different propensities to save out of profits and wages and implies conflict between growth and distributional equality. Recent developments have been concerned to explore how the Kaldor-Pasinetti-Kalecki model can be extended with different kinds of government intervention so as to avoid the trade-off.

The Marxist, neo-Marxist and dependency schools analyse development and underdevelopment in the context of the international capitalist system. The scattered references by Marx and Engels to dependency appear to indicate their belief that all backward countries would eventually become autonomous capitalist states.

Lenin's theory of imperialism as the highest stage of capitalism highlights the export of capital and the territorial division of the world as the prime features of the system, though the nature of this exploitative relationship is not clearly specified. In other writings Lenin followed Marx and Engels in arguing that backward nations (Russia) would eventually become full capitalist states, but there is an implicit recognition that future development would be fraught with difficulties due to (a) the weakness of the peripheral bourgeoisie, (b) the effects of competition from the centre, and (c) the survival of traditional structures.

Paul Baran (1957) provided the first major analysis of the effects of imperialism from the point of view of the less developed countries. Baran explains underdevelopment not as 'an original state of affairs' but as the result of a particular historical process. In this process developed countries became so by exploiting and colonizing the LDCs; independent industrialization was blocked by an alliance between local (comprador) elites and the metropolitan states. The analysis of A.G. Frank (1967) led to the 'impossibility thesis' and, subsequently, to the understanding that underdevelopment was part of the process of development itself. There were several other versions of neo-colonialism, but the common logic was that capitalism was the impediment and that de-linking or de-coupling was necessary. The central political message was the need for revolutionary national liberation.

In the 1970s criticism of both the structuralist and dependency approaches, as well as evidence of growth and industrialization in the less developed world, were used as arguments against protectionism and inward-directed development. The success of the NICs and other LDCs was used to justify the benefits to be reaped from outward-directed development. Marxist writers such as Warren (1980) used empirical evidence to argue that Marx was right to stress the progressive nature of capitalism; moreover, imperialism was in decline as capitalism advanced.

Such criticisms led to fragmentation among Marxists. Some disputed the evidence as superficial phenomena or explained the success of the NICs in terms of special factors and state involvement, while others emphasized the notion of distorted development and pointed to the growth of inequality, unemployment and impoverishment in the midst of growing wealth. Others, including some structuralists (partly as a response to criticisms of dependency theory), attempted to redefine dependency relations in terms of multinational corporations, technology, finance, aid and Third World debt. Another group of Marxists, including some feminists, turned their attention to gender issues and the subordination of women in the context of the spread of world market factories.

The Regulation school has its roots in debates of the late 1960s and 1970s between a number of French economists dissatisfied with existing theories of development. While retaining links with the Marxist approach to development, the school introduces new concepts to analyse the laws of capital accumulation. Thus in the work of Michael Aglietta (1979), the concept of 'mode of development' is used to distinguish four phases of capitalist development, each defined according to the 'regime of accumulation' and the 'mode of regulation'. Phases one and two were regulated by competitive markets, the former characterized by extensive accumulation and the latter by intensive accumulation. According to Aglietta, the third phase emerged out of the crisis of the 1930s and was characterized (1) by an 'intensive regime of accumulation' in new capital, embodying technical advance, and (2) by a monopoly 'mode of regulation' which provided for a rise in mass consumption. This regime of Fordism employing Taylorist modes of work organization resulted in a considerable rise in productivity and per capita incomes. Yet by the late 1960s Fordism was also in crisis, the nature of which was theorized by the Regulationists either in terms of unbalanced accumulation or the insufficiency of labour-productivity growth, with a consequent fall in the rate of profit.

The response of capital was to introduce a more flexible and fragmented system of work organization and to relocate primitive-Taylorist and Fordist labour activities in the periphery to exploit lower wage rates elsewhere and weaken the power of trade unions. In the 1960s the relocation took place in the less industrialized countries of the Mediterranean, Eastern Europe, Latin America and South East Asia. Unlike the dependency theorists, however, the Regulationists stress that a new pattern of autonomous local capital was being established in the periphery. This 'peripheral Fordism' allows for industrialization and growth in the periphery and is defined in terms of a regime of accumulation and a mode of regulation which are conditioned by the globalization of capital.

From the end of the 1970s peripheral Fordism was also entering a period of crisis which the Regulationists attempted to explain in terms of the consequences of central monetarism, the general recession and the resulting financial/debt crisis.

The Regulation approach has been criticized both in terms of its empirical validity and its theoretical adequacy. Nevertheless it has spawned attempts to understand the nature of post-Fordist society and, through the internationalization of capital, links with the developing world. Clearly this remains an important area of research.

RON AYRES

References

Aglietta, M. (1979), *A Theory of Capitalist Regulation*, London: New Left Books.
Baran, P. (1957), *The Political Economy of Growth*, New York: Monthly Review Press.

Frank, A.G. (1967), *Capitalism and Underdevelopment in Latin America*, New York: Monthly Review Press.
Kalecki, M. (1976), *Essays on Developing Economies*, London: Harvester Press.
Nurse, R. (1953), *Problems of Capital Formation in Underdeveloped Countries*, Oxford: Basil Blackwell.
Prebisch, R. (1950), *The Economic Development of Latin America and its Principal Problems*, New York: UN Dept. of Economic Affairs.
Rao, V.K.R.V. (1952), 'Investment, Income and the Multiplier in an Underdeveloped Economy', *Indian Economic Review*, **1**.
Rosenstein-Rodan, P. (1943), 'Problems of Industrialisation in Eastern and South-Eastern Europe', *Economic Journal*, **53**.
Warren, B. (1980), *Imperialism: The Pioneer of Capitalism*, London: New Left Books.

Dialectics

Dialectics or the dialectical method may be defined in contrast (but not in fixed and rigid opposition) to the analytical method. Although neither Hegel nor Marx characterized their method explicitly as dialectical, preferring other appellations such as the 'absolute', 'speculative' method (Hegel) or a 'genetical' or 'critical' presentation (Marx), the particular methodology used by both thinkers has historically come to be known as dialectical.

Superficially dialectics is often associated with 'holistic' approaches, i.e. those which attempt to deal with larger entities and whole systems in preference to parts. Dialectics has also been identified with a process which passes through the three stages of thesis, antithesis and synthesis. Hegel and Marx have rarely used the latter scheme since it is a misleading representation of dialectics. Both the holistic approach and the thesis-antithesis-synthesis scheme may be characterized as analytical approaches to dialectics. In a genuinely dialectical procedure, in contrast to analytical approaches, there is no fixed and rigid separation of wholes and parts, form and content, etc. which is a hallmark of analytical methodology. For instance, this is how Hegel discusses the whole/part dialectic:

> The relation of whole and parts, being the immediate relation, is one that is familiar to the analytic or reflective understanding. ... The limbs and organs, for instance of an organic body, are not merely parts of it: it is only in their unity that they are what they are, and they are unquestionably affected by that unity, as they also in turn affect it. ... The external and mechanical relations of whole and parts is not sufficient for us, if we want to learn about the truth of organic life. And if this be so in organic life, it is the case to a much greater extent when we apply this relation to the mind and formations of the spiritual world (Hegel, 1873, pp. 211–12).

Similarly in discussing the relation between form and content, Hegel states the following: 'Form and content are a pair of characteristics frequently employed by the reflective understanding, especially in the way of looking on the content as the essential and independent, the form ... as the unessential and dependent. Against this it must be noted that both are in fact equally essential; the two ... are distinguished by this circumstance, that matter, though implicitly not without form, still in being one thing or another manifests a disregard of form, whereas content, as such, is what it is only because *the matured form is included in it*' (Hegel, 1873, p. 209, emphasis added). This inclusion of the 'matured form' in the content makes the analytical separation of form and content impossible.

The following two examples are intended as an application of the above-mentioned points.

1. It was popular in the 19th century to subdivide treatises on political economy into parts dealing with production, exchange, distribution, etc. In the last few decades, it has similarly become popular to organize textbooks of economics around the three questions of what, how and for whom to produce. The implications of these practices have been that one can unambiguously divide an economy into distinct parts, that there is a linear chain proceeding from one part of the economy to another and that these divisions are common to every economy. Yet upon deeper reflection, these parts or problems of real economies are intimately connected with each other to the extent of defying any unambiguous division. For instance, neither the technology (how) nor the type of product (what) is indifferent to the distribution of income, as the pattern of development in many LDCs painfully demonstrates. Even if these divisions can be justified for taxonomic or didactic purposes, there is no question about the nonlinear relations between these sectors or problems. Furthermore it is naive to assume that the relations between these parts and problems of any economy will be identical regardless of the nature of socio-economic relations of particular real societies (see Shamsavari, 1991, Ch. 2 for more detailed analysis).
2. Mechanistic interpretations of Marx's theory of history tend to define forces of production in rigid and fixed opposition to the social relations of a mode of production. If we follow Cohen's interpretation, for instance, material forces of production are the content, and social relations are the form, of a mode of production, exactly in the same way as (following Cohen) one may say that the content of a statue (e.g. marble) is completely separate from and indifferent to the form of it (Cohen, 1979, pp. 91–2). Disregarding the fact that Cohen's analogy is false, Marx's actual investigations into the evolution of the capitalist system invalidate this interpretation. Marx's account of post-industrial revolution capitalism demonstrates that technology has been completely trans-

> formed to fit the requirements of mature capitalism. Here we may say, following Hegel, that the content (forces of production) includes the matured form. Thus the technology borrowed by LDCs from developed countries cannot be utilized efficiently without being considerably modified while the social (institutional) framework of these countries also requires change. In the former centrally-planned economies, the social form failed to transform the technology borrowed from capitalist countries in its own 'image'. In a way these countries, which are now also in the process of borrowing new social forms (e.g. markets), face the formidable task of transforming the entire techno-social structure of their economies (see Shamsavari, 1991, Introduction and Conclusion).

The scheme of thesis-antithesis-synthesis would represent the dialectical process only if it were understood that the true beginning is not thesis but synthesis, that the former already intimates the latter (although implicitly), that antithesis does not destroy the thesis but preserves it (transforms while retaining it) and finally that synthesis is a higher form of development that overcomes any fixed opposition between thesis and antithesis. Synthesis is essentially a restatement of the thesis, the result of a process in which thesis becoming 'another' (antithesis), has been mediated; this is not a simple 'immediate' but one which contains absolute mediation. The terminology that is preferred by Hegel is being-in-itself, being-for-itself and being-in and for-itself.

We shall now attempt to see if Hegel's *Logic* as well as Marx's *Capital* conform to the dialectical structure intimated above.

Some scholars have characterized the 'Doctrine of Being' in Hegel's *Logic* as the realm in which ideas merely exist or coexist without any relation to each other, and the 'Doctrine of Essence' as the sphere of relations where concepts are related to each other, e.g. as cause and effect or form and content. Finally, in the 'Doctrine of Notion', the fixed opposition between the categories of essence are overcome and resolved, i.e. the three doctrines represent cancellation, equilibrium and preservation, respectively. As I have shown elsewhere (Shamsavari, 1991, Ch. 4), this linear view of the *Logic* is not wrong but one-sided. According to Hegel himself:

> The Notion has exhibited itself as the truth of Being and Essence, which both revert to it as their ground. Conversely it has been developed out of being as its ground. The former aspect of the advance may be regarded as a deepening of being in itself, the inner nature of which has been truly laid bare: the latter aspect as issuing of the more perfect from less perfect. When such development is viewed on the latter side only, it does prejudice to the method of philosophy (Hegel, 1873, p. 244).

Marx's *Capital* (1976) exhibits a similar structure. For instance Marx begins by discussing the concept of commodity, analysing such forms of commodity as the commodity form, the money form, etc. The question as to why Marx begins with the commodity (presumably the common denominator of all commodity-producing economies) and not with capital (which is the specific feature of capitalism distinguishing it from other modes of production) has been debated extensively in the literature. Three responses to this question have emerged: (1) Marx begins with the commodity because historically it is the first form of human product developed for exchange and is thus an historical foundation of capitalism (the historicist approach); (2) Marx begins with the commodity because it is the basic elementary structure of capitalism (the structuralist approach); (3) by beginning with commodity, which is a form common to all commodity-producing economies, Marx intends to sidestep complicating features such as ownership of means of production in order to simplify the analysis of capitalism (the rationalist approach). Against all these approaches, I have argued (Shamsavari, 1991, Ch. 2) that Marx's beginning in *Capital* is neither the commodity as it appears in the dawn of history, nor the one which forms the elementary structure of capitalism; nor is it the simple model that, through a process of 'finite addition' (as Hegel would put it, see below) of complicating factors, leads to the developed model of capitalism. On the contrary, what forms the beginning of *Capital* is the commodity, not as it emerges under pre-capitalist conditions or as a simple substructure or thought construct, model, etc., but as it appears as a *result* (at the end rather than the beginning) of capitalist production. Thus Marx's discussion of the value form in the first chapter of *Capital* presupposes all the advanced features of capitalism. This is confirmed by Marx when he states:

> The commodity as it emerges in capitalist production is different from the commodity taken as the element, the starting-point of capitalist production. We are no longer faced with the individual commodity, the individual product. The individual product manifests itself not only as a real product but also as a commodity, as a part both really and conceptually of production as a whole. Each individual commodity represents a definite portion of capital and the surplus value created by it (Marx, 1971, pp. 112–13).

In order to lay bare the essence of dialectical conceptualization further, I will now discuss the pitfalls of the analytical method in general.

In the 1857 'Introduction' Marx, reflecting upon the methodology of political economy, makes a distinction between the method of pre-classical economists: while the former always began their inquiry 'with the real and concrete', such as the population of a country, and ended up with 'simple' relations such as labour, exchange-value and money, the latter economists began with simple relations and concepts and ended up with concrete wholes, such as the state and world market. The latter, observes Marx, is 'obviously the scientifically correct method' (Marx, 1973, pp. 100–101). I will now show that Marx's characterization of these two methods corresponds directly with Hegel's distinction between 'analytic' and 'synthetic' cognition.

According to Hegel, analytic cognition 'consists in the analysis of the given concrete object, in isolating the differences, and giving them the form of abstract generality' (Hegel, 1873, p. 315). He goes on to argue that 'the movement of the Synthetic method is the reverse of the Analytical method. The latter starts from the individual and proceeds to the universal; in the former the starting point is given by the universal (as a definition), from which we proceed by particularizing (in division) to the individual or theorem' (Hegel, 1873, p. 316). In short, the analytical method 'analyses' a given, say organic, whole into its constituent organs, parts and elements, which lend themselves to abstract definitions, concepts, etc. But this does not lead to knowledge of the original living thing unless a reverse journey takes place from the abstract elements to the concrete totality (the synthetic method).

Hegel's criticism of the analytic method is that it ends up with abstract (i.e. one-sided, contingent) universals, e.g. generic concepts that often stand in fixed and rigid opposition to each other. The synthetic method suffers from a similar deficiency. Synthetic cognition attempts to relate concepts yielded by the analytical method to each other, thus to overcome 'otherness'. Its aim is to overcome external or unrelated diversity by establishing, for instance, causal relations between phenomena. Its objective is to achieve the concreteness of Notion by subsuming diverse phenomena under a single law or concept. But it does not achieve this objective because these diverse phenomena 'only stand in relation to one another, or in the immediate unity, and just for that reason, not in the unity by which the Notion exists as subject' (Hegel, 1969, pp. 793–4).

Marx often criticizes classical economists on both grounds (see Shamsavari, 1991, Chs 3 and 4). For both Hegel and Marx the analytic and synthetic approaches, although deficient if pursued in a one-sided and self-external way, constitute necessary stages for science both historically and conceptually. At one point in *Theories of Surplus Value*, after criticizing classical political economists for their analytical approach, Marx concludes that the latter 'is the necessary prerequisite of genetical presentation, and of the understanding of the real, formative process in its different phases' (Marx, 1971, p. 500). Dialectics is both analytic and synthetic, although it cannot be reduced to either of these methods. This is made very clear in the following quotation where Hegel provides us with a succinct account of the dialectical (absolute) method and its concepts (Notions):

> The essential point is that the absolute method finds and cognizes the *determination* of the universal within the latter itself. The procedure of the finite cognition of the understanding here is to take up again, equally externally, what it has left out in its creation of the universal by a process of abstraction. The absolute method, on the contrary, does not behave like external reflection but takes the determinate element from its own subject matter's immanent principle and soul. This is what Plato demanded of cognition, that it should *consider things in and for themselves*, that is, should consider them partly in their universality, but also that it should not stray away from them catching at circumstances, examples and comparisons, but should keep before it solely the things themselves and bring before consciousness what is immanent in them. The method of absolute cognition is to this extent *analytic*. That it finds the further determinations of its initial universal simply and solely in that universal, is the absolute objectivity of the Notion, of which objectivity the method is the certainty. But the method is no less *synthetic*, since its subject matter, determined immediately as a *simple universal*, by virtue of the determinateness which it possesses in its very immediacy and universality, exhibits itself as an other (Hegel, 1969, p. 830).

Note that in the above quotation Hegel has criticized both methods, while confirming that dialectics is both analytic and synthetic. He has also provided us with the foundation of a dialectical critique of the application of quantitative methods in social sciences (e.g. econometrics, psychometry, etc.) which have become so prevalent since World War II.

ALI SHAMSAVARI

References

Cohen, G.A. (1979), *Marx's Theory of History: A Defence*, Oxford: Oxford University Press.
Hegel, G.W.F. (1873), translated by W. Wallace, Oxford: Clarendon Press.
Hegel, G.W.F. (1969), *Science of Logic*, translated by A.V. Miller, London: Allen & Unwin.
Marx, K. (1971), *Theories of Surplus Value*, Part III, Moscow: Progress Publishers.
Marx, K. (1973), *Grundrisse*, Harmondsworth: Penguin Books.
Marx, K. (1976), *Capital*, Vol. I, Harmondsworth: Penguin Books.
Shamsavari, A. (1991), *Dialectics and Social Theory: The Logic of Capital*, Braunton: Merlin Books.

Discrimination

Discrimination in the market for labour power occurs when economically identical workers persistently receive differential compensation. Empirical studies consistently find racial and gender differentials in the returns to the productive attributes of individuals. The fundamental theoretical difficulty in the economics of discrimination is the reconciliation of persistent earnings differentials with the competitive process.

Radical and Marxian economists have chosen at least three approaches in their attempts to reconcile the persistence of discrimination with the competitive process. They argue that economic theory must take account of the relationship between the variability of worker effort and racial inequality

(Reich, 1981); that both ceasing and continuing discrimination may be costly (Shulman, 1984), and that the economics of discrimination requires an alternative conceptualization of competition and accumulation (Williams, 1987; Mason, 1991).

Reich's thesis is a formalization of the notion that labour market discrimination is a tool used by capitalists to 'divide-and-conquer' the labour force. This model contends that output increases with the amount of work performed (*LD*), while costs are an increasing function of the amount of labour power purchased (*LP*). Therefore capital has a continuous incentive to increase the intensity of labour (*LD/L*), while workers have an obvious incentive to resist such pressures. Capital uses racial inequality as a mechanism to increase labour intensity.

This relationship is formalized in equation (1) where p = the price of output, w_B and w_w are the wage rates for black and white workers respectively, L_B and L_w are the employment levels of black and white workers respectively, and $Q = f(LD)$ is a short-run production function.

$$\text{Profit} = pf(LD) - w_B L_B - w_w L_w \quad (1)$$

$$LD = g(LP, BP), \text{ where } LP = L_B + L_w \quad (2)$$

$$BP = h(R_w, R_q), \text{ where } R_w = w_w / w_B,\ R_q = L_w / L \quad (3)$$

Equations (2) and (3) summarize the notion that the amount of labour performed depends on the amount of labour power purchased and the bargaining power (*BP*) of workers; further, the bargaining power of workers depends on the extent of inter-racial wage and employment inequality, R_w and R_q respectively.

Given $w_B > 0$, each employer selects R_w, R_q and L_B so as to maximize profits. Employers are willing to pay white workers a premium until the benefits (lower bargaining power) are just matched by increased wage costs. Discrimination then harms all workers by lowering the average wage rate and increasing profit; hence, workers have a class interest to unite across racial lines as capital continually seeks to divide-and-conquer workers in order to increase profit.

In addition to providing alternative theories of discrimination, the works of Shulman, Williams and Mason have also been the sources of radical and Marxian critiques of Reich's model. Collectively, these authors question the theoretical and empirical validity of the divide-and-conquer model.

Shulman (1984) recognizes that the demand for labour is a function of the price and quality of labour as well as 'certain behavioral characteristics which sustain capitalist control over the production process' (p. 115). On the one hand, managers adopt personnel and organizational policies designed to discourage worker solidarity and opposition to the prerequisites of capital. On the other hand, managers must adopt policies which encourage workers to cooperate with each other to facilitate production. Racial divisions play a role in maintaining this crucial mix of unity and disunity among the firm's work force.

The firm's cost of ceasing (continuing) employment discrimination is an increasing (decreasing) function of the aggregate unemployment rate. Accordingly, the extent of employment discrimination is a positive function of the net benefits of discrimination. The critical unemployment rate ($U_{c)}$ is where the net benefits to discrimination are zero.

A reduction in wage discrimination illustrates the contradictory nature of the discriminatory process. Any reduction in wage discrimination increases the cost of ceasing discrimination because managers will seek to use alternative forms of discrimination to create disunity among workers and to maintain managerial control; hence the cost of ceasing employment discrimination will increase for any given level of unemployment and thereby lead to a reduction in U_c. Therefore, a higher level of employment discrimination may occur in a slack labour market if the state has taken action to reduce wage discrimination.

No empirical information on critical inter- and intra-industry unemployment levels exists. This information would provide a definitive empirical evaluation of the race relations model.

The common elements of Marxian competition models of discrimination are: (1) persistent reproduction of the reserve army of unemployed; (2) micro-labour queues; (3) racial domination and class exploitation as equal factors in the discriminatory process; (4) job exclusion as the basic form of discrimination, and (5) the endogeneity of discrimination with respect to the competitive process.

First, at the highest level of abstraction – initially ignoring differences in units of capital, types of workers, types of work, levels of job control, remuneration and historical specifics – the structural possibility of discrimination arises because of the reserve army of unemployed. This persistent involuntary unemployment creates the possibility that jobs may be allocated on other than productivity-related characteristics of workers. Concomitantly, the immediate consequence of the use of non-economic criteria in the allocation of work is a material basis for labour-labour conflicts. And, as Reich suggests, such conflict reduces the bargaining strength of labour in relation to capital.

Second, within a unit of capital the work structure is hierarchical, not all jobs having equal strategic significance with respect to the production and appropriation of surplus value. The hierarchical structure of work implies that micro-labour queues (occupational reserve armies) will arise as workers queue for employment positions on their current levels of the occupational pyramid as well as positions that are higher up the occupational hierarchy.

For a given level of labour quality, the terms of employment (wages, working conditions and job control) increase with the strategic importance of the occupation. Hence, the creation of micro-labour queues and differential terms of employment provide a more concrete explanation for the possibility of allocating work on other than productivity-related criteria.

The third element in the theory of discrimination may be encapsulated as the principle of exclusion; this is an historically derived phenomenon which determines the probable targets and beneficiaries of unequal access to employment opportunities.

Fourth, wage discrimination is the most concrete expression of job exclusion. Extending the model to wage discrimination requires lowering the level of abstraction to include heterogeneous units of capital. At this level of abstraction, one can then construct an exceptionally robust theory of inter- and intra-industry wage differentials that is consistent with the competition of capitals within and between industries (Botwinick, 1993).

The essence of the Marxian competition theory of wage differentials is that the inter- and intra-industry competitive structure of capitals – capital intensity, size of the firm, location of regulating capitals (those firms using the best generally available means of production), special conditions of production, value of fixed capital investment, and cost differentials between regulating and subdominant capitals provides technical limits to wage increases between and within industries. The nature and extent of worker organization across capitals determine the capacity of workers to push wages towards these limits. Hence, it is likely that economically identical workers will receive different forms of compensation; wages, in this model, depend on the labour quality, the industry, firm and strategic location of the job, as well as the organization capacity of workers. Thus employment segregation and wage discrimination are not, in theory or in practice, separable phenomena.

Botwinick's analysis suggests that the upper bound on the wage rate of regulating capitals (w_R) is determined by a complex combination of the structural limits to wage differentials, a vector of labour quality (E), job desirability (D), market stability (Y) variables, and the bargaining power of labour. This relationship is expressed in equation (4). In turn, equation (5) relates the bargaining power of labour to the extent and quality of labour organization, where one measure of the extent of labour organization is the percent of workers unionized (U) and where the quality of worker unity is related in part to inter-racial wage and employment ratios as suggested by Reich.

$$w_R = R(S, E, D, Y, BP), \tag{4}$$

$$BP = G(U, R_q, R_w). \tag{5}$$

The job desirability vector (D) represents working conditions. The notion of compensating wage differentials has been a persistent theme in orthodox economics. Compensating differentials exist when capital, uncoerced by labour, pays a wage premium for work that is risky, dirty, disagreeable or otherwise undesirable.

No such notion exists in Marxian analysis. Under Marxian competition, wage premiums are paid for undesirable jobs only if labour has forced capital to increase the pecuniary returns for work. Under Marxian competition, disagreeable working conditions will not lead to higher monetary wages, but rather provide proxies for the degree of dominance of capital over labour. *Ceteris paribus*, poor working conditions are associated with low pay.

The wage rate is determined by the amount of socially necessary labour required to produce a family's consumption bundle. Therefore, increases (decreases) in the quality of labour power required to produce the output of regulating capitals will raise (lower) the wage rate. Similarly, demand pressures will tend to raise (lower) the wage rate of capitals growing above (below) their long-term planned rate of growth.

For a given occupation, the wage premium may be determined by

$$\mu = w_R - w_{min}, \qquad (6)$$

where w_{min} represents the minimum wage rate for the occupation.

Within the context of Mason's Marxian competition model, racial domination is expressed via the principle of exclusion – the use of ascriptive status (for example, race and gender) as labour allocation devices for scarce employment opportunities. As an historically derived phenomenon, the principle of exclusion will vary across societies.

Equation (7) summarizes the principle of exclusion:

$$R_q = H(\mu, D, U, Z). \qquad (7)$$

White employment relative to black employment (R_q) has a positive correlation with the wage differential (μ). R_q decreases as the extent of (industrial) unionization increases and as the level of racism within the union declines. Similarly, the working conditions vector (D) captures the often observed phenomenon that, as working conditions worsen, the exclusion of blacks decreases. Finally, Z captures the effects of state policy, community pressures, inter-racial wage differences and other exogenous variables.

Equations (6) and (7) reveal the interconnections between wage differentials, the inter-racial distribution of employment and the competitive structure of capitals. The class struggle equation (6) reveals the relationship between inter-racial employment levels and the wage differential. The racial exclusion equation (7) exhibits a positive relationship between the size of the wage differential and the inter-racial employment ratio. *Ceteris paribus*, firms (industries) with larger fixed capital investments, larger size or greater capital intensity will have larger wage differentials for a given inter-racial employment ratio.

Consider differences in fixed capital investment and inter-racial employments and employment ratios $E_2 < E_1 < E_0$. Regulating capitals will hire a combination of workers consistent with E_0. Less capital intensive firms (industries) will employ a racial mix up to E_1. The least capital intensive firms (industries) will employ a racial mix up to E_2. If there are any firms (industries) whose special conditions of production allow them to operate with a class struggle equation which dominates the class struggle equation of regulating capitals, these firms (industries) will not hire any black workers.

The Marxian competition model moves from the most abstract understanding of discrimination as a labour allocation device for determining service in the reserve army, to the most concrete understanding of discrimination as a device for determining access to high-wage jobs. It views discrimination as a multi-dimensional process whose elements are continuously reproduced and move in historically contingent directions in response to the initiatives of labour and capital.

This entry has evaluated the contributions of modern radical and Marxian economics to the understanding of discrimination and market competition. Towards that end, three models of discrimination in the market for labour power have been presented. The divide-and-conquer model is theoretically suggestive with respect to its discussion of bargaining power and racial inequality, but recent theoretical and empirical work has cast some doubt on its utility. The race relations model is an attempt to incorporate the aggregate state of the market for labour power as a mediating influence on the microeconomic decision making of firms. Future research on this model may explain the nature and extent of inter- and intra-industry differences in the critical unemployment rate. The Marxian competition model attempts to provide a logically consistent classical Marxist explanation of racial discrimination. Although this model is theoretically encompassing with respect to prior economic models, it has not been fully subjected to the fire of intense empirical investigation.

PATRICK L. MASON

References

Botwinick, H. (1993), *Persistent Inequalities: Wage Disparity under Capitalist Competition*, Princeton: Princeton University Press.

Mason, P. (1991), *Competition, Noncompensating Wage Differentials, and Racial Discrimination in the Labor Market*, New School for Social Research, unpublished dissertation.

Reich, M. (1981), *Racial Inequality: A Political Economic Analysis*, Princeton: Princeton University Press.
Shulman, S. (1984), 'Competition and Racial Discrimination: The Employment Effect of Reagan's Labor Market Policies', *Review of Radical Political Economics*, **16** (4), Winter, 111–28.
Williams, R. (1987), 'Capital, Competition, and Discrimination: A Reconsideration of Racial Earnings Inequality', *Review of Radical Political Economics*, **19** (2), Summer, 1–15.

Distribution: class and functional

The distribution of income and wealth has occupied economists for more than 200 years. (We shall not consider here the personal distribution.) We may identify two major approaches to the problem of income and wealth distribution within radical political economy: the classical approach (Ricardo in particular) and that of the Post Keynesians/neo-Ricardians. The question these theories try to resolve is the following: what are the laws which regulate the distribution of the product and wealth among factors of production, or among socio-economic classes? Classical, Post Keynesian and neo-Ricardian theories rely on an historical and institutional framework. This situation is the outcome of the particular visions of economic reality that these schools of thought endorse: in the case of classical and Post Keynesian theories, this vision encompasses the different behaviour, strength and bargaining power of socioeconomic groups within specific patterns of growth of the system.

Kaldor (1956) provides an excellent summary of the classical (i.e. Ricardian) functional theory of income and wealth distribution. Along traditional classical lines, Ricardo identifies three socioeconomic classes: the workers, who provide labour, receive a natural (higher than the subsistence) wage-rate and consume all their income; the rentiers, who provide the arable land, receive a (differential) rent and also consume all their income; and the capitalists, who earn the profits and who, by saving all of their income, provide the means for the accumulation of capital (which is the main source of economic growth). Growth is brought about by the accumulation of physical capital.

Until the stationary state is reached, the distribution of income is determined as follows: wages are equal to the number of workers times the natural wage-rate; rents are equal, for all different pieces of land, to the difference between actual and marginal productivity; while profits are the residual income (quite high at the beginning of the process). With the process of growth and the use of progressively less fertile land, rent becomes increasingly relevant at the expense of profits; then, at a certain point, capitalists will be discouraged from accumulating and the system will come to a standstill. The distribution of capital is straightforward in the classical model: human capital belongs to the working class; land, by definition, belongs to the rentiers, while physical capital (machinery) belongs to the capitalists. The progressive expansion of the economy tends to reduce the share of profits, while the share of rent in particular, as well as that of wages, tends to increase.

The analysis of income and wealth distribution in a growth model in which the economic behaviour of classes (or dynasties) is externally given was initiated by the Cambridge school. Kaldor (1956) and Pasinetti (1962) investigated the relationship between the steady-state rate of profits on the one hand, and the saving propensities of the social classes and the rate of growth of the economy on the other. Assuming two identifiable classes of individuals (on this point see Baranzini, 1991, Chs 1–4) who receive different factor payments (i.e. a working class which receives wages and interest payments, and a capitalist class which receives mainly interest payments), Pasinetti (1962) was able to show that the long-run equilibrium interest rate is equal to the exogenously given natural rate of growth divided by the capitalists' propensity to save: i.e. $P/K = n/sc$, where sc is the marginal and average propensity to save of the capitalist class. At the same time the share of profits in national income comes to be equal to $P/Y = nK/Ysc$, where (in most Post Keynesian models) K/Y is the exogenously given capital/output ratio, defined by technical conditions. In this way the behaviour of the working class (propensities to consume and to save, and patterns of capital accumulation) does not interfere with the distribution of income between profits and wages, nor with the determination of the profit rate (as well as the wage rate). In a certain sense we again find the classical proposition: the capitalist class provides most of the savings held within the system and defines the path of capital accumulation of the whole society; through its behaviour, it heavily influences the distribution of income among factors of production. Of course the non-capitalist classes (workers in this case) may, through their saving, consumption and accumulation behaviour, influence (as it seems more logical) the distribution of income among classes and their accumulation of savings path. The decisions relative to investment and growth of the productive system then come to be taken by a sort of 'entrepreneurial elite'. The case of our modern and industrialized societies is quite illuminating: public authorities, via their fiscal and monetary policies, try to reach a predetermined 'required' rate of growth for the nation which will allow them both to check public expenditure and to reach other economic policy goals.

The classical-Post Keynesian model of distribution briefly expounded above has been widely expanded in recent decades to include most aspects of modern economic systems, a development which proves that such a model (based on the coexistence of different socioeconomic classes) represents a serious alternative. At this point we may mention the lines of research which have been directly stimulated by this model of distribution (cf. Baranzini, 1991, pp. 56–73). They are:

1. the introduction of a differentiated rate of return for the various capitals of the system;
2. the introduction of a non-neutral monetary sector and of portfolio choice;
3. stability analysis and the long-term properties of the model;
4. the introduction of the public sector (various kinds of taxation) and of an external sector of the economy;
5. the extension of the model to include other kinds of socioeconomic classes; also other ways of closing the model and of determining equilibrium values of the main variables;
6. the introduction of the life-cycle theory into the model, providing a microeconomic framework, and
7. the analysis of the long-term distribution of wealth and of the income share of socioeconomic classes.

A total of 400 scientific papers and chapters or entire volumes and textbooks have been devoted to the above Post Keynesian and neo-Ricardian schemes of analysis, with the results proving quite interesting. From a general point of view, this specific research programme (for a partial bibliography see, again, Baranzini, 1991) has shown the following insights and conclusions:

1. The distribution of income among factors of production and among classes is no longer determined by technical factors only, as in the marginalist model, but also by demographic, institutional and historical factors. This aspect is much more in line with what happens in the real world and allows us to grasp the practical relevance of the analytical results obtained;
2. The strategic importance of the capitalist class in the process of accumulation, distribution and saving is confirmed. On the other hand the other classes, via their consumption behaviour, play a relevant role in determining the composition of demand, which in its turn (cf. Engel's Law) affects the composition and level of employment and production;
3. The relevance of the monetary factor, which is of course non-neutral in the process of distribution and accumulation;
4. The relevance of the distinction between life-cycle savings and intergenerational capital stock, as influenced by the historical process of accumulation. On this point we shall return below.
5. The analytical relevance of the equilibrium results obtained. The analysis of stability and convergence confirms the long-term properties of the system.
6. The possibility that the model has to generate new classes or to reinforce distinctions between the already existing classes.

The main drawbacks of the classical-Post Keynesian research programme of distribution and accumulation may be summarized as follows:

1. The constancy of the two propensities to save, exogenously given and hence independent of other variables as, for instance, the rate of return on capital and the rate of growth of population;
2. The assumption and identification of individuals who retain their class identity forever, i.e. classes which are inter-generationally stable;
3. The assumption of equality, in the long run, between the rate of profits which capitalists receive from their investments and the rate of interest received by workers on their accumulated savings (and hence lent indirectly back to active capitalists);
4. The assumption that classes can be almost entirely identified with given factors of production.

The first point above has raised considerable interest in the literature; in particular, it has been shown that the introduction of micro-foundations in the macro-model of distribution and accumulation may provide the following positive results (Baranzini, 1991, pp. 82–3):

1. More insight into the determination of the distribution of income among classes (at least when they all own a positive share of the capital stock) and into the determination of the equilibrium variables of the model.
2. An understanding of the sort of reasons that may lead to historical class differences, to a different accumulation of capital (both life-cycle and inter-generational), and to the particular conditions under which a class may start accumulating inter-generational assets.
3. An elucidation of the applicability of the Meade-Samuelson and Modigliani condition (according to which capitalists' capital share vanishes in the long run) or of the opposite condition (according to which workers' inter-generational capital share tends to zero). This should make it possible to determine when the equilibrium interest rate is the same for all classes of the system and when the possibility of multiple equilibria exists.
4. An assessment of the relative strength of the life-cycle versus the inter-generational capital stock and of the conditions which favour one or the other of the capital stocks.

It is clear that such a research programme is bound to link the marginalist approach (which provides the backbone for the microeconomic foundations via an intertemporal utility function for both consumption and bequest) and the Post Keynesian macroeconomic model (with its constant capital/output ratio and exogenously given rate of growth of population and of technical progress). In this way the problem of income distribution comes to be strictly related with the issue of capital accumulation and class differentiation, which are at the very basis of most physiocrat, classical, Post Keynesian and neo-Ricardian models. Actually the questions that one may ask in this context are of the following type. What are the consequences of the introduction (both in a deterministic and stochastic context) of the hypothesis of an imperfect capital market, which is rather appealing in a two- or multi-class model? Additionally, what are the consequences of the introduction of uncertainty on the optimal consumption and accumulation rates of the two classes? And how relevant is uncertainty in generating differences among classes, i.e. classes with a higher propensity to save (or to accumulate) than average? The results obtained are quite interesting (both analytically and empirically) and confirm the validity of the micro/macro approach obtained by combining a life-cycle framework with a post Keynesian macroeconomic model.

The short review that we have provided here has shown that the distribution of income and wealth (both functional and among social groups) cannot simply be reduced to a technological issue according to which the share of income is determined by the marginal productivity of factors of production times the quantity employed (as in the case of the marginalist approach), but is a function of a number of parameters, among which we find technology, demography, institutions, history and economic structures as being the most important.

MAURO BARANZINI

References

Baranzini, M. (1991), *A Theory of Wealth Distribution and Accumulation*, Oxford: Oxford University Press.

Harcourt, G.C. (1972), *Some Cambridge Controversies in the Theory of Capital*, Cambridge: Cambridge University Press.

Kaldor, N. (1956), 'Alternative Theories of Distribution', *Review of Economic Studies*, **23** (2), 83–100.

Pasinetti, L.L. (1962), 'The Rate of Profit and Income Distribution in Relation to the Rate of Economic Growth', *Review of Economic Studies*, **29**, 267–79.

Pasinetti, L.L. (1974), *Growth and Income Distribution: Essays in Economic Theory*, Cambridge: Cambridge University Press.

Division of labour

From the origins of modern economics, in particular in the work of Adam Smith, the division of labour (d.o.l.) was seen as central to the exchange economy. In classical political economy, where labour was considered the main factor of production, specialization in production was seen as the principal source of economic development and also as the source of exchange itself, in that consumption needs were generally seen as universal. Thus it was the move away from self-sufficiency in production that created the need for a market mechanism to reintegrate the now separated productive activities. In this context, Smith's famous maxim that the division of labour depends on the extent of the market can be seen as linking economic progress in general to the growth and unification of market economies. At the same time, the concept of the d.o.l. was central to the emergence of a sociological account of modernity: the distinctions between contract and status, between society and community, and between mechanical and organic solidarity can all be closely related to the contrast between a market organization of specialized producers and older economic systems with more self-sufficiency.

Already in Smith, as in other writers of the Scottish enlightenment, the social and human ambivalence of modern economic organization resting on the d.o.l. was perceived. Smith himself was aware of the inequalities that resulted from differential positions within the d.o.l. It is also significant that his own famous example of pin manufacture as an extreme case of subdivided tasks points to a d.o.l. within the enterprise and hence not organized by the market. Both the damage to the individual personality and the loss of social cohesion which can follow from an extreme d.o.l. were common themes in the critique of industrial society from the 19th century.

The work of Marx was crucial both in deepening and adding precision to the concept of the d.o.l. and in its use as an instrument of critical thought. Firstly Marx sets the d.o.l. in a different dynamic: capitalist economic development is now seen as multi-factor so that capital accumulation and technical change are more important influences than specialization of tasks; in fact, these latter processes continually shape and reshape the d.o.l.. Often, for example, the detailed subdivision of a task was the prelude to mechanization, so that the d.o.l. became a kind of preparatory analysis of the production process prior to its reintegration through machinery. The structure of industrial tasks continually changes in this perspective, with a long-run tendency for the replacement of directly productive labour by the supervision of machine processes. Nothing in these developments, however, reverses the functional separation of individual producers within an increasingly complex economic structure held together imperfectly by market exchange. Marx stressed the distinction between the *social* d.o.l. which existed among enterprises and the *technical* d.o.l. within the enterprise. The latter was not directly a market relation, but a micro-planned structure imposed by proprietors on employees by virtue of their asymmetric positions in the market. Consequences included one-sided development of workers who acquired mastery of only one or a few very specific functions, as well as a specific role for completely unskilled labour so that some workers specialized in 'the absence of all development'. Even those workers with valuable skills were threatened by continual accumulation and the associated recasting of the d.o.l. in a process where industrialists necessarily aimed to replace skilled by unskilled work wherever they could. The fate of handloom weavers in 19th century Britain can exemplify this aspect of the process: at first in great demand as the mechanization of spinning built up a mass market, the skills of the weavers were subsequently devalued by the mechanization of weaving itself which subjected them to a long and agonizing elimination. Early 20th century Marxist thought did not always develop the critical view of the d.o.l. since it was more concerned with distributional and other issues, though in the second half of the 20th century a revival of interest in these themes occurred.

Corresponding to the Marxian notion of a technical d.o.l. there developed a critique of 'scientific management' or *Taylorism*. The issue here was a very detailed division of operational tasks, together with the radical separation of the labour of execution from that of conception. Critical analyses led to the conclusion that the goal behind Taylorist work practices was in no sense 'efficiency' in any neutral or purely technical sense, but rather control over the labour process and its rhythm. The term Fordism was then used to denote, as a starting point, the reconstruction of the production process as a whole in ways which enforced Taylorist work organization, classically through the use of assembly line methods. The dynamic behind the introduction of these technologies thus becomes as much a question of conflict and control as of productive efficiency as such. Elsewhere critical analysis of labour market functioning led to notions of *dualism*: here the rationality and social efficiency of the market-controlled social d.o.l. was called into question by pointing out the structures of exclusion and privilege.

The international division of labour was a further aspect; this was examined in ways that tend to corroborate the view that the d.o.l. can be regarded as an imposed and hierarchical structure of relations, rather than one which follows from free market choice among agents in a basically symmetrical position. Of great importance in this context is *dependency theory*. Although some formulations of dependency theory have been criticized as excessively static, the insight of the importance of cumulative causation in determining the structure of trade has recently been confirmed by the *new international trade theory*, which points exactly to the advantages available to first entrants into any position in the world market (here again there is some precedent in Smith's famous infant industry argument).

Returning to the division of labour within economies, there have been important debates on both positive and prescriptive issues. The de-skilling debate centred on the tendency of capitalist development to eliminate existing skills and on whether or not counter-tendencies exist towards new forms of skill or even (in the most optimistic accounts) towards the emergence of multi-skilled or polyvalent workers. There have also been discussions on dualism, not that differentiation and fragmentation of labour markets are denied as such, but that the nature of segmentation and its dynamics has been disputed. Recent experience seems to point to relatively sombre assessments of both aspects of the d.o.l. On the one hand a certain widening of tasks is observed within many enterprises, but this is linked to attempts to integrate workers concerned into the firm to such a point that they identify their interests with those of the enterprise. Thus the technical division of labour may be less rigid but more controlled. Meanwhile high and persistent unemployment both intensifies existing patterns of differentiation and disadvantage and also inhibits any positive change in terms of worker autonomy within the firm, which now becomes a refuge from the immediate pressures of the labour market. Much recent work in the mainstream tradition of labour economies has tended to confirm the existence of this dilemma of the 'involved' worker, stressing the structural differentiation between the employed and the unemployed which follows from the nature of the employment relation itself.

Programmatic work by heterodox social scientists, whether in policy-oriented or utopian mode, has been characterized by related debates. At issue is whether the goals of equality and autonomy for all producers are best furthered by imposing constraints on the functioning of the market-controlled d.o.l. or by the development of a non-market sphere of free productive activity. Reconstruction of the d.o.l. in either direction seems to lead to a challenge to the more celebratory varieties of post-modernism which see actual autonomy (to the extent that it might exist) in the sphere of consumption and taste rather than in production.

Finally, feminist writing has forced a fundamental reassessment of the entire field of inquiry. Deep-rooted inequalities and oppression are found both in the status-linked hierarchies of the enterprise and in the systemic properties of labour markets. At the same time the division of labour within the home and in the reproduction of the population itself become necessary elements of the debate, with programmatic thinking having to be recast to include issues and conflicts often previously expunged as purely personal. In this way feminist contributions seem to validate many aspects of the heterodox approach to the d.o.l. which is again seen as unfree and unequal. However, this confirmation is linked to a change of perspective which clearly shows the limited and relative nature of the previous debates.

Contemporary economic developments in general suggest that the d.o.l. as such cannot be seen as the key to inequality and alienation within modern economies. On the one hand the real widening of tasks and responsibilities which is observed within many sections of advanced economies does nothing in itself to mitigate the fragmentation of interest and patterns of domination which stem from competitive individualism. Nor does such widening mitigate the isolation and separation of agency which, it is increasingly obvious, are related to the general complexity of the economic system, rather than simply to differentiations of the forms of labour. On the other hand, both within advanced economies and on a global scale, there are alarming tendencies to exclusion from economic life as a whole. These phenomena of exclusion are difficult to interpret within any functionalist framework, whether this is provided by optimistic neo-liberal accounts of the market or by classical Marxist views of imperialism and the industrial reserve army. A continuing erosion of status in economic life by the forces of market exchange leaves increasing numbers of individuals and even whole communities without the means to gain admission to the division of labour. This was the essence of original critiques of the d.o.l. during the enlightenment: exchange may offer an income to a butcher or a baker, but nothing is due to a human being as such; admission, even to a differentiated working society, is contingent on purely market forces.

The reinforcement of status as a basis of economic entitlement, however, poses critical problems in a modern society since it continues to be the case that the strongest and the most stable status relations arise from traditional and historically circumscribed forms of community, often with an ethnic or national basis. In this context notions of universal entitlement and of citizenship assume immense importance, as citizenship can be seen as a modern status relation rather than one dependent on particular and historically given social identities. The 'basic needs' approach to problems of underdevelopment seems fruitful here. In industrialized economies the notion of an economic citizenship points both to the gradual introduction of a right to work and to the reinforcement of professional status. Increasing access to broadly defined professions, where both rewards and working responsibilities are made relatively independent of market forces, seems a useful strategy for the reassertion of social control over the division of labour.

JOHN GRAHL

References

Beechey, V. (ed.) (1983), *Unequal Work*, London: Verso.

Blackburn, P., Coombs, R. and Green, K. (1985), *Technology, Economic Growth and the Labour Process*, London: Macmillan.

Braverman, H. (1974), *Labour and Monopoly Capital: The Degradation of Work in the Twentieth Century*, New York: Monthly Review Press.

Gorz, A. (ed.) (1976), *The Division of Labour: The Labour Process and Class Struggle in Contemporary Capitalism*, Brighton: Harvester.

Wilkinson, F. (ed.) (1981), *The Dynamics of Labour Market Segmentation*, Cambridge: Academic Press.

Dual labour markets (in Third World countries)

It is a remarkable fact that in almost all Third World countries an extreme degree of poverty of a major proportion of the population coexists with very low rates of open unemployment. Put in other words, it is amazing that hard-working *employed* people can be so poor. In very general terms, the reason for this apparent enigma is that the goods produced by the work of these people have a very low market value. Supply and demand factors account for this: the goods are cheap because the workers are extremely unskilled and have low productivity; there is excess supply of labour, and the potential supply of goods exceeds the level of actual demand.

In Third World countries, unskilled and low-paid workers live side by side with workers whose standard of life and working conditions mimic those of workers in the advanced industrialized economies. There is a very clear cleavage between the two groups of workers, but what really seems crucial is the dramatic economic and social abyss separating them within the same country, and the huge number of labourers working in very poor conditions.

Multinationals, state and large family-owned enterprises maintain fairly standard labour relations all over the world. There are differences across national experiences, but in general, workers in these enterprises are protected by labour legislation, have some degree of job security, are unionized, receive on-the-job training and are therefore qualified to perform certain specific tasks. For all these reasons, firms see these workers as important for the maintenance of their good performance, and pay them accordingly. Indeed, their wages are usually above the value of their marginal products or the 'competitive wage rate', for firms are prepared to share their economic rents with the workers.

In industrialized countries, apart from human capital attributes, race, gender and religion are the main factors behind the segmentation of the labour market. There is also segmentation due to seniority rules or the development of labour markets inside firms (Doeringer and Piore, 1971). Most workers are legally employed and have acquired a certain level of general education and specific skills. Furthermore, due to the development of welfare and unemployment benefit schemes, workers in the North have fairly decent reservation wages. The majority of the labour force therefore enjoys reasonably good working conditions and fairly high standards of living.

Segmentation in Third World countries has different properties. The term 'dual labour market' is quite appropriate, for it alludes to the notion of two separate and distinctive segments. In the formal sector, capitalist (or wage) labour relations are predominant; capital and labour are subject to legal constraints, while workers have specific skills and produce goods which satisfy minimum standards of quality. There is yet another important characteristic: workers in the formal sector are consumers of goods produced in the capitalist core of the economy. Hence, they consume most of the goods they produce.

In newly industrialized countries like Korea or Brazil, the bulk of workers in the formal sector belong to the first two or three generations of industrial workers. During the post-Second World War industrialization, they emigrated from the rural areas for lack of opportunities. When they came to the urban areas searching for a better chance, their levels of general education and skills were quite low. However, firms needed a stable labour force and therefore had to provide workers with the required skills. Once they had been trained, these workers became important for the firms which were then obviously prepared to pay more to retain them (Mazumdar, 1983). This is an important factor explaining wage differentials between workers in the formal and informal sectors in Third World countries. Mazumdar (1983, p. 256) mentions a study conducted in Bombay, where he found that 'workers in factories employing 500 or more workers earned two and one-half time the casuals, after controlling for (human capital) factors'.

Urban workers in the informal segment of the labour market constitute a stock of first- and second-generation immigrants coming from the rural areas who cannot find a job in a 'modern' capitalist firm. By modern capitalist firm, I mean one in which labour laws apply, where workers are paid at least the statutory minimum wage and can develop a career within the enterprise. The workers and their families do not return to the countryside, for the opportunities there are even worse than in the cities: the lack of access to land or to credit and capital prevents the development of any economically feasible rural activity. In the cities they become self-employed or find an illegal job performing tasks which do not demand any special ability. 'Illegal' in this context does not necessarily mean dealing with drugs or prostitution, but only the fact that labour legislation does not apply either to the employer or the employee.

Informal sector and low-paid formal sector workers and their families form an enormous sub-market which consumes a significant part of the goods and services produced in the informal sector itself. It is like an island within the country. Their incomes are too low to afford most of the manufactured goods produced in the modern sector; similarly, the quality of the goods they produce and the services they provide are usually too low to attract clients from the middle and upper layers of the formal sector, though personal servants are an exception.

There is a structural element which partly explains why some workers find a job in the modern capitalist core of the economy and others do not, or why some go to the formal sector and others end up in the informal sector. The long-run path of aggregate demand seems to play an important role in this connection. In essence, the development of huge informal labour markets of the kind described here results from a secular insufficiency of growth of demand for goods in the modern sector. If demand for labour in the modern sector could grow faster than the supply of labour, the excess of labour would gradually tend to vanish. However, the demand for labour can only grow faster if the demand for goods produced in the modern sector grows faster. The problem then is associated with the determinants of the volume and sectoral composition of aggregate demand, and their relation with the distribution of income.

A stagnationist-type argument found in classical economists like Lauderdale, Malthus and Sismonde de Sismondi applies quite well to this problem. The French political economist Sismondi (1819), for example, noted that 'the equality of enjoyment must always have as a result the continual extension of the market for the producers; their inequality must always make it shrink' (p. 331). In the same vein, he argued that 'by the concentration of fortunes in the hands of a small number of owners, the internal market is all the time shrinking' (p. 336). According to the stagnationist argument, a 'distributive trap' ensues when the propensity of the rich to consume is low, when the distribution of income is unequal and when the income of a vast majority of the population is low. These elements together imply a sluggish demand for goods and labour except if, for some reason, the levels of investment, exports or government expenditures compensate for the low level of consumption (see Dutt, 1984). In large closed economies like India and Brazil, it seems clear that the inequality in the distribution of income constitutes a hindrance to the growth of aggregate demand and employment.

The problem is not only one of global demand, but also of sectoral demand. The distribution of income affects the sectoral profile of supply by determining the types of goods for which there exists profitable demand. If the distribution of income is inequitable, potential demand will be biased towards the production of durable and luxury goods. Firms in the modern sector will direct their production to goods of greater sophistication. As this process evolves, a gradually smaller share of the population will have access to the goods, implying a reduction of the market. As noted already, the poorer workers in the formal and the informal sectors constitute a separate market in which cheap goods of lower quality are transacted.

An example of the relation between income distribution and the sectoral pattern of demand is given by De Janvry and Sadoulet (1983). They note that over the 1970s, electrical machines and transport equipment (cars in particular) were the most dynamic sectors – as measured by annual growth of output – in both Brazil and the US. In the US, the poorest 80 per cent were responsible for a significant share of the demand for the goods produced in those two sectors (64 per cent for cars and 69 per cent for electrical appliances). In

Brazil, by contrast, the contribution of the poorest 80 per cent was almost insignificant (6 per cent for cars and 21 per cent for electrical equipment). The conclusion drawn by De Janvry and Sadoulet is that, in Brazil, 'wage incomes do not create an important market for the key sectors' (p. 297).

Growth of aggregate demand, redistribution of income towards the poorer, and the redirection of supply to the production of wage-goods are necessary but not sufficient conditions for reducing the size of the informal sector in Third World countries. In the context of continuing technical progress and increasing international competition, education and training of the labour force seem imperative. In countries where the 'reserve army' is formed by uneducated and unskilled workers, even if (for whatever reason) the demand for labour started growing very fast, modern firms would have a hard time finding suitable workers. They would eventually hire unskilled workers for very low wages and start training them. When the level of formal primary and secondary education is very low, workers are slow to learn the techniques required to perform specific tasks. Hence, together with redistributive measures, there is the need to provide poorer families with basic and professional education.

It seems clear that poverty and the existence of the informal segment of the labour market are intimately related in Third World countries. Greater taxation of the rich and redistribution to the poor in the form of better public education and health services are required to reverse the situation. However, it goes without saying that the measures needed to reduce poverty and the size of the informal sector face enormous and very effective political opposition.

EDWARD J. AMADEO

References

De Janvry, A. and Sadoulet, E. (1983), 'Social Articulation as a Condition for Equitable Growth', *Journal of Development Economics*, **13**, 275–303.

Doeringer, P. and Piore, M. (1971), *Internal Labor Markets and Manpower Analysis*, Lexington, Mass.: D.C. Heath and Co.

Dutt, A. (1984), 'Stagnation, Income Distribution, and Monopoly Power', *Cambridge Journal of Economics*, **8** (1), 25–40.

Lewis, A. (1958), 'Economic Development with Unlimited Supplies of Labour', in A. Agarwala and S. Singh (eds), *The Economics of Underdevelopment*, London: Macmillan.

Mazumdar, D. (1983), 'Segmented Labor Markets in LDC's, *American Economic Review*, **73** (2), 254–9.

Sismonde de Sismondi, J.C.L. (1819), *Nouveaux Principes d'Economie Politique*, Paris: Delauny, 2 volumes.

Taylor, L. and Bacha, E. (1979), 'The Unequalizing Spiral: A First Growth Model for Belindia', *Quarterly Journal of Economics*, **XC.**

Econometrics

Econometrics is the process of using statistical methods to estimate economic relationships. It involves an interactive synthesis of economic theory, usually cast in mathematical form; measured data; procedures for statistical inference which provide the probabilistic framework for estimating parameters and testing hypotheses; and methods of computation. The end result of the interaction is an empirical econometric model which can be judged in terms of (1) its relevance for a particular purpose, such as forecasting, decision making or testing theories; (2) its consistency with other theoretical, historical or institutional information, and (3) its adequacy in representing the data. Econometrics is sometimes narrowly interpreted as being just the study of the methods of inference relevant to economic problems, particularly various types of regression, but it is the synthesis of the elements that is crucial. Since econometrics is a large, highly technical and very controversial subject, it is impossible to be comprehensive in 2,000 words; instead I will comment on some aspects that may interest radical political economists. A good discussion of the history, the techniques and the controversies that surround the subject can be found in Pesaran (1987), who also provides an extensive bibliography.

The fact that they are highly technical does not mean that econometric and statistical procedures are independent of ideology; for instance, Mackenzie (1981) shows how regression methods originated in eugenicist views of the world. Different schools of economic thought also have different attitudes to econometrics. The rapid growth in the use of econometrics, particularly between about 1950 and 1970, owed much to Keynesianism. Keynes himself was hostile, mounting a vitriolic attack on Tinbergen's econometric model of the trade cycle. However, Keynesian relations were straightforward to quantify, unlike supply and demand curves; Keynesian national income accounts provided plentiful data, and interventionist governments needed quantitative forecasts and estimates in order to manage the economy. Thus macroeconometrics flourished and macro-models proliferated. Those on the right shared Keynes's hostility. Monetarists, like Friedman, were sceptical of econometric techniques, though they used them on occasion. Many new classical economists rejected them outright: the Lucas critique provided a clear logical basis for the rejection of econometrics, while their calibrated real business cycle models did not rely on econometrically estimated parameters. Reflecting the right-wing shift in the profession, most macro-theorists are hostile to the large econometric models still widely used by government and business, e.g. see Mankiw (1990) and Summers (1991).

The Lucas critique starts from the observation that the behaviour of economic agents (as summarized in estimated relationships like the Phillips curve and the consumption function) will depend on their expectations about policy. If policy changes, then so will their expectations and thus their behaviour. As a result equations estimated from past behaviour will be unstable, likely to break down, and of no use in predicting the effect of any policy change. This is a specific example of a general problem of structural stability: why should we expect relationships observed in the past to persist into the future? Whether such structural instability is empirically important enough to destroy the basis of econometrics is a matter of heated dispute.

These are disputes within orthodoxy; beyond it, why should radical political economists be interested in econometrics? To the extent that most econometrics embodies orthodox economic theories, measures and methods of inference, they need only know enough to criticize and denounce it effectively. This has been a common response by radicals, including some established econometricians such as Zarembka and Rapping, who have renounced the subject. One basis for the critique of econometrics is provided by critical realism (e.g. Bhaskar, 1978). Using this approach Lawson has argued in a series of papers that there are inherent methodological (or more precisely ontological) limitations to the scope of application of econometrics (Lawson, 1989).

Lawson's critique generalizes the problem of structural instability. It argues that constant conjunctions of events – the empirical regularities presupposed by econometric analysis – neither exist in the social realm nor are necessary for scientific analysis. According to critical realism, stability exists in the social sphere, as in the natural sphere, not at the level of 'surface phenomena' such as events or states of affairs, but at the deeper level of the mechanisms (structures, relations and tendencies) that underlie those events and govern them. Strict empirical regularities, constant conjunctions of events, are a rare phenomenon even in natural science; they occur only in controlled experiments where the non-empirical mechanisms can be physically isolated and empirically identified. Outside experiments, any mechanism operates in conjunction with other countervailing mechanisms so that its operation is not directly manifest; likewise, any observed empirical event is a conjunction of numerous countervailing causes. Cases like planetary motion, where a single mechanism – gravity – almost completely dominates the observations, are extremely rare. On occasion, a particular mechanism may dominate sufficiently over a certain span of time or space to produce an apparent empirical regularity or 'stylized fact'. But such empirical patterns will in general be partial and non-persistent and, Lawson argues, cannot be refined into econometric relationships. They can, however, be a starting point for trying to understand the deeper structures or mechanisms that govern them and are being momentarily revealed. The aim is not to generalize specific empirical claims (induction), but to identify the non-empirical mechanisms that govern and condition them (retroduction). In this view, econometrics is, at best, limited to the initial illumination of the rough-and-ready empirical claims from which analysis takes off.

Even outside the orthodox tradition, few would go as far as Lawson, while others have tried to construct a radical econometrics which uses alternative theories, measures and methods to identify the underlying mechanisms. In a recent collection of papers, Dunne (1991) argues that much of Marxist theory can be cast into a form suitable for estimation and that data which corresponds to Marxist categories, e.g. measured in value terms or expressing more general social relations, can be constructed. Thus, given methods of statistical inference, it is possible to develop a quantitative Marxist econometrics which, they argue, need be neither empiricist nor incompatible with Marx's dialectical method.

In Dunne (1991), Desai quotes Marx in a letter to Engels in 1873 describing his analysis of data on prices, discount rate, etc. and saying, 'I have tried several times – for the analysis of crises – to calculate these ups and downs as irregular curves and thought (I still think that it is possible with enough tangible material) that I could determine the main laws of crises mathematically'. As Desai notes, there are still severe technical, mathematical and statistical obstacles to Marx's objective, although a number of contributors express some hope that the developing theory for chaotic systems may offer a route forward. Desai also makes the point that many aspects of the Marxist approach, such as the disjuncture between appearance and reality which is also central to Lawson's critique, are fundamental to statistical inference in econometrics too. The identification problem – the relationship between the unobservable structural form and the observable reduced form – is an example. Without a strong theoretical input, we cannot infer the structure from the observed data or determine the underlying mechanisms that govern events, even for such simple constructs as demand and supply curves.

None of the papers in Dunne (1991) addresses the nature of statistical inference itself. Although statistical inference raises deep philosophical and methodological problems, these tend not to be addressed by orthodox methodologists of economics, partly because of the technical level of the philosophy of statistics involved and partly because of the dominance of deductive logic in economics. Statistical methods involve probabilistic procedures for inferring general relationships from particular observations – that is, rules for induction. Since there is no philosophical basis for induction nor any agreement about the empirical definition of probabilities (beyond that they should satisfy certain axioms), it is not surprising that statistical inference is a matter of extreme controversy. This is most manifest between classical and Bayesian statisticians. Classical statistics, the type normally taught to social scientists, is (1) based on the notion of probabilities as the limit of a relative frequency as the number of observations becomes large, (2) treats parameters as fixed and (3) uses the Neyman-Pearson theory of significance testing, with its arbitrary use of some fixed probability of wrongly rejecting the null hypothesis. The Bayesian approach (1) views probabilities as subjective, (2) considers parameters as random variables and (3) uses the observed data to update some prior probability distribution for the parameters. These controversies between Bayesian and classical statisticians are reflected in econometrics, there being half a dozen conflicting approaches to the construction and evaluation of models. Darnell and Evans (1990) review and criticize these approaches. An important, though often implicit, element in the dispute involves different views of the purpose of econometrics.

Most practitioners have quite limited views of the purpose of econometrics. It is certainly not to establish economic laws of the sort Marx referred to in the quote above. Few would believe that economics generates well-established quantitative relationships of the sort provided by Newtonian natural science, laws which might be discovered by theoretical and empirical investigation. Even the strongest candidates – Gresham's law that bad money drives out good and Engel's law that the share of income spent on food declines with income – have to be heavily qualified. There would also be considerable scepticism about the weaker purpose of providing Popperian falsification of economic theories. The major difficulty this purpose faces is the Duhem-Quine thesis: theories are complicated composite constructs and it is never clear whether falsifying a particular model rejects a core element of the theory or some unimportant auxiliary assumption.

In principle, the Duhem-Quine problem is common to all science; in practice, it is far worse in econometrics. By their nature economic theories, orthodox or radical, are so general as to be non-operational. They come in the form of equilibrium conditions or dialectical interactions between unobserved variables, such as demand and supply or the class struggle. They merely say *ceteris paribus*, without specifying which other countervailing mechanisms are likely to be operating. The functional form of the relationship is usually undefined. To construct a model that represents a theory, the econometrician must undertake the following: choose observable proxies for the variables; specify functional forms; allow for expectation and adjustment processes; add extra factors to allow for other things not being equal, and make some assumptions about the distributions of errors. If the data then reject the model, is it the theory that is rejected or these auxiliary assumptions made by the econometrician? This uncertainty partly explains the ineffectiveness of econometric evidence to resolve issues like the Monetarist-Keynesian dispute.

One of the major developments in econometrics in recent years is in the testing of these auxiliary assumptions. When estimating a model, it is assumed, for instance, that the model is linear, that regressors are exogenous, that disturbances are independent, normally distributed with constant variance, and that parameters are stable. Since tests and inferences are only valid if these assumptions are true, it is important to investigate them. A battery of powerful misspecification or diagnostic tests is now available to do this. But while these diagnostics may reveal whether a particular estimated model is misspecified, and thus help to produce better models, they provide little help in testing substantive economic theories. Nonetheless, it remains a valuable discipline to have to ask whether a particular theory can be cast into the form of a model that is coherent with the data.

If econometrics will not reveal laws or falsify theories, if it rests on problematic notions of statistical inference, if it is vulnerable to endemic structural instability, what then is its purpose? The positive view is that econometrics can synthesize a large amount of information in an effective way. By using statistical methods to bring together data and theory, it provides a framework for systematic thought about economic phenomena. Within this framework it is possible to assemble and store information on data and relationships; to impose consistency, by ensuring that everything adds up properly for instance; to follow through complicated linkages' to use judgment and extraneous information in a coherent way; to ask clear questions and evaluate the answers, and all this very quickly on a computer. This framework can then be used, in a sympathetic rather than a mechanical way, to try to understand the economy, to provide forecasts or analyse policy.

RON SMITH

References

Bhaskar, R. (1978), *A Realist Theory of Science*, Brighton: Harvester Press.
Darnell, A. and Evans, J.L. (1990), *The Limits of Econometrics*, Aldershot: Edward Elgar.
Dunne, J.P. (ed.) (1991), *Quantitative Marxism*, Cambridge: Polity Press.
Lawson, A. (1989), 'Realism and Instrumentalism in the Development of Econometrics', *Oxford Economic Papers*, **41**, 236–58.
Mackenzie, D.A. (1981), *Statistics in Britain*, Edinburgh: Edinburgh University Press.
Mankiw, N.G. (1990), 'A Quick Refresher Course in Macroeconomics', *Journal of Economic Literature*, **28** (4), 1645–60.
Pesaran, M.H. (1987), 'Econometrics' in J. Eatwell, M. Milgate and P. Newman (eds), *The New Palgrave, A Dictionary of Economics*, Vol. 2, London: Macmillan, 8–22.
Summers, L.H. (1991), 'The Scientific Illusion in Empirical Macroeconomics', *Scandinavian Journal of Economics*, **93** (2), 129–48.

Effective demand

The term 'effective demand' is generally associated with the theory of output and employment determination proposed by Keynes in his *General Theory of Employment, Interest and Money*. The 'theory of effective demand' was intended to replace Say's 'Law of Markets' which states that there is no natural impediment to the operation of market forces in establishing full employment. Keynes traced the origin of this proposition to the quantity theory assumption of the long-run neutrality of money, building his own theory on the integration of monetary and real factors in the short period.

The development of Keynes's criticism of the quantity theory started under the influence of the 'Cambridge' school of monetary economics professed by Marshall and Lavington; this emphasized that money could not be considered as a commodity, but was at least partially endogenously determined by banks as a result of their lending activities. The possibility that there was no stable linkage between the quantity of commodity money and bank liabilities created by lending brought into question the independence and stability of the velocity of money.

In criticism of Irving Fisher's version of the quantity theory and stimulated by the work of Dennis Robertson on economic fluctuations, Keynes (1913) produced an early explanation of the cycle based on variations in credit creation by banks. If families hold temporarily unspent income as deposits which banks lend to business to finance investment of a larger amount because of the money multiplier, then current investment may exceed intended savings. This disequilibrium becomes visible in capital markets when firms try to sell long-term liabilities in order to repay loans from the banks and discover that savings are insufficient. This means that some bank loans are not repaid; banks then try to offset this illiquidity by reducing accommodation to business borrowers, causing excess supplies and a fall-off in investment. The divergence of saving and investment caused by endogenous money thus produces fluctuations in investment and prices.

Ralph Hawtrey (1913), working along similar lines, had argued that 'the manufacturer's efforts in producing ... goods depends upon there being an effective demand for them. It is only because the dealer anticipates this effective demand ... that he gives the manufacturer the order. ... The manufacturer ... accepting the order, and the banker discounting the bill, are both endorsing the opinion of the dealer. The whole transaction is based ultimately on an expectation of a future demand, which must be more or less speculative' (p. 78).

Thus, when Keynes started his *Treatise on Money* the idea of 'effective demand', linked to money creation of the banking system and based on expected future price and quantity conditions, was under general discussion. In his analysis of the two 'fundamental equations' for prices (based on unit labour costs) and the divergence of savings now joined the behaviour of nominal wages and labour productivity at the centre of the price determination process for consumption goods. The prices of capital assets were determined independently of the equations, by what Keynes called the 'bullishness and bearishness' of the public in deciding either to hold bank deposits or to finance capital projects directly through share purchase.

In *The General Theory*, Keynes noted that in the *Treatise* the prices of capital assets and bank deposits were determined by the same process. To remedy this deficiency (in a way which resembles Gunnar Myrdal's approach in his *Monetary Equilibrium*), the marginal efficiency of capital was formulated to deal with capital assets, with liquidity preference (bullishness and bearishness) reserved for the determination of financial assets, including bank deposits. Thus, in his new book Keynes argued that investment expenditure would be carried to the point which produces a marginal efficiency of capital, determined by expected net revenues over the life of the marginal investment, i.e. by expected consumers' expenditures on the output of the project less its expected costs of operation, discounted at the rate of interest, which is just equal to the rate of interest on money. The rate of interest, however, is determined independently of this relation by the liquidity preference of the public and the banking system and the policy of the central bank. Thus, 'effective demand is made up of the sum of two factors based respectively on the expectation of what is going to be consumed and on the expectation of what is going to be invested' (1973, p. 439). Therefore, the theory of effective demand is based on the combined influence of monetary (liquidity preference of the public and the banks) and real factors translated into expected future monetary sums (marginal efficiency of capital and propensity to consume).

The level of actual output and of employment was then determined by the 'point of effective demand' represented by the intersection of the aggregate supply price curve (a relation expressing the amounts of output and employment that entrepreneurs would offer for different levels of expected net monetary receipts) and the aggregate demand price curve (defined as the net receipts which entrepreneurs would expect to receive from alternative levels of output and employment). This intersection would determine the amount of labour entrepreneurs would hire to produce both investment goods and consumption goods and thus generate the actual level of income. The propensity to consume would determine households' actual expenditures out of income and the net receipts actually earned by investments undertaken. Expectations could be confirmed or disappointed. In equilibrium, short-term expectations concerning sales levels and profits on output from current capacity would be confirmed and would not raise doubts concerning long-term expectations of future capacity needs. Keynes thus states 'the *effective demand* is simply the aggregate income (or proceeds) which the entrepreneurs expect to receive … from the amount of current employment which they decide to give. … [It] is the point on the aggregate demand function which becomes effective because, taken in conjunction with the conditions of supply, it corresponds to the level of employment which maximises the entrepreneur's expectation of profit' (1936, p. 55).

Note that 'aggregate' demand is determined by the incomes produced by the expenditures generated by effective demand. Many economists interpreted Keynes's theory as relying on a divergence between effective demand and actual income (produced by aggregate demand) caused by mistaken expectations. Keynes argued that since long-term expectations would be little affected by short-term variations in output, they should be relatively stable in the face of disappointed short-term expectations; since long-term expectations determine investment expenditures, actual income should converge to the point of effective demand. Keynes's main point was not that entrepreneurs could make mistakes in predicting the future, but that even if short-term expectations were confirmed, there was no reason for the equilibrium determined by the unique point of effective demand to correspond to full employment output. Within Keynes's framework, Say's Law would be represented by the coincidence of aggregate supply price and aggregate demand price curves until reaching full employment, so that the only stopping point to an expansion was given by the supply of real resources.

Hayek, who had also been working on the relation between money and prices, criticized the *Treatise* for the absence of a theory of capital which formed the basis of his own approach. In the second volume of the *Treatise*, Keynes had employed what he called 'a simple relation' to explain relative prices based on analysis of spot and forward markets for foreign exchange in his *Tract on Monetary Reform*, extended to commodities. Sraffa (1932) developed this approach into 'commodity rates' of interest which he used to criticize Hayek's (1931) theory; Keynes in turn called this 'own rates' in his alternative expression of the theory of effective demand in Chapters 16 and 17 of *The General Theory*.

In the *Tract* Keynes had formulated what is now known as the interest rate parity theorem which states that, in equilibrium, the premium or discount of the forward price, F, of foreign exchange relative to its spot price, S, must be equal to the difference between the rate of interest paid on domestic deposits i, and foreign deposits i^*, of equivalent maturity, or formally $(F/S) - 1 = f = (i - i^*)/1 + i^*$. In simple terms, the foreign interest rate less the costs of insuring against a change in the value of foreign currency in the forward market will equal the domestic rate so that $i = f(1 + i^*) + i^*$. If the foreign rate is above the domestic, the insurance costs will be positive as foreign currency will have to be sold forward for domestic currency at a lower rate than it was bought (foreign currency is at a forward discount so f is negative), while in the opposite case they are negative since money is made by selling foreign currency forward at a higher price (a forward premium) than it was bought.

The importance of this relation is that it establishes an equivalence between rates of interest and inter-temporal prices. The interest rates in the formula are also relations between the spot and forward price of money for, as Keynes noted in his definition of the rate of interest on money in *The General Theory*, it is 'nothing more than the percentage excess of a sum of money contracted for forward delivery ... over what we may call the "spot" or cash price of the sum thus contracted for forward delivery' (p. 222). Writing F for the forward sum and S for the cash price, the rate of interest is $(F/S) - 1$. The marginal efficiency of capital, defined as the rate of discount which brings the flow of expected future net receipts of an investment project, F, into equality with its present production costs, S, normally written as $S = F/(1 + \text{mec})$ for a single period, may also be rewritten as $\text{mec} = (F/S) - 1$ to make it formally equivalent with the definition of the annual rate of interest (although Keynes warns against overlooking the fact that capital investments produce uncertain future returns over a number of periods and thus a net present value calculation in terms of demand and supply prices of capital is more appropriate).

The point of effective demand may then be defined by the equivalence of the forward premia of placing money in new investment projects and in lending money to buy financial assets. This approach may then be generalized by recalling the interest rate parity theorem which produces an equilibrium pattern of rates of return on holding domestic currency and $n - 1$ foreign currencies. Demand becomes effective at the point at which the rate of interest on money or the liquidity premium on money (as determined by the liquidity preference of the public and the banking system given the policy of the monetary authority) is equal to the rate of return to be earned on each of the $n - 1$ other types of investments (determined by their marginal efficiencies or their associated future premia or discounts determined by carrying costs and returns).

Any change in liquidity preference or monetary policy will thus change the rate of interest and shift the point of effective demand. A fall in the interest rate, for example, represents a fall in the forward price of money and shifts demand to other assets. This drives up the spot price of other assets and makes it profitable to initiate new investment. Income will increase, via the multiplier, by an amount sufficient to produce saving equal to the new investment. This will also produce a decline in the marginal efficiency of investment by influencing the forward premia on all assets until their spot prices relative to forward prices produce a rate of return equal to that on money. Both prices and quantities must adjust simultaneously for the economy to reach the new point of effective demand.

Just as in the interest rate parity theorem, where investment in foreign currencies is determined by the relation between the domestic and foreign interest rates, in this framework the only limitation on the level of output and employment is the relation between the rate of interest on money and the marginal efficiencies of capital investments. The failure of the interest rate on money to move automatically to the level required by full employment may also be interpreted as the failure of relative prices, as expressed in forward premia of different assets, to adjust to the proper level. However, the explanation for this failure, and thus for the predominance of unemployment as a quasi-permanent condition in capitalist economies, is not due to any failure of the operation of the free market price mechanism, but to the 'essential properties' of money which cause the money rate of interest to fall less rapidly than the rates on other assets when demand increases. Thus, Keynes's theory of effective demand not only integrates monetary and real factors, but it gives money the dominant role by also providing a theory of relative intertemporal money prices within the context of a monetary production economy which exhibits no spontaneous tendency to achieve full employment as a natural position of equilibrium.

J.A. KREGEL

References

Hawtrey, R. (1913), *Good and Bad Trade*, London: Constable.

Hayek, F. (1925), 'Die Wahrungspolitik der Vereinigten Staaten seit der Uberwinding der Krise von 1920', partially translated as 'The Monetary Policy of the United States After the Recovery from the 1920 Crisis' in Roy McCloughry (ed.) (1984), *Money, Capital and Fluctuations: Early Essays of F.A. Hayek*, London: Routledge & Kegan Paul.

Hayek, F. (1931), *Prices and Production*, London: Routledge.

Keynes, J.M. (1913), 'How Far Are Bankers Responsible for the Alternations of Crisis and Depression?', reprinted in *The Collected Writings of John Maynard Keynes, Vol. XIII, The General Theory and After: Part I, Preparation*, London: Macmillan for the Royal Economic Society, 1973.

Keynes, J.M. (1923), *A Tract on Monetary Reform*, London: Macmillan.

Keynes, J.M. (1930), *A Treatise on Money*, London: Macmillan.

Keynes, J.M. (1936), *The General Theory of Employment, Interest and Money*, London: Macmillan.

Myrdal, G. (1939), *Monetary Equilibrium*, London: William Hodge.

Sraffa, P. (1932), 'Dr Hayek on Money and Capital', *Economic Journal*, **42** (2), June.

Efficiency

It is generally assumed that 'efficiency' is something to be striven for, with the connotation that without it something desirable is lost or wasted. Nevertheless, whether efficiency is desirable depends upon implicit objectives and how they are defined and measured. No doubt all would like our school systems to be 'efficient' in the education of children, but there is much controversy over what constitutes a well-educated child. Peace-lovers might prefer their government's army to be inefficient. In this entry, efficiency will be considered in relation to purely economic objectives: the satisfaction of human needs through the production and consumption of goods and services.

Within production organizations, efficiency is defined in relation to both inputs and outputs. A mistake frequently made is to identify efficiency with maximum output, or dynamic efficiency with maximum growth. If, for example, a greater factory output is achieved by a reduction in workers' meal breaks, this in itself represents neither a rise nor a fall in productive efficiency because the input of worker-time has also increased. The correct way to define efficiency is via its converse – inefficiency. A system of production is inefficient if it is possible to produce more of any of its outputs without reducing any output or increasing any inputs; alternatively, it is inefficient if, without reducing any outputs, it would be possible to reduce one or more of the inputs while not increasing any other input. If production is not inefficient in either of these ways, it may be termed efficient. A corresponding definition applies to dynamic efficiency in the context of production over time, where current outputs are invested to produce future outputs. These definitions are common to both orthodox neoclassical and radical economics.

Within society, orthodoxy calls on the notion of 'allocative efficiency' based on the Pareto criterion: a system of societal allocation is efficient if it is impossible by some redistribution or reorganization to make some people better off without making one or more persons worse off. Under the abstruse assumptions of 'perfect competition', Pareto efficiency is guaranteed. There are however many well-known sources of market failure, including externalities and information asymmetries, which lead to inefficient allocations. While radical political economists recognize the importance of market failures, the fundamental objection is to the individualism inherent in the Pareto criterion as well as to the inherently conservative bias it supports: a societal transformation that supports greater efficiency in meeting human needs may require a reduction in inequality. 'Efficiency', then, is potentially one of those big issues, a critical discussion of which can be coextensive with a critique of capitalism. This article will however concentrate on narrower efficiency issues within productive institutions.

Orthodox neoclassical economics has, till recently at least, claimed that an organization which maximizes profits cannot be inefficient. The context for this strong claim is the 'black box' methodology with which production is analysed. Inputs are purchased in free exchange and 'transformed' into outputs which are then sold. This theory does not enquire into the economics of how the inputs are converted into outputs – that is assumed to be solely a technical datum. Thus the workplace is a 'black box' into which the economist need not peer.

The technical data may be summed up with a vector Z, the elements of which are the inputs and outputs of the production process, with inputs negative and outputs positive. Suppose it were claimed that a particular production system, Z_1, is inefficient. Then there must be another feasible production, Z_2, such that $Z_2 \geq Z_1$ with at least one element in Z_2 greater than the corresponding one in Z_1. With a positive price vector, P, it follows that $PZ_2 > PZ_1$; that is the net profits obtained from Z_2 are greater than those from Z_1. Hence Z_1 could not be profit maximizing.

An essential implicit assumption underlying this orthodox result is that the commodity-space in which commodities are exchanged (and P defined) is the same as the production-space of Z in which inputs are transformed into outputs. From Marx onwards, radical political economists have rejected this assumption as false with respect to the most important input – labour. Marx distinguishes between labour-power, that commodity which is bought on the labour market, and labour itself, the process of working to produce things or services of use. Labour-power may be thought of as the ability and willingness to work, the disjuncture between this and labour being gauged by work intensity or work effort. The process by which labour is extracted from labour-power – the management of labour – is not a technical datum, but a social relation which may be affected by both the external environment and the production technology. There is therefore no fixed mapping from commodity-space into production-space, proving the orthodox theorem to be incorrect (Green and Sutcliffe, 1987, Ch. 3).

These considerations may be exemplified by considering the advantages for capitalist firms of the division of labour. According to Adam Smith and subsequent orthodox economists, the benefits of the division of labour derive from technical facts such as the time saved by workers not having to switch between different tasks, for example, by walking between the field and the household: a production organization that does not take advantage of the division of labour is thus inefficient. However, the chief advantage for capitalists of the systematic fragmentation of work tasks advocated by the 'scientific management' philosophy of F.W. Taylor is that it increases management's control over labour and thereby raises the intensity of work (Braverman, 1974). The 'Taylorization' of production systems has undoubtedly raised both output and profits in many Western factories throughout this century, but this cannot be termed increased efficiency insofar as it is achieved through raising work intensity. Indeed, there are important respects in which Taylorism, as a system of production organization, is inefficient, not least in that it systematically suppresses the creative powers of workers themselves. Such powers cannot be harnessed to capitalist aims in the conflictual settings where Taylorism reigns, a fact exposed by the non-Taylorist methods of Japanese production systems. In addition, the rigid demarcations to which Taylorism has given rise are a source of inflexibility in times of uncertainty.

For a further example, consider the application of assembly-line production systems – often called the 'Fordist' production method. The specific efficiency gain of this system is that it reduces the time and energy required to move either the worker or the partly-completed product to the next stage. Yet this gain cannot account for the enormous increases in productivity that assembly-lines introduced, particularly in vehicle production. The main advantage for capitalists is the control over the pace of work that the technology allowed, and the concomitant ability to raise work effort. The modern computer has sometimes been found to perform a similar function in deskilling work tasks and controlling the work-effort of office workers (Barker and Downing, 1980).

The general lesson to be drawn is that innovations in production which lead to rises in labour productivity may not necessarily constitute a move to greater efficiency. Radical political economists have been able to explain many features of modern production in terms, not of what is most efficient, but of the outcome of conflict between management and labour, with the former dominant. These include the segmentation of labour markets, sexual and racial discrimination, the adoption of deskilling technologies and the hierarchical organization of workplaces.

In recent years neoclassical writers have also addressed these issues in ways that have some similarities with Marxist economists (Green, 1988). These modern neoclassical economists have broken with the tradition of assuming full information and, in particular, have recognized that the management of labour is both costly and imperfect. As a consequence the underlying notion of efficiency is re-cast. Workers are assumed to be self-interested (like all economic agents) and to dislike working, at least at the margin. Capitalists must therefore employ inputs (perhaps supervisory workers) to monitor worker performance. These supervisory inputs do not produce anything, and in a world of certainty their employment would be inefficient. But given the self-interested and 'opportunistic' behaviour of workers, supervisors are necessary. Therefore, the question has become: what form of organization and what form of feasible work contract lead to the most efficient production? It is now claimed that organizations with wage hierarchies and devoted to profit maximizing will necessarily be efficient, but little rigour attaches to such claims.

For radical political economists, these claims are false because they are based on an individualist approach to production organizations which assumes that workers' attitudes to work and their preferences are part of a fixed human nature, independent of the institutional and social context. On the contrary, there is considerable evidence that workers' propensity to shirk, or to perform with less than maximum effort, depends a great deal on whether they identify with and are fulfilled through their work. This depends on how far they are able to develop and use their individual potentials, how far their individual contributions are connected to the whole production process, how far they respect the authority of the production plan, whether it is seen as 'fair', and so on. Much of the study of management recognizes these facts, implicitly or explicitly, though they are ignored by neoclassical economics. For radical political economists the point is that the profit-maximizing firm may operate inefficiently and, conversely, that for an organization to operate efficiently, it need not have profit maximizing as its objective. This latter statement implies that production organized on more socialist principles has the possibility of being efficient. Indeed there is evidence that elements of socialist organization have led to greater efficiency in many areas within capitalist society; these include the impact of workplace democracy and cooperative participation (Hodgson, 1984, Ch. 9). This evidence cannot easily be universalized, however, and there is no suggestion that capitalism would be more successful if all firms operated as cooperatives. Nor is it claimed that a socialist enterprise would not have to find ways of making workers accountable for their efforts and contribution to production. The only safe conclusion we can draw is that the efficiency or otherwise of any production organization cannot be deduced *a priori* from its technical data: both its advantages for capitalists and its efficiency are contingent on social relations inside and outside the organization.

FRANCIS GREEN

References

Barker, J. and Downing, H. (1980), 'Word Processing and the Transformation of the Patriarchal Relations of Control in the Office', *Capital and Class*, No. 10, Spring, 64–99.

Braverman, H. (1974), *Labor and Monopoly Capital*, New York: Monthly Review Press.

Green, F. (1988), 'Neoclassical and Marxian Conceptions of Production', *Cambridge Journal of Economics*, **12**, 299–312.

Green, F. and Sutcliffe, B. (1987), *The Profit System*, Harmondsworth: Penguin.

Hodgson, G. (1984), *The Democratic Economy*, Harmondsworth: Penguin.

Employment relations and contracts

In *Capital*, Karl Marx made a distinction between labour (the activity of work) and labour-power (the capacity to work). It is labour-power, not labour, that is bought by the capitalist employer, perhaps by the hour. Marxian labour process theorists such as Braverman (1974) have addressed the specific social arrangements and practices concerned with the extraction of the maximum possible amount of labour from a given quantity of labour-power. They are able to do this by asserting that no predetermined quantity or quality of labour flows automatically from the sale of labour-power that is specified in the contract of employment. Instead, the outcome depends on a struggle and trial of strength between management and employees.

Nevertheless, there are problems with some of the formulations in this literature. For instance, Edwards (1979) writes: 'Workers must provide labour power in order to receive their wages, that is, they must show up for work; but they need not necessarily provide *labor*' (p. 12). However, we may object that if the worker remained idle, he or she would actually be in breach of the employment contract: neither labour nor labour-power would be supplied.

Furthermore and strikingly, much of Braverman's famous analysis can be turned against his own assertion of the distinction between labour-power and labour. In giving great emphasis to the methods through which it is ensured that the maximum labour is extracted from labour-power – such as hierarchical organization, incentives, discipline and managerial supervision – Braverman is implying that the amount of labour performed is essentially under capitalist control. As Littler and Salaman (1982) put it: 'the overall theoretical thrust of *Labor and Monopoly Capital* is to suggest that capitalists no longer face the problem of labour power as a variable and indeterminate component of the production process' (p. 252).

It is questionable whether recent work by Marxists is more successful in overcoming this problem. For instance, Samuel Bowles and his collaborators (such as Herbert Gintis, David Gordon and Thomas Weisskopf) also draw on the distinction between labour and labour-power. In their analyses they stress the possibility of a 'free lunch' – of extra output being obtained without an increase in inputs due to waste and slack in the economy. They also claim to explain variable productivity by reference to the balance of class forces within the firm. Thus Bowles's (1985) analysis focuses on the (costly) processes through which employers exercise power over labour, and the ability of workers to resist. Likewise, the amount of labour performed and consequently output achieved depend on factors such as the level of unemployment and the degree of unionization, both of which help to determine (positively or negatively) 'employer leverage' over workers.

Given the parameters that determine 'employer leverage', a fixed amount of labour will exude from a given amount of labour-power. Output is not simply a function of capital and labour, although a determinate (more complex) 'production function' exists nevertheless. One is left querying the purpose of the distinction between labour and labour-power in this analysis, especially given such orthodox features as the assumption of maximizing behaviour by both employers and employees which results in a predetermined equilibrium solution. Any 'extra' output must flow from a change in the parameters of a given function.

Arguably, what is not essential to a model of this type is the phraseology of class struggle; indeed, real struggle is actually excluded. Whilst in some sense there is a distinction between labour and labour-power – in that performed labour will depend upon factors which are additional to the employment contract – given those factors, the amount of labour is predetermined once the contract is agreed.

Braverman and others (like Marx before) fail to emphasize an essential element in the argument. To sustain the distinction between labour and labour-power, and indeed the basic conceptual autonomy of production from exchange, it is necessary to show that (within limits) the amount of labour extracted from labour-power is in some sense *indeterminate.*

The first theorist to give substantial attention to indeterminacy in the employment contract is Simon (1951). He attacks the traditional view in economic theory that labour is a 'passive factor of production', asserting that the orthodox view 'abstracts away from the most obvious peculiarities of the employment contract' (p. 293). This is seen to differ 'fundamentally from a sales contract – the kind of contract that is assumed in ordinary formulations of price theory' (p. 294). In a sales contract a 'completely specified commodity' is exchanged for an agreed sum of money. Even in cases where complete specification is absent, the details of the agreement are often regarded by law as implicit or 'understood'. In contrast, in the employment contract the worker agrees to perform one option from a mutually agreed and limited range of patterns of work, allowing the employer to select and allocate the tasks. In effect the worker agrees to accept the authority of the employer, notably concerning the specification of the particular work to be performed.

Whilst noting the frequency of contracts of this type in the real world, Simon does not examine the reasons why employers do not or cannot fully specify the work in advance. Fortunately, however, these reasons are fairly well understood today. Imperfectly specified employment contracts are widely attributed to the possibility of unforeseen changes in product demand or in the supply of materials or components, or of interruptions in production as a result of mechanical malfunctions or industrial disputes.

The pecuniary consequence of this indeterminacy, Simon argues, is that compared to a sales contract where the worker is contracted to supply a well-specified commodity or service), the capitalist will pay a higher wage for the privilege of asserting authority over the worker and of postponing the precise specification of the work to be performed.

The key indeterminacy in Simon's model is the fact that the outcomes (i.e. profits, work satisfaction, etc.) for each pattern of work are not known precisely at the time of contracting. Simon formalizes this by considering the probability density function of outcomes for each feasible pattern of work. At the time of contracting, both employer and employee are assumed to know the relevant probabilities, but not the precise outcomes.

While Simon advances our understanding of the employment contract by recognizing its essential indeterminacy, it is notable that he treats this as a matter of calculable probability. There is another problem here. If the probabilities are known, then it not only makes possible a complete specification of the contract from the start, but it also undermines the concept of authority that is central to Simon's argument. Given the probability distributions, the worker can compute the likelihood of each pattern of work being selected by the employer. Thus the acceptance of authority is not simply within the limits, but also within known probabilities, of employer behaviour. The ruling authority is not the employer but, as it were, the random throw of the dice. Given maximizing behaviour, the employer has no more power over the choice of outcome than the employee. The only significant difference is that the choice of pattern of work has the employer's utility as the maximand, given that the worker has maximized first.

In this context we may briefly note the more recent approach to the peculiarities of the employment contract, developed primarily by Williamson (1975). In his central thesis, the main purpose and effect of economic institutions such as the firm is to economize on transaction costs. However, the idea of transaction costs has been widely criticized as a catch-all phrase for multifarious deviations from the price mechanism. Furthermore, the typical formal representation of transaction costs among mathematical economists, as a fixed proportion of the value of the goods that are exchanged, differs in no significant way from a regular transportation cost.

Some writers have seen transaction costs as essentially informational in character. But it is important to recognize that the arguments of John Maynard Keynes in *The General Theory* have rendered the very idea of a rational calculus of information costs objectionable; in the normal circumstances of uncertainty we are forced to abandon full, rational calculation and are obliged to fall back on 'the convention' or 'average opinion'. Further, if such a rational calculus were possible, it is not clear why market contracting has been superseded by the organization of the firm.

It is proposed here that some degree of objective indeterminacy does exist in the production process, partly as a result of which agents are uncertain (in the sense of Frank Knight or John Maynard Keynes) as to the outcomes. Because the consequences of contracts pertaining to employment and production are not known precisely, even in terms of calculable probabilities and even when all contracts are concluded, real uncertainty is unavoidable and there is a functional distinction between production and exchange – a distinction that has eluded many orthodox theorists. Production is no longer an annex of the market because of the indeterminate outcome of production itself. All agents in the productive process confront the unforeseen and have to react to the unexpected. The forthright will engage with others to create stratagems and institutions to deal with the problems that are foreseen. But, essentially, the notion of an 'optimum' or an 'equilibrium' is without much meaning, for eventualities depend on imagination and expectation concerning an unfolding but uncertain future.

Of course, for Keynes the existence of uncertainty was crucial to his theory of macroeconomic behaviour. It appears that the concept of radical uncertainty is also crucial to the analysis of microeconomic institutions, such as the capitalist firm and the employment contract within it. In sum, the worker agrees to provide labour but to an imperfectly specified pattern, subject to some indeterminacy. Given the indeterminacy inherent in production, there must be choices and clashes of will: matters are not resolved *ex ante* by contractual or marketplace decisions, despite the orthodox assertion that the employment contract is subject to 'continuous renegotiation' during production.

What is suggested then, is that the distinctions made between employment and other contracts, between labour and labour-power, and between firms and markets, can be sustained only on the basis of the concept of true uncertainty. This suggests a fruitful amalgam between the economics of Marx and that of Keynes.

GEOFFREY M. HODGSON

References

Bowles, S. (1985), 'The Production Process in a Competitive Economy: Walrasian, Neo-Hobbesian, and Marxian Models', *American Economic Review*, **75** (1), March, 16–36. Reprinted in L. Putterman (ed.) (1986), *The Economic Nature of the Firm: A Reader*, Cambridge: Cambridge University Press.

Braverman, H. (1974), *Labor and Monopoly Capital: The Degradation of Work in the Twentieth Century*, New York: Monthly Review Press.

Edwards, R. (1979), *Contested Terrain: The Transformation of the Workplace in the Twentieth Century*, New York: Basic Books.

Littler, C.R. and Salaman, G. (1982), 'Bravermania and Beyond: Recent Theories of the Labour Process', *Sociology*, **16** (2), May, 251–69.

Simon, H.A. (1951), 'A Formal Theory of the Employment Relationship', *Econometrica*, **19**, July, 293–305. Reprinted in H.A. Simon (1957), *Models of Man: Social and Rational*, New York: Wiley, and in L. Putterman (ed.) (1986), *The Economic Nature of the Firm: A Reader*, Cambridge: Cambridge University Press.

Williamson, O.E. (1975), *Markets and Hierarchies: Analysis and Anti-Trust Implications*, New York: Free Press.

Equilibrium analysis

The following provides a stylized sketch of the evolution of 'equilibrium analysis' in macroeconomics. The limited number of references is allocated so as to highlight important conceptual changes.

In classical political economy the notion of equilibrium refers to abstract long-run or 'fully adjusted' positions, characterized by the equalization of inter-sectoral rates of return. Temporary disturbances are ruled out; relative prices are determined by production costs. Given the classical data set, such a position need not reflect a social optimum. It is, however, perceived as an attractor ('centre of gravitation') towards which the economy is pushed by inherent forces, mainly competition. Although an idealized position, describing the hypothetical result of identifiable economic forces, it is relevant to real-world analysis to the extent that permanent systemic forces can be isolated and their impact on the data set quantified.

Despite the obvious changes in *theoretical* content brought about by the marginal revolution, the *method* of long-run equilibrium analysis remained the same (Walras, 1977). With a different set of data, activity levels become endogenous. Discussion of the characteristics of the equilibrium position soon centred around the triad of existence, stability and optimality. New criteria, such as the absence of individual excess demands, became prominent, while the set of relative prices was now determined symmetrically by supply and demand; however, equalization of remuneration rates remained the condition *sine qua non*: the notion of equilibrium still describes an abstract long-run or fully adjusted position towards which the economy is pushed by forces inherent to the system. Equilibrium analysis as an attempt to disentangle permanent from transitory forces without ever implying an actual realization of the equilibrium configuration was shared by both schools (Garegnani 1976). A change in the method of *long-run equilibrium analysis* manifested itself only in the inter-war period.

At least two developments have to be distinguished here, both reflecting growing concern with the dynamics of the Walrasian system. The first refers to the notion of inter-temporal equilibrium used by Hayek *et al.* in attempts to find a systematic explanation for the business cycle. The other is the notion of temporary equilibrium put forward by Hicks (1939) which should become relevant for Keynesian macroeconomics. (Note, that neither the Cowles commission nor the Swedish school is discussed here.)

The aim in reconciling the business cycle – understood as *regular* co-movements of economic variables such as prices and outputs – with contemporary equilibrium analysis was not to explain the readjustment to a new equilibrium position following some initial disturbance. Rather it was to find convincing reasons to explain why activity levels should exhibit regular patterns of oscillation, including recurrent patterns *away* from the fully adjusted position. The deduction of regular fluctuations required either propagation mechanisms to account for regular and self-perpetuating overshooting (Hayek), or impulses not driven by 'sun-spots' but themselves the outcome of regular economic interaction (Schumpeter), or both (the Marxist tradition).

One possibility was to accept the Walrasian data set but to insist on structural feedback problems triggered by prices failing to perform their allocative function. The most important example of prices systematically conveying wrong signals, while important enough to cause repercussions for the system as a whole, is the distinction between the market and the natural rate of interest. However, the ultimate goal of deducing regular fluctuations by 'widening the assumptions' upon which equilibrium theory is based (Hayek) was never fully accomplished. The project fell into oblivion as the depression dragged on and, later, as Keynesian economics swept the profession.

The method of *temporary equilibrium analysis* was originally devised to partition the Walrasian time horizon into 'short' stretches where the trading period could be terminated before capital goods had fully adjusted. Strangely, the concept gained major importance as underlying IS-LM economics (including dynamic versions generated by multiplier-accelerator combinations): the device of temporary equilibrium, designed to open the way towards a more dynamic analysis, thus resulted in the notion of a short-run equilibrium, identified by the proverbial dictum 'no inherent tendency to change'.

To slip into the role of buttressing IS-LM equilibria with multiplier-determined activity levels, the efficiency postulates inherent in the notion of long-run general equilibrium analysis had to be tamed by performing aggregation with an incomplete set of markets or by introducing price rigidities (to justify 45-degree diagrams and the 'traps' of IS-LM theorizing). Thus, sub-optimal short-run equilibria came at a heavy theoretical expense (Kohn, 1986). One way out, namely to reintroduce the generality of the Walrasian system without falling for the need of perfectly coordinated outcomes, by further exploiting the distinction between notional and effective demand functions, was not taken.

The Keynesian-Monetarist debate prepared macroeconomics for future theoretical developments, but it does not loom large in a discussion of methods of analysis. Centred around the speed and likelihood of adjustment processes, the problems addressed were dynamic in nature. However, the short-run equilibrium concept was never questioned. The construct thus became exposed to more profound attacks – an easy target because the macromodels fashionable throughout the 1960s did indeed not represent fully specified equilibria.

The neoclassical growth model and the perfection of Walras's model in an atemporal setting provided by Arrow and Debreu (1954) both have to be taken into account for understanding the origin of the new classical criticism. The articulate Arrow-Debreu model, with complete contingency markets and strict informational requirements, at first sight could not have been perceived as all that relevant for macroeconomics; without it, however, the criticism of lacking microfoundations would not have mounted as it did. Likewise, the steady-state growth model, battered by the Cambridge critique, initially seemed to provide for little more than points of reference for comparative statics or attempts at endogenizing fluctuations via multiplier-accelerator interaction. But as a dynamic aggregated system, it became the 'dual' of the atemporal version, an attractor which expressed the optimality postulates of the latter in a much more workable manner. That left two venues: either to abandon the short-run equilibrium notion as untenable – which would have been a step back; or to find a device to incorporate observed fluctuations without losing the optimality properties associated with both the steady state *and* the atemporal version of modern equilibrium theory. The latter was accomplished by integrating the behavioural hypothesis of rational expectations into the structure of general equilibrium theory – replacing the full information assumption with mutual consistent beliefs, in effect continuously as people maximize objective functions subject to perceived constraints.

The result was a shift in method, from temporary or short-run to *continuous equilibrium analysis*. Though accompanied by theoretical conclusions reminiscent of monetarist imagination, labels such as 'monetarism mark II' (Tobin) are slightly misleading: it was this shift in method which had come to stay and not the initial set of economic theorems associated with it.

The greatest accomplishment of new classical macroeconomics is its reconciliation of equilibrium theory in a Walrasian tradition with mainstream macroeconomics. In a nutshell, its success relied on two simple devices: the replacement of the neoclassical synthesis with the dynamics of the neoclassical growth model, coupled with stochastic disturbances; and the replacement of ill-informed Keynesian agents with the representative geniuses of rational expectation models. With optimizing behaviour and mutual consistent beliefs, only the most convenient informational assumptions (asymmetries) are needed to allow for economic fluctuations – without giving up optimizing behaviour and consistent beliefs.

Another way of looking at this development is that new classical macroeconomics took up the pieces where the Austrians had left them. That would be a misunderstanding. The Austrians kept the equilibrium growth path as a point of reference because they attempted to explain systematic tendencies to move away from it. The new classical notion of continuous equilibrium and instantaneous adjustment relies on white noise to generate fluctuations. Neither a systematic explanation of technological or structural change, nor a systematic account of oscillations deduced from maladjustments in the price system, was ever part of the picture.

However, even with deviations perceived as the best possible responses to unforeseeable shocks (given information sets), it was soon realized that the optimal growth path itself need not be invariant to changes in the data caused by random shocks. As equilibrium business cycle theory moved from nominal to real impulses, the old concept of an exogenously determined growth path receded somewhat into the background, and with it the ancient notion of a long-run trend determined independently from short-run fluctuations. Economic development became contingent on stochastic vibrations of production functions, which in principle opens the way to reconsider uneven development over time as a result of structural adjustment processes.

The lasting legacy of new classical macroeconomics will consist in having redefined the notion of equilibrium from a position with no inherent tendency to change ('position at rest') to a state of affairs where 'no gains from trade are left unexploited'. In the process, macroeconomics has switched from old-fashioned equilibrium vs disequilibrium considerations and from (comparative) statics to dynamics, with the presumption of equilibrium as a situation of demand and supply moving continuously in line because excess demands are virtually instantaneously eliminated.

However, the notion of continuous equilibrium does not require representative agent models, just as it by no means precludes economic fluctuations. It also does not exclude the treatment of coordination failures as long as the latter are perceived to be equilibrium phenomena, i.e. framed as multiple equilibria which can be Pareto-ranked.

There are different ways of wrapping up the story to bring out these achievements. I choose a simple, stylized procedure (leaving aside any discussion of overlapping generation models). It starts with Lucas's statement that the hypothesis of rational expectations has to be understood as a consistency axiom, capable of being reconciled with different theoretical structures. This hints at the possibility of the exogenous growth path losing its importance and seems confirmed by the development of new Keynesian economics, essentially concerned with rationalizing price rigidities. The next step, then, is to focus on the hypothesis of rational expectations itself. The most prominent line of inquiry for that question became the criticism symbolized by the famous Keynesian beauty contest. But the consequence of showing that the use of the hypothesis is limited to instances where the behaviour of economic agents is guaranteed by strong assumptions generating mutual knowledge (consistent beliefs) was by no means to abandon the hypothesis. Instead, the Gordian knot, the impossibility of finding a solution once individual action depends on the *incomputable* expectation of other people's expectations, was simply cut. The possibility of deriving multiple rational expectations equilibria within the slightly modified mathematical structure of general equilibrium models followed. Soon not only structural features of the economy – externalities and non-convexities – but also beliefs ('sun-spots') could be held to provide reasons motivating the existence of multiple equilibria.

The theoretical possibilities revived by discarding the notion that uniqueness is a useful property of equilibrium analysis allows reconciliation with topics abandoned when macroeconomics first converted to the new notion of equilibrium. If multiple equilibria can be attached to structural features of the economy, such as increasing returns to scale, or to the systematic interaction of expectations formation, generating self-fulfilling prophecies, the claim to have reintroduced the coordination question becomes obvious. Small wonder that proponents of such a strategy have quickly approached the hallmark of textbook level (Azariadis, 1993).

Similarly, the literature on endogenous growth seems to result in closing a long-neglected gap – the distinction between growth and business cycle theories. And, again, it is concerned with neglected topics, such as attempts to endogenize technical and structural change and the observed pattern of uneven development. It will not take long for both approaches to merge.

The development of equilibrium analysis thus seems to portray a success story, with macroeconomic theory reverting to the old concern of how efficiently the system is coordinated in different circumstances, albeit on a higher technical level. The use of the equilibrium concept in economic analysis has become increasingly precise, allowing for better and better descriptions of distinct configurations of the economy. However, the perception that 'anything goes' does not mean we understand better. There is doubt as to whether enhanced modelling capacities have translated into clearer vision or, at least, more illustrative pictures; this criticism refers to the concept of unbounded rationality (Leijonhufvud, 1993).

To see where things may have gone astray, consider the most essential difference to older theories entailed in the shift in equilibrium analysis. This lies in the assumptions made about individual behaviour: no one asks so much of the cognitive abilities of 'representative' economic agents as does the modern theorist. Perhaps never in its history has theoretical macroeconomics been more divorced from the level of its daily applications. The question is whether these two observations are opposite sides of the same coin. If behaviour is incorrectly modelled, can one succeed in describing the systemic interaction of the elements that form the system we call 'economy'?

We have come a long way in making precise the concept of equilibrium in economic analysis – from long-run to temporary to continuous equilibrium. But several junctures along the way have never been explored. Somewhere en route we surely have given an overdose of cognitive endowments to rational economic man. At the same time he is situated in a model which, on the most basic level, has been artfully designed to deduct a well-defined optimal allocation of resources from an interactive system, using only few axioms. To say the least, macroeconomics' explanatory and predictive power has not kept pace with the increased formal sophistication needed to squeeze reasons for failure into this combination.

CHRISTOF RÜHL

References

Arrow, K. and Debreu, G. (1954), 'Existence of an Equilibrium for a Competitive Economy', *Econometrica*, **22**.
Azariadis, C. (1993), *Intertemporal Macroeconomics*, Oxford: Basil Blackwell.
Garegnani, P. (1976), 'On a Change in the Notion of Equilibrium in Recent Work on Value and Distribution' in M. Brown, M. Sato and P. Zarembka (eds), *Essays in Modern Capital Theory*, Amsterdam: North Holland.
Hicks, J. (1939), *Value and Capital: An Inquiry into Some Fundamental Principles of Economic Theory*, Oxford: Clarendon Press.
Kohn, M. (1986), 'Monetary Analysis, the Equilibrium Method, and Keynes's *General Theory*', Journal of Political Economy, **94** (6).
Leijonhufvud, A. (1993), 'Towards a Not-Too-Rational Macroeconomics', *Southern Economic Journal*, **60**.
Walras, L. (1977) [1926], *Elements of Pure Economics*, New York: Augustus M. Kelley; reprint of the English translation of the 4th definitive edition by W. Jaffe.

Expectations

Heterodox contributions on expectations in economic analysis tend to be set up in opposition to mainstream approaches. It is therefore useful to begin with the orthodoxy, against which some alternative (Keynesian) views can then be counterposed.

Perhaps the simplest way to model expectations is to assume that agents have 'perfect foresight' or correct point expectations of the relevant variables. This assumption simplifies analysis by allowing the theorist to abstract from the effects or disappointed expectations. It is probably most plausible where people have experienced stable conditions in the past and expect such conditions to continue in the future. For many purposes, however, the fact that expectations are usually subject to uncertainty of some kind or another cannot be ignored. By far the most widely used means to represent uncertainty in economic theory are different variants of the Doctrine of Mathematical Expectation (DME). Consequently, and despite the fact that the relevant temporal considerations are often left implicit, this device has also become most widely used means to represent expectations in economic theory. The basic idea is that expectations should be modelled as the probability-weighted sum or mathematical expectation of the uncertain outcomes q_i, or

$$\sum_{i=1}^{n} p_i q_i .$$

Where an agent must choose one from a number of actions with uncertain outcomes, the decision rule is to select the action with the highest mathematical expectation.

Modern microeconomics is dominated by the Subjective Expected Utility (SEU) model, a more sophisticated version of the DME. In terms of this model, the agent must choose one from a given set of 'acts' a_i $(i = 1, 2, \ldots, n)$, the consequences of c_{ij} of which depend on which of a set of exogenous and mutually exclusive 'states of the world' s_j $(i = 1, 2, \ldots, m)$ obtain. These ideas may be represented in the following payoff matrix:

		States of the world			
		s_1	s_2	$\cdots$	s_m
Acts	a_1	c_{11}	c_{12}	$\cdots$	c_{1m}
	a_2	c_{12}	c_{22}	$\cdots$	c_{2m}
	$\vdots$	$\vdots$	$\vdots$	$\vdots$	$\vdots$
	a_n	c_{n1}	c_{n2}	$\cdots$	c_{nm}

It can be shown that, subject to certain postulates of 'rational choice', a cardinal utility $U(a_i)$ may be attached to each act. There are two stages to the argument. First, numerical indicators of utility $u_i = u(c_{ij})$ are assigned to each consequence, and subjective probabilities $p(s_j)$ to each state of nature. Both sets of numbers may be elicited from the agent's choices concerning hypothetical gambles. Second, the utility of each act is expressed as the mathematical expectation of the utility of the final consequences.

$$u(a_i) = \sum_{j=1}^{m} p_j u(c_{ij}).$$

The decision rule is to select the act which maximizes expected utility. Point expectations (but not necessarily perfect foresight) are a special case of this theory, the expected consequence which corresponds to the state of nature being assigned a subjective probability of 1.

A somewhat stronger variant of the DME, the Rational Expectations Hypothesis (REH), has dominated recent discussion in macroeconomics. While agents are assumed to employ subjective probabilities in the SEU approach, rational expectations are assumed to correspond to the objective probability distribution of outcomes. Muth (1961, p. 316), who coined the term, writes:

'Expectations ... (or, more generally, the subjective probability distribution of outcomes) tend to be distributed, for the same information set, about the prediction of the theory (or the "objective" probability distribution of outcomes)'.

The REH may usefully be compared with the Adaptive Expectations Hypothesis (AEH) it superceded. The AEH may be written

$$ {}_tP^e_{t+1} = {}_{t-1}P^e_t + \lambda(P_t - {}_{t-1}P^e_t) \tag{1} $$

where ${}_tP^e_{t+1}$ denotes the current expectation of the price in the next period, P_t denotes the current price and λ is the adjustment coefficient ($0 < \lambda < 1$). In words, the current price expectation is equal to the price expectation of the preceding period plus some fraction of the amount that this last expectation was in error. By substituting for

${}_{t-1}P^e_t$, ${}_{t-2}P^e_{t-1}$, ... , (1) may be written

$$ {}_tP^e_{t+1} = \lambda \sum_{n=0}^{\infty} (1-\lambda)^n P_{t-n}. $$

In other words, the current expectation of the next period's price is wholly determined by the past history of prices. The closer λ is to 1, the more rapidly expectations adjust to a change in P.

The AEH came under fire on two counts. First, adaptive expectations are based on past observations of only the one relevant variable. This is implausible as agents would be expected to make use of all the information available to them. Second, when prices reveal a trend, the errors between actual and predicted values will be serially correlated. Adaptive expectations, in other words, lead to systematic forecast errors. The REH counters these two objections. Formally, the rational expectation ${}_tP^{re}$ of P is the mathematical expectation of P_{t+1} based on the information available at time t:

$$ {}_tP^{re} = E[P_{t+1} / I_t] $$

where $I_t = P_{t-i}, x_{t-i}$ ($i = 0, \ldots, \infty$), P_{t-i} are current and past values of P, and x_t is a vector of other variables that may help in predicting future values of P. The forecast error $z_{t+1} = P_{t+1} - E[P_{t+1}/I_t]$ has two important properties. First, the conditional expectation at time t of z_{t+1} is 0, since $E[z_{t+1}/I_t] = E[P_{t+1}/I_t] - E[P_{t+1}/I_t] = 0$. Second, forecast errors are orthogonal or serially uncorrelated over time:

$$ E[z_{t+1} \cdot z_t / I_t] = 0. $$

Rational expectations may be disappointed only if there is some unpredictable (unsystematic) shock to the system in which they are formed. Where agents' beliefs are point expectations held with certainty and in the absence of such shocks, rational expectations reduce to perfect foresight.

The AEH and the REH have very different analytical implications. For example, monetarists argue that deviations from the 'natural rate' of unemployment are the result of workers' underestimating their real wages by failing to take into account increases in the rate of inflation. These deviations are only temporary under the AEH, as workers' expectations of inflation gradually catch up to a (once-off) rise in the actual rate. A permanent trade-off requires workers systematically to overestimate their current real wage which, under the AEH, requires a constantly rising rate of inflation. This 'acceleration hypothesis' is ruled out by the REH, where rational expectations may be disappointed only as a result of random shocks. Whereas unanticipated rises in the price level still lead to temporary reductions in unemployment, systematic increases in the rate of inflation leave unemployment unaffected. This idea, formalized by Lucas (1972), precipitated the 'new classical' policy ineffectiveness literature of the 1970s and 1980s. Ironically, the subsequent discovery that speculative bubbles are consistent with the REH reinforces Keynesian doubts about prices reflecting 'fundamental' values on asset markets (Orléan, 1989).

There is little doubt that the DME is a tractable analytical device. For in Keynes's words (1973a, pp. 112–13), it reduces uncertainty about the future 'to the same calculable status as that of certainty itself'. Yet Keynes strongly opposes the DME in economic analysis on the grounds that it 'leads to a wrong interpretation of the principles of behaviour which the need for action compels us to adopt, and to an underestimation of the concealed factors of doubt, precariousness, hope and fear' (p. 122). Keynes's position may be traced to his 1921 *Treatise on Probability* (1973b), where he raises the following objections to the DME:

1. It is not always possible to attach a numerical value to the 'good' (the consequences) that might follow some course of action.
2. Probabilities are seldom numerically measurable (and often cannot even be compared in terms of more than, less than or equal to).
3. The DME ignores differences in the extent or 'weight' of the evidence on which probability judgments are based.
4. The DME makes no allowance for risk (e.g. where two distributions have the same expected values but different variances).

In effect, SEU theory constitutes a response to the first, second and fourth of these objections (the agent's 'attitude towards risk' being interpreted as a property of the curvature of his or her von Neumann-Morgenstern utility function). The critical literature on the normative and descriptive validity of these proposals is too large to consider here. For our purposes it is sufficient to note that SEU theory (and the REH) *assumes* precisely what Keynes is denying, namely that judgments of probability can in principle be mapped onto real numbers on the continuum [0, 1]. Moreover, SEU theory has no counterpart to Keynesian weight, considerations of which raise further questions about assigning probabilities which conform to the probability calculus (Anand, 1991).

Keynes continues to emphasize (2) and (3) above in his economic writings, using the DME as a foil against which to contrast his own views. He argues that, in practice, expectations are based on the 'convention' of projecting the existing situation into the future, except insofar as there are definite reasons to expect a change. He places particular emphasis on the degree of completeness of the information agents have in different situations, which depends heavily on the time-horizon of the expectations involved. These differences have methodological implications. Keynes abstracts from the effects of disappointed short-term (producers') expectations, on the grounds that they are revised gradually so that expected and realized results 'run into and overlap one another in their influence' (Keynes, 1973c, p. 50). Long-term expectations, by contrast, which form the basis of investment and liquidity preference decisions, 'cannot be checked at short intervals in the light of realised results' (p. 51). Although long-term expectations may be stable while existing conventions are maintained, they are prone to sudden revision (with a corresponding impact on the investment component of aggregate demand). This precariousness is exacerbated by mimetic and speculative behaviour on asset markets (Runde, 1991).

The writings of Keynes's followers show considerable diversity on the topic of expectations, ranging from the subjectivist/idealist side of the philosophical spectrum to the realist. Prominent amongst the former is Shackle whose theory of 'potential surprise' is designed to deal with situations in which agents cannot provide an exhaustive list of the possible consequences of their actions. Shackle's more recent work (1972) aims to display the tension inherent in attempts to capture expectations (which he regards as subjectively constructed surrogates for knowledge we do not have) in terms of the 'rational ideal' of formal economic theory. This has led both to his vision of a 'kaleidic' world in which the potential for novelty and sudden expectational shifts is ever present, and to charges of theoretical nihilism from his critics (who argue that his insistence on our 'unknowledge' about the future prevents him from saying much about the future consequences of current actions and, hence, about economic policy).

Recent realist contributions temper the scepticism associated with the Shacklean view. Lawson (1994), for example, a transcendental realist, distinguishes between events and the structures and mechanisms which give rise to and govern them. He argues that although it is impossible to form consistently accurate expectations of events in an open social world, we may nevertheless know a good deal about the structures and mechanisms which underlie those events. While individual agent's choices and actions could always have been other than they were, then, our knowledge of the more enduring structural aspects of social life (rules, social relations, positions and associated practices, etc.) may yet form the basis of expectations which lead to successful action in an uncertain world.

JOCHEN RUNDE

References

Anand, P. (1991), 'The Nature of Rational Choice and *The Foundations of Statistics*, *Oxford Economic Papers*, **43**, 199–216.

Keynes, J.M. (1973a), 'The General Theory and After. Part II: Defence and Development', *The Collected Writings of John Maynard Keynes*, Vol. XIV, New York: St Martin's Press.

Keynes, J.M. (1973b), 'Treatise on Probability', *The Collected Writings of John Maynard Keynes*, Vol. VIII, New York: St Martin's Press.

Keynes, J.M. (1973c), 'The General Theory', *The Collected Writings of John Maynard Keynes*, Vol. VII, New York: St Martin's Press.

Lawson, T. (1994), 'Expectations', in S.C. Dow and J. Hillard (eds), *Keynes, Knowledge and Uncertainty*, Aldershot: Edward Elgar (forthcoming).

Lucas, R.E. (1972), 'Expectations and the Neutrality of Money', *Journal of Economic Theory*, **4**, 103–24.

Muth, J.F. (1961), 'Rational Expectations and the Theory of Price Movements', *Econometrica*, **29**, 315–35.

Orléan, A. (1989), 'Mimetic Contagion and Speculative Bubbles', *Theory and Decision*, **27**, 63–92.

Runde, J.H. (1991), 'Keynesian Uncertainty and the Instability of Beliefs', *Review of Political Economy*, **3**, 125–45.

Shackle, G.L.S. (1972), *Epistemics and Economics*, Cambridge: Cambridge University Press.

Exploitation

The concept of exploitation is central to an understanding of Marx's economic analysis. According to Marx, labour is exploited in all class societies although the form of exploitation varies according to the social system. In a slave or feudal society, exploitation is open and obvious to all participants, as well as to social analysts. However, in a capitalist society with 'voluntary' exchange, exploitation is veiled both from the participants as well as from bourgeois (read non-Marxist) analysts. For Marx, the role of a social scientist is to get beneath the 'appearances' to the 'reality' or 'essence' of things. What is the Marxist concept of exploitation? What are its limitations or weaknesses? Is it possible to have a Marxist analysis of society without using this concept? Is the concept of exploitation simply a tool wielded for political and pejorative purposes? These are the questions addressed in this entry.

The *Shorter Oxford English Dictionary* defines exploitation as: '[T]he action of turning to account: the action of using for selfish purposes'. This rather opaque definition does not seem to capture the usually understood notion of exploitation as being an unfair/unethical (forced) extortion of someone else's labour for the benefit of a favoured group or class. Another common meaning is the exploitation of natural resources by the private or public sector.

Marx's concept of exploitation is set in his dialectical framework of a dynamic, growing society which progresses as a result of the conflict of opposing classes. In this framework profits which are accumulated (invested) provide the engine of economic development which is, in a capitalist society, driven by the capitalist class. What is the source of profits? Do they result from the process of exchange or the process of production? Marx's answer is unambiguous and forceful. Profits are *not* derived from exchange (circulation) as that would simply lead to a redistribution of gains between the different agents (capitalists). Exchange is a zero sum game: in aggregate, profits cannot be explained by exchange. Profits are derived from the nature of the production process where capitalists buy a unique commodity, namely labour-power, whose use value exceeds its exchange value. Labour-power creates *surplus value* which is appropriated by the capitalist and converted into profits through the process of circulation.

This appropriation of surplus value by capitalists comes about, not because of the existence of monopoly power or by cheating, but as a result of a normal capitalist process of production. The main difference between capitalist and pre-capitalist societies (like feudal or slave societies) is that this exploitation is not open and obvious, but veiled by market processes. He argued that in a feudal society exploitation was open, with serfs having to provide a certain amount of free labour for the lord of the manor. Similarly, in a slave society where slaves were simply provided their basic necessities like food and shelter and had to work long hours for their owners, there was obviously exploitation. However, in a capitalist society exploitation is similar in that workers are employed for long hours but paid only their exchange value which is less than their use value. The value of their labour-power in terms of hours or commodities is less than the value (in terms of hours) or the amount of the commodities produced by labour. A surplus is created. One of the main results in Marx's model, dubbed by Morishima as the 'fundamental theorem' of Marxian economics, is that positive surplus value is necessary and sufficient for positive profits in a competitive economy.

This exploitation, he argues, is a necessary concomitant of a capitalist society where the following assumptions hold: (1) competitive conditions exist and (2) capitalists and workers apparently meet on an equal footing and exchange their commodities at equilibrium prices. Marx stresses the point that exploitation is veiled, not only from the workers, *but also from the capitalists* who believe that they are both trading on an equal footing and exchanging equivalent amounts.

> The actual difference of magnitude between profit and surplus value … in the various spheres of production now completely conceals the true nature and origin of profit not only from the capitalist, who has a special interest in deceiving himself on this score, but also from the labourer. The transformation of values into prices of production serves to obscure the basis for determining value itself (*Capital*, Vol. 3. p. 168).

This exploitation is carried out in the process of production even though in the process of circulation there is apparently an equal exchange taking place, with competitive markets and voluntary trade. However, this exchange disguises the unequal relationship between capital and labour, described graphically thus:

> This sphere [circulation] we are deserting, within whose boundaries the sale and purchase of labour-power goes on, is in fact a very Eden of the innate rights of man. There alone rule Freedom, Equality, Property, and Bentham. Freedom, because both buyer and seller of a commodity, say of labour-power, are constrained only by their own free will. … Equality, because … they exchange equivalent for equivalent. Property, because each disposes only of what is his own. And Bentham, because each looks only to himself. On leaving this sphere of simple circulation … we can perceive a change in the physiognomy of our dramatis personae. He, who before was the money-owner, now strides in front as the capitalist; the possessor of labour-power follows as his labourer. The one with an air of importance, smirking, intent on business; the other timid and holding back, like one who is bringing his own hide to market and has nothing to expect but – a hiding (*Capital*, Vol. 1, pp. 175–6).

Further, Marx argues that the surplus labour that is exploited from workers is derived under *social compulsion*, even though it may appear to be freely provided:

> For this [surplus labour] to occur, the labourer must first be compelled to work in excess of the [necessary] time, and this compulsion is exerted by capital (*Theories of Surplus Value*, Vol. 2, p. 406; square brackets added).

There are several criticisms of this theory of exploitation; most of them based on criticisms of the labour theory of value – the transformation problem, joint production, etc. – which require some modification of the details of the concept of exploitation (for further details see, for example, Junankar (1982)).

A frontal attack on the Marxist concept of exploitation has come from Roemer (1982) and a vigorous debate has ensued in the pages of the journal

Philosophy and Public Affairs. Roemer argues that exploitation theory is not relevant to explain (i) the nature of profits or accumulation (accumulation theory); (ii) the unequal power relations in production (domination theory); (iii) alienation under capitalism (alienation theory); or (iv) the inequality of the ownership of the means of production (inequality theory). The main thrust of his argument is that because exploitation theory is based on the labour theory of value (LTV), and because the LTV is not valid or is redundant, hence exploitation theory is invalid. He claims that unequal exchange (LTV) is neither necessary nor sufficient for exploitation, which can be explained simply in terms of unequal property ownership *independently* of the LTV. Roemer contends that exploitation is interesting only from an ethical/justice viewpoint.

Reiman (1987) provides a critique of Roemer, beginning with a definition of society as exploitative 'when its social structure is organised so that unpaid labour is systematically forced out of one class and put at the disposal of another' (p. 3). Unpaid labour is defined as 'surplus labour' i.e. as the amount of labour that a worker provides to the capitalist in excess of the amount s/he receives in terms of wages (either in terms of labour time or in terms of commodities). Forced labour, he argues, is not incompatible with workers 'voluntarily' agreeing to work for a capitalist. The social system forces the worker to accept work simply to obtain an income, given that workers do not have other income-earning assets. He also makes the important point that the claim that capitalism is exploitative does not, *ipso facto*, make society unjust. Capitalism was praised by Marx for the great increases in productivity which followed accumulation. Unlike Roemer, Marx would argue that in spite of the exploitation that takes place in a capitalist society, *the worker may be worse off* (in terms of income or commodities s/he can consume) in a non-capitalist society, other things being equal.

As mentioned above, there are limitations to exploitation theory related to the shortcomings of the labour theory of value. However, the Marxist analysis of capitalist society places exploitation at the heart of the critique. The existence of exploitation in a capitalist society with free exchange of commodities, including labour-power – exploitation in terms of the unequal relationship of capital and labour and the dominance of the capitalist in the production process – shows that to 'clamour for *equal* or *even equitable retribution* on the basis of the wages system is the same as to clamour for *freedom* on the basis of the slavery system' (Marx, *Wages, Price and Profit*; Vol. I, p. 426). Exploitation clearly has pejorative overtones, but in his scientific enquiry Marx treats it as a neutral term. For political purposes it is clearly important to stress the problems of injustice and inequality in a capitalist society. But this inequality is not simply one of incomes or consumption, but also of the inequality of power in the production process which is disguised (veiled) by the process of circulation. It is important to remember that a social scientist is ultimately concerned about human relationships and not about the neatness of mathematical models. As Einstein is reported to have said:

> Concern for man himself and his fate must always form the chief interest for all technical endeavours ... Never forget this in the midst of your diagrams and equations.

Is it surprising that Marx had a labour theory of value, and that he was concerned about exploitation? Roemer's attempts to build an abstract theory of exploitation without surplus labour and surplus value, by claiming that all commodities can be said to be exploited, misses the point of the endeavours of Marx and his followers. By focusing on exploitation, Marx emphasized the problems of unequal relationships in (especially) capitalist societies, the problems not only of unequal income/wealth distribution, but also those of power at the (metaphorical) coal face where the capitalist confronts the workers.

P.N. JUNANKAR

References

Junankar, P.N. (1982), *Marx's Economics*, Oxford: Philip Allan.
Marx, K. (1977), *Capital*, Vols 1–3, London: Lawrence and Wishart.
Marx, K. (1865), *Wages, Price and Profit*, reprinted in K. Marx and F. Engels (1962), *Selected Works*, Vols. I and II, London: Lawrence and Wishart.
Reiman, J. (1987), 'Exploitation, Force, and the Moral Assessment of Capitalism: Thoughts on Roemer and Cohen', *Philosophy and Public Affairs*, **16**, 3–41.
Roemer, J. (1982), *A General Theory of Exploitation and Class*, Cambridge MA: Harvard University Press.
Roemer, J. (ed.) (1986), *Analytical Marxism*, Cambridge: Cambridge University Press.

Female employment and unemployment

Female employment and unemployment have been studied from three radical political economy perspectives: feminist, Marxist and institutional. Feminists and institutionalists have focused on the linked phenomena of occupational segregation and labour market segmentation to offer explanations of the persistence of gender divisions. Marxists have concentrated on historical shifts in female employment patterns in relation to the economic cycle and to long-run capitalist development. Each of the perspectives is outlined below. An overview of female employment in Britain since the Second World War is then given to show how the different perspectives throw light on this topic.

Marxists have characterized women in the 20th century as an industrial reserve army of labour comparable to peasants in 19th-century Europe. Women were initially latent reserves moving between the capitalist and domestic economies in response to cyclical changes; subsequently they were floating reserves, with a permanent attachment to the wage labour force (Humphries, 1983). The minority of women who still remain full-time housewives have been perceived as a hidden reserve of underemployed labour in a pre-capitalist sector, comparable with Marx's stagnant reserve of labour.

Capitalist production relations are expected ultimately to dominate the production of all goods and services previously produced within the domestic economy. Female proletarianization is an inevitable corollary of capitalist development. In time a secular substitution process should undermine the sex-segregated productive structure in which women act as an industrial reserve army. As women are taken into the wage labour force, their relatively low wages should encourage their employment in place of male workers. They should become, in representative proportions, 'primary' or 'core' as well as 'secondary' or 'peripheral' workers. Hence the sex-segregated employment structure and women's relatively low wages simply reflect the historic assimilation of the latest latent labour reserve which happens to be female and whose initial experience in paid labour is in secondary employment.

Consistent with this perspective, the exclusion of women from many working-class occupations in the course of the 19th century and the rise of the male family wage were the result of working class struggles to resist the capitalist drive to undermine the domestic economy and feminize the industrial wage labour force.

Feminists, on the other hand, argue that a system of patriarchal relations interacts with the system of capitalist relations to sustain gender inequality in the household and the wage labour force (Walby, 1986). Within the household, women's economic dependence gives men power over them whilst, in the workplace, men more or less consciously operate to exclude women from the more remunerative and prestigious occupations, rendering the tasks and occupations that women perform as low status, 'unskilled' work. Jobs are unskilled because they are feminized, not feminized because they are unskilled. Walby (1986) sees the systematic exclusion of women from more advantageous positions within paid work as the major device through which women are persuaded to remain in the patriarchal mode of production (household labour), because it makes it difficult for individual women to maintain independent households. The occupational structure is 'gendered' primarily as a result of male exclusionary practices in the public sphere rather than because women's domestic responsibilities place them at a disadvantage in the labour market. In explaining gender inequality, the emphasis is on women's exclusion from jobs rather than the quality of female labour.

Labour market segmentation theorists writing within an institutional framework argue that labour markets are and always have been structured by institutional arrangements for both the demand and the supply of labour. Contrary to the premises of neoclassical theory, these operate to discriminate between individuals and groups in the allocation of good jobs which are scarce relative to the numbers seeking them. The Cambridge Labour Studies Group investigated labour market segmentation and gender segregation in a range of industries (Craig *et al.*, 1982).

The ability of every society to generate supplies of low-paid labour, whatever its institutional structure, suggests that the existence of low-paid jobs is primarily demand determined. However, the structure of labour supply determines which groups are confined to low productivity sectors (e.g. women, racial minorities, immigrants) as well as the conditions under which labour is employed in low-paid sectors (e.g. reliance on immigrant labour is associated with long hours and shift work, whilst reliance on indigenous female labour is associated with part-time work).

Wage differences reflect differential bargaining power rather than differences in job content, skill or workers' potential productivity. Male and female workers of equal skill or ability are employed at widely different wage levels. Male workers organize to preserve their status as skilled workers and protect themselves from competition that would erode their earnings.

Women's position in the family structure and dependence on other sources of family income are the main explanations given for married women's availability for low-paid jobs. Employers take advantage of the lower supply price at which women are available, more than compensating themselves for the alleged higher costs of employing women with family responsibilities (e.g. the expectation that they will take time off to care for sick children or their unwillingness to work overtime).

Access to desirable jobs is carefully controlled through hiring and promotion rules and practices which act as a filtering process, rationing the available good jobs. Competitive labour markets, where jobs are accessible to all those with appropriate skills, are rare and characterized by low pay and poor working conditions. The notion of a dual labour market divided into a closed primary sector (white male workers) and an open secondary sector (female and other disadvantaged workers) is over-simplistic. There are merely different degrees of closure related to the methods by which employers target specific social groupings to fill particular jobs, while workers organize to protect themselves from competition and to exclude outsiders. For example, hiring procedures or racism may prevent black women from gaining access to certain secondary jobs.

In Britain the period after the Second World War can be divided into two phases: the post-war boom which lasted until the end of the 1960s and the phase of economic instability and mass unemployment continuing into the early 1990s. The feminization of the wage labour force in Britain during this period was initially demand-led, with most of the increased female employment accounted for by the expansion of both full-time and part-time jobs in traditionally female areas of employment. This process can be interpreted as the mobilization of a latent reserve. Married women did not yet generally identify themselves as permanent employees and were discouraged from seeking jobs during cyclical downturns. However, in many low-income families and most black families, women's earnings from employment were a crucial means of alleviating poverty.

In the 1950s and 1960s it was amongst relatively underemployed housewives (married, childless women who, prior to the war, had been excluded from employment by marriage bars, and women with older, school-age children) that activity rates rose most rapidly. Part-time jobs in both services and manufacturing industries were taken up, particularly by white, married women. Black women were more often forced to take full-time jobs to bring their families' income to an adequate level.

The post-war boom was based on new mass production industries which created new standards for working-class consumption, encouraging married women into employment to improve their families' purchasing power. Neoclassical economics portrays female labour force participation as a process by which women substitute market production for household production. As female wages and the relative efficiency of market production rise, it becomes rational for more women to spend time earning wages which they then use to purchase market substitutes for the goods and services previously produced at home. This model does not accurately reflect industrial development in the second half of the 20th century. Whilst a significant part of the industrialization process in the 19th century involved the substitution of factory production for household production (e.g. food and clothing), most of the expansion of industrial production in the second half of the 20th century has been in goods and services that were never produced in the domestic economy. The rise in married women's employment during this period did not involve a substitution of one type of labour for another so much as an addition to women's workload. Evidence from time budget studies in the US and other industrial countries indicates that time spent by both housewives and employed married women on housework and childcare did not decline in the post-war boom years. Although a proportion of the increased incomes of families was spent on household appliances that made certain domestic tasks easier and quicker, standards of family care rose simultaneously, while other changes in consumption patterns generated increased demands on household labour. Men did not significantly increase their share of domestic work.

By the time economic growth slowed and unemployment levels rose in the 1970s, family income and expenditure patterns across classes were generally premised, not on a male family wage, but on dual earnings, except in families with children under five where many husbands were working long hours to make up for their wives' lost earnings. However by the late 1980s the proportion of married women with children under five who were in employment was over one-third and rising rapidly. By 1990, 45 per cent of women had returned to employment within nine months of a birth.

Just as working-class expenditure patterns had adapted to a normal dependence on two wages, within the middle class the percentage of professional dual-earning families had risen significantly as the post-war generation of educated women established themselves in the labour market. The feminist movement arose out of and further reinforced rising aspirations amongst women in relation both to marriage and employment.

Married women were ceasing to be a latent reserve and becoming a semi-permanent floating reserve of wage labourers. On the one hand, they were still vulnerable to job loss or to exclusion from the labour market because of movements in and out linked to family formation. On the other hand, they were also relatively protected from job loss by the pattern of job segregation. Most of the expansion in female employment had taken place in the service sector, whereas job losses during the recessions of the 1970s and early 1980s were concentrated in manufacturing and other production industries.

The numbers of women in employment continued to increase during the 1970s and 1980s, despite changed labour market conditions. At an aggregate level women were not behaving as a pro-cyclical flexible reserve or buffer (Rubery, 1988). However, there is evidence that women in some manufacturing sectors and some public services were affected disproportionately by declining employment. Most of the expansion in female employment since the 1970s has been in part-time jobs. The utilization of female labour in the wage labour force has increased considerably less than the total number of female jobs. There is evidence to suggest that part-time female employment has been used as a buffer mechanism in some sectors (e.g. cyclical fluctuations were greater for part-time employment than for full-time employment in some manufacturing sectors). However there is also evidence in other sectors of part-time employment expanding and being substituted for full-time, especially female, employment. Part-time employment was commonly used by British employers during this period as a strategy for increased flexibility (i.e. reducing slack time) in areas of work in which women predominated. Overtime and short-time working remained the strategy for flexibility in male-dominated areas (Beechey and Perkins, 1987).

In Britain the growth of female employment in recessionary periods has been sustained, not because women are overcoming their relative disadvantage in the labour market, but because their preparedness to work for low wages and to take part-time work makes them a more attractive source of labour for particular jobs. New forms of labour-market segmentation and sex segregation develop in periods of industrial restructuring. Women have penetrated new areas as well as traditional ones.

In this period the rise in activity rates came to affect increasing numbers of mothers with young and pre-school children. The burden of domestic work was much greater for these women than had been the case for most of the married women drawn into the labour force in the earlier phase. In some countries this period saw a significant expansion of state-subsidized childcare provision to accommodate the needs of working parents. In Britain, however, most mothers used a combination of part-time employment and childminding by relatives and private childminders. Although husbands of married women working full time were taking a greater share of housework and childcare by the 1980s, in less than a quarter of families was domestic work said to be shared equally. Where women had part-time jobs, husbands' contributions remained minimal. In this phase the new groups drawn into the labour force were again substituting employment for leisure, but also, where they could afford it, buying goods and services to substitute for their own household labour (e.g. convenience food, nursery care).

Sex segregation has been sustained and recreated to a much greater extent than predicted by Marxist theory. Men and women work in different types of jobs (horizontal segregation) and different grades of occupation (vertical segregation). Occupational segregation pre-dates capitalism and has survived wars, economic crises, restructuring and technological revolutions. Small-scale localized studies indicate that it is the active engagement of male employees, both unionized and non-unionized, that is most significant in sustaining sex segregation. Sometimes employers also have an interest in maintaining sex-typing of jobs. At other times they are indifferent or see an advantage in changing the sex-typing of occupations (e.g. the British newspaper industry in the 1970s and 1980s).

Male exclusionary practices are significant in denying women access to particular jobs. Skill divisions between men and women have been generated and sustained through the struggle of unionized men, often in craft-based unions, to retain their craft dominance at the expense of women. Individual men also move out of spheres penetrated by women. Men's employment is even more segregated than women's (see Cockburn in Walby, 1986).

Established patterns of horizontal segregation at the lower levels of the occupational structure are the most resistant to radical change. Black women and women in manual and 'unskilled' jobs are the most vulnerable to unemployment and the least likely to have access to education and training opportunities. The female labour force has itself become more differentiated. As women gain appropriate qualifications, they achieve greater access to professional and managerial positions. However gender segregation within these occupational groups persists and women continue to be under-represented in the highest paid jobs.

Marxists provide powerful insights into historical shifts in female employment patterns. However they have overestimated the decline of the domestic economy and underplayed the persistence of gender segregation and inequality. Feminism, whilst providing the most developed analysis of the maintenance of gender inequality, needs to be linked into a broader institutional framework to explain diversity and change in gender divisions.

JEAN GARDINER

References

Beechey, V. and Perkins, T. (1987), *A Matter of Hours*, Cambridge: Polity Press.
Craig, C. Rubery, J., Tarling, R. and Wilkinson, F. (1982), *Labour Market Structure, Industrial Organisation and Low Pay*, Cambridge: Cambridge University Press.
Humphries, J. (1983), 'The Emancipation of Women in the 1970s and 1980s: From the Latent to the Floating', *Capital and Class*, **20**, 6–28.
Rubery, J. (ed.) (1988), *Women and Recession*, London: Routledge & Kegan Paul.
Walby, S. (ed.) (1986), *Gender Segregation at Work*, Milton Keynes: Open University Press.

Finance capital

The concept and theory of finance capital first appeared in print in 1910 in Rudolf Hilferding's famous book of the same name, *Das Finanzkapital*. Finance capital was the theoretical centrepiece of Hilferding's book; indeed, it is difficult to separate the concept from the book. At the time the book was hailed as a major achievement by Hilferding's political allies, Bauer and Kautsky, who claimed it as the fourth volume of Marx's *Capital*. Moreover the concept was shortly to be popularized by Lenin in his 1920 booklet on imperialism. This ensured that the concept of finance capital gained wide currency from the outset.

Hilferding described the object of his book as an attempt '... to arrive at a scientific understanding of the *economic characteristics* [my emphasis] of the latest phase of capitalist development' (p. 21; hereafter all references are to the Bottomore (1981) edition). It follows from the above that one way of viewing finance capital is as the latest stage in capitalist development.

In any historical epoch a particular articulation or configuration of fractions of capital prevails, and many economists (as diverse as Marx, Walras, Keynes and Schumpeter) have given prominence to the links between industry and finance. Hilferding sketches a musical chairs picture of the links between fractions of capital since the beginnings of capitalist production. In the era of early capitalism, *pre-capitalist* fractions (like usurers' and merchants' capital) played an important role in accumulation. The next stage, heralded in by the Industrial Revolution, was one in which industrial capital subordinated bank and money-dealing capital to its needs. The latest or modern stage is finance capital in which bank capital is the hegemonic fraction which dominates industrial and other fractions of capital.

Hilferding identifies the basis of the hegemony of bank capital as stemming from two processes of concentration which:

1. lead to the formation of cartels and trusts and thus to the elimination of free (perfect) competition;
2. bring bank and industrial capital into an ever closer relationship which he characterized as finance capital.

These processes of concentration and their interplay form recurring themes throughout Hilferding's analysis. On one hand, they are related to the growing power of bank capital and, on the other, to an analysis of finance capital as a stage of capitalism. The elimination of perfect competition through concentration is not as controversial as the alleged power of bank capital. However the privileged position of bank capital has aroused controversy even within radical economics.

Under capitalism, industry and finance have always interacted, but Hilferding highlights relationships with banks and interprets them in a novel light. For Hilferding the three major functions of bank capital form the basis of the power and influence which he claims bank capital exerts under modern capitalism. These three functions are concerned with the roles which bank capital plays in relation to money, credit and fictitious capital (this is capital represented by securities such as equities and bonds).

Since credit money (as represented by bills of exchange or banker's drafts) arises in circulation, Hilferding called it circulation credit. Because the bulk of payments between capitalists takes the form of credit money, a system for netting out or clearing payments and receipts is necessary. Bank capital operates such payments and clearing systems as one of its major functions. Initially credit money took the form of commercial credit (or bills), but Hilferding noted a tendency for bank credit, such as bankers' acceptances, to replace commercial credit as the major form of credit money.

How could the control of the payments mechanism and of the supply of bank credit enable bank capital to exert influence over industrial capital? Hilferding believed that this function conferred no specific power over bank capital. Lenin on the other hand stressed how the operation of the payments mechanism enabled banks to ascertain the exact financial position of other capitalists. This would have been true in Lenin's day when most companies relied on just one bank for banking services. Today the monitoring of a company's financial position is complicated by multi-bank relationships.

Bank capital's second main function is the supply of capital credit or loan finance facilities. This is called capital credit since it involves a transfer of capital between capitalists. By contrast, credit money or circulation credit is merely a payment in the exchange of equivalents. Hilferding notes that historically capital credit has tended to replace circulation credit, thus reinforcing the near monopoly of bank capital in the spheres of money and credit.

Crucially for Hilferding, capital credit implies long-term relationships between banks and enterprises, as compared with the essentially short-term nature of circulation credit. However both his and Lenin's conception of the power conferred on bank capital by the supply of capital credit is couched in terms of the competition for *access* implied by a developed credit system. While access to credit is important, they both overlooked the *conditionality* of such credit facilities which to be fair to them, has only developed in recent decades. In other words capital credit today is advanced subject to detailed conditions inscribed as restrictive covenants in loan agreements which may limit and circumscribe the activities of the enterprises concerned.

One of Hilferding's insights is the distinction which he develops between money and credit on the one hand and fictitious capital on the other. The latter arises from the mobilization of capital or the issuing of securities by the modern joint stock company. In the individually owned enterprise, the industrial capitalist or entrepreneur owns and controls the means of production. By contrast, in the corporation, the raising of equity becomes the domain of money capitalists, including bankers, who become the owners of the corporation's equity stock. This implies that these money capitalists are the owners, not of the corporation's means of production (except, *in extremis*, on liquidation or receivership), but of claims to potential dividends. Hilferding describes shareholders as money capitalists rather than industrialists since they can in principle convert their shares into money capital at any time on the stock exchange.

Hilferding, unlike Lenin, emphasizes the role of banks in the raising of new or additional equity capital. In this investment banking function, Hilferding envisages banks earning a new source of revenue which he calls promoter's profit. In the modern corporation, profit of enterprise is no longer appropriated by the industrialist, but rather is divided into dividends paid to shareholders and promoter's profit paid to banks. He also argues that the role of banks is further enhanced in modern capitalism by the demise of the stock exchange and the appropriation of its functions by banks.

To sum up, bank capital's major functions place it in a relatively powerful position *vis-à-vis* industrial capital. Both Hilferding and Lenin stress that this can lead to interlocking directorships and cross shareholdings between banks and industry. An important point stressed only by Lenin is that the power of bank capital is predicated on the combination of all its functions. Thus in both the US and Japan, for example, investment and commercial banking functions are segmented (although deregulation is eroding segmentation in both cases); this limits the relative power of both types of banks as compared with some of their European competitors.

A number of caveats must be added at this stage. First, the subordinate role of the stock exchange *vis-à-vis* bank capital is specific to Germanic countries or those following the Hanseatic tradition. In most other advanced economies the Anglo-Saxon tradition implies that the stock exchange plays an important role, although the role of banks has increased in the wake of various deregulatory measures known as big bangs. Second, Hilferding seems to have overlooked the role of other financial institutions in relation to fictitious capital. In countries such as the UK and US, pension funds and insurance companies dominate the ownership of equity claims on the stock exchange. Finally it it curious that both Hilferding and Lenin saw power relations between banks and industry as unidirectional; they both appear to have overlooked Marx's view that bank capital ultimately depends on industrial capital for its profits. It is only in the latter context that one can appreciate the current bad debt problems facing many leading commercial banks.

Hilferding stressed that one of the major secular tendencies of modern capitalism was that of concentration through the formation of cartels and trusts. However these processes are selective rather than general. Hilferding's elaboration of cartels and trusts appears confined to industry; this contrasts sharply with Lenin's (1920) account of concentration within banking and industry. Marx's distinction between the concepts of centralization and concentration of capital is echoed in Hilferding's differentiation between the concentration of ownership of property and of production.

One problem with Hilferding's concept of concentration is that he appeared to countenance no effective limits to the process. Indeed, he explicitly mentions 'tendencies towards the establishment of a general cartel and … a central bank' (p. 234). This seems unsatisfactory for the following reason, which Lenin was later to formulate in terms of inter-imperialist rivalries.

Even in a world dominated by the export of capital, it fails to take account of ongoing competition between corporations based in different national economies or groups of economies, as in the case of the European Community's plans for a single market by 1992.

To turn to crises, Hilferding's somewhat controversial view was that they stem from disproportionalities in the course of the cycle. Crises arise from disturbances in the price structure when market prices deviate excessively from prices of production. If the rate of profit begins to fall, the exacerbation of these disproportionalities can lead to crisis. The development of cartels intensifies disproportionalities although, in Hilferding's view, the credit system obscures such disproportionalities during the business cycle. The upside of these developments is the elimination of 19th century style monetary crises. The concentration of power in the hands of bank capital, combined with the absence of monetary crises, safeguard against banking and stock exchange crises. With the benefit of hindsight one can see that Hilferding was overly optimistic concerning the possibility of ending financial crises. The Third World debt crisis and the October 1987 stock market crash are vivid reminders of the latter.

Despite the centrality of fractions of capital in his analysis of finance capital, it is somewhat ironic that Hilferding concludes that the phase of finance capital unifies all fractions of capital and the opponents of finance capital. This unity means that capital is able to exert coordinated political pressure on the state to support its policies. These include measures relating to domestic protective tariffs for cartels and those designed to promote the export of capital. This is a relatively disappointing conclusion but, in Hilferding's defence, it must be said that the theory of the capitalist state was underdeveloped at the time of writing.

The concept of finance capital raises separate issues *vis-à-vis* radical economics and orthodox economics. For the former, the issue raised by Hilferding's concept of finance capital is whether it is a valid characterization of a separate stage of capitalism. Sweezy (1942) was confidently able to assert that Hilferding had mistaken a transitional phase of capitalism for a lasting one. This initiated a debate on the historical and contemporary power of bank capital which is well summarized by Harris (1983). In retrospect the debate may well have been misguided since the issue at stake is whether the Anglo-Saxon or Hanseatic financing tradition (or some combination of both) will prevail in the future as financial markets become increasingly integrated at the international level.

In Hilferding's defence it may be argued that he was employing the concept of bank capital in its broadest sense of the Hanseatic tradition of universal banks. These banks supply a wide or universal range of bank services, including those associated with both commercial and investment banks. It is common for such banks to hold significant equity stakes in companies and to be directly represented on the board of directors. Countries such as the US, Canada and Japan have segmented financial systems where commercial and investment banking are legally separate. In recent years the barriers within such systems have been subject to deregulatory pressures and are being eroded. Interestingly the concept of universal banking underpinned the European Commission's Second Banking Directive for the creation of a unified banking market within the European Financial Area by 1992. Moreover the principal rationale behind the whole 1992 project was to promote concentration within the Community so that EC-based blocs of capital could compete with their US and Japanese rivals. In that context, Hilferding's discussion is still relevant today.

By and large the theory of finance capital raises issues which orthodox economics overlooks. In the finance literature, the famous Modigliani-Miller (1958) proposition states that the method of financing a corporation does not matter, whereas the theory of finance capital would suggest otherwise. Not only that, but finance capital favours the role of banks *vis-à-vis* industry. In the orthodox theory-of-the-firm literature, the role of the stock exchange rather than that of banks is given prominence. This neglect of the role of banks is probably a reflection of the predominance of the stock market in the Anglo-Saxon financial tradition as the backcloth against which leading Western economists theorize.

JERRY COAKLEY

References

Coakley, J. (1982), 'Hilferding's Finance Capital', *Capital and Class*, No. 17.

Harris, L. (1983), 'Finance Capital' in T. Bottomore (ed.), *Dictionary of Marxist Thought*, Oxford: Basil Blackwell.

Hilferding, R. (1910), *Das Finanzkapital*, Vienna. Edited from translations by M. Watnick and S. Gordon with an introduction by T. Bottomore (ed.) (1981), *Finance Capital: A Study of the Latest Phase of Capitalist Development*, London: Routledge & Kegan Paul.

Lenin, V. (1920), *Imperialism the Highest Stage of Capitalism*, Moscow: Progress Press.

Modigliani, F. and Miller, M.H. (1958), 'The Cost of Capital, Corporation Finance and the Theory of Investment', *American Economic Review*, **48**, 261–97.

Sweezy, P. (1942), *The Theory of Capitalist Development*, New York: Monthly Review Press.

Financial instability hypothesis

The financial instability hypothesis has both empirical and theoretical aspects. The readily observed empirical aspect is that from time to time capitalist economies exhibit inflations and debt deflations which seem to have the potential to spin out of control. In such processes the economic system's reactions to any movement of the economy amplify that movement – inflation feeds upon inflation and debt – deflation upon debt-deflation. Government interventions aimed to contain the deterioration seem to have been inept in a number of historical crises. These historical episodes provide evidence supporting the view that the economy does not always conform to the classic precepts of Smith and Walras – that economies can best be understood by assuming that at all times they are equilibrium-seeking and-sustaining systems.

The classic description of a debt deflation is by Irving Fisher (1933) and that of a self-sustaining disequilibrating process by Charles Kindleberger (1978). Martin Wolfson (1986) not only presents a compilation of data on the emergence of financial relations conducive to financial instability, but also examines various financial crisis theories of business cycles.

As economic theory, the financial instability hypothesis is an interpretation of the substance of Keynes's *General Theory* which also places the latter historically. As *The General Theory* was written in the early 1930s, the great financial and real contraction of the US and other capitalist economies of that time was part of the evidence *The Theory* aimed to explain. The financial instability hypothesis also draws upon the credit view of money and finance of Joseph Schumpeter. The key work for the financial instability hypothesis in the narrow sense is, of course, Hyman P. Minsky (1975).

The theoretical argument of the financial instability hypothesis starts from the characterization of the economy as capitalist, with expensive capital assets and a complex sophisticated financial system. The economic problem is identified (following Keynes) as the 'capital development of the economy' rather than the Knightian 'allocation of given resources among alternative employments'. The focus is on an accumulating capitalist economy that moves through real calendar time.

The capital development of a capitalist economy is accompanied by exchanges of present money for future money. Present money pays for resources that go into the production of investment output, whereas future money is the 'profits' that will accrue to the capital asset-owning firms as capital assets are used in production. As a result of the process by which investment is financed, control over items in the capital stock by producing units is financed by liabilities; these are commitments to pay money at dates specified or as conditions arise. For each economic unit the liabilities on its balance sheet determine a time series of prior payment commitments even as the assets generate a time series of conjectured cash receipts.

This structure was well stated by Keynes (1972):

> There is a multitude of real assets in the world which constitutes our capital wealth – buildings, stocks of commodities, goods in the course of manufacture and of transport, and so forth. The nominal owners of these assets, however, have

> not infrequently borrowed *money* [Keynes's emphasis] in order to become possessed of them. To a corresponding extent the actual owners of wealth have claims, not on real assets, but on money. A considerable part of this financing takes place through the banking system, which interposes its guarantee between its depositors who lend it money, and its borrowing customers to whom it loans money wherewith to finance the purchase of real assets. The interposition of this veil of money between the real asset and the wealth owner is an especially marked characteristic of the modern world (p. 151).

This Keynesian *veil of money* is different from that of the quantity theory of money. According to the quantity theory veil of money, the exchanges in trading in commodity markets are of goods for money and money for goods. The Keynesian veil implies that money is connected with financing through time. A part of the financing of the economy can be structured as dated payment commitments in which banks are the central players. The money flows are first from depositors to banks and from banks to firms and then, at some later date, from firms to banks and then from banks to their depositors. In the first instance, the exchanges are for the financing of investment; in the second, they fulfil the prior commitments that are stated in the financial contract.

In a Keynesian veil of money world, the flow of money to firms is a response to expectations of future profits, and the flow of money from firms is financed by profits that are realized. In the Keynesian set-up, the key economic exchanges take place as a result of negotiations between generic bankers and generic businessmen. The documents 'on the table' in such negotiations detail the cost and profit expectations of businessmen who interpret them as enthusiasts: the bankers as sceptics.

It follows that in a capitalist economy the past, the present and the future are linked, not only by capital assets and labour force characteristics, but also by financial relations. The key financial relations link the creation and ownership of capital assets to the structure of financial relations and changes in this structure. Institutional complexity may result in several layers of intermediation between the ultimate owners of the community's wealth and the units that control and operate that wealth.

Expectations of business profits determine both the flow of financing contracts to business and the price in the market of existing financing contracts. Profit realizations determine whether the commitments in financial contracts are fulfilled, whether financial assets perform as the pro formas of the negotiations indicated they should.

In the modern world the analysis of financial relations and their implications for system behaviour cannot be restricted to the liability structures of businesses and the cash flow they entail. The current performance of the economy either validates or does not validate the liability structures of households (in terms of their ability to borrow on credit cards for expensive consumer goods such as automobiles, house purchases and to carry financial assets), governments (with their large floating and funded debts) and international units (as a result of the internationalization of finance).

The system may behave differently than in earlier eras due to, first, an increasing complexity of the financial structure and, second, a greater involvement of governments as refinancing agents for financial institutions as well as for ordinary business firms, both of which are marked characteristics of the modern world. In particular the much greater participation of national governments in assuring that finance does not degenerate as in the 1929–33 period means that the down-side vulnerability of aggregate profit flows has been much diminished. However the same interventions may well induce a greater degree of up-side (i.e. inflationary) bias to the economy.

In spite of the greater complexity of financial relations than was true in the past, the key determinant of system behaviour remains the level of profits. The financial instability hypothesis incorporates the Kalecki (1965)–Levy and David (1983) view of profits in which the structure of aggregate demand determines profits. In the skeletal model, with highly simplified consumption behaviour by receivers of profit, incomes and wages, in each period aggregate profits equal aggregate investment. In more complex though still highly abstract structures, aggregate profits equal aggregate investment plus the government deficit. As expectations of profits depend upon investment in the future and as realized profits are determined by investment, whether or not liabilities are validated depends upon investment. Investment takes place in the present because businessmen and their bankers expect investment to take place in the future.

The financial instability hypothesis therefore is a theory of the impact of debt on system behaviour and the way debt is validated. In contrast to the orthodox quantity theory of money, the financial instability hypothesis takes banking seriously as a profit-seeking activity. Banks seek profits by financing activity; like all entrepreneurs in a capitalist economy, bankers are aware that innovation assures profits. Thus using the term generically for all intermediaries in finance (whether they be brokers or dealers), bankers are merchants of debt who strive to innovate in the assets they acquire and the liabilities they market. This innovative characteristic of banking and finance invalidates the fundamental presupposition of the orthodox quantity theory of money to the effect that there is an unchanging 'money' item whose velocity of circulation is sufficiently close to being constant so that changes in this money's supply has a linear proportional relation to a well-defined price level.

Three income-debt relations for economic units – labelled as hedge, speculative and Ponzi finance – can be identified. Hedge-financing units are those which can fulfil all of their contractual payment obligations by their cash flows: the greater the weight of equity financing in the liability structure, the greater the likelihood that the unit is a hedge-financing unit. Speculative finance units are those that can meet their payment commitments on 'income account' on their liabilities even though they cannot repay the principal out of income cash flows. Such units need to 'roll over' their liabilities; i.e. issue new debt to meet commitments on maturing debts. Governments with floating debts, corporations with floating issues of commercial paper and banks are typical hedge units.

For Ponzi units the cash flows from operations are not sufficient to fulfil either the repayment of principal or the interest due on outstanding debts by their cash flows from operations. Such units can sell assets or borrow in order to pay interest; dividends on common stock lower the equity of a unit even as they increase liabilities and the prior commitment of future incomes. Each unit that Ponzi finances lowers the margin of safety that it offers the holders of its debts.

It can be shown that if hedge financing dominates, then the economy is an equilibrium-seeking and deviation-containing system, whereas the greater the weight of speculative and Ponzi finance, the more likely that the economy is a deviation-amplifying system. The first theorem of the financial instability hypothesis is that the economy has financing regimes under which it is stable and financing regimes under which it is unstable. The second theorem is that, over periods of prolonged prosperity, the economy moves from financial relations that make for a stable system to those that make for an unstable system.

In particular, over a protracted period of good times, capitalist economies tend to move from a financial structure dominated by hedge-finance units to one dominated by units engaged in speculative and Ponzi finance. Furthermore, if an economy with a sizeable body of speculative financial units is in an inflationary state and the authorities attempt to exorcise inflation by monetary constraint, then speculative units will become Ponzi units and the net worth of what were previously Ponzi units will quickly evaporate. When this happens, units with cash flow shortfalls will be forced to try to make position by selling out position. This is likely to lead to a collapse of asset values.

The financial instability hypothesis is a model of a capitalist economy which does not rely upon exogenous shocks to generate business cycles of varying severity: the hypothesis contends that business cycles of history are compounded out of the internal dynamics of capitalist economies as well as out of the system of interventions and regulations designed to keep the economy operating within reasonable bounds.

HYMAN P. MINSKY

References

Fisher, I. (1933), 'The Debt Deflation Theory of Great Depressions', *Econometrica*, **1**, 337–57.

Kalecki, M. (1965), *Theory of Economic Dynamics*, London: Allen and Unwin.

Keynes, J.M. (1936), *The General Theory of Employment, Interest and Money*, New York: Harcourt Brace.

Keynes, J.M. (1972), 'Essays in Persuasion' in *The Collected Writings of John Maynard Keynes*, Vol. IX, London and Basingstoke: Macmillan/St Martins Press, for the Royal Economic Society.

Kindleberger, C. (1978), *Manias, Panics and Crashes*, New York: Basic Books.

Levy, S.J. and David A. (1983), *Profits and the Future of American Society*, New York: Harper and Row.

Minsky, H.P. (1975), *John Maynard Keynes*, New York: Columbia University Press.

Wolfson, M.H. (1986), *Financial Crises*, Armonk, New York: M.E. Sharpe Inc.

Firms and corporations

The central challenge of radical political economy has been to reject the orthodox notion of the firm as an efficient form of economic organization, whilst retaining the behavioural assumption that firms seek to maximize profits. In conventional neoclassical theory the firm is assumed to be cost efficient, selecting from amongst technically efficient production techniques those which minimize costs and, given competitive product markets, maximize profit. More recently, the new institutional economics has viewed firms in terms of minimizing the costs of transactions, or transactional efficiency (Williamson, 1985). Radical economic analyses stress the central role of considerations of power and control in maximizing the firm's profits. Two main strands can be identified: the first focuses on the character of the employment relationship, the second on the nature of competition in the product market.

In the employment relationship, the special character of the employment contract – whereby employers purchase workers' capacity to work rather than a specified amount of performed labour – means that employers can secure more output by working employees more effectively or more intensively for a given wage. Profits are increased by the exercise of more effective control by the employer, but because labour input has increased as well as output, no improvement in efficiency has necessarily occurred. In the product market, the ability to exercise a degree of control over market conditions – market power – enables firms to mark up prices over cost and thereby increase profits. Again no improvement in efficiency has necessarily occurred.

Radical economic analysis of the employment relationship is usefully viewed in the context of the treatment of the issue provided by transactions costs economics (TCE), which has dominated recent orthodox work on the firm. TCE argues that hierarchy within the employment relationship is in the mutual interests of both workers and employers. This is because employers use their authority to curb opportunistic behaviour by individual workers, to the benefit of broader organizational goals. Any conflict within the firm is between self-interest and the common good. Moreover, the evolution of the firm is argued to result from the successive displacement of less transactionally efficient modes of labour management, by modes with superior efficiency properties. Because employers and workers are seen to have a common interest in reducing the scope for opportunistic behaviour, the overall welfare effects of these successive innovations are presumed to be positive (Williamson, 1985).

Radical economists have challenged these conclusions. In a seminal contribution, Marglin (1974) argued that neither the emergence of the putting-out system, nor its subsequent displacement by the centralized factory, can be attributed to efficiency considerations. The putting-out system deprived producers of their control over the product, and the factory deprived them of their control over the production process. As a result, workers were coerced into seeking work in factories because they no longer had direct access to the market. The factory did not represent a more efficient means of organizing work, but offered employers a superior capability to extract increased labour effort through direct surveillance and enforcing longer working hours. Output and profits increased, but so too did labour input. The subsequent evolution of modes of labour management within the firm has been seen by radicals to be motivated by employers' search for ever more effective means of extracting effort from the workforce. Particular emphasis has been placed on the role of employer strategies aimed at creating divisions amongst the workforce (Bowles, 1985). Thus, whereas TCE views the bureaucratic mode of employment relations as having desirable efficiency properties, radicals interpret it as a means by which employers attempt to enhance their control by creating divisions amongst the (external and internal) workforce.

Radical economists characterize the employment relationship as involving an inherent conflict of interest between employers and workers. Workers are motivated by the need to attain an adequate standard of living, and to exert control over the pace and content of their work. Employers are motivated by the need to accumulate profit, which requires cost minimization and control over the production process, including workers' effort and task adaptability. Because employers do not purchase a specified quantity of work performed, scope for conflict exists both over the terms of the (incomplete) contract and, subsequently, over the precise labour which workers are required to perform. Employers are able to use the authority which the incomplete nature of the labour contract vests in them to try to secure an outcome to this conflict favourable to their interests. Workers, for their part, develop their own forms of organization – notably trade unions – in order to exercise countervailing power against the use of authority by the employer. In turn, employers will try to shape the form of workers' organizations in order to minimize any challenge to their dominance.

Bowles (1985) provides a formal treatment of the radical approach to the firm by supplementing the orthodox neoclassical production function with a third term representing labour effort. It is assumed that employers are able to compel workers to act in ways that they would not themselves choose, but that doing so is costly. This takes two forms: (1) the use of direct supervision and (2) the payment of a wage premium above the market rate to secure commensurate behaviour. Assuming decreasing returns to both of these will generate a lower profit maximizing level of output than in the absence of such costs. Further assuming that capitalist employers select forms of work organization and technology that best enable them to extract labour effort, Bowles demonstrates that although these will maximize the private return to the employer, they will also necessarily be socially inefficient.

A second main strand of radical analysis has departed from the conventional assumption that firms are price takers, to investigate the consequences when firms attempt to exercise a degree of control over their product market environment. The focus of analysis thereby shifts away from the small firm of the neoclassical model to large corporations. Power in markets for products and services enables firms to mark up prices over costs, thus increasing profitability. Cowling (1982) shows that such market power is a function of concentration in the industry and of the ability of firms to collude. But inter-firm collusion will be unstable, as the possession of market power is itself subject to competition between firms. Firms will incur expenditures on advertising, product development and excess capacity in order to protect their established market positions (Cowling, 1982). Importantly, competition is viewed as a process and not as an (equilibrium) state of the world. Indeed the competitive process can result in monopolistic outcomes. This perspective is shared by radical economists who otherwise differ on the priority that should be accorded to the opposing tendencies of competition and collusion.

Thus, in contrast to the static nature of the neoclassical firm, radical analyses of firm behaviour are dynamic in character. Firms are viewed as active economic agents seeking to shape the conditions under which they operate. In a tradition that goes back to Marx, the conditions for securing longer-run profitability are seen to rest on the successful expansion of the firm and its markets. This involves transforming constraints encountered in markets for products, raw materials, capital (and labour). The development of the large corporation is thus driven by the need both for new markets and to exercise control over those markets in the face of competing firms – a process vividly charted for the United States by the business historian Alfred Chandler (1977). The means by which constraints are overcome periodically require innovations in the internal organizational structure of the firm. Chandler's analysis of the emergence of the multi-divisional form of internal organization emphasizes its role in facilitating strategies of market expansion and diversification.

The growth of large corporations has raised questions concerning who exercises effective control within them. Radicals have differed over the managerialist thesis that a separation of ownership from control has occurred within the large corporation, resulting in the dominance of managerial goals. Recent writing, however, has increasingly questioned why owners should ever relinquish control in the first place, drawn attention to the increasing importance of institutional ownership and demonstrated the feasibility of exercising control through relatively small shareholdings. Relatedly, it has also been proposed that the large firm should be defined, not as a legal entity, but in terms of its ability to exercise strategic control over production units, whether directly owned or not.

The two main themes of radical work on the firm have been extended into the analysis of transnational companies. The drive to expand markets has led firms to open up markets overseas. Moreover in order to secure a degree of control over overseas markets, in the face of competition from indigenous producers or rivals from outside the local market, firms have established local operations and thereby become transnational (Hymer, 1976; Cowling, 1982). Market imperfections in the transfer of intermediate goods (such as technology and management skills) together with the extension of market power lie at the heart of Hymer's pathbreaking thesis on transnationals. Local production is itself seen to be a marketing advantage – in part because of the ability to tailor products and services to local requirements – and thereby contributes to market power.

In terms of exercising labour control, transnational companies are seen to possess substantial power advantages when compared with firms operating in a single country. These lie in the ability to 'divide and rule' across borders, for example by threats to switch production to alternative locations or through the ability to withstand local industrial action by dual sourcing products from sites located in different countries. Workers, and their organizations, can only counter the exercise of such power by establishing effective cross-border organization – a response that has been shown to be fraught with difficulty. Most dramatically, some radicals have argued that a 'new international division of labour' is being generated by transnationals, in which production is located in the lowest labour cost economies of the developing world. There are, however, limits to this process: the productivity of cheap labour may be far less than that of more expensive labour in industrialized countries; moreover, product market considerations drive transnationals' locational decisions, as well as those relating to production costs.

PAUL MARGINSON

References

Bowles, S. (1985), 'The Production Process in a Competitive Economy: Walrasian, Neo-Hobbesian and Marxian Models', *American Economic Review*, **75**(1), 16–36.
Chandler, A.D. (1977), *The Visible Hand*, Cambridge, Mass.: Harvard University Press.
Cowling, K. (1982), *Monopoly Capitalism*, London: Macmillan.
Hymer, S. (1976), *The International Operations of National Firms: A Study of Direct Foreign Investment*, Cambridge, Mass.: MIT Press.
Marglin, S.A. (1974), 'What Do Bosses Do?', *Review of Radical Political Economics*, **6**, 33–60.
Williamson, O.E. (1985), *The Economic Institutions of Capitalism*, New York: Free Press.

Fordism and post-Fordism

Fordism and post-Fordism have become stock reference points in the research literature on industrial and economic restructuring, yet their status as analytical and empirical categories remains highly controversial. The terms are commonly used to delineate two qualitatively distinct phases of capitalist economic development in the twentieth century. Fordism refers to the age of mass production and consumption, big business, and the Keynesian welfare state, while post-Fordism signals the collapse of this system and the emergence in the 1970s and 1980s of new systems of economic and industrial regulation, production, consumption and social institutions.

As with earlier attempts by political economists to periodize the capitalist economy, this approach has been judged deficient in several important respects. Critics argue that the core concepts are poorly specified and fail to properly represent the complex and uneven patterns of industrial and social change which have characterized the advanced capitalist economies this century.

The concept of post-Fordism is especially elusive. Most writers that invoke the term do so in order to record a radical departure from Fordist patterns of economic and social organization, rather than to specify the precise character, dimensions and dynamics of what is said to be the new paradigm. Hence any proper evaluation of post-Fordism must first address the issue of the coherence and historical relevance of Fordism.

In its most restricted sense, Fordism is used to denote a series of technical innovations in production, thought to have been pioneered in Henry Ford's River Rouge plant in Detroit in 1913, but subsequently generalized throughout manufacturing industry. Ford thus is most immediately connected with the introduction of the moving assembly line, although the evidence reveals that mechanical transfer lines were used in the slaughterhouses by companies such as Swift and Armour before Ford harnessed them to the car manufacturing process. Nevertheless Ford did spearhead significant changes in the social organization of work which allowed such technical innovations to be exploited to the full.

Paramount among these changes was the erosion of craft workers' skills and their unions, through the determined application of Frederick Taylor's principles of 'scientific management'. By standardizing components and finished products, and decomposing the assembly process into myriad routine operations, Ford was able to divide mental and manual labour, bolster managerial control and intensify the labour process. The initial results, in terms of productivity advance and cost cutting, were impressive, but Ford's system of labour control merely tended to displace rather than eradicate shop floor conflict. When competitive pressure from rival companies, notably General Motors, led to further attempts by Ford to cut costs by intensifying the labour process and trimming wages, the limits of his system of social control were clearly exposed.

Contemporary observers, most notably Gramsci (to whom the concept of Fordism is usually credited), focused their attention on the relationship between Ford's manufacturing system and the wider social structures in which it was embedded. In the *Prison Notebooks* (1971), Gramsci argued that Fordism represented the 'ultimate stage' of the socialization of the forces of production, and derived 'from an inherent necessity to achieve the organization of a planned economy'. The high standards of individual discipline and social morality required to sustain Ford's industrial and social project could, in his view, only be achieved in a classless society (see Clarke, 1990).

The historical record suggests that Gramsci was wide of the mark. But his belief that Fordism and class society were fundamentally incompatible has been a dominant theme of the contemporary analysis and debate which stresses the internal contradictions of Fordism as a mode of social and industrial regulation under capitalism. Especially influential in this respect has been the work of the French regulation school particularly Aglietta (1979).

Fordism, according to Aglietta, 'marked a new stage in the regulation of capitalism. It denotes a series of major transformations in the labour process', which were accompanied by broader structural changes in the 'conditions of existence of the wage earning class' (Aglietta, 1979, p. 116). Crucial in this respect was the growth of trade unionism and collective bargaining, which provided a mechanism for translating productivity gains into wage rises, extensions in the credit system and the emergence – particularly after 1945 – of the Keynesian welfare state.

Aglietta's analysis of Fordism is situated in respect of a preceding phase – which he calls 'Taylorism' – in which innovations in the productive sphere, notably the elaboration of the detailed technical division of labour, facilitated rapid productivity gains. These gains outstripped the growth of the means of consumption and hence eventually undermined the dynamics of capital accumulation. The crisis of the inter-war years, which culminated in the Great Crash and mass unemployment, is thus interpreted by Aglietta as stemming from unchecked disproportionalities between the spheres of production and consumption.

Such disproportionalities were averted under Fordism, through the generalization of commodity relations and the rapid growth of markets for mass produced consumer goods, which in turn fuelled the growth of productive capacity. But, after two decades of rapid and crisis free capital accumulation between 1945 and 1965, the Fordist era allegedly fell into crisis. According to Aglietta, and other members of the French regulation school (see entry on 'Regulation theory'), the crisis was triggered by the build-up of technical and social obstacles in the labour process, resulting in a productivity slowdown and a profits squeeze, first manifest in those industries producing means of production, but generalized thereafter. The wave of labour unrest which spread throughout the advanced capitalist economies in the 1960s is traced by these writers to the futile attempts by capital to restore profitability by further degrading the conditions of labour.

The 1970s and 1980s are correspondingly seen by the regulationists as a period of increasing social and economic upheaval and experimentation, during which time the major economic forces (transnationals and national and international state agencies in particular) sought to resolve the crisis of Fordism on terms favourable to capital. The term neo-Fordism, rather than post-Fordism, is invoked by regulationists to signify a deepening and extension of Fordist structures which took place during these years.

Significant innovations in production included the automation of previously mechanical processes, aided by the application of micro-electronic technologies, and the use of more flexible modes of work organization and regulation to yoke workers to the new technological systems. Beyond production, leading edge companies embraced more fluid organizational forms (subcontracting, franchising, joint ventures and licensing arrangements) in order to escape from the high fixed costs of maintaining large corporate bureaucracies and integrated complex production systems at a time of increasing market volatility.

The French regulationists grounded their analysis of the stages of capitalist development within a Marxian framework. Thus the three successive stages highlighted by Aglietta (Taylorism, Fordism and neo-Fordism) are treated as distinct forms of an accumulation regime underpinned by the dominance of relative surplus value extraction in production. In short there is no implication that capitalism, and capitalist forms of worker exploitation, were being transcended, despite significant changes in the institutional and technological structure of the economy.

By contrast, the concept of post-Fordism has become associated with the idea that there are new economic and social dynamics at work which are leading ultimately to the break up of traditional capitalist relations. Thus, for example, Lash and Urry (1987) speak of a new era of 'disorganised capitalism', while Jacques and Hall (1989) refer to the construction of a new pluralistic politics based on diverse social and economic movements rather than traditional class antagonisms.

Post-Fordism, as noted, is defined in opposition to Fordism. Most commonly it is identified with the renaissance of craft work in small and medium sized firms, decentralized production systems, and increased product specialization. These trends in production organization are traced to the early 1970s when the crisis of Fordism supposedly took hold. Mass markets are said to have become saturated and hence the principles of mass production were rendered redundant. Moreover traditional patterns of labour organization and control, based on deskilling and rigid hierarchy, are deemed inappropriate to the so-called 'new times' and the new production and economic paradigm which is taking root in the advanced industrial countries.

Post-Fordism is used interchangeably in some writings with the narrower concept of flexible specialization, but critics suggest that the latter term is far more specific and has greater coherence (Hirst and Zeitlin, 1991). Flexible specialization, like post-Fordism, refers to the emergence of significant changes in the technical and social organization of industry, specifically in manufacturing, but makes no claim to any broader structural shifts in the character of society.

But the analytical force of both concepts hinges on the argument that there was a basic technical paradigm shift in production, reflecting the collapse of mass markets for relative cheap, consumer goods in the 1970s. Advocates of flexible specialization suggest that Fordism (mass production) is but one of a number of competing production paradigms, which became dominant in the early twentieth century because of the strategic choices of key actors in a contingent environment, and not for reasons of technological superiority. Likewise the revolution in manufacturing – the so called 'Second Industrial Divide' (Piore and Sabel, 1984) – that is supposedly currently taking place in some regions of the advanced world economy also reflects specific, historically contingent circumstances. Advocates of this mode of analysis, quite rightly, stress that the term post-Fordism is far too indiscriminate in proposing universal changes in the structure of society on the basis of scant evidence.

Yet both approaches have failed to demonstrate convincingly that the categories Fordism and mass production provide a secure theoretical and empirical point of departure for the analysis of both past and present trends in industrial restructuring. Attempts to analyse the contemporary weakness of economies such as the United States and Britain, in terms of their failure to make the transition from Fordism (mass production) to post-Fordism (flexible specialization) have been shown to be flawed in important respects

(Nolan and O'Donnell, 1991). It is questionable that British industry was ever dominated by the principles of mass production, and hence it is difficult to sustain the view, put forward forcibly by Hirst and Zeitlin (1989), that Britain's current economic crisis is the product of a continued commitment to these outmoded methods.

Equally, the indiscriminate application of the terms Fordism and post-Fordism to the other major advanced capitalist economies has proved untenable: consequently there has been a proliferation of terms such as 'flawed Fordism', 'flexible Fordism', 'state Fordism', 'blocked-Fordism', and so forth, in order to capture the complex and diverse histories of these different regions of the world economy. The analytical status of these terms thus remains highly questionable. At best they offer a convenient and superficially attractive way of periodizing complex patterns of industrial and economic change; at worst they present a misleading, crude and rigid taxonomy which obscures the critical dynamics of change and continuity in the capitalist economy.

PETER NOLAN

References

Aglietta, M. (1979), *A Theory of Capitalist Regulation: The US Experience*, London: New Left Books.

Clarke, S. (1990), 'New utopias for old: Fordist dreams and Post-Fordist fantasies', *Capital and Class*, **42**.

Gramsci, A. (1971), 'Americanism and Fordism', *Prison Notebooks*, London: Lawrence and Wishart.

Hirst, P. and Zeitlin, J. (1989), 'Flexible specialisation and the competitive failure of UK manufacturing', *Political Quarterly*, **60** (2).

Hirst, P. and Zeitlin (1991), 'Flexible specialisation versus post-Fordism: theory, evidence and policy implications', *Economy and Society*, **20**.

Jacques, M. and Hall, S. (eds) (1989), *New Times*, London: Lawrence and Wishart.

Lash, S. and Urry, J. (1987), *The End of Organized Capitalism*, Cambridge: Polity.

Nolan, P. and O'Donnell, K. (1991), 'Flexible specialisation and UK manufacturing: a comment on Hirst and Zeitlin', *Political Quarterly*, **62** (1).

Piore, M. and Sabel, C. (1984), *The Second Industrial Divide: Possibilities of Prosperity*, New York: Basic Books.

Gender and political economy

Gender was not explicitly discussed within the neoclassical or Marxist paradigms. In both cases there was an element of universality and of gender neutrality which disguised the unequal position of women in the social and economic domains.

Marxist theory analysed relations of production within a capitalist system where exploitation was based on the private ownership of the means of production and therefore assumed a class form. Women were exploited only as members of a social class not specifically as women.

Engels (1968) attributed inequality between the sexes to the existence of private property and the consequent need for heirs. The absence of private property thus safeguarded working-class women against male repression. In this sense sexual oppression had a class element. The destruction of capitalism and the subsequent elimination of property would ultimately liberate all women.

The oppression of women within different institutional arrangements and class environments showed that class alone was not a sufficient explanation, so that alternative theories became necessary. Marxist feminists attempted to reconcile the Marxist theory with feminism, while radical feminists sought an explanation for gender inequality in the domination and subordination of women by men. A reconciliation of the two approaches was attempted in 'dual theories'.

Radical feminists singled out the male sex as the main agent of women's oppression. *Patriarchy*, the system of male domination over women, is independent of any particular social system. It had preceded capitalism, and subsequent social and economic changes had not succeeded in dislodging it. The claim that '*personal is political*' summarizes their position. Politics is not only fought at a class level, within the traditional means of class struggle or other political practices, but also on the level of day-to-day experience. Power is exercised through a number of different means including psycho-cultural ones. Thus, 'personal is political' represents an attempt to raise consciousness and provide a programme for action. For radical feminists the main preoccupation was with sexuality rather than economic aggregates. Rape and male violence against women were the focus of their attention since they considered these incidents not simply as isolated events but as the means of exercising social control over women. One of the main criticisms against this concept of patriarchy is that it is ahistorical and not analytic, thus providing only a partial explanation for men's behaviour.

In contrast to the radical feminists, *Marxist feminism* seeks an explanation of women's inequality within the class structure of capitalism. There is a dual oppression based on class and sex/gender. The *domestic labour debate* arose out of the need to provide an explanation for the role of women in a capitalist system. The family was regarded as the site of production of consumption goods. Women contributed towards the reproduction and maintenance of the male worker and their children through the production of use-values at home. There is disagreement whether this action creates value or not. Gardiner (1975) argues that, as this process takes place outside the market mechanism, it cannot create value but leads instead to the creation of surplus value. By making goods fit for consumption, domestic labour allows workers to enjoy higher levels of living at a lower wage. This activity benefits male workers and capitalists. The benefit to capitalists arises since the value of labour power can be maintained below the actual subsistence level of the working class, thus leading to higher levels of profits. As long as women's consumption is less than the use-values they produce, they contribute to surplus value.

There is a further claim that women create value. As a worker's wages are destined to support him and his wife, the second part of the wage represents her contribution to value which is 'equal to the value she consumes in her own upkeep' (Secombe, 1974, p. 89). Further, he argues that the family plays an important ideological role in socializing the future generation of workers: in this way he sees that the exploitation of women favours capital as a whole more than it does individual men.

Particular problems of the domestic labour debate are, first, that it concentrated on the domestic field while most of women's problems arose specifically out of their dual involvement in domestic duties and in the labour market. Second, it reduced women's predicament to the performance of housework, implying that a solution could be found if the latter were eradicated. Capitalism and the development of consumer durables have indeed facilitated this process. Third, as Molyneux (1979) claims, the domestic labour debate concentrates too closely on the role of women as 'wives' and does not examine sufficiently their overall position within the family. Although child-bearing and rearing is a more arduous work than wifehood, this aspect is not sufficiently developed in the debate. The ideological dimension of the family was not tackled.

Despite its pitfalls, the close examination of housework delved into areas which had not been considered before. Further, it led to discussion of a *family wage and wages for housework*. The former expresses, implicitly at least, the recognition that the family is the source of production, where the husband is directly involved in the production process and the wife in the domestic one. One payment covers both activities, both the needs of the male worker and those of his family, assuming that the wife is totally involved in the domestic arena. The presupposition of a 'typical family' is a fundamental weakness of this approach, as it justifies discrimination in favour of men as 'breadwinners' and is prejudiced against unmarried people. Related to the domestic labour debate and aiming to avoid the pitfalls of a 'family wage', a demand was made by some feminists for a wage for housewives. This thesis was criticized widely as it aimed to maintain women within the domestic arena, completely overlooking other advantages available to them through work.

The *dual-system theories* provide a synthesis of Marxism and radical feminism, with present relations being shaped by the forces and influences of both patriarchy and capitalism. There is a symbiotic relation between them which is impossible to separate. Capitalism provides the material basis of operation, while patriarchy provides a system of control. The two systems are kept relatively separate in the work of Hartmann (1979). Within a capitalist framework, patriarchy leads to the appropriation of both domestic and wage labour by men. At work, patriarchal attitudes lead to the segregation of jobs and the appropriation of the best ones for men. Similarly, at home women do more housework, even when they also undertake a paid job.

Walby's (1990) analysis, although within the dual-systems approach, is critical of parts of Hartmann's work, particularly as the latter does not bring out sufficiently the conflict between capitalism and gender. For Walby, this relationship is not an harmonious one but is characterized, instead, by tensions arising out of the exploitation of women's labour. She distinguishes between *private and public patriarchy*, arguing that such a distinction allows for historical changes: 'In private patriarchy it is the man in his position as husband or father who is the direct oppressor and beneficiary, individually and directly, of the subordination of women' (Walby, 1990, p. 178). Public patriarchy, on the other hand, arises when women have access to both public and private arenas but are subordinate to men within both. The expropriation of women is performed collectively and not by any individual patriarch. The household is one location of women's oppression, but not the most important one in a modern capitalist state. Walby further distinguishes six key structures which are present in both private and public patriarchy: the patriarchal mode of production; patriarchal relations of paid work; patriarchal relations in the state; male violence; patriarchal relations in sexuality, and patriarchal relations in cultural institutions. Patriarchy is therefore characterized by the interaction of those six structures with the strategies of segregation adopted in the public and private domains. As they move from private to public patriarchy, women experience problems of segregation and exclusion which explain their exploitation in the labour market. Women's involvement in domestic labour is the result of lack of opportunities in the labour market. Walby's analysis is quite powerful, although it has been criticized by some as emphasizing patriarchal structures at the expense of the structures and development capital; despite her protestations to the contrary her ahistorical approach has also been decried.

The early discussion of the domestic labour debate later subsided because of its inherent weaknesses, although its contribution to feminist thought was very significant. The emphasis among feminist economists and sociologists in the 1970s was to analyse further the structures of the labour market and explain the secondary position of women within it. This analysis developed along the lines of the *reserve army of labour* (RA) approach, and the *segmented labour market theory* (SLM). For a further discussion in this area, see the entry Female employment and unemployment in this handbook.

The reserve army of labour approach was used by Marx in a gender-neutral form to analyse the effects of capital accumulation on labour. As accumulation proceeds, capital displaces labour, thus creating a pool of unemployed workers. Feminists saw women playing the role of the reserve army i.e. a pool of unemployed and flexible workers which could be drawn into the market in times of labour shortages and then asked to return home in periods of recession. As women's wages tend to be lower than men's, some Marxist and neoclassical economists argue that a rational entrepreneur would not undertake such policies. An explanation of this behaviour would need to be complemented by a theory of patriarchy. On an empirical basis, it seems that although there have been periods in the past, such as the immediate post-war period, where policies consistent with the RA hypothesis were used, the empirical evidence from recent years is not very supportive of this hypothesis.

The SLM theory, in its first form of the dual-labour market, distinguishes between a primary and a secondary market. In the primary one, which is composed mainly of white men, there is a hierarchical structure and vertical mobility, while the secondary one, composed mainly of women and people from ethnic minorities, is characterized by people with low training and skills, low pay and horizontal movement. These markets are segregated as there is no (or very limited) mobility between them. Although this analysis did not explicitly address women's employment, the gendering of the labour market, the deskilling of the labour force and the social construction of skills are closely related to this analysis.

ELENI PALIGINIS

References

Engels, F. (1968), 'The origin of the family, Private Property and the State' in K. Marx and F. Engels, *Selected Works*, Lawrence & Wishart.

Gardiner, J. (1975), 'Women's Domestic Labour', *New Left Review*, **89**.

Hartmann, H. (1979), 'The Unhappy Marriage of Marxism and Feminism: Towards a More Progressive Union', *Capital and Class*, **8**.

Molyneux, M. (1979), 'Beyond the Domestic Labour Debate', *New Left Review*, **116**, July/August.

Secombe, W. (1974), 'The Housewife and her Labour under Capitalism', *New Left Review*, **83**.

Walby, S. (1990), *Theorizing Patriarchy*, Oxford: Blackwell.

Global political economy

Global political economy does not constitute a single field or, still less, a unified theoretical viewpoint of the same order as neoclassical, Keynesian or Sraffian economics. The term signifies a location (global) and a subject matter (politics and economics). Within this broad structure, a number of different, often competing, traditions are housed. I will first define global political economy and then discuss two approaches to it – realist and Marxian.

Global political economy can be defined as the interaction between politics and economics at the global level. Depending on the analyst, politics may refer to the state (the central institution), to power (the means or currency), or to public policy (the outcome). Similarly, economics may refer to the market (institution), to voluntary exchange (the means) or to wealth (the outcome). Different meanings of politics and economics obviously imply different kinds of political economy. Classical political economy focuses on wealth and associated ideas of subsistence, surplus and accumulation. Marxism focuses on class and class processes. The treatment of particular economic concepts as central creates different opportunities and constraints in relation to politics.

The realist approach starts with state power and wealth as analytically coequal categories. Wealth is the basis of national power; power is critical for the pursuit of wealth. Notwithstanding short-term trade-offs, power and wealth are mutually supportive in the long term.

From this general starting point, there are many different routes. One direction is inspired by the 'economics of protection' literature. States are conceptualized as organizations 'producing' protection and organized violence. They take (through taxes) social wealth and convert it into objects of state power (tanks, missiles, trained soldiers, military leaders). The technology for converting wealth into the instruments of power is characterized by varying levels of efficiency; in other words, there is a production function for violence.

What are the implications for economic exchange? If two states have different technologies of violence, firms competing globally will be affected. If state *A* is more efficient than state *B*, firms within *A* will enjoy a 'protection rent'. In this way the costs of protection become relevant for economic competition.

A second route relating power and wealth asks how states can create and maintain international 'influence structures' – patterns of interaction that are easily exploited for power purposes. In a diversified trade structure that does not rely on single partners and where substitution possibilities (partners and products) are not costly, it is difficult to be influenced. States interested in exercising influence attempt to tie others to themselves and to make it costly for them to break free.

Hirschman (1945) was one of the first to recognize the power potential in Ricardian arguments regarding gains from trade. These gains describe the incremental consumption that takes place through international specialization compared to autarky. Hirschman argued that, when formulated in opportunity cost terms and inverted, the classical gains from trade describe a country's vulnerability. This opportunity cost idea, concretized in the form of trade, points the way to a connection between power and economic exchange.

A third theme of realist political economy attempts to link the global distribution of power to trade. Power may be distributed in many ways, but multipolarity, bipolarity and unipolarity are three ideal types. Changes in the distribution of power are typically used to explain war, but they are also relevant for economic exchange.

Gowa (1989) argues that trade is more likely to be open (free trade) under bipolarity (within blocs) than under multipolarity. This is so because security externalities (the positive effect of economic exchange on security) are captured by bloc partners; also, under bipolarity, there is a higher degree of certainty about who one's partners are. Multipolar international systems are demonstrably more fluid than bipolar systems. The relative stability of bipolarity provides incentives to value the future more than under multipolarity. If this theory is true, we should expect greater trade openness in bipolar systems, greater success of regional integration efforts when unions are nested within a stable bipolar structure, and partial reversibility of success (such as the European Community) when the systemic distribution of power changes.

There are numerous strands within Marxian global political economy. Marx and his followers have inspired work on imperialism, global class conflict, dependency theory, world systems theory, unequal exchange and the political preconditions for global production and exchange. Among different analysts, the core of Marxism has been represented, alternatively, as power relations and as class process. On the one hand (e.g. dependency theory), world inequalities are explained as results of power-bargaining relations among rich and poor states and classes. On the other, these same inequalities are explained by class processes, i.e. as results of the production, realization and appropriation of surplus value. Power and class are not the same. They identify two directions for Marxian theory.

I will comment on three areas of work in Marxian global political economy: the internationalization of capital, unequal exchange theory and the Gramscian approach.

Modern Marxists seem less interested in deducing imperialism from the laws of motion of capitalism than exploring a variety of motives and consequences. Firms 'go abroad' for many reasons: to preserve market shares, oligopolistic rivalry, cheap labour, etc. Marxists have studied European integration, economic competition among major economic blocs (Western

Europe, East Asia, North America), and the changing international division of labour. Some scholars analyse the relation between transnational economic integration in the European Community (EC) and national/international democratic forces. Some see capital as moving easily within Europe from one location to another, depending on changing incentives, while democratic checks are largely undeveloped. Picciotto (1990) sees this imbalance as a recreation at the global level of the structural advantages of capital in general. He is not optimistic about removing the 'democratic deficit' through democratic action and class struggle globally.

Unequal exchange theory tries to answer questions of the type: why are some countries rich and others poor? Why are there rich and poor zones (centres and peripheries) in all parts of the world economy? While different explanations are offered, the common point of departure is the belief that part of the explanation has to do with interactions among countries or, more precisely, among different classes and different countries. This focus links the concerns of dependency theory, world systems theory and unequal exchange theory.

Unequal exchange is broadly consistent with a number of surplus drainage mechanisms, among them worsening terms of trade, profit repatriation, licensing fees and interest on debt. Terms of trade theorists generally argue that less developed countries experience declining export revenue (per unit – this is not a balance of trade argument) and increasing costs for imports. These changing costs may reflect power-bargaining variables (oligopolistic vs competitive industries) or, more likely, different market returns to particular classes of goods. Prebisch (1950) argues that poor terms of trade for LDCs have to do with their position in the global division of labour (exporters of primary goods, importers of manufactured goods). As global income rises, demand for manufactures will rise faster than demand for primary goods, thus causing differential price increases.

Since the 1950s contributions have been made based on departures from Prebisch's elasticity argument. Emmanuel (1972) provides one example. In technical Marxian terms, what is unequal in Emmanuel's theory is not exchange *per se*. The source of inequality lies in cross-national variations in class power. Workers in the core are organizationally stronger, producing a rent that in turn results in higher wages than in the periphery. Since wages are a component of costs, goods produced in the core will be priced higher than those produced in the periphery, quite apart from considerations of productivity, product quality or degree of competition. Differential, intra-systemic (i.e. domestic) class power results in an unequal international outcome, with no power wielded among international actors.

The Gramscian approach rejects the primacy of economics and instead considers politics, economics and culture as co-equal categories. The work of

Cox (1983) may be taken as representative of this approach. Cox's three categories are social forces (including material forces), state forms and ideas. These concepts can be used to illuminate numerous global phenomena such as global cooperation.

The Gramscian approach does not view international cooperation among capitalists in terms of strategic interaction within an overarching structure of anarchy. Employing a concept of transnational culture, Cox sees cooperation emerging out of contacts among national ministries (Trade, Industry and Finance) and in the "non-political" culture of bankers, academics and international consultants. The key points of contact are not so much the official external arms of states (Departments of External Affairs or Defence) as the economic ministries. International organizations such as the European Community and the IMF are important, as are less formal associations such as the G–7.

In summary, the Gramscian approach substitutes a conception of international governance as informal rule in place of world government traditionally conceived as the dominance of international political structures with lines of authority running from the top down.

Space limitations do not allow us to mention exhaustively all the other approaches to global political economy. Nevertheless, both Marxism and realist proponents have fostered rich traditions of theory and a full research agenda for the years ahead. They are thus good indicators of what global political economy is about.

JAMES A. CAPORASO

References

Cox, R.W. (1983), 'Gramsci, Hegemony, and International Relations Theory', *Millenium*, **10** (2), 126–55.

Emmanuel, A. (1972), *Unequal Exchange: A Study of the Imperialism of Trade*, London: New Left Books, and New York: Monthly Review Press. (First published in French, 1969).

Gowa, J. (1989), 'Bipolarity, Multipolarity, and Free Trade', *American Political Science Review*, **83** (4), 1245–56.

Hirschman, A.O. (1945), *National Power and the Structure of Foreign Trade*, Berkeley and Los Angeles: University of California Press.

Picciotto, S. (1990), 'The Internationalization of the State', *Review of Radical Political Economics*, **22** (1), 28–44.

Prebisch, R. (1950), *The Economic Development of Latin America and Its Principal Problems*, Lake Success, NY: United Nations Department of Economic Affairs.

Growth poles

The notion of growth poles was first put forward by François Perroux. Operating mostly on the basis of synthesis and intuition, Perroux created the notion of growth poles as an integral part of a general economic theory of dynamic change. Perroux's approach is compatible with, but also different from, classical and Marxian sectoral analyses because the engine of sectoral transformations is represented by the dominant firm. His views on the subject are largely contained in the well-known book *L'économie du XXe siècle*, first published in 1961 (Perroux, 1991). In this respect Benjamin Higgins is correct in pointing out that Perroux's work – written sometimes in a rather convoluted way – is not on regional economics as such, but about pure theory. Instead, economists working on issues of regional planning 'converted it into a totally different theory which treated growth poles as urban centres, and spread effects as being generated in a particular geographic space, namely the region adjacent to the urban center itself' (Higgins, 1988, p. 44).

In contrast to the geographical and functionalist utilization of the growth poles concept, Perroux conceived it as an instrument to convey and explain the elements of power and domination which characterize the asymmetric relations governing any dynamic process. The growth pole is the abstract location where the interaction between active and passive units takes place, thereby unleashing a process of growth and structural change (Perroux, 1975). Economic growth must occur through growth poles, not for geographical reasons, but because certain factors (such as technical progress, the concentration of resources necessary to overcome indivisibilities in capital formation, etc.) cannot be uniformly spread over all firms. In Perroux's view, growth is seen as a discontinuous process. Technical progress is not like manna from heaven falling uniformly on all productive units. Instead – like new investments – it requires a hot-house situation. These hot-house conditions represent the framework containing the growth poles; i.e. they constitute the space or the overall environment of the growth pole. In other words, this environment will have to produce an input-output structure as well as a set of institutions consistent with the activities of the growth-generating units.

A growth pole can be a particular area within a country, a whole state and even a whole continent. The theoretical and abstract nature of Perroux's concept is evidenced by Higgins's remark according to which, in Perroux's eyes, the growth pole of Latin America was located in Europe and the US. Today we could say that the growth pole of Australia is in East and Southeast Asia, which gives a vivid picture of the asymmetrical character of economic relations in a dynamic setting. In Perroux's jargon, the manifestations of these asymmetries are called *domination effects*.

For Perroux the need to think in terms of economic domination stems from the shortcomings of the theory of competitive general equilibrium, as well as from the identification of basic stylized facts. He defines perfect competition as a situation in which '*all elements of domination are excluded*, or as a world in which contracts are arrived at without struggle' (Perroux, 1991, p. 75; my translation). In turn, the stylized facts are derived from a Schumpeterian reading of economic history. Each major phase of development is marked by a set of activities generating impulses for the rest of the system, such as the expansion of railways, steamships, autos, etc. The construction of these branches depends in a crucial manner on particular sectors such as steel, aluminium, mechanical industries, etc. In this sense Perroux anticipated a thesis which became fashionable among American economic historians many years later; namely that each historical period is characterized by a set of relevant sectoral relations.

These dominant sectors exercise leadership over other branches both directly, by using some of their products and, indirectly, by compelling them to adjust to the new macroeconomic environment. The core of the dynamic and innovative activities is represented by the dominant firm, which is defined as such because it exerts non-reversible changes on other units. More specifically, the activities of the dominant firm are felt by different types of units: by those which are linked to the leading firm through an input-output relation, as well as by those which fall into its orbit, although initially their activities may have had little or nothing to do with those of the dominant unit. The connection between dominant firms, leading sectors and innovations implies that growth impulses come mostly from large consolidated units exercising power, thereby acting as a gravitational force over weaker, yet necessary, units.

Before going any further, it appears necessary to clarify why growth requires a set of dominant firms. Indeed, theorists like Smith and Schumpeter conceptualized the process of competitive accumulation as a state in which no unit can obtain permanent advantages. Moreover, the concept of the dominant firm has got nothing to do with Marx's views about the centralization and concentration of capital. In my opinion Perroux's conception of the dominant firm is the result of an intellectual procedure whereby the neoclassical notion of externalities is reversed and put into a Schumpeterian framework. If it is accepted that growth and innovation imply a significant degree of discontinuity *vis-à-vis* the surrounding environment, then those firms capable of setting up the said discontinuities will emerge as the dominant ones.

This means that in determining prices, output and investment decisions, leading firms will have to influence the environment in such a manner that its shape and structure remain in a consistent relation with their plans. From a strict microeconomic point of view, externalities will always exist, so that dominant firms will not be able to internalize them. Yet, precisely because they do not just maximize a programme under some constraint, but undertake developmental plans instead, they are bound – if they are to succeed – to exercise a systemic influence over their environment. Externalities comprise the challenge facing dominant firms; the creation of a growth pole is the manner in which leading units intervene and either overcome or exploit such externalities.

In this context, the existence of firms cannot be dissociated either from their role or from an economic space in which units are formed on a necessarily unequal footing. To put the matter differently, Coase's ontological question of why firms exist has no *raison d'être* in Perroux's approach. The Schumpeterian emphasis on innovations, discontinuity and growth leads Perroux to explain the function of firms in terms of their physiological differences. It is these differences which in turn explain the formation of poles in any concrete situation. The dominant firm tends to be a monopolistic unit, since the discontinuous processes it gives rise to require the absorption of larger quantities of inputs than do those of the more passive units. Hence, the dominant firm will have a certain degree of freedom in setting prices which must be consistent with its growth plans. We will see, however, that the analysis of the role of the dominant firm within a growth pole is fraught with major theoretical limitations because of the static Chamberlinian frame of reference chosen by Perroux.

A growth pole is characterized by the presence of a leading industry which acts as the key industry. Its central role is determined by whether or not the increase in turnover it induces for all the other (passive) industries is significantly larger than its own increase. Perroux is quick to point out that 'one cannot write down once and for all the list of the key industries on the basis of their features and techniques'. Furthermore, the 'decisive factor is that there should be industries acting as *privileged foci for the application of the forces or dynamisms of growth.* When these forces engender an increase in the turnover of the key industries, they will cause a strong rise in the turnover of a much larger set' (Perroux, 1991, p. 185). The key industries therefore perform the function of generating spillover effects to other branches of the economy.

Perroux's approach does not try to reconcile disproportions with equilibriating factors. Poles are structured around uneven relations between the leading and the passive units. The destabilizing nature of these relations may indeed have a positive effect, insofar as the dominant oligopolistic units generate a higher rate of growth of productivity and of accumulation than would have been the case in a more competitive regime. The benefits of oligopolies are expressed in even stronger terms when he observes that, in modern times, there are two ways for an economy to be strong. The first is when it is able to finance its best technical units as well as provide markets for them, even when facing opposition from its trading partners. The second is to operate in a regime of competition with many small and medium units which, by producing at low costs, will expand national incomes. He concludes that 'the best way to be dynamically strong is the first' (Perroux, 1991,

p. 223). By the same token, an economy can grow on a competitive as well as on a monopolistic basis. In the competitive case, if world demand is highly elastic, the economy will expand its sphere of influence by reducing costs and prices. Yet it can also grow by forming monopolistic industries which reduce costs and undertake direct investment abroad. This will be to the benefit of the national economy because it creates external areas dependent upon it. In the general process of development, the spread effects stemming from the growth pole are a prerequisite for the formation of a coherent national economy. The stronger its monopolistic forces, the stronger the economy.

We can begin the assessment of Perroux's contribution from this precise issue. The question of monopoly or oligopoly is two faceted. The creation of monopolistic industrial structures does, indeed, imply a growing economic strength for the countries or areas where it has occurred. Japan and Germany, for instance, did not start from a competitive basis. They moved directly into large-scale industries, bypassing competition altogether. Yet, a mature oligopolistic situation is by no means conducive to sustained growth, as argued, *inter alia*, by Kalecki, Steindl, Sylos-Labini and Sweezy. The point is that the analytical formulations of this group of authors are stronger than the intuitive ones produced by Perroux. The strength of a country organized around oligopolistic structures may actually imply that it is strong enough to export its stagnationist tendencies abroad. From this perspective a growth pole attaining mature oligopolistic status can become a source of stagnation if, for instance, it manages to obtain a persistent balance of payments surplus with the rest of the world. Chamberlin's study of monopolistic competition stimulated Perroux's thinking on domination effects, but the more dynamic approaches linking oligopoly to maturity and maturity to excess capacity did not seem to influence his analysis.

It is indeed in relation to questions concerning hierarchy and domination that Perroux's approach is at its best. The hierarchical relations inside the growth pole are seen as determined only by the existence of dominant firms belonging to key sectors, thereby avoiding any *a priori* classification of what these sectors might be. By contrast, the other theory emphasizing structural linkages (i.e. the Marxian one) singled out the capital goods sector or 'heavy industry' as the only growth-inducing branch of activity.

In the light of historical experience, Perroux's method of moving from the role of the dominant firm to the intersectoral environment necessary to sustain the dynamism of the firm and of leading industries, is more far-sighted than the categorical nature of Marxian growth models centred on the predominance of the capital goods sector (Halevi, 1992). Investment priority in 'heavy industry' does not define the formation of appropriate linkages needed to keep up the momentum of growth. For example, the priority given to the capital goods sector in the industrialization of Malaysia has produced markedly different outcomes from the same priority given in countries like Romania. This means that the linkages were in fact very different, with the 'heavy industry' model unable to offer any explanation as to why the results differed so much.

The 'heavy industry' model was intended to be both expansionary and equilibriating, the latter being mostly a long-run policy objective which never materialized, but operated as the ideological justification for the investment strategies of the so-called socialist countries. This dual function of the model can be found in even the most distinguished and refined Marxist thinker of the post-war era, Maurice Dobb.

More importantly still is that binomial growth and equilibrium are replaced by the polarization of growth processes and the spread effects which ought to follow at a later stage. Without such spread effects, growth poles would lose their economic viability – absorbing rather than generating resources. Yet, in Perroux's theory there is no mechanical way to ensure the implementation of the spread effects. The technical capacity of dominant firms in this context should not be translated into an ability to organize the social process required for the formation of a growth pole. Institutions, not firms, can structure social processes. This is because the uneven distribution of power between dominant and non-dominant firms will never by itself create the meeting grounds needed to establish the necessary interrelations. It is the task of institutions to enable the uneven power structure to operate coherently in a developmental direction. At this point the viability of a growth pole is gauged on the basis of its also being a developmental pole in the socio-institutional sense. Thus, forward and backward linkages are not only (or just) technical and physical phenomena, but also refer to the social aspects of development.

In France, Perroux's analysis of the connection between space and growth has found a novel dimension in the theory of regulation developed in a Marxian vein by de Bernis. Here the central idea is the articulation of the productive system in a specific productive space. The consistency of the productive system is then analysed in terms of Marxian reproduction conditions (de Bernis, in GRREC, 1991).

JOSEPH HALEVI

References

GRREC (1991), *Crise et Régulation*, Grenoble: Université Pierre Mendès France.

Halevi, J. (1992), 'Asian Capitalist Accumulation: From Sectoral to Vertical Integration', *Journal of Contemporary Asia*, **22** (4).

Higgins, B. (1988), 'François Perroux' in B. Higgins and D. Savoie (eds), *Regional Economic Development: Essays in Honour of François Perroux*, Boston: Unwin Hyman.

Perroux, F. (1991), *L'Economie du XXe Siècle*, Grenoble: Presses Universitaires de Grenoble.

Perroux, F. (1975), *Unités Actives et Mathématiques Nouvelles*, Paris: Dunod.

Growth theories (Keynesian growth)

Modern growth theory has its origins in the work of Roy Harrod and Evsey Domar in the 1930s and 1940s. Using Harrod's terminology, their analysis suggested that a 'warranted growth path' may exist, but that there may be no mechanism to ensure equality between the warranted growth rate and the growth of labour supply (the 'natural growth rate'). Secondly, the analysis indicated that, most likely, the warranted growth path would be unstable. To many economists both mainstream and heterodox – these conclusions appeared to be at odds with the empirical evidence, and following a description of Harrod's analysis and the neoclassical response, this entry considers some alternative Post Keynesian and Kaleckian models of economic growth.

Harrod's basic argument is straightforward. Assume constant returns to scale and let the given technique be represented by a constant maximum output-capital ratio, σ. If the average saving propensity is s and u denotes the rate of utilization of capital, the Keynesian equilibrium condition $I = S$ can be rewritten as

$$g_w = \hat{K} = I / K = S / K = sY / K = su\sigma. \quad (1)$$

In a static Keynesian analysis, the accumulation rate is the exogenous variable which determines the short-run equilibrium value of the utilization rate. A long-run dynamic analysis, however, must allow for feedback effects of aggregate demand on firms' investment decisions. The feedback effects may be complex, but the steady growth implications are quite simple. Firms invest in order to achieve a desired capital capacity, and it seems reasonable to suppose that the desired capacity is proportional to the expected level of future demand. These demand expectations should be satisfied (on average) under the tranquil conditions of (hypothetical) steady growth. It follows that the rate of utilization must be at the desired level: if it differed from the desired level, firms would try to correct the discrepancy and the rate of accumulation would not remain constant.

Assuming a given desired rate of utilization and reading the equation from right to left, equation (1) defines the (steady-state) warranted growth rate. The equation specifies the particular rate of accumulation which – taking into account the multiplier effects of investment on output – would make firms achieve the desired rate of utilization so that, even with hindsight, there would be no incentive to change the rate of accumulation. The growth path is 'warranted' precisely because of the consistency (on average) between expectations and outcomes; warranted growth implies that (on average) firms have rational expectations. Outside steady growth the analysis becomes more complicated, but at any moment and for any given initial conditions, there are warranted paths of investment which, if executed, would turn out to be justified in the minds of investors by the paths of demand that they generated.

The warranted paths are benchmark cases. Expectations are not always satisfied, and actual growth therefore need not be warranted. But disappointed expectations – a discrepancy between actual and warranted growth – lead to changes in expectations and investment; in fact, interactions between the actual and warranted growth rates were at the centre of Harrod's attempt to develop a general framework of economic dynamics. He argued, in particular, that there would be no tendency for the two rates to become equal. Expectations may change in response to past mistakes, but this learning process (in modern terminology) does not imply convergence to a rational expectations equilibrium of warranted growth.

In order to illustrate this instability, we may assume that initially there is steady growth along the warranted path described by equation (1), but that the accumulation rate is then subjected to a shock which temporarily raises it above the warranted rate. Reading the equation from left to right in the standard Keynesian manner, this rise in accumulation *above* the warranted rate implies a high utilization rate and hence a *shortage* of capacity. The shortage of capacity induces firms to *increase* the rate of accumulation, but the multiplier effects of aggregate investment on aggregate demand then imply a further rise in utilization and an exacerbation of the disequilibrium. In the absence of policy intervention, stability would require firms to reduce investment in response to a shortage of capacity. This response would only be individually rational if each firm expected all other firms to react to the shortage by curtailing their investment spending as well. The implausibility of this assumption makes it safe to conclude that, without policy intervention, the warranted growth path will be (locally asymptotically) unstable.

Assuming that instability problems can be overcome through fiscal and monetary policy, a second problem remains. The warranted growth rate in equation (1) is fully determined by the variables s, u and σ. If these three variables, as well as the growth rate of the labour force, are given exogenously, the rate of growth of employment will differ from the growth rate of the labour force (the natural growth rate) except by coincidence. Accommodating changes in one or more of the variables could, in principle, equalize the warranted and the natural growth rates, but Harrod saw no reason to expect any such automatic adjustments. The choice of technique, for instance, may depend on the rate of interest, but an attempt to derive a rate of interest 'which brought the warranted growth rate into equality with the natural growth rate ... really makes no sense' (Harrod, 1973, p. 173).

Not all Keynesians accept Harrod's analysis, and a number of Post Keynesian theories of economic growth have been developed. Since their starting point has been the equilibrium condition for the product market, specification of the saving and investment functions has been crucial. Disregarding monetary and financial issues and assuming a given technique, a general formulation assumes that both *I/K* and *S/K* depend on the utilization rate u and the profit share π. Algebraically,

$$I/K = i(u,\pi);\ i_u > 0,\ i_\pi > 0 \tag{2}$$
$$S/K = s(u,\pi);\ s_u > 0,\ s_\pi > 0 \tag{3}$$

and the equilibrium condition becomes

$$i(u,\pi) = s(u,\pi). \tag{4}$$

Equation (4) does not suffice to determine both u and π, but in some special cases the equation may yield a unique solution for the growth rate. One such case arises if *I/K* and *S/K* depend exclusively on the profit rate (that is, on the product $u\pi\sigma$ where, by assumption, the technical coefficient σ is constant). This specification, used by Robinson (1962), implies determinate equilibrium values of both $u\pi$ and *I/K*; assuming a constant rate of utilization, the growth rate of output is equal to the accumulation rate. Furthermore, if saving is more sensitive than investment to changes in the profit rate, then an increase in 'animal spirits' (an upward shift in the investment function) raises both growth and profitability, while increased thrift (an upward shift in the saving function) leads to lower growth and reduced profitability.

In general, however, additional assumptions are needed to close the model, and Kaldor's (1957) solution was to impose full employment,

$$\hat{L} = n. \tag{5}$$

With a fixed coefficient function and in the absence of technical progress, the change in utilization is then given by

$$\hat{u} = \hat{L} - \hat{K} = n - i(u,\pi). \tag{6}$$

Assuming that equation (4) defines π as a function of u (by imposing weak restrictions on the partial derivatives of i (,) and s (,)), we get

$$\pi = \pi(u), \tag{7}$$

and the evolution of u can be determined by the differential equation

$$\hat{u} = n - i(u,\pi(u)) = h(u). \tag{8}$$

If $h' < 0$, $h(0) > 0$ and $h(1) < 0$, this equation has a unique and stable equilibrium solution with $0 < u^* < 1$.

Kaldor also introduced endogenous technical progress into the model. This innovation, in the form of a technical progress function, complicates the analysis slightly but does not alter the qualitative results in (8): a steady growth equilibrium at full employment (at a constant rate of employment) exists and, depending on parameter values, will be asymptotically stable. The full employment assumption, however, was imposed by Kaldor without (convincing) theoretical justification, and it is unclear why a Keynesian economy should generate continuous full employment. Furthermore, accommodating variations in the output-capital ratio (the utilization rate) are used to equalize the warranted and natural growth rates in the model. Despite the inclusion of an independent investment function, Kaldor's analysis thus shares key assumptions with the neoclassical argument.

A Kaleckian mark-up specification provides an alternative closure of the model in equations (2)–(4) (Rowthorn, 1981; Dutt, 1984). Ignoring raw materials and intermediate inputs and assuming a fixed coefficient production function, a constant mark-up on variable cost is equivalent to a constant profit share:

$$\pi = \pi_0 \tag{9}$$

With π_0 given by firms' pricing behaviour, the equilibrium condition for the product market now determines the utilization rate of capital and hence the growth rate. Only by change will this rate equal the natural rate of growth, so that one of Harrod's problems remains. But the other problem, the instability of the warranted path, is usually assumed away.

A standard Keynesian analysis of income determination presupposes the stability of short-run equilibrium: changes in income must affect saving more than investment if the multiplier is to be positive. The Kaleckian literature retains this standard short-run assumption, but extends it to the long run by positing the same specification of the saving and investment functions for both the short and the long term. This exclusion of lagged effects of past utilization and profitability on current saving and investment rules out the possibility of an unstable warranted growth path.

A Harrodian analysis, by contrast, assumes that there is a well-defined desired rate of utilization and that persistent deviation from this rate leads to changes in the accumulation rate. These endogenous shifts in the short-run investment function imply that the steady-growth investment function becomes perfectly elastic at the desired rate of utilization (and hence that $\frac{\partial i}{\partial u} \to \infty$). Arguably, the desired utilization rate may itself depend on a number of factors, including the rate of growth of demand, but plausible extensions of Harrod's analysis in this direction leave the instability result unchanged (Skott, 1989). The Kaleckian literature therefore (implicitly or explicitly) rejects the existence of a desired rate of utilization.

This rejection and the reversal of the relative long-run sensitivities of investment and saving to changes in utilization affect the comparative statics of changes in distribution. Thus, when $s_u > i_u$, equation (4) implies that

$$du/d\pi \gtreqless 0 \text{ for } i_\pi \gtreqless s_\pi. \tag{10}$$

These inequalities capture the traditional stagnationist argument associated with the work of Steindl and Baran and Sweezy. If the short-run stability condition is satisfied and if saving is more sensitive than investment to variations in the distribution of income ($i_\pi < s_\pi$), then a rise in the profit share – an increase in the degree of monopoly as reflected in the mark-up – will reduce utilization. Depending on the precise values of the partial derivatives with respect to both profitability and utilization, the result may also be a decline in the rate of growth. If, on the other hand, $i_\pi > s_\pi$ then an increase in the degree of monopoly stimulates both utilization and economic growth. The Kaleckian framework (including the short-run stability condition $i_u < s_u$) thus allows different scenarios, and Marglin and Bhaduri (1990) explore the properties of both the stagnationist case and 'exhilarationist' regimes in which $du/d\pi > 0$.

Sectoral and geographical aspects of the growth process, institutional change, technical progress and increasing returns, environmental problems and the role of natural resources, financial and demographic issues – these and other important elements have been ignored here. Space limitations provide a partial explanation of these omissions, while other entries cover some of the issues. But it should be emphasized that the abstract models in this entry give a partial and in some respects distorted view of a growth process that is both immensely complex and poorly understood. Simple as the models may be, however, they may help to structure the analysis. The Harrodian, neoclassical and Kaleckian models differ with respect to both theoretical perspective and policy implications, but they highlight some of the Keynesian questions that must be addressed by any theory of economic dynamics.

PETER SKOTT

References

Dutt, A.K. (1984), 'Stagnation, Income Distribution and Monopoly Power', *Cambridge Journal of Economics*, **8**, 24–41.

Harrod, R. (1973), *Economic Dynamics*, London and Basingstoke: Macmillan.

Kaldor, N. (1957), 'A Model of Economic Growth', *Economic Journal*, **67**, 591–624.

Marglin, S.A. and Bhaduri, A. (1990), 'Distribution, Capacity Utilization, and Growth' in S. Marglin and J. Schor (eds), *The Golden Age of Capitalism*, Oxford: Oxford University Press.
Robinson, J. (1962), *Essays in the Theory of Economic Growth*, London and Basingstoke: Macmillan.
Rowthorn, R.E. (1981), 'Demand, Real Wages and Economic Growth', *Thames Papers in Political Economy*, Autumn.
Skott, P. (1989), *Conflict and Effective Demand in Economic Growth*, Cambridge: Cambridge University Press.

Growth theories (neo-Marxian growth)

The dynamic interaction between distribution and accumulation is at the centre of neo-Marxian growth theory. This entry describes some recent attempts to formalize this interaction and also considers the possibility of integrating both Marxian and Keynesian insights within the same model.

Accumulation depends on profits, and the extraction of surplus value in turn depends on the balance of power between workers and capital. High rates of accumulation may reduce the reserve army of labour and increase the strength of workers *vis-à-vis* capital, but in the simplest neo-Marxian specifications the balance of power is taken as an exogenous variable. Marglin (1984), for instance, assumes that there is a 'conventional wage' which reflects 'community standards' and 'class power'. Algebraically, this assumption can be expressed as

$$w = w(z_0),\ w' > 0 \tag{1a}$$

where w is the share of wages in income and z_0 represents (working) class power and community standards.

Marglin explicitly excludes the level of employment as an influence on workers' strength. The capitalist sector, he argues, does not comprise the whole economy, and even if the growth rate of the total labour force is exogenous, the supply of labour to the capitalist sector may be perfectly elastic at a given real wage. The growth rate of employment cannot permanently exceed the growth rate of the labour force; however, the exhaustion of all hidden reserves of unemployment, Marglin argues, belongs to a future so remote that it can be disregarded even in long-term analysis.

The existence of non-capitalist production in most economies – and certainly at the world level – is indubitable, but the mere existence of a non-capitalist sector does not imply an exogenous real wage rate. The real wage may well be related to conditions in the non-capitalist sector, but both the supply of labour to the capitalist sector and the demand for capitalistically produced goods will in general depend on the sectoral composition of output. This composition changes over time depending on the rate of accumulation. Real wages cannot therefore be taken as exogenous and, ideally, the interactions between the different sectors should be explicitly included in the analysis.

Sectorally disaggregated models quickly become analytically intractable, but in one-sector models of pure capitalism, the gradual influence of accumulation on distribution can be captured by allowing the size of the reserve army of labour to affect the relative strength of workers. Workers are strong when the reserve army is small; in a static formulation, the wage share therefore becomes positively related to the rate of employment, so that

$$w = w(e, z_1), w_e > 0 \; w_z > 0 \tag{1b}$$

where e is the employment rate and z_1 represents the effects of other exogenous influences on workers' strength.

The efficiency wage literature offers a possible formalization of the influence of the reserve army on distribution (Bowles, 1985). A firm cannot, in general, monitor the work effort of its individual workers continuously, but even with imperfect monitoring, a worker has to consider the effects of effort on the risk of dismissal. As a result, the worker's choice of effort depends on the 'cost of job loss'. The cost of job loss, in turn, depends on the firm's wage offer. If effort is sufficiently sensitive to variations in the wage, it will be optimal for a profit-maximizing firm to pay a higher wage than is required to attract workers. Assuming that all firms are identical, this framework implies an equilibrium real wage rate which depends on the rate of employment. (Unemployment benefits also influence the real wage and should thus be included among the z-variables if equation (1b) is justified along these lines.)

The choice of effort can be derived from a standard utility-maximizing framework, and in a neoclassical formulation, the utility function is viewed as exogenous. From a Marxian perspective, however, the attitude towards work is not 'simply a manifestation of human nature, but in part the result of the social institutions in which the production process takes place' (Bowles, 1985, p. 33). Furthermore, 'work intensity' may reflect collective as well as individual reactions (viz. strikes and other forms of industrial action). The relation between the cost of job loss and work intensity therefore depends on a range of social and institutional factors including worker organization, wage aspirations and militancy, factors which from a long-term perspective cannot be regarded as exogenous.

The work on 'social structures of accumulation' represents an ambitious attempt to incorporate social and institutional effects on the process of accumulation in both theoretical and empirical analysis. Less ambitiously, Goodwin's (1967) formalization of Marx's 'general law of accumulation' can be interpreted along these lines. The gradual effect of labour market conditions on worker strength and militancy implies that the z-variables, z_1 in equation

(1b) and z_0 in (1a), follow a dynamic path. It may be assumed, more specifically, that high employment leads to a cumulative rise in militancy:

$$\frac{dz}{dt} = \gamma(e);\ \gamma > 0. \tag{2}$$

Equations (1a)–(2) and (1b)–(2), respectively, yield the following reduced-form expressions for the rate of growth of the wage share,

$$\hat{w} = \phi(e, z_0) \tag{1c}$$
$$\hat{w} = \psi(\hat{e}, e, z_1), \tag{1d}$$

while the simple 'real wage Phillips curve' used by Goodwin (1967) emerges as a special case:

$$\hat{w} = f(e);\ f' > 0. \tag{1e}$$

Equations (1a), (1b) and (1e) represent three common neo-Marxian specifications of the distribution of income, but the dynamic behaviour of the economy also depends on the determination of saving and investment. With respect to this latter question, there is near unanimity among neo-Marxian writers that the rate of accumulation is positively related to the rate of profits, and if both the capital-output and the capital-labour ratios are constant, the rate of growth of employment is equal to the rate of accumulation. It follows that both these growth rates are inversely related to the share of wages in income:

$$\hat{K} = \hat{L} = g(w);\ g' < 0. \tag{3}$$

The combination of (1a) with (3) implies steady growth at the rate $g(w(z_0))$, and an increase in the wage share following a rise in militancy thus reduces the growth rate.

Using (1b) instead of (1a) produces a simple differential equation describing changes in the employment rate:

$$\hat{e} = \hat{L} - n = g(w(e, z_1)) - n;\ g'w_e < 0. \tag{4}$$

Assuming that there is an equilibrium solution $g(w(e^*, z_1))=n$ with $0 < e^* < 1$, it follows from equation (4) that the economy converges to this (unique) equilibrium, and in equilibrium the rate of growth is equal to the growth of the labour force. If n is exogenous, an increase in militancy thus has no permanent effects on the growth rate but merely increases the equilibrium rate of unemployment.

Similar conclusions apply to the model described by (1e) and (3). This two-dimensional system of differential equations represents a slightly generalized version of Goodwin's (1967) growth cycle. In contrast to the specification with (1b) and (3), this system produces persistent fluctuations in employment and income shares. However, the average rate of growth is equal to n, and an increase in militancy leads to a rise in the average rate of unemployment.

The Marxian models described so far share a common weakness: they pay no attention to the 'conditions of realization' in the product market. Keynesian aggregate demand problems have been excluded, and the real wage rate has been determined by conditions in the labour market without any consideration of firms' pricing and output decisions.

Equation (1b), for instance, describes an equilibrium *real* wage that may not be realized. Wage bargaining, which determines nominal wages, takes into account the expected general price level, but since the actual price level emerges as the weighted average of firms' individual price decisions, such expectations may turn out to be mistaken. If, say, firms are identical and have excess capacity and if unit labour costs are constant below full capacity, the application of a constant mark-up implies an actual real wage that is constant and fully determined by the mark-up. For a given value of z_1, the equilibrium real wage in (1b) will thus only be realized for a unique value of the rate of employment. Employment rates above (below) the equilibrium value imply product prices that are higher (lower) than expected; with standard assumptions about the formation and revision of expectations, the equilibrium describes a unique NAIRU (non-accelerating inflation rate of unemployment).

Using a different terminology, Rowthorn (1977) reaches similar conclusions. He assumes that the income claims of both workers and capitalists increase with increases in demand and that as a result, the claims become mutually incompatible at both high and low levels of demand. If demand is given at some arbitrary level, the resulting (positive or negative) 'aspiration gap' generates unanticipated (positive or negative) inflation. But this resolution of the conflict is only temporary. Effective demand, he argues, may determine employment in the short term, but actual and anticipated inflation must coincide along a steady growth path; thus Marxian conflict over distribution determines the rate of unemployment in steady growth. The 'over determination' resulting from the integration of different theoretical approaches within the same model is resolved by restricting Keynesian forces to the short term. In the long run, aggregate demand adjusts endogenously – possibly through monetary and fiscal policy – to eliminate the aspiration gap.

Marglin's (1984) synthesis of Marx and Keynes exhibits a similar problem of overdetermination. Unlike Rowthorn, however, Marglin does not impose a long-run consistency between actual and anticipated inflation; thus Keynesian factors may play a role even in the long term. Overdetermination is avoided in Bowles and Boyer (1988) who combine a Marxian efficiency-wage determination of the distribution of income with a (Post) Keynesian equilibrium condition for the product market. However, their analysis focuses on short-run issues and they treat firms' mark-up decisions as an accommodating variable: labour market conditions dictate an optimal ratio of money wages to the expected general price level, and it is assumed – implicitly – that the pricing behaviour of individual firms validates these price expectations.

Keynesian demand, however, may influence long-run employment even if firms set prices and even if persistent expectational mistakes are ruled out in steady growth. The neo-Marxian determination of the (expected) real wage in equation (1b) includes social and institutional factors as well as the rate of employment. The possibility of endogenous changes in these factors implies that equation (1b) in combination with a mark-up equation will be insufficient to determine the long-run equilibrium. A period with unexpectedly high wages, for instance, is likely to produce an upwards shift in wage aspirations as workers gradually come to regard the new level as normal. If income aspirations contain historical and conventional elements of this kind, the competing-claims equilibrium ceases to be independent of (the history of) aggregate demand (Skott, 1991).

The integration of Keynesian and Marxian elements in Skott (1989) therefore allows both effective demand and worker militancy to play a role in the long-run determination of the distribution of income and the rate of employment. An increase in militancy, for instance, reduces the rate of employment in this model, while an increase in 'animal spirits' raises both the share of profits and the rate of employment. The model suggests that the interaction between saving and investment decisions determines a Harrodian 'warranted growth path' which is locally unstable. The neo-Marxian influence of labour market conditions and worker militancy on firms' production and investment decisions transforms this instability into persistent cyclical fluctuations. The resulting cyclical growth path has similarities with Goodwin's (1967) model, but the underlying cyclical mechanism differs significantly.

All of these models have severe limitations. Single-sector models of a closed capitalist economy may capture some Marxian insights into the growth process, but Marx's own analysis of the 'schemes of reproduction' suggested that 'disproportionality' problems would be the rule rather than the exception. The distinction in the schemes of reproduction between investment, consumption and luxury goods may not, however, represent the most pressing need for disaggregation. The inability of the simple models to address questions of 'uneven development' is arguably much more serious: both spacial disaggregation and the explicit consideration of technical change will be needed to overcome this limitation.

A mechanical introduction of exogenous and disembodied Harrod-neutral technical progress implies slight notational complications, but the qualitative conclusions of most models remain unaffected by this extension, while the gains in terms of realism or explanatory power are limited. Technical progress, however, is neither constant nor exogenous, and the endogeneity of technical change may be a powerful force behind 'uneven development'. Discussions of the unevenness of the growth process abound in the Marxist literature, but other traditions have also made important contributions in this area. The spatially destabilizing effects of learning-by-doing (and other forms of increasing returns and endogenous technical change) have been emphasized by Kaldor and Myrdal as well as by many development theorists; recently these issues have also been recognized by mainstream writers.

The question of uneven development is related to the traditional Marxian concern with the interaction between the economic sphere and the wider network of social and political institutions. It is always questionable whether the institutional framework may be taken as given in long-run analyses, but unstable economic processes will almost inevitably lead to political intervention and put pressure on existing institutional structures. A narrow economic analysis is therefore likely to be particularly misleading in the presence of important sources of economic instability.

It should be noted finally that neo-Marxian theory has been conspicuously silent with respect to environmental aspects of economic growth. This silence underscores the limitations of the abstract models in this entry. The models may illuminate some Marxian insights, but they provide a very partial picture of the growth process.

PETER SKOTT

References

Bowles, S. (1985), 'The Production Process in a Competitive Economy: Walrasian, Neo-Hobbesian and Marxian Models', *American Economic Review*, **75**, 16–36.

Bowles, S. and Boyer, R. (1988), 'Labour Discipline and Aggregate Demand', *American Economic Review Papers and Proceedings*, 395–400.

Goodwin, R.M. (1967), 'A Growth Cycle' in C.H. Feinstein (ed.), *Socialism, Capitalism and Growth*, Cambridge: Cambridge University Press.

Marglin, S.A. (1984), *Growth, Distribution and Prices*, Cambridge, MA: Harvard University Press.

Rowthorn, R.E. (1977), 'Conflict, Inflation and Money', *Cambridge Journal of Economics*, **1**, 215–39.

Skott, P. (1989), *Conflict and Effective Demand in Economic Growth*, Cambridge: Cambridge University Press.

Skott, P. (1991), 'Efficiency Wages, Mark-up Pricing and Effective Demand' in J. Michie (ed.), *The Economics of Restructuring and Intervention*, Cheltenham: Edward Elgar.

Human motivation

Why do people act the way that they do? A simple answer, embodying the idea that people are instrumentally rational, is that agents act because they wish to achieve certain ends. Thus, when agents maximize utility or profits in economics, it is the objective of utility or profit which motivates and it is the calculating capacity of (instrumental) rationality which informs the agent of the action best likely to satisfy those aims. The origins of this thought are in Hume (who famously cast reason into the lowly position of 'the slave of passions'), though the idea has proved extremely influential in economics, in radical political economy and in other social sciences. Nevertheless, radical political economy usually eyes the argument somewhat suspiciously because it seems to give only a partial account of human motivation.

Before I explain those radical suspicions, it may be helpful to say a word about the modern axiomatic approach to decision making found in mainstream economics. This approach again suggests that people act because they are rational, but it associates rationality with choices which satisfy certain conditions (like reflexivity, completeness, transitivity, etc.).

At first sight, this may seem rather different from the instrumental hypothesis that people act to maximize utility. However, first impressions can be deceptive. Choices satisfying the axioms can be represented 'as if' they came from a process of maximizing a utility function (or expected utility in the more general case). The utility function representation is arbitrary in the sense that any number of utility functions which are positive monotonic transformations (or linear transformations, in the general case) of each other could be used to represent these choices. In this way, 'utility maximization' is a heuristic gloss on action which accords with the axioms of rational choice.

This is an important observation because it helps to sever the traditional and controversial connection between mainstream economics and classical utilitarianism. However, it should not be thought that it thereby dispenses with the need for an instrumental account of motivation. To appreciate why this still might be needed, consider what it is about rationality under the axiomatic approach which makes it rational to follow an axiom like 'transitivity'. The point of the question is that it is difficult to think of an answer which does not rely on an instrumental conception of rational motivation. After all, intransitivity is obviously worrying when you have objectives which you wish to satisfy, because it means you could be traded into poverty and this would undermine your capacity to achieve those ends. (A person starting with bundle C, who prefers A to B, B to C and C to A, rather than A to C as would be demanded by transitivity, will pay to swap C for B, B for A, and A for C; he/she thus pays at each stage in a cycle which returns him or her back to holding C.)

It would be wrong to suggest that radical political economy eschews the instrumental account of motivation (either in its maximizing or axiomatic form). For instance, it is at play when profit maximizing behaviour is attributed to firms. Likewise, it is central to so-called 'rational choice' or 'analytic' Marxism (see Roemer, 1988). Nevertheless, with the important exception of the latter, radical political economists have typically criticized theories which rely *exclusively* on this account (particularly in relation to individual decision making).

On descriptive grounds, the broad criticism is that there is more to action than individual intentions. This criticism can be read in a variety of ways, depending on the sense in which there are 'things going on behind the backs' of individuals. A simple, but powerful, way of reading the point is that individual action is always constrained; moreover, it often seems that the constraints are more important than the individual calculation of what to do given those constraints. For instance, Marx was quite withering about those who argued, in effect, that an individual 'chooses' to supply labour as a result of a utility maximizing decision. To say this is to miss the crucial point – which is that the individual often has no alternative but to sell his or her labour in order to survive.

The point, however, needs careful handling because many constraints on an individual's action come from the actions of others. Thus to make the point really tell, one has to demonstrate that the constraints on action are not simply the consequence of instrumentally rational actions undertaken by other individuals. If this can be done, then 'something' genuinely is going on behind all individuals' backs which is missed when one relies only on the instrumental model. Of course, in a simple sense, there is always a legacy of history in the form of resources and their distribution which constrains individuals at any moment in time. But in general, it will not suffice to appeal to this form of constraint because it can always be argued that these inheritances are still constraints supplied by the actions of others, albeit those of a previous generation. Instead, the decisive claim of radical political economy is that there are rules, conventions and institutions that guide individual action and which cannot be understood simply in terms of (previous) interactions between instrumentally motivated individuals (see, for instance, Hodgson, 1988).

The argument here for a form of social irreducibility has been made in a variety of ways. One which turns on a recognition of uncertainty is finding a fresh warrant from developments in game theory. To be specific, post Keynesians, following Keynes, have argued that it is often the existence of conventions or institutions which enable agents to form expectations under conditions of uncertainty. In this sense, conventions serve instrumental agents. But this does not mean that they can always be explained with reference to those instrumental concerns, because there will often be more than one convention or institution which could act as an anchor for expectations. Thus the use of *one* convention rather than another requires the acknowledgement that there is something other than individual intentions at work. Furthermore, since the use of one convention rather than another may affect the distribution of the gains from economic activity, this irreducible component can be rather important.

This is no more than a quick sketch of one argument (see Hargreaves Heap, 1989, for an extended discussion). Nevertheless, it is worth mentioning because, perhaps somewhat paradoxically, the mainstream is coming to similar conclusions. In particular, in game theory the growing doubts over the applicability of the Nash (and related perfect equilibrium) solution concept, together with the problem of multiple equilibria once it is accepted, suggest that there is precisely the same sort of indeterminacy of action in games which is characteristic of the Post Keynesian understanding of uncertainty (see Binmore, 1990).

Radical political economists have also criticized the instrumental view because it fails to take account of processes that operate on individual preference formation. Even if we are born with some broad desires which translate into a need for things like food, clothing and shelter, it stretches credulity to imagine that this inheritance is fine tuned to the level at which we actually consume (i.e. Citroen 2CVs rather than Ford Escorts, or Levis 501s rather than heavy blue cotton trousers). Instead, to explain our fine-grained preferences in this sense we need to introduce socialization processes, the stimulae we receive later in life from advertising, peer groups and the like, and the (often peculiar) ways in which we process new information.

Much might be said on these topics as well as on the earlier argument with respect to conventions. I will restrict myself to four brief comments. Firstly, there is an obvious connection between socialization and the earlier comments on conventions because much socialization often entails the transmission of the rules of the 'social game' between generations. Once this is noted, it may be tempting to cast socialization as an amplification of that earlier argument rather than as a point about preference formation. Actually, it is both because the rules of the social game often supply reasons for action (just as it is the rules of chess which supply reasons for moving knight in a particular way and not some antecedent preference for moving wood about a board in a somewhat strange fashion).

Secondly, by definition, conventions are shared rules for doing things and as a result they yield shared patterns of behaviour amongst those who follow them. In this way, radical political economy finds a licence for collective constructs like class, gender and ethnicity when analysing individual behaviour.

Thirdly, the danger of this radical critique is that it may propel us from one extreme (the instrumental, where the individual appears to be in charge of his or her own decisions) to its opposite (a kind of social dope, where everything goes on behind the individual's back). Both extremes, it might be added, also offer strangely mechanical notions of individual agency. One way of avoiding both dangers is through the introduction of a richer notion of rational motivation. For instance, one might argue that reason is as much concerned with the selection of the ends which we pursue as it is with how best to achieve given ends (see Earl, 1986, for an application to consumer behaviour). Reason in this sense may not shine brightly, but at least it may motivate us to grope towards different ways of acting in the world. And we do need some sense of this groping if we are to account for change (whether it be of an entrepreneurial variety or the sort that has us escaping from 'false consciousness').

Finally, whatever the disputes (and there are plenty) over the significance of irreducible conventions, of advertising, peer groups and the like, it would be difficult to claim that, in the presence of such processes, our preferences and actions are in any simple sense our own. This is important because it helps to explain why radical political economy tends to value the 'negative' sense of freedom rather less than its 'positive' counterpart. The 'negative' sense is concerned with being able to act on given preferences and it fits rather well with an instrumental account of motivation. In contrast, the 'positive' sense, which is concerned with enabling individuals to become autonomous, seems more appropriate to those who for one reason or another doubt the authenticity of individual action. For instance, once the existence of irreducible conventions and institutions is admitted, it is tempting to suggest that we should attempt to bring these institutions within the domain of (collective) choice since we have something here which affects individual choice but which is not the product of it.

Of course, this is but the first move in what is a long argument, but to note even this first move is helpful because it suggests a reason for the heated nature of discussions concerning human motivation. Quite simply models which purport to explain why we act are indissolubly linked to questions of how we should act.

SHAUN HARGREAVES HEAP

References

Binmore, K. (1990), *The Foundations of Game Theory*, Oxford: Basil Blackwell.
Earl, P. (1986), *Lifestyle Economics*, Brighton: Wheatsheaf.
Hargreaves Heap, S. (1989), *Rationality in Economics*, Oxford: Basil Blackwell.
Hodgson, G. (1988), *Economics and Institutions*, Cambridge: Polity Press.
Roemer, J. (1988), *Free to Lose*, London: Radius.

Hysteresis

Economists use the term 'hysteresis' to denote the persistent influence of past economic events. This usage recalls the origin of the term in the physical sciences. The 19th-century physicist James Alfred Ewing coined 'hysteresis' to denote the persistent effects of the temporary exposure of ferric metals to magnetic fields: subsequent states of the metal were best understood by reference to the past. The general idea was that a transitory disturbance of a system can cause a persistent change in the description of that system. More specifically, the current value of an endogenous variable can depend on past rather than present values of some explanatory variable.

To anyone accustomed to modelling dynamic interactions with systems of ordinary difference or differential equations, the general notion of hysteresis does not seem exceptional: past and present states of such systems are always related by the rules of motion of the system. One may also readily accommodate the specific notion of dependency on the past. Consider the problem of modelling a transitory disturbance of a dynamic system characterized by autonomous (time independent) rules of motion. Given a disturbance that occurs during the time interval $[t_1,t_2]$, one might model the persistent effects of this transitory disturbance in at least two ways. First, the disturbance may be incorporated directly into the description of the system in order to yield a non-autonomous system. Second, the autonomous system can simply be analyzed subsequent to the disturbance; the state of the system can then be explained in terms of its state at t_2 and the passage of time. In the first case, the resulting description (solution) of the post-disturbance system will involve a direct reference to the disturbance. In the second case, the persistent influence of the disturbance is felt through the lasting importance of the state at t_2. In these contexts, using the term 'hysteresis' accomplishes little more than emphasizing that a system is truly dynamic.

When economists use 'hysteresis' simply to contrast dynamic with static systems, they employ a rhetorical device to draw attention to a perceived novelty. For economists accustomed to the inherently static general equilibrium framework deriving from Walras, perhaps any notion of important historical linkages will be novel. However, economists do not generally consider the influence of lagged income in popular modifications of the Lucas supply curve to constitute hysteresis. In contrast, dependence of the 'natural' rate of unemployment on the history of unemployment *is* considered hysteretical: it is a particular influence of the past on the present that is generally absent in economic models. Similar considerations are involved in Elster's discussion of the relationship between the superstructure and the economic basis. Elster (1976) suggests that the standard interpretation of historical materialism links the current superstructure, s_t, to the current economic basis, b_t. He contrasts this with an hysteretical variant, $s_t = s^1(b_t, s_{t-1})$, wherein the current superstructure depends not only on the current economic basis but also on the past superstructure, s_{t-1}.

Although the formalisms of discrete time analysis may seem to suggest otherwise, hysteresis is not a matter of unmediated action at a temporal distance. The past can influence the present only through traces left in the present, for the very nature of causal explanation implies that an event at time t_1 cannot affect events at time t_2 unless it also affects events at all $t \in (t_1, t_2)$. A complete description of the present – without reference to the past – is *logically* adequate for prediction in any causal dynamic system. However, such a description may not be practicable. In the terminology of Elster (1976), epistemological hysteresis characterizes dynamic systems for which no ahistorical description is feasible. The impossibility of ontological hysteresis, in the sense of unmediated action at a temporal distance, does not rule out the possibility of epistemological hysteresis, in the sense of the fundamental historicity of the system from the perspective of the investigator.

In applied work, epistemological hysteresis is pervasive and important. For example, a researcher studying the wage determination process can observe the past history of aggregate unemployment but not the expectations and current human capital of all the individuals in the labour force. In this case, as in James Alfred Ewing's original work, the researcher can refer to the macro-past of a system but not to its current micro-state. When appropriate causal links exist between the observable past and the non-observable current state, an hysteretical description of the macro-system is useful for explanation and prediction. Theoreticians, in contrast, do not generally model hysteresis in this way. Indeed, *prima facie* such a project appears to conflict with the very notion of a formal model of hysteresis. Perhaps for this reason, the concepts of hysteresis current in the social sciences are weaker than epistemological hysteresis.

Explicit social science models of hysteresis involve dynamic systems that – through appropriate redefinition of the state variables – may readily be expressed entirely in terms of the contemporaneous state. Motivations for not expressing the dynamic system in this way include the desire both for presentational simplicity and, most importantly, for a useful interpretation of the system under investigation. A dynamic system is said to display hysteresis by an investigator who judges that the current state of the system is best understood in terms of its past. In such cases the natural description of the state of the system will include explicit reference to the past. This suggests that whether or not one characterizes a system as hysteretical depends not only on its technical characteristics but also on individual judgments about the adequacy of various descriptions to the understanding of the phenomenon under investigation. To illustrate this point, recall Elster's hysteretical relationship between basis and superstructure. Elster (1976) suggests that one might eliminate the appearance of hysteresis in the superstructure by summarizing in the current culture, c_t, the influence of the past superstructure, s_{t-1}. If $c_t = c(s_{t-1})$, we can introduce culture as a new state variable and write $s_t = s^2(b_t, c_t)$. Such algebraic manipulation does not yield a non-hysteretical system, however, *unless* one finds that the reformulation leads to the judgment that the superstructure is best understood without reference to its past.

Interest in hysteresis represents a belief in the importance of the past for our understanding of the present. Applications pervade the social sciences. Hysteresis can be important in explaining the evolution of institutions, organizations, and technological systems. A classic example is the adoption of the QWERTY keyboard, which suggests that standards for technological compatibility may not evolve efficiently. Current norms and institutional structures, which contribute to the feasible range of economic activity, cannot be understood without reference to the past. Random historical events can influence the collusive success of oligopolies that can monitor each other only imperfectly, the locational commitments of firms and households in the presence of agglomeration externalities, and the behavioural rules of thumb adopted in circumstances of bounded rationality. Past consumption patterns are important influences on current and future consumption: habit formation is hysteresis in preferences. Current production levels depend on the historical paths of factor inputs, not just on current inputs. The trade balance may be permanently affected by a large, transitory real exchange rate shock if entry into foreign markets involves significant sunk costs. The social mobility of individuals may depend on the class history of previous generations. False trading (disequilibrium exchange) can influence equilibrium prices and quantities. The 'natural' rate of unemployment appears to depend on the history of unemployment. Hysteresis effects on human nature deriving from the history of capitalism may be crucial considerations for those who wish create social institutions that rely on altruism or feelings of community.

Hysteresis may even be relevant to questions of distributive justice, since justice may best be pursued through reference to past actions. From a natural rights perspective, the current distribution of wealth and income may be judged to be just if it arose without violating individual rights. Similarly, if the distribution of income and wealth should respond to merit, and if merit is seen as deriving from past actions, then judgements of justice will refer to past actions. To refer simply to current merit is possible but less informative.

In many of the examples above, the past is so persistent that different initial states generate divergent long-run outcomes. David (1988) suggests that we can think of path-dependent systems as those that are unable to sever their links with the past no matter how much time passes. In general accord with the current hysteresis literature, one may consider such path dependence in the context of globally stable systems. Every solution of a globally stable system converges, so path dependence in this context bespeaks multiple equilibria. Multiple equilibria are associated with the presence of null (unit) characteristic roots in linear systems of differential (difference) equations. In non-linear systems, multiple equilibria can be generated in a variety of ways. Many social scientists have reserved the term 'hysteresis' for situations displaying this path dependence of equilibrium outcomes. As David notes, the implications of such hysteresis for applied work in economics are radical: when the influence of the past persists strongly in the present, good applied economics will generally require good economic history. Hysteresis implies that a careful description of the past is crucial for understanding the present and predicting the future. In the presence of pervasive hysteresis, economics must become a truly historical science.

ALAN G. ISAAC

References

David, P.A. (1988), 'Path-dependence: Putting the Past into the Future of Economics', IMSSS Technical Report No. 533, Stanford University, November.

Elster, J. (1976), 'A Note on Hysteresis in the Social Sciences', *Synthese*, **33**, 371–91.

Industrial policy

In the absence of a well-accepted general definition of industrial policy, it makes sense first to divide policy actions into a broad trio of different *types* of intervention which generally come under the 'industrial policy' banner. The first of these is policy to deal with market power, although there is some merit in a further subdivision between 'natural' and 'unnatural' monopoly. The second group of policies consists of 'proactive' interventions aimed at pushing industrial development in certain desired directions. The third group of policies is 'reactive' and arises in response to problems of structural change (generally unemployment) in declining industries located characteristically in peripheral regions.

Considering possible *rationales* for such interventions, it is once more useful to identify three broad approaches to the understanding of industrial policy. The first is rooted in the neoclassical concept of 'market failure'. The second is associated with the Austrian school which raises the market to the status of an icon and is consequently hard-pushed to admit the possibility of market failure. The third, which again might warrant further subdivision, relates to the role of the state in directing industrial development. These three rationales are now considered in turn.

The *market failure* approach, which fits more or less neatly into the overall neoclassical analysis of economic activity, attempts to identify the conditions which preclude a competitive equilibrium. This approach is essentially pluralist with a neutral state and suggests that government intervention has the potential to correct such market failures and improve the functioning of markets. Recent developments have focused attention on informational asymmetries as a source of market failure.

Under a market failure approach, monopolies and restrictive practices distort competition and cause deadweight welfare loss. The usual remedy is for some clearly defined and consistently applied set of competition rules which affects the competitive environment for all firms. The problem of natural monopoly is of particular interest, with solutions directed towards re-establishing and utilizing market disciplines wherever possible.

The market failure approach is generally less comfortable with both proactive and reactive interventions. There has been some intellectual support for state finance of R&D where externalities affect the ability of private firms to appropriate the results of investment in information. Social benefits from research spending typically exceed private benefits, and the case for state funding for basic research is sometimes extended to encompass applied research as well. Reactive industrial intervention is seen as an interference with the process of market adjustment but, where assistance *is* countenanced, preference is for measures which ease the process of transition rather than those which preserve outdated and uneconomic capacity.

The *Austrian* approach to intervention can usefully be described as coming from the radical right. It is appealing in its simplicity but ultimately barren theoretically as it elevates what is at best a useful characterization of market processes to the status of a mechanism which by definition produces the most desirable outcomes. The approach identifies the competitive market process as the mechanism by which economies develop over time. The key players in the process are entrepreneurs motivated by the prospect of personal gain. Rewards flow to those entrepreneurs who have best identified or guessed what the public is willing to buy. By their actions, both successful and unsuccessful, they inform other players about the market. By imitation and arbitrage the market develops over time, but never to the static equilibrium of orthodox economics. The process of change is perpetual.

The policy prescriptions of the Austrian approach are straightforward: the market must be allowed to operate free of statutory restrictions. In its most extreme form, the implication is that governments have simply to dismantle state ownership and statutory restrictions on market entry to achieve this benign outcome. Conventional competition policy, aimed at restrictive practices, barriers to entry and the abuse of monopoly power, is unnecessary as the high profits earned in such cases are a vital signal to other entrepreneurs who will invariably and inevitably find ways to enter the market and compete away the profits.

Both proactive and reactive industrial intervention from the Austrian viewpoint is misguided and counterproductive. The free market system will ensure that firms take up profitable opportunities to invest in research. Subsidies to ailing firms and industries, typically categorized as 'lame ducks', are harmful because they interfere with the signals generated by the market.

The *state intervention* approach is the third broad rationale for industrial policy and (in contrast) comes generally from the radical left, although a strongly interventionist state has also been found within corporatist models. Leaving aside for the moment debates over the role of the capitalist state, the interventionist state forms particular objectives for industrial policy in a narrow national context. Key firms or industries within the manufacturing sector receive state support to provide the basis for future national economic development (Cowling, 1987).

This third rationale typically sees a role for competition policy, but generally involves rather more pragmatism in policy application than does the market failure approach. Some large firms may be constrained if consumers are disadvantaged, but it is equally possible that other large firms will be actively encouraged. Each case will be viewed on its merits in relation to the overall economic strategy. In some contexts competition will be welcomed;

in others it will be castigated as 'wasteful duplication'. In such a system, where the role of the state is viewed positively, public ownership becomes an acceptable instrument for addressing the problem of natural monopoly.

Proactive policies are readily explained within the interventionist state approach. Key sectors will be identified for support, which may be in the form of R&D assistance, export aid, preference in government procurement and import restrictions. Sometimes, in 'picking winners', governments have selected particular private sector firms as 'national champions' to be the vehicle for state development plans. Reactive intervention to ameliorate the impact of structural adjustment can also fit within the interventionist state approach, as it admits the principle that the state can *choose* to direct economic development, rather than being passive in the face of market forces. Support can thus be justified for the retention of strategically or politically sensitive firms which are in decline.

Turning to recent experience within the developed economies, the thrust of industrial policy making within an international context has seen the interventionist state pushed aside in favour, arguably, of a version of the Austrian approach. Tentative moves towards a US industrial policy in the face of the pressures of deindustrialization have withered. Policies in the UK and the US have been aimed to 'make the market work better', for example by reducing personal and corporate taxes as a way of improving incentives and by removing irksome government controls on industrial behaviour. The dismantling of Eastern European command economies has been accompanied by an exhortation to follow the true path of the market. State-owned enterprises in many countries have been privatized or deregulated. Industrial planning is widely seen as inimical to developed capitalism. At the same time, however, it is widely recognized that perhaps the most successful developed economy of recent times, Japan, has clearly pursued a very directive industrial policy supported by protectionism (Thompson, 1989).

While such contradictory developments highlight shortcomings in the orthodox and Austrian approaches to industrial policy, the state intervention approach outlined above is not itself without weaknesses. This perhaps indicates a need to consider matters from a wider radical perspective. Such an understanding in turn relates to two broad issues: the first concerns the underlying tendencies of the developed capitalist economy; the second relates to how the state operates within the context of the advanced capitalist economy.

There is much debate about the underlying dynamics of capitalism. Within Marxian analysis the competitive process plays an important role within capital accumulation, requiring capital to reinvest surplus in a perpetual struggle to survive. Marx identifies two important tendencies in this process: the concentration and centralization of capital. The first tendency concerns an increase in the size of necessary capital for production to take place; the second tendency concerns the aggregation of larger amounts of capital under particular ownership groups. The impact of such tendencies is likely to be manifest in increasing industrial concentration and increasing diversification.

There is further debate about how the nature of capitalist production will change over time, again fuelled by a competitive process between internationally active capitalist enterprises. But recent analysis has generally moved away from Marx. At a certain stage of capitalist development, production has been characterized as 'Fordist' – a reflection of the predominant mass production methods of manufacturing. This dominant organizational model is said to be giving way to the 'post-Fordist' model of manufacturing under conditions of flexible specialization. It is argued that the nature of industrial competition has shifted from 'big business' to networks of smaller firms, often located within industrial districts. This 'new competition' is characterized by the Schumpeterian model. Within this setting there is a need for nationally-based strategic industrial policies to promote conditions under which such competition can operate (Best, 1990).

This contrasts with an important feature of Marxian analysis – the irrelevance of national boundaries to capitalist production and capital accumulation. In Marxian analysis, the growth of international capital is an inevitable stage in the development of the capitalist mode of production. This raises a fundamental issue for industrial policy, which is a manifestation of national interests within an increasingly globalized economy. Central to this issue is the role of Multinational Enterprises (MNEs). In particular, radical analysis generally sees the development of international capital embodied through MNE activity as being 'beyond the control' of national and even international governments. From this perspective the state is subservient, an agent of international capital acting to ensure the conditions under which accumulation can take place. Industrial policy is thus driven by the needs of capital which has no national allegiance.

A further refinement of this approach involves a distinction between industrial capital and finance capital. At certain times in particular national economies, the needs of finance capital are seen as more important than those of industrial capital, leading to a systematic downgrading in the importance of a traditional industrial policy aimed at manufacturing. Within the UK, it is argued that the needs of the City of London as a financial centre have dominated economic policy making to the alleged detriment of productive industry (Fine and Harris, 1985).

In contrast, the interventionist state approach generally believes that the state can be 'recaptured' by democratic means to represent the interests of labour; nor is it so pessimistic about the potential power of the state in response to the problems posed by international capital. Various means are suggested by which governments, either nationally or internationally, can exercise control and direction over the activities of the MNEs. But in considering the possibilities of such international action, some contradictions remain. The creation and extension of regional trading blocs, rather than providing the framework for a combined response to the problems embodied by MNE activity, generally exhibit the tensions between the different national interests of trading partners. Within this setting can arise the paradoxical outcome of different national governments pursuing the interests of their 'own' MNEs in the face of other MNEs. Partly in response to such contradictions, it is sometimes suggested that democratic influences should now be encouraged at the local rather than national or international levels.

On the surface, the development of industrial policy will always be driven by the needs of individual governments in particular circumstances. Industrial policy was not regarded as important while Keynesian demand management policies were working. Only as this post-war success began to crumble has the search for policy widened to encompass increased industrial intervention. And while there may be links between particular interventions and specific economic theories, it is more frequently the case that economic theory is used simply to provide *ex post* justifications for actions which have been undertaken for pressing political reasons. This suggests that for a theoretical understanding of industrial policy a model is required which comprehends the wider interactions between state, industry and the economy.

PETER MOTTERSHEAD

References

Best, M. (1990), *The New Competition*, Cambridge: Polity Press.

Cowling, K. (1987), 'An Industrial Strategy for Britain: The Nature and Role of Planning', *International Review of Applied Economics*, November.

Fine, B. and Harris, L. (1985), *The Peculiarities of the British Economy*, London: Lawrence and Wishart.

Thompson, G. (ed.) (1989), *Industrial Policy – USA and UK Debates*, London: Routledge.

Inequality

Rousseau ('All men are created equal ...') was keen on the rights of men but not quite so sure about women – which is a good starting point for discussing inequality. The presumption of a natural equality, if only in the eyes of God, has a long tradition in Western thought. But defining equality and explaining whom it refers to and what it means in practice are more difficult since it encompasses three rather different debates. Firstly, there is the question as to whether people are naturally equal in essence? Secondly, if people are similar in their capabilities but face very different life chances, does some form of natural rights justify redistribution from rich to poor? And thirdly, if it does, then how far can any such redistribution be justified without infringing on other natural rights? Does the promotion of equality threaten liberty?

Taking the first question: does the distribution of income reflect natural ability? Is it the quality of the seed or the soil in which it is sown that determines the outcome? Various studies have attempted to show that genetic or biological factors underlie the superior position of a particular class, group or race (typically the one to which the investigator belongs). Both the methodology and research material of such studies have been challenged; suffice to say that no firm conclusions have been reached. (For a comprehensive account see Green, 1981.)

The second question asks whether, if people are naturally equal in essence but unequal in terms of social and economic outcomes, the State should intervene to offset those market forces which lead to economic inequality?

The Western tradition, embedded in Christianity, is based on the presumption that an equal humanity does imply some basic equality in the form of minimum subsistence and common legal and political rights. In Western democracies the adult franchise is universal for citizens, and there is a minimum income guarantee for recognized household units. Equality of opportunity is accepted as a desirable objective and laws have been passed to eradicate overt discrimination.

In reality, the modern welfare state probably owes more to concepts of economic efficiency than to views about social justice. There is general recognition that equality of access to such fundamental goods as education, health care and housing is necessary if the nation's talents are to be suitably harnessed. But how far can this go? What is fair?

Equity, as opposed to equality, recognizes that since economic resources do not arrive like manna from heaven, a fair distribution would need to give most to those who contribute most. An enforced more equal distribution would not only be unfair, but also self-defeating, since it would destroy the incentives that are necessary to encourage the additional work which increases total output. However, equity can also be interpreted in terms of whether the resulting income distribution is basically an accurate reflection of relative inputs into national economic well-being or the distillation of social judgments. Do the relative shares of merchant bankers and nurses truly reflect their contributions to social welfare?

These fundamental questions of rights, the role of the State and equality versus equity have been explored by various schools of philosophy.

Utilitarianism, which underlies much of neoclassical microeconomic theory, can be criticized for concentrating solely on the total sum of economic resources and ignoring distribution. The greatest happiness of the greatest number and its modern economic equivalent – utility maximization – both assume that an increase in the total is synonymous with an improvement in overall social welfare.

Utilitarianism recognizes the impossibility of actually measuring individual utility (happiness) and hence of making interpersonal comparisons. But if a pound is worth as much to the rich as to the poor, then total welfare cannot be increased by income redistribution alone. Policies which increase overall Gross Domestic Product are desirable even if they leave the rich richer and the poor poorer.

Alternative concepts of social justice are dependent on whether it is the outcome that matters or the process by which it arrives. Libertarians are concerned with the conflict between liberty and equality. Equality, however minimally defined, implies that the State should intervene in private resource allocation decisions via either taxation or regulation. Both impinge on individual freedom of action and lead to a resulting distribution of economic resources which is different from a pure market solution.

The 'natural rights' libertarians, such as Nozick (1974), see such intervention as unjust. He argues for the primacy of property rights and the importance of an historical context. Individuals have the right to use as they see fit any resources justly acquired or transferred. His view implies that social justice is determined by the legitimacy of acquisition and not by any resulting inequality. Redistribution via voluntary transfers (e.g. charity) is just, but taxation to provide anything more than the 'minimal state' necessary to enforce property rights and defence is unjust. Anything more implies forced labour.

In contrast, Rawls (1971) avers that our ideas about social justice are influenced by the resulting distribution of economic resources. His 'maximin' rule suggests that whilst all citizens should have maximum liberty concomitant with equal rights for others, individuals under a Lockean veil of ignorance (who did not know where they would end up in the economic hierarchy) would freely choose a distribution which maximized the position of the least well off, even at the expense of their own potential income. His view implies that redistributive taxation to improve the position of the poor is just since such an outcome would be accepted by the majority.

Neither of these views is egalitarian since both stress the primacy of liberty in preference to equality. Critics argue that the concept of liberty being employed here is very narrowly defined. Can a right be meaningful if the power to exercise it is lacking? We may all have the right to sleep at the Ritz but, for some, sleeping outside on the street may be all that is realistically available.

Measurements of inequality are similarly dependent on views as to what equality or equity actually means. Can such measures be objective (positive) or only subjective (normative)? In reality, the measurement process itself, as well as interpretations of the data, are affected by value judgments.

In any comparison of income or wealth distribution, decisions have to be made about what unit to use (e.g. individual, family or household) and what time period (e.g. week, month, year or lifetime). In general the larger the unit and the longer the time period, then the more equal any distribution will seem to be. One implication is that, within the chosen unit, resources are distributed equally. Another is that relative poverty is the same irrespective of whether it is a prelude to future wealth (e.g. students) or a culmination of a lifetime's experience (e.g. pensioners). These are value-ridden assumptions.

In measuring inequality, decisions also have to made as to what actually constitutes income or wealth. Some components such as earnings, investment returns and cash benefits are straightforward. But fringe benefits, ranging from subsidized canteens to the company car, private medical insurance and generous pension contributions are less easy to quantify. Should capital gains and losses be regarded as part of income in a given year? And how do you compare the income of *X* who owns a house with *Y* who has to rent? Given the same basic income, are they equally well-off in any meaningful sense? And is the individual who can produce a lot of his/her own needs from private resources, such as a farmer, in the same economic position as someone without these advantages?

It would not matter if such additional components of income were equally distributed and comprised a constant proportion over time. But evidence suggests that the unincluded components accrue disproportionately towards the better off and have increased in importance over time (Atkinson, 1975).

Finally, comparisons over time or between countries are susceptible to socio-demographic differences such as age structure or labour force participation rates. Pensioners and students are low earners. Working wives bolster the household income of middle-earning units. Even if the share between different sections of income-earners were to remain the same, the changing composition of household units would affect the overall distribution of income.

Even if there were universal agreement about data, conflict would still exist over interpretation. The positive measures of inequality assume objectivity. The one most typically employed is the graphical representation of the Lorenz curve which shows the actual distribution of income or wealth compared to an equal distribution. However both this and its associated summary statistic, the Gini coefficient, which encapsulates the information as a single number, are subjective in interpretation.

In comparing distributions over time or between countries, problems arise in interpreting changes that have different effects on various parts of the distribution. At its simplest, if both the richest and the poorest lose out in favour of middle income groups, does this suggest that the distribution has become more or less equal? The mathematically-based positive measures assume that, if the middle gains more from the top than from the bottom, then the resulting distribution is obviously more equal. However, a more egalitarian approach would question whether a change which led to the poorest actually receiving less of the total could be described as more equal.

The normative measures are more Rawlsian in approach. They assume that there is diminishing marginal utility of income. Thus Atkinson (1975) bases his inequality measure on the assumption that society might be prepared to accept a loss in total income if the resulting distribution were more equal.

Sen (1973) believes that the meaning of inequality data cannot be encapsulated into a graph or summary statistic since interpretation is dependent on the full range of available information. His 'weak equity axiom' suggests that if society as a whole thinks that person *A* has a lower level of welfare than *B*, then in comparing two income distributions, the one which gives a relatively higher share to person *A* should be seen as the more equal.

The distribution of income and wealth is only one aspect of inequality. Alternative approaches use other social indices, arguing that health status or educational attainment is a better guide to the distribution of social welfare. However, much recent work suggests that health status in developed countries actually depends on the distribution of income.

Taking this approach, Quick and Wilkinson (1991) show that while there is no correlation between mortality statistics and average income per capita in developed countries, there is a positive relationship between mortality and proportion of income received by the lower half of the income distribution. Furthermore, they show that improvements in mortality accrue across the whole income spectrum, suggesting that society as a whole benefits from a more egalitarian distribution.

According to Quick and Wilkinson, Great Britain and Japan had similar mortality profiles in the early 1970s when their income distributions were broadly similar. But increasing income inequality in Britain since the mid-1970s has been accompanied by a divergence in mortality statistics between the two countries. The underlying argument suggests that more equal societies will tend to create social institutions (such as public health measures, public transport and affordable housing) that in the long run are beneficial to the whole population. While there are enormous difficulties in making comparisons between countries with very different social structures, there are good reasons for believing that questions about the inequality of income are still of genuine importance.

RIMA HORTON

References

Atkinson, A.B. (1975), *The Economics of Inequality*, 2nd edition, Oxford: Clarendon Press.
Green, P. (1981), *The Pursuit of Inequality*, Oxford; Martin Robertson.

Nozick, R. (1974), *Anarchy, State and Utopia*, Oxford: Blackwell.
Rawls, J. (1971), *A Theory of Justice*, Cambridge, A: Harvard University Press.
Sen, A.K. (1973), *On Economic Inequality*, Oxford: Clarendon Press, and New York: Norton.
Quick, A. and Wilkinson, R. (1991), pamphlet, London: Socialist Health Association.

Inflation

The persistence of inflation in all industrialized countries during the post-war period has caused considerable debate about its potential causes. In radical political economy, inflation is invariably seen as a symptom of underlying conflicts among different groups in society, particularly between labour and capitalists, over the distribution of income. The central thesis of the conflict approach to inflation is that workers and employers have a desired or target income share. If the actual wage share of income is below the target share, workers will respond by demanding higher pay rises in order to move closer to their target share. This creates a 'core' wage inflation which is passed on to consumers, since employers strive to maintain their target profit share by adding a mark-up on unit costs. This leads to leap-frogging of wages and prices due to conflicting claims between workers and capitalists over available income, and to the reluctance of either group to concede a fall in its income share which might result from disturbances, such as rising import costs. Another important feature of the conflict theory is the endogeneity of money.

The broad thrust of the conflict approach to inflation has been modelled in the literature in two slightly different ways. Rowthorn (1977) starts by assuming that firms follow a pricing policy aimed at giving them a target profit share Π^*. On the other hand, workers and employers agree through bargaining on a certain money wage (which makes an allowance for anticipated inflation $\hat{P}^a$); this gives workers a negotiated wage share W^n and capitalists a negotiated profit share Π^n. If the negotiated and target profit shares are different, there will be conflict. This conflict or aspiration gap is measured by $A = \Pi^* - \Pi^n$ and indicates the extent to which the aims of firms' pricing policies are inconsistent with what was agreed in wage negotiations. Hence the actual rate of price inflation is given by

$$\hat{P} = \lambda(\Pi^* - \Pi^n) + \hat{P}^a \quad (1)$$

where a 'hat' above a variable indicates rate of change.

According to Rowthorn the aspiration gap is determined by the market power of workers and capitalists, as well as by their willingness to use it. He argues that a major determinant of this market power is the level of demand which imposes a discipline on workers and firms. During periods of recession, rising unemployment will weaken the bargaining strength of trade unions and demoralize their members, while excess capacity will make firms follow a cautious pricing policy. As employment gradually expands and the surplus of capacity is reduced, the discipline of demand is relaxed, workers and firms become more confident and aggressive, using their power to force up wages and prices. Both workers and firms also resist increases in taxes and import costs, since these reduce the income share available for wages and profits. Hence Rowthorn makes the wage share W^n and the target profit share Π^* increasing functions of the demand for labour D^l, capacity utilization D^c, the state share T, and the foreign share F. It is important to notice that the role of demand in this model is to act as a regulator of conflict. Another significant aspect of the model is the role played by the burden effects T and F. Refusal by both workers and capitalists to accept any reduction in their real income (implied by a rise in taxes or import costs) will lead to greater distributional conflict and a rise in inflation as each group attempts to shift the burden onto the other.

Sawyer (1982) and Taylor (1987) have modelled the conflict theory of inflation in a somewhat different way, though the thrust of their analysis remains similar to that of Rowthorn. It is assumed that in developed industrialized economies, production is dominated by oligopolistic firms. Under such conditions of production and market organization, the mark-up pricing rule urged by Kalecki (1971) becomes the norm. In open economies, the mark-up τ is defined over the prime (or average variable) cost of labour and imported intermediates, inclusive of interest costs for the financing of working capital. Hence the overall price level P is given by

$$P = (1+v)(1+\tau)(1+iz)[bW + \alpha EP^m] \tag{2}$$

where v is the rate of indirect taxation on the prices of final goods, i the nominal interest rate, z the period over which prime inputs must be financed as working capital, W the money wage, b the labour-output ratio, E the nominal exchange rate, P^m the price of imported intermediate inputs in foreign currency, and α the input-output coefficient for imported intermediates.

Equation (2) suggests that an increase in either the nominal wage, the exchange rate, the price of imported intermediates, the interest rate, the indirect tax rate or the mark-up rate will drive up the price level, while an increase in productivity will reduce the price level. In reality, most components of costs do not occur instantaneously but rather are spread over time; thus equation (2) will also hold in growth rate form. While the growth rates of v, i, b, and α can legitimately be treated as exogenous, the dynamic evolution of the mark-up and of wage rates requires further investigation.

The treatment of the mark-up rate has been the subject of considerable debate. Kalecki (1971), among others, has argued that the mark-up rate is approximately constant, determined by the degree of monopoly. This assumption has important policy implications. When the mark-up and average costs are constant with respect to output, it follows that changes in demand will have very little effect on price inflation. On the other hand, Sawyer (1982), using a short-run profit maximization model of oligopoly, shows that the mark-up rate depends on four factors: (a) the elasticity of demand; (b) the perceived reaction of other firms to output changes; (c) the level of industrial concentration; and (d) the degree of effective collusion. The first two factors depend on the level of output, while factors (c) and (d) are equivalent to Kalecki's degree of monopoly power and can be treated as constant. This analysis implies that the mark-up rate τ becomes a continuous variable which affects both the price level and its growth rate. Eichner (1979) argues that the mark-up rate is influenced by the need for internally generated funds for investment, where the latter is determined by the secular growth of output. Taylor (1987) treats the mark-up as a variable which is predetermined in the short run, while its dynamic evolution depends upon the discrepancy between the actual level and a reference level of capacity utilization at which firms hold mark-ups steady (i.e. the level that reconciles the conflicting income claims of workers and capitalists). Taylor's equation can be further expanded to incorporate the influence of international competitiveness on the growth rate of the mark-up factor.

In modern industrial economies, wages are determined by collective bargaining. As Sawyer (1982) and others have pointed out, this does not necessarily imply that all workers need to be fully organized in trade unions, for many crucial features of collective bargaining would also apply to non-unionized workers. The central aspect of the conflict approach to wage inflation is that workers have a strong idea of what would constitute a satisfactory wage to aim for in their pay negotiations. This wage reflects three fundamental objectives: first, further improvement of their living standards (this implies that workers have some notion of a desired or target share of income, which in turn implies a target real wage); second, maintenance of their existing real wage; third, restoration of differentials relative to other comparable groups. Rowthorn (1977) and Sawyer (1982) argue that the ability of workers to achieve their desired money wage is likely to be constrained by the level of real economic activity on the basis that high and especially rising unemployment tends to demoralize workers and weaken their bargaining position. These ideas on wage formation imply the following equation for the rate of wage inflation:

$$\hat{W} = a_0 + a_1(LS^* - LS) + a_2\hat{P}^e + a_3(W^{ag} - W) - f(U, \Delta U) \tag{3}$$

The first term measures the influence of conflicting income claims. When the actual wage share of income (LS) is below the desired wage share (LS^*), workers respond by demanding larger pay rises, thus leading to conflicting claims over output. The influence of expected price inflation ($\hat{P}^e$) reflects the workers' objective of maintaining their current real wage. The third term reflects the demand for restoring the differential between the current actual wage and the average wage of comparable groups (W^{ag}), which provides an additional source of conflict. The final term captures the influence of the aggregate demand constraint.

A major problem that arises in applications of this model is the measurement of the desired wage share. Various explanations have been suggested for this variable. The Marxist view is to relate the determination of the target real wage (and hence of LS^*) to the existence of a 'subsistence' bundle of goods representing the value of labour-power, workers' average skill levels and the quality of working conditions. A second view is that the desired wage share reflects popular aspirations about prosperity and the quality of life. These aspirations depend on a variety of factors such as high growth rates of income and stable employment experienced in the past, the growth of relative needs and income gains (both of which are strongly influenced by greater mobility, improved communications and increased advertising), the degree of social acceptance of profits, and the provision of social services by the state. A third view is that the target wage share emerges from the optimal solution to the trade unions' problem of balancing the benefits of achieving a desired real wage or wage share against the costs associated with demanding a higher real wage. The limitation of all these explanations is that they tend to be rather ambiguous. What is needed is an analytical model of the individual as citizen, worker and consumer and a more realistic view of the relationships among individuals. Furthermore, they all fail to provide any guidance on the most appropriate measure of the desired wage share of income.

The inflationary process described by such price and wage equations implies that the ability of restrictive demand management policies to achieve a permanent reduction in the inflation rate combined with sustained economic growth is limited, due to constraints imposed by the distributional conflict which is the essence of the modern inflationary process. Since this conflict reflects fundamentally diverse aspirations among the different income groups in society, it is obvious that it is not a purely economic problem, but also a social and institutional one. Agreements between workers, firms and government on 'planned income growth', as well as on measures to achieve a more equitable income distribution, would thus seem essential for resolving the distributional conflict.

NICHOLAS SARANTIS

References

Eichner, A. (1979), 'A Post-Keynesian Short-Period Model', *Journal of Post Keynesian Economics*, **1**, 38–63.

Kalecki, M. (1971), *Selected Essays on the Dynamics of the Capitalist Economies*, Cambridge: Cambridge University Press.

Rowthorn, R. (1977), 'Conflict, Inflation and Money', *Cambridge Journal of Economics*, **1**, 215–39.

Sawyer, M. (1982), 'Collective Bargaining, Oligopoly and Macroeconomics', *Oxford Economic Papers*, **34**, 428–48.

Taylor, L. (1987), 'Macro Policy in the Tropics: How Sensible People Stand', *World Development*, **15**, (12), 1407–35.

Input–output analysis

The production subsystem where virtually everything is produced is at the core of a truly viable economy. The flow of goods and services among the producing industries (inter-industry flows) is best captured by an input–output model. Since Nobel prize-winner Wassily Leontief (1941) first developed such a model, input–output analysis has been greatly expanded in many ways.

To place such a common-sense notion of what is important into 'radical' political economy seems at first strange. However, as the theory unfolds, it clearly does violate some wonderfully treasured views of what properly comprises economics. In the static or timeless input–output model, the relationship between inputs and output (the technical coefficients) is fixed. The cost of production of each unit of a product is thus set as if in concrete at all levels of output so that constant costs prevail, much as in classical economic theory. Unlike the presently fashionable neoclassical theory, marginal products (the extra output from an extra unit of input) do not decline as output rises.

A complete understanding of the *mathematics* of input-output modelling would require knowledge of matrix algebra, a daunting task for the uninitiated. My goal for the reader is less ambitious: I aim only to convey a feeling for the topic and its most important implications. For this, we need simply define a 'matrix' as a table comprised of rows and columns and a 'vector' as either one row or one column. A square matrix is one with an equal number of rows and columns. From these, all things flow.

The input–output table's *inner matrix* is comprised of the rows showing the flow of each industry's output to other industries and the columns showing the source of each industry's inputs from the same other industries. Coal flows to the steel industry and is received by the steel industry. It is a perfectly square picture of the inter-industry structure of the economy. The technical coefficients are calculated from these flows. A technical coefficient relating coal to steel, for example, would be the amount of coal needed to produce a ton of carbon steel. (In 1978, 0.95 tons of coal were required to produce a ton of US carbon steel. The technical coefficient was 0.95.)

There is a second way of viewing the inner matrix. It also comprises the *intermediate output* of the economy. These are outputs used strictly as inputs. It is the output–input aspect of input–output! If, for example, we consider the entire output of the lumber and woods products industry and subtract all its intermediate outputs (used by other industries in *their* production), the balance will be the lumber and woods products available to final consumers.

In a third perspective, the inner matrix (if in money value) includes all the outlays by industries for the materials used in production. The difference between total expenditures by these industries (the same as the value of total output) and the outlays for materials is equal to the industries' *value added* or income generated for the economy. This value added is the sum of wages, salaries, interest, rent and profits in the economy. In this way the value of national output will equal the value of national income. The national input-output table has been used as a periodic check on the reliability of national income accounts separately estimated.

Although the government data-crunchers construct the inner matrix in money or value terms (i.e., *PXQ*), some major theoretical breakthroughs are based upon models in which economists have sorted out the real (i.e., *Q*) values from the nominal values (the *P*s). The technical coefficients are in real or *Q* terms – tons of coal, iron ore, steel scrap or mbtus of energy. A square matrix of technical coefficients is called the *A* matrix, the list of ingredients required by the economy's technological recipes.

We can always reconstruct the inner matrix by multiplying the *A* matrix by a price or *P* vector. Once final demand is also expressed in quantities, that vector can be multiplied by the *P* vector to obtain the value of final demand, the same $C + I + G$ or aggregate expenditures of conventional Keynesian economics.

The value added (income generated) by each industry can be divided into its two major components: labour income and a residual, usually treated as 'profits'. Labour, like materials, can be expressed as technical coefficients. Continuing our earlier example, in 1978 the production of a ton of carbon steel required 8.14 manhours. This labour requirement multiplied by the wage rate for steelworkers ($11.66 per hour) and, in turn, by total carbon steel production gives us the total wage bill for the industry. If materials costs per ton and the wage bill per ton are subtracted from the price of carbon steel, we have the residual income or unit 'profits' ($29.92 per ton that year).

The reader is no doubt relieved to know that we have covered the basics. Only now does the devout technician experience enjoyment. The complete system can be solved in terms of various things, but especially quantities and prices.

The key to these and other solutions is found in the 'Leontief inverse'. The *Leontief inverse* gives not only the direct but also the indirect materials requirements for each industry. The technical coefficients included only the *direct* requirements for production such as the 0.95 tons of coal, the 1.65 tons of iron ore, the 0.10 tons of steel scrap and the 11 mbtus of energy per ton of carbon steel.

The *indirect* requirements include the tons of coal required to produce the 1.65 tons of iron ore in order to produce the ton of carbon steel, as well as the mbtus of energy to produce the 0.95 tons of coal to produce the ton of steel, and the amount of transportation to get the 0.10 tons of steel scrap to the carbon steel plant to produce the ton of steel, and so on. You can begin to understand what I mean by enjoyment.

Suppose we solve for prices. The income payments per unit of product that become price include not only the value added of those industries providing direct inputs, but also of those industries providing indirect inputs. Therefore, the prices which must prevail in the long period if each industry is to cover its costs of production will be based on directly and indirectly incurred costs of production and income payments. These prices, or the 'dual price solution' to the Leontief model of production, comprise the value added vector properly multiplied by the Leontief inverse.

What can be done for quantity and price requirements can also be done for labour requirements. The labour vector (comprised of the technical labour coefficients) can be multiplied by the omnipotent Leontief inverse to provide the hours of labour required, directly and indirectly, to produce a single unit of output for each and every industry. Moreover, we can give residual income or 'profits' the same treatment to find out the profits earned both directly and indirectly by each industry.

Can the intermediate output supplied by all industries constituting the production system be reduced to only one type of fundamental input? This central issue in value theory has divided economists from the beginning. Karl Marx, relying on a labour theory of value, believed labour to be the only source of value and thus he would multiply the Leontief inverse by the labour vector and be done with it. The neoclassicals come closer to the opposite: they would focus on the Leontief inverse times profits. The neoclassicals take the extra step of associating profits with the proper return on capital. Hence, the neoclassical theory is more a capital theory of value.

For now, let us consider the total value added required of the economy in terms of both labour value and profits. This problem was solved by Pasinetti (1981) in his vertically integrated model of production. Having derived the required hours of labour and amount of profit (both direct and indirect) per unit of production, Pasinetti multiplied these sets of values by the demand vector. Independently, Canterbery (1979, 1994) developed a similar model without sensing the vertically integrated nature of the production system.

The results are surprising. Since the direct material requirements are now reflected in larger values for the labour and profits coefficients, the inner matrix disappears. The industries producing intermediate goods also are no longer needed; this only leaves those industries that are producing for final consumption.

Of course, advanced economies actually do have vertically integrated industries. In the United States, cinema producers own both the distribution companies and the theatres in which films are shown. But the vertically integrated model of production is nonetheless hypothetical. Despite its fanciful nature, however, the model usefully shows the direct relationship between basic inputs such as labour and the net or final output of the economy. And, as we shall see, Canterbery's version serves other real world purposes as well.

Once the wage rate (unit labour cost) is known in the Pasinetti or Canterbery models, we only need to find 'profits' in order to derive the price solution. In this way the full cost of production necessary for replication or continuous expansion of the economy can be found. In this regard Sraffa (1960) has provided some wonderful insights.

Sraffa counters the neoclassical view in which the wage rate measures the marginal product of labour and the profit rate measures the marginal productivity of capital. As in Leontief, the ingredients in production in each industry are defined by technology. The total value added by the economy or national income is fixed. What is so for the nation is only so-so for any particular industry; its value added is not immutable.

The value added in the auto industry will vary as the wage rate and thus its wage bill (with those fixed technical coefficients) move relative to the profit rate. In turn, since price depends upon value added, the relative price of autos will change. (Technological improvements will also change prices.) In violation of all things held sacred by the neoclassicals, price changes alter the income distribution even as the income distribution alters prices!

Neoclassical prices allocate resources in an efficient way. Sraffian prices do not, but rather are the vehicle for redistributing income between workers and capitalists as wage rates move relative to profit rates. Since efficiency depends only on technology – not on relative prices – income is left free to be allocated by class struggle, administered wages and relative bargaining power. Also, total national output is above the fray and out of harm's way.

The printing of this book, for example, is accomplished with a computer, a printing press and a binder. The money values of capital, however, depend upon the price times quantity of all these capital goods (and others) combined. The printing press, the computer and the binder all sell at varying prices. These prices, or the 'rentals' for the services from these capital goods, in turn depend upon the distribution of income between workers and capitalists. Therefore, the value of capital (its price times its quantity) is not decided by capital's productivity after all.

Sraffa dealt value or price theory a damaging blow. By the neoclassicals' own devices, either the wage rate or the profit rate must be a 'given' that cannot be determined by the production system. If it is the wage rate that is set outside the system, then profits comprise a residual unrelated to the rate of return on capital.

Pasinetti's price solution to the vertically integrated economy highlights the dependency of prices on wages and profits. Canterbery (1979) presumes prices to be set by a percentage mark-up placed by each industry upon its wage bill, on its direct and indirect materials requirements, and on its direct and indirect profits from all industries. Canterbery makes no distinction between the mark-up and the profit margin. Later, Eichner (1987), who long before had a fully developed theory to explain mark-ups, employs Leontief, Pasinetti, Sraffa and Canterbery to build a dynamic or economic growth version of this genre. What enables the economy to grow are the introduction of investment in excess of what the economy requires simply for its reproduction, as well as the inclusion of business savings as part of industry profits. Eichner (1987, pp. 355–8) proves that we need make no distinction between the mark-up and the profit margin, even for a growing economy.

E. RAY CANTERBERY

References

Canterbery, E.R. (1979), 'The Mark-up, Growth and Inflation', Paper presented at the Eastern Economic Association Meetings.

Canterbery, E.R. (1994), 'A General Theory of International Trade and Domestic Employment Adjustments' in Khosrow Fatemi and Michael Landeck (eds), *International Trade: 1992 Regional and Global Management Issues*, London: Macmillan.

Eichner, A.S. (1987), *The Macrodynamics of Advanced Market Economies*, Armonk, N.Y.: M.E. Sharpe.

Leontief, W. (1941), *The Structure of the American Economy, 1919–1929*, Cambridge, MA: Harvard University Press.

Pasinetti, L.L. (1981), *Structural Change and Economic Growth*, London: Cambridge University Press.

Sraffa, P. (1960), *Production of Commodities by Means of Commodities*, Cambridge: Cambridge University Press.

Interest rates

Theories of the rate of interest can be classified into two broad categories: real and monetary. Real theories of the rate of interest postulate that real factors, such as time preference (in the form of the propensity to consume) and the productivity of capital, determine real rates of interest. Within the tradition of real theory, nominal or monetary rates of interest are treated as irrelevant to the decisions of rational agents. By contrast, monetary theories of the rate of interest postulate a role for nominal or monetary variables as decision variables in the choices of rational agents. Monetary theories of the rate of interest also allow a role for apparently non-economic factors in the determination of interest rates.

Real rates of interest are of two types, one theoretical and the other empirical. The theoretical variety of real rates are commodity rates, while the empirical variety are inflation-adjusted nominal rates. Furthermore, the relationship between the two concepts has never been satisfactorily explained. Commodity real rates are encountered in Walrasian theory, where interest rates are defined in terms of inter-temporal relative rates of exchange, i.e. a quantity of jam today can be transformed into a known quantity of jam tomorrow. Empirical real rates of interest are inflation-adjusted nominal rates – a nominal rate of interest adjusted for the actual or expected rate of inflation.

In monetary theories, there is no distinction between the theoretical and empirical definitions of the rate of interest. The money or nominal rate of interest is nothing more than the 'percentage excess of a sum of money contracted for forward delivery' (Keynes, 1936, p. 222).

Contrasting Keynes's liquidity preference theory (a monetary theory) with the classical loanable funds theory (a real theory) suggests how the two can be distinguished. However, until recently this distinction has been difficult to draw and the literature is replete with demonstrations of the apparent equivalence of the two approaches.

The failure to draw a distinction between liquidity preference and real theories of the rate of interest is explained at one level by the fact that the evaluation of the two competing views proceeds within the confines of a theoretical structure conducive only to real theories of the rate of interest. In most cases the analysis is conducted within the context of models in which money itself cannot be given a meaningful role. Specifically, money is neutral, superneutral and/or an inessential addition to these models; moreover, the existence of a monetary equilibrium cannot in general be established (Rogers, 1989; Hoover, 1988, pp. 120–23). Monetary variables such as the nominal rate of interest therefore play no role in the decisions of rational agents who see through the veil of money and make decisions taken on the basis of monetary variables reflect 'money illusion' and are *prima facie* evidence of irrational behaviour.

The latter conclusion points to an additional and more fundamental issue relevant to the distinction between real and monetary theories of the rate of interest. The issue was, it seems, first alluded to by Hugh Townsend (1937) who noted that Keynes's liquidity preference theory required a broader approach to value theory than the utility maximizing analysis employed in real theory (what Keynes referred to as the 'Benthamite calculus'). Recent research on the relationship between Keynes's philosophy and economics by Lawson (1989, 1990) and O'Donnell (1989), for example, has shed further light on the nature of value theory underpinning liquidity preference theory in particular, and monetary analysis in general. Developments in this area can be introduced to provide the value theory foundations for a monetary theory of the rate of interest as proposed by Rogers (1989). That analysis rests on the use of conventions to establish rational opinion concerning the 'normal' behaviour of nominal rather than real rates of interest.

The comments which follow outline the relationship between the value theory proposed by Lawson and O'Donnell, and the monetary theory of the rate of interest examined by Rogers (1989). These issues illuminate Keynes's liquidity preference theory, although discussion focuses on the general principles underlying a monetary theory of the rate of interest.

The need for a generalized value theory in monetary analysis is highlighted by the perennial puzzle facing monetary theorists: the coexistence of money and interest-bearing assets. As is well known, Keynes's (1936, p. 168) answer to this question is based on the existence of uncertainty. Uncertainty as to the future rate of interest is a necessary condition for the holding of money rather than interest-bearing assets. To understand a monetary economy, it is therefore sensible to begin with an appreciation of what is meant by uncertainty.

Exponents of real analysis restrict the domain of application of economic theory to that range of uncertainty to which quantifiable probability and mathematical expectation apply. Beyond that, it is argued, economic theory has nothing to say (Hoover, 1988, part v). But as Lawson and O'Donnell in particular have documented, uncertainty is far more pervasive. If anything, only a minority of cases fall within the quantifiable range, while the vast majority fall outside it. This, it seems, was Keynes's view.

Raising the question of uncertainty immediately forces us to come to some conclusion as to the limits of economic analysis. In particular, any value or monetary theory with a claim to generality must be capable of dealing with the case of non-quantifiable uncertainty. Starting with this observation, it can be argued that the concept of rational behaviour must be broadened beyond that of the utility maximizing calculus. But in the absence of certainty and/or quantifiable probabilities, what constitutes rational behaviour? As Lawson (1989, 1990) and O'Donnell (1989) have explained, in such circumstances rational agents rely on conventions and other inductive regularities as a basis for decisions.

From the perspective of monetary theory, such a suggestion is not as startling as it may seem. On reflection, it is apparent that money itself, in whatever form it takes, is a convention; it is acceptable in exchange because it is generally acceptable. Many commodities can, and have, performed the role of money, but once a particular convention (form of money) has been widely accepted, it is not readily abandoned even in the face of significant inflation. In the case of fiat money, the existence of a credible sovereign power would seem to be a necessary condition for the general acceptance of the currency.

Although money is a ubiquitous convention which is usually taken for granted, it cannot be introduced into 'monetary' models of real analysis where conventions have no role. (This is another way of explaining why real analysis has encountered such difficulty in accommodating money.) The monetary theory of the rate of interest sketched in Rogers (1989) relies on the role of more subtle conventions at key points in the analysis. These conventions cannot be analysed *a priori*, but only in particular historical instances where their existence is essential for rational decision making in the face of unquantifiable uncertainty. Faced with a world in which the knowledge necessary to apply utility maximization and mathematical expectation is not available, rational agents form expectations and make rational decisions on the basis of conventions. Decisions taken on the basis of existing conventions are rational in the sense that they are purposeful, objective and not based on whim or 'animal spirits' (Lawson, 1990). Conventions are not subjective because their value to a particular agent arises from the fact that they are widely held and acted upon. Also, the existence of durable conventions provides the stability and continuity without which economic theory would be impossible. As Keynes (1936, p. 152) explained: 'the ... conventional method of calculation will be compatible with a considerable measure of stability in our affairs, *so long as we can rely on the maintenance of the convention*'. Given the existence of durable conventions, the Marshallian static method can be applied because some durable or persistent forces are at work in the economy. Without the existence of this durability, it is hardly possible to bring economic theory to bear.

The argument can now be illustrated by contrasting some key characteristics of the real or classical theory of the rate of interest with the monetary theory of the rate of interest that emerges from a re-assessment of Keynes's liquidity preference theory.

The classical or real theory of the rate of interest postulates that real forces of productivity and thrift combine to determine a real or natural rate of interest (a commodity rate not to be confused with an inflation-adjusted nominal rate). These real forces dictate the pattern of financial flows (loanable funds) such that the nominal rate of interest adjusts to the real or natural rate compatible with full employment long-period equilibrium.

By contrast, the monetary theory of the rate of interest postulates the existence of an additional margin to time preference. In the world of non-quantifiable uncertainty, time preference is composed of the propensity to consume (thrift) and liquidity preference (Keynes, 1936, p. 166). Liquidity preference in turn requires the introduction of the historically relevant conventions (by contrast, real theory aims to be ahistorical). For example, at the time of the *General Theory*, Keynes identified the role of opinion concerning the 'normal' rate of interest as an important convention in financial markets. In terms of this convention, agents could make rational decisions in the face of non-quantifiable uncertainty. More recently, conventions relating to the achievement of money supply or exchange rate targets have performed a similar function (conventions are influenced by prevailing economic theory). Without the existence of such conventions, rational agents have no alternative but to fall back on whim or animal spirits.

In the context of a monetary theory of the rate of interest, nominal interest rates may take on a causal role in the determination of long-period monetary equilibrium. Rogers (1989) argues that the conventions relating to the nominal rate of interest play a central role in Keynes's equilibrium version of the principle of effective demand as well as the demonstration of the existence of a long-period unemployment equilibrium. The behaviour of the money rate of interest is determined by existing conventions; given those conventions, a monetary equilibrium may exist but is not inevitable. As Keynes (1936, p. 168) put it, liquidity preference is a 'potentiality or functional tendency'. The existence of durable conventions (and expectations) turns this potentiality into something akin to a functional relationship amenable to analysis with the tools of economic theory. The existence and stability of a monetary equilibrium therefore depend on the durability of existing conventions and institutions that define the 'rules of the game'.

In monetary analysis 'the' nominal rate of interest (in the sense of the term used by Keynes, 1936) may determine long-period equilibrium. This analysis reverses the direction of causation between the monetary and real or natural rate of interest postulated by real analysis. In particular, the marginal efficiency of capital adjusts to the 'normal' money rate of interest. Furthermore, as there is no automatic market mechanism driving conventions in financial markets to produce the unique long-period equilibrium of real analysis, long-period equilibrium with full employment must be a fluke. In monetary analysis, non-uniqueness is the norm and multiple long-period equilibria are inevitable. Consequently, a long-period equilibrium with unemployment is not a surprise or an anomaly.

To summarize. It is now clear that liquidity preference theory in particular, and monetary theory in general, require the support of the broader value theory identified by Townsend and recently examined by Lawson and O'Donnell. In that context, the Marshallian static method can be applied and a monetary theory of the rate of interest begins to make sense.

COLIN ROGERS

References

Hoover, K.D. (1988), *The New Classical Macroeconomics*, Oxford: Basil Blackwell.

Keynes, J.M. (1936), *The General Theory of Employment, Interest and Money*, London: Macmillan.

Lawson, T. (1989), 'Keynes and Conventions', mimeo, Faculty of Economics and Politics, University of Cambridge.

Lawson, T. (1990), 'Keynes and the Analysis of Rational Behaviour', mimeo, Faculty of Economics and Politics, University of Cambridge.

O'Donnell, R.M. (1989), *Keynes: Philosophy, Economics and Politics*, London: Macmillan.

Rogers, C. (1989), *Money, Interest and Capital; A Study in the Foundations of Monetary Theory*, Cambridge: Cambridge University Press.

Townsend, H. (1937), 'Liquidity-Premium and the Theory of Value', *Economic Journal*, **47**, 157–69.

International finance

The profound structural problems of the international financial system over the past two decades are a result of the confrontation between a rapidly changing pattern of asset type and ownership in an increasingly global capital market on the one hand, and the relics of a system of international monetary regulation established in the last years of the Second World War on the other. The divergent investment and savings trends in key regions of the world market continue to cause acute instability, despite the neoclassical belief that, given a well-functioning world capital market, national savings and investment need not be correlated. This is because the gap between domestic savings and investment can always be financed by acquiring foreign assets or liabilities to cover the current account surplus or deficit.

In terms of the neoclassical paradigm, the matching capital account imbalances mainly reflect differential rates of return on (corporate) investment and differing (household) savings rates across countries, with a risk-adjusted single interest rate clearing the world capital market. However the correlation remains, indicating less capital movement than might be supposed theoretically. There are also strong indications that most capital flows take place between OECD economies, while the capital account drives the current account of the balance of payments outside the OECD. Moreover, large and persistent current account imbalances frequently lead to sudden and unpredictable changes in macroeconomic policies – or in variables such as exchange rates, interest rates or the prices of financial assets – and thereby induce large adjustment costs.

In fact, until relatively recently, the classical 'specie flow' paradigm (established by Hume and formalized by Ricardo) – of international capital flows adjusting to trade imbalances, followed by monetary effects on domestic prices and eventual trade balance – was the basis of international financial theory. It was only with the collapse of the gold standard and the German reparations debate between the wars that the direct income and wealth effects of international capital movements came to be theorized. However, the agenda established in the Keynes–Ohlin debate was suspended during the Second World War and did not seem relevant in the subsequent three decades. This was because the Bretton Woods system appeared to represent a substitute for the gold standard which (albeit imperfectly) would permit an effective payments system based on fixed exchange rates and assisted adjustment. However, the de-linking of the dollar from gold, the oil and debt shocks, and the emergence of rival core currencies all helped to force the debate back onto the agenda tabled half a century earlier.

Modern mainstream macroeconomics (based on Hicks's interpretation of Keynes) has addressed these problems with some effect. International finance theory in this tradition is mainly derived from Meade, and has developed in various fruitful directions, among which are the following: the analysis of asset-acquisition behaviour based on the relationship between real balances, incomes and interest rates pioneered by Tobin; the analytical modelling of the link between exchange rates, interest rates and portfolio decisions developed by Dornbusch; and the extension of liquidity-preference theory into a monetarist theory of the balance of payments by Mundell. In marked contrast to the depth and breadth of these mainstream approaches, which have produced a plausible account of some crucial aspects of international finance, few critical economists – whether of post Keynesian, Kaleckian or Sraffian persuasion – appear to have addressed the central issues of international finance. Just why this should be so is not clear, in view of both the evident theoretical and practical importance of the subject on the one hand, and the strong post Keynesian tradition of domestic monetary analysis and the notable critical contributions to international trade theory from the Sraffian viewpoint on the other.

Paul Davidson is virtually the only radical economist to have attempted any sustained theorization of international finance. He suggests (1982; pp. 9–17) that a post Keynesian approach to the topic should regard the economic system as moving through historical time (rather than towards an abstract equilibrium), where expectations in an uncertain world affect the decisions of economic and political institutions that make up financial markets. Davidson argues that a correct reading of Keynes requires (1) the explicit inclusion of the distribution of income and power in economic analysis, (2) a clear distinction between the economic roles of real and finance capital, and (3) recognition of the fact that income effects dominate substitution effects in both creating and resolving international monetary problems in the real world. He proceeds to extend the Keynesian monetary analysis of the closed economy beyond the corresponding open economy model developed by Meade in order to allow for international finance as such in what he terms a 'non-unionized monetary system' (NUMS) after the collapse of Bretton Woods.

Davidson's analysis thus focuses on an adjustment process involving the theory of reserve asset holdings for open economies derived from Keynes's liquidity preference theory, including the 'finance motive'.

Davidson's theoretical work contains important insights, but is based on a fairly rudimentary accounting system which limits its analytical depth and in particular prevents a formal treatment of financial stocks as opposed to flows (understandable in Keynes's 1930 *Treatise on Money*, but hardly so today). This approach limits the modelling of the dynamics of adjustment under uncertainty and thus ultimately of the role of money (as opposed to other assets) itself. Gray and Gray (1988–89) provide an appropriate post Keynesian flow-of-funds format, as opposed to the traditional balance of payments accounts, which emphasizes the interdependence of the balance sheet components. This allows for multiple inter-country flows (as opposed to the 'open economy' versus the 'rest of the world' construct in most theories of international finance) as well as for explicit asset-liability portfolios; these in turn permit global investment-savings imbalances to be reflected in changing net wealth positions. This approach demonstrates how the budgetary and transfer consequences of the US position as a world debtor have contributed to the fragility of the post-Bretton Woods system. Gray and Gray suggest that trade adjustment to eliminate the mismatch between illiquid assets and liquid liabilities (which underlies world financial instability) may be preferable in the long run. Meantime, increased cooperation among national monetary authorities, whereby both the mismatch and the adjustment speed are reduced by deliberate policy, is essential in a world with political constraints on rapid fluctuations in current balances and thus activity levels.

The construction of a critical theory of international finance probably requires the extension of neo-Ricardian trade theory to include financial flows. Most analytical models of the world economy in the Sraffian or structuralist tradition either assume that net capital flows automatically adjust to the trade solution in terms of pricing rules, income flows and production technology, or that capital flows can be inserted exogenously, as in the case of development aid. Even the introduction of Kaldorian savings functions within trading countries in order to integrate trade with growth does not constitute the base for a theory of finance as such. This is because the current account remains dominant and the stock valuation criterion in terms of expected flows (first established by Fisher) is ignored. In particular, the way in which institutional sectors (such as governments, banks, corporations or households) adjust their net wealth positions towards desired levels in response to changes in the international economy, and the consequences that arise therefrom, have yet to be explored.

An important first step in linking international bank credit and debt into the formal structure of critical trade and accumulation theory is provided by

Darity (1987), who combines a Kaleckian accumulation scheme with the comparative statics of a world model based on the Sraffian 'surplus' approach. Finance is introduced by including the indebtedness of each region with an international banking sector as a prior claim on current surplus. There are public and private sectors in each of the two producing regions, the production of and trade in capital goods being a crucial element linking investment and finance. The international banking sector creates credit as a multiple of deposits, and nominal interest rates are set by the 'northern' monetary authorities as a policy instrument; rate spreads and credit allocation are endogenous. Although Darity assumes a single currency area (and thus exchange rate movements cannot affect the balance of payments) he does generate a wide range of plausible financial situations by including segmented credit markets and a private sector capable of building up unsustainable asset positions. Further work on international crises resulting from structural asymmetries and the failure of interest rates to clear global capital markets would logically follow from this approach.

The institutionalist theory of international capital movements provided by Kindleberger (1987) systematizes the insights that historical events provide into market response to uncertainty. Financial crises are evidently far more frequent than trade crises and follow periods of what the classical economists called 'overactivity' (credit-based speculation leading to price 'bubbles'). These occur when all financial agents attempt to liquidate their positions at once, leading to a sharp fall in asset values (which of course are based on expected returns) independently of current flows (e.g. of profits), leading to mass bankruptcy. Whether such financial crises have serious consequences depends upon the response of the monetary authorities who must exercise their role as lenders of last resort while avoiding moral hazard. In other words, some degree of uncertainty is essential for prudential regulation of banks and the creation of an orderly financial market. Kindleberger suggests that multilateral institutions such as the International Monetary Fund and the Bank of International Settlements did have some success in managing the debt crisis, but that this was due more to their mobilization of support funds from northern governments and commercial banks than to the stabilization programmes imposed on southern debtors. Moreover, the political capacity of these two multilateral financial institutions effectively to exercise the role of world monetary authority, abandoned by the US some 50 years after taking it over from the UK, is clearly still very limited.

The remaining element required in order to construct a critical theory of international finance would be an explicit consideration of the financial activities of the modern transnational corporation. It is their capital accumulation decisions which underpin the process of global investment and even savings, to the extent that the bulk of investment is financed out of retained profits. The pioneering work by Dunning (1988) provides an appropriate (albeit explicitly 'eclectic') model of foreign direct investment from which such an element might be fashioned. As such investment is essentially an intra-firm phenomenon, it can best be explained by industrial organization theory and the analytics of corporate capital structure. In this context, it is of some interest to note that the literature on this subject not only discounts the national economy (although not the nation state) as a relevant analytical category, but also seems to presume that finance is not an effective constraint on corporate investment decisions, along effectively Kaleckian lines.

Finally, despite the evident fact that over the past two decades flexible exchange rates have not facilitated orderly trade adjustment (but on the contrary have stimulated speculative capital movements, price volatility and new forms of protectionism as forces of instability), there has been little radical interest in the original Keynesian proposals for supranational credit money or a world central bank. Guttman (1988), for instance, updates the original Bancor proposal in an interesting way for the post-Bretton Woods world, so as to go beyond its original restricted role as an official reserve asset. However, he does not address the microeconomic underpinning of the prudential regulation required to control global private banking (where recent theories of public action might be usefully applied), nor the wider political economy issue of participation and transparency in the social control of such an institution. This neglect by radical economists may well be the result of widespread criticism of the 'Bretton Woods institutions' (i.e. the IMF and the World Bank) for their failure to prevent or resolve the debt crisis and for the welfare consequences of the adjustment programmes they imposed on debtor countries as a condition for access to further credit. Much of this criticism is misplaced, because the Bank and the Fund have limited powers and in any case should logically be evaluated, not as global welfare agencies, but on their capacity to restore sustainable capitalist growth. In particular, the record of the Bank and the Fund in developing domestic and international capital markets as a means of promoting efficient payments systems and as vehicles for private investment has been disappointing in both capitalist LDCs and formerly planned economies. This 'failure of global governance' should be the central agenda item for critical economists concerned with international finance.

E.V.K. FitzGerald

References

Darity, W. (1987), 'Debt, Finance, Production and Trade in a North-South Model: The Surplus Approach', *Cambridge Journal of Economics*, **11**, 211–27.

Davidson, P. (1982), *International Money and the Real World*, London: Macmillan.

Dunning, J.H. (1988), *Explaining International Production*, London: Unwin Hyman.

Gray, H.P. and Gray, J.M. (1988–89), 'International Payments in a Flow-of-Funds Format', *Journal of Post-Keynesian Economics*, **XI** (2), 241–60.
Guttman, R. (1988), 'Crisis and Reform of the International Monetary System' in P. Arestis (ed.), *Post-Keynesian Monetary Economics*, Cheltenham: Edward Elgar, 251–98.
Keynes, J.M. (1930), *Treatise on Money*, London: Macmillan.
Kindleberger, C.P. (1987), *International Capital Movements*, Cambridge: Cambridge University Press.

International trade

The standard approach to international trade theory in both the radical and the orthodox traditions is, first, to model the relevant factors of a non-trading economy and to describe the resulting autarky equilibrium, and then to consider how that equilibrium would differ if, instead, the economy were allowed to trade freely with some other 'similar' economy. The economies are 'similar' insofar as they differ only in some quantitative sense (for example, in technical coefficients or factor endowments), displaying no qualitative or structural asymmetry. The patterns of trade and the consequences of trade are then inferred by comparing autarky economies with their trading *alter egos*. Such an approach, needless to say, is static and ahistorical and fails to capture the diversity of economic structures that are found in the trading world. As a consequence, economists of most persuasions have been increasingly attracted to the development of North-South (or centre-periphery) models where structural asymmetries are recognized from the beginning and where the emphasis is less on comparing states and more on the way outcomes evolve over time. It is thus necessary to consider radical contributions both within the standard methodology and to the more recent developments in the North-South literature.

Radical theories within the standard approach, like their orthodox counterparts, are inspired by the celebrated chapter 7, 'On Foreign Trade', of Ricardo's *Principles*. Here Ricardo purported to show how international specialization according to comparative advantage would lead to aggregate welfare gains for participating nations. For orthodox economists this remains the central message of international trade theory and is the ideological underpinning of many 'liberal' policy prescriptions (such as favouring export promotion over import substitution, devaluation over quantitative restrictions as a development strategy, not to mention the entire thrust of GATT).

But Ricardo's illustrative example, widely reproduced in elementary textbooks, scarcely does justice either to the remaining analysis of chapter 7 or to the general spirit of the *Principles*. In general terms, Ricardo's vision was a dynamic one, stressing the importance of growth through the accumulation of capital. In chapter 1 of the *Principles*, Ricardo discussed in detail how the existence of capital impinges on the determination of relative prices. He concluded that, in the face of a positive rate of profit and unequal 'capital:labour' ratios, prices would diverge from labour values. However, reasoning on the basis of simple numerical examples, he argued that these divergences were not significant. Hence in chapter 7 he felt justified in illustrating his argument with a story wholly consistent with the simple labour theory of value – the forerunner of today's textbook 'one-factor' model.

From this base, trade theory has developed along three distinctive routes. The neoclassical route has been to extend the one-factor model to two factors, the second called 'capital'. The pricing problems of capital have been side-stepped by treating 'capital' as a primary factor on the same footing as labour. This allows Ricardo's 'gain-from-trade' conclusion to proceed unimpeded and has given rise to the famous 'factor endowments' or Heckscher-Ohlin (HO) explanation of trade patterns. For neo-Marxists, the divergence of price from labour cost (value) was seen to imply the possibility of 'unequal exchange' (see separate entry) the implication being that relative labour costs are, in some sense, 'true' or 'just' prices. The problem for this theory, however, is that it is possible to show that the victims of unequal exchange may nevertheless gain from trade in the conventional sense of having enlarged consumption possibilities. The third, 'neo-Ricardian', route provides a more robust alternative to neoclassical theory and it is this on which I shall concentrate. (For an account of both neoclassical and non-neoclassical theories that is both comparative and eclectic, see Evans (1989). The major early contributions to the neo-Ricardian literature are collected in Steedman (1979); for a compact and simplified survey of the issues, see Steedman and Metcalfe (1985).)

Neo-Ricardian theory is based on Sraffa's approach to pricing and consequently deals rigorously with the problems thrown up by the existence of capital. Sraffa, of course, was the inspiration for the radical critiques in the capital theory controversy (see separate entry) and it is not surprising that the spirit of criticism should have extended to HO theory, based on the neoclassical concept of 'capital'. The early contributions of Steedman and Metcalfe and Parinello were in this vein. The central point is that, in the presence of heterogeneous capital goods, one can no longer assume a monotonic relationship between the rate of profit (interest) on one hand, and relative commodity prices or factor intensities on the other. The consequence is that the HO theorem and the associated Stolper-Samuelson theorem are no longer valid. The critique was also extended to embrace the factor-price equalization theorem.

The neo-Ricardians made their constructive contributions by reworking Ricardo's original analysis, but making full allowance for the effects on prices of the existence of a positive rate of profits. Beginning with Sraffa it is possible to derive, for a given autarky technique, a relationship between the wage rate (in terms of some numeraire) and the uniform, competitive rate of profit – the *w–r* relation. Each point on this relation is, in general, associated with a distinct set of relative prices. The actual outcome depends on the level of the exogenously given distribution variable (*w* or *r*); if, for example, *w* is fixed, then *r* and prices follow. If price-quantity duality holds (requiring the assumption of constant returns), the *w–r* relation is identical to the relation between per capita consumption and the rate of growth (*c–g*); given the capitalist savings propensity, σ, $g = \sigma r$ and *c* follow directly. If autarky relative prices in one economy differ from those in a potential trading partner, it is possible to show that specialization will lead to an outward shift in the *w–r/c–g* possibilities in the neighbourhood of the initial *w,r* combination. Thus free trade is profitable and will be undertaken if permitted. Elsewhere, however, the *w–r/c–g* possibilities may shrink and, if $\sigma < 1$, the relevant *c–g* point may be inferior to the autarky one. In this strictly comparative sense, there arises the possibility of a loss from trade. The failure of a profit-maximizing choice of technique (i.e., the choice of specialized versus non-specialized production) to maximize per capita consumption is a consequence of the violation of the golden rule of accumulation (which implies that $\sigma = 1$).

This loss-from-trade conclusion inspired a neoclassical interest in what Samuelson called 'time-phased systems' (i.e., those with a Sraffian production structure) in an effort to reconcile the outcome with the orthodox standpoint. This was done by arguing that the correct approach to evaluating gains from trade was to consider the consumption profile of an economy which had undergone an actual transition from autarky to free trade, rather than merely comparing equilibrium outcomes (a distinction which had not previously troubled neoclassical theorists). If that were done, it could be shown that where an economy had suffered a 'comparative' loss from trade, it had also gained a 'transitional' consumption boost. If the entire consumption stream is discounted at a rate equal to *r*, then it turns out that the present value of the transition-plus-trade stream is always greater than the autarky stream, thus restoring the neoclassical position.

Whilst this argument is logically unassailable, it has to be remembered that the assumptions on which it is based (the concession to heterogeneous capital notwithstanding) are largely neoclassical. The point about neo-Ricardian theory (which its advocates, perhaps mistakenly, saw no need to spell out) is that it is a classical theory, one in which profits are regarded as a surplus dependent on technology and the wage rate, and not a return to abstinence or a reward for overcoming time preference. That being so, there is absolutely no reason to equate *r* with the social rate of time preference and to use it as the appropriate rate for discounting alternative consumption streams. Thus in a country where the social discount rate is less than r, greater weight would be put on future consumption losses so that the loss-from-trade outcome is sustained (see Mainwaring, 1991, Ch. 2 for a fuller explanation). It may be worth mentioning that a similar result holds in the case of international investment, but this is not disputed by neoclassicals who have developed their own 'immiserizing investment' result.

In the last ten years or so, the more interesting developments in international trade theory have taken place in the context of North-South models which emphasize structural asymmetries and analyse dynamic processes. In some ways the classical approach, in which prices depend on exogenous distribution, lends itself well to this method because asymmetry can be introduced by allowing different 'closures' (i.e., ways of determining w or r) in each global region. Thus Mainwaring (1991) considers a North in which r is determined exogenously and a South where w is given from outside. The approach is most fully exploited by Dutt (1990) who considers various combinations of closure (which he labels neoclassical, neo-Keynesian, Kalecki-Steindl and neo-Marxian) in the two regions and analyses the corresponding outcomes. The result is a bewildering set of alternative global development stories (including uneven and underdevelopment), the lesson being that economists must first be sure of appropriate structures before reaching practical conclusions.

A feature of Dutt's approach which is shared with many other North-South analyses is that the pattern of specialization is predetermined (an assumption which is at least as justifiable as beginning with wholly notional autarky economies). This is the case not only in the neoclassical model of Findlay, but also in its more radical counterparts such as Taylor's structuralist (Kalecki-based) model, Vine's Kaldorian model and those models due to Krugman and Conway-Darity which hinge on increasing returns (see Dutt, 1990, for references). More recently consideration has been given to ways in which the regional pattern of specialization may be endogenized to some degree. In the Conway-Darity model (which is 'Kaldorian' in a different way from that of Vines), including international capital movements allows investment in Southern manufacturing to become profitable in the course of global development. A similar outcome is discussed more extensively in Mainwaring, the argument briefly running as follows.

Suppose that the North specializes in manufactures, the South in food, and that the Northern capitalist savings propensity is greater than the Southern: $\sigma_n > \sigma_s$. Without international investment, $r_s > r_n$ and so there is an incentive for Northern capitalists to invest in food, thus equating the rates of profit. This means that part of the profits earned in the South will be saved at the ratio σ_n so that the aggregate savings ratio on Southern-earned profits will rise. Indeed, the world average savings rate will rise tending, if undisturbed, to σ_n. This is the 'international Pasinetti process'. If, initially, labour is not a constraint in either region, so that the wage rates are fixed, the average profit rate follows from global technology and is also fixed. Thus with a rising average savings rate, the world growth rate rises, as do the two regional rates. It is then conceivable that the Northern rate will come to exceed the rate of growth of its labour force, bringing accumulation up against a full-employment barrier. This can be relieved to some extent by increasing overseas investment in food, although the possibilities here are limited by declining terms of trade for food. Thus at some point it becomes profitable to divert part of overseas investment into manufacturing so that Southern production becomes diversified. Once introduced, manufacturing could become indigenized through various channels including demonstration effects. Symmetrically, the exhaustion of land/natural resources in the South could stimulate diversification in the North. In this way, existing patterns of production and trade are explained as evolutionary outcomes. In the process the South may grow very fast, but this growth is concentrated in the investment or manufacturing enclaves, the remaining part of the economy stagnating. The South may also become increasingly indebted. This is only one of a number of evolutionary or 'stages' approaches which attempt to explain trade patterns in historical and structural terms. Further refinements in this direction can be expected.

We may conclude that radical economics has made important contributions to international trade theory within both the standard and the more recent North-South methodologies. If there is one conspicuous failing, however, it is in the theory of trade policy. There are few, if any, rigorous and detailed non-neoclassical analyses of the impact of various forms of protection, with or without externalities and other market failures. Indeed, apart from expressions of scepticism concerning the global optimality of free trade – soundly based on a rigorous demonstration of the possibility of loss from trade – commercial policy is an area all but abandoned to orthodoxy. This failing probably stems from the absence of a complete non-neoclassical theory of demand, which suggests that advances in this area of trade theory will have to await more profound developments in radical political economy.

LYNN MAINWARING

References

Dutt, A.K. (1990), *Growth, Distribution and Uneven Development*, Cambridge: Cambridge University Press.

Evans, H.D. (1989), *Comparative Advantage and Growth: Trade and Development in Theory and Practice*, Brighton: Harvester Wheatsheaf.

Mainwaring, L. (1991), *Dynamics of Uneven Development*, Aldershot: Edward Elgar.

Steedman, I. (ed.) (1979), *Fundamental Issues in Trade Theory*, London: Macmillan.

Steedman, I. and Metcalfe, J.S. (1985), 'Capital Goods and the Pure Theory of Trade' in David Greenaway (ed.), *Current Issues in International Trade*, London: Macmillan.

Investment theory and radical perspectives

Joan Robinson once likened theoretical constructions to maps. Some are very detailed, but often ones showing the main routes are more important. In practice more or less all economic variables have an influence on each other. Theory amounts to identifying the strongest influence or in identifying conditions under which different influences operate strongly.

It should be clear from what has been said that radical and orthodox theories of investment cannot be counterposed at the level of a single set of causal influences operating on investment. There are of course issues to be discussed here, but they are subsidiary to the question of structure.

Most schools of thought agree that, viewed as a company decision, investment involves a trade-off between foregone expenditure opportunities today and future benefits tomorrow. It is a trivial matter to express investment demand as a function of proxies for expected future benefits (output, profits, etc.) and proxies of opportunity cost (interest rates, liquidity measures, takeover pressure, uncertainty, etc.). At this level the disagreement between the neoclassical and other persuasions is the following: how flexible is capital adjustment to relative prices (including profitability). Theories with perfectly flexible production functions, perfectly competitive markets for products, inputs and finance, and zero adjustment costs may be contrasted with a world of putty-clay production models (possibly vintage models), downward-sloping demand curves, sticky prices, preference for internal finance, delivery lags, supply constraints and irreversibility. The empirical literature is broadly supportive of the latter models rather than the former, but the number of plausible models is very large and econometricians have great trouble in estimating investment equations that are stable: we will return to this problem of instability below.

Traditional interpretations of the Keynesian investment function centre on translating a demand curve for the capital stock (parameterized by the rate of interest) into an investment demand function, relating investment to the rate of interest. There is considerable dispute as to how this should be done consistently. Usually the assumption is made that the price of capital goods rises to choke off sudden demand. But is this anticipated at the micro level, making the demand function dependent on supply conditions? This problem with Keynes's theory, explored by Asimakopulos (1971), has been formally addressed in a restrictive setting. But the more general point raised by Asimakopulos was that the investment decision is much more complicated than either Keynes or orthodox economists have suggested; this is because investment changes the conditions under which profit is generated, including the amount of existing capital, utilization, technology and prices. In Keynes's approach, the 'impact of a higher rate of investment on prices of capital goods is included, but not its effect on expected profits' (Asimakopulos, p. 384). This line of argument reflects the view that profits depend on investment, a stand championed by Kalecki and Joan Robinson.

For Kalecki and some post Keynesians, there is another point at issue. Capitalists, if rational, would only wish to add sufficient capacity to the capital stock so as to be consonant with the prevailing degree of monopoly (market power/class relations). There is thus an ambiguity to investment behaviour. Investment itself, by raising demand, generates the profits and expectations which fuel further investment. However, by adding to capacity, investment will threaten profitability – most clearly in the case of new entry. This is the basis of the various investment models set out in Kalecki's works. If investment runs ahead of what is required to maintain profitability, there is both a positive expansion effect and a negative 'kickback' effect. Put differently, investment enhances profitability on the demand side, but runs the risk of reducing profitability if supply enhancement is excessive.

Kalecki combines a number of elements to get a determinate expression for investment. According to the two-sided relationship above, investment depends on the liquidity effect of past savings (profit flow or, more correctly, accumulated flows), on change in profits (reflecting expectations of profitability) and on the kickback effect. Profits in turn are regarded as determined by investment. Substituting for profits, one obtains a difference equation for investment and a steady-state solution. Kalecki downgrades the kickback effect in his early formal models, arguing that the capital stock shows only mild fluctuations. In later writings he allows for the kickback effect by modelling it with respect to new capital only. This issue seems relatively unexplored, both theoretically and empirically.

The formalism of these models may obscure their central focus. Kalecki's basic idea is already implicit in Marx's *Capital* and is reflected in later writings such as those of Schumpeter. Competition between capitalists forces the pace of accumulation and results in over-investment relative to desired profitability. Crisis follows, which in Kalecki takes the form of cycles and potential excess capacity – even under growth conditions.

Followers of Sraffa have attempted to deny the possibility of a falling profit rate induced by accumulation unless accompanied by a rising wage rate. However this criticism suffers from restricted formalism, and even competent orthodox economists have shown that over-investment is possible in a world of dynamic oligopolistic competition.

Nevertheless, the extent to which this form of boom and bust investment scenario dominates modern economies must remain in question. Coordination of investment appears to proceed relatively smoothly in some tight oligopolistic industries such as chemicals. Insofar as this is true, Kalecki's points about over-capacity must either be independently established or be formulated in terms of rent-dissipation inherent in maintaining barriers to entry (where over-capacity is a chosen strategy). The latter appears to be the position taken by Cowling (1982); there is also qualified support for this in empirical studies.

Independent theoretical development of the underconsumption argument has emerged in a series of papers by Kaldor, Steindl and Rowthorn, referenced in an encompassing model set out in Marglin and Bhaduri (1990). The basic model consists of two curves relating profit share to capacity utilization. The degree of monopoly curve reflects a constant mark-up over variable costs. Intersecting this is the realization condition that savings (retained earnings) equal investment. Depending on the formulation of the investment equation and the relative strengths of savings and investment propensities, there can be full employment or stagnation. More interestingly, the model suggests another distinction between cooperative regimes (wage-led growth favourable to capital and labour) and conflictual regimes. The latter may exist even under stagnation if the accelerator effect is weak, as when confidence is shaken by a series of shocks such as financial instability. Marglin and Bhaduri (1990) suggest that the 'stagnationist game of wage-led growth could turn out the only game in town' (p. 183), but they omit to consider increased public control of investment. A deficiency of these models is that investment is narrowed down to its role as a constituent of demand, whereas a richer model would show the effect of investment on capital stock. It would also seem desirable to consider excess capacity as planned, as in Cowling (1982); his discussion of the mechanics of oligopoly behaviour in respect of capacity formation is richer than in the formal model of underconsumption.

Although most of the developments of Kalecki's work on investment are underconsumptionist, the more orthodox Marxian view of crisis as due to over-accumulation is also clearly present in Kalecki, though it fits somewhat uneasily with the notion of a constant degree of monopoly. A cogent version of a modern-day Marxist model is Wood (1975), presented as a theory emerging from the microeconomics of the firm. Profits and investment are linked via an internal finance function (distribution is not, therefore, reflected in an *ex-ante* mark-up), while growth and the profit share at the level of the firm are negatively related (corresponding to Kalecki's diminishing returns to capital). In Wood, there is no 'degree of monopoly' constraint on distribution to close the model; thus there is one extra degree of freedom in that the capital output ratio is determined endogenously by growth maximization; a higher capital-output ratio improves the growth/profits trade-off. Individual firms are therefore led to accumulate by the Marxian imperative of growth. At the aggregate level this increases the capital-output ratio, with repercussions for profitability. This model is clearly at variance with the underconsumptionist approach above. It captures one aspect of firm behaviour, although the growth maximization hypothesis is probably not relevant to firms in mature industries.

Wood's model is often linked to that of Alfred Eichner (1976), because in both, price and investment are jointly determined. An accelerator theory of investment replaces the variable capital-output ratio in Eichner's framework. Contrasts with the basic Kalecki model are that only long-run cyclically averaged variables are relevant to pricing, and the mark-up is flexible. The pricing rule generates stable cyclical surpluses and deficits. Eichner suggests that the surpluses could be translated into faster growth if expectations of instability could be countered by planning the evolution of wages or investment.

Investment depends on expectations. For a significant number of investments in fixed capital or R&D, the formation even of probability distributions of returns may be difficult. Unless there is some form of coordination, expectations may not be consistent in a decentralized economy. Such a view underpinned Keynes's observations on investment in Chapter 12 of *The General Theory* and later writings. Investment depends on long-term expectations which are exogenous in the sense of not being necessarily related to any current economic variable. Although Keynes believed that current variables exerted a disproportionate influence on long-term expectations, these were liable to be at first sticky under the force of convention and then to change dramatically in response to some news shock. Clearly this marks investment out as a *causa causans* and is consistent with the notion of causality running from investment to profits.

Post Keynesians tend to mix up two features of the uncertain investment climate. On the one hand, there is the 'state of confidence' or 'animal spirits' which is rightly regarded as a measure of the bullishness of decision makers. But this should not be equated with the notion of uncertainty which reflects the degree of forecast confidence investors have irrespective of the state of animal spirits. Keynes himself sometimes used the concepts interchangeably though they are distinct.

The issue is important if uncertainty has a life of its own – connected, say, with structural change or technology. This variable could then influence animal spirits, while being relatively uncorrelated with most of the variables normally assumed to capture this (such as capacity utilization, current profitability, etc.). Recent work on investment under uncertainty (summarized in Driver and Moreton, 1992) confirms that uncertainty can have a serious depressing effect on capital formation, particularly under conditions of low profitability and irreversibility. As Keynes emphasized, liquidity is a natural response to uncertainty. This view complements the stagnationist models mentioned earlier. It raises the possibility that major technical and structural change (which create uncertainty) necessarily transform the economic regime to a stagnationist one, a situation which can be overcome only by public coordination. This view is consistent with the theory of long-wave development.

CIARAN DRIVER

References

Asimakopulos, A. (1971), 'The Determination of Investment in Keynes's Model', *Canadian Journal of Economics*, **4**, August, 382–8.

Cowling, K. (1982), *Monopoly Capitalism*, London: Macmillan.

Driver, C. and Moreton, D. (1992), *Investment, Expectations and Uncertainty*, Oxford: Blackwell.

Eichner, A.S. (1976), *The Megacorp and Oligopoly*, Armonk: M.E. Sharp.

Kalecki, M. (1991), 'Theories of Economic Dynamics', Part V in J. Osiatynski (ed.), *Collected Works of Michal Kalecki, Vol. II: Capitalism: Economic Dynamics*, Oxford: Clarendon Press, 203–348.

Marglin, S.A. and Bhaduri, A. (1990), 'Profit Squeeze and Keynesian Theory' in S.A. Marglin and J.B. Schor, *The Golden Age of Capitalism*, Oxford: Clarendon Press, 152–86.

Wood, A. (1975), *A Theory of Profits*, Cambridge: Cambridge University Press.

Labour process debate

Since Adam Smith observed workers in a pin-making factory, the role of labour in the production transformation process has been subject to much debate. This debate has taken the form of historical as well as on-going contemporary research in which certain organizing concepts are presented as having validity in explaining the economic and institutional conditions which affect the labour process.

In general terms these organizing concepts attempt to describe the relations between capital and labour and, following from this, examine the conditions of work for the employee. It is the unequal power relation between the interests of capital and labour which establishes the terms and conditions of the labour process debate. The employee sells labour time to the employer who is free (subject to certain institutional constraints) to manage that employee's labour time in the productive process. It is this relation between the management of capital and the use of labour time which is the subject of the ongoing debate on the labour process.

In order to develop an understanding of the labour process debate, it is important to consider the dominant organizing concepts which have been used historically to explain the relation between capital and labour. In the classic work by Braverman (1974), the organizing concept used to examine the relations between capital and labour has subsequently been represented as a Fordist control of labour time. For Braverman the management of production involved the construction of a particular stereotype of mass production. Mass production systems (of a Fordist type) involved, firstly, a process of deskilling the workforce through the application of Taylorist work study methods which established the division of labour tasks into a set of repetitive operations; secondly, the use of dedicated fixed technology in which worker conception is separated from execution and, finally, a moving assembly line which set the pace of work for a semi-skilled workforce.

For historians and social scientists the importance of this organizing concept cannot be underestimated. It provided an organizing foundation upon which most of the literature on the labour process has since been based or set against. For historians the moving assembly line established at the Ford Highland Park plant is used to represent all that is bad about production and the management of the labour process. The moving assembly line is the metronome through which Ford, and those who followed, established control of working time and improvements to labour productivity. For social scientists, the Fordist model provided a checklist which could then be applied to establish the presence or absence of particular features of the Fordist model in case-study material.

More recently the Fordist model has again been invoked as a means to explain what is often perceived as 'a general crisis of the industrial system'

(Piore and Sabel, 1984). Here it is argued that 'the present deterioration in economic performance results from the limits of the model of industrial development that is founded on mass production'. Mass production of the old Fordist type is now an inappropriate means to organize production, especially when market and institutional conditions have changed.

Piore and Sabel present an alternative model of industrial development which they term 'flexible specialization'. This system is presented as the polar opposite of mass production and the Fordist system of mass manufacture. Flexible specialization is a type of production organization based on skilled workers who produce a variety of customized goods. Some have further argued that a culture of post-Fordist capitalism is now emerging in which consumption has a new place. As for production, the key word is 'flexibility' of plant and machinery, as well as of products and labour.

For Piore and Sabel, post-Fordist manufacture is not only a new paradigmatic form of productive organization, but also one which can be historically realized in the type of economy where one kind of production system dominates a geographic area. For the UK, in particular, it is argued that mass manufacture of the old Fordist type is unable to respond to the changing characteristics of the market and consumer demand. The post-war Keynesian consensus has been unable to regulate and sustain aggregate demand to levels which can fully load old-style Fordist systems of mass manufacture. Productivity growth has not only been frustrated by market instability, but by worker resistance in the workplace and poor levels of training.

More recently the work of Womack, Jones and Roos (1990) constructs another alternative organizing concept – that of 'lean production'. Here the economic success of Japanese car assemblers is explained by the fact that Japanese lean producers take half the labour hours to manufacture a car, making their productivity twice that of their competitors. The promise to those wishing to imitate is one of transformed performance; the recommendation which follows is that all should (and can) adopt lean production systems. The conditions of transferability are not questioned because techniques and systems are viewed as both neutral and multinational in nature.

Womack, Jones and Roos do not examine the structural conditions which operate in Japan to promote cost reduction or the difficulty of replicating these unique institutional conditions elsewhere. The underlying message of lean production is that management is the key social actor in social and economic transformation, though it disregards the fact that different types of social settlements operate beyond the realm of management action.

As with the Fordist explanation of success in an earlier period, so now lean production together with flexible specialization are promoting successive eras of new and different organizing concepts. The productivity benefits which are assumed to flow according to the new paradigm(s) are used to delegitimize the prevailing national social settlements of the unsuccessful who can and must change their ways if they are to succeed against the new competition (Williams et al., 1992b).

Considering more recent critical work in the labour process debate, the tendency is to assimilate the conclusions drawn from the efficiency of lean production or the nature and attributes of Fordism. These authors accept the conclusions concerning the efficiency of lean production within a critical leftist framework.

The classic work by Nichols (1986) reviews the managerial bias which saturates the literature on productivity and which, in an earlier period, blamed British workers for poor economic performance. Yet Nichols welcomed the National Institute Studies as aspiring to more precise and rigorous investigations.

Cutler's (1992) review of the National Institute productivity studies and William's *et al.* (1992a) review of the IMVP lean production case show that such supposedly exemplary studies can always be criticized for a failure to control or consider relevant variables which affect the conclusions drawn. More generally, productivity studies are fundamentally flawed. They attempt to explain deficiencies in productivity by invoking an X factor – be it management, training, management accounting or factor input deficiency; by identifying such diverse factors, all cannot be right.

Within the labour process debate the choice is either to continue to accept that organizing constructs and productivity analysis are useful theoretical tool(s) against which to assess or investigate economic development, or to accept that, if the evidence does not fit the construct, then it is time to abandon the construct.

In the work by Williams (1992b) on the production of the Model T, the authors argue that there is a contradiction between the stereotype and the reality of Henry Ford's manufacturing practice. Using archive material, the authors describe the activity of manufacturing at Ford Highland Park, arguing that this factory in no way represents a stereotype of single-product output, of dedicated production characteristics or of a de-skilled workforce. On the contrary the product was continually redesigned and the factory continually reorganized, resulting in the need for a constant recomposition of labour tasks. Improvements to flow in repetitive manufacturing operations such as that at Highland Park were a necessary means to reduce value added conversion costs. The prominence of labour within the manufacturing conversion process is therefore of vital importance when, in most advanced economies, labour accounts for over 70 per cent of conversion costs.

The implication of formal reflection rather than *ad hoc* criticism is that it helps to override organizing constructs like Fordist practice or lean production systems with an historical understanding which stresses the importance of continuity and discontinuity over time. The management of labour costs is and has always been the overriding problem, but the techniques applied to reduce labour's share of conversion costs do change to meet particular circumstances.

New forms of work practice and organization offer the promise of economic regeneration. Organizing concepts are presented as providing the solution to firm specific problems which, in aggregate, transform national economic performance. There is a failure, however, to recognize the implications for the labour process; preexisting conditions of employment and social settlement have to be challenged.

Furthermore, it is not at all clear that the adoption of new forms of work organization can take enough labour hours out of production so that the market and financial positions of firms are preserved. International competition is more concerned with the relation between differing social settlements than with forms of organizational best practice. Competition exposes one form of social settlement (shorter working hours at higher pay per hour) to another (long working hours at lower pay per hour).

At a national level it is not possible to abstract the firm or enterprise from peculiar national institutional conditions which may materially affect its behaviour. In the UK and the US the institutional conditions operate to facilitate the use of assets for value in exchange rather than for productive organic growth. Here productive virtue is subordinated to the requirements of financial engineering, while dividends are issued at the expense of employment and internal investment.

In much of the labour process debate, the firm is represented as an essentially productionist entity when clearly alternative behavioural typologies exist. In Britain and America financial engineering or changes in the ownership of corporate assets generates increases in shareholder value at the expense of employment. The outcome is a hollowed out manufacturing base which becomes subordinated to the primary activity of dividend distribution and dealing in assets.

At a supranational level the deepening and widening of the EC has more general implications for the European labour process. The 1992 programme and European monetary integration are concerned with freeing up market relations rather than with regulating institutional conditions. The absence of a strong industrial and regional policy results in a negative form of European integration which reinforces the persistence of unequal income distribution and conditions of employment within Europe. Within this weak institutional framework it is open for firms to transfer from an existing social settlement and locate in low labour cost economies which surround the central regions of Europe.

This brief summary of the labour process debate cannot cover all the issues in detail because these are wide and diverse. However a range of issues has been raised which we hope will stimulate further debate.

COLIN HASLAM

References

Braverman, H. (1974), *Labour and Monopoly Capital*, New York: Monthly Review Press.
Cutler, A. (1992), 'Vocational Training and Economic Performance', *Work, Employment and Society*, July.
Nichols, T. (1986), *The British Worker Question*, London: Routledge.
Piore, M. and Sabel, C.F. (1984), *The Second Industrial Divide: Possibilities for Prosperity*, New York: Basic Books.
Williams, K. *et al.* (1992a), 'Against Lean Production', *Economy and Society*, August.
Williams, K. (1992b), 'Ford versus Fordism – The Beginning of Mass Production?', *Work Employment and Society*, December.
Womack, J., Jones, D. and Roos, D. (1990), *The Machine That Changed the World*, New York: Rawson Associates/Macmillan.

Labour theory of value

For Marx, an analysis of the development of capitalist society – to lay bare the economic laws of motion of modern society – has to begin with an analysis of the production of commodities; that is, products produced for sale. The property that all commodities have in common, that creates the relationship of exchange, is that they are the product of labour. Capitalism is generalized commodity production where goods are produced, not for the immediate consumption by the producers, but for exchange for profit: Henry Ford did not make cars because he liked cars, but because he liked money. Even the ability to work – labour-power – becomes a commodity under capitalism, bought and sold. But this act of buying labour-power is quite separate logically and in time from the act of labouring. It is this difference – between the value created during the labour process on the one hand, and the value of labour-power on the other – which for Marx is the source of surplus value. From surplus value comes the mass of profits, interest, rents and dividends, as well as the income of unproductive labourers under capitalism.

Marx's labour theory of value has been criticized for being redundant. Since agents respond to wages, prices and profits (not the value of labour-power, values and surplus value), it is the former categories which should be used directly rather than negotiating the unnecessary detour of labour values. The relevance of such criticisms depends on what a labour theory of value is being used for. If the sole aim is to calculate relative prices and if this can be done without the use of a labour theory of value, then the criticism would have some force. However, this is clearly not the purpose (and certainly not the sole purpose) of Marx's use of a labour theory of value.

Marx's method of analysis involves abstracting from the mass of secondary conflicts and events in order to focus on the key determinants of the objects being analysed:

> in the analysis of economic forms ... neither microscopes nor chemical reagents are of use. The force of abstraction must replace both. But in bourgeois society the commodity form of the product of labour – or the value-form of the commodity – is the economic cell-form (*Capital*, Vol. I, p. 19).

Thus he was well aware of conflicts between different sections of capital over, for example, industrial profits and rents, but thought that these could only be properly understood on the basis of an analysis of the key conflict between labour and capital, since this is the source of the surplus value over which the different sections of capital then clash. Similarly, Marx was well aware that capitalists might cheat, over-price and under-pay, but argued that such influences on profitability must be secondary, in a logical sense, to the explanation of the fundamental source of profits in general under capitalism. He argued that unless we can explain the existence of profits under capitalism by abstracting from these secondary influences – unless profits can be explained in a situation where nothing is over-priced, where everything exchanges for its full value – then we cannot claim to have achieved anything like an adequate explanation of profits.

Marx was well aware that prices deviated from values according to the capital intensity of the sector, and that there would be continuous further deviations of day-to-day market prices. He considered that the redistribution of profits between sectors, and between individual capitalists, is secondary to the process of profit generation under capitalism as a whole. An analysis of this needs to focus on the conflict between labour and capital for which the assumption of goods being sold at their values allows an abstraction from the continuous redivision of profits between sectors of capital (industrial and financial) and between individual capitals.

However, Marx's own explanation of the transformation of values into prices of production (transformed values, taking account of different compositions of capital, rather than actual prices) is incomplete. His illustration in Volume III of *Capital* has sectors with different compositions of capital marking up total costs by a uniform rate of profit (so that labour-intensive sectors sell at prices of production less than values), but without those input costs themselves having been transformed into prices of production. Although this point has been made in criticism of Marx, it was one which he himself had raised.

> We have seen how a deviation of production from values arises from:

1. adding the average profit instead of the surplus-value contained in a commodity to its cost-price;
2. the price of production, which so deviates from the value of a commodity, entering into the cost-price of other commodities as one of its elements, so that the cost-price of a commodity may already contain a deviation from value in those means of production consumed by it, quite aside from a deviation of its own which may arise through a difference between the average profit and the surplus-value (*Capital*, Vol. III, pp. 206–7).

Marx's phrase 'We have seen' is somewhat hopeful; it presumably refers back to a previous discussion of this issue which concludes that 'Our present analysis does not necessitate a closer examination of this point' (p. 165). Nevertheless, it is clear that he was well aware of what was required.

A separate criticism focuses on Marx's assertion that total prices of production would equal total values and that total profits would equal total surplus value whereas, if the former holds, then the relation of profits to surplus value will be influenced by the value composition of capital of the various sectors and on whether the sectors producing the goods accounted for by surplus value happen on average to have prices of production greater than, equal to or less than value.

Such criticism of Marx's presentation has led to the argument that there is nothing necessarily special about labour. All goods can be measured against any standard one might wish to choose, not necessarily labour. And certainly it is true that all exchange relations could be expressed in terms of some other measure; one could indeed have a 'jelly theory of value'. It has been proven that 'Marx after Sraffa' can be presented as a theory of price without recourse to a labour theory of value. What such a presentation tells us specifically about the capitalist mode of production, its origin and its laws of motion is less clear. For Marx, the transformation of values into prices of production was not just a logical abstraction (although it is also that), but to some extent took place historically as capitalist commodity production developed:

> The exchange of commodities at their values, or approximately at their values, thus requires a much lower stage than their exchange at their prices of production, which requires a definite level of capitalist development. … Apart from the domination of prices and price movement by the law of value, it is quite appropriate to regard the values of commodities as not only theoretically but also historically previous to the prices of production (*Capital*, Vol. III, p. 177).

More generally, Marx is concerned with economic relations in material practice – how surplus is produced, appropriated and redistributed. The question of (equilibrium) prices is not of central concern nor interest.

For Marx, capital is self-expanding value, not a thing but a social relation of production. Thus the last chapter of Volume I demonstrates that 'capital' will fail to act as self-expanding value unless it has in place the necessary exploitative relations of production, whereby people become 'free' to sell their labour-power (free to choose which particular capitalist to be exploited by, but also historically freed or divided from their access to the means of production and hence from any alternative to selling their labour-power). It has been suggested that this chapter on colonization concludes Volume I in order 'not to attract the attention of the censor by finishing on too resounding a note' (McLellan, 1977, p. 350, note 1). But it would be wrong to downplay its importance: Marx had been arguing in Volume I that capital had to expropriate people from the land in order to make them dependent on capital for work (this need not involve any geographical shift, just a separation of them from the means of production). That this is what capital had had to do in Western Europe was denied by Marx's contemporary political economists (as it has been since: Chambers, 1953, and Chambers and Mingay, 1966, argue that the class of dependent wage-labourers had been provided by population growth). So Marx took the example of the colonies where 'population ... increases much more quickly than in the mother-country, because many labourers enter this world as ready-made adults, and yet the labour-market is always understocked. The law of the supply and demand of labour falls to pieces' (p. 720). The dependence of labourers on capital had not yet been established.

Marx cites the example of a Mr Peel who took with him from England to Western Australia means of subsistence and of production to the amount of £50,000. Surely, then, this Mr Peel was exporting capital – self-expanding value? No: those means of production can only be self-expanding value if there are wage workers compelled to (voluntarily) sell their labour-power. Mr Peel did, however, have the foresight to bring with him, besides, '3,000 persons of the working class'. But these workers on arrival were no longer separated from the means of production as they had been via the enclosures in Britain; hence they could choose not to work for Mr Peel, which is precisely what they did. Thus Mr Peel discovered that capital is not a thing, but a social relation between persons. Unhappy Mr Peel, Marx concludes, who provided for everything except the export of English relations of production to Western Australia! (*Capital*, Vol. 1, p. 717).

Marx's labour theory of value abstracts, then, from the superficial and transitory influences on prices and the rate of profit in order to uncover the underlying determinants of the system. It does certainly focus attention on the appropriation by the exploiting class from the exploited.

The debates concerning Marx's labour theory of value referred to above centre on the following. First, is such a theory necessary for the calculation of relative prices? And against this, would a theory of prices stated in relation to other prices alone (or some arbitrarily picked alternative to labour, such as a 'jelly' theory of value) be particularly illuminating as to the origin and development of the capitalist mode of production? Second, is Marx's theory flawed by errors? And against this, are the alleged errors genuine limitations to Marx's theory? Finally, is the theory not simply a metaphysical abstraction? And against this, is it possible to proceed to an understanding of all surface phenomena without first abstracting from some of the detail? Is it accurate to describe as metaphysical a theory which expresses definite facts about material life? (Fine, 1989, p. 10).

A quite separate debate around the labour theory of value has in the past concerned the issue of whether the 'law of value' would continue to operate under socialism. The law of value, for Marx, ultimately determines how much of its disposable working time society can expend on each particular class of commodity. Following the collapse of the Soviet Union and the socialist countries of Eastern Europe, it is perhaps fitting to recall that Marx had warned that

> ... after the abolition of the capitalist mode of production, but still retaining social production, the determination of value continues to prevail in the sense that the regulation of labour-time and the distribution of social labour among the various production groups, [and] ultimately the book-keeping encompassing all this, become more essential than ever (*Capital*, Vol. III, p. 851).

JONATHAN MICHIE

References

Chambers, J.D. (1953), 'Enclosures and Labour Supply in the Industrial Revolution', *Economic History Review*, V (3), 319–43.

Chambers, J.D. and Mingay, G.E. (1966), *The Agricultural Revolution*, London: Batsford.

Fine, B. (1989), *Marx's Capital,* 3rd edition, London: Macmillan.

Marx, K., *Capital*, references from Lawrence and Wishart editions of Volume I (1977) and Volume III (1974).

McLellan, D. (1977), *Karl Marx*, St. Albans, Herts: Paladin.

Liquidity

Liquidity is a *general* quality or characteristic of individual assets, portfolios or economies, and incorporates several *dimensions*. The amount of liquidity possessed by an asset is a function of the characteristics of the asset itself, but is also influenced by external factors such as general economic conditions and various subjective factors. While the term is usually applied at the micro level to a particular asset or portfolio, it may also be applied at the macro level to describe the liquidity of an economy as a whole.

The term liquidity applied to a particular asset signifies one that may be quickly converted to the medium of exchange or to legal tender, at low transactions costs and little loss of value. Thus, in the *Treatise*, Keynes defined liquidity as 'certainly realizable at short notice without loss' (Keynes, 1971, p. 59). In *The General Theory* (*GT*), Keynes emphasized that liquid assets have low or negligible costs of storage and safekeeping (Keynes, 1964, p. 217). Thus, wheat is fairly illiquid, as storage costs and losses due to wastage may be significant; a demand deposit is more liquid than a certificate of deposit that requires a penalty for early withdrawal.

Those characteristics which impart high liquidity to an asset include: good secondary markets; government guarantees standing behind the asset to ensure that it will maintain parity with legal tender; time to maturity (generally, shorter-term assets are more liquid); the wealth, credit-worthiness and other characteristics of its issuer; negligible elasticities of production and substitution; and 'stickiness' of value relative to money wages and to the unit of account in which debts are written. These last points will be discussed below.

General economic conditions also help determine the liquidity of an asset. When confidence is high, the amount of liquidity embodied within privately-issued assets rises. Thus, Marx argued that in an expansion, bills of exchange are sufficiently liquid to be used to circulate commodities. However, when confidence collapses, they suddenly become illiquid and will no longer circulate, with holders trying to 'liquidate' them in exchange for legal tender. In the modern period, commercial paper may be quite liquid in a boom, but lose its liquidity when pessimism reigns. Finally, subjective or institutional and conventional factors also play a role in determining the liquidity of an asset. An asset may become liquid merely if conventional wisdom holds it to be so. Thus, Keynes argued that land has frequently (but primarily in the past) been regarded as highly liquid (Keynes, 1964, p. 241).

A liquid portfolio contains a substantial portion of liquid assets. Davidson (1986) defined a liquid position as one which ensures the ability to meet contractual obligations as they come due. Thus, a portfolio is liquid if it contains media of exchange (legal tender, bank deposits), government debt (which can be liquidated quickly), lines of credit (an off-balance-sheet item used to obtain loans of bank deposits should the need arise), and other liquid assets. A liquid position would also be one for which expected income flows exceed contracted payments on debt (Minsky, 1986). Thus, an economic agent who committed half of expected income flows to payments on debt has a more liquid position (all else equal) than does an agent who similarly committed 80 per cent of income. Likewise, a bank with higher reserves-to-loans and equity-to-loans ratios has a more liquid position than does a bank with lower values for these ratios.

Finally, liquidity may be applied at the aggregate level. An economy with a greater ratio of government debt (including high-powered money) to private debt, or with a higher ratio of government debt to gross national product

(GNP), is more liquid. It has also been argued that an economy with more money relative to GNP is more liquid (Cramp, 1989). However, there is some circularity of reasoning in this application of the term, for if we define money as the most liquid of assets, we cannot obtain this measure of liquidity until we have identified those assets that make up the money supply. As Marx and many Post Keynesians have argued, the liquidity of an economy is reduced over the course of an expansion as spending is financed by the creation of private liabilities whose growth rate generally exceeds that of government debt or narrowly-defined money (Minsky, 1986).

Money is frequently defined as the most liquid asset. Keynes argued that the division between money and other liquid assets may be made on the basis of convenience; in the *GT*, he arbitrarily included as money those assets that retained general purchasing power, with a time to maturity of less than three months (Keynes, 1964, p. 167). Money is also frequently identified (primarily by orthodox economists) with those assets that function as media of exchange. Post Keynesians have tended to define money very broadly: Minsky (1986) describes it as a promise to pay; as such, money includes any debt that transfers purchasing power from the future to the present. Alternatively, money can be defined as a social relation: Schumpeter argued that the social purpose of credit money is to place purchasing power into the hands of entrepreneurs; as such, we might define money as the social creation that gives control over society's resources to the capitalists (Wray, 1990). Finally, money might be defined as the generalized, social unit of value in which accounts are kept; Keynes, for instance, emphasized that the most important function of money is as a unit of account. As both Keynes and Marx argued, the purpose of production in a capitalist economy is to end 'with more money than it started with' (Wray, 1990). Thus, money is the unit of account in which we measure success at accumulation. If we take this approach, money as a social measure of value is separated from those assets that *function* to varying degrees as money. The degree to which each functions as money will depend on its relation to the idealized money of account – a degree which will be at least partially determined by the liquidity of each.

In summary, there is no absolute standard of liquidity, even with regard to individual assets; Keynes argued that liquidity is merely a multidimensional scale that can be applied to rank assets (Keynes, 1964, p. 240). The quantity of liquidity embodied in assets, however, may be fairly accurately measured by the liquidity premia, or the differential interest rates paid by each. Thus, if the rate on a demand deposit is 3 per cent, but that on a certificate of deposit is 6 per cent, then the demand deposit is more liquid and the premium paid by the certificate of deposit is a measure of its illiquidity. Each asset has a return that may be measured by $q–c+l$, where q is the expected yield, c is the carrying cost (or wastage), and l is a measure of liquidity. In the case of capital goods, $q–c$

would be significant, but l would be negligible. In the case of a liquid asset, however, q would be low, c would approximate zero, and l would be significant. That is, most of the return from holding a liquid asset would be due to its liquidity. In equilibrium, the expected returns (including the return to liquidity) of all assets must be equalized so that each may find a home.

In the *GT*, Keynes actually devoted little space to a discussion of liquidity; instead, he concentrated on liquidity preference. This may be defined as the desire to hold liquid assets, which exists because of uncertainty about the future. Keynes emphasized that one exercises liquidity preference with regard to a stock of savings (Keynes, 1964, p. 194). By doing so, he separated the decision to save from the decision regarding the form in which savings are to be held. The former would be determined primarily by income, the latter primarily by liquidity preference. Thus, given a stock of wealth, liquidity preference determines the portion to be held in the form of immediate, liquid command (Keynes, 1964, p. 166). An increase in liquidity preference raises the return to liquid assets (l) relative to that of illiquid assets (q–c). However, given a stock of assets, rising liquidity preference does not lead to adjustments of the quantity of liquid assets held in portfolios; rather, the prices of all assets adjust until those desiring a greater quantity of liquid assets become satisfied with the existing composition. Thus, rising liquidity preference lowers the prices of illiquid assets (raising yields) and raises the prices of liquid assets (lowering yields) until quantities demanded equal the (fixed) quantities supplied.

Liquidity preference theory is a theory of value since it determines the prices of all assets. Through its effects on demand prices over the whole spectrum of assets, liquidity preference influences the economy. Keynes argued that the return on money, the most liquid asset, sets the standard that must be achieved by all assets which are to be newly produced. Furthermore, in the case of most assets, expected returns tend to fall as the quantity produced rises. However, the return to money (l) does not fall nearly so rapidly as the return to all other assets as accumulation proceeds. This is due to the 'peculiar' characteristics of money, characteristics shared to a lesser degree by other liquid assets. These include a small elasticity of production; a small elasticity of substitution; low carrying costs; and relative stickiness of the value of money with regard to wage and debt contracts. Since carrying costs are low, an increase in the volume of money will not raise total carrying costs (c); holding liquidity constant, the return to money (l–c) will not fall significantly as the quantity of money increases. Since wage and debt contracts are written in money terms, holding money always increases one's ability to meet contractual obligations; thus, money always provides a positive return (l) regardless of the quantity held, as long as nominal wages (and other nominally valued contracts) are relatively sticky. Given a low elasticity of substitution, as the prices of other (more illiquid) assets fall, one will not substitute out of money. Finally, given a low elasticity of production, as liquidity preference rises, there is no tendency to move to full employment merely by allocating more labour to the production of money, which becomes a 'sinkhole' of purchasing power.

Although Keynes used the terms liquidity preference and money demand interchangeably, it is useful to distinguish between them. Rising liquidity preference indicates a desire to move to a liquid position, either by liquidating assets, by retiring debts or even through necessitous borrowing. Under these conditions, the money supply (narrowly or broadly defined) is not likely to increase; indeed, it shrinks if debts are retired. Instead, asset prices adjust. One might define money demand as a willingness to issue liabilities (borrow) in order to increase spending. Thus, optimism leads to greater planned spending, which must be financed. As long as banks and other financial institutions share in the optimism, this demand for finance ('money demand') will lead to a greater supply of finance ('money supply'). Given these definitions, money demand and liquidity preference will normally move in opposite directions: when liquidity preference is low and expectations are high, both money demand and money supply are expanding; but when liquidity preference is high and pessimism reigns, both money demand and money supply are falling (Wray, 1990).

Liquidity plays an essential role in non-orthodox thought: economists from Marx to Keynes recognized that the preference for liquidity must rise as confidence falls and that this generates unemployment. This insight was lost by orthodox economists who dropped uncertainty from their theories and replaced it with calculable probabilities. Thus, neither liquidity nor liquidity preference can play any significant role in conventional approaches. As Keynes exclaimed, no one outside an insane asylum would hold money in a neoclassical world. Furthermore, Keynes argued that in the real world, it is the desire for liquidity and the existence of assets whose return from liquidity exceeds carrying costs that prevent capitalist economies from achieving full employment. According to Keynes, nothing 'is more anti-social than the fetish of liquidity' since 'there is no such thing as liquidity of investment for the community as a whole' (Keynes, 1964, p. 155). He goes on to argue that:

> Unemployment develops, that is to say, because people want the moon; – men cannot be employed when the object of desire (i.e. money) is something which cannot be produced and the demand for which cannot be readily choked off. There is no remedy but to persuade the public that green cheese is practically the same thing and to have a green cheese factory (i.e. a central bank) under public control (Keynes, 1964, p. 235).

L. Randall Wray

References

Cramp, A.B. (1989), 'Liquidity' in J. Eatwell, M. Milgate and P. Newman (eds), *The New Palgrave: Money*, New York and London: Norton, p. 185.

Davidson, P. (1986), 'A Post Keynesian View of Theories and Causes for High Real Interest Rates', *Thames Papers in Political Economy*, Spring.

Keynes, J.M. (1964), *The General Theory of Employment, Interest and Money*, New York and London: Harcourt Brace Jovanovich.

Keynes, J.M. (1971), *A Treatise on Money* in D. Moggridge (ed.), *The Collected Writings of John Maynard Keynes, Volume VI*, London and Basingstoke: Macmillan.

Minsky, H.P. (1986), *Stabilizing an Unstable Economy*, New Haven and London: Yale University Press.

Wray, L.R. (1990), *Money and Credit in Capitalist Economies: The Endogenous Money Approach*, Aldershot: Edward Elgar.

Long period

Being well aware of the significance of, and the complexity arising from, the element of time in economic theory, Marshall adopted a four-fold division of time (in accordance with his general methodology of *ceteris paribus*): the market period, the short period, the long period and the period of secular movements of normal values. In fact, the last three divisions all refer to 'normal values' – those values implied by 'the predominance of certain tendencies which appear likely to be more or less steadfast and persistent in [economic] action over those which are relatively exceptional and intermittent' (Marshall, 1920, p. 28). The market period refers to a situation where the stock of a commodity supplied to the market is fixed, so that the price in that market is determined by the accidental states of demand and supply on the market day. The period of secular movements is one in which the demand-determining factors such as 'fashion or taste' and 'new substitutes' (p. 285) – together with other factors such as the state of technological knowledge, the level of population and (as we shall argue in more detail below) the level of capital in the economy as a whole (p. 315) – are assumed to change gradually. Under the assumption that these factors remain little changed, short-period and long-period 'normal values' are determined. The dividing line between short and long periods is whether 'the supply of specialized skill and ability, of suitable machinery and other material capital, and of the appropriate industrial organization has not time to be fully adapted to demand' (pp. 312–3) through 'investments of capital and effort'.

Marshall's concept of long period is a partial equilibrium development (and a modification) of the older general equilibrium concept of long period which originated in the classical political economy. For classical economists such as Smith and Ricardo and for Marx, the long period is defined (as for Marshall) by the existence of some persistent factors and, in the general equilibrium setting, by the tendency of the rate of profit on the supply price of capital goods to be uniform across all branches of production in the economy. This tendency implies the adjustment of productive equipment (not only its composition, as in Marshall, but also its aggregate level) to demand. The distinction between 'natural prices' (or 'prices of production') and 'market prices' is the result of such reasoning. The natural price of a commodity is the price corresponding to the uniform rate of profits and is ascertained when the quantity brought to the market of that commodity matches the 'effectual demand' for it – in Smith's words, 'the demand of those who are willing to pay the natural price of the commodity'. The market price, determined by temporary forces in the day-to-day marketplace, is considered to gravitate gradually towards the natural price. This gravitation is assumed to be achieved by the free competition of capital; namely, by the free movement of financial capital in search of a higher return. The validity of the classical picture of gravitation, in which a higher market price is associated with a higher rate of profits and in which the level of 'effectual demand' is assumed to be unchanged during the gravitation, is a question to be settled. However, the essence of the classical concept of long period, defined by the uniformity of the rates of profit, is the analysis of the configurations which result from the *persistence* of some determining factors (distinguished from the accidental influences of temporary forces) and the implication that the conditions of production *adjust* themselves to demand.

Those factors conceived as having permanent influences are reflected in the choice of what is taken as given in a specific analysis; this choice may be a matter of economic perspective within the scope of the analysis, varying from theory to theory. The classical theory of value and distribution takes as given the level and composition of output (the 'effectual demand'), the real wage rate and the technological state, since these factors are considered to be determined by relatively more complicated social and accumulation processes. For marginalist theory, which uses demand and supply analysis to determine prices, output quantities and distribution simultaneously, the givens are individual preferences, capital endowment (whether as a value magnitude or as a set of given physical quantities) and the state of technology (see Marshall's conditions above). Any long-period theory which intends to analyse the determination of output along a line not incompatible with the classical theory of value and distribution (where output is given) may choose a different set of data (to which we shall return below).

Although the *specifications* of the long period differed widely from one theory to another, the classical *method* of the long-period position (associated with the uniform rate of profits) had nonetheless been universally accepted – until the advent of the inter-temporal and temporary equilibrium theories during the inter-war period. Since then, the classical concept of the long period has either been increasingly associated with the stationary or steady state, or has been abandoned as not providing a useful method of economic analysis (Garegnani, 1976).

The association of the long period with the stationary or steady state unduly restricts the scope of the method of long-period positions as adopted even by such early marginalist economists as Wicksell, Walras and Marshall; along with classical economists and Marx, they did not confine their analysis of long-period normal values to such states. Such an association reflects the change in the general method of economic analysis from the classical long period to the 'post-Walrasian' short period (Garegnani, 1976). One of the data in the marginalist theory of value and distribution is capital endowment. For such economists as J.B. Clark, Menger, Böhm-Bawerk, Wicksell, Jevons and Marshall, capital endowment was given as a single value magnitude called 'capital'; the measurement of 'capital' varied from one author to another, but one requisite for such measurement was that this magnitude be independent of the rate of profits (it is now well known that this requisite cannot in general be satisfied; Sraffa, 1960). Walras, a notable exception, took capital endowment as a set of given physical quantities. But as Walras himself was soon to realize and Wicksell was quick to point out, the uniformity of the rates of profit on the supply price of capital goods implies that the endowments of various capital goods cannot be given in predetermined proportions. (Taking capital endowment as a single value magnitude – 'capital' – could avoid this contradiction, because 'capital' was conceived to change its physical composition through the process of saving and investment.) Logical consistency required a choice between the uniformity of the rates of profit and the given physical endowments; 'post-Walrasian' theorists chose the latter.

The inter-temporal general equilibrium theory, developed into a rigorous form by Debreu, Arrow and Hahn, assumes the existence of complete futures markets in which the coordination of decisions by all traders over the whole time horizon is achieved at a single period. In other words, a full system of prices discounted by the 'own rates of return' between two adjacent periods is assumed to exist for each commodity type. It can then be shown (Bliss, 1975) that, if all the elements of a vector of input and output quantities in a given production set grow at a common rate and steadily in each period, and if no other vector of input and output quantities in that production set yields a higher profit, then one can find a vector of prices such that the 'own rates of return' are uniform across commodity types and over time. This uniform 'own rate of return' is not larger than the uniform growth rate of input and output quantities.

Logically correct as this argument is in its own setting, it should be mentioned that the method of long-period positions does not necessarily refer to the sequence of equilibria over time. Two different non-steady-state notions of a long-period position can be identified in the literature. First, a long-period position is deemed to refer to a situation *at a point of time* to which the configuration of an economy tends to approach over time in order to achieve uniformity in the rates of profit. At that position, the level and composition of productive capacity will have been adjusted in such a way as to match that of aggregate demand. That particular position would not be reached in reality, however, because of various disturbances – including (slow) changes in those persistent forces which determine the long-period position. Be that as it may, a long-period position plays the role of a 'centre of gravitation' which 'regulates' the actual movements of the economy. Secondly, a long-period position is conceived rather as the configuration of *average* values, on the assumption of the persistence of certain determining factors. The rates of profit need not be uniform at any moment of time, but would tend to be so *on average* over a sufficient run of time should there be no change in the given determining conditions. The prices of commodities at any moment of time will be different from the prices determined by the condition of the uniform rate of profits, but would approach to them *on average* over a sufficient run of time. The *average* stock of capital goods is endogenously determined, through investments over time, in proportions compatible with the uniform rate of profits. These two different notions of a long-period position will have different analytical implications. But they in common represent the gist of the long-period method; that is the identification of the effects of those (changing) fundamental forces which define a 'centre of gravitation' towards which actual values are constantly attracted; in particular, the isolation of the effects of the adjustment of productive equipment to demand (or, in general, the interactions between aggregate demand and aggregate supply).

The denial of the existence of such fundamental and persistent forces, independent of accidental and transient influences, constitutes the basis of the recent rejection of the long period as a useful method of analysis. Such rejection comes from two sides: from Joan Robinson and her followers on this subject and from temporary general equilibrium theory.

Temporary equilibrium theory avoids the main shortcoming of intertemporal equilibrium theory – the assumption of the existence of complete futures markets. In the newer theory, the state of the economy at the current period is determined by the expectations of its future state made by all traders in the current period; in turn, these expectations are formed on the basis of past states of the economy. We then have a sequence of temporary equilibria, each equilibrium being determined by expectations which are in turn revised by the realized states of previous periods. This sequence would thus not show any significant tendency; hence the rejection of the method of long-period positions. Garegnani (1976), however, finds two shortcomings in this theory: one is that the very impermanence of the determining factors, which causes the changes in equilibrium, does not allow those factors to be distinguished from accidental causes; the other is that the introduction of unobservable quantities – expected prices – deprives the theory of any definite results. Both shortcomings make the theory incapable of being a useful guide to the behaviour of the economy and thus to any policy recommendations. (Attempts to show that the sequence of temporary equilibria with exogenous random shocks may tend to a stationary state over an infinite time horizon have not been very successful.)

The criticism of the classical concept of long period by Joan Robinson is based on her methodology in which uncertainty, expectations and the irreversibility of historical time (typified by that of committed investments) assume the central role in economic analysis. The long period is, for her, a sequence of short-period positions which reflect 'historical processes' (reminiscent of Kalecki's now famous dictum: 'the long-run trend is but a slowly changing component of a chain of short-period situations; it has no independent entity'). But as Garegnani (1976) argues, if Robinson's criticism is actually directed to the tendency of the economy to the full employment of labour in the long period and to the unrealistic assumption of the stationary or steady state, this criticism does not apply to the classical method of long-period positions. This is because those targets of her criticism are familiar features, not so much of the classical method, as of the demand and supply analysis of marginalist theory. In developing Robinson's criticism, others argue that, as in Chapters 5 and 12 of Keynes's *General Theory*, unrealized short-term expectations do influence long-term expectations, such influences being effective enough to shift the equilibrium implied by previous long-term expectations. Thus the concept of the long-period position as a 'centre of gravitation' loses ground. However, apart from the question of whether Keynes's 'long-term expectations' represent one of the fundamental forces compatible with the classical concept of long period, we find that this description of the economy is not very distant from that of temporary equilibrium theory. Even if such 'shifting equilibrium method' (Kregel, 1976) is taken for granted, what is still needed is a full development of the analysis of short-period positions as representing (short-period) *normal values* in the Marshallian sense, possibly complemented with a long-period analysis, though not necessarily of the classical type.

The full employment or otherwise of labour in a long-period position is a result of the specifications of the long period, rather than of the long-period method itself. This leads us to the recent debate on whether Keynes's employment theory presented in and around *The General Theory* is a long-period theory in the sense used in classical political economy (Eatwell and Milgate, 1983). The dust seems to have settled, if only lightly, on the proposition that Keynes did use the concept of long period in the Marshallian sense (that is, where the effects of capital accumulation are put aside) and that he also provided some limited analysis of such long-period positions, though his main concern was with the short period.

Whilst it is generally agreed among post Keynesians that the full employment of labour is not a necessary feature of the long period, some debates have recently been sparked among them on whether the long-period position – in which the uniform rate of profits implies the adjustment of productive equipment (its level and composition) to the state of demand – will necessarily imply the realization of the full (or, more generally, an exogenously given 'normal') utilization of productive capacity (see, for example, *Political Economy – Studies in the Surplus Approach*, Vols 2 and 3, 1986–87). The real issue at stake is whether the degree of utilization implicit in the long-period position is determined endogenously or otherwise. Different conclusions derive from the different economic perspectives of the groups involved, which are reflected in their choice of factors considered persistent in the long run of time. Those who insist on the necessary fulfilment of the given normal degree of utilization seem to consider that there are no such things as either long-period investment functions or long-period mark-up rates in pricing which can be maintained over the long run of time: investment behaviour and/or mark-up rates are subject to such changes in direction as to ensure the (given) normal degree of utilization. Those who argue for the opposite case, in contrast, accept the existence of such sustainable long-period investment functions and mark-up rates, and deduce that they are generally not compatible with the achievement of an exogenously targeted degree of utilization. The truth seems to be that both groups place themselves at opposite extremes: interaction between the planned degree of utilization and planned long-term investment behaviour seems a nearer approximation to reality; this means that the 'normal' degree of utilization, which is taken into account when long-term investment is planned, is in general endogenously determined. However, this degree of utilization, reflected in the methods of production in a long-period position, will be achieved through changes in long-period prices as well as in quantities. It is noted, in addition, that the group which denies the fulfilment of the given normal degree of utilization envisages the long period as a steady state, whilst the opposite group has a non-steady state in mind, more in line with the classical concept of the long-period position which seems capable of accommodating the endogenous determination of the normal degree of utilization.

MAN-SEOP PARK

References

Bliss, C. (1975), *Capital Theory and the Distribution of Income*, Amsterdam: North Holland.
Eatwell, J. and Milgate, M. (eds) (1983), *Keynes's Economics and the Theory of Value and Distribution*, London: Duckworth.

Garegnani, P. (1976), 'On a Change in the Notion of Equilibrium in Recent Work on Value and Distribution: A Comment on Samuelson' in M. Brown, K. Sato and P. Zarembka (eds), *Essays in Modern Capital Theory*, Amsterdam: North Holland (reprinted in Eatwell and Milgate, 1983).
Kregel, J. (1976), 'Economic Methodology in the Face of Uncertainty', *Economic Journal*, **86**, June, 209–25.
Marshall, A. (1920) [1961], *Principles of Economics*, London: Macmillan, eighth edition.
Sraffa, P. (1960), *Production of Commodities by Means of Commodities*, Cambridge: Cambridge University Press.

Long waves

Long 'waves' or 'cycles' are usually defined as regular variations in economic growth and price movements longer than the short business cycle. Their existence has been acknowledged for a long time. As early as 1847, Hyde Clarke referred to a 54-year cycle linked to astronomical and meteorological variations. In *Capital* Marx spoke of 'fluctuations extending over very long periods' and implicitly related them to investment in buildings, roads and other fixed capital with a low turnover period. The concept of long waves only became more firmly established in the literature through the works of N.D. Kondratieff in the 1920s. His 1925 study – the best known in the English-speaking world – was the first to amass substantial empirical evidence on the long-wave hypothesis. Kondratieff's test for the existence of long waves consisted of fitting ordinary least squares trends to a number of output and price series and then taking a nine-year moving average of the deviations from trend. Based on these filtered deviations, Kondratieff claimed that the world capitalist economy displayed long cycles with the following periodization:

1st long wave:	upswing	1780 – 1810/17
	downswing	1810 – 1844/51
2nd long wave:	upswing	1844/51 – 1870/75
	downswing	1870/75 – 1890–96
3rd long wave:	upswing	1890/96 – 1914/20
	downswing	1914/20 – ?

Kondratieff's 1925 paper lacked an explanation for the long wave, being mainly concerned with describing the phenomenon. In this connection, five stylized facts were noted:

1. During the upswing phases, years of prosperity are numerous, whereas years of depression predominate during downswing phases;
2. The problems of agriculture are particularly severe during long-wave downswings;

3. Innovations (what he called inventions) cluster during downswing phases, with their large-scale application being observed during the next long upswing;
4. Gold production increases during the beginning of the long upswing, and the world market for goods is generally enlarged by the assimilation of new and (especially of) colonial countries;
5. Wars and revolutions occur during upswing phases.

All these five characteristics he saw as endogenous to the long-wave process rather than exogenous causal explanations for the long wave. Kondratieff's theory of the causes of long waves was developed later, in a paper read before the Economics Institute in Moscow in 1926. The basic causal mechanism was the replacement of capital goods with a long lifetime *à la* Marx. Discontinuities in reinvestment were explained by Tugan-Baranowsky's theory of free loanable capital. In this framework, the conditions needed for the upswing were as follows: a high propensity to save; a large supply of loan capital at low interest rates; the accumulation of loan capital at the disposal of powerful industrial and financial capitalists, and a low price level in order to induce saving. The downswing is triggered by the increase of interest rates and the resulting capital shortage.

Kondratieff's theory of long waves is clearly defective in a number of ways. His view of a strict separability between the trend and the 40 to 60 year cycle implies the assumption of an unchanged equilibrium structure for the world capitalist economy during 1780–1920. His theory of the cycle leaves unexplained the lower turning point and fails to consider credit expansion as an alternative to savings. His view of long waves as an internationally synchronized phenomenon is also problematic; the existence of relative backwardness in the world economy has important implications for the long-wave generating mechanism. Through international capital movements, funds can move to higher growth peripheral regions during downswings in the leading economies and vice-versa. In this sense, Kondratieff's assumption of a closed capitalist system is not valid for the period he analysed.

A more refined and influential theory of long waves was developed by Schumpeter (1939). The main driving force behind the Schumpeterian long wave is investment in 'major' innovations (e.g. cotton textiles and iron during c. 1790–1815; railways, steam and steel during c. 1845–73; electricity and industrial chemistry over c. 1895–1913). The cycle starts from a position of equilibrium with full employment, when a group of entrepreneurs borrow to invest in basic innovations. This bids resources and factors away from old activities through rising prices. The long gestation lags of new investment imply that output remains constant during this process. Meanwhile the demand for more producer goods to introduce innovations leads to structural change, increasing the weight of the producer goods sector. This characterizes the 'prosperity' phase of the cycle. As the new investment gets into operation, the innovative entrepreneur reaps extra profits, thus inducing a number of 'imitators' to enter the market. This leads to a diffusion of innovations and rapid output growth, so that the price level starts to fall. Deflation, combined with greater uncertainty, hampers the introduction of innovations and sets off the 'recession' phase of the cycle. Whether the economy will return to its equilibrium or descend further into depression depends on what happens during the prosperity phase. In his 'first approximation' scheme, Schumpeter assumes that only new firms take part in the innovation wave. In this case, over-investment does not take place. Once the recession is over the economy is back to a new equilibrium position, where the level of money income is the same as that of the previous equilibrium, but the level of output and of capital stock is higher. Hence, the cycle evolves along an upward trend.

In his more realistic 'second approximation', Schumpeter assumes that old firms also participate in the innovation wave. Excessive optimism accompanying the innovation process leads to over-investment and speculation. As a result, the economy does not return to its equilibrium position after the recession but descends further into depression. Abnormal liquidation of less efficient firms and the faster decline of money wages and interest during the depression nudge the economy back to a new equilibrium. Hence the four-phase long cycle of prosperity, recession, depression and recovery.

By jointly explaining the trend and the cycle, the emergence of new industries and structural changes between the producer and consumer goods sectors, Schumpeter's model constitutes a major advance over previous long-wave theories. Nonetheless, two crucial questions are left unanswered: first, it is not clear why major innovations should cluster every 50 years or so; secondly, long gestation lags and an inverse price-output relationship of about 25 years or so have not been observed by economic historians.

These issues are central to the long-wave debate which has emerged since the mid-1970s. As the debate now stands, there are serious empirical objections to the existence of the 40–60 year long waves. First, the methodology employed by Kondratieff and many other long-wave analysts is flawed: the use of least squares deterministic trends and moving averages tends to generate artefact long cycles. Secondly, there is no sound theoretical reason to expect a regular bunching of major innovations either during the depression or in the upswing phase of the cycle. Statistical analyses of the distribution of major innovations over the last hundred years or so rejects Schumpeter's swarming hypothesis (Solomou, 1987). Finally, both Kondratieff and Schumpeter concentrated their analysis on price trends. The relationship between price and output trends is by no means straightforward. As such, their case for long waves as a *real* phenomenon is weak. Evidence for the 'core' of the world economy (UK, US, France and Germany) based on a more sound statistical methodology and more extensive production data has rejected the existence of 40–60 year cycles (Solomou, 1987). Recent research on 'peripheral' economies has also reached similar conclusions (Catão, 1991).

This does not imply that economic growth has been steady in the long run. Wave-like fluctuations longer than the short business cycle have been observed for a number of economic variables during specific historical epochs. For instance, world prices and trade displayed a wave-like pattern from 1873 to 1933. Strong evidence also exists of 15–20 year swings in output, investment, money stock, terms-of-trade and migration during 1870–1913. These so-called 'Kuznets' or 'long' swings have been observed for a number of 'core' and 'peripheral' economies and were caused by a complex interaction of labour migration, terms-of-trade, monetary shocks and weather variables upon an historically specific economic structure (Kuznets, 1930; Abramovitz, 1968; Solomou, 1987; Catão, 1991).

To sum up, long-wave analysts such as Kondratieff, Schumpeter and their followers have rightly pointed out the existence of dramatic long-term fluctuations in economic growth which are associated with discontinuities in long-term fixed investment and major innovations. Yet the empirical evidence they have provided in support of the 40–60 year cycle is weak. Moreover, their view of long waves as stemming from a single cyclical mechanism operating throughout the history of capitalism is not valid. Causation processes behind economic fluctuations usually result from the complex interaction of a number of variables – the depreciation of basic fixed capital and technological innovations being just two. As recent research on economic history has shown, autonomous monetary shocks, population movements, weather changes and relative backwardness across countries are also important in explaining long-term economic fluctuations. Monocausal mechanistic views are unlikely to help us understand the historical path of modern economies.

L.A.V. Catão and S.N. Solomou

References

Abramovitz, M. (1968), 'The Passing of the Kuznets Cycle', *Economica*, **XXXV**, 349–67.

Catão, L.A.V. (1991), 'The Transmission of Long Cycles between "Core" and "Periphery" Economies: A Case Study of Brazil and Mexico, c. 1870–1940', Ph.D. dissertation, University of Cambridge.

Kondratieff, N.D. (1979) [1925], 'The Major Economic Cycles', in translation; *Review*, **II** (4), 519–62.

Kuznets, S.S. (1930), *Secular Movements in Production and Prices: Their Nature and Bearing upon Cyclical Fluctuations*, Cambridge, MA: Harvard University Press.

Schumpeter, J.A. (1939), *Business Cycles: A Theoretical, Historical and Statistical Analysis of the Capitalist Process*, Vols I and II, New York: McGraw-Hill.

Solomou, S.N. (1987), *Phases of Economic Growth 1850–1973: Kondratieff Waves and Kuznets Swings*, Cambridge: Cambridge University Press.

Markets

The term 'market' is so widely used in popular and academic discussions of economic phenomena that it has come to embody a multifarious set of concepts. It is often used abstractly, as when leaders of the former Soviet Union speak about a transition to a market economy. In this case the adjective 'market' merely indicates the kind of relations between enterprises that are characteristic of advanced capitalist economies.

By contrast, a second sense in which the term 'market' is used is quite literal, as in the case of a mediaeval fair. The imagery contained in the latter usage has been quite influential, as may be seen in the work of Walras and in contemporary orthodoxy. A deleterious effect of this imagery is to be found in the notion of an invariant 'law of supply and demand': the farmer supplying food to 'the market' on a given day will receive a higher price if demand is strong than if it is weak. In a world of continuous production, however, strong demand may manifest itself by depleting inventories; when volume effects are present, the result may well be lower, rather than higher prices.

A further pernicious effect of this imagery may be seen by contrasting it with a third usage of the term 'market'. The question, 'Is there a market for this good?', asks whether there is sufficient consumer demand in a given sector to sustain viable profitability. From the marketing manager's perspective, the imagery of the mediaeval fair in which the market for the good is already 'there' is irrelevant. It may be precisely the manager's task to *create* a market for this product by, for instance, persuading or manipulating a catchment of potential consumers or by creating products which appeal to a need which these consumers may not even be aware *exists*.

The presumption that markets invariably and always exist is a commonplace of orthodoxy:

> the operation of the market costs something and by forming an organisation and allowing some authority (an 'entrepreneur') to direct the resources, certain marketing costs are saved. The entrepreneur has to carry out his function at less cost, taking into account the fact that he may get factors of production at a lower price than the market transactions which he superseded, *because it is always possible to revert to the open market if he fails to do this* (Coase, 1937; emphasis added).

But, as will be seen below, it is a myth to presume the invariant existence of a market to which 'it is always possible to revert'. Historically, the evolution and development of markets – of their extent and their depth – have been contingent on the actions pursued by traders and other economic participants. The presumption from orthodox theory of the ubiquitous existence of 'things' with well-defined boundaries called markets is unfounded. Markets are in fact not *things* but behavioural relations between economic actors.

This leads us to the fourth sense in which the term 'market' is used in economics: a market for a product is said to exist when the conditions sufficient to sustain (perfect) competition are present; that is to say, when products are interchangeable as commodities (or are at least roughly commensurate) and therefore compete on the basis of price. Governments in capitalist economies often have an important role to play in the development of markets in this sense by promoting product standardization. Periodically, with the emergence of new technologies, difficulties arise in capitalism which block the inherent tendency to commodify production. In the 1890s in the US, for instance,

> the market was flooded with competing types of electrical apparatus and chemical products peddled by the new companies, in addition to the plethora of machined goods and machinery itself. Since each company was concerned above all with promoting its own products, and devised unique means of evaluating their quality and performance, *comparison between competing products was difficult.* And since each manufacturer used its own specially machined parts, *replacement by those of another was virtually impossible* (Noble, 1979, pp. 69–70; emphasis added).

In the 1920s, it was administrative action by the Department of Commerce (under the future president Herbert Hoover) and by trade associations which imposed uniformity of standards and specifications on machine tools and electrical equipment. It was this planned and coordinated activity – sometimes by firms working through trade associations and sometimes through the mediation of government – which created the prerequisites for market competition between firms producing commensurate commodities with uniform specifications. Thus administered, planned action by central authorities made possible the development of markets and the commodification of these products. For any individual firm, the heterogeneity of performance specifications stood as an obstacle to expansion and development plans and thus to profitability, but only a central administrative body could plan and coordinate the conflicting interests of enterprises.

Thus, the richness and extent of markets are contingent on the kinds of planning decisions made by central administrative agencies and by individual firms. In orthodoxy, as we have seen, the presumption exists that the conditions for sustaining markets of all kinds are readily available in the absence of interference by government. But, in fact, there may be an important role for governments and other administrative organizations to play in the promotion of markets which otherwise might not readily exist: aspirins and milk have the possibility of becoming commodities when governmental specifications are set and the public is informed that all such products are functionally identical; even aspiring monopolists may be unwittingly instrumental in the development of markets, as for example when IBM standardized the PC in order to realize the potential economies from the creation of a fully-fledged market for the good.

The fifth sense in which the term 'market' is used is to designate the domain of competition for a product delineated geographically and qualitatively (i.e. by whether the product can be separated from others of a similar kind). Once again the mediaeval imagery of Walrasian economics is deceptive: there is often casual talk about the market 'or' the industry for a given product. But in the real world of continuous time, there is no necessary reason why the 'market' for a particular good, as delineated by actual and potential substitution on the part of consumers, should correspond geographically and qualitatively with the 'industry' for that particular good, in which actual and potential suppliers must be delineated.

This fifth usage of the term 'market' is of the greatest significance for the economic theory of competition. But it is notorious that objective and consistent criteria to delineate markets for the purpose of cross-sectional comparisons do not exist. This is a critical weakness in the orthodox theory of competition. The central methodology emerging from orthodox theory for comparing two competitive situations (i.e. two 'industries') is to compute an index of market concentration (for instance a Herfindahl index) for each of them and to declare the industry with the higher index to be less competitive. But if objective and consistent criteria for market delineation do not exist even in principle, the resulting indices have little meaning. This makes a mockery of the orthodox claim to exceptional precision compared with alternative approaches to the analysis of competitive processes. It is as if the relative population densities of cities were to be calculated in the absence of any basis, even in principle, for delineating the boundaries of 'a city'. Empirical work using the relative population densities of different cities would ultimately have to rely on officially given delineations of city boundaries; in applied work in industrial economics, the most commonly used measure of industrial boundaries is based on data from the Standard Industrial Classification of the census. Measures of market extent derived from this source have no more theoretical justification than do the boundaries of a town set by the City Fathers.

There are many reasons why it is difficult, if not impossible, to establish a principled criterion for the delineation of the market. However, the most significant reason for this failure is that the boundaries of a market cannot be specified independently of the behaviour of the participants in that market, as is demanded by the structure-performance model of orthodox theory (Steiner, 1968, Auerbach, 1989, Ch. 3). The boundaries of a market – qualitative, spacial and temporal – are inherently linked to the behaviour of the participants involved in that market: in the steel industry, it is largely a result of the long-range planning by Japanese producers and the competitive response of others that what was once a series of nationally insulated oligopolies has become a unified world industry. To have attempted to predict the behaviour of steel producers in the 1960s and 1970s in the context of constraints imposed by existing 'market structures' would have been fruitless, since it was the behaviour of the producers themselves which reshaped these very market structures. In sectors experiencing even more rapid change, such as electronics, attempts to predict behaviour on the basis of exogenously specified market constraints become even more pointless. At present even the most sophisticated orthodox approaches to competitive processes offer little else than the analysis of optimal strategies in the context of an exogenously specified environment. In a current and extremely influential book we may read, 'For the purposes of the present book, the *empirical* difficulty of defining a market will be ignored. It will be assumed that the market is well defined' (Tirole, 1988, Introduction; emphasis added). Small wonder, then, that orthodoxy has so little to offer in public policy considerations of industrial questions.

Thus, orthodox approaches to the question of the market make two key related presumptions. The first is that markets are naturally ubiquitous, and that only specific instances of 'market failure' can justify their non-existence in cases where they are otherwise desired or desirable. Secondly, their extent and depth – the 'structure' – of this market can be described independently of the actual behaviour of the participants, so that competitive behaviour can be predicted on the basis of structural characteristics. The inappropriateness of these notions is an important aspect of the failure of the orthodox theory of competition.

PAUL AUERBACH

References

Auerbach, P. (1989), *Competition*, Oxford: Basil Blackwell.
Coase, R. (1937), 'The Nature of the Firm', *Economica*, New Series, **IV**, 386–405.
Noble, D. (1979), *America by Design*, Oxford: Oxford University Press.
Steiner, P. (1968), 'Markets and Industries', entry in the *International Encyclopedia of the Social Sciences*, New York: Macmillan.
Tirole, J. (1988), *Theory of Industrial Organization*, Cambridge, MA: MIT Press.

Methodology in Economics

Traditionally within philosophical discourse the term methodology has denoted the study of method, an activity concerned with the procedures and aims of a particular discipline, along with an enquiry into the manner in which the discipline is organized. In economics, especially in recent years, the term methodology has been employed both in a narrower and in a broader sense than this. The narrow usage, prevalent especially amongst econometricians and other 'modellers', but which will not be considered further here, is merely a heading given to a brief statement of techniques applied in specific analyses. The second, broader, interpretation adopted by most contributors to explicitly methodological texts is essentially *philosophy of science* as applied, or as of concern, to economic issues (see, for example, Caldwell, 1982). This interpretation is wider than the study of method *per se* in that, among other things, it allows explicit attention to and elaboration of ontological issues – a questioning of the nature of being, of the object of analysis – an activity that is presupposed by, but which cannot be reduced to, the study of methods and procedures.

Now why should economists bother with methodology so conceived? This is the question that is often asked. Essentially the task of methodology or philosophy of science is, in the manner of Locke, to act as an under-labourer for science. It cannot licence any particular substantive theory, but serves instead as a ground-clearing device. Within economics, methodology is concerned, for example, with critically assessing self-interpretations and claims to scientificity made by economists of whatever hue. The aim is to facilitate a set of perspectives on the nature of the economy and society and how to understand them. However, although methodological reasoning cannot support any particular substantive claim, and always remembering that methodological analysis is as corrigible as any other, the current state of malaise in economics is such that extensive ground-clearing through explicit, sustained and informed methodological analysis and debate may be just what the subject most needs.

What, then, are the main perspectives so far provided or supported via methodological reasoning in economics, and their strengths and limitations? And what, currently, is the orientation that is most sustainable? More specifically, what are the traditionally prominent conceptions of social science found within economics and how, if at all, can recent methodological insights improve upon the perspectives they entail?

With some stretching, economic methodology (i.e. philosophical discussion of all issues bearing upon the actual or ideal nature of economic analysis) has, over the last 50 years or so, been dominated, at least until quite recently, by two broad traditions. The first, a naturalistic tradition, which has been by far the more dominant of the two, has viewed science, actually or ideally, as an activity grounded in positivist principles based ultimately on the Humean notion of laws and causality. This tradition (see Bhaskar, 1979) is rooted in the Humean dismissal of the possibility of any account of being or of ontology, and specifically in a denial that it is possible, rationally, to hold to an account of the independent existence of things or the operation of natural necessity. Instead, all we have is sense-experience or impression.

Now, contra Hume, any theory of knowledge, including positivism, presupposes some ontology, some account of being. For it must be assumed, even if only implicitly, that the world is such that it could be the object of knowledge of the required or specified sort. The Humean theory, in fact, presupposes an ontology of experiences constituting atomistic events. And if particular knowledge is of events sensed in experience, any conception of general (including scientific) knowledge must be of constant patterns that such events reveal in space and over time. It is these constant conjunctions of events, of course, that constitute the Humean account of causal laws.

The positivist or Humean theory of knowledge, then, presupposes an ontology of atomistic events and their constant conjunctions. But equally any theory of knowledge presupposes (in addition to an ontology) a social theory, an account of human agency and institutions. For clearly these must be of a form that enables knowledge of the specified type to be produced. Thus, if again implicitly, the Humean theory entails a conception of human agents as the passive sensors of given events and recorders of their constant conjuctions.

Further still, any theory of knowledge also presupposes (in addition to an ontology and a social theory) some philosophical method, some account of how its characteristic results are obtained. In positivism, because events are given in experience, they are taken to constitute all that is real, while experience, because in effect constituative of the world, is in consequence held to be certain. Science, then, is viewed as monistic, the accumulation of incorrigible facts. In addition, the implicit ontology of atomistic events, and specifically their constant conjunctions, entail that scientific method is deductive in structure.

Now while it is doubtful that many economists accept the sort of analysis upon which these Humean or positivist results rest, it is clear that the results themselves have been accepted in economics quite pervasively (if usually selectively). Thus economic science is interpretated almost universally as the search for constant conjunctions of events. Econometrics (at least as interpreted by most econometricians) provides an obvious case in point, but the Humean scientific image can, I think, be seen to underpin most orthodox substantive positions (amongst others). Even orthodox 'pure theory', to the extent that it constitutes substantive economics at all, is rooted in this tradition. Although the emphasis here is not always on the empirical, the deductivism upon which it rests presupposes, as noted, the ubiquity of constant event conjuctions, while any lack of immediate empirical content is sustained, when it is, only on a promissory note. In similar fashion, orthodox economic theory posits agents as passive sensors of events ('signals'), a conception allowing that knowledge can always be analysed in a purely individualistic way. In its turn, of course, philosophical discussion in contemporary mainstream economics reduces almost entirely to the questioning of the relative advantages of methods of induction versus deduction in the process of elaborating (revealing, estimating, testing, constructing, etc.) the sought-after constant event conjuctions. Notice too that since all knowledge is sensed, the cognitive claims of theory, meta-theory, metaphysics, morality and politics etc. can be summarily rejected. In short, positivism, whether or not explicitly acknowledged, functions as an ideology for economics, encouraging, by injunction or by resonance, various conceptions of the nature of science, nature, society, economy, persons and their interconnections.

Now, although this naturalist tradition rooted in Humean analysis has dominated methodological discussion and prescription in economics over the past 50 years or so, it has not been exclusive. Some prominence has also been attained by other traditions, most notably by a broadly anti-naturalist position which can be referred to as subjectivist or hermeneuticist. The latter, in contrast to the more dominant naturalist approach, has asserted a radical distinction between the natural and social sciences stemming from identified distinctions in their subject matters. The lineage of this tradition is traceable back through Hayek, Weber and Dilthey to the transcendental idealism of Kant, and is most prominent amongst certain modern Austrians and Shakelians.

The starting point of the hermeneutic or subjectivist tradition is an emphasis upon the conceptual nature of social phenomena coupled with an insistence upon taking seriously the fact of human agency, including choice. Its aim, as noted, has been a distinct anti-naturalistic science of economics. However, its presupposition that the natural sphere is subject to laws conforming to the Humean specification – its acceptance of the Humean conception of science – coupled with a recognition that such laws, if operative in the social sphere, would leave no space for human agency, have in consequence often encouraged a total voluntarism along with an impoverished role for social science. An example is provided by a collection of influential contributions of Hayek (1942–44), who perhaps has been the most prominent subjectivist writer on economic methodology in modern times. In Hayek's (1942–44) writing the recognition that society is concept-dependent encourages the conclusion that it is concept-determined, that society is exhausted by its conceptional component (see Lawson, 1994). The latter conclusion in turn gives rise to a conception of social science as involving little more than *Verstehen*, or the grasping of how lay-agents themselves grasp their own existence. The upshot is that, in attempting to escape positivist naturalism in social science, Hayek, in parallel with the positivist reduction of physical reality to experience, succeeds merely in reducing society, including the economy, to self-interpretation. Social science in turn is reduced to grasping or understanding but without the possibility of explanation or criticism.

Much of the history of the philosophy of economics, then, can be viewed as a kind of to-ing and fro-ing between these basic conceptions – though with the positivist tradition usually the more dominant. However, recent developments in the philosophy of social science, systematized under the heading of *critical realism* (see Bhaskar, 1979; Lawson, 1989a, 1989b), provide an alternative conception of economics as science – identifying problems with *both* the positivist and hermeneutic positions and providing a means for their transcendence.

According to critical realism, the positivist tradition is correct to view all science (including economics) as unified in its essential method, while the hermeneutic tradition is correct to view science as differentiated in ways governed by, or specific to, its object. But just as critical realist and positivist conceptions of the shared essential method of science are drastically opposed, so significant differences between critical realist and hermeneuticist conceptions are evident.

In viewing science as unified in its essential method, critical realism rejects the Humean view (shared by the positivist and Hermeneutic traditions alike) that natural science is concerned with seeking out, or with testing claims formulated as, constant conjunctions of events. According to critical realism the world – both natural and social – is, among other things, structured and open. It is structured in the sense that underlying manifest phenomena at any one level are irreducible structures, powers, necessary relations, mechanisms and tendencies etc. which govern them. It is open in the sense that manifest phenomena are typically governed by various countervailing mechanisms simultaneously, so that the deeper structures can rarely be directly 'read off'.

According to critical realist analysis, then, science is unified in its essential movement from manifest phenomena, at any one level, to the deeper structures and relations that govern them. Note that the essential mode of inference supported or required here is neither induction (particular to general) nor deduction (general to particular), but *retroduction* or *abduction* (manifest phenomenon, at any one level, to 'deeper' conditioning structure). For example, this essential movement of science is captured not by starting from, say, the observation of a few black ravens and inferring that all ravens must be black (induction), nor by starting with the claim that all ravens are black and deducing that the next one to be observed must be black (deduction), but by starting with the observation of one or more black ravens and identifying a causal mechanism intrinsic to ravens which disposes them to being black.

Now from this critical realist perspective, positivism can be seen to rest upon the illicit generalization and inadequate analysis of a special case – of the closed system. This is a situation in which a non-empirical stable mechanism is physically isolated and thereby empirically identified. Typically this case only arises in situations of experimental control (see Bhaskar, 1979; Lawson, 1989a, 1989b). Critical realism of course can accommodate and, unlike positivism itself, explain this case too. But it is a case that is far from being essential to science or even generally available within the natural realm. And it appears to be without any non-trivial or significant application whatsoever in the social sphere. Consequently the whole positivist project is found, through realist argument, to be largely beside the point for economic analysis.

If critical realists, as against hermeneuticists, conceive of science as unified in its essential method, they share with the hermeneutic tradition the understanding that economics, unlike natural science, deals with a pre-interpreted reality, a world already conceptualized by lay-agents in their activities. And like that tradition, they acknowledge the epistemological consequences of this. But while accepting that social material is concept-dependent, critical realists part company with the hermeneuticist/subjectivist tradition in insisting that social material is not exhausted by its conceptual component. Moreover critical realists also recognize that social reality exists intransitively, being both social and yet inadequately conceptualized by lay-agents – and thus prone to rational conceptual critique. Critical realism, then, views economics as potentially revelatory, just like any other science, being concerned to identify the unacknowledged (in part material) conditions, tacit skills, and unconscious motivations that are necessary for some activity to take place, as well as the unintended consequences of such activity. And being potentially revelatory, it also lays the basis for emancipatory development – rather than the mere amelioration of states of affairs.

To sum up, the task of methodology in economics is essentially to act as an under-labourer for economic science, being concerned to sweep away existing debris through elucidating a set of perspectives on the nature of the social world and on how to understand it. In this sense methodology, or philosophy, or meta-theory – wherein critical realism appears currently to be the most sustainable position – can certainly make a difference to the conduct of economic science, always remembering, of course, that it constitutes at most a necessary (and never a sufficient) condition for enlightened change and development.

TONY LAWSON

References

Bhaskar, R. (1979), *The Possibility of Naturalism: A Philosophical Critique of the Contemporary Human Sciences*, Brighton: Harvester Press.

Caldwell, B. (1982), *Beyond Positivism, Economic Methodology in the 20th Century*, London: Allen & Unwin.

Hayek, F.A. (1942–44), 'Scientism and the Study of Society', *Economica* (various issues). Reprinted in *The Counter Revolution of Science*, Indianapolis: Liberty Press, 1979.

Lawson, T. (1989a), 'Abstraction, Tendencies and Stylised Facts: A Realist Approach to Economic Analysis', *Cambridge Journal of Economics*, **13** (1), March, 59–78. Reprinted in T.

Lawson, G. Palma and J. Sender (eds) (1989), *Kaldor's Political Economy*, London and San Diego: Academic Press.
Lawson, T. (1989b), 'Realism and Instrumentalism in the Development of Econometrics', *Oxford Economic Papers*, **41** (1), 236–58. Reprinted in N. De Marchi and C. Gilbert (eds) (1990), *The History and Methodology of Econometrics*, Oxford: Oxford University Press.
Lawson, T. (1994), 'Realism and Hayek: A Case of Continuing Transformation' in M. Colonna, H. Hagemann and O. Hamouda (eds), *Capitalism, Socialism and Knowledge: The Economics of F.A. von Hayek*, Aldershot: Edward Elgar.

Modes of production

The concept of the *mode of production* is one of the basic – if not *the* basic – concept of Marx's historical materialism. It occurs in most, if not all, of the major works of the 1840s in which Marx and Engels gradually worked their way towards the materialist conception of history. It also occurs in various purely polemical newspaper articles of the 1848–50 period, testifying to the political, rather than purely theoretical, significance that Marx attached to it. But the most complete, the classic, formulation of the concept occurs in Marx's brief, compact statement of the theory of historical materialism, in the famous three-page 1859 'Preface' to the *Contribution to the Critique of Political Economy*. For capturing the genuine flavour of the concept, no substitute to reading the actual text of the 'Preface' exists.

In modern terminology, 'economic system' is perhaps the term which comes closest to Marx's 'mode of production'. He envisaged the history of human society as an evolutionary process, consisting of a discontinuous sequence of increasingly productive stages of economic growth. To each stage, a specific mode of production, a different economic system, corresponded whose character was determined by the level of productive potential attained at the given epoch. 'The hand-mill gives you society with the feudal lord; the steam-mill society with the industrial capitalist', as the oversimplified but strikingly effective formulation in *The Poverty of Philosophy* (1847) put it.

This evolutionary process tended to the achievement of conditions of material affluence sufficient for making possible the establishment of a non-exploitative, classless society. In the 'Preface', Marx identified five specific modes of production, four of them belonging to the past or present and being exploitative in character, and one – socialism – predicted to emerge in the non-too-distant future and mark an end to the open or disguised enslavement of labour:

> In broad outlines Asiatic, ancient, feudal, and modern bourgeois modes of production can be designated as progressive epochs in the economic formation of society. The bourgeois relations of production are the last antagonistic form of the

> social process of production – antagonistic not in the sense of individual antagonism, but of one arising from the social conditions of life of the individuals; at the same time the productive forces developing in the womb of bourgeois society create the material conditions for the solution of that antagonism. This social formation brings, therefore, the prehistory of human society to a close.

These various modes of production each with a different level of productivity, Marx distinguished by, 'the direct relationship of the owners of the conditions of production to the direct producers' (*Capital*, Vol. III, Ch. XLVII). On this basis, slavery was the central socioeconomic institution of antiquity, serfdom of feudalism and wage labour of capitalism, while the Asiatic mode was described as a peculiar hybrid of village communities resting on communal ownership of land and an overarching absolutist state that dominated and exploited them.

In addition to such historically specific analysis, Marx attempted in the 'Preface' to sketch out a general theory of modes of production, attributing to each of them a common mechanism of rise and decline. To this effect, he constructed the general concept of the mode in a dialectical fashion, as a unity of two polar or antagonistic opposites: the *forces of production* and the *relations of production*. Forces of production included natural resources, the accumulated material means of production, technology, labour and, in modern jargon, 'human capital'. Relations of production referred to the division and allocation of functions in society with respect to productive activity. In exploitative societies they were relations of class domination: in non-exploitative ones they were based on cooperation among individuals. In all cases they were expressed through the prevailing system of legal ownership of productive assets.

The antagonism between forces and relations of production arose from the fact that their correspondence, which lay at the foundation of each mode of production, was never perfect or unconditional. The historical career of each mode was divided into two phases. In the first phase the relations of production acted as a stimulus, encouraging the growth of the forces of production. In the second, these very same production relations turned into obstacles to the further development of production forces.

> At a certain stage of their development, the material productive forces of society come into conflict with the existing relations of production, or – what is but a legal expression of the same thing – with the property relations within which they have been at work hitherto. From forms of development of the productive forces these relations turn into their fetters. Then begins an epoch of social revolution.

The development of antagonism between forces and relations of production can be explained on the grounds that forces are seen as inherently dynamic while relations, on which the vested interests of the ruling class are based, are by nature static within each economic system. This is because ruling classes defend them irrespective of the harm they may be causing to society as a whole. (Relations are, of course, subject to change in periods of transition, but it takes a revolution to replace them.) In this interpretation, the role of the forces of production in economic development would always be progressive, while that of the relations of production would change from being progressive to regressive. Alternatively, a conservative aspect may be identified in the development of the forces of production themselves if they prove unresponsive to the stimulus from a new system of relations of production, and thus slow down the pace of economic and social progress. In either case, it is the interplay between forces and relations of production that generates movement in each specific mode of production, leading eventually to its replacement by a superior mode, better adapted to new productive conditions in a manner vaguely reminiscent of Darwinian evolution. This dynamic character which Marx has imparted to the mode of production concept is an essential part of its definition.

The mode of production – 'of material life' as Marx often stressed – was used by him intensively to shift the focus of the debate on social structure and change from the ideological sphere to that of material interests, from politics, law and religion to the economy – without, however, losing sight of the crucial importance of the ideological element in all social and political strife. In his effort to be consistent with the materialist interpretation of history without ignoring the importance of ideology, he was led to formulate his famous base-superstructure doctrine:

> The sum total of these relations of production constitutes the economic base of society, the real foundation, on which rises a legal and political superstructure and to which correspond definite forms of social consciousness. The mode of production of material life conditions the social, political and intellectual life process in general. It is not the consciousness of men that determines their being, but, on the contrary, their social being that determines their consciousness. ('Preface', p. 503–4).

Some definite type of causality, described recently by Cohen (1978) as 'functional causality', is associated with the concept of the mode of production. It runs from the forces to the relations of production, and from those to the ideological superstructure and to human consciousness. It is not unidirectional; the importance of feedback effects from the relations of production to the development of production forces, and from the superstructure to the base, is certainly acknowledged. This occurs in the 'Preface' itself with regard to relations, and by Engels in his oft-quoted 1890 letter to Joseph Bloch with regard to the superstructure.

The concept of the mode of production has enjoyed a very active political life. In the necessity of replacing a lower by a higher type of production relations, Marxist political parties have sought to justify their revolutionary socialist aspirations. Communist orthodoxy, however, did not always benefit from the related analysis. In an unwitting tribute to the liberating potency of the 'Preface', Stalin purged Marx's text by excising from Soviet editions published under his regime any reference to the Asiatic mode of production, presumably in order to discourage the drawing of dire analogies between that and his own brand of collectivist tyranny. The mode of production analysis has also been attacked as 'mechanistic' or 'economistic' by a section of the Marxist left. They perceived in it a kind of economic determinism incompatible with the exercise of the revolutionary class initiative implicit in the opening sentence of the Communist Manifesto: 'the history of all hitherto existing society is the history of class struggles'. This particular objection, whatever its merits, had been anticipated by Marx when he wrote: 'but class contradictions are based on economic foundations, on the existing mode of material production and the conditions of commerce resulting from it' (*Collected Works*, Vol. III, pp. 494–5).

Still in the political arena, it has been claimed that Marx's insistence in the 'Preface' that 'no social order ever perishes before all the productive forces for which there is room in it have developed; and new, higher relations of production never appear before the material conditions of their existence have matured in the womb of the old society itself' (p. 504) was falsified by the successful outcome of a socialist-oriented revolution in backward Russia of 1917. It has since been claimed that this insistence was vindicated by the failure, in the end, of the Soviet experiment.

In the scholarly field many philosophers, historians, sociologists and economists, not necessarily Marxist, have drawn inspiration in their research from the forces-relations, base-superstructure scheme. Its influence has been so pervasive as to make the quotation of specific examples difficult. But whole branches of economics, like the study of economic systems or individual contributions like Rostow's 'stages of economic growth', Gerschenkron's study of the interplay between economic backwardness and the degree of institutional centralization in industrial revolutions, or Galbraith's studies of what he called 'the new industrial state' provide examples of the, perhaps unconscious but undoubtedly fertile, diffusion of Marx's broad idea throughout the scholarly community.

In addition there has been a remarkable and explicit development of his line of research in the form of a quest in history for modes of production unknown to himself. Based on certain intuitions of Marx in the *Grundrisse* and on anthropological discoveries published after Marx's death, Engels proposed a regime of primitive tribal communism as being present at the very beginning of the sequence of modes of production given in the 'Preface'. Wittfogel (1957) has constructed the concept of 'oriental despotism' and of the 'hydraulic civilization' as variants of the Asiatic mode of production in his analysis of the great riverside societies of Ancient Egypt, India and China. Finally, modern economic development specialists, grappling with the problems of Third World societies, have proposed definitions of a colonial mode of production and a peasant mode of production in attempts to move away from the capitalism/socialism dichotomy they found too restrictive.

Critics have also been active. Popper has characterized the mode of production theory as impervious to the test of falsifiability and therefore as unscientific. A more common criticism has insisted on its excessively economic determinism and on the thesis of unilinear progress that the 'Preface' appears to impose on historical evolution. In response to some of these criticisms the French Althusserian Marxist philosopher, Etienne Balibar, has attempted a thorough-going reformulation of the relevant concepts. To the charge of excessive economic determinism he responded by arguing that the economy dominated society, not only directly, but also by determining which level (e.g. religious, political) was dominant at each historical epoch. Economic determinism (or reductionism) may be diluted this way, but only at the cost of laying historical materialism wide open to Popper's strictures of lack of falsifiability. Balibar (1920) is on stronger ground with his construct of the 'socioeconomic formation', a mixed regime containing elements of an old declining and a new rising mode of production. This is actually what we observe in history, rather than the ideal forms listed in the 'Preface'. The mixture, however, is on each occasion dominated by one main institution, typical of only one of the modes that make up the mixed formation. In that sense the socioeconomic formation can be identified as a form of appearance of some specific, ideally defined mode of production (e.g. capitalism, socialism), thus averting the dissolution of the basic concept of the mode into an unsystematic proliferation of special cases.

Despite its shortcomings and the critical fire it has drawn, Marx's 'mode of production of material life' has been one of the few, really influential great ideas to emerge in social science over the last two centuries. It has offered a robust vehicle for the materialist interpretation of history which has fundamentally changed the way Marxists and non-Marxists alike today understand human society.

GEORGE CATEPHORES

References

Balibar, E. (1970), 'The Basic Concepts of Historical Materialism' in L. Althusser and E. Balibar (eds), *Reading Capital*, London: New Left Books.

Cohen, G.A. (1978), *Marx's Theory of History: A Defence*, Oxford: Oxford University Press.

Marx, K. (1847) [1976], 'The Poverty of Philosophy', in *Collected Works*, Vol. 6, London: Lawrence & Wishart.
Marx, K. (1859) [1971], 'Preface' to *A Contribution to the Critique of Political Economy*, London: Lawrence and Wishart.
Marx, K., *Collected Works*, Vol. I (1967), New York: International Publishers; Vol. II (1970), London: Lawrence & Wishart; Vol. III (1972), London: Lawrence and Wishart.
Marx, K. and Engels, F. (1969), *Selected Works*, Vol. I, Moscow: Progress Publishers.
Wittfogel, K.A. (1957), *Oriental Despotism: A Comparative Study of Total Power*, New Haven: Yale University Press.

Monetary circuits

Over the last 20 years, a theory of the monetary circuit has been developed, mostly in the French and Italian literatures (Graziani, 1989; Messori, 1985). By and large, the theory aims at emphasizing that the fundamental structural properties of economic equilibrium – such as income distribution, the rate of accumulation, the rate of growth – are determined, not by the preferences of single agents coupled with their initial endowments, but by decisions of those agents who enjoy command over money.

An immediate consequence is that the theory cannot consider the aggregate money stock or its initial distribution as given magnitudes. In fact, a vital point of the models of the monetary circuit is the careful reconstruction of the process of creation, circulation and final destruction of money, which is considered a strictly endogenous variable. As a further consequence, the agents of the model must include (along with households, firms and government) the banking system as a fundamental decision maker.

Long before the present-day theory of the monetary circuit was developed, a monetary macroeconomic theory had been elaborated by leading economists of the Swedish and German schools; they included Wicksell, Schumpeter, Mises and Hahn. All these authors had provided a rigorous analysis of the process of money creation and circulation, while Schumpeter more than any other had emphasized the vital role of decisions taken by bankers. The distinction between the above mentioned authors and present-day circuit theorists lies in the fact that what was considered by Wicksell and his followers (with the possible exception of Schumpeter) as a disequilibrium situation is now taken to be the regular working of the capitalist process. As for the theory of income distribution, present-day authors tend to follow the presentation given by J.M. Keynes in the *Treatise* (not in *The General Theory*), by M. Kalecki and by the early Post Keynesians, such as Joan Robinson, Nicholas Kaldor and Richard Kahn. Again, the distinction is that, in the Post Keynesian approach, investors are considered to be the agents who take the final decisions and, in contrast to what happens with circuit theorists, the role assigned to banks is a totally passive one.

The theory of the monetary circuit is now represented in France by two main groups. Of these, the so-called Dijon school (B. Schmitt and A. Cencini; see for example, Schmitt, 1975) tends to concentrate on theoretical problems; the Paris group (led by A. Parguez; see for example Parguez, 1985) is mostly concerned with policy problems.

Mainstream economics identifies the supply of the monetary base in a closed economy with a Government deficit not covered by public debt. Circuit theorists tend to adopt the opposite assumption and consider the money stock as entirely created by means of debt and credit operations taking place between the Central Bank, commercial banks and private agents. The basic model of the theory thus resembles very closely the Wicksellian pure credit economy.

The theory of the circuit considers a monetary economy as inconsistent with the presence of a commodity money. Any economy using a commodity as money is considered to be a barter economy. The usual belief about the historical origins of money evolving from a commodity money into a modern paper currency and into bank deposits is thus rejected. According to the theory, money is created by means of a triangular transaction involving the payer, the payee and a bank. Money comes into existence the very moment a payment is made. At that moment, in one and the same act, the borrower becomes a debtor and the agent receiving a payment becomes a creditor of the bank. Money is therefore credit money, even if no direct debt and credit relationship is created between the payer and the payee.

The so-called monetary circuit consists of three different phases, extending from the initial creation of money to its final destruction.

The first step is the decision taken by banks of granting credit to firms in order to enable them to start production. If we consider firms as a whole, their only external purchase is labour, which means that credit requirements are determined by the scale of production and by the money wage rate prevailing on the labour market. Negotiations between banks and firms determine the amount of credit actually granted and the rate of interest charged by banks. Circuit theory assumes credit to be created by banks (loans make deposits and not the other way round) and considers the banking system taken as a whole to be endowed with unlimited credit potential.

The second step is given by production and expenditure decisions. Firms enjoy total independence in making decisions concerning real aspects of production. Wage earners can only decide how to spend their money wages, how much to save, how to allocate savings between securities issued by firms and money balances. Money spent on the commodities market or on securities goes back to firms and is available for repaying debts to the banking system.

The third and final step, coinciding with the final destruction of money, is the repayment of debt. If households spend the whole of their wages (no matter whether on commodities or on securities), firms are able to repay their debt to the banks (abstracting from interest) and the circuit is closed without losses. If households decide to keep part of their savings in money balances, a portion of the money initially created remains in existence as a debt of firms and a credit of households to the banking sector (some authors prefer to say that money proper exists only in the fleeting moment a payment is being made, while money balances are wealth and not money). This shows that money is in the nature of credit money and that its existence coincides with a disequilibrium situation.

A basic tenet of circuit theory is that employment and real output (consumption and investment) are determined by independent decisions of producers. The decisions of households concerning consumption and saving can only determine the level of money prices. Circuit theorists thus follow the model of income distribution first outlined by Keynes in the *Treatise*, elaborated by Kalecki and later utilized by the Post Keynesian school.

Circuit theorists emphasize the fact that since producers have access to bank credit, they can also acquire whatever share of real output they have decided to buy. Therefore they subscribe totally to the Kaleckian principle that wage-earners spend what they earn and capitalists earn what they spend. Neither taxes nor government expenditure modifies this conclusion. Taxes, even if levied on profits, do not reduce the purchasing power of capitalists, which depends solely on bank credit. The consequence is that, even if taxes are levied, firms will still be able to buy the same amount of commodities as they would without paying taxes, so that real profits are not touched. On the other hand, if subsidies are paid to households, this will only increase the level of money prices without increasing real consumption, at least insofar as firms do not revise their own output plans.

If government expenditure takes the form of the direct purchase of commodities, crowding out will only occur at the expense of households whose real consumption will be reduced, whereas firms whose purchasing power is in principle unlimited will still be able to buy the same amount of real goods.

Finally, since the price level depends only on aggregate demand and not on the existing quantity of money, the inflationary impact of deficit spending will depend only on its amount and not on how it is financed, whether by debt or by money creation.

At the end of each period, firms must pay interest at the agreed rate on sums borrowed from the banks. Insofar as government expenditure is absent – so that the only money present in the market is that which firms themselves have injected by paying wages – what firms can get back by selling goods or by issuing securities can equal, at most, their initial expenditure. This means that, in the most favourable case, firms will be able to repay the principal of their debt, but money will never be available for the repayment of interest.

The problem of interest payments is solved if banks spend their interest earnings on commodities produced by firms (or on wages and salaries paid to their employees who spend their incomes on commodities), thus enabling firms to pay their interest debt. In substance what takes place is a sort of barter, with firms paying interest in kind. What share of real output firms will have to yield to banks depends on the interest rates charged by banks and on the level of prices charged by firms. High interest rates may induce firms to protect their real profits by charging higher prices, thus becoming a possible source of inflation.

The basic idea of the theory of the monetary circuit is that, in a monetary economy, the ownership of resources as such, be it in the form of material wealth or working ability, does not entitle the owner to a share of real income. Ownership of wealth only entitles one to a money income, the real content of which escapes any possible negotiation. Even financial wealth, while being a possible source for increasing consumption of single individuals at the expense of others, is not real wealth to households as a whole. Firms, in contrast, are able to acquire any quantity of real goods as a consequence of having access to bank credit, something which endows them with unlimited purchasing power. Banks and firms alone determine activity levels, the rate of accumulation and the rate of growth.

The analysis of money creation makes clear that money is initially created in order to cover current costs of production. The circuit approach thus helps to dispel a recurring mistake in the literature, according to which finance supplied by banks is confused with the financing of fixed investment. Of course investment needs to be financed in the sense that capital goods currently produced have to be sold to some agent wanting to keep them as real wealth. Investment finance can be supplied by household savings as well as by profits. In no case is it supplied by banks. The role of banks is to supply credit and to finance the formation of money balances, not of financing investment.

The principle of consumers' sovereignty (even in its milder form of consumers' preferences being relevant to the decisions of firms) is unknown to the theory of the circuit. Households can have an influence on the decisions of firms by acting at the social and political level, not as agents negotiating in the market. Equilibrium as defined in the theory of the circuit is not necessarily unique. It is in fact in the nature of circuit analysis to allow, within limits set only by social constraints, for a multiplicity of possible equilibria depending on the strategies of banks and firms.

AUGUSTO GRAZIANI

References

Graziani, A. (1989), 'The Theory of the Monetary Circuit', Thames Papers in Political Economy, Spring.

Messori, M. (1985), 'Le circuit de la monnaie: acquis et problèmes non résolus' in R. Arena and A. Graziani (eds), *Production, circulation et monnaie*, Paris: Presses Universitaires de France.

Parguez, A. (1985), 'La monnaie, les deficits et la crise', *Economies et Sociétés*, Series *Monnaie et production*, 2.

Poulon, F. (1982), *Macroéconomie approfondie*, Paris: Cujas.

Schmitt, B. (1975), *Théorie unitaire de la monnaie, nationale et internationale*, Albeuve, Switzerland: Castella.

Money and credit

There is wide agreement on the subject of money and credit among non-orthodox authors. What, in this context, will be called the Post Keynesian view of money is broadly endorsed by all followers of the various schools of radical political economy, be they Kaleckians, neo-Marxists, French circuitistes, Institutionalists and neo-Ricardians. Despite their apparent lack of interest in money matters, even neo-Ricardians have a vision of money which is similar to that of other non-orthodox monetary theorists (Pivetti, 1985). Historically, the views of Thomas Tooke and the Banking School, together with the non-orthodox monetary ideas of authors such as Marx, Wicksell, Schumpeter and Keynes, have constituted the common heritage of this Post Keynesian theory of money. Post Keynesians theorize about a monetary system which has been developed by bankers for centuries, one based on scriptural means of payment, but which has been neglected by the mainstream as a result of its obsession with commodity money.

Money and credit are closely intertwined in the post Keynesian approach. Indeed its authors often refer to the creation of credit-money. The works of Kaldor (1982) and Moore (1988) are most representative of the standard view of the post Keynesian theory of credit-money. The modern origins of this view must however be found in an article of Jacques Le Bourva (1959, pp. 717–25). In his paper Le Bourva outlines with precision all the main elements of a theory of endogenous credit-money which, compared to those of the neoclassical view, are as follows: (1) money enters the economic system through the activity of production rather than exchange; (2) money must mainly be understood as a flow, rather than as a stock; (3) the importance of money arises from the creation of new liabilities within the process of income expansion, rather than from its existence as an asset within a portfolio; (4) money is a social convention and the interest rate, rather than being market determined, is one of these conventions; and finally (5) money is fundamentally an endogenous variable which can be created and destroyed, as in the efflux and reflux principle of the Banking School, rather than an exogenously determined variable. The first two characteristics have been mainly developed by the exponents of the theory of the monetary circuit. The next two have been discussed in particular by followers of Minsky. Since these four characteristics are discussed in the entries on Monetary circuits, Financial instability and Liquidity, the focus of the present analysis will be on the endogeneity of the money creation process.

Causality is an important feature of non-orthodox economics. The causal chain within a monetary production economy can be specified in the following fashion. Firms make production plans according to their expectations. They demand advances from the banking system to implement these production plans. The demand for loans generates the creation of a flow of money identical to the flow of income. The expenditure and portfolio decisions of households lead to the emergence of residual stocks of credit and of money. The central bank provides the required base money corresponding to the outstanding money stock, at the price of its choice. The supply of money is endogenous, in the sense that it is determined by its demand – conditional on output, prices, interest rate levels, and the bankers' opinion of the creditworthiness of borrowers.

This endogeneity can be seen at three levels. First, there is endogeneity at the juncture between the firm and the private bank. When firms worthy of credit ask for a loan, banks create one. A flow of money is created as soon as a new loan is awarded to a firm. Secondly, there is endogeneity at the juncture between the household and the bank. The demand for deposits of households is necessarily accommodated by the commercial banks. When households take a portfolio decision with respect to their wealth, the money balances that they desire to hold have already been created at the production financing stage. Thirdly, there is endogeneity at the juncture between the commercial bank and the central bank. The latter must provide the high-powered money that the former needs. Again, the loans inducing such exigencies have already been made when reserve requirements come into effect. The monetary authorities are constrained to provide the required base money, but at the price of their choice – at the interest rate that they see fit to set.

The main institutional feature of modern monetary systems is the presence of the overdraft. In pure overdraft economies, firms overall are indebted towards the banks, while banks overall are themselves indebted towards the central bank. The existence of predefined overdraft arrangements guarantees a smooth functioning of the monetary system. At the juncture of the firms and the banks, the unutilized portions of lines of credit provide the required flexibility. All modern economies exhibit this feature. At the juncture of the banks and the central bank, the discount window plays the role of the bank overdraft, providing the flexibility of liability management. Even financial systems that seem to be based on the textbook base money multiplier and asset management, such as that of the US, contain important features of the overdraft economy, as shown by Moore (1988).

A major implication of credit-money based on the overdraft system, in contrast to commodity money, is that there can never be any excess of money. If banks were to retrieve excess reserves, they would use them to reduce their debt towards the central bank. Similarly if firms or households were to hold money balances in excess of what they desire to hold, they would deplete them by paying back past loans (Kaldor, 1982, p. 70). This principle of reflux, dear to the Banking School, extends to open economies. With pegged exchange rates and when countries are running trade surpluses, the supply of money need not rise. Exporters will use the proceeds of the sale of foreign currency to reimburse their past loans, while banks will use the foreign currency to diminish their needs in base money or to decrease their debt towards the central bank. This particular reflux phenomenon is called the 'compensation principle'.

Briefly, the main post Keynesian view of endogenous money can be presented as follows. Money is credit driven. Banks first make loans and then search for the required base money; that is, loans make deposits and deposits make reserves. The supply of and the demand for credit-money are interdependent. The control instrument of the central bank is not a quantity, but a price – the rate of interest.

In orthodox monetary theory, the supply of new loans depends on the availability of free reserves. The stock of high-powered money set by the central bank determines the stock of money and eventually the amount of outstanding loans through the standard money deposit multiplier. This can be represented as $M = mH$. Causality must be read from right to left, the independent and causal variable being the amount of base money or high-powered money H under the control of the central bank, with the dependent variable being M. The multiplier m is a supposedly stable function of the proportions of money held under various forms, given their relevant reserve ratios.

As is well known, this standard neoclassical view can be represented by a graph in the money/interest rate space, where the supply of money is a vertical line, hence the expression *verticalists* used by Moore (1988). The orthodox assumption, that with proper management the central bank would be able to set the level of the money stock as it wishes, is a legacy of gold. Money is seen as a commodity, the supply of which is constrained by the current stock of gold.

The Post Keynesian view assumes reverse causation. Banks first make loans and search later for the appropriate funds and reserves to cover the increase in their assets. The demand for loans is the causal factor. Following

Le Bourva (1959, p. 720), we may represent the so-called money supply and supply of credit curves as horizontal lines (Kaldor, 1982, p. 24). Hence the name *horizontalists* put forth by Moore (1988) to designate the proponents of the standard Post Keynesian view. Banks provide the necessary credit or the necessary deposits at a given price, while the central bank provides the amount of base money induced by the creation of money. The latter relation can be represented by a credit *divisor*, which replaces the standard money deposit multiplier. The credit divisor d is represented by $H = dL$. Causality must be read again from right to left, the demand for loans, here called L, being the exogenous factor, while the quantity of base money is the dependent variable.

We now come to some of the main theoretical and policy implications of the hypothesis of endogenous money. Concerning non-orthodox theories, despite the importance it is accorded by proponents of the theory of endogenous money in the Minsky and Rousseas tradition (Wray 1990), the theory of liquidity preference clearly falls into the background. The base rate of interest is determined by the decisions of the central bank and is thus of a conventional nature. In that context, liquidity preference will merely affect the structure of interest rates. Liquidity preference is consequently mainly relevant in the short run, when rentiers or financial institutions have not yet endorsed the money rates that the central bank wishes to impose upon the economy. In the long run, as the neo-Ricardians would have it, liquidity preference, strictly defined, plays little role. The interest rate set by the central bank is then considered to be normal, in that it is permanent rather than transitory. This implies that in long-run models of growth and distribution, the real world can be tamed by abstracting from liquidity preferences and by assuming that the rate of interest is a given.

Neoclassical economists sometimes wonder why post Keynesians attach so much importance to the endogeneity of money. However, the fact that money is endogenous and demand-led, rather than supply-led, has clear destructive implications for the mainstream. In particular, if monetarism stands with exogenous money, it necessarily falls with endogenous money, as was recognized from the outset by Friedman. Since today's neoclassical synthesis is constituted of variations centred around the old monetarist model, all neoclassical macroeconomic theories are affected by the theory of endogenous money. The most obvious impact is on the theory of inflation. Since the supply of money is not an exogenous variable, it cannot be held responsible for initiating a general increase in prices. Inflation cannot be caused by an excessive rate of growth of the money supply due to incompetent central bankers; nor can it be due to a balance of payments surplus, as the compensation principle shows. The standard distinction on this issue between fixed and flexible exchange rates is thus challenged.

A credit-led theory of endogenous money has other crucial consequences. It allows a reassertion of fundamental Keynesian causality running from investment to savings, as well as fundamental opposition to the neoclassical concept of scarcity. Furthermore, since a monetary policy is best expressed by the level of the rate of interest (real or nominal) and since the stock of money is endogenous, all wealth effects, real balance effects or other similar Pigou or Patinkin effects may be ignored. This justifies the post Keynesian focus on distributional issues in the analysis of effective demand, including the role played by interest rates in redistributing income.

Finally, because the creation of credit-money is initiated by private agents in their business transactions and not by the central bank, it follows that the effects of any monetary policy can never be ascertained beforehand with precision. Monetary policy is like gliding.

MARC LAVOIE

References

Kaldor, N. (1982), *The Scourge of Monetarism*, Oxford: Oxford University Press.

Le Bourva, J. (1959), 'La théorie de l'inflation, le rapport des experts et l'opération de décembre 1958', *Revue Économique*, **10** (5), September, 713–54. This has been partially translated in J. Le Bourva (1992), 'Money Creation and Credit Multipliers', *Review of Political Economy*, **4** (4), 447–66.

Moore, B.J. (1988), *Horizontalists and Verticalists: The Macroeconomics of Credit Money*, Cambridge: Cambridge University Press.

Pivetti, M. (1985), 'On the Monetary Explanation of Distribution', *Political Economy*, **1** (2), 73–103.

Wray, L.R. (1990), *Money and Credit in Capitalist Economies: The Endogenous Money Approach*, Aldershot: Edward Elgar.

Monopoly capitalism

Monopoly capitalism refers to the stage of capitalist development once the process of concentration and centralization of capital has led to the emergence of oligopoly in significant sectors of the economy and also to stagnation in the macroeconomy. Though other dissenters, most notably Thorstein Veblen, have worked on what could be called a theory of monopoly capitalism, this is mainly a development and revision of Marxian economics. Karl Marx himself anticipated the emergence of industrial monopoly, but provided only broad generalizations about its consequences for the theoretical analysis of capitalism.

The first Marxian economist to develop a detailed theory of monopoly capitalism was Rudolf Hilferding, in his *Finance Capital* (1981). This focused on the idea of the domination of industrial by financial capital in the era of large joint-stock companies, combinations and cartels which arose towards the end of the 19th century. The joint-stock method of organization overcame limits on the size of units of capital, but made these dependent in Hilferding's eyes on sources of finance. Some of Hilferding's ideas, such as restrictions on the mobility of capital leading to unequal profit rates across industries, have continued to be hallmarks of monopoly capital theory, though his notion of financial control of industry has generally dropped out. His arguments about the desirability of capital export leading to imperialism were endorsed and adapted by Nikolai Bukharin and V.I. Lenin.

The modern Marxian theory of monopoly capitalism is associated mainly with the names of Paul Baran and Paul Sweezy, due to their classic *Monopoly Capital: An Essay on the American Social and Economic Order* (1966). The theory underlying their exposition in turn owes much to the work of Michał Kalecki and Josef Steindl. Following suggestions in the writings of Marx and Rosa Luxemburg, Kalecki (1939) developed the major theme of macroeconomic effective demand failures in the context of 'imperfect' competition. Steindl (1976) related this to longer-term stagnation in the industrialized capitalist economies. Baran and Sweezy saw that the consequences of this work pointed to twin phenomena: a tendency for the potential economic surplus to rise and the problem of absorbing that surplus.

The potential surplus (which includes profit, interest, rent, surplus employee compensation, government spending and other wasteful expenditures) rises as productivity growth allows production costs to fall relative to prices. This potential fails to be fully realized, however, since investment spending stagnates when excess productive capacity is not eliminated by margin-squeezing price competition. Thus the existence of monopolistic conditions and so downwardly rigid mark-ups lead to inadequacy in effective demand by weakening the inducement to invest while maintaining the profit share and so restricting the growth of consumption.

Baran and Sweezy (1966) examined the ability of various types of private and social spending to maintain effective demand by 'absorbing' the potential surplus; also the effects of developments associated with this stage of capitalism on the quality of life in the US. In the absence of significant 'epoch-making innovations' they argued that private investment is not an adequate source of expenditure. Wasteful selling costs and useful government expenditures help to some degree, but they found that military spending, particularly that associated with maintaining the American empire, was the preferred method of surplus absorption, with baleful consequences.

The question of what precisely determines prices under oligopolistic arrangements has never been satisfactorily resolved either in mainstream or radical economics. Kalecki held that a firm's price mark-up over direct costs depended on its 'degree of monopoly', which he came to see as a question of the degree of concentration in the firm's industry, the level of selling costs and the level of overheads. Kalecki also allowed that strong trade unions could cut into the mark-up, given limits on the ability of firms continually to accept money wage increases and to raise prices. Steindl emphasized the level of cost differentials across firms in an industry as the primary consideration affecting pricing strategy. Large cost differentials enable lower-cost producers to gain overall from slimmer profit margins when they find it possible to price below the costs of their smaller rivals. Small cost differentials, occurring once the smaller firms in an industry have been eliminated and oligopoly achieved, instead limit the attractiveness of price competition. In this stage of 'maturity' Baran and Sweezy argued that conditions would obtain of price leadership approaching joint profit maximization or, at the very least, of downward price rigidity.

Critics of the theory of monopoly capitalism from within Marxian economics have argued that monopoly capitalism wrongly explains the production of surplus value by behaviour in the product market, rather than as due to the exploitation of labour arising from conditions in the labour market. Some have also claimed that monopoly capitalism implies a cessation of competition and have criticized the idea that a tendency for profit rates to become equalized across industries should not apply. Others have raised alternative explanations for macroeconomic stagnation, resting either on a revival of Marx's argument for a falling tendency of the rate of profit or on a profit squeeze due to rising labour costs.

Though the stage of monopoly capitalism is seen to have superseded an earlier stage of competitive capitalism, Kalecki held the view that capitalist competition was always to some degree imperfect. The difference between the two stages may thus not be a tendency towards equal profit rates under competitive capitalism on the one hand, and no such tendency under monopoly capitalism on the other. Steindl's argument concerning maturity does describe different stages of development, but the emphasis in both stages is on intra-industry competition, not the migration of capital among industries (which is always somewhat problematic when capital takes a specifically fixed form).

None of these authors has ever declared the death of competition; they have said rather that competition takes different forms in the stage of maturity. As in the mainstream industrial organization literature, it is seen that price competition comes to be replaced by product competition, involving such things as advertising and product differentiation. When new products are developed or new entrants break into a previously closed market (as with new international interpenetration), however, price competition may break out again for a time. Baran and Sweezy held that the effect of monopoly capitalism was to retard somewhat the impetus of innovation and to ensure that the tendency towards stagnation would always eventually reassert itself.

The existence of monopolistic effects on profits does not overthrow the Marxian idea that workers are paid less than the value they create. This surplus value is distributed across industries in accordance with differential market power. The effect of the conditions of the wage bargain on the rate of surplus value is not ignored. It is recognized that the rise of oligopoly may bring stronger bargaining power against workers and so increase the total amount of surplus value, and that this may in turn be countered by the force of organized trade unions. The effects of oligopoly and of the level of effective demand on the magnitude of surplus value are not factors which Marx took into very much account, but they do logically belong to the analysis.

The macroeconomic question has to do with a critique of 'Keynesian' explanations of stagnation associated with the theory of monopoly capitalism. When critics considered the industrialized economies in the 1970s, they identified an observed fall in profit margins and the profit share (not inclusive of all of Baran and Sweezy's surplus) at a given level of capacity utilization and associated this with the theory of the falling rate of profit or another version of a profit squeeze by labour costs. According to the 'underconsumptionist' view (taken to be that of the monopoly capital school), this should, however, have increased aggregate demand rather than contributed to the stagnation experienced in this period.

Many defenders of the notion of monopoly capitalism argue that this dip in price-cost mark-ups has mainly been due to increased international competition. This has also contributed to greater concern for keeping wages and prices down and so greater willingness on the part of governments to use demand-restricting policies, supported further by inflation fears aroused by Vietnam war spending in the US in the late 1960s and supply shocks in the 1970s. We have thus seen stagnation by policy, as Kalecki had predicted.

Keith Cowling (1982) has contributed to the theory of monopoly capitalism, first, by developing Kalecki's notion of the degree of monopoly and, second, by relating the theory to various developments in industrial organization and managerialist theory. He has also treated the question of the effect of greater internationalization on mark-ups, arguing that such an effect depends upon whether there are significant asymmetries in competition between the penetrators' domestic and foreign markets. Where international penetrators are protected at home, they foresee more benefits from price-cutting abroad than otherwise. Cowling also makes the point that greater internationalization of production can lead to greater downward competitive pressure on wages, depressing aggregate demand, other things being equal.

Thus the post-1970 period need not be taken as a contradiction of monopoly capital theory. The stagnation coinciding with slightly shrinking mark-ups can be seen, not as a matter of a profit squeeze by labour costs or a rise in the organic composition of capital, but rather as a combination of several factors: international predation in some markets, capital flight to cheaper cost jurisdictions, and austerity policies by governments fearing inflation and labour cost disadvantages.

Baran and Sweezy rejected Hilferding's association of monopoly capitalism with control of industry by financial capital as an unwarranted generalization from the case of turn-of-the-century Germany. Recently, however, Sweezy has reassessed the importance of finance capital. He sees the greater use of debt and financial speculation to be a consequence of the post-1970 era of stagnation, with important implications for the behaviour of firms and the economy. This may represent a new form of financial influence over industry. Stagnation decreases the profitability of investment in physical capital, which at the same time creates both inadequate outlets for the investment of the surplus which is realized and dependence upon debt by firms and households struggling to maintain production and living standards respectively. Speculation and finagling with 'creative' financing arrangements become sources of profit. Transferring financial and physical assets becomes more desirable than creating them. The economy becomes more inflation-prone, and institutions become more supportive of restrictive demand policies to fight inflation.

Monopoly capitalism is a stage of capitalist development. Though it engenders a type of stagnation, it is not itself immune to change. State policies to prevent severe stagnation became acceptable but again problematic in the context of the contradictions of capitalism. We cannot be certain of what new developments await, but recognizing our present epoch as an era of monopoly capitalism has been significant for our understanding of the forms which its stagnationist tendencies have taken.

TRACY MOTT

References

Baran, Paul and Sweezy, Paul (1966), *Monopoly Capital: An Essay on the American Social and Economic Order*, New York: Monthly Review Press.

Cowling, Keith (1982), *Monopoly Capitalism*, New York: John Wiley and Sons.

Hilferding, Rudolf (1981) [1910], *Finance Capital: A Study of the Latest Phase of Capitalist Development*, edited by Tom Bottomore, London: Routledge & Kegan Paul.

Kalecki, Michal (1939), *Essays in the Theory of Economic Fluctuations*, London: Allen and Unwin.

Steindl, Josef (1976) [1952], *Maturity and Stagnation in American Capitalism*, New York: Monthly Review Press.

Multinational/transnational corporations

Multinational or transnational corporations (TNCs hereafter) are firms which have transcended their national borders by undertaking and controlling foreign production. Although there exist historical examples of firms without an original home base (which would justify the title *multinational*), most firms have undertaken activities such as direct foreign investment (DFI) after having first established themselves within the home base of a nation-state. For this reason we favour the term *transnational*. The TNC phenomenon dates back to the end of the 19th century, but has acquired momentous proportions since the end of the Second World War, initially through the expansion of American firms in Europe. It is estimated that now over 50 per cent of total exchanges in market economies take place within TNCs. The largest TNCs have an annual turnover which outstrips the annual gross national product of all but a handful (around 15) of nation-states. These figures are indicative of the potentially very important global economic (and political) role of TNCs.

The first serious attempt at economic analysis of the TNC was Hymer's doctoral thesis in 1960 (first published in 1976 by MIT Press). Some of Hymer's best papers have been collected in Cohen *et al.* (1979). There have been many interpretations of Hymer's contribution as well as extensions and critiques of his work. The most widely held interpretation centres around the concept of 'ownership-oligopolistic or monopolistic-advantages'. According to this, TNCs-to-be will decide to undertake DFI activities in foreign ('host') countries if they possess advantages over indigenous firms; these could include access to capital, product differentiation, managerial skills, etc. The existence of such factors helps TNCs to offset the natural disadvantages they face *vis-à-vis* host country rivals, in terms of language, culture, etc. The exploitation of such advantages will allow firms to earn a higher rate of return than firms which do not possess them, *ceteris paribus*.

A second interpretation of Hymer's identifies a 'removal of conflict' theory, according to which TNCs pursue collusive practices in order to increase their profits. It is worth pointing out that the two interpretations are not mutually exclusive, and indeed follow from the same basic concept that firms seek maximum possible profits. To achieve this they could exploit 'ownership advantages' to obtain a competitive edge *vis-à-vis* rivals (and/or offset existing advantages of rivals) *and* collude with rivals to raise profits.

In his various contributions Hymer has also mentioned factors strongly reminiscent of what is today known as the internalization-transaction costs theory (the idea that hierarchy can lead to reductions in market transaction costs, such as costs of information, negotiation and contracting). He also referred to the ability of TNCs to 'divide and rule' workers, to locational factors, and to factors related to the product life cycle as reasons explaining their existence. To these he added the ability of TNCs to play off one nation-state against another and the overall advantages of 'multinationality' *per se*. All these were to be developed into distinct theories of the TNC. In particular, the now well-known 'market power', 'internalization' and 'eclectic' theories all build on Hymer's contribution.

The 'market power' theory has been developed by among others Hymer's Ph.D. thesis supervisor Charles Kindleberger. There exists now a whole industry of writings emphasizing the market power-type aspects (collusion, barriers to entry, increased concentration and prices) of TNCs. Some authors in this tradition are critical of TNCs. Others (notably Kindleberger) believe that their advantages (transmission of technology, creation of employment, etc.) more than offset any disadvantages due to increased market power.

The 'internalization' theory has been associated with the work of Buckley and Casson (1976), although related arguments have appeared before and (independently) after, particularly in the work of Oliver Williamson and other writers in this 'markets and hierarchies' tradition. The Buckley and Casson contribution was concerned with failures in the markets for intermediate products (know-how, management skills, etc). Their main claim was that such failures could be solved by internalizing the market for such goods; that is, by choosing DFI to market-type modes of foreign operations such as exporting, licensing, etc. In the Williamson version, DFI is explained in terms of bounded rationality, opportunism and asset specificity problems of market-type international operations such as licensing. The internalization theory's focus on natural market failures leads to the implication that TNCs should be seen as efficiency-enhancing solutions to market failures.

The 'eclectic' theory (or 'eclectic paradigm' or OLI – Ownership, Location, Internalization framework) involves the claim that international production (not just the choice of institutional form, such as DFI vs licensing) can be explained in terms of the factors identified by the two previous theories, plus locational factors. This has been developed by John Dunning. Product life-cycle issues have been stressed by Raymond Vernon, while an explicitly 'divide and rule' theory was developed by Roger Sugden. Other theories focus, for example, on the 'oligopolistic interaction' type arguments of Hymer's 'removal of conflict' approach (see Pitelis, 1991, for more details).

There are ongoing debates concerning the concepts developed by all these theories, of which a few can be mentioned. Are ownership advantages always a necessary condition for overseas operations? Can asset specificity explain DFI? Can transaction cost reductions be separated from market power increases? Are 'ownership' advantages realized by internalization? Are locational factors independent from internalization? It is not my aim here to discuss these in any detail. I only wish to claim that, although each of the theories develops a particular aspect of Hymer's work, taken separately each compares unfavourably, I believe, with Hymer's own contribution, not only in terms of generality, but also in terms of dynamics and historical richness.

Albeit mainstream originally, Hymer's views gradually moved in favour of the Marxist tradition. In this tradition, a theory of the TNC has been proposed by Palloix (1976), who linked the TNC with an inherent tendency towards

the self-expansion of capital due to competition. This tendency was said to lead to the internationalization of the three circuits of capital – commodity capital, money capital and productive capital. The internationalization of the first is associated with world trade, of the second with international capital movements and of the third with the TNC. In this sense the TNC is seen as an aspect of a more general inherent tendency towards the self-expansion of capital and (thus) its internationalization.

All the theories mentioned so far focus on supply-side aspects of the problem (with the exception of aspects of the product life cycle), ignoring macroeconomic demand-side considerations. This is hard to explain considering the near unchallenged dominance of Keynesian (demand-side) macroeconomics during this era. One exception is the other Marxist theory of internationalization of production and TNCs, by Baran and Sweezy (1966). They proposed that a tendency exists for an increasing 'surplus' which is the Marxian notion of surplus value (profit, rent, interest and income from self-employment) plus 'wasteful expenditures' from governments and firms (such as armaments and advertising). *Ceteris paribus* this implies reduced effective demand of the underconsumption type (in crude terms, falling consumption resulting from redistribution of income towards the rich). Investment, they claimed, fails to fill the 'gap', resulting in a 'realization failure'. This is only partly offset by increasing wasteful expenditures and provides an overall general incentive for demand-starved firms to look for overseas markets.

A problem with these Marxist theories is that they do not explicitly address the issue of the 'choice of institutional forms'. For example, why should a firm choose a fully owned plant and not licensing or a joint venture? (Note that licensing and joint ventures do not necessarily fall outside the definition of the TNC if, for example, the focus is kept on control rather than ownership. In this case, the critique of Palloix and Baran and Sweezy becomes a milder one; i.e. a failure fully to discuss the forms that TNC activities can take.) On the other hand, while Palloix (and Hymer) investigate the production-side of the problem (capital expansion due to conflict with labour), this is ignored by most other theories. In turn, all theories but Baran and Sweezy's ignore the demand-side.

It is possible to build upon all these contributions to develop a production cum exchange, demand- *and* supply-side based theory of the TNC, which also adopts a dynamic approach. In brief, starting from the concept of competition between capital and labour (conflict) and between firms (capitals) themselves (rivalry), it can be suggested that conflict with labour will necessitate an expansion of the productive base of firms, while rivalry will oblige firms to look for sources of competitive advantage, new technologies, organizational forms, products, etc. The two types of competition will tend towards maximum possible profits through cost reductions and expansion-growth.

Removal of the constraints to growth (e.g. 'financial constraints', through share issues and the compulsory socialization of capital through pension funds, and 'managerial constraints' through the multidivisional (M) form of organization) will generate a tendency towards increasing firm size, thus increasing concentration within national economies – a tendency facilitated by the conscious strategies of firms to obtain and maintain monopoly positions. Monopolization (in part achieved through shareholding) will generate increasing profit margins, thus *ceteris paribus* increasing surpluses and effective demand problems, and eventually declining profit rates. These will increase excess capacity and reduce output and investment domestically. Firms faced with the coexistence of 'ownership advantages' (abundance of profits, access to capital, the M-form organization, etc. – all these obtained in the very process of firms becoming national oligopolies) *and* declining effective demand and investment prospects domestically, will have a supply *and* demand side incentive to go overseas, an incentive heightened by the prospect of emerging foreign rivals. The form of international operations (e.g. licensing versus fully-owned subsidiaries) will depend on a host of supply-side factors, including transaction costs-related, and 'divide and rule'-type, issues.

The above crude account suffices to make the point that the main insights of production- and exchange-based supply- and demand-side theories of the TNC are synthesizable and that there is something to be gained by taking this route. Important in this approach is that it dispenses with the efficiency *or* inefficiency focus of the more specific theories in favour of an emphasis on efficiency *and* inefficiency due (and giving rise) to TNCs.

The relationship between economic crises and TNCs, and the efficiency versus inefficiency aspects of their existence and operations, are more complex than allowed for in this short comment. The role of these and other factors becomes more pronounced when one enters the important issues of the impact of TNC operations on the global economy, in particular on the following relationships: TNCs and nation-states (developed and less developed); TNCs and international state apparatuses; TNCs and international capital markets; TNCs and the 'new international division of labour'; TNCs and 'deindustrialization' and/or 'relative decline', etc. Debates on these issues are often very emotive, but also far too long to be given any serious treatment here (see Pitelis, 1991, for more details). For the purposes of this entry it is worth mentioning that the recognition of the importance of TNCs by nation-states has arguably led to a situation where the latter have to cultivate their (and foreign) TNCs in order to attract investment to their soil (competitive bidding). In this sense international competition of nation-states trying to support their own TNCs (so as) to attract foreign TNCs can be viewed as an additional reason for TNCs. Similarly the ability of TNCs to

extract benefits by playing off different nation-states could be elevated to the status of an additional reason for (theory of) TNCs.

CHRISTOS N. PITELIS

References

Baran, P. and Sweezy, P. (1966), *Monopoly Capital*, Harmondsworth, Pelican.
Buckley, P. and Casson, M. (1976), *The Future of Multinational Enterprise*, London: Macmillan.
Cohen, R.B., Felton, N., Van Liere, J. and Nkosi, M. (eds) (1979), *The Multinational Corporation: A Radical Approach: Papers by Stephen Herbert Hymer*, Cambridge: Cambridge University Press.
Hymer, S.H. (1976), *The International Operations of National Firms: A Study of Foreign Direct Investment*, Cambridge MA: MIT Press.
Palloix, C. (1976), *L'internationalisation du Capital – Elements Critiques*, Paris: François Maspero.
Pitelis, C.N. (1991), *Market and non-Market Hierarchies*, Oxford: Basil Blackwell.

Peripheral Fordism in Europe

The notion of 'peripheral Fordism' in the European context is a fairly new development (Lipietz, 1987). European peripheral Fordism is very much related to post-war capitalist developments – what has come to be known as the Fordist era. In what follows we begin with the latter development which we label as 'core Fordism' before we deal with 'peripheral Fordism' in general and its European developments in particular.

The core Fordist model describes a situation whereby, in the post-war period, capital was concentrated in large multiplant enterprises, thus taking advantage of the economies of scale provided by big markets. An historical compromise manifested itself in the relationship between capital and labour. Productivity gains produced steady improvements in workers' real incomes, institutionalized as an 'inflation plus' norm for wage deals. At the same time, the Keynesian welfare state expanded the social wage along with the private wage. The institutions of collective bargaining, the relation between banks and industry, and the role of the state were all central issues in core Fordism. Dynamic economies of scale, important productivity growth and the specialization prompted by the creation of new markets clearly implied 'circular and cumulative causation' (Myrdal, 1957; Kaldor, 1972). The dynamic interplay between investment and productivity growth reinforced inequalities which were thus explained by endogenous factors in the process of historical development, rather than by exogenous 'resource endowment'.

By the late 1950s the development of the manufacturing sector in the core European countries, together with the dependence of the Mediterranean countries and Ireland on a backward agricultural sector, led to a substantial increase in differentials between these two sets of countries. These differences were in terms of standards of living, employment and the ability to generate growth. Core countries enjoyed the competitive advantages and the dynamic increasing returns to scale that the manufacturing sector normally generates. These further induced higher productivity and rate of profit in the faster-growing countries, which made it progressively harder for the slower countries to compete. An inflow of capital and skilled labour into the former ensued, along with further expansion of production and the reaping of greater economies of scale, higher productivity and rate of profit. These results, labelled as 'backwash', were thought to be contained by certain advantages accruing to the slower countries. These were the 'spread' effects, which resulted, for example, from expanded markets, the transfer of new technology from the advanced regions, etc.

The 'spread' effects were not thought to be strong enough to outweigh the negative effects emanating from 'cumulative causation'. Large migration of labour from the South to the North, as guest workers, relieved pressures in the labour market in both core and peripheral countries. As these workers were not permanent immigrants in the core countries, most of their income was remitted home, thus bringing some improvements in the balance of payments of the peripheral countries. These 'spread' effects were very weak and completely inadequate to bring any real and positive effects to the economies of these countries.

Even if by chance the 'spread' and 'backwash' effects are in balance, this would not be a stable equilibrium, since any change in the balance of the two forces would be followed by cumulative movements. There is also the idea that 'cumulative causation' in economic terms generates inequalities in non-economic terms, such as political power, cultural domination, etc. (Cowling, 1985). It is thus expected that those countries which are relatively rich dominate, not just in the economic power sense, but also in terms of their ability to exert political superiority. In this way they are in a position to impose their policies and culture over the less powerful countries.

But this Fordist era came to an end by the late 1960s. The problems of over-accumulation and declining rates of profit, the enhanced bargaining power and political weight of the trade unions, the development of the affluent consumer who rejected standardized, mass-produced, commodities, etc. created a crisis which caused capital to develop new strategies. From about the early 1970s onwards, it is argued, there began a dramatic change in terms of the organization of production, including the manufacturing sector, and the development of the service sector. Keynesian economic policies, which had worked reasonably well prior to the late 1960s, proved completely unable to resolve the new crisis.

Several attempts have been made to explain developments following the collapse of the Fordist model. There is the post-Fordist theory and what is sometimes called 'flexibility' theory or 'flexible specialization' theory, as well as the neo-Fordist theory and the 'regulation' theory, both of which represent the natural development of the Fordist thesis. A more relevant development from the point of view of this entry is, of course, what we referred to above as 'peripheral Fordism'.

The crisis in Fordism caused by the collapse of profitability is seen as producing a new pattern of capitalist development. In their attempts to recover profitability, multinationals in particular sought refuge in the peripheral countries of Europe, East Asia as well as in Latin America. A large and low-paid working class in these countries created an important basis for improvements in profitability, while the removal of high tariffs and quotas by moving production there gave multinationals the opportunity to penetrate these new markets and take advantage of the thirst for consumer goods of their rising bourgeoisie. This development is precisely what Lipietz (1987) has labelled 'peripheral Fordism'. It is Fordism inasmuch as it involves intensive accumulation and mass consumption, especially of consumer durables. It is peripheral in that some centres of 'periphery manufacturing' are now located in the periphery. Exporting cheap manufactured goods to the centre is the other dimension of local markets. Thus an obvious difference between peripheral Fordism and Fordism itself is that, unlike the latter, the former cannot regulate demand or indeed adjust it to local Fordist branches, given that world demand is involved in this case.

Industrialization is achieved through imports from the centre which are paid for by exporting cheap manufactured goods to the centre. But ultimately peripheral Fordism should only be contemplated 'when growth in the home market for manufactured goods plays a real part in the national regime of accumulation' (Lipietz, 1987, p. 80). The finance of peripheral Fordism has taken the form of borrowing on the international capital and money markets. Such financing in the pre-peripheral Fordist period had been channelled through direct investment. Following the emergence of peripheral Fordism, however, financing through direct investment became inadequate and international bank finance began to replenish the shortfall.

There are two constituent elements of what comprises Fordism – regulation and accumulation (see, for example, Aglietta, 1979; Lipietz, 1987) and the way they are linked to each other – which are very different in core and peripheral European countries. Fordist accumulation in the core countries is the result of an historical process essentially determined by developments that took place within them. The necessary institutional framework was in place or indeed developed to support this process. In particular, the state as the mediator and arbitrator of social conflicts facilitated accumulation. The process was supported by a strong trade union movement and large powerful corporations, thus giving rise to the notion of 'corporatism' which provided a fertile ground for Keynesian policies to operate upon and for regulation to become feasible and in some respects successful.

This process of accumulation does not appear to exist in the case of peripheral European countries, however, due to the internationalization of the process of accumulation resulting from the emergence of the multinational corporation. Peripheral accumulation is facilitated by forces that operate beyond the state, while regulation remains within the realm of individual economies. But even in the sphere of regulation, the ingredients necessary for success are not apparent in the peripheral countries. This difference between accumulation and regulation in core and peripheral countries requires analysis beyond the confines of both core and peripheral Fordism. This is what we have discussed elsewhere (Arestis and Paliginis, 1993), arguing that the appropriate analysis should emphasize indigenous industrialization. We might label the type of model that emerges from this analysis as 'post-peripheral Fordist'.

Greece, Ireland, Portugal and Spain are considered the peripheral countries of the EC. Their 'peripherality' is determined by a lower than average per capita GDP, a large and inefficient agricultural sector and a late developing industrial sector, partly controlled by multinational capital. In 1992, per capita GDP in Greece was 52.1 per cent of the EC average, in Ireland 68.9 per cent, in Portugal 56.3 per cent and in Spain 79.9 per cent. Looking at previous levels of relative per capita GDP, the 1992 situation represents an improvement for Ireland and Portugal from their 1980 levels; however, Spain's per capita GDP was higher in 1975 than it is now and in Greece there has been a definite and continuous deterioration since 1980. The rate of growth of output in all the three countries except Ireland has been consistently lower in the post-EC membership period than it was from 1961 to 1973.

Similarly, looking at investment as a per cent of GDP, all peripheral countries experienced higher levels in their pre-EC era than they now enjoy. This is of further significance, given the importance of the manufacturing sector in the developmental process. It may not be unrelated to the fact that, despite the increase in the level of employment for the Community as a whole in the 1980s, Spain and Ireland experienced historically very high levels of unemployment.

In all these peripheral countries the agricultural sector is large and inefficient, its modernization, reform and reduction in size being vital for any long-term development. At present, despite a considerable reduction in the level of employment in this sector, agriculture still commands a share in employment well above the EC average. In 1992 its share of employment was c. 27 per cent in Greece, 19 per cent in Portugal, 15 per cent in Ireland and 13 per cent in Spain, while the EC average was 7 per cent. Further, as a result of large inefficiencies in this sector, its contribution to GDP is disproportionate to its share in employment. This high level of employment in the agricultural sector is the result of the inability of the manufacturing sector to absorb the surplus labour force. While the development of the agricultural sector cannot provide the basis for a long-term development of the periphery, expansion of the secondary sector could play this role. The industrial sector provides large-scale employment, balance of payments benefits and, through backward and forward linkages, could create the basis for long-term employment. However, adverse historical events prohibited these countries from developing this sector and kept them as predominantly agrarian.

The inflow of capital to these countries in the 1970s in the form of multinationals and the protection that their products enjoyed in the local markets, through tariffs and quotas, allowed some industrial sectors to develop. Despite the usual negative aspects of peripheral Fordism, multinationals had a positive effect upon the peripheral economies of Europe in that they led to some industrial expansion. However, the creation of the Single European

Market removed the protection enjoyed by local industries in the whole of the periphery. Greece, for example, experienced a period of economic stagnation in the 1980s because her incorporation into the EC gradually removed the benefits of tariff protection (Arestis and Paliginis, 1993). These developments may bring back the initial advantages of core economies and may lead to the premature de-industrialization of the periphery.

PHILIP ARESTIS AND ELENI PALIGINIS

References

Aglietta, M. (1979), *A Theory of Capitalist Regulation: The US Experience*, London: Verso.

Arestis, P. and Paliginis, E. (1993), 'Divergence and Peripheral Fordism in the European Community', paper delivered at the International Conference on Economic Integration Between Unequal Partners (Athens, 20–22 August 1992), and also at the 1993 Annual ASSA meetings (Anaheim, California). To be published in the proceedings of the Athens International Conference.

Cowling, K. (1985), 'Economic Obstacles to Democracy' in R.C.O. Matthews (ed.), *Economy and Democracy*, London: Macmillan.

Kaldor, N. (1972), 'The Irrelevance of Equilibrium Economics', *The Economic Journal*, **82** (4), December, 1237–55.

Lipietz, A. (1987), *Mirages and Miracles*, London: Verso.

Myrdal, G. (1957), *Economic Theory and Underdeveloped Regions*, London: Duckworth.

Planning

All conscious economic activity, whether undertaken by individuals, firms or governments, involves planning in some form. But for the purposes of this entry, planning is defined as deliberate action taken by the state in order to shape the operation of the economy over the medium to long term, normally at the sectoral level.

Enthusiasm for planning has fluctuated markedly over the past 50 years. In the 1940s economists were quick to associate their proposals for intervention with this term. Since the 1970s and particularly since the collapse of the formerly centrally planned economies, however, the name has acquired much less favourable connotations; those proposing comprehensive intervention at the central level are now more inclined to characterize it as industrial policy rather than planning.

While anticipating the collapse of capitalism, the elimination of the private ownership of capital and the replacement of production for use by production for profit, Marx remained reticent about the form of economic organization which would succeed capitalism, confining himself to the observation (in *The Civil War in France*) that 'united co-operative societies are to regulate national production upon a common plan', replacing the anarchy of the market.

On seizing power in Russia in 1917, the Bolsheviks accordingly had to construct their own blueprint for socialism and did so in various stages.

In the period of War Communism (1918–1921), emergency measures to win the Civil War were clothed in the language of planning and of an abrupt movement to a high stage of socialist society. However, this approach was significantly reversed under the New Economic Policy (1921–1928) which restored market relations and led to significant denationalizations. During NEP, the GOELRO plan for the electrification of Russia went ahead and the State Planning Commission began publishing 'control figures' – sectoral forecasts for the economy, initially for one year and subsequently for five.

Central planning of the Soviet economy really began at the end of NEP with the adoption of the first Five-Year Plan. The first two Plans (1928–1937) contained explicit sectoral targets rather than forecasts. They provided for the wholesale industrialization of the economy, with an emphasis upon investment, heavy industry and the infrastructure. Their targets revolved around the completion of a relatively small number of giant construction projects, to which resources were channelled on a priority basis. Annual plans adjusted resource allocation to meet changing priorities and to respond to the uneven pattern of fulfilment.

The result was a dramatic transformation involving the development of new heavy industry, a massive transfer of population from countryside to town and significant declines in both rural and urban living standards. The Soviet system in this period has perceptively been described as a *sui generis* war economy, the phrase capturing the concentration upon a relatively few priority sectors and the willingness of the regime to use almost any means to achieve its ends.

Following the Second World War and the long period of reconstruction, the planning system settled down into a more routine phase. The Soviet Union and other countries in Eastern Europe (to which the Soviet system was transplanted after the war) constructed long-term (10 to 20 year) plans intended to express the aspirations of the Government for long-term development; Five Year Plans, which focused particularly upon investment projects; and annual Plans, which specified detailed and legally binding directive targets addressed to individual enterprises.

The essence of *directive planning* is the substitution of hierarchical (authority) relations for the horizontal 'market' relation found in decentralized economies. At the apex of the hierarchy is the Council of Ministers (itself often overshadowed by the leadership of a hegemonic party). At the base lie the individual production units and households. Between apex and base exists a range of bureaucratic organizations whose task is to construct and monitor plans for production units. In an extreme form, all resource allocation, including the assignment of consumption goods to households and of household labour to firms, could be undertaken directively. In practice, centrally planned economies allowed the demand side of the consumption goods market and the supply side of the labour market to function on market lines: that is, households could sell their labour at fixed wages to enterprises and use the resulting incomes to buy consumption goods at fixed prices.

Directive planning hinges upon the collection and aggregation of information. Whereas in a simple market model all information is captured in prices (offer prices or demand prices), in a directively planned economy information on output capacity has to be collected from production units, aggregated and transmitted to planners who then identify targets which are transmitted down the hierarchy to plan executants. The process can be an iterative one, with provisional targets going down and revised information coming up.

The huge informational burdens of directive planning are thus reduced by aggregation of information. Tractable volumes of information at the top are thus combined with highly detailed targets at the bottom, but at the cost of loss of information along the way and the emergence of errors in the plan. The informational complexity of central planning is also reduced by the stability of the economy's total output, with planning focusing mainly upon the disposition of additional resources arising from economic growth. This facilitates planning, but the economy may vegetate.

A directive plan requires consistency, or the equality of supply and demand in all sectors. Initially, planned economies used for this purpose a very rudimentary balancing technique which ignored most interactions among the various sectors of the economy. The later application of input-output models had the potential to produce consistent plans if the information underlying them had been accurate, but it was not. Directive plans were sustained by incentive systems which rewarded managers in accordance with their degree of plan fulfilment. This introduced an incentive to conceal productive capacity. As a consequence, the full potential of the economy was not realized.

A proper evaluation of directive planning must recognize its capacity to mobilize resources and achieve radical economic transformations. Against this are set a lack of long-term dynamism and an incapacity to adapt to technical change and to more sophisticated patterns of demand.

Beginning in the late 1950s, a number of attempts were made to decentralize planning in ways which would make it more efficient. This was sometimes linked to a desire to introduce more democracy into economic decision making.

A theoretical blueprint for wholly price-guided *decentralized planning* had been set out by Oscar Lange in the 1930s, but reform proposals normally took the form of amending the existing system by substituting horizontal links between enterprises for vertically imposed quantitative targets. This relaxation could in principle be applied to all sectors, but planning was often relaxed differentially. In some countries major investment decisions were made centrally, while decisions relating to minor investments and consumption were determined through a decentralized process. In others (notably in China) a proportion of output was centrally allocated, while the rest was distributed on a price-guided system.

Unfortunately, these attempts at reform met with generally disappointing results. There were doubts about the political commitment to economic reform; influential administrators in central ministries – as well as political leaders – resisted proposals which diminished their powers; in many cases the reforms were inadequately considered and incompetently implemented; industry was highly concentrated and often behaved monopolistically; and, finally, macroeconomic disequilibria made it difficult to relax central control without inflation.

Thus a cycle of decentralization and recentralization can be perceived. Economic performance deteriorated and popular dissent grew. The one economy which appears to have enjoyed a degree of success from partially decentralized planning is China, where it survives.

Indicative planning is a distinctive variant principally applied in economies where the dominant form of ownership of property is private. The major illustrations are France and Japan, but other European economies have attempted indicative planning too, as – arguably – does the European Union.

The standard theoretical approach to indicative planning is based upon a distinction between environmental and market uncertainties. The former lie outside the policy makers' control, but the latter are based upon ignorance about the course of conduct likely to be undertaken by firms within the same country or region. Indicative planning thus seeks to disseminate to each firm information about others' intentions. Environmental uncertainty is dealt with through alternative plan variants.

There are, however, serious doubts about whether this conception of indicative planning can reduce uncertainty. As environmental uncertainties multiply, the number of scenarios requiring investigation increases alarmingly. Moreover, recent theoretical work in futures markets, expectations and strategic behaviour suggests that firms can make reasonable forecasts or insure against uncertainty; also that outside a competitive environment they will furnish misleading information. This supports a different role for indicative planning as an organizing framework for the Government's own macroeconomic and industrial policy interventions. Indeed, historical analysis of French planning shows that it was most effective when the French economy was less open to trade and when the Government had a substantial direct role in resource allocation. The Japanese experience also suggests that most of the benefits from the system accrue from the Government's capacity to coordinate the pre-competitive phase of research and development.

The reputation of national economic planning now stands at a low ebb. The regimes of the centrally planned economies in Europe have collapsed, and indicative planning now has few adherents. Central planning is now restricted to China (in a modified form) and to a small number of developing socialist economies.

However, forms of *quasi-planning* are on the increase. After a decade of neglect in the UK and the US, industrial policy is enjoying a revival. The coordinating powers of the European Union are being expanded. The governments of the formerly planned central economies are undertaking a radical and, in some cases, planned restructuring of their economies. Governments have also collectively agreed plans to control the emission of certain environmental pollutants. These developments suggest a move away from the individual economy as a natural focus for planning, in favour of either sectoral interventions or coordination at supranational level. While the days of national economic planning appear to be over, the incentives to coordinate economic activity still remain strong.

MARTIN CAVE

References

Brada, J. and Estrin, S. (eds) (1990), 'Symposium on Indicative Planning', *Journal of Comparative Economics*, **14**, 521–812.

Eatwell, J., Milgate, M. and Newman, P. (1991), *Problems of the Planned Economy*, London: Macmillan.

Hare, P. (1991), *Central Planning*, London: Harwood Academic.

Kornai, J. (1992), *The Socialist System: The Political Economic of Communism*, Princeton: Princeton University Press.

Power in economic theory

The concept of 'power' is absent from neoclassical economic theory. One can peruse the indexes of dozens of economics texts without encountering the term. More surprising, there is no entry for 'power' in the encyclopaedic *New Palgrave*; nor is the concept given more than passing attention in many recent treatises on Marxian economic theory. Only the institutionalist tradition has consistently taken the issue of economic power seriously, as the work of such great institutionalist economists as Veblen, Commons and Galbraith attests. In contrast to the neglect of power in economic theory, the term plays a central role in political discourse and in many critiques of the hierarchical and undemocratic nature of the capitalist economy.

A compelling economic theory of power is implicit, however, in recent developments in microeconomic theory. Our purpose here is to make this new theory explicit. We treat power as the capacity of some agents to influence the behaviour of others in their favour through the threat of imposing sanctions. In our usage, power may be exercised over the formation of the preferences of others, as well as over more traditional objects of economic conflict such as the distribution of income (Lukes, 1974).

The liberal tradition in political philosophy and economics affirms the notion that, in an idealized liberal capitalist society, the state is the sole agent capable of imposing sanctions and hence is the sole repository of power. According to this view, power is absent in the competitive economy, though economic power may of course be wielded over state policy through the influence of campaign contributions, lobbying and the like (Przeworski, 1990). What is termed purchasing power in common parlance is not power at all in our usage, for the ability to acquire goods and services in a competitive economy in no way involves the use of sanctions.

But power – in the everyday sense of command over others implied by our definition – is transparently present in the economy, whether in the hands of bankers allocating credit or capitalist employers directing the activities of working people. The hiatus between rudimentary observation and liberal economic theory in this case may be traced to a peculiarity of the (until recently) hegemonic general equilibrium model associated with the neoclassical tradition and particularly with Leon Walras. This peculiarity is the assumption that the terms of exchanges can be written into contracts enforceable at no cost to the exchanging parties, thereby obviating any role for the exercise of power by economic actors in the enforcement of the contracts into which they have entered. Perhaps the most notable political implication of the Walrasian model, strikingly counter-intuitive, is that the location of decision-making authority within the enterprise (its political structure) has neither allocative nor distributive effects in competitive equilibrium, and hence may be considered irrelevant to economic theory. Samuelson (1957) has expressed the matter more succinctly: 'In a perfectly competitive model,' he wrote, 'it really doesn't matter who hires whom; so let labor hire "capital"' (p. 894).

The absence of power in the Walrasian model is based on the presumption that supply equals demand in competitive equilibrium for, when markets clear, each agent's transaction is equivalent to his or her next best alternative. From this it follows that each agent loses nothing by abandoning his or her current or most preferred transaction in favour of the next best alternative. In this situation, no agent can impose sanctions on another. For instance, if the labour market clears, the manager of a firm cannot use the threat of dismissal to control the behaviour of an employee, since a discharged worker can find equally desirable employment elsewhere.

Yet as we shall demonstrate, post-Walrasian developments in the microeconomics of information, transactions costs and principal agent relationships have demonstrated that, even in competitive equilibrium, a market economy sustains a system of power relations and that such power relations explain otherwise inexplicable aspects of the capitalist economy (see, for example, Bowles and Gintis, 1993; Williamson, 1985).

Consider agent A who purchases a good or service from agent B. We call the exchange *contested* when B's good or service possesses an attribute which is valuable to A, is costly for B to provide, yet is not fully specified in an enforceable contract. Exogenous enforcement is absent in the following cases: when there is no relevant third-party enforcer (as when A and B are sovereign states); when the contested attribute can be measured only imperfectly or at considerable cost (work effort, for example, or the degree of risk assumed by a firm's management); when the relevant evidence is not admissible in a court of law (such as an agent's eye-witness but unsubstantiated experience); when there is no possible means of redress (e.g. when the liable party is bankrupt), or when the number of contingencies concerning future states of the world relevant to the exchange precludes the writing of a fully specified contract.

In such cases the *ex post* terms of exchange are determined by the monitoring and sanctioning mechanisms instituted by A to induce B to provide the desired level of the contested attribute.

An employment relationship is established when, in return for a wage, the worker B agrees to submit to the authority of the employer A for a specified period of time in return for a wage w. While the employer's promise to pay the wage is legally enforceable, the worker's promise to bestow an adequate level of effort and care upon the tasks assigned is not. Work is subjectively costly for the worker to provide, valuable to the employer, and costly to measure. The manager-worker relationship is thus a contested exchange. The endogenous enforcement mechanisms of the enterprise, not the state, are responsible for ensuring the delivery of any particular level of labour services per hour of labour time supplied.

Faced with the problem of labour discipline, the employer may adopt the strategy of contingent renewal; that is, promise to renew the contracts of employees if satisfied with their level of work, but dismiss them otherwise. To be effective, such a strategy requires two things: the employer must adopt a system of monitoring to determine with some degree of accuracy the work effort levels of employees, and must also be able to deploy a costly sanction against those whose effort levels are found wanting.

The imposition of a costly sanction requires that the worker be paid a wage sufficiently high that he or she would prefer to retain the job, given the alternatives available (unemployment insurance and job search followed by a new job, for example). For any given wage, the worker will determine how hard to work by trading off the marginal disutility of additional effort against the effect that additional effort has on the probability of retaining the job and thus continuing to receive the employment rent. As a result of this employer wage-setting strategy, in competitive equilibrium the expected well-being (measured in income or utility or some other metric) of the employed worker must exceed that of the worker without the job. The difference between the two is termed an employment rent; it must be positive for a contingent renewal strategy to be effective, otherwise the sanctions are without force.

The employer will determine the optimal wage by trading off the cost of increasing the wage against the additional work effort which the employment rent elicits from workers, or perhaps the reduced monitoring costs which a higher wage allows.

Where employers adopt contingent renewal strategies, two results will follow. First, employees will work harder than they would have in the absence of the threat of the sanction. And second, workers without jobs would prefer to be employed but cannot obtain a job by the promise of working as hard as the currently employed for lower wages (the promise is not believable). The first result indicates that A's enforcement strategy is effective. The second indicates that the labour market does not clear in competitive equilibrium: workers holding jobs are not indifferent to losing them, since there are identical workers either involuntarily unemployed or employed in less desirable positions.

Does employer A have power over worker B? As we have seen, in equilibrium there will exist unemployed workers identical to B who would prefer to be employed. Thus A's threat to dismiss B is credible and dismissal is costly to B. Hence A can apply sanctions to B. In addition, A can use these sanctions to elicit a preferred level of effort from B, and thus to further A's interests. Finally, while B may be capable of applying sanctions to A (e.g. B may be capable of burning down A's factory), B cannot use this capacity to induce A to choose a different wage, or to refrain from dismissing B should A desire to do so. Should B make A a take-it-or-leave-it offer to work at a higher than equilibrium wage, or should B threaten to apply sanctions unless A offers a higher wage, A would simply reject the offer and hire another worker. Thus A has power over B.

Models of non-clearing markets have traditionally been viewed as disequilibrium models. In the contested exchange model, however, non-clearing markets are characteristic of competitive equilibrium defined in the standard manner: actors are incapable of improving their position by altering variables over which they have control.

The employer's power is clearly based on his or her favourable position in a non-clearing market. We say that employer A, who can purchase any desired amount of labour and hence is not quantity constrained, is on the *short side* of the market. Where excess supply exists (as in the labour market), the demand side is the short side; conversely, suppliers of labour are on the *long side* of the market. When contingent renewal is operative, the principle of *short-side power* holds: agents on the short side of the market have power over long-side agents with whom they transact.

Despite the clear disparity in the positions of A and B in this case, both parties gain from A's exercise of power over B. Short-side power is not a zero-sum game, since if A did not exercise this power, the best mutual agreement would involve a wage/effort pair that is strictly inferior to the contingent renewal arrangement for both parties. Short-side power is thus not purely distributive, but also productive.

What is the connection between the ownership of wealth and the exercise of economic power? The Walrasian model answers that, through the process of exchange, property rights confer on their holders no advantages other than the greater consumption, leisure or capacity to bequest made possible by, and in proportion to, the value of one's holdings: the power of wealth is purchasing power. Yet where claims are endogenously enforced and short-side power obtains, the connection of wealth to power is both more extensive and less direct.

Access to wealth, either through ownership or favourable location in capital markets, often confers the advantages of short-side power. The reason for this is straightforward: capital markets are as much arenas of contested exchange as are labour markets. In return for a sum of money from lender A today, borrower B contracts to repay the loan, together with a specified debt service, at some given time in the future. This promise is enforceable in a court of law, however, only if B is solvent at the time the repayment is called for. The borrower's promise to remain solvent is no more amenable to exogenous enforcement than is the employee's promise to supply a particular level of work effort.

Just as the employer is not obliged to accept the level of work effort offered by the worker in the absence of the threat of sanctions, so the lender can devise incentives which induce a more favourable level of performance than borrowers would spontaneously exhibit. The lender will generally have a motive to do so, since there is a conflict of interest between lender and borrower concerning the choice of risk: the profits from choosing a high-risk, high-expected-return investment strategy accrue to the borrower, while the costs of such a strategy – increased chance of default – are borne by the lender. If the borrower's choice among investment projects involving different profiles of risk and rates of return could be contractually specified and effectively third-party enforced, the exchange between lender and borrower would be Walrasian in character. But this is not the case. Not only are the actions of borrowers too subtle to be subjected to effective contractual specifications, but penalties imposed on a reckless borrower are limited by that borrower's exposed assets. Thus capital markets involve contested exchange.

The central enforcement strategy open to the lender is that of requiring the borrower to contribute equity capital to the project. Since this equity is lost in the case of the borrower defaulting, the incentive incompatibility between borrower and lender, as well as the adverse selection problem, are considerably attenuated.

The observed relationship between wealth and command in a capitalist economy thus flows from the fact that only those who possess wealth can contribute equity to a project. The wealthy are thus in an advantageous position to make offers characterized by reduced incentive incompatibility.

Since even perfectly competitive markets involve power relations among economic agents, it follows *a fortiori* that the exercise of power is ubiquitous in real capitalist economies characterized by market structures ranging from competitive to oligopolistic. Thus political philosophy, which has traditionally limited the study of democratic accountability to the sphere of government, has an important role in analyzing economic relationships. We obtained this result by relaxing a single assumption of the Walrasian model: the existence of costless third-party enforcement. Indeed, we have seen that state power and short-side power are in a sense substitutes: the power associated with advantageous market position comes into play precisely where the state cannot be called upon to enforce contracts.

SAMUEL BOWLES AND HERBERT GINTIS

References

Bowles, S. and Gintis, H. (1993), 'The Revenge of *Homo Economicus*: Contested Exchange and the Revival of Political Economy', *Journal of Economic Perspectives*, **7**(1), Spring, 83–102.
Lukes, S. (1974), *Power: A Radical View*, London: Macmillan.
Przeworski, A. (1990), *The State and the Economy under Capitalism*, Chur: Harwood.
Samuelson, P. (1957), 'Wages and Interest: A Modern Dissection of Marxian Economics', *American Economic Review*, **47**, 894–905.
Williamson, O.E. (1985), *The Economic Institutions of Capitalism*, New York: Free Press.

Prices and pricing

Theories of pricing are concerned with explaining how individual firms arrive at the prices they charge their customers. Theories of prices refer to a body of analysis concerned with what are variously referred to as 'prices of production', 'long-period prices', 'natural prices' or 'classical prices' (of production). The prices set by individual firms will not usually be equal to the prices of production; the relationship between the two different concepts will be considered subsequently.

In examining how individual firms arrive at their prices, it is useful to adopt a distinction between those commodities whose price changes are largely cost-determined and those whose price changes are largely demand-determined. The distinction, attributable to Kalecki (1954), bears a superficial similarity to – but is distinct from – the more orthodox dichotomy between fixprice and flexiprice markets. The Kaleckian distinction reflects the fundamentally different conditions under which prices are determined. For many primary products production, at least in the short period, occurs under conditions of relatively inelastic supply. Consequently, fluctuations in demand often lead to price fluctuations. The existence of production lags, in conjunction with the process of expectations formation and the fact that supply tends to be more elastic in the long period, often serve to exacerbate price fluctuations, as do the activities of speculators.

Institutional conditions within manufacturing, and to an extent within other non-primary sectors, are very different. Industries are typically dominated by large public corporations, generally producing a variety of products, often under production conditions where minimum efficient scale is a sufficiently high proportion of industry demand to warrant only a few major producers. Oligopolistic interdependence thereby follows. It is from this empirically substantiated position that a number of models have been developed, from various methodological standpoints, that focus on the decisions of firms as price setters. These represent attempts to fill the void left by the rejection of the neoclassical, perfectly competitive, short-period, profit maximization model in which individual firms are price takers.

From a behaviourist perspective, one might focus on the actual behaviour of the firm, where attention is paid to the information available and the costs of processing it. From such a standpoint, it is the existence of uncertainty which led many economists to eschew the model of short-period profit maximization under perfect information. Kalecki (1954) proposed the pricing equation.

$$p = mu + n\bar{p}$$

where p is the individual firm's price, $\bar{p}$ is the average price in the industry, u is unit costs and m and n are price-fixing parameters which characterize the 'degree of monopoly' of the firm's position. Kalecki's own way of expressing this relationship went through a number of phases whose differences need not concern us here. The important point is that the firm is assumed to set its price, taking into account its unit prime costs and the prices set by others, but in the context of the particular institutional environment as reflected in the parameters m and n and summarized by the term, 'degree of monopoly'. By dividing both sides by u and aggregating over all firms in an industry, Kalecki's equation can be rearranged to show how the industry mark-up depends on m and n. Hence, by relating the mark-up to the various determinants of the degree of monopoly, the model can be empirically tested.

A number of radical economists have been seduced by Kalecki's attempt at relating price setting to the industrial environment and have attempted to incorporate (or derive) this feature within models which do not suffer from the perceived drawbacks of the simplistic behavioural relationship set out above. Cowling and Waterson (1976) proposed a model which has been both embraced and modified by some Kaleckian, as well as many more orthodox industrial, economists. Individual firms are assumed to maximize their own short-period profits, explicitly taking account of the reactions of their rivals. This leads to an industry mark-up which depends on several factors: the Herfindahl index of industrial concentration, the industry price elasticity of demand and the 'reaction coefficient', representing the expected output change by one firm in response to a change in output by another.

One potential drawback of Cowling and Waterson-type models is the assumption of short-period profit maximization. One way to avoid this is by formulating the pricing decision in a way which incorporates consideration of a target rate of return on investment, thereby providing an analytical framework whereby firms' pricing and investment decisions are simultaneously considered. Although antecedents can be traced, a number of complete models of this genre were published in the early 1970s. A stylized version, based on Eichner (1973) but sharing many features with other models in this class, can be summarized as follows. Oligopolistic interdependence is captured by assuming price leadership, where the oligopoly price leader aims to maximize the growth of sales. Investment opportunities are represented by a Marginal Efficiency of Investment (MEI) schedule. Funds to finance investment projects can be obtained externally, at an interest rate, i, or may be generated internally by increasing the mark-up on existing product lines. This latter alternative is not costless: Eichner identified a substitution effect, whereby customers switch to alternative products; an entry effect, whereby custom is lost to new entrants; and a government intervention effect, which is that high prices could result in government legislation which ultimately would be costly to the firm. This analysis can be extended to include an 'uncertainty effect' whereby the price leader might be concerned with the possibility of other firms not following, and conceivably also a 'trade union effect' if the oligopolist feared that mark-ups beyond a certain level might precipitate a demand for wage increases. The losses resulting from these effects can be reduced to and represented by an implicit rate of return, R, associated with the investment funds.

Investment occurs up to the point where the MEI is equal to the cost of funds. If the cost of internally-generated funds, R, is less than the cost of borrowed funds, i, then any additional funds required are generated internally by increasing the mark-up. This leads to increases in R. Once this implicit interest rate becomes as high as the cost of borrowing, any additional funds are borrowed from external sources. Thus, the level of investment, mark-up and breakdown of funds between internal and external sources are determined simultaneously, but in a model in which 'uncertainty' – if considered at all – is reduced to 'risk'.

In proposing these models, one of the objectives of Eichner and others was to provide microeconomic foundations for post Keynesian macrodynamic analyses of growth. Since growth models, by their very nature, concern long-period relationships, a question of great interest is the relationship between short-period prices, resulting from the pricing procedures just outlined, and the long-period prices of production which can be obtained from a disaggregated steady-state model.

We now set out a model of 'prices of production', based on Piero Sraffa's *Production of Commodities by Means of Commodities* (1960). For ease of exposition, we consider an economy which produces just three commodities, where these three commodities are also used as inputs into the production of themselves and each other. The analysis is focused on one clearly-defined time period, for which the outputs A, B and C of the three commodities are taken as given. Defining A_a, B_a and C_a as the inputs of commodities A, B and C used in the production of A, and defining p_a, p_b and p_c as their respective prices, the total value of the commodity inputs into the production of A – collectively referred to as the Means of Production of A – can be written as:

$$(A_a p_a + B_a p_b + C_a p_c).$$

The other production input is homogeneous labour, with the labour requirements for the production of A defined as L_a. The wage rate and profit rate – defined as the ratio of the value added to the value of the means of production – are defined as w and r respectively, so that the complete production equation for A is given as:

$$(A_a p_a + B_a p_b + C_a p_c)(1 + r) + L_a w = A p_a.$$

Equations for the production of two other commodities are written using equivalent notation. It is assumed that the profit rate is equalized throughout the economy so that a three-commodity economy is represented by the three following equations:

$$(A_a p_a + B_a p_b + C_a p_c)(1 + r) + L_a w = A p_a.$$
$$(A_b p_a + B_b p_b + C_b p_c)(1 + r) + L_b w = A p_b.$$

$$(A_c p_a + B_c p_c + C_c p_c)(1 + r) + L_c w = A p_c.$$

This system of equations has two degrees of freedom, which is reduced to one once a numeraire is specified. One of Sraffa's contributions was to define a numeraire which is invariant with respect to changes in prices. However, many of the most important insights of this analysis can be appreciated by adopting the much simpler procedure of defining one of the prices as unity. Whichever convention is chosen, the fact remains that the system of equations still has one degree of freedom. Solution for prices (or relative prices if one price is used as numeraire) requires one more of the prices, or one of the distribution variables, w and r, to be predetermined.

This leads to a major insight: any change in this one predetermined variable affects the value taken by all of the others! Prices and income distribution are solved for simultaneously. Provided that the wage rate and profit rate are the same throughout the economy, there is one unique configuration of income distribution and relative prices that permits the exchange of output for inputs necessary for such an economy to reproduce itself. Prices cannot be determined independently of income distribution and vice versa. This important result – which applies for a system of any number of commodities – has provided the basis for a far-reaching critique of the entire edifice of neoclassical value theory. If prices cannot be determined independently of income distribution, this has fatal consequences for concepts of aggregate capital, particularly for the idea that w and r are determined by the marginal products of labour and capital as specified in an aggregate production function.

In terms of its positive contribution, Sraffian analysis has stimulated research – and controversy – in at least two directions. From the specification adopted above, any profits can be perceived as a surplus over and above what is strictly required for the system to reproduce itself. This point is in common with much Marxian analysis, where profits arise from the exploitation of workers. The Sraffian analysis of prices offers the potential for building economic analysis around the notion of exploitation, but based on a price theory which does not suffer from the major weaknesses associated with the labour theory of value.

Other economists have been investigating the potential for integrating a Keynesian analysis of effective demand with Sraffian price theory, pursuing the holy grail of an integrated approach to both short-period and long-period analysis which avoids the major weaknesses of neoclassical orthodoxy.

The final question to consider here is what, if any, is the relationship between the pricing decisions taken under oligopolistic conditions in the short period and the long-period prices which would have to exist if the economy were to be in a mythical situation of perpetual reproduction. Unfortunately, this question must be answered separately for each individual pricing theory proposed. Since, as already indicated, Eichner's model was proposed explicitly to provide the microfoundations for macrodynamic analysis, the question can most readily be considered for this model. If we were to place an Eichnerian model into a steady-state world where the MEI and the cost of internal and external funds were both equal to the rate of profit, then the objective of maximizing the rate of growth would be met and the growth rate would be equal to the profit rate, *r*. However, if such a steady-state position does not exist to begin with, it is yet to be demonstrated that it would be achieved. An alternative and less ambitious perception is to consider the configuration of long-period prices as some form of 'centre of gravity' which, although probably never attained, provides some indication of the nature and general magnitude of what the relationship between the prices of individual commodities would be if the effects of temporary fluctuations were removed.

PETER J. REYNOLDS

References

Cowling, K. and Waterson, M. (1976), 'Price-Cost Margins and Market Structure', *Economica*, **43**, August, 267–74.
Eichner, A.S. (1973), 'A Theory of the Determination of the Mark-Up under Oligopoly', *Economic Journal*, **83**, December, 1184–200.
Kalecki, M. (1954), *Theory of Economic Dynamics*, London: Unwin University Books.
Sraffa, P. (1960), *Production of Commodities by Means of Commodities*, Cambridge: Cambridge University Press.

Productive–unproductive labour in Marxist economics

For Marx, productive labour is labour employed by capital which produces surplus value. This includes all labour which is necessary to the production process, and therefore includes service labour (such as transportation and warehousing), the labour of management and supervision, as well as labour directly responsible for physical output. On the other side of the coin stands productive consumption. 'Production is consumption and consumption is production. … All investigations of the former are concerned with productive and unproductive labour, those of the latter with productive and unproductive consumption' (Marx, 1970b, p. 198).

Marx did not invent the distinction between productive and unproductive labour, but reworked it from early political economists, especially Sir William Petty, from the physiocrats and of course from Adam Smith. Part I of his notebooks *Theories of Surplus Value* (1969, Vol. I) is largely devoted to this task. The essential feature of these early theories was their focus on the production and measurement of a net or surplus economic product and its investment. But Marx strongly disagreed with his predecessors' view that the historical origins of capital lay in the primitive accumulation of surplus product generated by the mediaeval-feudal economy and circulated as merchant capital. This idea implied that any source of surplus – the land, labour or even labouring cattle in the case of Adam Smith – could be productive of capital.

On the contrary, Marx insisted, capital is nothing more than unpaid or surplus labour in its surplus value form; moreover, as a mode of production, capitalism accumulates only by transforming petty commodity producers (unproductive) into wage-labourers (productive). 'The so-called primitive accumulation, therefore, is nothing else than the historical process of divorcing the producer from the means of production' (1970a, Vol. I, p. 714). In this context, unproductive labour and unproductive consumption are important features in Marx's *Capital* only when he is dealing with the disappearing remnants of pre-capitalism and pre-capitalist social classes.

But in expropriating the mediaeval economy, its land, its materials and its supplies of labour, capital was also taking over the costs of production and reproduction of these resources. To offset these additional burdens, capital's inner drive to raise productivity and cut the direct and indirect costs of production was geared to a new level of intensity. On the one hand science, technology and new methods of work organization were recruited to the side of capital to effect the shift from absolute to relative forms of surplus value. On the other hand, capitalists sought ways to reduce the length of time capital is tied up in the production and circulation of commodities. The money and commodity circuits of capital were speeded up.

Marx regarded capital involved in the process of circulation as not productive of surplus value at all. 'The process of circulation is a phase of the total process of reproduction. But no value is produced in the process of circulation, and, therefore, no surplus value' (1970a, Vol. III, p. 279). But he also regarded circulating capital as merely a form through which total social capital rotates. Circulating and industrial capital are but 'two different and separate forms of existence of the same capital', while commercial capital, which deals directly with commodity exchange, 'is nothing but a transmuted form of a part of this capital of circulation constantly to be found in the market' (1970a, Vol. III, p. 268).

The activities of finance (circulating) and merchant (commercial) capital arise first and foremost out of the need to develop capital and money markets to aid the circulation of money capital from low- to high-profit investments, and also the circulation of commodity capital to realize embodied surplus value as profit. The profits of financial and commercial capital are therefore depicted as expenses to industrial capital and as part of the share-out of surplus value. On the one hand, capital strives to maximize surplus value in production while reducing costs to a minimum. On the other hand, a large sector of non-productive finance and merchant capital arises, which demands its share of surplus value and therefore enters into the determination of the general average rate of profit, $S/C+V$, constituting part of the denominator.

The cost savings arising from the more efficient circulation and turnover of capital will, in principle, outweigh the additional costs of a growing commercial sector. However, this sector develops and operates with relative autonomy and even becomes an arbiter between capitals in the cycles of boom and slump. And because commercial capital stands on the same footing with regard to the rate of profit as industrial capital, the argument of some writers – that commercial capital is unproductive because the labour employed is not subject to the same competitive determinants of productivity as industrial capital – cannot hold up.

In Marx's analysis, unproductive labour and unproductive consumption are minimal, reflecting the importance he attached to their role within the capitalism of his day. The unproductive consumption of kings and landlords was marginal compared with the rising productive might of industrial capitalism, and even the consumption of capitalists *qua* capitalists was confined by the walls of their stomachs. The unproductive labour required to service these wants could be found 'from whores to popes', but he added that 'the honest and "working" lumpen proletariat belongs here as well' (1973, p. 272). On the other hand, labourers who produced goods or services for unproductive class consumption, but were employed by capital to do so, were productive of surplus value. Neither the nature of the goods or services, nor the nature of the consumption, reflected upon the capitalist nature of the production process. Rather, what is produced by wage-labour may be unproductively consumed, but at a price which includes capital's profit. This implies that a transfer of value takes place from the savings of the unproductive consumer to the revenue of capital. These savings can come from accumulated property incomes of past surplus value or from pre-capitalist stocks of wealth. If the latter, the transaction is tantamount to adding money to circulation without adding to the circular flow of commodity capital, since unproductive consumption represents a leakage. Other things being equal, this would induce inflation.

The 1970s saw a revival of interest and debate by Western Marxists concerning the productive–unproductive distinction, a short summary of which can be found in Fine and Harris (1979). One contribution came from the women's movement and centred around the role of domestic labour. Feminists argued that unpaid housework and mothering supplied capital with reduced reproduction costs of labour-power, and in that sense should be considered indirectly productive of surplus value. The terms 'productive' and 'unproductive' were seen as ideological in the sense that they falsified and undervalued the role of domestic labour. But this is reminiscent of Marx's initial reaction to the labour theory of value as found in Ricardo's writings, which he rejected on the grounds that it demeaned labour's productive role by treating it as a commodity to be bought and sold like any other. After further reflection, Marx came to the view that Ricardo had scientifically and correctly represented precisely what capitalism did in reality.

Another debate arose concerning the structural changes overtaking contemporary capitalism, including changes in social class and the prospects for socialism. Assuming, for brevity, that the socialist project would replace capitalist society with one no less productive but more egalitarian, Marx argued that the proletariat was the necessary social agency because it, and it alone, was productive of capital's life-blood – surplus value. The rise of public sector employment, the decline of the agricultural and industrial sectors together with the rise of the commercial and service sectors led to the argument that there had been a dramatic shift in the balance of employment to occupations traditionally thought of as unproductive. Yet workers in many of these occupations were collectively organized and still capable of struggle against the predations of capital. They were therefore just as much part of the modern working class as the archetypal industrial worker, and just as capable of being the agents of social, and socialist, change. If, under Marx's definition, they were not all strictly speaking productive of surplus value, then the distinction had lost its use-value.

But there were confusions in this debate. Many of the services offered, both business and consumer, are productive in terms of Marx's criteria of being employed by capital and also productive of surplus value. The majority of so-called service-sector jobs should be regarded as part of the collective productive labour necessary to organize capitalist production more efficiently and more productively. They are, in reality, as much a part of industrial capital as traditional manufacturing jobs. Official industrial and occupational classifications are not constructed to differentiate productive (investment) activities from non-productive (transfer) or from unproductive (disinvestment) activities.

The same applies to many state activities, some of which are merely transfers of value and some of which are reproductive and therefore represent a common cost to capital, though many are productive for and of capital either indirectly or directly. The political nature of the state may remove its sphere of employment from the immediate effects of market competition, but the sharpening of capitalist competition on a global scale does not leave national state sectors immune for long. Furthermore, as a warfare state, the public sector has become an unproductive consumer on an historically unprecedented scale.

Another related school of thought, influenced by the work of Sraffa, argued from a slightly different premise, namely that the labour theory of value was itself redundant; therefore no distinction could sensibly be drawn between different types of labour using surplus value as its basis. Any surplus product produced for the system could be considered productive; also any work that contributed, directly or indirectly, to that surplus could be considered productive. In effect this abolished the distinction almost entirely because any output which is an input into any sector of the economy (including itself) can be considered indirectly productive simply by stretching output into the indefinite future. But by the same token, any output which is wasted today implies, by infinite backwards regression, that all the past inputs which indirectly contributed to its present existence were unproductive. This does not render the distinction very useful.

Yet it is not just Marxists who continue to employ the distinction. Even some economists quite hostile to the Marxist tradition have been unable to ignore the activities of whole armies of corporate lawyers, accountants, speechwriters, lobbyists and so on, who find very lucrative employment doing little more than shuffling the pack of profits, causing the cards to favour one corporation over another, or the capital of one nation over another. They have invented their own term for this productive–unproductive distinction, for labour which does not add value to the national product. This is 'Directly Unproductive Profit-Seeking Activities' or DUP, defined as labour employed in profit-seeking activities which are directly unproductive in the sense that 'they yield pecuniary returns but do not produce goods or services that enter a utility function directly or indirectly via increased production or availability to the economy of goods that enter a utility function' (Bhagwati, 1982, p. 989).

The productive–unproductive labour distinction has not lost its relevance. On the contrary, there are many aspects of contemporary global capitalism that can be analysed with its help. For example, how far do the recent migrations of labourers from the South offer modern capitalism new opportunities to unburden itself of labour reproduction costs? What are the implications for capitalist development and class relations of the partial withdrawal of labour from capitalist commodity production into underground petty commodity economies, a phenomenon common to developed and developing economies alike? The productive–unproductive distinction remains fundamental both to the classical tradition of political economy, which focuses upon the production of a net or surplus product, and particularly to Marx's labour theory of value.

JOHN URE

References

Bhagwati, J.N. (1982), 'Directly Unproductive, Profit-Seeking (DUP) Activities', *Journal of Political Economy*, **90**, October.

Fine, B. and Harris, L. (1979), *Rereading* Capital, London: Macmillan.
Marx, K. (1969, 1972), *Theories of Surplus Value*, Volumes I–II, III, London: Lawrence & Wishart.
Marx, K. (1970a), *Capital*, Volumes I–III, London: Lawrence & Wishart.
Marx, K. (1970b), *A Contribution to the Critique of Political Economy*, London: Lawrence & Wishart.
Marx, K. (1973), *Grundrisse: Foundations of the Critique of Political Economy*, Harmondsworth: Penguin Books.

Profits

The literature of political economy exhibits many different perspectives on profits. So far as formal analysis in contemporary economics is concerned, however, only three types of theory are evident: neoclassical, neo-Ricardian and Post Keynesian. Despite important criticism by the neo-Ricardians and the Post Keynesians in the last 40 years, neoclassicism remains predominant in the treatment of profits, as in all other areas of economic discourse. There are also great similarities among the three approaches, which stem from the increasing attention paid to the rigorous formulation of models in modern economics. Each theory typically operates at a high level of abstraction, focusing primarily upon the equilibria of competitive, closed economies, with homogenous labour and without scarce natural resources. Their differences centre on how they dichotomize variables into exogenous and endogenous components, and thus on how they represent causation. This, in turn, reflects differences of 'vision' as to how economic processes operate.

Neoclassical theory takes consumers' preferences, producers' technologies and agents' asset endowments as exogenous and shows how these determine the pattern of prices and quantities traded in equilibria of supply and demand. Consumers each maximize a utility function defined by their preference ordering and subject to a budget constraint specified by their ownership of assets. The solutions to these optimization problems constitute consumers' demands and supplies for commodities, including consumer goods and supplies of labour. Producers maximize profits subject to the constraints of technology; the solutions to these maximization problems specify their demands for inputs and supplies of outputs. The price vector which simultaneously satisfies all the consumers' and all the producers' optimizations is the equilibrium set of prices, corresponding to which is a set of trades which clear all markets. The values of these endogenous variables are sufficient to specify the pattern of profits and rates of return. These distributional magnitudes are thus held to be ultimately caused by the three exogenous components of the analysis: preferences, technology and asset endowments. Neoclassicals have sometimes truncated this story by arguing that the principal factors underlying profits are 'time preference' and 'capital productivity'.

The bias of consumers for present consumption over future consumption requires the payment of a premium to encourage saving, which is necessary for the capital formation that will provide the resources from which profits can be paid. A further specialization is possible when savings behaviour and labour supplies are exogenized so that capital productivity is highlighted as governing the level of profitability. Modern neoclassical economists, however, would emphasize that these are only particular applications of their more general models. Bliss (1975) provides an excellent account of all these issues.

Neo-Ricardian theory dichotomizes economic phenomena into exogenous and endogenous components differently. The wage, technology and outputs are taken as given, and thus represent the determinants of the endogenous variables – commodity prices and the rate of profit. An illustration can be provided by the following model of an economic system producing only two goods:

$$\begin{aligned} a_{11}\, p_1(l + r) + l_1\, w\, p_2 = p_1 \\ a_{21}\, p_1\, (l + r) + l_2\, w\, p_2 = p_2 \end{aligned} \qquad (1)$$

where the a_{ij} represents the inputs of commodity j required to produce one unit of commodity i; l_i are the inputs of labour in the production of i; p_i are prices; w is the wage and r is the rate of profit. Once w is specified exogenously and the unit of price measurement is chosen, the technical parameters (the a_{ij}s and l_is) are sufficient to determine commodity prices and the rate of profit. Alternatively if, instead of the wage, the rate of profit were assumed to be given exogenously, the commodity prices and the wage would likewise be determined (see Equation (4) below). Typically, profits are regarded as surplus, corresponding to no exchange of equivalents, and therefore amenable to being conceptualized as a form of exploitation. This explains why neo-Ricardianism is sometimes referred to as 'surplus theory' and is associated with Marxism. Sraffa (1960) is the classic text of modern neo-Ricardian economics.

Post Keynesian theory, like the other two approaches, takes technology as given but in addition postulates the pricing policy of firms (the mark-up, reflecting the 'degree of monopoly'), the savings behaviour of different groups, the money wage and investment outlays of capitalists as the exogenous determinants of profits. This can be shown for an economy composed of only two classes, capitalists and workers, assuming, first, that workers do not save and capitalists' savings propensity is s_c and, second, that there are sufficient unemployed resources to allow variations in economic activity without price changes. The following relationships must hold between incomes and expenditures

$$Y = P + W = I + (l - s_c) P + W \qquad (2)$$

where Y is national income, P is profits, W is wages and I is net investment. Simple manipulation of equation (2) yields

$$P = I/s_c. \qquad (3)$$

Profits are thus determined by capitalists' expenditures and savings behaviour. Once data on firms' mark-ups and the money wage rate are added, the sectoral distribution of profits and the level of employment will also be determined. The pivotal idea is expressed in the dictum attributed to Michal Kalecki: 'workers spend what they get and capitalists get what they spend.' In other words, without spending flows that do not correspond to costs of production (investment and capitalist consumption), profits would necessarily be zero. Robinson (1956) is perhaps the most famous text of Post Keynesian theory which develops and elaborates on this basic notion.

Neoclassical and neo-Ricardian economics have long lineages in intellectual history. Each can be traced back to pre-Smithian ideas, and both are evident in Adam Smith's own work. Indeed, historians of thought like Maurice Dobb and Ronald Meek have argued cogently that the analysis of value and distribution since the 18th century can be represented as the development and interaction of these two traditions. The works of Ricardo, Marx, Dmitriev, Bortkiewicz, Leontief, von Neumann and Sraffa constitute the principal contributions to surplus theory. Neoclassical ideas, on the other hand, are clearly evident from Smith onward, although the watershed in their formulation is usually traced to the 'marginal revolution' of the 1870s and 1880s. During the 20th century the Walrasian version of neoclassicism has become dominant, and this dominance has been reinforced by the devastating neo-Ricardian attack on the alternative Austrian and aggregative forms of neoclassical profit theory during the 'capital controversies' of the 1960s and 1970s. Post Keynesianism is of later vintage, originating in the 1930s with the work of Kalecki and Keynes, although anticipations of some of their ideas can be found much earlier in the work of Marx and others.

Drawing on these historical backgrounds, each of the three approaches to the analysis of profit in modern economics has constructed more complex models which depart from the simplifications outlined earlier. Heterogenous labour, scarce natural resources, international trade and the public sector have all been incorporated in their analyses. Every school of thought also recognizes the importance of market power and disequilibria for a full understanding of profits. The ideas of Joseph Schumpeter and Frank Knight on innovation and uncertainty have been assimilated in all these types of theory, despite the fact that their original formulations were essentially neoclassical in orientation. Nevertheless, the basic distinctions between the three types of economics can still be represented analytically by the alternative partitioning of phenomena into exogenous and endogenous subsets as indicated above.

Behind this formal difference, however, there lies a diversity of vision as to how capitalist economies function, as well as disparate views on the methodologies by which they should be studied. The neoclassical position is essentially that of classical liberalism, in which economic phenomena are constituted by contracts formed from the optimizing choices of agents. In consequence, neoclassical economists show a pronounced bias in favour of methodological individualism and the search for microfoundations cast in choice-theoretic terms. The structuralism of the neo-Ricardians lies at the other extreme. Actions are understood as resulting from systemic properties, and agents' subjectivities are considered to be dominated by class relations. As a result, 'individuals' make no explicit appearance in the formal theory. Post Keynesianism, on the other hand, represents a convex combination of these two poles and is best regarded as a form of modern institutionalism where convention, habit and 'rules of thumb' predominate as devices to handle the uncertain environment in which all economic agents have to operate.

There have been various attempts to integrate neo-Ricardianism and post Keynesianism, particularly in the context of steady-state growth models. Typically, capitalists' expenditures on investment and savings propensities are the variables used to determine the rate of profit, which is then incorporated into the equations determining commodity prices and the other distributional variables of neo-Ricardian theory. Thus, for example, dividing through by K (the capital stock of the economy), equation (3) becomes

$$r = g/s_c \tag{4}$$

where r is the rate of profit (P/K) and g is the rate of accumulation (I/K). Assuming constant returns to scale, equation (4) can be added to equations (1) in order to determine the commodity prices and wage rate (which is now taken as endogenous). However, there is some tension between the two streams of thought. Post Keynesians give far more importance both to the economic relations of the 'short period', and to volatile expectations, than do neo-Ricardians; they have also tended to view integrated models as dealing with those unusual circumstances in which the causal significance of these considerations are dominated by the long-run structural forces on which the neo-Ricardians focus. For their part, neoclassical theorists have viewed both Post Keynesian and neo-Ricardian theories as dealing with forms of economic relationships which their own analysis shows to be 'special cases'.

All three paradigms can formulate logically coherent theories of profit, and can do so in a wide variety of models of different complexity. Each type of analysis can also launch critiques of its rivals, as is shown in Howard (1983). Consequently it is not clear by what criteria choice can be made between them, especially in an era where all forms of scientific positivism are under siege. So far as radical economists are concerned, they have preferred neo-Ricardian and Post Keynesian economics to neoclassicism, but the rise of 'rational choice Marxism' in the 1980s indicates that ideological stance has no clear-cut implications for the mode of analysis.

M.C. HOWARD

References

Bliss, C. (1975), *Capital Theory and the Distribution of Income*, Amsterdam: North Holland.
Howard, M.C. (1983), *Profits in Economic Theory*, London: Macmillan.
Robinson, J. (1956), *The Accumulation of Capital*, London: Macmillan.
Sraffa, P. (1960), *The Production of Commodities by Means of Commodities*, Cambridge: Cambridge University Press.

Public expenditure

It is useful to distinguish three different approaches to public expenditure which are identified with different strands of thought on the nature of the state. In general terms, it can be said that the Marxist, radical-left approach to public expenditure is dictated by the view that the state serves the long-run interests of capital and that its actions are directed towards creating the conditions for the survival of the capitalist system. The social democratic and/or democratic socialist approach recognizes that the state can play an important role in improving the social and economic conditions of a society and identifies areas and ways for this role to be pursued. Finally, proponents of economic liberalism, as exemplified by the Austrian school and the radical right, are hostile to the role of an interventionist state other than as a provider of defence and security.

As one would expect in centrally planned economies, the state's role in the economy is pervasive so that public expenditure is a large percentage of national expenditure. Countries with a relatively long history of social democratic or democratic socialist government, such as the Scandinavian countries, are associated with high levels of public expenditure in relation to Gross Domestic Product (GDP) – often well over 50 per cent and in some cases in excess of 60 per cent. Such countries, often called mixed economies in the 1950s and 1960s, have entrusted governments to play an important role in both the production and the distribution of national income. On the other hand in countries where the capitalist spirit of free market economics rules high, such as the US, the economic role of the state is more limited and public expenditure is a relatively small percentage of GDP, e.g. 30–35 per cent. These percentages vary substantially over the business cycle but on the whole for most developed countries, they exhibit an upward trend.

The most important single item of public expenditure in industrially developed countries is social welfare payments. Their importance has increased substantially over time, both in absolute and relative terms. Welfare payments are considered as a means of achieving a number of objectives: to relieve poverty through various income support schemes; to prevent individual/household living standards from falling below a socially acceptable level during periods of economic distress (e.g. unemployment benefits, health-related benefits); to assist individuals in achieving an efficient distribution of consumption patterns over their life cycle through, for example, appropriate pension schemes; in terms of equity, to redistribute income towards lower income groups of individuals/households; to preserve individual dignity and foster social solidarity (e.g. free education and medical care). Barr (1992) argues that in addition to the above objectives, welfare payments can be, at least partly, rationalized and explained on the basis of market failures, especially information imperfections, and can be viewed as the outcome of processes that conform to the pursuit of efficiency objectives. This approach to the welfare state in effect supports the extension of economic-theoretic arguments in explaining public expenditure to the domain of welfare state payments. Such arguments were extensively used in the past to explain the role of the state in the provision of public goods and to support countercyclical policies in the presence of non-clearing markets. For the sake of completeness it should be added that the public choice theory has developed arguments suggesting that the growth in government activity can be explained, at least partially, in terms of the objective functions of governments and bureaucrats.

The Marxist approach to public expenditure is very much dictated by the view of the state as a creature of a particular mode of production. Gough (1979), for example, although not dismissing alternative approaches as useless, suggests that it is only through a Marxist political economy approach that we can fully understand the contradictory nature of the welfare state. He claims that

> [i]t simultaneously embodies tendencies to enhance social welfare, to develop the powers of the individuals, to exert social control over the blind play of market forces; and tendencies to repress and control people, to adapt them to the requirements of the capitalist economy. Each tendency will generate counter-tendencies in the opposite direction; indeed, this is precisely why we refer to it as a contradictory process through time (p. 12).

Marxist writers suggest that the expansion of the welfare state in the post-war period was to a large extent the outcome of class conflict and the ability of the working class to press for measures that mitigate hardship or modify the blind play of market forces. The same policies may serve the long-term interests of capital as long as they help to reduce working class discontent, diffuse and de-orientate working class power, and assist in integrating and controlling the working class. In this context O'Connor (1973) distinguishes three types of state expenditure: social investment in projects and services that increase the productivity of labour; social consumption, including projects and services that lower the reproduction costs of labour power; and social expenses, which consist of projects and services which are required to maintain social harmony – to fulfil the state's legitimization function. The contradictory nature of social consumption and social expenses, and the observed tendency of such expenditure to grow faster than the rest of the economy, has posed a number of questions concerning their effect on the future of capitalist economies. O'Connor (1973) has emphasized the problems of financing an ever-growing level of welfare expenditures, suggesting that capitalist economies are faced with what he refers to as 'the fiscal crisis of the state'. The same issue was raised by non-Marxist economists. Bacon and Eltis (1978), for example, put forward the view that the growth of public expenditure was at the core of the reasons for the poor performance of the British economy. They suggested that the growth of the state was mainly at the expense of capital which was finding it increasingly difficult to maintain adequate levels of capital formation. In other words the increase in the 'social wage' was seriously encroaching on profitability and marketed output.

The Bacon and Eltis (1978) thesis on public expenditure is a particular aspect of the general proposition that any attempt by government to stimulate aggregate demand is futile in that any effect on the economy of the extra public spending is fully offset by a displacement or 'crowding-out' of an equivalent amount of private spending. Over the years the 'crowding-out' debate has taken a multitude of forms, its importance having been argued on both theoretical and empirical grounds. The staunch proponents of the full force of 'crowding-out' support that it can be physical and direct, or financial and indirect; that it applies to both current and capital expenditure by the state, and that it is valid irrespective of the degree of utilization of the productive resources of the economy. The 'crowding-out' thesis is presented as an additional critique against an active economic role for the state: the public sector is not only inefficient and incapable of stabilizing the system – which is fairly stable anyway – but it is also utterly ineffective in influencing overall aggregate demand and the level of economic activity in the real sector of the economy. And although some aspects of this ongoing debate have provided valuable insights into the effects of different categories of public expenditure and of alternative ways of financing such expenditure, the case for a complete 'crowding-out' is far from being proved, either on theoretical or empirical grounds. More important, perhaps, the present experience of a prolonged and deepening economic contraction in many capitalist economies appears to have swung the pendulum towards a resurgence of the Keynesian view that, without direct government intervention, an economic recovery may take a very long time to materialize.

Political concern with the size of the public sector and interest among economists in the role of public expenditure were heightened in the 1970s because of the well-documented strong tendency of the growth of public expenditure to outpace the growth of Gross National Product. To the radical right this was a matter of vital concern as it was assumed to pose a great risk for the viability of the capitalist system. The main criticism was directed against Keynesian economic policies that were seen as the intellectual basis providing the green light for government to run budget deficits. The main thrust of public choice theory was that the state is prone to excessive and growing intervention in the economy. Being supporters of a minimal state, public choice theorists have advocated radical constitutional changes aimed at an effective diminution of the ability of the state to exercise discretion in the economic sphere. Theoretical arguments in favour of the balanced budget doctrine, of a constant rate of growth of money supply, of an independent central bank and of the denationalization of money are manifestations of this school of thought.

Although none of these policies has been fully adopted in the 1980s, the bulk of economic policies pursued by a number of governments of developed economies, especially those of Thatcher in the UK and Reagan in the US, were largely dictated by the intellectual force of such arguments. Large-scale privatizations, the abandonment of the commitment to full employment, the reduction of public sector employment, substantial reforms in industrial relations legislation and a number of other similar measures were presented as a means of rolling back the frontiers of the state. The tendency by governments to accept the principle of a more limited role of the state has had the effect of arresting the growth of public expenditure as a ratio of GDP. In the case of the UK this effect went further in that the public expenditure ratio was substantially reduced in the period 1983–89. This development should not be considered as irreversible, however, since there are already signs that under the unusually long contraction of the 1990s, the ratio of public expenditure to GDP is once more on an upward trend. On the basis of earlier experience over the business cycle, it can reasonably be argued that, in the absence of growth in the economy, the public expenditure to GDP ratio is likely to reach the post-war peak registered in 1975. Barr (1992) suggests that the re-examination of the role of the state in the 1980s was, to a large extent, motivated by ideology and macroeconomic stringency. However, he points out that, despite the new ideology, neither the Thatcher nor the Reagan administrations actually succeeded in rolling back the boundaries of the welfare state.

The Marxist left shares the radical right's view that the tendency of the relative size of public expenditure to grow is a source of some serious problems for the capitalist system. The analysis of the issues involved, the general disposition towards the problem as well as policy prescriptions are, of course, different between the two camps. As already explained, the right's solution amounts to a substantial shrinkage of state activity and a reduction in its ability to 'undermine' free markets or replace a free-market economy with governmental institutions. The left, on the other hand, suggests that while increasing public expenditure (in the form of social capital and social expenses) is a means of ensuring a continuous reproduction of the capitalist system, the parallel need to fund such expenditure is itself a source of new problems. It claims that the contradictory nature of the system cannot be transformed either through a shrinkage of state activity or a gradualist, reformist, social democratic agenda. It appears, however, that despite the historical swings of the political and economic pendulum, the social democratic state has a remarkable capacity to survive.

The history and experience of the last 15 years provide considerable *prima facie* evidence that doctrinaire positions of either the right or the left on the economic role of the state are untenable. Stiglitz (1989) adopts an eclectic position and provides a painstaking record of cases where the state has an important role to play. Keynes's (1936) advocacy of a large extension of the traditional functions of government to include a substantial socialization of investment as a means of securing an approximation to full employment is the classic example of the beneficial extension of state activity. The seriousness of the present economic recession is a strong reminder that markets are imperfect, that the capitalist system is bedevilled by business cycles, and that the unique powers of the state can be put to good economic use.

GEORGE HADJIMATHEOU

References

Bacon, R. and Eltis, W. (1978), *Britain's Economic Problem: Too Few Producers*, 2nd edition, London: Macmillan.

Barr, N. (1992), 'Economic Theory and the Welfare State: A Survey and Interpretation', *Journal of Economic Literature*, June.

Gough, I. (1979), *The Political Economy of the Welfare State*, London: Macmillan.

Keynes, J.M. (1936), *The General Theory of Employment, Interest and Money*, London: Macmillan.

O'Connor, J. (1973), *The Fiscal Crisis of the State*, New York: St Martin's Press.

Stiglitz, J.E. (1989), *The Economic Role of the State*, Oxford: Blackwell.

Rate of profit

A surprisingly uniform notion of the role and importance of the rate of profit in a competitive capitalist economy underlies almost every major school of economic theory. Abstracting from uncertainty, risk and barriers to competition, there is general agreement about the role of the rate of profit, defined as the ratio of net income per time period of a private enterprise to the total invested capital.

Profit theory is the intellectual arena in which radical critiques of economic theory have been the most successful. In the capital debates of the 1960s and 1970s it was clearly acknowledged by all participants that the attempt to define the rate of profits by appealing to traditional notions of marginal productivity and/or time preference was hopelessly mired in internal inconsistencies (Harcourt, 1972). Despite this critical success, though, the debate failed to supplant the use of marginalist theories of profit in mainstream economic analysis. In fact, for much of the economics profession, there is today little apparent awareness of the extent to which such comfortable notions as the aggregate production function and the marginal productivity theory of distribution can rightfully be appealed to only on purely ceremonial grounds.

Most serious debate in economics is of a highly internal nature, and it is evident that the main sources for alternative views on the theory of profits – the longstanding body of Marxist economics and the more recent Sraffa-based theories – have not themselves yet been capable of supplying a sound and widely accepted theoretical alternative to the reigning orthodox theory, not even amongst those dissatisfied with that orthodoxy. After much internecine warfare in the 1970s, Marxist theory was supplanted, at the level of high theory, by the more exacting logic of the Sraffian interpretation of an objective materialist rate of profit, centred around the classical notion of a surplus. Yet this notion itself has not proved to be immune from criticism. From a technical standpoint, the precise justification of the notion of 'equalized' rates of return upon which Sraffa's system rests has been particularly troublesome. Recent literature has shown that it is quite difficult to illustrate whether, and how, simple Sraffian systems might 'gravitate' to a position of long-period equilibrium in which all sectors exhibit an equal rate of return.

Even if the questionable validity of the basic assumption of Sraffian economics – that profit rates will tend to equalize across all sectors – is ignored, there is still little explanation in the Sraffian literature of what actually does determine this (presumed general) rate. Given the relative infancy of the attempts to construct a positive account of the economic process along the lines suggested by Sraffa (as opposed to the critical work it has inspired), most of the debates have been less about actual theories of the rate of profit than about the proper object and method by which the analysis of distribution should be pursued. At a simplistic level, the question can be posed as a choice between setting the rate of profit or the wage rate as the independent variable that closes the Sraffa model prior to the simultaneous endogenous determination of the other distributive variable and prices. Some have taken a cue from Sraffa's own brief comment (1960, p. 33) that since the 'rate of profits, as a ratio, has a significance which is independent of any prices and can well be "given" before the prices are fixed, it is accordingly susceptible of being determined from outside the system of production, in particular by the level of the money rates of interest'. In such models, as the rate of money interest changes with financial conditions and central bank policy, profits and wages lay claim to varying levels of the surplus created in the Sraffian production system. On the other hand, others (most prominently Garegnani) have argued that such 'non-persistent' forces as characterize the uncertainty and financial considerations appropriate to the determination of the rate of money interest are an insufficient grounding for a theory of distribution. Alternatively, they suggest 'closing' the Sraffian system by accounting the wage rate as logically prior to prices, not the profit rate. In so doing, Garegnani claims to be resurrecting the method of classical economists in their emphasis on the social and historical determinants of wages and in their reluctance to cast wages into a supply and demand framework.

These debates within the classical/Marxian camp will no doubt continue. However, it is worth noting that the insight Marx offered into profit cannot be exclusively confined within the theoretical concerns of the Sraffians or the neoclassicals. That is to say that both of these approaches consistently operate within an ahistorical abstract point of view in which neither the historical development of the system nor the concrete social positions of the system's agents (along with the relations of power and dominance that exist between them) plays any role. On an altogether different level is Marx's analysis of the social conditions which make the existence and level of profits possible. Thus, Marx's general theory of *exploitation*, as laid out in the first nine chapters of Volume I of *Capital*, presents the *origin* of profit as at once more abstract and more historical than is implied by the more traditional question of the relation of prices to the rate of profit. By Marx's account, the origin and fundamental point about profit is that it arises from the exploitation of labour, defined quite simply as a social setting in which the exchange value of labour time is less than the exchange value of that labour time's product. Thus for profit to exist requires a distinct, historically given, organization of production in which the roles and power of workers and capitalists are clearly defined. Moreover, this characterization of the process of production, and the associated distribution of the economic surplus of such a society, provide the fundamental locus of the characteristic Marxian view of inherent distributional conflict in a capitalist economy.

There is an important flaw common to all of the radical traditions noted so far, as much as to the neoclassical tradition that they so effectively undermined in the capital debates. So long as all of the dominant schools of thought on the rate of profit continue to assume that the phenomena of profit rate determination and equilization can be adequately situated purely within the production side of the system – in what Marx called the material basis of society, Sraffa the technical conditions of production, and the neoclassical theory the conditions of productivity and thrift – then so long will economic theory neglect the crucial roles of *financial* influences on the rate of profits. A truly radical view of profits, one that is alternative to the dominant outlook shared by the modern Marxist, Sraffian and neoclassical schools, would thus be one that recognized the large role played by financial considerations in modern investment and distribution, and which elevated these financial spheres of the economic process to an equal status with the 'real' forces emphasized by all the previously mentioned traditions of profit theory. The formidable nature of such a task can be recognized by considering the extent to which this also calls for a reformulation of the conceptual basis of value theory and of competitive behaviour generally. Elements of such a theory are nevertheless to be found lurking beneath the surface in the deep underworld of economic discourse; i.e. in non-orthodox radical economics.

When competition is viewed as fundamentally a financial process, it becomes evident that many of the traditional notions that have survived down to this day from the classical conception of the economic process are also in need of updating. The works of Keynes, Schumpeter, Kalecki and Veblen all represent various attempts to make this point. Schumpeter and Keynes are perhaps less likely to be accounted as 'radical' theorists, but the extent to which their basic insights are consistent with 'post-capital critique' economics has recently begun to be noticed (see Rogers, 1989). Kalecki is more likely to be counted in the radical camp; his work is particularly relevant in this regard in the sense that his approach to Marxist theory is so breathtakingly progressive when compared to the sometimes tawdry scholasticism into which the capital debates and the internal Marxist controversies of the 1970s often descended.

Kalecki (1968) can be seen as attempting to reorient Marx's analysis of profits away from a strict grounding in labour values and relative prices and towards a macroeconomic theory of aggregate profits defined in money terms. Thus his inspiration is Marx's suggestive analysis of the capitalist circulation process in Volume II of *Capital*. Yet rather than attempt, as Marx does, to reduce this process to labour value categories, Kalecki reinterprets profits as a monetary magnitude which is determined in circulation, not production. His own specific theory of the amount of aggregate profits (that they are determined as investment, minus workers' saving, plus the trade surplus with other economies, plus the government's budget deficit) is less important than the fundamental reorientation of profit theory he thereby achieved. Profits so determined are not seen as an index of surplus value, but as a *claim* on the surplus social product. Note that this does no violence to the basic notion, common to Marx and Sraffa (and the whole classical tradition, for that matter), that the characteristic feature of capitalist distribution is the struggle over this surplus. Nor does it rule out, or depend upon, any particular theory, such as Marx's Volume I account, of the *origin* of this surplus. But it does make quite explicit that the struggle over distribution will be carried out, not only on the Marxist's proverbial 'shop floor', but also in the boardrooms of financial institutions, the halls of central banks and even, in this day of mutual funds and pension plans, in the front rooms of wage earners themselves. Thus the financial arena becomes crucial to determining how the final claims over the social surplus will be exercised.

But perhaps the most subversive point of view on profit theory was that offered by Veblen (1904) at the turn of the century. Put simply, Veblen challenged the orthodox view of profits on the *a priori* grounds of ignoring the sense in which the source of the rate of return to ownership of the industrial facilities of a modern economy have changed since Adam Smith's day. According to Veblen, only in the 18th century, when the original classical writers set the imprint of future economic theory, did it make sense to conceive of the return to the businessman's or 'capitalist's' part in industry as purely a reward for their immediate supervision of the productive concern. This worldview was irretrievably altered with the rise of large-scale industrial capitalism, organized along the lines of the modern corporation. In these more modern times, Veblen argued, the pace and extent of technological advance (as Schumpeter was later to illuminate in his theory of profit), and the organization of markets where ownership claims can be traded with ease, liquidity and anonymity (which Keynes was to make so much of in *The General Theory*), have replaced the personal nature of classical competition with an impersonal financial process in which the motivating force is pecuniary gain through strategic purchase and sale.

The extensive revision in the categories of classical economic theory that this entails is thoroughly discussed by Veblen and used to weave his own highly original *Theory of Business Enterprise*. Here it is sufficient to note a few of the modifications to the classical view of the competitive process that Veblen suggests. First he takes explicit issue with the materialist concept of the 'uniform' rate of profit, arguing that what is now important in conditioning competitive capital flows is a much more expectational and immaterial 'prospective profit yielding capacity' of any given decision (p. 90). Such a process of competition is much less likely to foster the productive efficiency of the industrial system, he argues, than the common-sense view of the normal rate had in earlier times. This is because such trading profits are divorced from the classicals' underlying assumption that profits are earned by the capitalist-cum-undertaker pursuing productive activity as a way of life. Furthermore, industrial organization based on large corporations fosters the growth of monopoly factors that are more firmly entrenched than is usually presumed. To compete, these large enterprises are forced to resort to management of their markets through large-scale advertising (pp. 35–65). At the same time it becomes a competitive necessity to resort to 'credit finance' increasingly to leverage the firms' operations so as to speed up the financial turnover of capital (pp. 92–104). All of this results in a redefinition of the 'capital' upon which profits are made. No longer is capital just the aggregate market value of a firm's productive assets, as in the materialist theories of both the old and the new classical traditions. In modern business enterprise, argues Veblen, the predominant part of a firm's capital is the immaterial 'goodwill' felt towards it by the community of traders. Thus – and note the Keynesian vision emerging – the final point is that the very basis upon which profits are calculated becomes a question of the largely irrational process witnessed daily on the world's stock exchanges.

MICHAEL SYRON LAWLOR

References

Harcourt, G.C. (1972), *Some Cambridge Controversies in the Theory of Capital*, Cambridge: Cambridge University Press.
Kalecki, M. (1968), *The Theory of Economic Dynamics*, London: Monthly Review Press.
Rogers, C. (1989), *Money, Interest and Capital: A Study in the Foundations of Monetary Theory*, Cambridge: Cambridge University Press.
Sraffa, P. (1960), *Production of Commodities by Means of Commodities*, Cambridge: Cambridge University Press.
Steedman, I. (1976), *Marx After Sraffa*, London: New Left Books.
Veblen, T.B. (1904), *The Theory of Business Enterprise*, New York: Charles Scribners.

Regulation theory

The regulation approach has enjoyed remarkable popularity for over a decade as one of the leading paradigms in the revival of institutional and evolutionary economics. Although this is due in part to growing interest in Fordism, a topic with which the regulation approach is closely associated, this body of theory has much deeper and wider implications. It is best understood as a general research programme within radical political economy; as such it embraces several schools with similar approaches to the socially embedded and socially regulated nature of the capitalist economy. All these schools are interested in the historically contingent ensembles of complementary economic *and extra-economic* mechanisms and practices which enable capital accumulation to occur in a relatively stable manner over long periods despite the fundamental contradictions and conflicts generated by the capital relation itself. In particular, whilst far from neglectful of the essentially anarchic role of exchange relations in mediating capitalist reproduction, regulationists also stress the complementary role of other mechanisms (institutions, norms, conventions, networks, procedures and modes of calculation) in structuring, facilitating and guiding (in short, 'regulating') capital accumulation. Thus one could suggest that regulationists regard the structure of capitalist economies as a complex ensemble of social relations comprising an accumulation regime embedded in a social structure of accumulation; and that they analyse accumulation dynamics as a complex process consisting in the self-valorization of capital in and through regulation. Hence the regulation approach goes well beyond a narrow concern with production functions, economizing behaviour and pure market forces to investigate the wide range of institutional factors and social forces directly and indirectly involved in capital accumulation.

These concerns are especially clear in the Parisian school, which has styled itself the *école de la régulation* and is often regarded as co-terminous with this approach. The school comprises political economists such as Aglietta, Boyer, Delorme, Lipietz and Leborgne; has produced the most extensive body of regulationist work, and has been widely acclaimed in many disciplines (cf. Aglietta, 1979; Boyer, 1990). But even in France, one can find two other self-proclaimed regulation schools: a Research Group on the Regulation of Capitalist Economies (GRREC) and some communist economists associated with Paul Boccara. Moreover, if one looks outside France, further theoretical currents exist which operate with similar assumptions and acknowledge an affinity with the Parisians. Here one could mention an Amsterdam school of international political economists; a West German current concerned with states and societal regulation; a Nordic school interested in the specificity of the small open economies in that region; a radical US current interested in social structures of accumulation, as well as a significant number of radical geographers interested in the spatial dynamics of accumulation. In addition, many theorists and schools now employ such core Parisian concepts as 'accumulation regime' and 'mode of regulation' or invoke purportedly regulationist, substantive concepts such as Fordism and post-Fordism.

Given both the pioneering work of Aglietta and the current prominence of the Parisian approach, it is worth focusing on this school. It developed in the mid-1970s in opposition to structural Marxist and neoclassical views of the mechanistic *reproduction* of capitalism. From quite different assumptions, both perspectives claimed that capitalism somehow reproduces itself automatically, impersonally and immutably. To this essentially static account, Aglietta and other Parisian theorists counterposed the dynamic notion of *régulation*. This notion highlights the historically contingent economic and extra-economic mechanisms which lead specific economic agents to act in specific circumstances in accordance with the unevenly changing, objective requirements of capitalist reproduction. Aglietta's initial work focused on the changing structural forms of regulation in America, but other Parisian theorists studied developments in France and/or other European economies. By the mid-1980s they had elaborated the core concepts deemed most appropriate for exploring these changes. Each stage of capitalism is analysed as a long wave of economic expansion and contraction with its own distinctive structural forms; together these endow it with its own cyclical patterns and forms of structural crisis. Moreover, as advocates of a long *wave* (rather than long *cycle*) theory, the Parisian school treats the succession of stages as essentially discontinuous, creatively destructive and mediated through class conflict and institutional change.

There are four key terms in this approach. Firstly, an *industrial paradigm* is a model governing the technical and social division of labour. One such model is mass production. This concept is primarily microeconomic. Secondly, an *accumulation regime* is a complementary pattern of production and consumption which is reproducible over a long period. Accumulation regimes are sometimes analysed abstractly in terms of their typical reproduction requirements but, specified as national modes of growth, they can be related to the international division of labour. This concept is broadly macroeconomic. Thirdly, a *mode of regulation* is an emergent ensemble of norms, institutions, organizational forms, social networks and patterns of conduct which can stabilize an accumulation regime. This is a more meso-level concept embracing both economic and extra-economic factors. It is generally analysed in terms of five dimensions:

1. the wage relation: labour markets and wage-effort bargaining, individual and social wages, life styles;
2. the enterprise form: its internal organization, the source of profits, forms of competition, ties among enterprises, links to banking capital;
3. the nature of money: its dominant form and its emission, the banking and credit system, the allocation of money capital to production;
4. the state: the institutionalized compromise between capital and labour, forms of state intervention, and
5. international regimes: the trade, investment, monetary settlements and political arrangements that link national economies, nation-states and the world system.

And, fourthly, when an industrial paradigm, an accumulation regime and a mode of regulation complement each other sufficiently to secure for a time the conditions for a long wave of capitalist expansion, the resulting complex is analysed as a *model of development*. This is an holistic concept that attempts to depict the economy in its most inclusive or integral sense. All four concepts are typically defined to take account of the conflictual and antagonistic nature of capitalism.

Using such concepts, early Parisian work identified two main stages in capitalist development: an extensive accumulation regime associated with liberal, competitive capitalism, and an intensive regime accompanying monopoly capitalism. An unstable transition period intervened between these stages in the inter-war years when the intensive regime emerged without a suitable mode of regulation. Likewise the stagflation of the 1970s was held to signify the structural crisis of intensive accumulation and its mode of regulation. At first the school examined attempts to resolve this crisis and restabilize the intensive regime through 'neo-Fordist' techniques. More recently, its work has re-examined the conditions underpinning the post-war model of development (now explicitly treated as Fordist rather than as monopolistic), as well as considering possible new development models under the rubric of post-Fordism.

Of the other regulationist currents, the 'social structure of accumulation' school comes closest in broad outline to the Parisian approach. Developed mainly by radical political economists in the US in the late 1970s, it seeks to explain the alternation of rapid economic expansion and stagnation in capitalist economies in terms of the successive creation and collapse of a whole set of institutions and institutionalized compromises – economic, political and ideological – which, at least for a time, promote long-term economic growth. This is an important approach with great potential, backed up in several cases with detailed empirical work and sustained critiques of orthodox neoclassical approaches (e.g., Kotz *et al.*, 1993).

The most distinctive features of the other schools mentioned above can be briefly stated. The other French schools share a much narrower focus on the economic mechanisms that regulate the self-valorization of capital, with the GRREC putting more emphasis on the pluri-national character of modes of growth than is normal for Parisian theorists, and the PCF school stressing the potential of self-management to re-regulate capitalism in the interests of workers (GRREC, 1990). The Amsterdam school is distinctive for its emphasis on the generic conflicts between alternative industrial and financial concepts of control (or strategies of regulation) and its interest in the internationalization of such control (for example, in Atlantic Fordism; cf. Overbeek, 1993). The Nordic school is also concerned with the international dimension, but has a strong economic policy orientation (e.g. Mjøset, 1987). German work draws on the Parisian school for many concepts but its primary foci are state intervention, struggles for hegemony and the broader societal implications of regulation (e.g., Demirovic *et al.*, 1992). Lastly, radical geographers have been particularly interested in the contrasting spatial scales on which regulation (in whatever form) occurs.

The regulation approach has been criticized on several counts. Firstly, it is accused of functionalism, i.e., of assuming that modes of regulation emerge in order to meet certain functional needs of pre-given accumulation regimes. A regulationist might respond that modes of regulation are actually chance discoveries which co-evolve with, and thereby co-determine, different accumulation regimes. Secondly, the regulation approach is alleged to believe in objective and immutable laws of capitalism: it thereby ignores class struggle or reduces it to a ruse of capitalism's self-development. But almost all regulationists regard economic laws as mediated in and through specific institutions and practices and argue that no mode of regulation can contain class struggles for ever. Thirdly, it is sometimes said that regulationism is too simplistic, reducing post-war history to an inevitable transition from a stable Fordism to a stable post-Fordist era. This criticism would be better aimed at its superficial reception outside regulation theory proper. It also ignores the regulationist emphasis on historical specificity, as well as the increasingly broad empirical scope of recent regulationist work. Fourthly, the very idea of 'regulation' is said to imply that conscious action (notably state intervention) can somehow suspend capital's contradictions and guide accumulation without crises. This criticism is rooted in anglophone confusion between *régulation* (social regularization) and legal or state regulation. Finally, it is alleged that, because regulation theorists have speculated about new forms of compromise which might help to restabilize a post-Fordist capitalism, they are mere political reformists. There is no obvious single political message entailed in the regulation approach, however, and it would quite wrong to sacrifice its major heuristic potential because of secondary disagreements over political issues.

Indeed, regulation theorists have made major contributions both to the overall analysis of accumulation as a socially embedded, socially regulated process, and to more detailed accounts of the following: Fordism, the various conditions making for post-war growth, the causes of inflation, changing forms of internationalization, the state as a subject and object of regulation, the specificity of East Asian capitalism, the temporality of accumulation and many other issues. It thus remains a progressive research paradigm with many themes still to be explored.

Bob Jessop

References

Aglietta, M. (1979), *A Theory of Capitalist Regulation: the U.S. Experience*, London: Verso (first published in French 1976).

Boyer, R. (1990), *The Regulation School: A Critical Introduction*, New York: Columbia University Press (first published in French 1986).
Demirovic, A., Krebs, H.-P. and Sablowski, T. (eds) (1992), *Hegemonie und Staat: kapitalistische Regulation als Projekt und Prozeß*, Münster: Westfälisches Dampfboot.
GRREC (1990), *Crise et régulation: recueil de textes, 1983–1990*, Grenoble: DRUG.
Kotz, D., McDonough, T. and Reich, M. (eds) (1993), *Social Structures of Accumulation: The Political Economy of Growth and Crisis*, Cambridge: Cambridge University Press.
Mjøset, L. (1987), 'Nordic Economic Policies in the 1970s and 1980s', *International Organization*, **41** (3), 403–57.
Overbeek, H. (ed.) (1993), *Restructuring Hegemony in the Global Political Economy*, London: Routledge.

Rent

In the preface to his *Principles of Political Economy and Taxation* (1821), David Ricardo credits Thomas Malthus and an unnamed pamphleteer (whom we now know to have been Edward West) with the discovery of 'the true doctrine of rent'. A clear understanding of this doctrine, Ricardo observed, is indispensable to the analysis of how economic growth influences distribution, and to a correct assessment of the impact of taxation on different social classes. Within the classical theory of value and distribution associated with Ricardo, Marx and, in the 20th century, Piero Sraffa, rent represents an appropriation by landowners of a portion of the social surplus. It originates from two causes which may, but need not, operate simultaneously: land is, first of all, scarce, and is not of uniform quality.

The special nature of rent is obscured within the neoclassical analysis of distribution, which treats land no differently from labour and capital. Rent, like the real wage and the profit rate, is viewed as a market-determined price that reflects the relative scarcity of a particular category of productive factor; moreover, it is regulated by precisely the same substitution mechanisms that govern the prices at which labour and capital are hired.

By contrast, classical theory views wages, profits and rents as determined by distinct, though not independent, mechanisms. The real wage might be explained, for example, in terms of cultural and biological norms; then prices and the profit rate would depend upon the real wage and the technical conditions of production, given the economy's gross output vector. (Outputs are treated as data in the classical analysis of distribution; they are presumed to reflect historical consumption patterns, population, the level of economic development, etc.) Since neither labour nor the capital stock functions as a parametric constraint on the economy's production possibilities, the wage and the profit rate cannot be interpreted as indices of factor scarcity. Classical theory addresses the issue of scarcity exclusively in connection with the analysis of rent of land, where the latter is understood to represent all non-produced inputs other than labour. That is to say, *rent theory explains the consequences of resource scarcity for distribution and prices in a classical, or Sraffian, framework.*

A distinction can be drawn between extensive and intensive rent (or, alternatively, between differential and absolute rent). When land is so abundant that (i) only the highest quality land needs to be used, or (ii) society can increase outputs by bringing into use additional land of uniform quality in combination with the quantities of other resources that maximize the output per worker on each parcel (so that diminishing returns to labour and capital are not incurred), then there is no basis for the payment of rent. If, however, the demand for agricultural products is such that land of inferior quality must be brought into use, then higher quality (more productive) land will command a premium which is called differential, or extensive, rent; this premium will equal the difference between the value of the output produced on the higher quality land and the value of the output harvested on the least productive piece of land brought into use. Intensive, or absolute, rent emerges as a consequence of diminishing returns to the application of successive doses of labour and capital to a given quantity of land of uniform quality.

An important result associated with the classical theory of rent is the proposition that differential rent is not an element of a commodity's normal cost of production and therefore does not enter into its price. Ricardo demonstrated that the price of a commodity that requires the use of land as an input is regulated by the cost of production on marginal land, *i.e. on land that pays no rent*. This proposition might seem counter-intuitive. But its validity becomes evident when we recognize that, if a commodity's price *were* equal to the sum of the wages, profits *and rents* generated on average by the production of a unit of that commodity, then capital operating on less productive land – on land earning little or no rent – would yield higher rates of return than capital operating on more productive land, an outcome that is not only counter-intuitive itself but also patently absurd. The price of a commodity, then, can be resolved entirely into wages and profits.

This analysis was the basis for Ricardo's belief that capitalistic accumulation would be accompanied by a tendency for the profit rate to fall. As accumulation proceeds, the economy must bring into cultivation progressively less fertile land to feed a growing labour force. The increased difficulty of production in agriculture raises the price of food relative to manufactured goods, and accordingly necessitates (if we follow Ricardo in assuming the real wage to be given by historical circumstances) the payment of a higher money wage. On the supposition that the prices of manufactured goods remain unchanged in terms of money, the increased wage entails a diminution of the rate of profit. This process would be accompanied by increasing rents, and Ricardo therefore concluded that the interests of landowners are opposed to those of capitalists. His opposition to the Corn Laws was motivated by a concern that restrictions on the importation of grain would lead to an extension of the margin of land under cultivation in England, and thereby cause a decline in profits, with harmful consequences for economic growth. (He recognized, of course, that this tendency is counteracted to some degree by increasing returns in manufacturing and by technical progress in agriculture.)

Ricardo also concluded from this analysis that the burden of a tax on rents falls entirely on landlords, and that such a tax would therefore have no impact on prices or the profit rate.

A more rigorous analysis of rent than that presented by Ricardo is now available as an outcome of Sraffa's investigations. The discussion which follows is a condensation of Sraffa (1960, Chapter 11), Montani (1975) and Kurz (1978), to whom the reader should refer for thorough treatments. Ricardo's principal conclusions are confirmed, but some important results unknown to him concerning the connection of rental rates and land productivity to distribution, will emerge.

Consider an economy that produces $(n–1)$ manufactured goods and a single agricultural good (corn), the nth product. Manufactured goods are produced without the use of land, under conditions of constant returns, in given quantities $q_1, \ldots q_{n-1}$. Corn is produced on k parcels of land, each of different quality, in the amount $q_n = q_{n(1)} + \ldots + q_{n(k)}$, where $q_{n(z)}$ represents the quantity of corn grown on land parcel $\Lambda^{(z)}$. We adopt the following notation: a_{ij} and l_j $(i = 1, \ldots, n; j = 1, \ldots, n–1)$ are respectively the amounts of commodity i and labour required to produce q_j units of manufactured good j; $a_{in(z)}$ and $l_{n(z)}$ are the amounts of commodity i and labour used to produce corn on land $\Lambda^{(z)}$; p_j is the price of commodity j; w and r are the real wage and the profit rate; and $\rho^{(1)}, \ldots, \rho^{(k)}$ are the rents paid on each of the k parcels of land. We assume that all sectors are basic in the sense of Sraffa. The price equations for the economy can then be written:

$$(p_1a_{11} + \ldots + p_na_{n1})(1 + r) + wl_1 = p_1q_1$$

$$\cdot \quad \cdot \quad \cdot \quad \cdot \quad \cdot \quad \cdot \quad \cdot$$

$$(p_1a_{1,n-1} + \ldots + p_na_{n,n-1})(1 + r) + wl_{n-1} = p_{n-1}q_{n-1}$$

$$(p_1a_{1n(1)} + \ldots + p_na_{n,n(1)})(1 + r) + wl_{n(1)} + \rho^{(1)}\Lambda^{(1)} = p_nq_{n(1)}$$

$$\cdot \quad \cdot \quad \cdot \quad \cdot \quad \cdot \quad \cdot \quad \cdot$$

$$(p_1a_{1n(k)} + \ldots + p_na_{n,n(k)})(1 + r) + wl_{n(k)} + \rho^{(k)}\Lambda^{(k)} = p_nq_{n(k)}$$

The system contains $(n + k - 1)$ equations and $(n + k + 2)$ unknowns: n commodity prices, k rental rates, the real wage and the profit rate. One of the commodities may be designated as numeraire and its price set equal to unity. As in the classical literature, the real wage is determined exogenously. The remaining degree of freedom can be eliminated by introducing the condition that one parcel of land, the marginal parcel, generates no rents. This condition gives an additional independent equation: $\rho^{(m)} = 0$.

To solve the system we need only identify the marginal parcel of land. Note first that once the real wage is given, relative prices and the profit rate will depend upon the technical coefficients in manufacturing and in the process that produces corn *on marginal land*. The $(n\text{–}1)$ manufacturing sector equations, together with the single equation describing the process of corn production on no-rent land, form a self-contained system capable of determining the $(n\text{–}1)$ relative prices and the profit rate; the remaining equations serve only to determine the $(k\text{–}1)$ non-zero rents. It is possible to construct k such self-contained systems, each distinguished by the supposition that a different parcel of land is the one that pays no rent. Since each of these systems has a different n^{th} equation, there will be k different solutions for the profit rate. The parcels of land can then be ranked in order of profitability; that is, in order of the profit rate each yields when it is presumed to be the marginal parcel. Land will be brought into use in decreasing order of its profitability. As the demand for corn expands, capitalist-farmers will first make use of the land that yields the highest profit rate, then the parcel that yields the second highest profit rate and so on. The marginal parcel, then, is the land that yields the lowest profit rate given the real wage and the required level of agricultural output.

The model presented above is the starting point for modern discussions of rent from the Sraffian standpoint. Two significant, and unexpected, results have emerged from the analysis of this model. The first is that the productivity ranking of land is sensitive to distribution; that is, when the real wage is altered, the ordering of parcels of land in terms of profitability is also liable to change. Thus contrary to what Ricardo, and indeed virtually all economists, had taken for granted, productivity is not a purely physical attribute of land. No *a priori* comparison of two parcels of land with respect to quality can be made on the basis of their physical properties alone; the real wage (or the profit rate) must be known *before* a ranking can be established. This result is explained by the fact that changes in distribution give rise to highly complex patterns of changes in relative prices. It is therefore possible that wage rate changes might alter the costs of cultivation on different parcels of land in such a way that parcels that had been associated with low-cost (more profitable) processes at the initial wage are associated with high-cost (less profitable) processes at the new wage, and vice-versa.

A second result is that the ranking of lands of different quality in order of profitability need not coincide with their ranking in order of rent per acre. The two rankings *would* coincide if each acre utilized labour and the means of production in the same proportions; but in general the condition that entrepreneurs adopt the least-cost technique requires that inputs be used in different proportions on different types of land. A decline in the profit rate due to the extension of cultivation might therefore induce variations in production costs on different acres such that lands with improved productivity rankings at the new profit rate actually fall in the ranking of rent per acre.

Intensive rent comes into existence when more than one method of production must be employed on homogeneous land in order to meet demand. So long as unutilized land of given quality is available, the economy will accommodate increases in demand by bringing more land under cultivation with the technique that incurs the lowest unit cost per acre. But once all homogeneous land has been brought into use, further increases in demand can be accommodated only by the adoption of a second, more productive, technique. This more productive technique will be costlier than the technique that had been in use at lower levels of demand (otherwise the more productive technique would have been adopted first). Additional quantities of any commodity that requires land as an input will then be produced by two techniques operating simultaneously on different parts of the available land, in proportions determined by the level of demand, according to the criterion that unit cost of production be minimized for that level of demand. Since the higher-cost process regulates the price of the product, the lower-cost process will yield a rent which must be paid by entrepreneur-capitalists at a uniform rate per acre (because land is, by assumption, homogeneous). The commodity's price will adjust so that capitalist-entrepreneurs operating the second process are able to pay the required rent while earning the same rate of profit as capitalist-entrepreneurs operating the lower-cost process. Analogous reasoning applies if further increases in demand require the activation of still more costly techniques.

The relevance of rent theory extends beyond questions concerning the fertility and scarcity of land. The analytics outlined above constitute the foundation of a non-neoclassical approach to resource scarcity in general. Problems connected with the use and depletion of non-renewable resources, such as fossil fuels and old-growth forests, fall within the purview of rent theory. The return to obsolete machines and to monopolized technical knowledge (e.g. patents) can also be understood as forms of rent.

GARY MONGIOVI

References

Kurz, H. (1978), 'Rent Theory in a Multisectoral Model', *Oxford Economic Papers*, **30**, 16–37.
Montani, G. (1975), 'Scarce Natural Resources and Income Distribution', *Metroeconomica*, **27**, 68–101.
Ricardo, D. (1821) [1951], *On the Principles of Political Economy and Taxation*, edited by P. Sraffa, Cambridge: Cambridge University Press.
Sraffa, P. (1960), *Production of Commodities by Means of Commodities*, Cambridge: Cambridge University Press.

Savings

In the early 19th century the role of savings was one of the most hotly debated issues of political economy. Whereas most authorities, following Adam Smith and the Physiocrats, emphasized the beneficial role of savings as a source of finance for investment, some dissenters, of whom the best known is Thomas Malthus, regarded excessive saving as a potential source of deficient effective demand. It was on this basis that Keynes commended Malthus for his opposition to Say's Law although, other than his instinct, there was little else correct in Malthus's criticism.

Nevertheless, the question posed by Malthus has been a persistent theme in 'unorthodox' or 'radical' economic theory. This is not surprising, since savings are simply the part of income that is not consumed, and consumption is the largest and most visible component of expenditure. Moreover it is easy to persuade oneself that investment expenditure is in some sense subordinate to consumption, since investment decisions must depend on expected future demand. If there is one strand that runs through radical political economy on the subject of savings, it is the influence of income distribution, and especially the split between profits and wages. Marx suggested that the productive powers of capital would eventually come into conflict with the underconsumption of the masses; indeed, the potential for underconsumption created by an excessive share of profits in income has been a recurring story in radical political economy. The theory is quite straightforward: the (marginal) propensity to consume out of wages is less than out of profits so that, for the same level of income, a redistribution of income towards profits implies more savings and less consumption demand.

Radical political economy has been much more concerned with long-run tendencies in historical development than has orthodox thought. As a consequence it has tended to interpret particular episodes as manifestations of these tendencies rather than as a conjunction of special circumstances. Moreover the generally optimistic view of market systems in orthodox economics accentuates the tendency to see depressions, such as that of 1929–33, as unusual, whereas in radical political economy such experiences have stimulated the development of crisis theories that emphasize the transient nature of the preceding boom. Whether these crisis theories focus on the role of savings rather than other factors depends very much on the circumstances which the theories are attempting to explain. For example, in the 1930s underconsumption theories were popular because, during the 1920s' boom in the US, profits appeared to have grown significantly more than wages, thus increasing their share of national income. However the end of the long post-war boom in the 1970s did not create a fashion for underconsumption theories, but for crisis theories of other types, based on themes such as the over-accumulation of capital. The reason was that, if anything, the share of profits in income was being squeezed in the later boom years, partly as a result of trade union militancy; thus the underconsumption story was not a plausible one.

Formal analysis of the role of savings in economic development did not begin until the post-war period. In 1955 Kaldor published an article in which he treated investment as exogenous, as in a basic Keynesian model, but treated the *level* of income as constant, allowing the *distribution* of income to bring planned savings and investment into equality through changes in the profits share. He regarded this as a long-run model, arguing that normally income was fairly close to its full-employment level. However the treatment of investment as exogenous severely limits the relevance of the Kaldor model. Joan Robinson, in her *Accumulation of Capital*, tried to flesh out the model by allowing investment to be an increasing function of the profit rate. This produces a two-way causal relation between investment and profits, and may generate both stable and unstable equilibria, or no equilibrium at all, depending upon the precise specification of these relations.

In the 1980s there has been some interest in a more formal investigation of underconsumptionist arguments. Whether these arguments have any validity depends very much on the specification of the investment function. If investment is an increasing function of capacity utilization and the profit rate, then a redistribution of income from profits to wages has contradictory effects on aggregate demand. Consumption increases because of the greater marginal propensity to consume out of wages but, at a given level of capacity utilization, investment falls because of the reduction in the profit rate. If, however, the stimulus to consumption outweighs the reduction in investment, then effective demand grows and the increased capacity utilization may, in certain circumstances, actually cause investment to increase. Whether in practice a reduction in the profits share stimulates demand depends on the numerical parameters of the model, specifically the difference between the marginal propensities to consume out of profits and wages and the profits share coefficient in the investment function. If investment is very sensitive to the profits share, then the squeeze on savings through a redistribution towards wages will actually reduce effective demand.

A key point in the Post Keynesian theory of savings is the dual consumption function, whereby the consumption-income relationship varies according to the source of income: wages or profits. A consumption function of this type also appears in the work of Kalecki and was implicit in the writings of the classical period when it was generally assumed that real wages were at or close to subsistence level, so that saving was scarcely an option for workers. This specification of the consumption function sharply differentiates Post Keynesian theory from the more orthodox variety. However the difference is more apparent than real. Orthodox theory is concerned with consumption out of *household* income; since firms determine what proportion of profits reach households through their policy on dividend payments, the aggregate savings rate out of profits will reflect the decisions of firms as well as households. In the UK firms have tended to distribute about half of their profits to households, so the orthodox assumption of a unique household consumption function still implies a higher savings rate out of profits than out of wages, as assumed by Post Keynesians.

Do households save a larger proportion of income as they get richer? Budget studies of households on different income levels at the same date suggest that the answer is 'yes', which would imply that the aggregate propensity to save would rise over time as average incomes rose. However this has not happened at all in the US and only to a mild degree in other countries, the concern of much orthodox consumption theory being to resolve this paradox.

In many countries the savings ratio (the proportion of household income saved) has fluctuated significantly over the last 25 years, leaving macroeconomic forecasters with egg on their faces. For example in the 1970s there was a general tendency for savings ratios to rise at a time when inflation was relatively high and post-tax real interest rates were negative. Conversely, savings ratios have tended to fall again in the 1980s when real interest rates were positive. This is difficult to explain because it is precisely the opposite pattern to that which would be predicted by economic theory. One possibility is that higher inflation creates uncertainty in people's minds about future real incomes, either because their real income fluctuates more (given an unchanged frequency of salary adjustments) or because peaks in inflation have tended to be associated with recessions and significant increases in unemployment as a result of the oil price shocks of 1973–74 and 1978–80.

In the 1980s a major issue in some countries, such as the US and particularly the UK, has been the impact of financial deregulations on savings behaviour. Financial deregulation increases competition in financial markets and tends to lead to a relaxation of borrowing conditions as lenders compete for market share. In the case of assets such as houses, the increased demand that results from relaxation pushes up the price, encouraging further speculative buying; the increased wealth of house-owners stimulates further consumption which is often financed by borrowing against the increased value of the house. Institutional factors affecting the availability of mortgages for house purchase and other loans go some way towards explaining why some countries, such as Japan and Italy, tend to have particularly high savings ratios: in these countries consumers find greater difficulty in borrowing against their income and so need to save a larger proportion of the price before purchasing consumer durables or houses.

In the UK consumption expenditure began to exceed forecasts by a substantial margin from 1984 onward. The consumption boom came in the wake of financial deregulation and was accompanied by a bubble in house and share prices. The ratio of household debt to income doubled over the 1980s. Financial deregulation certainly contributed to the rise in house prices because of the relaxation of lending conditions, with a larger proportion of the house price advanced and higher multiples of income used to calculate the borrower's loan limit. Financial deregulation also led to a relaxation of restrictions on lending for the purchase of consumer durables. The consumption boom can be regarded either as a direct response to the removal of liquidity constraints or as an effect of the increase in housing wealth which, according to the life-cycle theory of consumption, should lead to a reduction in current saving.

The rise in consumer debt was unsustainable, particularly in view of the very high real interest rates being paid, the turning point coming with the end of the 1980s' boom. In both the UK and the US the subsequent recession has been prolonged by the reluctance of consumers to increase their spending in the face of a large burden of debt. This in turn has spilled back on the financial system, with an escalation of bad debts as households fail to service their loans and as the price of the assets (notably houses) used as collateral falls. Those countries which did not go in for wholesale financial deregulation avoided this 'boom and bust' in the household loan market and have experienced less fluctuation and greater predictability in their consumption behaviour.

Thus the recent behaviour of savings is not well accounted for by either orthodox or radical theory. However it has provided interesting evidence about the behaviour of deregulated financial systems. In good times, financial institutions become incautious and vie with one another for market share, matching the lending conditions of the most generous. Faced with unrestrained offers of credit, many households fail to foresee the implications of the accumulation of debt at high real interest rates. When economic conditions worsen, the whole house of cards collapses. But will the banks avoid the same mistake next time? They failed to learn from the excessive international lending of the 1970s, so why should they learn from the excessive domestic lending of the 1980s? Perhaps the one factor that will rescue the bankers from themselves is that there is no longer any apparently safe sector left to lend to.

MICHAEL BLEANEY

References

Guiso, L., Jappelli, T. and Terlizzese, D. (1992), 'Savings and Capital Market Imperfections: The Italian Experience', *Scandinavian Journal of Economics*, **94**, 197–213.

Kaldor, N. (1955–56), 'Alternative Theories of Distribution', *Review of Economic Studies*, **24**, 83–100.
Maddison, A. (1992), 'A Long-Run Perspective on Saving', *Scandinavian Journal of Economics*, **94**, 181–96.
Shafer, J.R., Elmeskov, J. and Tease, W. (1992), 'Savings Trends and Measurement Issues', *Scandinavian Journal of Economics*, **94**, 155–76.
Taylor, L. (1985), 'A Stagnationist Model of Economic Growth', *Cambridge Journal of Economics*, **9**, 383–403.

Sectoral balance

While the rate of economic growth in an economy is often explained in terms of aggregative determinants such as savings, investment and technical change, the importance of a proper balance between sectors is also recognized. Different sectors in the economy may be said to be in balance when they grow in relation to each other in such a way that the overall growth of the economy is not hindered. In contrast, when some sectors become relatively large or small so as to undermine the growth process, we may say that sectoral balance has been disrupted.

Interest in the question of sectoral balance in radical political economy has arisen from several important influences. First, classical political economists (and even some of their predecessors) – who emphasized accumulation and growth, and for whom sectoral distinctions were important characteristics of the economy – focused on the relation between sectors such as agriculture and industry. Marx developed his analysis of reproduction in terms of the relation between consumption and investment sectors, and discussed the possibility of crises as a result of sectoral disproportion. Second, models developed by some of the main modern inspirers of radical political economy have emphasized the role of multisectoral analysis. Sraffa has used a multisectoral model with intersectoral capital mobility where commodities enter into the production of other commodities. Pasinetti has extended this framework to examine accumulation over time, pointing out the difficulties associated with attaining balanced growth with full employment; this is due to changes in consumption expenditure shares of different sectors with income growth, and to differential sectoral rates of technical change. Kalecki has stressed the differences between industrial sectors with cost-determined prices, and primary sectors with demand-determined prices. Finally, the rise of development economics has revived old questions and raised new ones concerning sectoral interaction. An early concern of the subject was with the question of balanced growth; subsequently, questions on the interaction between agriculture and industry, consumption and investment sectors, and luxury and wage goods became central issues in the sub-discipline.

Much of the interest in the question of sectoral balance within the radical political economy tradition has taken the form of focusing on the role – positive or negative – of particular sectors in the growth process. The sectors receiving most attention include agriculture, investment goods, exports, luxury goods, services, non-market and unproductive sectors.

The relation between agriculture and the rest of the economy was an important issue for the physiocrats, Smith, Ricardo and Malthus, and has been revived with the rise of development economics. Two main approaches to the issue can be discerned within the radical political economy tradition.

One derives from Ricardo and sees the agricultural sector primarily as a source of wage goods for industry: agricultural stagnation improves the terms of trade for agriculture, increases the industrial product wage and thereby reduces profits and accumulation. Lewis's model (although it emphasizes the capitalist-peasant rather than the industry-agriculture distinction) pioneered a large literature which takes labour from the agricultural sector to be in unlimited supply at a given agricultural wage. A model of this type has been developed by Kaldor and presented as an alternative to the neoclassical equilibrium theory. It emphasizes the dynamic aspects of this relation between the two sectors, stressing the saving-investment processes in each sector; in dynamic equilibrium, the two sectors grow at the same rate so that an equilibrium terms of trade emerges. This framework has not only been applied to less developed economies, but also to the international economy in which the North produces industrial goods and the South primary products (see Dutt, 1990b).

The second approach, deriving primarily from the work of Kalecki, is reflected in models developed by Taylor (1983, 1991), among others: in the industrial sector, mark-up pricing prevails and output is demand-determined, whereas in agriculture, output is capacity-constrained and price is demand-determined. In the long run the two sectors grow at the same rate, sometimes at the exogenously-fixed rate of growth of agriculture, as in some of Kalecki's work on development economics. In the short run, agricultural expansion (or, consistent with Malthus's view, an improvement in the agricultural terms of trade) can help to solve the market problem for industry by increasing the demand for industrial goods. However, if Engel effects are strong, a higher agricultural price may necessitate greater spending on agricultural goods by wage earners, thereby squeezing industrial demand, as in Ricardo's story.

The relation between investment and consumption goods sectors was emphasized by Marx in his models of simple and expanded reproduction. An imbalance between these sectors due to over-investment in one could violate the balance conditions of smooth reproduction, result in excess supply and a fall in the rate of profit in the relevant sector, and bring about a disproportionality crisis. Subsequent work on the balance between these sectors has taken other directions. First, a literature which has developed around the Feldman–Mahalanobis–Domar model has shown how a closed economy (and also an open economy with limited export growth) has to allocate a higher share of its investment to the investment good sector to have (ultimately) a higher rate of balanced growth, implying that a small investment good sector reduces the rate of growth. The issue of how sectoral investment should be allocated on the traverse – the path to a long-run configuration – has also been examined by Lowe. While this literature investigates planned growth, a second set of models has been developed examining Marx's analysis of expanded reproduction under conditions of surplus labour (see Dutt, 1990b). These examine a variety of issues, including conditions under which the economy converges to a long-run balanced-growth equilibrium with intersectorally-equalized rates of profit.

Stagnation in export sectors can obviously retard growth in foreign exchange-constrained and demand-constrained economies. However, a relative expansion of export sectors can, in certain situations, create problems of the Dutch-disease type. Structuralist models of mineral-exporting countries have shown (see Taylor, 1983) that an expansion in mineral production (which is entirely exported) draws away non-traded infrastructure, in inelastic supply, from the manufacturing sector. The rise in the price of infrastructure may reduce both the production and export of manufactured goods, thereby reducing diversification in both production structure and exports, retarding economic growth in the long run.

The importance given to social class and income distribution in the radical political economy tradition has implied a strong interest in the role of the luxury goods sector. One means of examining the issue is to follow Sraffa's distinction between basic and non-basic goods (where the latter can be identified with luxury goods), arguing that technical change in an economy with a large luxury goods sector does not have favourable inter-industry effects. Another route, which has produced a rich crop of models, is the structuralist development literature. For instance, Taylor and Bacha (see Taylor, 1991) have shown how greater inequality (relatively more income going to skilled workers) results in a relative expansion in the luxury sector, which can excite investors into investing more in the luxury goods sector, implying greater inequality (since skilled workers obtain a higher income flow from the luxury goods sector). Other models, however, show that a relative expansion of the luxury goods sector may imply a lower rate of growth, because this expansion reflects a more regressive income distribution, which (given that richer sections of the economy have higher saving rates) reduces overall purchasing power and, hence, output and investment. If luxury goods also have lower labour requirements, this tendency will be exacerbated.

The remaining sectors have attracted much attention in the analysis of stagnation and de-industrialization in the US and UK, although echoes have also been heard in relation to developing economies.

Baumol has argued that a relative expansion in services reduces the rate of growth of the economy because the potential for growth in productivity of the services sector is far more limited than is the case for goods: thus service sector expansion, by drawing away labour (and other productive factors) from goods production, reduces the overall rate of productivity growth. An alternative argument – proposed by Kaldor and others – points out that manufacturing sector growth generates technological change due to learning by doing which has spinoff effects in other sectors: service sector expansion frustrates manufacturing from performing as this engine of growth.

Marx's distinction between productive and unproductive labour (where the former is involved in production proper and the latter in circulation activity) has been revived by Wolff and others. It is argued that an over-expansion in unproductive sectors (which do not experience technical change) diverts resources away from productive sectors which experience productivity growth. While this contention is similar to Baumol's neoclassical argument with fully-employed resources, a more Marxian approach emphasizes the reduction of the investible surplus due to spending on unproductive activity. Bringing in effective demand considerations, however, may support the arguments of Baran and Sweezy: expansion of unproductive activity will, by generating more consumption demand, increase the demand for goods, the actual surplus and, hence, the rate of growth of the economy.

Bacon and Eltis have drawn attention to the unfavourable consequences of growth in the non-market sector, which produces goods provided by governments rather than sold in markets. They have claimed that non-market sector expansion has crowded out productive investment (given resistance by workers in reducing consumption) under conditions of full capacity or full employment. Individual sectors such as defence have also been singled out for blame. Others, however, have pointed out that under conditions of excess capacity and unemployment, where effective demand considerations are important, non-market sector expansion can 'crowd in' (rather than crowd out) productive investment and thus stimulate economic growth; moreover, such expansion, through its positive effects on education and technology, can have further positive effects on growth.

This review of contributions on sectoral balance in the radical political economy tradition shows that we have learned much about the effects of a relative over-expansion or decline of particular sectors on the overall growth process. This literature has shown us that these effects depend on two key issues. First, they depend on the precise nature of sectoral differences – such as (for instance) how their products are used (for consumption or investment), income elasticities of demand, technical production conditions (differences in rates of productivity growth) and the technological implications of production (differences in learning and spinoff effects). Second, they depend on the macroeconomic characteristics of the economy: the implications of the relative expansion and contraction of particular sectors will have different effects on the economy depending on whether it is best described as a neoclassical economy which fully employs all its resources and invests all its savings, a Marxian one with surplus labour and in which all saving is automatically invested, or a Keynes-Kaleckian one where effective demand constrains the rate of growth. Much careful attention needs to be given to these issues before we can decide whether the relative expansion (or contraction) of one particular sector leads to economic stagnation.

AMITAVA KRISHNA DUTT

References

Dutt, A.K. (1990a), 'Sectoral Balance in Development: A Survey', *World Development*, **18** (6), 915–30.
Dutt, A.K. (1990b), *Growth, Distribution and Uneven Development*, Cambridge: Cambridge University Press.
Taylor, L. (1983), *Structuralist Macroeconomics*, New York: Basic Books.
Taylor, L. (1991), *Income Distribution, Inflation and Growth: Lectures on Structuralist Macroeconomic Theory*, Cambridge, MA: MIT Press.

Segmented labour market theory

Segmented labour market theory owes a debt to a number of sources. Theoretically, it is dependent upon a critical stance to human capital theory. It rejects the notion that the position of workers in (or out of) the labour market is primarily determined by their working potential, whether innate or acquired through training or experience. Rather, labour market position is structured economically and socially by factors that are entirely independent of the skills and preferences of individuals. Also, rewards and hierarchies in employment may not reflect the intrinsic demands of the jobs concerned.

A second theoretical component derives from the idea that capital itself is structured, most simply into a dual economy of monopolistic and competitive sectors – the primary (or core) and secondary (or periphery) sectors of the economy respectively. From this *industrial* structure, there is presumed to be a corresponding labour market structure, with primary jobs to be found in the highly profitable, monopolistic sector and secondary jobs in the competitive, low-profit sector. Primary labour markets are assumed to include secure, well-paid jobs, unionized with long-term career prospects, whereas secondary jobs are casualized, unorganized and low paid. There is limited mobility between primary and secondary employment.

This second theoretical element has been described as labour segmentation from the demand-side, i.e. either from what capitalists want or arising systemically out of duality in the industrial structure. From the demands of capital, there follows a labour market structure. To complete the analysis of segmentation, it is necessary to specify who gets to fill what are the otherwise empty places in the labour market structure – whether these be advantaged or disadvantaged jobs. It is generally presumed that the privileged, such as white male trade unionists, occupy the primary jobs, whereas the disadvantaged are confined to secondary markets. This borders on the tautologous, although there is the implicit assumption that whatever disadvantages a particular 'socioeconomic group' (such as ethnic minorities or women) filters through to assign them to inferior labour market positions.

This is what might be termed the supply side of the labour market. It has been associated not only with overt discrimination, but also with a range of socioeconomic variables such as trade unionism, differential access to education, and the constraints imposed on women as a consequence of their primary responsibility for domestic labour.

Initially, the theory had its modern origins in the work of Doeringer and Piore who argued in terms of a dual labour market, with some emphasis on internal labour markets and upward mobility being available only to those in primary employment. From that point onwards, in response to empirical acknowledgement of the extreme complexity of the structuring of labour markets, dual labour market theory had to give way to segmented labour markets in which the latter are both more numerous and potentially overlapping.

There have also, subsequently, been two separate main schools of thought. One is associated with Reich, Edwards and Gordon, US radicals for whom US labour markets are currently segmented, reflecting a particular phase in the development of US capitalism (its having previously been through the two phases of labour market formation and homogenization). Their analysis is predominantly supply-side oriented with segmented labour market structures corresponding to the imperatives of capitalist production and control of the workforce. Demand-side factors, such as race and sex, assign workers to the predetermined labour market structures.

The Cambridge (England) school takes this as its point of departure and adopts a more general approach. Primarily concerned with the causes and incidence of low pay, they argue, partially in criticism of the other school, that both the formation of labour market segments and assignation to them are dependent upon supply-side factors. Skills and corresponding grading, for example, are socially constructed and are not simply a reflection of job requirements. Trade unions have the ability to affect the definition of the skill structure and not just who gets what jobs within it.

With this approach, segmented labour market theory adopts an analytical structure that has a surprising parallel with traditional neoclassical labour market theory. In its simplest versions, the latter does not generate labour market structures, although these could be rationalized on the basis of informational and contractual imperfections, but it does depend on the interaction of supply and demand (as the interaction of the marginal product and the marginal disutility of labour). Segmented labour market theory also depends upon the interaction of supply and demand, but the factors making up these draw upon a wider compass. Also the outcome is perceived differently, giving rise to overlapping dynamic labour market structures rather than an allocatively efficient equilibrium, rewarding each individual according to his/her productivity and disutility.

This raises the problem of the exact nature of the theory involved and how it gives rise to labour market structures. There seems no doubting the empirical evidence for the existence of labour market structures, nor of the relevance in explaining this by variables drawn from the industrial structure (demand-side) and the social reproduction of labour (demand-side). But these two sets of variables tend to be counterposed to one another empirically, as if their theoretical connections were transparent.

This is borne out by the treatment of segmented labour market theory within industrial sociology where it has, unsurprisingly, occupied a prominent place. Here, as in radical economics, the status of the analysis as theory is far from explicit. There is a commitment to the notion that labour markets are structured and that the corresponding segments and occupation of them are determined by socioeconomic variables. The problem is, however, to what extent this moves beyond organized description, even if motivated by a general antipathy to human capital theory.

This observation is borne out by reference to the empirical work that has been done on segmented labour markets; this has been both extensive and invaluable, but also weakly rooted theoretically. Studies fall into two sorts. First, there are micro studies which identify particular segments, usually of the low-paid, whose wages and conditions are informally associated with indices of socioeconomic disadvantage and industrial structure. Taken together, these studies suggest an ever-increasing range of variables to be taken into account.

Second, there are studies of the economic structure and the segmented, labour market structure as a whole. On the demand side, this might use techniques such as factor or principal component analysis to identify an industrial structure which is then used to explain the presence of corresponding labour market structures. Conversely, in an analysis that has close affinities with the estimation of discrimination as the unexplained residual left after taking account of the variables from human capital theory, the same techniques can be used with socioeconomic variables on the supply side to grind out labour market segments. Here, again, there is an analogy with neoclassical economics, especially as the two approaches – one from the supply side, the other from the demand side – tend to have many variables in common; high capital intensity, for example, is both an index of industrial structure and of labour market skill. Essentially, the identification problem recognized in orthodox supply and demand analysis has been overlooked in placing emphasis on segmented labour market theory on either the supply or the demand side in macro-empirical analysis.

This reflects the previously noted absence of sound theoretical foundations for segmented labour market theory. In a survey of the literature, Fine (1987) has thus been led to suggest that the theory falls within the methodology of a middle-range analysis. For this, intermediate, abstract concepts such as labour market structure and supply- and demand-side variables are employed with only an implicit connection to more fundamental theoretical analysis (of capital or accumulation, for example). The middle-range variables are then readily translated into more concrete empirical observation to identify and explain labour market structures and inequality between them. By the same token, a labour market segment that has already been identified appears to be immediately explained by reference to the more abstract intermediate concepts.

In short, segmented labour market theory essentially belongs to an institutionalist tradition applied to labour markets, initially through the industrial structure, but subsequently in conjunction with other variables from the supply side. On this basis, appropriate and contingent explanatory variables are selected according to what appear to be the primary causal factors. These are only loosely linked to more abstract theoretical determinants.

BEN FINE

References

Doeringer, P. and Piore, M. (1971), *Internal Labor Markets and Manpower Analysis*, Lexington: Heath Lexington Books.

Fine, B. (1987), 'Segmented Labour Market Theory: A Critical Assessment', *Birkbeck Discussion Paper in Economics*, no. 87/12; reproduced in shortened version as a Thames Paper in Political Economy, Spring, 1990.

Gordon, D., Edwards, R. and Reich, M. (1982), *Segmented Work, Divided Workers: The Historical Transformation of Labor in the United States*, Cambridge: Cambridge University Press.

Loveridge, R. and Mok, A. (1979), *Theories of Labour Market Segmentation*, Amsterdam: Nijhoff.

Wilkinson, F. (ed.) (1981), *The Dynamics of Labour Market Segmentation*, with Introduction, London: Athlone Press.

Short period

The modern analytical treatment of time in economic models originated with Alfred Marshall's *Principles of Economics* (1920). Classical political economy had approached the economic system as a set of social relationships evolving over historical time. Thus their laws of motion could only be established after observing the system for a sufficient length of time. As authors such as Piero Garegnani and John Eatwell have proposed, a crucial methodological feature of classical political economy was the attempt to sort out the essential aspects of the system from among the accidental mass of facts that constituted the everyday operation of the economy. The assumption was that, if the operation of the system could be studied long enough, the accidental influences would cancel each other out and only the essential relationships would survive the passage of time. As a consequence, economics should be concerned only with long-run trends. For those focusing on the short run, anecdote would prevail over theory since agents would operate under misperceptions and temporary restrictions, exhibiting behaviours that would not be sufficiently systematic to be generalized to theoretical propositions.

Marshall's fundamental innovation in this field was to separate two aspects of the classical approach. On the one hand, he postulated that agents act in rational (intelligible) ways in the face of given known circumstances. If goals are known and the relevant features of the environment can be specified, one should be able to predict actions. On the other hand, the circumstances under which decisions are made are assumed to have specific durabilities, being themselves (at least in part) shaped by the actions of agents. Any situation is intelligible once agents learn the restrictions imposed over their choices, assuming they are rational – that is, that they consistently pursue their objectives. In this context, time matters insofar as it allows the environment to change, forcing agents to modify their choices so as to take advantage of new circumstances and thereby changing still further the environment itself.

In strictly analytical terms, all that Marshall was proposing was the possibility of developing a *decision* theory under specified restrictions. The temporal aspect of it was added through the intuitive proposition that, if time is allowed to pass, at least some of the relevant circumstances that restrict the options of agents may be considered to be changeable. If the environment is changing, one could then take the set of decisions corresponding to each context as temporary. Decisions define equilibrium situations since they are compatible with the perceived restrictions on the choices of agents. However, they are short-period equilibria, since at least a subset of the circumstances themselves may be considered to be temporary. Given the specific questions that concerned Marshall, he took these restrictions to be mainly represented by the quantity and nature of capital assets available at a given moment of time:

> For short periods people take the stock of appliances for production as practically fixed; and they are governed by their expectations of demand in considering how actively they shall set themselves to work those appliances. In long periods they set themselves to adjust the flow of these appliances to their expectations of demand for the goods the appliances help to produce (Marshall, 1920, pp. 310–11).

If enough time is allowed to pass, the environment itself (the stock of appliances) can be modified to shape a new context where the most advantageous decisions can then be made. The specification of short-period restrictions (in terms of the quantity and type of capital goods) was largely adopted in both the micro and the macroeconomic literature. Thus, Keynes presented his general theory of employment in terms of employment decisions made by entrepreneurs restricted by their existing productive capacity, while Kalecki's business cycle models consist of a description of a suitably defined sequence of short-period disequilibria in which decisions are made based on the 'wrong' data concerning the existing capital stock. This is because entrepreneurs are assumed to suffer from a 'perception lag' in their evaluation of the quantity of capital in existence at each moment (Kalecki, 1971). These developments allowed economic analysis to be applied to less persistent processes than those which concerned classical political economy, differentiating classes of phenomena according to their degrees of permanence.

The notion of periods, however, is still an attribute of an equilibrium concept; one is still talking about consistency with a given environment. As general equilibrium theorists remind us, to be able to conceive and describe an equilibrium situation does not mean that this specific situation may be reached by any actual process taking place through time. To achieve consistency, one has to learn the relevant features of the environment, and learning takes a run of time. If the circumstances change while learning is taking place, the agent may have to begin the whole process again before reaching the chosen period equilibrium.

Thus, in reality, the concept of period involved notional or logical time, not calendar time. If one thinks of equilibrium as actually attainable situations, to every chosen *period* (market, short, long, secular) – to every listing of restrictions on agents' decisions – there must correspond some definition of a *run* of time over which those restrictions should remain valid in order for the economy to move towards them. One should be able to define the run of time required to reach a short-period equilibrium, and the same for any other period. However, once one considers uncertainty as implying the possibility of sudden and unpredictable change in the relevant circumstances, one has to admit that equilibrium configurations may never be reached, even if they can be theoretically conceived.

These radical implications for the usefulness of the concept of equilibrium are not unanimously shared. Neo-Ricardians, and many of the variants of

Marxian economics, assume that although random disturbances may impact the economy in the short run, they are not powerful enough to lead to deviations from its path towards long-period equilibrium. Thus, short-period equilibrium is not a useful subject of analysis because in the short run disturbances may prevail. Only in the long run will the elements that determine a long-period equilibrium dominate over these random influences. In contrast, Post Keynesians and some variants of Marxian economics, such as the French regulationist school, admit that the longer the time horizon considered, the more unknowable (the more uncertain) the future becomes. It is only in the short run that the world may be assumed to be stable enough to allow learning. If this is so, one can define a *short run* as the lapse of calendar time necessary for the economy to move towards *short-period equilibria* because the latter may portray the actual scenario in which informed decisions may be made. This was precisely Keynes's point when he explained his concentration on short-period models:

> Thus we are supposing, in accordance with the facts, that at any given time the productive processes set on foot, whether to produce consumption goods or investment goods, are decided in relation to the then existing capital equipment. But we are not assuming that the capital equipment remains in any sense constant from one accounting period to another.
>
> If we look at the productive process in this way, we are, it seems to me, in the closest possible contact with the facts and methods of the business world as they actually exist (Keynes, 1979, pp. 64–5).

The view that short-period models can have more than merely notional interest, serving as a stylization of actual (empirically identifiable) situations and behaviours, was shared by Joan Robinson and was part of her legacy. Time and the concepts proposed to model it were some of Robinson's favourite subjects, especially in her later works. Already in *The Accumulation of Capital*, however, Robinson proposed the following:

> Everything that happens in an economy happens in a short-period situation, and every decision that is taken is taken in a short-period situation, for an event occurs or a decision is taken at a particular time, and at any moment the physical stock of capital is what it is; but what happens has a long-period as well as a short-period aspect. Long-period changes are going on in short-period situations (Robinson, 1969, p. 180).

Kalecki follows the same method of trying to reproduce the conditions under which entrepreneurs make their decisions by concentrating on short-period conditions. Differently from Keynes, however, Kalecki opted for treating explicitly the feedback of short-period *disequilibria* on the set of restrictions themselves. Instead of taking the capital equipment as given and describing behaviours compatible with that stock of capital, Kalecki chose to show that the decisions of capitalists to invest change the environment from one moment to the next, making any past choice obsolete in the face of the new-found conditions. Kalecki then conceived a system in which short-period disequilibria lead to a chain of situations that exhibit cyclical behaviour. Harrod explores a similar feedback of decisions on short-period restrictions to show that short-period equilibria can be linked to describe an equilibrium path to the economy.

FERNANDO J. CARDIM DE CARVALHO

References

Kalecki, M. (1971), *Selected Essays on the Dynamics of Capitalist Economies*, Cambridge: Cambridge University Press.
Keynes, J.M. (1979), *The General Theory and After: A Supplement, The Collected Writings of John Maynard Keynes*, Vol. XXXIX, edited by D. Moggridge, London: Macmillan and Cambridge: Cambridge University Press for the Royal Economic Society.
Marshall, A. (1920), *Principles of Economics*, London: Macmillan, 8th edition.
Robinson, J. (1969), *The Accumulation of Capital*, London: Macmillan, 2nd edition.

Social contracts

The development of social contracts in post-World War II Western Europe has been strictly connected with the rise and decline of the Keynesian welfare state. On the one hand, Keynesian policies and the growth of social expenditures made public institutions a primary source of allocation of economic resources. This led organized interests gradually to shift their action from the market to the state in order to influence its policies and to negotiate over the way public resources were allocated. On the other hand, the very decline in the ability of politicians to manage Western economies – dramatically shown by the stagflation of the 1970s – led many governments to seek support from the large interest organizations by involving them in economic policy-making. This happened for two basic reasons. First, to try and compensate for their weak political legitimacy as public authorities responsible for national economic performance by means of a social legitimacy provided by the major interest associations. Second, to use these associations as their main allies in fighting economic crisis, under the assumption that a basic instrument in this fight was the latter's willingness to subordinate their demands to this common imperative.

It is in this context that social contracts developed in several European countries, accompanied by the diffusion in the social sciences of such concepts as 'political exchange' (Pizzorno, 1978), 'neo-corporatism' (Schmitter, 1974) and 'concertation' (Lehmbruch, 1977). Both in this rapidly growing literature and among several policy-makers, one could detect a common belief during the 1970s that can be summarized in three points. First, social contracts provide the most efficient solution to economic policy problems in advanced industrial democracies, as is shown by the fact that 'neo-corporatist countries' have the best economic and political performances. Second, precisely for this reason, attempts to follow this path are – or soon will be – at work in several other European countries as well. Third, for these attempts to succeed, however, some institutional, organizational and cultural conditions are needed that are beyond the control of participants in social contracts.

The first belief may stem from value options favouring an orderly participation of trade unions in public policy-making, but in the 1970s it also seemed to find empirical support in comparative quantitative studies of the consequences of concertation on the performance of Western economies. Such highly corporatist countries as Austria, Sweden, Norway, Switzerland and Germany were shown to be the best equipped to face the various aspects of economic crisis, including inflation, recession, unemployment and decline in industrial productivity (Lange and Garrett, 1985). Also, they were shown to be the least vulnerable to 'ungovernability problems'. Some doubts on these general conclusions were cast by more qualitative analyses showing that, in each of these countries, there was a different trade-off between good performance in some of these indicators and bad performance in others, depending on the strategic choices made by their governments (Scharpf, 1984). Nevertheless the overall impression remained that social contracts were indeed the most adequate form of economic management in advanced industrial democracies.

The second phenomenon is easily explained by the former. The relative success of the first group of countries in facing problems common to all Western democracies led the political elites of other countries to experiment with institutionally similar solutions. In the late 1970s and early 1980s, three major European countries with traditionally non-corporatist policy-making systems engaged in several attempts at centrally-negotiated social pacts (Regini, 1984). Great Britain took the lead in 1974 with the 'social contract' negotiated between the TUC and the Labour party, which lasted (with diminishing success) while the latter remained in office, never to be revived after 1979 by Conservative governments. Italy followed with the so-called 'bargained laws' during the 'national solidarity' period in 1977–79 and with tripartite national agreements signed in 1983 and 1984. In Spain, either bipartite or tripartite national 'framework agreements' were signed almost every year well into the mid–1980s, after the 'Moncloa pacts' of 1977 had helped stabilize the new democratic regime.

All these attempts, however, were halted or even reversed during the 1980s when political elites all over Europe became either more suspicious of participation in economic policies by organized interests, or overtly hostile to organized labour, as in Britain. This loss of ascendancy of the social contract ethos of the 1970s was mainly explained by a lack of the organizational, institutional and cultural features that were regarded as necessary preconditions by the neo-corporatist literature. Among these, one should list the organizational centralization and concentration of the interest associations and their monopoly of representation; the presence of a pro-labour government in office, and a cultural tradition of cooperation and mutual confidence between private and public actors. While some of these features were present even in the cases mentioned above, no doubt very few countries (perhaps only Austria and Sweden) met the majority of conditions required by the neo-corporatist model.

Even in the latter countries, however, the situation slowly changed, calling for different explanations of the limited success which social contracts were enjoying. In particular, the new more unfavourable attitude by the European political elites stressed the need for a better understanding of the role that social contracts could play in their strategies, hence of the conditions under which governments might be willing to involve organized interests in economic policy-making.

Such conditions may result from two unintended consequences of the Keynesian welfare state. The first one is the growth in wage pressures (and, in some cases, in industrial conflict as well) that stem from full employment and the related increase in workers' market power, as Kalecki had foreseen some decades ago. Where governments cannot resort to authority to check the undesired effects of such power, they may try to transfer the distributional conflict from the economic to the political system, where they can compensate unions' self-restraint with welfare provisions and other benefits. The second unintended consequence is the greater incentive for a plurality of dispersed social interests to organize in order to put pressure on state institutions and to take advantage of the resources allocated by them. Where effective mechanisms for selecting and excluding demands are not easily available to governments, they run the risk of being 'overloaded' and of reaching a 'governability crisis'. Providing the large interest organizations with privileged access to state resources and involving them in the policy-making process may then be seen as precisely such a mechanism, one that also prevents these organizations from using *ex post* their veto power.

Besides these reasons for involving interest associations which relate to the unintended consequences of the Keynesian welfare state, one should recall that in the 1970s the fight against inflation had the highest priority in the economic policy agendas of most European countries. Before monetarist policies attracted a growing number of political elites, consensual incomes policies were generally seen as the major instrument in such a fight. Thus social contracts in that period inevitably revolved around voluntary incomes policies in one form or another, which the large interest organizations agreed to, often in exchange for more generous welfare provisions or state support to industry.

Remarkably, these defining conditions of the 1970s to a large extent disappeared in the following decade, when labour became far weaker, state resources significantly decreased and inflation lost its status as the preeminent problem in economic policy agendas. Here undoubtedly are the main reasons for the general shift in European government strategies during the 1980s.

Even before, however, the trend to concertation and social contracts could hardly have been seen as a generalized one. In different periods and countries, different solutions have been found to the common problems discussed above. Governability has long been achieved in Italy, especially in the south, via forms of patronage that provided an 'atomistic' consensus. In France, labour exclusion – rather than involvement – has been the key to controlling distributional conflict. And pluralist pressure politics has always dominated the North American political economies, characterized by little (if any) participation of weak and competing interest associations in state policy-making.

The extent of experimentation with social contracts can thus be seen as dependent not only on pre-existing institutions, but also on the changing interests and varying cultures of the public and private actors. In contrasting the countries in which social contracts have had a long and rather stable history with the ones where late attempts basically failed, one should not overlook major differences even among the former. The content and the outcomes of the political exchange taking place in the different experiences of social contract have in fact showed wide variations. What the neo-corporatist literature has generally called 'concertation' actually covers quite different institutional arrangements corresponding to different power relations among its actors. It is precisely the diversity in their relationships of political power that accounts for the differences in the formative process, the content and the outcomes of these arrangements.

With this perspective, one can distinguish three main groups of experiences of social contract. The first one, characteristic of Sweden, Norway and Austria, has been a long-lasting, highly stable concertation under the relative hegemony of labour. Strong and (in Sweden) initially militant trade unions have imposed a generalized social contract as part of their own strategy, and have largely succeeded in shaping its content. The second one has been equally stable, but can better be described as a subordinate incorporation of labour in economic policies. Examples are Switzerland and Holland, where weaker trade unions have been offered a status in public policy-making but have not been able to influence it effectively, as shown by the more limited expansion of the welfare state and of redistributive policies in these countries. Finally, Britain and Italy in the 1970s, together with Denmark, experienced a highly unstable type of concertation. Trade unions were in these countries strong and militant but, for various reasons, the possibilities for them to achieve substantial results in the political arena were limited, leading them to enter only short-term social pacts while resisting more generalized forms of cooperation.

One can, in conclusion, discern both general trends and major differences in the diffusion of social contracts among European countries. While it is fair to say that the 1970s was the decade of most dramatic expansion and that the 1980s witnessed a generalized decline, one should not overlook the wide variations within both trends. Should European governments be tempted to look to social contracts again in the 1990s, it is safe to predict that their chances of success will be quite uneven and will probably depend on their history in each individual country.

MARINO REGINI

References

Lange, P. and Garrett, G. (1985), 'The Politics of Growth: Strategic Interaction and Economic Performance in the Advanced Industrial Democracies, 1974–1980', *Journal of Politics*, **47** (3).

Lehmbruch, G. (1977), 'Liberal Corporatism and Party Government', *Comparative Political Studies*, **10** (1).

Pizzorno, A. (1978), 'Political Exchange and Collective Identity in Industrial Conflict' in C. Crouch and A. Pizzorno (eds), *The Resurgence of Class Conflict in Western Europe since 1968*, London: Macmillan, Vol. 2.

Regini, M. (1984), 'The Conditions for Political Exchange: How Concertation Emerged and Collapsed in Italy and Great Britain' in J. Goldthorpe (ed.), *Order and Conflict in Contemporary Capitalism*, Oxford: Clarendon Press.

Scharpf, F. (1984), 'Economic and Institutional Constraints of Full-Employment Strategies: Sweden, Austria and West Germany, 1973–1982' in J. Goldthorpe (ed.), *Order and Conflict in Contemporary Capitalism*, Oxford: Clarendon Press.

Schmitter, P. (1974), 'Still the Century of Corporatism?', *Review of Politics*, **36**.

Social conventions

It is well known that orthodox neoclassical economic theory does not provide a satisfactory logic to explain the many and important instances of collective action involving many persons and therefore characterized by the prisoners' dilemma and the associated free-rider incentives. An alternative approach to the explanation of collective action has been built on the concept of social customs, developed originally by Akerlof (1980), to provide a microfoundation for a theory of unemployment. Akerlof defines a social custom as an 'act whose utility to the agent performing it in some way depends on the beliefs or actions of other members of the community' (p.749). This approach is grounded in utility theory but introduces the possibility of interdependence across individuals' actions and beliefs.

In recent years, the social custom framework has been applied to the problem of collective action. Booth (1985) is concerned with providing an explanation for the existence of the open-shop trade union. Booth observes that UK workplaces are often characterized by union membership in the absence of compulsory closed-shop agreements, arguing that such membership is costly to the individual and yet cannot be explained by incentive private goods. As all workers in these unionized establishments are paid a uniform wage independent of the individual worker's union status, any gains secured by the union have the characteristics of a public good. Booth is able to show how a simplified version of the social custom model is able to provide an explanation for the existence of voluntary union membership. Membership is driven by each individual's sensitivity to 'reputation' effects: individuals derive utility from conforming with the behaviour of others. Thus, both zero and 100 per cent membership are stable equilibria.

Naylor (1989) develops a more general social custom model to explain the existence and persistence of collective action. In this approach, an individual chooses whether or not to join in a collective action not only according to reputation effects, but also according to whether the individual is a believer in the social custom or not. In the context of collective action, the social custom is best thought of as the appeal to individuals within the community to refrain from free-riding. For any given level of belief in the social custom, and taking account of other parameter values (such as the cost of action to the individual and the extent of individual sensitivities to reputation effects), there will be some level of adherence to the social custom. So far the approach is based firmly on the principles of individual optimization. But the outcome is defined as stable only if the resulting *degree of adherence* to the social custom is equal to the initial and given *extent of belief* in the social custom. If this condition is not satisfied, then it is assumed that the proportion of the population believing in the social custom will change until it generates an equal degree of adherence. This is then the steady-state self-supporting equilibrium. To assume that, out of equilibrium, it is the proportion of the population believing in the social custom which changes may be arbitrary, but this can be justified in various ways. For example, a cognitive dissonance argument would be consistent with a shift to belief in the social custom by those individuals previously not believing, but nonetheless joining in the collective action on the strength of the reputation or solidarity effects.

In this approach, then, individuals choose optimally whether or not to adhere to the social custom, but they do not make an optimizing decision regarding their belief in the social custom: this depends both on their own adherence decision (itself influenced by the actions and beliefs of others) and on such other socio-psychological characteristics as relate to the cognitive dissonance argument. In sum, an explanation of the degree of support for a given social custom – or of the existence of a particular social norm – rests on neither 'structureless agency' nor 'agentless structure'. The social custom approach incorporates important elements of rational choice theory, but is not based exclusively on the assumption of optimizing agents with exogenous preferences: the socioeconomic environment (itself only partly explained within the model) and the psychological responses of individuals are other crucial features of the model. This suggests that the framework developed by the school of rational choice Marxists may be an appropriate one for analyses in which social norms and customs are important only if this framework relaxes the assumption of fixed and exogenous individual preferences. If this is so, then whilst there is a valid, if limited, role for rational choice theory, methodological reductionism to the level of the individual will be seen as unproductive.

The foregoing begs an important question: 'What is the origin of the social customs whose existence we have so far taken as given?' As examples, why might there be social customs evoking individuals to join unions, to pick up litter, to give blood, to pay taxes or more generally to refrain from free-riding?

Let us consider, then, the issue of the emergence of social norms. Within rational choice theory, we have already distinguished between, on the one hand, an economic agent whose preferences are given and self-regarding and, on the other, a socioeconomic agent whose goals and choices are likely to be influenced by the actions and beliefs of others. We shall now argue that it is possible to explain the emergence of what Sugden terms a 'social convention' within a model built on the assumption of rational economic agency. But we shall argue, with Sugden, that a social convention is different from a social norm, and that the emergence of the latter takes us outside the narrow scope of rational economic agency.

Sugden (1986) develops a game-theoretic explanation of the emergence of social conventions. He presents conventions as rules regulating social life and as evolving spontaneously to become self-enforcing once established. More formally, a convention is defined as any stable equilibrium in a game that has two or more stable equilibria. Sugden distinguishes between three broad categories of conventions (conventions of coordination, of property and of reciprocity). The convention of reciprocity is the most relevant to our foregoing discussion of collective action problems, as Sugden shows how repeated public-good games provide one context for the evolution of such conventions. In such games individuals choose between strategies of cooperation (e.g. of joining a collective action) and defection (free-riding); whilst cooperation is not in individuals' immediate interests, a stable strategy (such as tit-for-tat) of cooperating with other cooperators can arise under appropriate circumstances. One condition for this is that the probability of the game finishing after any given round is sufficiently small. The crucial assumption here, of course, is that the game is not being played anonymously. If a fellow player is either unlikely to meet you again, or unlikely to either recognize you or remember your deed in the future, then there is little scope for the evolution of a convention of cooperation.

Enforcements can be classified into two categories. In the repeated game literature, the 'folk theorem' provides a formal model of personal enforcement occurring when the same set of agents frequently play the same stage game ad infinitum. A second mechanism is community enforcement which can generate social norms of cooperation when facilitated by the labelling of defectors. Yet cooperation also exists in circumstances under which labelling is not feasible. There are a number of possible reasons for this. The first is often dismissed as tautological. It is the argument of the in-process benefits of giving: this widening of the interpretation of utility can always be offered in defence of rational choice theories. A second answer adds some psychological flesh to the bones of the rational economic agent, suggesting that individuals have basic emotional responses of resentment and guilt to the breaking of established conventions. This case is developed by Sugden (1986, Ch. 8). In this way it could be argued that an apparently unsustainable social norm of cooperating in a one-shot prisoners' dilemma can evolve from a social convention of reciprocal cooperation when the latter acquires a moral force through the psychological reactions of individuals. As a corollary of this view, one could justify the social custom approach discussed earlier.

Economic rationality, then, can account for the evolution of social conventions, but some socio-psychological structure is needed to explain the development of the social norms which are capable of sustaining cooperation in the face of a dominant free-rider incentive. The inclusion of a role for social norms is likely to be most relevant in circumstances favourable to the evolution of social conventions. This is more likely when a group of individuals is homogeneous and highly interactive. This approach also provides an economic underpinning for the sociological argument deriving from Kerr and Siegel (1954) who distinguish between the 'isolated mass' and the 'integrated individual'. The isolated mass is said to possess its 'own codes, myths, heroes and social standards' and consequently to be the more capable of sustaining collective action. It might be argued that individuals whose social development has been within such an environment are more likely to contribute towards public good provision. Thus, in some sense, apparently altruistic behaviour is a backward-looking or learned response. The argument which started out as a rational choice micro-foundation for social conventions has acquired a behaviouralist element through the inclusion of a role for psychological responses such as guilt and resentment.

It would appear, then, that traditional rational-choice economic theory can explain the evolution of social conventions of reciprocal cooperation. Unreciprocated or altruistic cooperation is explicable as the behaviour of an individual who has attributed a moral force to those social conventions through his/her proneness to guilt or resentment, amongst other psychological responses. Thus do social norms or customs evolve. Importantly, we should note that there is no reason to suppose that the particular convention or the norm which becomes established will be the one which maximizes social welfare. So what does determine the selection of a particular convention? Sugden contends that versatility is an important criterion. Schelling (1960) argues in favour of prominence which 'depends on time and place and who the people are'. One is 'dealing with imagination as much as with logic' (p. 58). This leaves an important role for the analysis of how individuals interpret their environment within which they then make their behavioural choices.

To this point we have stayed within the tradition of methodological individualism in discussing the spontaneous evolution of social conventions and norms pertaining to the logic of collective action. However, a further possible influence on the selection of social conventions is the exertion of power by groups of agents with both influence and vested interests in the arrangement of such conventions. For example, by capturing political power, groups or classes can seek to shape the environment in which social conventions evolve. Our analysis would suggest that governments wary of the development of communities capable of organizing effective collective action would have an incentive to avoid the generation of 'isolated masses' of individuals. To the extent that collective provision is an alternative to market provision, the interests of profit-seekers would imply the same incentive. More generally, the argument that individuals' preferences are influenced by social and psychological factors provides a channel through which commercial forces originating in the objectives of producers can be seen to shape individual behaviour. Once it is established that the wants to which capitalist production is responding are, at least in part, determined directly or indirectly within a capitalist system of production, then the whole structure of that system is invertible.

To conclude, then, it is argued that social attitudes (such as those captured by social conventions) are likely to influence individual economic behaviour in the spheres of both public good and private good provision. To some significant extent the persistence of social conventions can be explained by rational individual behaviour – although there need be no presumption that the conventions which survive will be the most efficient. We have drawn a distinction between social conventions and social norms, arguing that the latter are not wholly explicable in a rational choice analysis, but motivate the social custom framework for the economic analysis of collective action problems.

ROBIN NAYLOR

References

Akerlof, G. (1980), 'A Theory of social Custom of which Unemployment may be one Consequence', *Quarterly Journal of Economics*, **94**, 749–75.

Booth, A. (1985), 'The Free Rider Problem and a Social Custom Model of Trade Union Membership', *Quarterly Journal of Economics*, **100**, 253–61.

Kerr, C. and Siegel, A. (1954), 'The Inter-Industry Propensity to Strike – an International Comparison' in A. Kornhauser, R. Dubin and A. Ross (eds), *Industrial Conflict*, New York: McGraw-Hill.

Naylor, (1989), 'Strikes, Free Riders and Social Customs', *Quarterly Journal of Economics*, **104**, 771–85.

Schelling, T. (1960), *The Strategy of Conflict*, Cambridge, MA: Harvard University Press.

Sugden, R. (1986), *The Economics of Rights, Co-operation and Welfare*, Oxford: Blackwell.

Social policy

The term 'social policy' is a comparatively recent one in British academic life. Like industrial relations, social policy is still typically regarded as an area of study rather than a clearly defined and established discipline *per se*. Certainly, like industrial relations, it draws upon a number of academic disciplines. However, despite a continuing viewpoint in favour of inter-disciplinary inquiry, the clear tendency has been towards specialized discipline-based studies. In this multi- rather than inter-disciplinary milieu, sociology and social administration have predominated; however, from the late 1960s onwards, academics in these disciplines have been increasingly forced to concern themselves with both economic factors and the contributions of economists.

In general the invasion of economics into social policy has been undertaken by those of a neoclassical persuasion. Certainly most of the work in specific policy areas has been within this framework. Non-orthodox economists have largely concentrated on overviews of the welfare system. Consequently in what follows attention will be focused on the broader issues such as the functions of, and the constraints upon, social provision, and especially the nature of the inter-relationships between social policy and the economy.

In the period since 1945, the dominant social policy tradition in the UK has been a pragmatic, empirically oriented and values-based Fabianism epitomized by the work of Richard Titmuss. Titmuss emphasized only the value conflicts between social and private market provision. During a period of steady economic progress and high employment, he and other defenders of state social provision were untroubled by the need to present a systematic analysis of the economic consequences of welfare provision. In the more troubled times of the 1970s, however, the idea of conflict between economic and social goals was forcefully raised by the New Right. Defenders of social provision reacted to this by producing empirical work testing the validity of New Right claims, and by reformulating and elaborating the economic and social case for the welfare state.

As regards the former, important work has been done by the Swedish researcher, W. Korpi, whose work does not substantiate the claims that social provision has had a negative effect on productivity and the growth of output. Korpi's analysis indicates no strong negative correlation between the size of social security expenditures and economic growth rates. Furthermore, the severity with which different countries were hit by post-1973 economic crises does not seem to be related to the size of their public sectors or of their welfare states (Korpi in Bulmer *et al.*, 1989).

As regards detailed defences of welfare policies by economists, neo-institutionalists in the US have been very much to the fore. From Hamilton through Ayres to Klein and Dugger, social provision has been defended on instrumental grounds. The strong underconsumptionist tradition within institutionalism has meant that redistributive policy has been seen as important to the achievement of a continuously rising effective demand essential to the steady growth of output and the maintenance of high employment levels. Recently, galvanized by the work of the New Right, Dugger has attacked neoclassicism's failure to recognize the vital role of welfare policies and progressive tax regimes as automatic stabilizers in capitalist societies which have tendencies towards underconsumption and cyclical instability.

Dugger, however, argues not just that there is no fundamental conflict between equity and efficiency in the conventional sense, but also that welfare policies serve, to use P.A. Klein's terminology, the 'higher efficiency': they are, he argues, part of a complex matrix of institutional arrangements that humanize and give coherence to society (Dugger in Lutz, 1989).

Unlike the institutionalists, Marxists have agreed with much of the New Right's economic critique of the welfare state, although they query the neo-conservatives' understanding of its socio-political role and criticize their failure to perceive the basic contradictions at play. Utilizing the now familiar accumulation versus social legitimization approach, they have argued that the provisions of the welfare state impose regulations on capital and constitute rights to labour that can reduce the possibilities for, and assist the ability to resist, exploitation. Curbing social provision therefore can assist accumulation, but will tend to create legitimation problems. Thus the fundamental contradiction of welfare capitalism is seen to be that while it cannot do without a detailed network of social policy, it cannot happily subsist with it.

From this viewpoint a strategy of privatization and restriction of social expenditures might appeal to the New Right, but it is one beset with problems.

The apparent attempts by neo-conservative governments in the 1980s to carry out such a strategy have generated considerable debate. One of the most discussed aspects of this strategy has been its distributional impact. Most writers have emphasized the ways in which inequality of outcome and opportunity widened in the decade, but Papadakis and Taylor-Gooby have argued that policy changes in the UK in the 1980s have added to the complexity of, rather than merely uniformly exacerbated, pre-existing inequalities. An important aspect of this process, it is alleged, is that attempts to restrict state involvement in welfare may only succeed in redirecting it. Even in housing, by common consent the most affected area in the UK, it has been argued that reduction in direct council housing provision has been partially balanced by an expansion of indirect state subsidy directed away from council house tenants but towards the very poor (on housing benefit) and the better off (receiving mortgage tax relief). Hence it has been concluded that a simple 'rolling back the frontiers of the state' is not easy in welfare areas and has not been systematically achieved in the UK (Papadakis and Taylor-Gooby, 1987).

In a recent interesting analysis of the impact of economic events upon welfare provision, T. Davies has presented a picture of economic crisis leading to attempts to improve efficiency (restructuring) which, in turn, produces a downgrading or reversal of redistributive objectives, efforts to get 'more policy for less money', and labour market policies designed to 'meet the needs of employers'. For many this picture would appear to fit the circumstances of the UK and other Western capitalist countries in the 1980s.

Davies's work, however, is based on the experience of Hungary and leads him to conclude that, in a period of world economic crisis, countries are faced with rather constrained choices in the formulation of social welfare policy. How one interprets this analysis will no doubt be affected by one's perception of the nature of pre-reform Eastern European economies. Even if they are viewed as state capitalist rather than socialist or communist societies, however, one still has to take account of the fact that several of them adopted a strategy for the achievement of welfare goals that was quite different from those pursued in Western countries (Davies in Millard, 1988).

A perspective on the successes and failures of this strategy in her native Hungary has been provided by Z. Ferge. The prevailing view in Hungary was that, under socialism, social policy in its Western manifestation became redundant. Instead, social objectives were to be carried out through the operation of the economy. Ferge suggests that some degree of success was achieved via this strategy in that, whilst wages remained low, the distribution of income was markedly levelled and the impact of low wages was offset by a system of price controls that gave wide access to the basic necessities of life. Further, the commitment to full employment, a goal achieved in the late 1960s, facilitated a significant reduction in the incidence of poverty.

Old structural inequalities, however, were replaced by new ones, Ferge argues, and the relationship between the economic and social spheres was neither genuinely organic nor harmonious. In Ferge's view the gains of the strategy were achieved at the cost of economic backwardness which eventually caused social harm. It did so by the reproduction of low-skill jobs, by ultimately leading to the under-financing of so-called 'unproductive' social services, and by creating a severe shortage of resources for those unable or unwilling to work. Ferge concludes therefore that, whilst the political process forced some important social functions onto the economy, the economy was damaged by the scale and type of political intervention; ultimately, its ability successfully to achieve social purposes was compromised (Ferge in Bulmer *et al.*, 1989).

A greater awareness of the pressures on welfare provision, and perhaps a diminished confidence in it, have provoked recurring talk of the 'crisis of the welfare state'. Certainly the alleged shortcomings of the system of welfare have been extensively aired. For those on the left one such failure has been the inability to achieve a more significantly progressive redistribution of income and life opportunities. Indeed, it has become apparent that governmental fiscal activity in areas such as transport, housing and education has often differentially favoured the better off. Faith in the 'strategy of equality' underlying the welfare state has in consequence been weakened. Furthermore, the usefulness of any strategem geared exclusively towards secondary interventions has been called into question. For example, drawing on the experience of LDCs, Steward argues that whilst, in theory, any secondary income distribution can be achieved via redistributive policies, in practice the socioeconomic conditions that produce a highly unequal primary income distribution are likely to constitute fundamental barriers to redistribution. As social policy in itself is unlikely to be significantly successful in the promotion of egalitarian objectives in such circumstances, attention naturally shifts towards a consideration of how primary distributions of income may be altered (Steward in Bulmer *et al.*, 1989).

Commentators from all parts of the political spectrum have in recent years rounded on centralized, bureaucratic welfare provision, arguing that public welfare services have been seriously deficient in a number of areas, especially those of efficiency, quality of service and accountability. Certainly those on the left have increasingly argued for a more decentralized, democratic and community controlled system of provision. For such writers, of course, equity is a key issue: here recently-published work on bureaucratic allocation in Britain, Poland and Hungary suggests that such allocation does not automatically achieve the aim of equity. Indeed, it may often favour the less needy (Le Grand and Winter in Millard, 1988).

Given the high income elasticity of demand for the services provided by the state in the West, however, some argue that it is possible, and in some cases highly probable, that the better off would be more favoured by the market than by bureaucratic allocation (Le Grand and Winter in Millard, 1988). Radicals certainly retain a commitment to universal provision of social services and allocation according to need rather than means. They, of course, are looking for more effective and democratic systems of non-market allocation, and they reject the privatization strategy of the New Right.

Finally, there has been growing criticism of the failure to analyse social policy in the context of the development of a patriarchal and racially structured society. In F. Williams's view, for example, the British welfare state has to be understood as an entity which developed not just within a capitalist society, but in a capitalism which absorbed and recreated the social relations of imperialism and of patriarchy. As regards the latter, Williams argues that women's interests need to be seen as central, not additional, to economic strategies and the provision of welfare if the nature of work and welfare is to be transformed in ways conducive to the achievement of greater gender equality. As Williams points out, recent research in Scandinavia suggests that even in the most advanced welfare states this has not been satisfactorily achieved (Williams, 1990).

M.G. MARSHALL

References

Bulmer, M., Lewis, J. and Piachaud, D. (eds) (1989), *The Goals of Social Policy*, London: Unwin Hyman.
Lutz, M.A. (ed.) (1989), *Social Economics: Retrospect and Prospect*, London and Boston: Kluwer Academic Publishers.
Millard, F.A. (1988), *Social Welfare and the Market*, London: Suntory-Toyota International Centre for Economics and Related Disciplines, London School of Economics and Political Science.
Papadakis, E. and Taylor-Gooby, P. (1987), *The Private Provision of Public Welfare*, Brighton: Wheatsheaf Books, New York: St Martin's Press.
Williams, F. (1990), *Social Policy: A Critical Introduction*, Cambridge: Polity Press.

Social structure of accumulation

The Social Structure of Accumulation (SSA) is a theory (1) of institutional structure, (2) of institutional formation, (3) of institutional change, (4) of crisis and long waves, and (5) of the historical development of capitalism.

As Schumpeter and Keynes argued, the 'creative destruction' of capitalism causes constant change and uncertainty, which provides a problematic context for long-term investment. Institutions are developed to reduce uncertainty and improve the business climate. The SSA analysis goes further, identifying the class conflicts of capitalism as the key source of new institutions, the shape they take and their unravelling.

The capitalist economy is riddled with conflicts between classes and class factions. These include class conflict between employers and employees, the conflict born of competition between new immigrants and natives, small business and large corporations, finance and industry, whites and racial or ethnic minorities, etc. There is also the conflict between capitalists and classes from other sub-dominant modes of production: feudal remnants, tribal societies, patriarchal family structures, etc. While these conflicts cannot be eliminated, they can be managed. Institutional arrangements can promote non-disruptive avenues for expressing conflict and for working out particular remedies. Laws, courts and administrative practices may provide measures for resolving specific conflicts.

Beyond shaping the *form* which conflicts take, institutional mechanisms legitimize certain *objects* of conflict. When certain structures are set in place, they treat some issues as settled. Thus the post-war structure of labour relations outlawed strikes in sympathy with other workers, making it difficult to organize new workers. Conflicts between financial sectors were limited to issues about what interest rate (and inflation rate) should prevail, rather than who could enter which markets, which was strictly defined by law.

The SSA approach differs from another long-wave approach to institutions, the Regulation school, because of its focus on class conflict as the source of institutional development. Within the SSA framework, there are two competing views of how a new SSA comes into being. One argues that in any given historical period, some class conflicts are more salient than others. Once these particular conflicts are channelled by new institutions, a core is established on which other institutions must build (Kotz, forthcoming). This helps explain the uneven development of any new SSA and its degree of internal coherence.

In the alternative view, given the break-up of old institutions, class factions experiment with new forms of conflict in order to address new objects of concern. These competing experiments represent different world views (Naples, 1986). The very essence of capitalism may even come into question. Then, instead of a new SSA, an entirely new political-economic structure may be promoted. The state is the key arena for institutionalizing some experiments since it establishes the meta-rules of the game; it is also the ultimate protector of private property and ensuing right to profits. When some world view comes to dominate state policy, its advocates use the coercive power of the state to repress recalcitrant advocates of alternative views. Thus, for example, once labour-management negotiation and accommodation became the model and ongoing workplace struggle was deemed illegitimate, President Truman repeatedly called in the National Guard to mine coal when the United Mine Workers struck in the late 1940s.

The theory of Regulation, unlike SSA theory, attributes the success of any institutional framework to what is functional for accumulation. Thus, Regulationists argue, unions were accepted in basic industry because they would stabilize wages, which would stabilize consumer demand and help prevent the return of the underconsumption crisis which Regulationists consider a major cause of the Great Depression. SSA analysts argue that, in a world in which old institutions do not 'work' any more, it is anyone's guess which new institutions will be functional for accumulation. The very functionalism of institutions is contingent on their success in shaping class conflicts, which can only be discovered by trial and error, both by class antagonists and by creative state agents.

It is not even possible for some perceptive government leader to impose a new 'functional' structure. Coercion is inadequate; it is costly for the state continually to have to enforce laws which are considered unfair. Instead the laws and institutions which emerge must be seen to be in the interests of a sufficient number of citizens, including preferably both sides of any conflict, so that the need for expensive enforcement will be minimal. This requires education about the new ways of life, whether through direct experience with new institutions or by propaganda to sell the new ideas.

Early proponents of the SSA view treated institutional change as exogenously generated. For instance, several authors argued that international competition undermined both oligopolistic arrangements in product markets and unionism in basic industry. But more powerful arguments identified the SSA itself as the source of such events, or explained why the SSA was vulnerable in a particular period (Naples, 1986). It is now recognized that it was the very success of the SSA in structuring post-war international trade and finance which provided the opportunity for Germany and Japan to recover to the point of out-competing US corporations. That is, a successful SSA creates conditions which may bring about its demise.

The SSA structures conflict without eliminating it. The underlying competition between class factions, for instance, is embedded in institutional arrangements. While any market may have a large market leader, that firm may still face challenges from renegades who undercut price, and may have to retaliate to teach this and other firms a lesson. The oligopolistic structure is not necessarily threatened by this behaviour, as ongoing tacit cooperation is in competitors' interests. But because such conflicts surface, it takes work and resources to reproduce institutions over time.

Furthermore, the application of the logic of particular institutional arrangements on an expanding scale illustrates the limits of that approach. Thus the productivity bargain in basic industry meant that shopfloor complaints would be handled through a grievance procedure while work continued. But industrial accidents and widespread disease from occupational hazards were found to be treated the same as a complaint about a work-rule change. Workers started circumventing the procedure by walking out over safety and health, as well as over other issues which could have readily been handled by the grievance mechanism.

SSA analysis is not deterministic. Many contradictions may surface and undermine an SSA, and many possible SSAs may emerge in a crisis. In light of the impossibility of eliminating all class conflicts, it is likely that an SSA will unravel over time. But that tendency has counteracting tendencies, in the resilience of the SSA itself and its own conflict-management provisions.

In Gordon's (1978) original formulation, the SSA was a theory of the resolution of economic crisis rather than a theory of crisis *per se*. It was therefore consistent with other purely economic theories of crisis including Schumpeter's technological waves of innovation, Regulationists' technology paradigms and Marx's rising organic composition of capital. But the endogenous nature of the breakdown of an SSA qualifies it as a *bona fide* source of crisis. Since the SSA's existence helps to render the economy more stable and predictable, its demise creates a problematic environment for corporate planning. Firms make decisions which prove to be mistakes, reducing average profitability further.

Moreover, the same events which erode the SSA often directly confront profitability or accumulation. Thus domestic challenges to the Vietnam war undermined the US's ability to serve as a world police force and enforce Pax Americana (Bowles *et al.*, 1990). This allowed for the formation of OPEC, with little fear of retaliation: OPEC then redistributed profits away from capitalists in the advanced countries.

The crises which SSA theory addresses are long-wave crises, 40–60 year periods of boom and bust, each of which has culminated in a great depression. The phases of the long wave, distinguished by their associated rates of accumulation, have corresponding phases of development of the SSA, each of which is qualitatively distinct. During the crisis phase, new elements of different possible SSAs are experimented with. In the early expansion, the meta-rules are worked out by actors sharing a common view of what the world will look like in the coming era. Some world view or core of institutions becomes hegemonic, and other visions or behaviours are no longer tolerated; this was manifest in the McCarthy witch-hunts. During the boom the SSA develops in a 'normal' way, with steady application of the general framework to the particular case. At the same time, the contradictions embodied in the SSA start to surface as sustained accumulation, high profits and low unemployment provide an opportunity for economic actors to challenge perceived abuses under the SSA.

In the stagnation phase, continued challenges to the terms of the truce undermine its ability to be reproduced. An accelerating decline in profitability and income formation lead to efforts to reduce the resources going into conflict management. In other words, deregulation ensues. In the crisis phase the institutional structure is very much in flux, and possibilities which seemed remote in the expansion phase become manifest. For instance, proto-Nazi political efforts have returned in many advanced countries, while certain sectors of the media are treating the 1963 assassination of President Kennedy as a conspiracy whose cover-up implicates the military in a *coup d'état*.

The concept of SSA was devised to explain the shape of institutions and their importance for accumulation in advanced capitalist countries, especially the US. Yet recent events in the former Soviet Union uncannily dovetail with the historical periodization characteristic of an SSA. Stalin's consolidation of power and of his vision for Soviet development occurred during the Great Depression of the advanced countries. The recent crisis of profitability in the Soviet Union and failure of planning again provided a context wherein democratic movements could take root. Even the world crisis of planning has First World counterparts – for instance IBM's failure to keep pace with competitors in light of the rigidity of its top-heavy organization, and its consequent move to a more decentralized structure. In fact the merger movement has eliminated middle layers of management in many industries, reflecting the demise of bureaucratic control (Edwards, 1979) as a method for managing personnel. Both US and Eastern European confidence that decentralization and subcontracting will correct the problem are naive from an SSA perspective: by increasing flexibility, such a structure will increase the pace of change and instability rather than providing a new mechanism for reducing any capitalist's uncertainty.

Marxists have often periodized history into stages in the development of capitalism. The SSA provides a radical alternative to such older stage-theories as Lenin's imperialism and Baran and Sweezy's monopoly capital. Like these, the SSA links institutions to economic dynamics. Since it is more general, the SSA framework may be used to analyse future stages of capitalism and the possibilities of socialism, as well as past events.

MICHELE NAPLES

References

Bowles, S., Gordon, D.M. and Weisskopf, T.E. (1990), *After the Waste Land*, Armonk, New York: M.E. Sharpe.

Edwards, R.C. (1979), *Contested Terrain*, New York: Basic Books.

Gordon, D.M. (1978), 'Up and Down the Long Roller Coaster' in *US Capitalism in Crisis*, Economics Education Project, Union for Radical Political Economics, New York: URPE, 22–35.

Kotz, D. (forthcoming), *Essays in the Social Structure of Accumulation*, New York: Cambridge University Press.

Naples, M.I. (1986), 'The Unravelling of the Union-Capital Truce and the US Industrial Productivity Crisis', *Review of Radical Political Economics*, **18** (1 & 2), Spring–Summer, 110–31.

Socialism

There are two general conceptions of socialism, one 'idealistic' and the other 'scientific'. Conceived in the first of these two forms, socialism is a vague notion without a structured ideological corpus, although it is on this terrain that it continues to be viable. Of the three ideals of the French Revolution of 1789 – freedom, equality and brotherhood – this form of socialism is the extension into the economic sphere of the two principles of equality and brotherhood (on the validity of these ideals, even for the modern thinker, see Martinelli *et al.*, 1989). This variety of socialism has existed and still exists in a number of versions where the term 'socialism' is qualified in various ways to indicate other, related bodies of ideological thought: the French utopian socialism of Proudhon, the Christian socialism of the papal encyclicals 'Rerum Novarum' and 'Centesimus Annus', liberal socialism in the Italian version of Piero Gobetti and the Rosselli brothers and as the English Fabianism of Sydney and Beatrice Webb, and the democratic socialism of the Scandinavian and German traditions. The concept of socialism also includes the cooperative ideology and movement that grew in some sectors of Western economies and which Yugoslavia experimented with as a system of firm management with state ownership of the means of production and market connections among firms.

The second definition of socialism is that of 'scientific socialism'. As a structured ideological corpus with its origins in the thought of Karl Marx, scientific socialism also has its roots in the ideals of 1789 and in French utopian socialism, although it was born to supersede the latter on the levels of analysis and of politics. These two levels – analysis and project – were assumed to be closely interconnected: in his XI Thesis on Feuerbach, Marx argued that it was not enough to interpret the world; one also had to change it.

This pattern has been the glory and the downfall of an ideology which, for a century and a half, has dominated the thought and actions of thinkers, intellectuals, citizens and political militants of every race and every country in the world. Although this grand design brought important social advances and cultural enrichment, it failed to accomplish its overall objectives. When, in this century, Marxists began to change the world, especially where they had the power to bring radical change and not just to alter the course of events, the results they achieved were invariably and increasingly disappointing. And this was because the second two objectives of 1789, equality and brotherhood, conflicted with its first objective of freedom.

Not only was scientific socialism unable to attain equity at the expense of efficiency (see the essay by Martinelli *et al.*, 1989, for a discussion of the trade-off between equity and efficiency); in fact, it proved incapable of achieving either of these two objectives (Laski and Brus, 1989, discuss the evolution of the socialist economic structure). Privileges did not disappear in the command economy; they were merely demonetized, taking the form of direct access to affluence and power.

Is it possible today to draw a connection, which was the foundation of scientific socialism, between the scientific analysis of the capitalist economy and the political will to overcome it? The answer is undoubtedly no, and for at least three reasons, which I seek to set out below.

The first reason is the unreliable nature of the laws of economics. A positivist faith in science led the scientific socialist to claim that it was possible to detect the laws of motion, the laws of unavoidable crisis, and the reasons for the collapse and the superseding of the capitalist mode of production. As far as economic 'laws' are concerned, certain 'regularities' do exist, but they emerge in only some spatio-temporal contexts and not in others. Indeed, these regularities are often identified as such only because they have been generated by models that a particular observer constructs to account for phenomena which he or she takes to be stylized facts in a multiform and confused reality (Myrdal, 1953).

The second reason why the scientific analysis of capitalism and the political will to overcome it cannot be linked is that there is no 'one' capitalism. It comes in many forms. An economic system is the outcome of numerous interweaving factors, three of which deserve particular attention: firm, market and the state. Different kinds of firms in terms of organization and ownership may exist in different economic systems; there is no necessary two-way relationship between the predominant system of firms and the overall economic system. The same applies to the market. The economic system may consist of markets of varying degrees of competitiveness. The market may be regulated or otherwise by institutions which guarantee its transparency and which forbid the use of insider information. An economic system will also comprise forms of state intervention of varying intensity and type. Some countries seek to achieve redistributive equity principally by means of taxation; others also provide the universally available social services (welfare, health, education, etc.) which form the basis of the modern welfare state. Full employment was not on the state agenda prior to World War II; it then moved to the top, and is now again of secondary importance for many governments. In some countries, the state participates in and guarantees agreements among non-state economic subjects, an example being the so-called neo-corporative tripartite arrangement among state, trade unions and employer organizations of the European social democratic governments. In other cases the government is decidedly hostile to any state intervention in bargaining among private subjects. Clearly, since the Second World War, in different countries and in different periods, the balance between public and private power and between collective and individual action has altered (see Armstrong *et al.*, 1984, for a historical perspective).

Today socialism faces a further problem. In the past, when 'market failures' occurred, there was a tendency to believe that it was automatically the state's duty to intervene in areas where the market had miscarried. Today, however, 'market failures' are matched by a long list of what by analogy have been called 'state failures': bloated bureaucracies, corruption and waste in the production of goods and services. These two kinds of failure impose a comparative-cost analysis of state and market.

The third reason for the failure of scientific socialism is not just that Western thought refuses to countenance violence – and therefore class struggle – as a means to achieve a classless society; there are other important problems of equity which cannot be solved by abolishing class differences. These problems are manifest, among countries and within countries, in various areas including sexual, racial and intergenerational equality (see Sen, 1973, for a discussion of the problem of inequalities and ethics).

Furthermore, a serious shortcoming of Marxism was that it stressed the consequences of the *social* division of labour (because of property rights) while underestimating the consequences of the *technical* division of labour (dependent or independent, hierarchical or in cooperative teams, physical or mental, etc.), which depends much less on whether a country is capitalist or socialist and much more on other factors: the development of technology (as has been pointed out by Marcuse and the so-called Frankfurt school of sociology), the organization of the firm, and the relationship between the firm and the social environment.

The limits and failures of scientific socialism do not preclude the possibility of socialist thought even after the fall of the Berlin Wall. Of the many areas in which its development is still possible and still necessary, I shall limit myself to the strictly economic. Without presuming to be exhaustive, I shall single out four areas in which one can still meaningfully employ the idea of socialism – defined as a form of social organization and/or of coordination of the economic decisions of subjects, firms and state which differs from the market (but is not necessarily counterposed to it). These four areas are the North-South economic relationship, ecology, international Keynesianism and distributive justice.

As regards the first of these economic areas, the North-South relationship, I believe that one should be able to distinguish, in non-Manichaean manner, between the following: cases where the underdevelopment of the South is the result of deliberate political strategies pursued by firms and governments in the North; cases where the problem is systemic and the South's underdevelopment is of no benefit to the North; and cases (not a few) where the fault lies entirely with the South. Socialism in the third case means, not the nationalization of the economy, but a policy which overrides the shortsighted selfishness of classes and privileged interest groups in order to pursue the objectives of long-term development which benefit (albeit to varying extents) all members of society.

On the other hand, there are also numerous cases where responsibility for failed economic development lies outside the country concerned and is caused by the impersonal mechanisms of the international market or by the self-interest of the more industrialized countries. I shall give two of many possible examples. The first concerns the management of the flows of international credit that derive from past or present disequilibria in trade balances. As well as being unstable, the present system is also unfair, because it is not in the interests of countries with a trade surplus to invest in the poorer areas of the world. The second example is the customs barriers raised by the North to protect its economy against goods from the South. A recent study by the World Bank calculated that the loss of income due to these barriers is higher than the monetary value of the transfers for aid and cooperation from the world's North to its South.

What socialism means today should by now be clear: the international political bodies must be strengthened so that they are able to govern on a world scale, given that many systemic inefficiencies can be resolved and many conflicting interests reconciled at this level.

There is a second area, that of ecology, where socialist doctrine acquires new significance as a sort of counterweight to the idea of the free market. The goal is to alter patterns of consumption and investment by introducing incentives for the production of certain goods or the adoption of certain techniques, and disincentives for others, which the market on its own cannot generate. Markets for environmental goods do not exist; commonly-owned resources (commons) have no price and are exploited indiscriminately and irrationally. The market must be 'corrected' by means of tax instruments to make the use of exhaustible resources costly and also to provide financing for the technological innovation and scientific research by which exhaustible resources may be conserved. The problem at the moment is that modern phenomena of environmental breakdown (the hole in the ozone layer, acid rain, the pollution of the seas, etc.) are by their nature phenomena on a world scale. The ever closer interconnection between ecology and development urges the creation of supranational institutions equipped with the authority and instruments to regulate the environment on this scale.

The third area in which socialist institutions should govern the economy in harness with the market is that of international Keynesianism. The crisis of Keynesian economics has in large part been due to the obsolescence of much of the theory and policy of economic control developed for closed economies. Such theory and policy are no longer applicable to very open economies when taken individually (one thinks here of the difficulties involved in pursuing an independent interest rate policy at the single-country level). This does not mean that it no longer makes sense to pursue a 'Keynesian' policy at the world level: it is still relevant when there is a worldwide lack of effective demand, when inflationary pressures arise because of tensions on markets for primary commodities or because destabilizing speculation affects international financial markets. That a policy of this kind is urgently needed is demonstrated by the fact that, for more than ten years now, around 10 per cent of the labour force of the leading industrialized countries of major changes in production techniques, which have sent entire industrial sectors into rapid decline, and the insufficient growth rate of the economy as a whole.

As regards the final area, distributive justice, I conclude these reflections with the following consideration. Being a socialist economist does not mean that one dismisses budget constraints as non-existent. Instead, the socialist economist reacts to the plight of the poverty-stricken not by saying that 'they are poor because they choose to be', but that 'they are poor because there is a malfunction in the system'.

FERDINANDO TARGETTI

References

Armstrong, P., Glyn, A. and Harrison, J. (1984), *Capitalism Since World War II*, London: Fontana.
Laski, K. and Brus, W. (1989), *From Marx to the Market: Socialism in Search of an Economic System*, Oxford: Clarendon Press.
Martinelli, A., Salvati, M. and Veca, S. (1989), *Project 89: Three Essays on Freedom, Equality and Brotherhood*, Milan: II Saggiatore.
Myrdal, G. (1953), *The Political Element in the Development of Economic Theory*, London: Routledge and Kegan Paul.
Sen, A. (1973), *On Economic Inequality*, Oxford: Clarendon Press.

Socialization of investment

To the modern neoclassical economist trained in the tradition of Friedman and Lucas, the term 'socialization of investment' conjures up Hayekian fears of the collectivist state with public ownership of the means of production. While being instinctively suspicious of Keynesian ideas, few of these neoclassical economists would recognize that this radical conception of the state as a direct player in the organization of investment was very much at the heart of Keynes's thinking. Indeed, together with Keynes's support of the 'euthanasia of the rentier', it constitutes the only explicit long-term policy proposal to be found in *The General Theory*. This radical view of socialized capital formation would be especially surprising since, throughout the post-war period, students of economics have generally been taught to think that Keynesian stabilization policy entails nothing more than short-term contra-cyclical spending measures along the lines of Lerner's principle of functional finance, regardless of whether government net spending is for investment or consumption purposes. During times of recession, in particular, the state should directly stimulate aggregate demand, even if this may involve little else than paying workers to fill old bottles with banknotes. Over the longer term, however, the net flow if these public expenditures ought to be zero so as to ensure the long-run neutrality of the state in the private affairs of the market. This caricature of Keynesian policy of economic stabilization, which has merited so much criticism with the rise of monetarism during the 1970s, runs somewhat counter to the long view of economic policy held by Keynes, who explicitly favoured the so-called socialization of investment.

Apart from Chapters 12 and 24 of *The General Theory*, the other main reference source for Keynes's 'long view' is to be found in the less well-known *Treasury Memoranda* of 1943–44 (Keynes, 1980, pp. 264–419) though, as pointed out by Kregel (1985, pp. 36–7) and Smithin (1989, p. 211), the seeds were sown as early as in his 1926 monograph, 'The End of Laissez-Faire' (Keynes, 1972, pp. 272–94). Keynes's critique of laissez-faire capitalism, found scattered in these various writings, rested on the view that, if left to itself, a modern monetary production economy would face recurrent problems of market coordination and the chronic underutilization of resources. This state of underemployment equilibrium, with its related instabilities, was the inevitable outcome of a fundamental conflict between industry (enterprise) and finance (the rentier sector) that characterizes the mature phase of laissez-faire capitalism. Recognizing the crushing burden of finance on the productive activities of industrial enterprises, Keynes was to infer that, in a world of uncertainty, the short-run speculative behaviour of rentiers tends to prevail in the market for financial securities. The ability of rentiers to impose a constraint on the liquid funds to be made available for the long-term financing of enterprises and their strong desire for liquidity would together result in effective rates of investment in long-term projects being far below the socially optimum rate necessary to attain full employment. In such a speculative economy, entrepreneurs have generally lost their 'spontaneous urge' to invest in longer-term projects (their 'animal spirits') and have themselves developed a rentier-like appetite for liquidity and for short-run capital gains. The only logical alternative, then, is to view 'the State, which is in a position to calculate the marginal efficiency of capital-goods on long views and on the basis of the general social advantage, taking an ever greater responsibility for directly organising investment ...' (Keynes, 1973, p. 164). According to Keynes only an enlightened state, impervious to the speculative game of finance, can provide for the necessary 'make-weight' projects 'so as to preserve as much stability of aggregate investment ... at the right and appropriate level' (Keynes, 1982, p. 387).

Indeed when pressed by fellow economists in 1943 to identify how far he would be willing to go in socializing investment, Keynes envisaged that in his proposed system as much as 'two-thirds or three-quarters of total investment' would be directly influenced by public and semi-public bodies (Keynes, 1980, p. 322) whose activities would be guided by the traditional 'motive of private exchange' as well as 'technically social' motives that have normally justified investment in social infrastructure (cf. Kregel, 1985, p. 37). However, Keynes fell short of suggesting a precise mechanism for implementing such a policy measure so as to achieve his long-term economic goal, spelled out in the last chapter of *The General Theory*. Much like Marx, Keynes had more to say about the drawbacks of the existing system than about how actually to put into practice his policy proposal for the socialization of investment.

Keynes did leave us with some useful hints as to how the process of socializing would possibly take place. A careful reading of Keynes's writings would suggest that at least two interpretations of his radical proposal can be legitimately corroborated. These have formed the basis of a broader post Keynesian agenda for economic policy. The first is connected with his support throughout most of the 1930s and early 1940s for the establishment of a National Investment Board (NIB). The purpose of such a Board was to achieve full employment by strategically regulating the aggregate flow of investment expenditures through the appropriate control of long-term financing. This proposal for a NIB had already been in the political platform of the British Labour party during the early 1930s. While rejecting the original Labour party position that the creation of such a Board should necessarily be accompanied by the nationalization of the banking system, Keynes agreed that the NIB should be pooling the enormous funds accumulating in the hands of public and semi-public bodies. The NIB would then ensure 'an adequate demand for them, partly by making them available at a rate which would attract a sufficient demand and partly by stimulating the undertaking of particular investment propositions' (Keynes, 1982, p. 137). This Board would behave much like a large publicly-run investment bank, whose purpose is primarily to engage in the longer-term financing of investment projects in order to provide the necessary 'make-weight' in the system. By means of the NIB, Keynes was thus advocating the direct control of a substantial portion of available funds in the capital markets so as to ensure a socially optimum level of employment.

Keynes's specific proposal of direct intervention in the capital markets through the NIB has been echoed in more recent times by those advocating the democratic control of capital formation, sometimes described as the doctrine of pension-fund socialism. In countries such as Sweden and to a lesser extent Canada, it is also referred to as the policy of promoting Meidner-type employee investment funds. If such employee funds were to be included in funds of 'public and semi-public bodies', a collective decision-making body set up to regulate these huge funds for more socially-desirable investment purposes could be construed as a mechanism of socializing investment. The position defended by Arestis (1986, p. 709) is that the Swedish investment strategy of encouraging wage-earner funds exemplifies very well what Keynes and Post Keynesians really mean by socialization of investment.

There is however an alternative interpretation of Keynes's view prominent in the literature. This has to do with his related proposal for a separate 'capital budget' for government so as not to confuse investment expenditures with the consumption expenditures of the state. While at first glance this may appear to be merely a question of presentation, both Kregel (1985) and Smithin (1989) point to Keynes's mechanism of capital budgeting as playing a pivotal role in his long-term programme for socializing investment.

Although Keynes did admit that 'at one time I had conceived that this [capital budgeting] should be the task of a semi-independent statutory authority to be called the National Investment Board' (Keynes, 1980, p. 408), the proposal for a NIB and his view on capital budgeting are for him quite distinct in nature. Keynes had long recognized that a policy of direct public investment, whether administered through the NIB or not, would pay for itself and would also be the most efficient means to achieve full employment of resources over the longer term. If accounted for correctly by means of a capital budget, this public expenditure policy would under normal circumstances generate persistent surpluses in the current operating or 'ordinary' budget of government. Indeed as Kregel (1985, p. 32) also points out, chronic operating deficits in the 'normal' or 'ordinary' budget would instead be the visible sign of a failure on the part of governments to remain committed to an active public investment policy of achieving full employment.

Keynes's position was that, in an expenditure-led high growth economy, governments should aim at obtaining surpluses in the ordinary budget with these current surpluses being, in turn, 'transferred to the capital Budget, thus gradually replacing dead-weight debt by productive or semi-productive debt ...' (Keynes, 1980, p. 277). Hence just like a private investment ultimately bears fruit for business enterprise, any comprehensive public investment policy would inevitably pay for itself over time by engendering a surplus in the operating balance of government. However unlike a private firm, the state should utilize this surplus, not to extinguish its debts, but strategically to expand further its capital expenditures. The effect of this feedback mechanism of transferring operating surpluses to the capital budget of the state would be that a growing proportion of total investment expenditures in the economy would become socialized.

This view of capital budgeting, however, should not be construed as trying to attain, in the final analysis, the state ownership of all the means of production in conformity with Marxian principles. Keynes's proposal in favour of public investment has to do with the *composition* of government expenditures and not about whether the share of *total* government expenditures out of GNE should rise so as ultimately to monopolize all investment spending in the economy. Yet Keynes did believe that these public capital expenditures should be significant enough to stabilize overall investment spending over the business cycle; in the long run, they should also be 'maintained at a level which will allow the growth of capital to the point where it ceases to be scarce' (Keynes, 1973, p. 376). Perhaps this is why he had proposed that as much as two-thirds or three-quarters of total investment should be under the influence of the public authorities. In this light, moreover, as has been discussed elsewhere (cf. Seccareccia and Lavoie, 1989), Keynes's policy of socializing investment is intimately connected with his prediction concerning the ultimate withering away of rentier income whose existence depends on capital being scarce.

While his latter view of capital saturation has found little support in modern discussions, Keynes's concept of the capital budget and the importance he attributed to public investment have been taken up by numerous modern writers, especially subsequent to the influential work of American economist Robert Eisner during the last decade. Staunchly opposed to the orthodox 'crowding out' hypothesis, there has emerged a complete body of literature that deals with the composition of government spending. Instead of being inimical to private sector growth, public investment on social and material infrastructures raises private sector output and productivity. Hence a policy of socializing investment by means of an enlarged rate of public capital formation would enhance over the long term private sector economic performance and lead to higher levels of growth of output and employment. After all, the original implementation of such Keynesian public investment policies in most Western countries during the first two decades of the post-war period was associated with the longest wave of economic growth in the modern economic history of the Western hemisphere. This golden age of the 'mixed economy' came to an end only with the rise of monetarism when the state began to relinquish its post-war Keynesian role of socializing investment and to favour, once again, the rentier control of the investment process.

Mario Seccareccia

References

Arestis, P. (1986), 'Post-Keynesian Economic Policies: The Case of Sweden', *Journal of Economic Issues*, **20** (3), September, 709–23.
Keynes, J.M. (1972), *The Collected Writings of John Maynard Keynes*, Vol. IX, London: Macmillan.
Keynes, J.M. (1973), *The Collected Writings of John Maynard Keynes*, Vol. VII, London: Macmillan.
Keynes, J.M. (1980), *The Collected Writings of John Maynard Keynes*, Vol. XXVII, London: Macmillan.
Keynes, J.M. (1982), *The Collected Writings of John Maynard Keynes*, Vol. XXI, London: Macmillan.
Kregel, J.A. (1985), 'Budget Deficits, Stabilisation Policy and Liquidity Preference: Keynes's Post-War Proposals', in F. Vicarelli (ed.), *Keynes's Relevance Today*, London: Macmillan, 28–50.
Seccareccia, M. and Lavoie, M. (1989), 'Les idées révolutionnaires de Keynes en politique économique et le déclin du capitalisme rentier', *Economie appliquée*, **42** (1), 47–70.
Smithin, J.N. (1989), 'The Composition of Government Expenditures and the Effectiveness of Fiscal Policy' in J. Pheby (ed.), *New Directions in Post-Keynesian Economics*, Aldershot: Edward Elgar, 209–27.

Speculation

The subject of speculation is unloved: it did not even rate an article in the *New Palgrave* (1987) – though that was put right in the later *New Palgrave Dictionary of Money and Finance* (*NPMF*) (1992). There are good reasons for its rejection: speculation is difficult to define; it is based on subjective evaluations; it is a threat to many propositions dear to the hearts of neoclassical economists, such as efficient and stable markets and the identity of the rate of interest and the rate of profit. In the face of a rich history of speculative excesses (see Kindleberger, 1978) and the revelations by the enormously successful speculator George Soros of his activities during the sterling crisis of 15 September 1992, who would deny that it exists as a profitable economic activity and therefore ought to have a place in economic analysis? The obvious answer to this rhetorical question is 'no sane person'; but economists, at least until very recently, have resisted developing a theory of speculation and incorporating it into the main body of economic theory. The reasons for this failure lie only partly in a rational calculation of the damage speculation would cause to the mainstream economist's picture of the world, for it is widely ignored by non-mainstream economists too. The idea of speculation carries an emotive, and very negative, charge: it is perceived as *unfair*, even wicked or semi-criminal.

Much has been done, therefore, to tame speculation, starting even with the way it is defined. For example, Tirole (*NPMF*, 1992) defines a purely speculative market as one 'where the aggregate monetary gain is zero and insurance plays no role'. This definition is fairly standard amongst neoclassical explorations of speculation; most notably, it is shared by Friedman, Baumol and Telser in their famous debate (about which more later) and modern work on 'bubbles'. (Tobin's famous article 'Liquidity Preference as Behavior toward Risk' is all about insurance and therefore, even by neoclassical standards, not about speculation.)

Speculation takes place within financial markets and is self-referential. These properties are shared by arbitrage. However, at least one way of distinguishing between arbitrage and speculation is that arbitrage takes place across 'space' and refers to other parts of a market (e.g. arbitrage between assets of different maturities) in contrast to the intertemporal reference of speculation.

Within the intertemporal domain, Keynes (1936) made the distinction between speculation and enterprise in terms of motive: enterprise seeks a stream of profit, earned by producing output for market sale, while the motive of speculation is to capture capital gains in financial markets. Capital gains may be generated not only by expectations of profit from actual production and sale, but also by the cumulative effects of speculative opinion. Speculation is 'the activity of forecasting the psychology of the market', while enterprise is 'the activity of forecasting the prospective yield of assets over their whole life' (Keynes, 1936, p. 158).

Brockway (1983) added a third category to Keynes's, using two criteria: the pay-off of the activity and its wealth-creating potential. Brockway identifies zero-sum games which are not wealth-creating but merely redistributive as gambling. Enterprise is positive-sum and wealth-creating. Speculation lies between these extremes: it is like gambling in producing no new wealth, but it is non-zero-sum because new money may enter the market. This latter property is crucial to the non-neoclassical approach to speculation. Money which flows into speculative markets may be lost to production and investment in real capital; speculative markets may serve as an 'infinite sink of purchasing power' which in a depression starves the economy of a much-needed stimulus. It can also disturb the relation between real assets and their financial counterparts, as for example in the UK housing market since the late 1980s, when house prices, after a speculative boom, fell below the value of mortgages established in the boom, leaving householders with 'negative equity'.

Most authors are clear that speculation involves forecasting, but the famous debate between Friedman and Baumol and Telser (see bibliography in Chick, 1990) has foundered on the question of whether speculators must *anticipate* peaks and troughs, or whether it is sufficient for them to buy cheap and sell dear, even after turning points. Friedman took the first position and it is this – coupled with his implicit assumption that the game is zero-sum – which led to his well-known and comforting conclusion that speculation must be stabilizing. Despite the considerable doubt cast on this conclusion by Baumol and Telser, Friedman's conclusion is taken in some quarters to be an article of faith: witness the 'definition' of speculation in the Routledge *Dictionary of Economics* (1992): 'buying and selling ... in order to make a capital gain. It has been described as "arbitrage through time". Although much condemned as an unreal activity [?] for private gain, it does contribute to price stability' (p. 433). Quite the opposite conclusion is reached by the followers of Keynes: speculation, because of its self-fulfilling and cumulative character, is typically a destabilizing influence, a force for amplifying price variations.

Whether speculation is stabilizing or destabilizing can be viewed as a matter of theory. But the importance of speculation is a matter of empirical judgment. There are times when speculation is a major force to be reckoned with, and times when it is quiescent: times when it is merely a 'bubble on the steady stream of enterprise', and times when 'the capital development of a country [becomes] a by-product of the activities of a casino'. In the latter event 'the job is likely to be ill-done' (Keynes, 1936, p. 159).

In what sense and by what criterion would the job be ill-done? The implicit proposition is that, even allowing for the problems attached to allocating resources according to profitability (and there is no evidence that Keynes had as many reservations on this issue as does the present author), profit is a far better guide to suitable allocation than the rate of return on assets subject to speculation. Whether the effect of speculation is stabilizing or otherwise, both the theoretical and practical significance of speculation lies in its ability to drive a wedge between the rate of return on financial assets (the rate of interest) and the rate of return obtained by owning and operating real capital which produces goods for market sale (the rate of profit; see Chick, 1987). Stock market prices have a major influence on the ability of firms to find the finance for expansion, and these prices are influenced by speculation.

If the demand for financial assets were governed only by profitability, and profitability were governed exclusively by 'real' factors, then the return on financial assets would become a perfect reflection of 'the forces of productivity and thrift' which are supposed, in neoclassical theory, to govern accumulation. The existence of financial assets then does not change the conclusions of neoclassical economics. This neutrality theorem has been a leitmotiv from Walras to Modigliani and Miller. By contrast, in the Keynesian frame of reference, even if speculation were stabilizing in the sense of damping fluctuations in interest rates, it would still interfere with the exclusive sway of 'real' factors. Stock and bond market prices have a major influence on the cost and availability of finance for accumulation, and these markets are influenced by speculation. Furthermore, the effect of speculation on these markets in Keynes's analysis is assumed to be, more likely than not, both destabilizing and procyclical. Its effect is to make investment even more volatile than it would be by virtue of the uncertainty surrounding future profits.

From a Keynesian perspective, the whole notion of whether speculation is stabilizing or otherwise is problematic. Such a notion presupposes that non-speculative, 'real' factors – the 'fundamentals' – remain ultimately unaffected by the speculative process itself, for only by reference to unaltered fundamentals can the notion of stabilization have meaning. An assumption of independent fundamentals lies behind the interesting and valuable, but limited, neoclassical work on 'bubbles' (see the article by Kindleberger in the *New Palgrave*); this work is deeply concerned with the question of whether the speculative series converges to the fundamentals. In Keynes's framework, by contrast, the fundamentals are permanently affected by speculation: speculation in part determines the rate of interest, the rate of interest in part determines investment, and investment is an irreversible change in the capital stock. This change may embody new techniques, but even with unchanged techniques, productivity is altered. Thus there is no hard and fast separation between the speculative and non-speculative part of the market; there are no fundamentals to converge to. The study of speculation properly involves path-dependency (Chick, 1990).

The speculative demand for assets was put forward by Keynes as part of his theory of the rate of interest. With the Modigliani-Miller theorem now occupying the high ground, the non-neutrality of speculation needs to be re-emphasized. It is not just a matter of realities like the tax laws which invalidate Modigliani-Miller: there are reasons for buying and selling financial assets which do not correspond to the forecast return on the real assets to which they are a claim. If money flows into financial markets, the return on financial assets may diverge substantially from 'real' returns. When that happens, 'economics finds itself entangled in the ancient conflict of opinion and truth, the medieval conflict of nominalism and realism, the modern conflict of appearance and reality' (Brockway, p. 518). (Recall the description of speculation, above, as an 'unreal' activity.)

Unpleasant though we may find it, speculation is a fact of economic life, and it therefore deserves as much recognition and searching analysis as other economic activities.

VICTORIA CHICK

References

Brockway, G.P. (1983), 'On Speculation: A Footnote to Keynes', *Journal of Post Keynesian Economics*, **4**, Summer, 515–22.

Chick, V. (1987), 'Speculation, the Rate of Interest and the Rate of Profit', *Journal of Post Keynesian Economics*, **10** (1), Fall, 124–32.

Chick, V. (1990), 'Some Methodological Issues in the Theory of Speculation', in D.E. Moggridge (ed.), *Perspectives on the History of Economic Thought*, Vol IV: *Keynes, Macroeconomics*

and Method, Aldershot: Edward Elgar for the History of Economics Society, 113–24. Reprinted in V. Chick, *On Money, Method and Keynes: Selected Essays* (1992), edited by P. Arestis and S.C. Dow, London: Macmillan.
Keynes, J.M. (1936), *The General Theory of Employment, Interest and Money*, London: Macmillan. Reprinted as Volume VII of *The Collected Writings of J.M. Keynes*, edited by D.E. Moggridge, London: Macmillan.
Kindleberger, C.P. (1978), *Manias, Panics and Crashes: A History of Financial Crises*, New York: Basic Books.
The New Palgrave Dictionary of Money and Finance, (*NPMF*) (1992), edited by J. Eatwell, M. Milgate and P. Newman, London: Macmillan. See especially the article on 'Speculation' by J. Tirole.
The New Palgrave: A Dictionary of Economics (1987), edited by J. Eatwell, M. Milgate and P. Newman, London: Macmillan. See especially the article on 'Bubbles' by C.P. Kindleberger.

Structuralism

Structuralism is a methodological approach to the social sciences which emphasizes interactions occurring between various components of a social system, as opposed to a focus on the individual components themselves. While these structures may not always be directly observable, their presence is detectable by virtue of the concrete social and economic phenomena generated by them. Variants of structuralist methodology are found in literary criticism, linguistics, aesthetics and the social sciences, both Marxian and non-Marxian. The main structuralist current within Marxism has its origins in the writings of Althusser, and stands in opposition to the versions of Marxism developed by Lukacs, Gramsci and the Frankfurt school.

In the context of contemporary economics, structuralism usually refers to macroeconomic theories which explicitly recognize the heterogeneity of conditions in different countries and between sectors within countries. Originally formulated as a critique of orthodox growth theory, particularly with reference to trade and stabilization policies in developing countries, the term encompasses a wide range of views; for this reason, it is difficult to speak of a single or coherent set of structuralist analyses or policy positions. Nevertheless, in contrast to their neoclassical counterparts, structuralists share a common concern to formulate theoretical models which take account of characteristics specific to the country or sector under study.

Three prominent streams of structuralist thought are discernible. These are (1) the ECLA (United Nations Commission for Latin America) school of the 1950s and 1960s (particularly the work of the organization's first director, Raúl Prebisch), (2) the 'neo-structuralist' theories which emerged in Latin America in the late 1970s, and (3) the structuralist macroeconomic theory closely associated with the work of Lance Taylor.

The point of departure for ECLA economists was the idea that the world economy is composed of two poles, the centre and the periphery, and that the structure of production differs markedly between the two. While production in the centre is both homogeneous and highly diversified, with strong interlinkages between sectors and industries, the structure of production in the periphery is heterogeneous and specialized, combining economic activities with significant differences as to labour productivity (such as primary commodity exports and subsistence agriculture). These structural differences between centre and periphery cannot be understood in isolation, but instead reflect the roles adopted by each pole in the emerging international division of labour. Developments in the periphery are therefore conditioned by interactions with the centre in the context of a single, dynamic world economic system.

ECLA analysis emerged over a period of years (mostly in the 1950s and 1960s) in the form of numerous documents focusing on specific problems and regions (see Prebisch, 1961, for example). In retrospect, however, ECLA-inspired analyses achieved a degree of theoretical concordance and internal coherence often overlooked by earlier critics. The nucleus of ECLA analysis is a critique of the conventional theory of international trade (as expressed in the Heckscher-Ohlin-Samuelson version of Ricardo's theory of comparative advantages), which attempts to show that the international division of labour seen as a 'natural' product of world trade by conventional trade theorists in fact benefits the centre to a much greater extent than the periphery.

We can identify three main implications of the core-periphery framework for economic change in developing countries: structural unemployment of the labour force, external disequilibrium, and secular deterioration in the terms of trade (see Rodriguez, 1980).

1. *Structural unemployment.* Building on two-sector models of capitalist development, ECLA analysis assumes that employment growth in the periphery is proportionate to the rate of investment in the modern sector. Full employment at adequate levels of labour productivity can therefore only be achieved if capital accumulation in the export and import-substitution sectors is sufficient to absorb new entrants into the modern-sector labour force, such entrants originating both from the traditional sector and from additions to the economically active population resulting from population growth. Structural unemployment will therefore arise as a product of imbalances between investment in the modern sector, of levels of employment-shedding in the traditional sector and of population growth.
2. *External disequilibria.* Specialization in primary product exports and low levels of inter-industry integration in the periphery produce a pattern of demand for manufactures strongly oriented towards imports. An income elasticity of demand for manufactures greater than that for primary commodities implies that imports of the periphery will grow more rap-

idly than those of the centre. Since in the long run, given Marshall-Lerner conditions, there must be a balance between the reciprocal demand for imports of the centre and periphery, the higher income elasticity of imports of the periphery imposes a limit on the rate of economic growth in these countries which is less than that obtainable by the centre. From this point of view, in the long term, rapid and sustained growth in the periphery can only be obtained through a reorientation of highly income-elastic demand for manufactures to domestic industries through import substituting industrialization and a diversification of exports towards more income elastic goods.

3. *Deterioration of the terms of trade.* Given the differences in income elasticities of imports in core and periphery countries, higher income levels in the latter will increasingly orient the 'consumption path' in these countries towards imports. From the point of view of supply, specialization in primary commodity exports also generates a 'production path' which is equally trade dependent. As higher shares of aggregate demand and output are linked to trade, the disparity in income elasticities will tend to raise prices of imports while depressing export prices for the periphery countries taken as a whole: thus the tendency towards declining terms of trade for the periphery. As in the case of employment and trade disequilibria considered above, countries of the periphery can only escape this vicious circle through industrialization policies which redirect demand for manufactures to domestic producers, and which will eventually provide a source of price-elastic exportables. In other words, industrialization is viewed as a necessary (and, in some ECLA writings, a sufficient) condition for accelerated growth.

However, the ECLA school does not assume that industrialization will take place spontaneously as a result of market forces. In the absence of government intervention to encourage private sector accumulation in this sector, in fact, structural obstacles (such as the international division of labour and internal sectoral imbalances) will work to inhibit the development of manufacturing. Policies proposed by ECLA writers include protection for infant industries, exchange controls, incentives for foreign direct investment in industry, and state-led investment in industries providing essential goods and services or to ease supply bottlenecks (particularly large, slow-gestating projects which are unlikely to be undertaken by the private sector).

Thus implicit within ECLA analysis is the assumption that there exists an ideal model of sectoral growth which, if properly implemented, will give rise to a process of *balanced economic transformation* that will progressively lift the constraints on growth associated with structural unemployment, trade disequilibria and deterioration of the terms of trade. It is here that the great strength of the ECLA approach – its examination of the structural impediments to development in the periphery – is also its greatest weakness. For even when the 'structure of production' is interpreted in the widest possible sense, it must be recognized that economic performance over the long term involves more than sectoral balance and inter-industry linkages. In particular, while ECLA analysis explores some aspects of the development of the forces of production, it addresses neither the transformation of relations of production, nor the social and political implications (both domestic and international) or changing production relations to promote the evolution of the system as a whole.

ECLA has attracted criticism from across the ideological spectrum, not least because of the willingness of authors of this school to go beyond theory to suggest concrete policy measures. From the left, ECLA was criticized both for failing to condemn the mechanisms of exploitation inherent within the world capitalist system and for rejecting the notion that international trade is exploitative (see entry on Dependency theories). Orthodox economists predictably attacked ECLA for its departures from conventional trade theory (see Haberler, 1961). On the political front, the right was also wary of structuralism as a 'Trojan horse of Marxism' owning to similarities between the two approaches. Both sets of analyses, for example, identified the international division of labour and traditional power elites as the main obstacles to growth, and both proposed interventionist policies to promote domestic industrialization. The tendency to identify structuralism with Marxism was also encouraged by the simultaneous reformulation of both approaches during the 1960s.

Another crucial area of divergence between structural and conventional economic theories concerns the analysis of inflation in developing countries. Structuralists distinguish between the 'initial' upward pressure on prices on the one hand and monetary 'propagation mechanisms' through which price increases feed back upon themselves on the other. This view of inflation, closely associated with the work of Kalecki and with Keynes's analysis of inflation during the Second World War, locates the 'initial' causes of inflation in the inelastic nature of agricultural supply, in conflict over income and wealth distribution, in rigidities in public finances and in foreign sector constraints.

Structuralist thinking underwent important changes towards the end of the 1970s, responding to growing disillusionment with the dependency school and the need to counter a resurgent neo-liberalism in Latin America. A key characteristic of 'neo-structuralist' theories (see Lustig, 1988) is the attempt to shift the focus of analysis from the long-period issues addressed by ECLA to short-period problems; the latter include stabilization and acute trade imbalances associated with the debt crisis and resulting stagflation of the 1980s. The immediate concern was to formulate stabilization policies which were less recessive and regressive (in terms of income distribution) than orthodox 'shock therapy' approaches. As a result of this emphasis on the short period, neo-structuralism is largely bereft of discussion of long-term economic strategies which have consistently been the hallmark of traditional structuralist thinking.

Events during the 1970s and 1980s – particularly the heterogeneous nature of capitalist development in Latin America – also shaped the evolution of contemporary structuralist models, the most prominent proponent of which is the North American economist Lance Taylor. Like the ECLA structuralists, Taylor's arguments are formulated as a critique of orthodox optimization theories, particularly the uniform application of exchange rate devaluation and monetary targets to control trade disequilibria and inflation in developing countries. Unlike ECLA, however, Taylor attempts to construct formal models of the macroeconomy as an alternative to those on offer from more conventional theorists.

New structuralist models relax several key assumptions of the orthodox model (see Taylor, 1991). First, since adjustment does not always take place through changes in relative prices, provision must be made for mark-up pricing in certain sectors. Second, the neoclassical separation between growth and distribution is discarded in favour of a more historically realistic approach examining the role of shifts in income and wealth distributions on the adjustment process. Third, the money supply under certain conditions is endogenous to the level of activity on the 'real' side of the economy, with the result that tight money policies may restrict production while failing to control price inflation. Finally, the precise nature and level of development of financial institutions in specific developing countries will feature prominently in interactions between the 'real' and 'financial' sides of the macroeconomy.

Much of the content of new structuralist models is descended from Keynes, Kalecki, Kaldor (1956) and other economists of the Cambridge school, although reoriented to account for pricing and production conditions peculiar to developing countries. Nevertheless, like neo-structuralists before him, Taylor has emphasized the need for flexible approaches to macroeconomics and stabilization, advocating more orthodox approaches where economies are overheated or where the exchange rate is substantially overvalued. Although this tendency towards eclecticism has drawn criticism from non-orthodox economists searching for a generally applicable alternative to the standard neoclassical model, it is possible to view this flexible approach as a realistic response to the seemingly limitless heterogeneity of conditions in developing countries. At the very least, the new structuralism represents a needed corrective to both the highly schematic core-periphery framework of the ECLA school and to the universalism of conventional macroeconomic theory.

GABRIEL PALMA AND JONATHAN PINCUS

References

Haberler, G. (1961), 'Terms of Trade and Economic Development' in H.S. Ellis (ed.), *Economic Development of Latin America*, New York: St Martin's Press, 275–95.

Kaldor, N. (1956), 'Economic Problems of Chile', ECLA, mimeo; reprinted in N. Kaldor (1964), *Essays on Economic Policy II*, London: Duckworth.

Lustig, N. (1988), 'Del Estructuralismo al Neostructuralismo: La Busqueda de un Paradigma Heterodoxo', Colección de Estudios CIE-PLAN, no. 23, March.

Noyola, J. (1956), 'El Desarrollo Económico y la Inflación en Mexico y Otros Paises Latinamericanos', *Investigación Económica*, fourth quarter.

Pinto, A. (1968), 'Raices Estructurales de la Inflación en América Latina', *El Trimestre Económico*, January–March.

Prebisch, R. (1961), 'Economic Development or Monetary Stability: The False Dilemma', ECLA, *Economic Bulletin*, no. 1.

Rodriguez, O. (1980), *La Teoría del Subdesarrollo de la CEPAL*, Mexico: Siglo XXI Editores.

Taylor, L. (1991), *Income Distribution, Inflation and Growth: Lectures on Structuralist Macroeconomic Theory*, Cambridge, MA: MIT Press.

Surplus approach

'Surplus approach' is the expression often used to indicate the economic theory which has its roots in the works of the classical authors (mainly represented by Smith and Ricardo) and of Marx. More specifically, the term refers to the view of distribution held by those economists, where incomes other than wages result as the 'surplus' of the social product above wages, wages being taken as known prior to other incomes. In turn, this conception flows from the explanation of the real wage rate which characterizes this approach.

According to this explanation, the real wage is determined by a complex of social and economic circumstances which can be divided into two basic groups. A first group is constituted by those institutional and customary elements that are believed to set the level under which the real wage cannot fall at any particular period and in any particular society. This *minimum* wage, which the classical authors refer to as a 'subsistence' wage, consists of the kinds and quantities of commodities that society has historically come to regard as necessary to the worker. It therefore includes not merely what is needed for physical subsistence, but whatever else which, in the common opinion, is considered indispensable for the worker.

A second group of factors affect what can be termed the 'bargaining position' of workers *vis-à-vis* employers. These factors determine whether the position of workers is so weak that the real wage just coincides with the minimum, or strong enough so as to enforce a higher than minimum wage. This group includes all the circumstances that are able to affect the solidarity and degree of organization of workers, including especially the level of unemployment and factors influencing that level.

Though for analytical purposes it is useful to distinguish between these two groups of circumstances, interactions between them are obviously possible. Thus the bargaining position of workers may have an influence on the minimum wage (once the real wage has stayed above the subsistence level long enough to permeate the institutions and conventions of society), causing an increase in the minimum wage itself. In turn, the minimum wage that workers are confident of obtaining may affect their bargaining position – for instance, by influencing their capacity for resistance in any struggle with employers.

In terms of this explanation, it is natural to treat the real wage as *given* in the determination of other incomes. The latter therefore result as the residual of a social product which in turn is taken as a datum together with the prevailing methods of production, in this part of the theory.

The determination of shares other than wages involves the question of determining the relative prices of commodities, to which neither the classical economists nor Marx gave a satisfactory solution. The analytical difficulties met in this respect were one of the reasons why this approach was progressively abandoned in favour of marginalist theory (more often referred to as *neoclassical* theory, an expression that – after Sraffa's edition of Ricardo – appears to be a misnomer, implying a false continuity between the two approaches). In relatively recent times, however, a general solution to the determination of relative prices in the classical framework has been provided by Sraffa (1960). This has produced a revival of the surplus approach which has proceeded in parallel with an assessment (mostly by the same economists) of basic difficulties in marginalist theory.

The determination of surplus incomes and relative prices, which has been defined as the *core* of classical theory (Garegnani, 1987, para. 4), occurs, as hinted above, by taking as given the real wage, the social product and the technical conditions in use. Of course, the theory also investigates these three groups of circumstances, but this is done at a separate stage of analysis. This separation is the natural consequence of the different characteristics of the relations that are included in the core with respect to those outside it. Whilst relations inside the core possess known general properties, the same is not true for the relations that link the real wage, the social product and the methods of production to the various factors that are believed to determine them. This is exemplified by the nature of the influences that in this theory affect the real wage. Other instances are provided by the interrelations that may exist between the three groups of *data* relating to the core, such as the influence that output levels exert on technical conditions when returns to scale are not constant; or the complex of influences that the level of the real wage has on aggregate demand, and therefore on the level of the social product. (Examples of such different influences on aggregate demand are provided by the positive influence that the height of the real wage exerts on the general propensity to consume, and by the negative influence it may have on the incentive of profit earners to invest.) Thus, although these relations are quite general in kind, no universal principle can be established with respect to their individual properties (including, in some cases, even the direction in which they work). Therefore they are better studied by means of a 'case-by-case' analysis, in which the conditions specific to each particular situation can be taken into account. Nevertheless, any such analysis presupposes the relations that constitute the core; in this sense it can be seen that the latter constitutes the basic part of classical theory.

On the basis of what has been argued so far (see Garegnani, 1987, for more details), we are able to consider some recent developments that have taken place within this approach and that concentrate on the role of effective demand in the analysis of accumulation. In contrast to marginalist theory, the classical approach does not explain distribution in terms of demand for, and supply of, available resources. Therefore this approach is compatible with levels of production which need not ensure the full employment of labour. This opens the way to a determination of aggregate output which fully takes into account Keynes's principle of effective demand: i.e., the multiplier and the role of income in adjusting savings to investment.

Joining the principle of effective demand with the classical theory of distribution frees Keynes's analysis from the elements of marginalist theory it contains, with special reference to the decreasing 'marginal efficiency of capital' and the associated notion of an interest-elastic investment demand. These analytical fragments have in fact been the Trojan horse by which the so-called 'neoclassical synthesis' has reduced Keynes's argument to a particular, short-run case of orthodox theory. But these fragments are actually unnecessary to the principle of effective demand; moreover, they are open to the criticism made against the marginalist notion of a function of demand for 'capital' (and its flow counterpart, investment; Garegnani, 1978–79, Part II, paras 5 and 6).

Once it is associated with the classical theory of distribution, Keynes's basic idea – that what governs the level of output is effective demand, rather than the availability of resources – can be freely applied to the determination of long-run levels of output and therefore to the analysis of growth. This appears to be the meaning Keynes himself attributed to his theory, though it was presented in a short-period analytical framework.

The essence of the principle of effective demand is the independence of investment from saving decisions, so that the latter bear the burden of adjustment to the former. In the short-period context of Keynes's analysis, this adjustment takes the form of a level of income which can be lower than that corresponding to the full utilization of capacity and to the associated employment of labour. It might seem, however, that when we turn to long-run analysis, there is less scope for an adjustment relying on the level of income. Indeed, changes in capacity utilization are commonly seen merely as a short-run phenomenon, while in the long run the normal rate of capacity utilization should prevail. Given the usual assumption that the share of savings out of profits is higher than that out of wages, the adjustment of savings to investment would accordingly be committed not to the level, but rather to the distribution, of income – as reflected by the level of the real wage. It would follow that in the long run the independence of investment from savings could not fit with the classical explanation of distribution, since the way in which income divides between wages and profits would be exclusively determined by the need for savings dictated by the pace of accumulation. This is what we find in some versions of the so-called 'Cambridge theory of distribution', in which the real wage depends inversely on the rate of capital accumulation.

The position just summarized has been rejected on the basis of two arguments. The first one relies on the consideration that, in the long run, the size of capacity varies precisely as a result of investment. Through this route, additional amounts of savings can be obtained independently from any permanent change in capacity utilization, and without any need of change in distribution. Thus, larger savings corresponding to a higher investment trend could be generated by operating the additional capacity that investment itself progressively brings to existence (Garegnani, 1992, paras 4 and 5).

The second argument is that there appears to be no foundation for the belief that the flexibility of the rate of utilization of overall capacity is limited to the short run only. No precise theoretical support has ever been provided for this belief, however commonly it is held. Experience perhaps suggests that large excess capacity does not last indefinitely; this, however, appears to be largely irrelevant to the issue. On the one hand, once the questions of the size and utilization of capacity are properly set into a long-run perspective, large margins of increase in actual utilization are available, even above the *normal* rate of utilization, and therefore quite apart from the existence of any excess above the desirable amount of capacity (Ciccone, 1986, paras 3 and 4). On the other hand, the Keynesian view that demand is determined independently from potential output means that, to the extent it takes place, the elimination of excess capacity is obtained, not by the adjustment of demand to existing capacity but, on the contrary, through the destruction of part of the latter – typically by abstaining from replacements. On its own, this adjustment of capacity to demand does not affect the cause of excess capacity – the lack of demand – but merely cancels out its visible traces. Therefore it does not set any long-run limit to possible falls in demand and income, whatever its effectiveness in clearing the signs of those falls in the ratio of capacity to actual output.

At any rate, the reduction in the size of overall capacity *relative* to that of demand is likely to be slowed down and contrasted by the negative feedbacks that falls in the levels of gross investment will have on demand. One can reasonably expect, therefore, that unless autonomous upswings in the trend levels of demand intervene, capacity utilization will stay below the normal rate for long periods of time. Not only that: it has been argued that, though the attempt to adjust capacity to demand is continuously at work, the independent determination of demand is actually *inconsistent* with the maintenance of capacity utilization at the normal rate, even on average over the long run (Garegnani, 1992, para. 13).

The conclusion can thus be reached that, in the long run, output is liable to respond to demand through changes both in the size and in the utilization of productive capacity. It follows that, from a long-run point of view, the level of income appears to be even more powerful in adjusting savings to investment than in the short run, when existing plant constitutes a tighter limit on the expansion of output. That long-run adjustment, therefore, sets no necessary constraint on the level of the real wage, so that the view of capital accumulation as determined independently from savings decisions appears to be perfectly consistent with the classical framework and the explanation of distribution proper to it.

ROBERTO CICCONE

References

Ciccone, R. (1986), 'Accumulation and Capacity Utilization: Some Critical Considerations on Joan Robinson's Theory of Distribution', *Political Economy – Studies in the Surplus Approach*, **2** (1), 17–36.

Garegnani, P. (1978–79), 'Notes on Consumption, Investment and Effective Demand', *Cambridge Journal of Economics*, **2** (4), December 1978 (Part I); **3** (1), March 1979 (Part II).

Garegnani, P. (1987), 'Surplus Approach to Value and Distribution' in J. Eatwell, M. Milgate and P. Newman (eds), *The New Palgrave: A Dictionary of Economics*, London: Macmillan, Vol. 4, 560–73.

Garegnani, P. (1992), 'Some Notes for an Analysis of Accumulation' in E. Nell, D. Laibman and J. Halevi (eds), *Beyond the Steady State*, London: Macmillan, 47–71.

Sraffa, P. (1960), *Production of Commodities by Means of Commodities*, Cambridge: Cambridge University Press.

Surplus labour

As Marx demonstrated in *Theories of Surplus Value*, the concept of surplus labour is implicit in all the principal texts of classical political economy from Petty through Quesnay and the Physiocrats, to Smith, Ricardo and Richard Jones. An early critic of classical economics, Charles Hall, had everything but the name when he wrote, in 1805, that 'eight-tenths of the people consume only one-eighth of the produce of their labour; hence one day in eight, or one hour in a day, is all the time the poor man is allowed to work for himself, his wife, and his children. All the other days, or all the other hours of the day, he works for other people' (cited by King, 1983, p. 350). Probably the first explicit reference to 'surplus labour' was made, however, in 1821 by the anonymous author of a pamphlet on 'The Source and Remedy of the National Difficulties': 'Whatever may be *due* to the capitalist, he *can only receive the surplus labour* of the labourer; for the labourer *must* live ... the interest paid to the capitalists, whether in the nature of rents, interests of money, or profits of trade, is paid out of the *labour of others*' (*ibid.*). Several of the so-called 'Ricardian' socialists, like William Thompson, Piercy Ravenstone, John Gray, Thomas Rowe Edmonds and John Francis Bray, endorsed the idea and even attempted to quantify it, without invoking the term itself (ibid., pp. 349–55).

Marx encountered the work of the early socialists in the mid-1840s, the notion of surplus labour being (once again) implicit in some of his own writings later in the same decade. Almost certainly, though, his first references to 'surplus labour' were made in the *Grundrisse* manuscripts in 1857–58, after which the concept became a cornerstone of his mature economic analysis. For Marx surplus labour is defined as the difference between the total living labour performed and what he termed *necessary labour*, which is the labour required to produce the goods and services that are consumed by producers and their families. Surplus labour can thus be found in any type of society other than the most primitive. It is in fact a condition for the existence of class societies, since without it there would be no *surplus product*, and no one who did not work would be able to survive. Marx used the method by which surplus labour was extracted as the defining characteristic of different modes of production: 'The essential difference between the various economic forms of society, between, for instance, a society based on slave-labour, and one based on wage-labour, lies only in the mode in which this surplus-labour is in each case extracted from the actual producer, the labourer' (Marx, 1867, p. 217).

In the slave and serf modes of production, surplus labour was a palpable and undeniable fact, being imposed upon the producers by the extra-economic coercive power of the slave-owners and feudal lords. Under capitalism, where the human capacity to work has become a commodity, bought and sold on the market at its value like any other, there appears to be no surplus (or unpaid) labour, since the worker receives a wage for each hour that is worked. This, Marx explains, is one of the most tenacious illusions engendered by capitalist competition. But an illusion it is: so long as part of the net output of society accrues to non-producing classes – so long, that is, as there is a surplus product – surplus labour is being performed. In capitalism this surplus labour takes the form of *surplus value*: the difference between the value created (that is, the total labour-time performed) by the working class and the value of its own labour-power. Rent, industrial and commercial profit, and interest are all paid out of this surplus value, as too are the wages of domestic servants and all other unproductive workers (Marx, 1867, part III).

Some of the problems inherent in the concept of surplus labour will already have become apparent. The definition of necessary labour depends crucially on the theory of wages that is adopted. For the most part Marx did not assert a physiological subsistence theory of wages, arguing instead that there was a 'moral and historical element' in the value of the labour-power. Coupled with the substantial increase in real wages that has actually occurred in advanced capitalist economies over the last 150 years, this has led some Marxists, as well as Ricardian theorists like Piero Sraffa, to conclude that at least some sections of the working class may share in the surplus product with capitalists. This however renders the distinction between necessary and surplus labour very much less sharp than it originally appeared. Similar implications follow from the controversial question of demarcating productive from unproductive labour, a problem which is especially acute where workers employed in commercial and financial sectors are concerned, as well as in the context of state employees. Marx himself regarded the transport and storage of goods as productive operations, while bookkeeping and selling activities were unproductive. These distinctions, however, are very difficult to defend, and the boundaries between these supposedly distinct types of labour have in any case become somewhat artificial. Marx would probably have counted workers in state-owned trading enterprises as performing productive labour, while denying that status to nurses, teachers and librarians. In a society where the health and education of the labour force are essential preconditions for efficient production, this is hard to justify; also the increasing use of information as a productive input renders suspect any suggestion that clerical and managerial employees are *ipso facto* unproductive.

Despite these difficulties, the concept of an economic surplus has proved profoundly influential in the 20th century in the analysis, not only of the crisis-prone nature of advanced capitalist societies, but also (and more especially) of the causes of economic backwardness. In both cases it is the magnitude of the surplus and the uses to which it is put which determine the economic dynamics of the system. Thus Paul Baran and Paul Sweezy invoked the growth of the surplus as a proportion of net output to explain the strength of stagnationary tendencies in modern capitalism (Howard and King, 1992, Ch. 6). In addition, Baran's remarkably influential analysis of underdevelopment – and the theories of imperialism derived from it by Baran himself, by Andre Gunder Frank and by Immanuel Wallerstein – hinge on the extraction of surplus from poor peripheral regions by the rich, metropolitan centres of world capitalism (*ibid.*, Chs 9, 11). At a higher level of abstraction, Sraffa's meticulous reconstruction of the Ricardian system has suggested to many that a revived 'classical-Marxian' or 'surplus' economics represents a serious alternative to orthodox theory since it permits profits to be explained, and their movements charted, quite independently of the neoclassical forces of supply and demand, marginal productivity and utility maximization (*ibid.*, Chs 12–15).

The crucial word in all of this, however, is 'surplus' not 'surplus labour', the integrity of the latter concept having recently been threatened by two (closely-related) Sraffian challenges. One denies the need to conceive of the surplus product in terms of embodied labour, while the other points to further serious deficiencies in the conventional Marxian definitions of both necessary and surplus labour. On the first point, critics of Marxism note that the surplus has a tangible existence as a surplus product; that is, as a collection of useful objects (the treatment of services in this context is fraught with difficulties). It can be evaluated in current market prices, long-run equilibrium or 'natural' prices (the Marxian 'prices of production'), or in quantities of embodied labour. The first of these standards is of little theoretical interest, while the second – so Marx maintained – can be derived only from the third. But this claim is incorrect, since knowledge of the physical and social conditions of production, together with information about the distribution of the net product between capital and labour, are together sufficient to determine equilibrium prices without any reference to labour values. The concepts of surplus labour, and surplus value, are therefore redundant (Steedman, 1977). While this conclusion is often denied as a matter of principle by those surplus theorists like Sweezy who regard themselves as orthodox Marxists, in practice they often acknowledge its validity by themselves measuring the surplus in terms of market prices. It is significant that surplus labour plays no explicit role in either the theoretical or the empirical analyses of Baran and Sweezy.

The second problem arises from the possibility that conventionally-defined labour values may sometimes be negative in systems of joint production where profits are positive. This raises the further prospect of negative surplus value, which in turn entails that surplus labour is negative. Yet the notion that negative surplus labour can be the source of positive profits is paradoxical: if the labour force spends less time at work than is required to produce its own means of subsistence, even what Marx termed the 'simple reproduction' of the economic system should be impossible, and there should be no question of maintaining a non-producing class. To avoid this possibility, values must be redefined in the minimum-labour terms proposed by Michio Morishima, so that necessary labour is measured by the number of hours that would have been needed to produce the specified bundle of wage-goods had the technical processes of production with the lowest labour requirements been employed, rather than those actually used. Surplus labour is then defined as the difference between total labour and necessary labour *redefined in this manner*. Then, and only then, can the so-called 'Fundamental Marxian Theorem' be established: positive surplus value (and hence also positive surplus labour) is a necessary and sufficient condition for positive profits, and vice-versa (Morishima, 1973). One important consequence of this revision of the Marxian analysis is that surplus labour can no longer be defined at the level of the individual enterprise or industry; the concept is meaningful only in aggregate, for the entire economy.

These criticisms are not universally accepted. Orthodox Marxists like Fine (1982) continue to assert the merits of Marx's original analysis of surplus labour, on the grounds that his critics employ a faulty (often Ricardian) methodology and fail to appreciate the critical, Hegelian basis of the Marxian problematic. Thus the future status of the concept of surplus labour will depend on the outcome of much broader controversies in Marxian political economy.

JOHN E. KING

References

Fine, B. (1982), *Theories of the Capitalist Economy*, London: Edward Arnold.

Howard, M.C. and King, J.E. (1992), *A History of Marxian Economics, Volume II: 1929–1990*, London: Macmillan, and Princeton: Princeton University Press.

King, J.E. (1983), 'Utopian or Scientific?: A Reconsideration of the Ricardian Socialists', *History of Political Economy*, **15** (3), Fall, 345–73.

Marx, K. (1867) [1961], *Capital, Volume I*, Moscow: Foreign Languages Publishing House.

Morishima, M. (1973), *Marx's Capital: A Dual Theory of Value and Growth*, Cambridge: Cambridge University Press.

Steedman, I. (1977), *Marx after Sraffa*, London: New Left Books.

Tax incidence

Neoclassical public economics is the amalgamation of what had been two increasingly discredited branches of economics – welfare economics and applied public finance (principally tax incidence theory). Recently, however, there have been significant improvements in each, to such an extent that leading public finance economists now claim that neoclassical tax incidence theory represents all that is best in economics by offering important insights which contradict initial casual impressions. They consider the study of tax incidence to be fun because it offers such surprising findings, and also very important due to its implications concerning the impact of government policies. This marks a return to the spirit of Kalecki's (1937) seminal paper in Post Keynesian public economics. Kalecki's opening sentence reads: 'Mr Keynes' theory gives us a new basis for the enquiry into the problems of taxation. The analysis of the influence of various types of taxes on effective demand leads, as we shall see, to quite unexpected results, which may be of practical importance'. This survey continues in the same vein by offering conclusions which may be as surprising to Post Keynesians as to neoclassicals.

The three taxes Kalecki considered were on commodities, income and capital. His basic assumptions were of a closed economy with unemployed capital and labour, a worker's propensity to consume of zero and a balanced budget. First, an *ad valorem* tax on wage goods is introduced. Capitalists are profit maximizers and the effect of the tax is to increase marginal costs. But since the tax revenue is spent on unemployment benefits and salaries for public employees, demand also rises. Thus, output, profits, capitalists' consumption and investment are unchanged and the only real effect is a redistribution of income from employed to unemployed workers. Next, introduce a tax on profits. The profit maximizing level of output does not change, nor do investment or capitalists' consumption. Workers' consumption rises and so too must gross profits. The increase in workers' consumption will be reduced by the increase in prices brought about by the increase in output. Finally, a tax on capital is introduced. The effects largely correspond to those for the profits tax, except that an increase in capital taxation will not lower net profitability or raise the rate of interest. Capital taxation is not a cost of production in the long term, so that the incentive to invest is even stronger than before the introduction of tax. Kalecki concluded that capital taxation is the best way to stimulate business and reduce unemployment, but he doubted if any government would have the political will to adopt it as an anti-recessionary policy.

Kalecki's paper made little impact until the 1970s when it was expanded and developed by Asimakopulos and Burbidge (1974) (hereafter AB). The AB paper has remained until recently the most fully articulated Post Keynesian statement on tax incidence. Theirs is a short-period model in which investment is taking place, but is assumed to be largely predetermined. The marginal propensity to save out of wages is assumed to be zero; all saving is done out of profit income. The economy is assumed to be in a position of trade and budget balance and is in equilibrium when predetermined investment is realized and is equal to what firms have chosen to save. These assumptions are sufficient to determine post-tax profits in real terms as a function of the savings propensities and the rate of investment in real terms. If the government then introduces, say, a higher rate of profits tax at the beginning of the short period and spends the extra tax revenue, post-tax profits will be unaffected by the tax if short-period equilibrium is re-established. This conclusion holds in both competitive and non-competitive market conditions because government expenditures have an expansionary effect via the balanced budget multiplier. In competitive markets, the expansion is accompanied by lower real wage rates because the increased demand leads to higher prices relative to wages and hence to costs. The resulting higher pre-tax profits make it possible for post-tax profits to be unchanged even though the rate of profits tax is higher. In non-competitive markets, the multiplier effect will lead to an increase in output and employment. Because firms are assumed to have set prices by adding a mark-up to standard costs calculated at less than full capacity output, short-period fluctuations in demand are met by changes in output so that profits can rise substantially with no increase in price because of higher sales and the spreading of fixed costs over a larger volume of output.

This example from the AB model demonstrates that in Post Keynesian terms, the legal and economic incidence of taxes can differ even in the short period. This result is not possible in neoclassical models because of their assumptions of full employment, profit-maximization and wage and price flexibility. Thus, a major difference between Post Keynesian and neoclassical tax incidence theory is that the former recognizes that the legal and economic incidence of broad-based taxes can differ even in the short period, a conclusion precluded in the latter.

Mair and Damania (1988, 1992) have extended the AB model to include a property tax and to analyse the differential incidence effects of substituting a poll tax for a property tax. Neoclassical theory sees the main effect of a local property tax as being equivalent to a profits tax by reducing the return to capital by the average national rate of tax. However, Mair and Damania reverse this result by demonstrating that the principal effect of a local property tax will be on workers' incomes, i.e. on consumption. They show that the macroeconomic effect of introducing a poll tax to replace a property tax will be deflationary by redistributing income away from workers, thereby reducing consumption.

The AB model, however, has quite severe limitations. In its competitive form, prices are assumed to be completely flexible and the economy to be at full employment. In the non-competitive version, AB assume prices are set in some unspecified way by price leaders and are held unchanged over the business cycle. Thus, tax-induced demand changes lead only to variations in output, with the aggregate supply curve implicitly assumed to be perfectly elastic. This is an over-simplified approach to the forces determining prices in non-competitive markets and provides no explanation of the dynamic process through which non-competitive prices are determined or sustained over the business cycle. Damania and Mair (1992) use supergame analysis to model the non-competitive sector in terms of a strategic process in which firms interact continually over time. This supergame model brings Post Keynesian theory back to Kalecki's original insight that price wars are more likely to occur in the upswing of a business cycle than in a recession. Damania and Mair reverse many of the results of the AB model and demonstrate that, in general, the burden of taxes is on real wages; thus Post Keynesian tax incidence theory may be more properly seen as a theory of the cyclical determination of the real wage.

Laramie (1991) has fully integrated the structure of taxation into Kalecki's theories of income distribution at the industrial and macroeconomic levels, thereby addressing one of the major limitations of Kalecki's macroeconomic analysis. His contribution is to recognize that, as tax revenues change, so too will the factors determining the distribution of income, depending on the method of tax finance used. The impact of taxes will depend on the type of tax levied, on how firms treat the tax (as a prime cost or an overhead cost), and on the effect of the tax on firms' mark-ups. Work by Laramie and Mair (1993) shows that for UK manufacturing industry, business property taxes are treated by firms as an overhead cost and do not influence any of the parameters determining the distribution of income.

Laramie brings out the obvious but often ignored role of taxation in Kalecki's theory of income distribution. The stability of the wage share in national income is not simply the outcome of opposing movements in the mark-up, k, and the materials-to-wages ratio, j, but also depends on the stability of the tax structure. Laramie has reintroduced the political dimension into the analysis of the conflict over the distribution of income. Whereas Kalecki and other post Keynesians have focused on the class struggle of trade unions to reduce the mark-up, Laramie has extended the analysis of class struggle to other activities of the state, particularly the revenue side of the budget.

This integration by Laramie of tax incidence theory into the framework of Kaleckian macroeconomics provides an opportunity for a rapprochement between 'bourgeois economists' (such as Post Keynesians) and radical economists on the issue of the fiscal crisis of the state. The recent advances in Post

Keynesian analysis now provide a basis for the development of a broadly based radical approach to public economics which may produce yet more 'unexpected results'.

DOUGLAS MAIR

References

Asimakopulos, A. and Burbidge, J. (1974), 'The Short Period Incidence of Taxation', *Economic Journal*, **84**, 267–88.
Damania, D. and Mair, D. (1992), 'The Short Period Incidence of Taxation Revisited', *Cambridge Journal of Economics*, **16** (2), 195–206.
Kalecki, M. (1937), 'A Theory of Commodity, Income and Capital Taxation', *Economic Journal*, **47**, 444–50.
Laramie, A.J. (1991), 'Taxation and Kalecki's Distribution Factors', *Journal of Post Keynesian Economics*, **4**, 583–94.
Laramie, A.J. and Mair, D. (1993), 'The Incidence of Business Rates: A Post-Keynesian Approach', *Review of Political Economy*, **5** (1), 55–72.
Mair, D. and Damania, D. (1988), 'The Ricardian Tradition and Local Property Taxation', *Cambridge Journal of Economics*, **12** (4), 435–50.
Mair, D. and Damania, D. (1992), 'A Post Keynesian Approach to the Incidence of Taxation' in P. Arestis and V. Chick (eds), *Developments in Post Keynesian Economics: Essays on Methodology, Pricing, Distribution and Policy*, Aldershot: Edward Elgar.

Taxation

According to orthodox economics, the role of the state in a market economy should be limited to the appropriation of revenues to correct for market failure in the attainment of efficiency, equity and stabilization objectives. In radical economics, by contrast, the role of the capitalist state is to appropriate revenues to finance the two functions often thought of as contradictory: accumulation and legitimation. The accumulation function seeks to promote the production and realization of profits or surplus value; the legitimation function to conceal the inherently antagonistic nature of capitalism. The effects of taxation are considered here in light of these two functions. The relationship between taxation and the functions of the state is established; the economic effects of taxation are discussed, and the relationship between the accumulation and legitimation functions re-evaluated.

Given that the functions of the capitalist state are accumulation and legitimation, it follows that labour bears the burden of taxation in the same manner as it bears the full burden of the creation of profits; also that the capitalist state, through its powers of taxation, is a principal agency of exploitation. As a consequence, taxation may be thought to epitomize the contradiction between accumulation and legitimation. In raising revenues to promote the accumulation of capital, the state raises class antagonisms; similarly in attempting to legitimize class relations by, for example, redistributing income through the tax system, the state also undermines the accumulation process.

Following the work of O'Connor (1973) and Kalecki (1971), the contradiction between accumulation and legitimation is considered below in light of the following: (1) the expenses necessary to maintain a 'legitimate' tax system, and (2) the economic effects of redistributive taxation.

At the political level, as O'Connor (1973) so aptly describes, tax systems have been designed to conceal the distribution of the tax burden through a myriad of taxes and definitions of what is taxable. As such, tax systems perceived to be progressive, because of a progressive income tax rate structure, may actually be regressive because of the definition of taxable income and because of the existence of other tax bases. The cost of this obfuscation is one of the legitimation expenses both incurred and imposed by the state.

The legitimation expenses incurred and imposed by the state are minimized by the extent to which tax ideologies are effective. Given the exploitive nature of taxation, tax ideologies are necessary to support the development of and compliance with tax systems. These tax ideologies are represented in the methodological approach presented to mainstream public finance textbooks. In this methodology, the political and the economic are separated. The state is an altruistic institution which has the goal of maximizing social welfare subject to some constraints. The study and analysis of tax systems are therefore relegated to social welfare criteria where the existence of class domination and conflict is denied (see O'Connor, 1973).

The failure of tax ideologies causes legitimation crises which pave the wave of tax 'reforms'. However, the process of class domination for example as described by O'Connor (1973), causes anti-tax sentiments and movements to be coopted and translated into the dominant interests within the state apparatus. For example, in the 1980s in the US, a tax revolt led to an increased reliance on regressive forms of taxation under the semblance of increasing economic efficiency through some archaic notions of 'trickle down' or through some far-reaching rationale, e.g. to reduce the exploitation of capital.

The pervasiveness of commodity fetishism, tax ideologies and the complexity of the tax system may thus conceal the true distribution of tax burdens. But beyond this, what impact does taxation have upon accumulation and what can be said about taxation's impact on the relationship between accumulation and legitimation? To begin, the existence of legitimation expenses necessary to maintain the legitimacy of the tax system, whether publicly or privately borne, consumes capital necessary for the expansion of the capitalist mode of production. As such, these legitimation expenses impose a trade-off between accumulation and legitimation. In contrast, redistributive tax policies impose no such clear contradiction between accumulation and legitimation. As will be shown below, redistributive tax policies to promote legitimation may paradoxically have no impact on (or perhaps actually promote) accumulation; again, the pursuance of the accumulation function may undermine the conditions necessary for legitimation while having no impact on (or perhaps actually hindering) accumulation. To illustrate this argument, the economic effects of taxation are considered.

The economic effects of taxation depend upon (1) the structure of taxation and the relationship between the type of tax revenue and the direction of government spending, and (2) the power which economic classes can exert in reaction to being taxed. Each of these will be considered briefly and then the dynamic effects of taxation will be discussed in light of the accumulation and legitimation functions.

As noted above, the state derives and reports tax receipts from a variety of bases such as personal income, business and personal property, corporate profits and sales. These tax bases represent sources of tax revenues derived from various economic classes – labour, capital, rentiers and the unemployed. The distribution of tax liabilities within and between classes is the outcome of conflict at the political level and reflects the relative degrees of power each exercises within the state apparatus. The functional distribution of taxation and income is not accurately known since the state does not typically publish such information.

The inter-class distribution of taxation is important in determining the macroeconomic effects of taxation, given that different classes derive income from different sources, pay different average tax rates and have different propensities to spend. This is illustrated by Kalecki (1971) when he demonstrates the economic effects of taxation. Kalecki shows that neither increases in profit taxes used to subsidize the consumption of the unemployed or wage earners, nor increases in the wage tax used to finance government purchases (see O'Connor, 1971), has any impact on the aggregate level of profits. Under these conditions, the state's pursuance of the legitimation function does not hinder accumulation, whereas its pursuance of the accumulation function undermines the conditions for legitimacy without promoting accumulation. As Kalecki (1971) suggests, opposition to legitimation expenses through redistributive tax policies is therefore political, although expressed in economic terms.

These conclusions are predicted on the standard Kaleckian assumption (see Kalecki, 1971) that labour spends all its income, and also on the assumption that the aggregate mark-up is constant with respect to a change in the tax structure. The former assumption can be relaxed while still maintaining much of the force of the argument, but if the latter assumption is relaxed, the state may be unable to carry out its legitimation function through redistributive tax policies.

Whether change in the tax structure is regressive or progressive in nature, arguments can be made that the aggregate mark-up may be variable with respect to changes in the functional distribution of tax liabilities, depending on the power of the various classes to react and the specific economic conditions underlying the determination of the mark-up (see Damania and Mair, 1992). These reactions are likely to be asymmetrical. With class warfare, attempts will be made to shift tax increases but not tax decreases. Following an increase in taxation on labour income, workers may seek higher wages which may reduce the aggregate mark-up (see Kalecki, 1971), or capitalists may pass on a hike in taxes on profits through higher mark-ups. Rentiers may react to an increase in taxation by attempting to shift the term structure of interest rates upwards. If successful, profits will be redistributed from capitalists to rentiers. To offset this loss, capitalists may attempt to raise mark-ups. Thus the rentier tax may ultimately be shifted onto labour. If capitalist and rentiers are able to shift taxes, these taxes become equivalent to a tax on wages. Assuming that capitalists and rentiers are able to shift taxes onto labour, the state, in the absence of income policies, is impotent in fulfilling the legitimation function through redistributive tax policies. In all likelihood, some degree of shifting takes place which depends on the factors that determine the degree of monopoly and how these are affected by the tax system. The extent to which shifting takes place is as yet unresolved.

In addition to tax shifting effects on the mark-up, an intra-class income distribution effect might also be considered. This effect arises when the state redistributes income within economic classes (see O'Connor, 1973). For example, if the government increases corporate profits taxes to finance purchases of social capital, the government is redistributing profits from some industries paying taxes but not receiving the benefits provided by the social capital. As O'Connor (1973) describes, industries receiving benefits may be able to 'bottle up' the gains provided by the state through adjusting mark-ups relative to costs. The state therefore promotes accumulation within specific industries at the expense of other industries. The bottling up of benefits compounds inter-class conflict with intra-class conflict; as a consequence, crises of legitimation may take on new dimensions where inter-class alliances are formed.

To summarize, three problems arise in considering the impact of taxation on the relationship between accumulation and legitimation. First, the 'true' functional distribution of taxation and income is not known. Second, the nature of the dynamic processes, both short run and long run, through which various economic classes will react to the imposition of new taxes is uncertain and not yet completely understood. Third, the redistributive impact of the state's budget on specific industry mark-ups and on the aggregate mark-up is also not fully understood.

Recently an attempt has been made by Laramie and Mair (1992) to consider the dynamic effects of taxation on investment using a Kaleckian model.

Kalecki (1971, pp. 165–83) showed that new investment depends, among other things, on the level of entrepreneurial savings and on the relationship between investment that generates the standard rate of profit and actual investment, where the former is the reciprocal of the pay-off period. According to Kalecki, if investment that generates the standard rate of profits is greater than actual investment, then the actual rate of profits is greater than the standard rate and business will seek external sources of funds to finance investment. Laramie and Mair have analysed the impact of taxation on investment in this theoretical framework with and without a government budget constraint. With no budget constraint, a decrease in the tax rate on wages is shown to increase profits and investment (depending upon the economy's long-run growth trend and business cycle stage). By contrast, a decrease in the tax rate on profits is shown to have an uncertain impact on investment and will depend upon the sizes of the two opposing effects. The decrease in the tax rate on profits reduces the rate of depreciation (the rate at which profits are lost to existing capital as the consequence of technical progress) and thus reduces new investment, but simultaneously increases after-tax profits, thereby stimulating new investment. The effect on investment will thus depend on which of these two factors is the larger. With a budget constraint, by contrast, a decrease in the tax rate on wages will result in increased profits and in new investment, depending on the parameters in the model, but a reduction in the tax rate on profits will simply reduce the rate of depreciation and net investment (over much of the business cycle), assuming a positive long-run growth trend. These conclusions are still tentative and depend on the assumption of a constant mark-up, but nonetheless add some insight into the relationship between accumulation and legitimation. Under some circumstances, the state, in pursuance of its legitimation function, actually promotes accumulation. This conclusion contrasts with that of Kalecki's static approach, where redistributive tax policies were shown to have no impact on accumulation.

Kalecki's insights into tax incidence and the logical extensions that follow therefrom allow a re-evaluation of the contradiction between the accumulation and legitimation functions of the state. As demonstrated above, the state's legitimation function, which may involve the redistribution of income, need not necessarily hinder accumulation and may potentially foster it. However, Kalecki (1971, pp. 138–45) did recognize that in the long run, political changes may result from the pursuit of full employment policies which may diminish the political power of business leaders and lead to a decline in their ability as a class to accumulate wealth. Thus, the contradiction between accumulation and legitimation is not economic *per se*, but political with economic consequences. Given that Kalecki first published his ideas on taxation as long ago as 1937 (see Kalecki, 1971), more interest in this topic might have been expected. However, relatively little attention has been paid in the radical literature to the effects of taxation, in particular to the dynamic effects. While the recent work referred to above has taken Kalecki's analysis out of a short-period framework, many issues remain unresolved.

ANTHONY J. LARAMIE

References

Damania, D. and Mair, D. (1992), 'The Short-Period Incidence of Taxation Revisited', *Cambridge Journal of Economics*, **16**, 195–206.

Kalecki, M. (1971), *Selected Essays on the Dynamics of a Capitalist Economy 1933–1970*, Cambridge: Cambridge University Press.

Laramie, A.J. and Mair, D. (1992), 'Taxation, the Rate of Depreciation, the Trend and the Business Cycle', Working paper, Heriot-Watt University.

Mair, D. and Laramie, A.J. (1992), 'The Incidence of Business Rates on Manufacturing Industry in Scotland and the Rest of the UK', *Scottish Journal of Political Economy*, **39**, 76–94.

O'Connor, J. (1973), *The Fiscal Crisis of the State*, New York: St Martin's Press.

Technological change

The phrase 'technological change' has recently become much more fashionable in the economics literature. Certainly it appears more centrally than it did 20 years ago when Rosenberg characterized 'technological change' as (occupying) a curious sort of underworld in economics. Even if 'it was not totally ignored' by the classical economists, nevertheless 'it played ... the role of a kind of afterthought which modified somewhat the dimensions of an analysis which was undertaken without it, and in which other variables ... were regarded as more important' (Rosenberg, 1971, p. 9). The argument I should like to make in this short definitional entry is that the relatively late appearance of technological change in legitimate economic discussion actually relates to the intellectual context in which it is embedded. The mainstream of economic theory is essentially a static discipline which explores the behaviour of economic agents over relatively short time periods. Conversely the notion of *change* - carrying with it concepts such as *structure* and *function* – really does not appear, at least not in pure theory. Hence the marginality of technological change.

Conventional economic analysis defines 'technology' or 'technique' in terms of the act of production; i.e. the act of adding value to resources. In terms of a simple production function, this is written as

$$Q = A(t)F(K, L)$$

where K is capital flow, L is labour flow, Q is output flow, and $A(t)$ is technology at time t. The two concepts are defined differently. 'Technology' [$A(t)$] represents an efficiency frontier in the given state of knowledge. 'Technique' represents a precise ratio of inputs for a given production level *at time t* and hence defines the capital and labour intensity of production. Conversely 'technological change' represents a shift in the production function; i.e. a shift in what is technically feasible over time. In addition, it is then straightforward to define relative factor saving and augmenting biases as properties of the shift.

So far so good! But it is here that the problems begin because all we have really done is to define two states of nature. Nothing has been said about how the economic system has moved from one to the other. It is rather akin to the problems of classical physics in explaining the movement of an electron from one energy level to a higher one, since it clearly does not pass through an intermediate space/time trajectory. Electrons are never observed in intermediate positions.

In the 19th century, economists argued that 'economic growth' – the rate of change of output of the whole (macro)economic system – could be explained simply by the rate of investment, which in turn was determined by the rate of savings. Technological change occurred as a by-product but, beyond a passing mention, it was not something that warranted a lot of thought. The difficulties really began in the middle of the present century, in my view due to two factors.

The first was the statistical discovery by Solow, Abramowitz and others that only a very small percentage of observed changes in national output could be explained by investment differentials. The second was the growing interest in varying international rates of economic growth, particularly with respect to Third World countries – an important practical issue.

Regarding the first, for example, Solow's conclusion that c. 87 per cent of US non-farm output/head change over the first half of the 20th century could *not* be explained by changes in investment/head, was a shock to established thinking. The unexplained portion, the 'residual', was labelled technological change, with subsequent efforts made to ascribe values to likely causative variables such as education, scale factors, R&D, employment, participation rates, etc. For example Denison (in Rosenberg, 1971, p. 363), probably the best example of this genre, 'explained' 2.00 per cent of a 2.93 per cent US growth rate between 1929 and 1957 as follows: 0.43 per cent was due to an increase of capital stock; 0.58 per cent to advances in knowledge; 0.12 per cent to R&D expenditures; and 0.87 per cent to education. However, it is not clear why these causes are independent of each other (as they must be if each is given a separate value). It seems far more likely that they act together as part of an evolutionary process. For example, increases in the capital stock usually mean 'advances in knowledge', requiring more 'educated workers' to attend the new machines and often involving a lot of trouble-shooting R&D, leading to more 'knowledge', etc.

The second difficulty relates to the notion of *structural change*. Interesting questions, like how new technologies/industries appear on the economic scene and within what type of institutional context, simply cannot be explored directly by mainstream theory. An important reason contributing to this difficulty, I suggest, is the rigid separation between microeconomics and macroeconomics. In reality, of course, observed *macroeconomic* change actually originates from *microeconomic* fluctuations.

It is for reasons such as these that technological change has remained on the professional periphery, allowed to appear largely as an exogenous influence on more 'tractable' economic relationships, such as the conditions underlying the relative stability of specific growth paths. In a sense, professional values appear to have proved stronger than an important set of economic issues.

Over the last 10 to 15 years or so, the neo-Schumpeterian school of economics has begun to take the concept of technological change more seriously. The reason why they are called neo-Schumpeterians is that they all take inspiration from the Austrian economist Joseph Schumpeter, who in a series of books and papers in the first half of this century, sought to explain how economic systems grow. For Schumpeter (1934, p. 9), the inspiration for growth was *innovation* which he defined in terms of *novelty* – new products, new processes, new markets, new resources and new organizational forms. Innovations occurred as a result of 'entrepreneurial' behaviour on the part of business people, who in turn were activated by competition and by the lure of monopoly profits. It was the entrepreneur who was the creative force driving the economic system on to greater heights of achievement. Provide conditions appropriate for entrepreneurship and the economy would flourish.

Implicitly therefore, although Schumpeter did not express it in this way, he was describing a process through which the macro evolves out of the micro. The collective behaviour of individual people in exploring 'economic possibility space' would drive the economic system as a whole to ever greater heights of productive possibility. It is this micro-macro interface that the neo-Schumpeterians have begun to explore (Dosi *et al.*, 1988).

They argue that technological change arising in this way is not exogenous, but is actually determined by the organizational context within which it occurs. A convenient means of expressing the concept is that any one productive agent (say a firm) operates with a specific 'technological system' which is peculiar to its own operations and which in a sense encapsulates the knowledge necessary for production to be maintained. Such a system defines and orchestrates the range of competence that the firm possesses and summarizes the economic efficiency with which it converts inputs into outputs. Another way of looking at the same phenomenon is as the *information* available to the firm – *contextualized* into routines, work schedules, machinery, management control systems, production programmes and people-embodied skills, which together underlie the production process as a whole at any point in time.

But this technological system is at the same time the focus of change because of economic competition from other firms that threatens to take away market share and reduce profits. In addition, creative forces within the firm have a similar effect in bringing about change. In this way the firm's technological system is perpetually in a state of flux (at least potentially) due to environmental competition and internal creativity. In order to 'manage change', firms establish specific institutional mechanisms through which they focus resources and attempt to control events in a reasonably ordered way, since clearly continuous change would lead to great inefficiency. The most important such mechanism is the R&D laboratory, but it is not the only one. Examples of others are the dedicated 'project team' set up to engineer a new investment project, personnel appraisal schemes designed to improve man-power efficiency and periodic buying-in of external management consultancy services.

Elsewhere a colleague and I have tried to extend this idea of a technological system into something rather like a 'technological field', somewhat akin to the notion of an electric field in physics but without Maxwell's equations to give the idea substance (Clark and Juma, 1992). Perhaps the easiest way to describe it is in terms of information flows. Within any industrial sector, the firm's technological system is constantly being potentially destabilized by new information, as best practice improves throughout the sector. This wider 'technological field' (or 'paradigm') does not improve linearly but, like Kuhn's scientific paradigm, goes through periods of relative quiescence (normal technology) punctuated by sudden radical upheavals.

In its relatively calm state, the 'field' represents a set of standard practices for production, embodied in the skills and competences of relevant people and organizations. It is often science-based and enshrined in specific engineering standards and codes of conduct which prescribe best practice. And in a dynamic sense it embodies a strong prescription regarding which directions of technical change to pursue and which to neglect. In short it describes a technological system in 'cognitive space', providing the ruling heuristic for good technological practice. In its revolutionary state there are usually two or more major technologies competing for economic application, and so the 'field' becomes much more fluid, with greater uncertainty on the part of the firm about which economic directions to pursue.

The problem with this approach is that no matter how realistic it may appear to be, its conceptual analysis fits more easily into different theoretical traditions based on non-economic disciplines. My own view is that this will continue for as long as economics remains wedded to its mechanistic roots and until it begins to engage more directly with the uncertainties and complexities of economic dynamics.

NORMAN CLARK

References

Clark, N.G. and Juma, C. (1992), *Long Run Economics*, London: Pinter Publishers.
Dosi, G. *et al.* (1988), *Technical Change and Economic Theory*, London: Pinter Publishers.
Rosenberg, N. (1971), *The Economics of Technological Change*, Harmondsworth: Penguin.
Schumpeter, J. (1934), *The Theory of Economic Development*, Cambridge MA: Harvard University Press.

Technological unemployment

Shortly before his death, Schumpeter pronounced '[t]he controversy that went on throughout the nineteenth century and beyond, mainly in the form of argument pro and con "compensation" ... dead and buried' (Schumpeter, 1954, p. 684). However, in the recent past, against the background of the microelectronics revolution, the old controversy between labour displacement pessimism and compensation optimism was revived. The spectre of technological unemployment has entered the stage again. Technological changes are both heroes and villains in modern legend. Some regard the modernization of the economy, the development and diffusion of new technology and rapid structural change as the most efficient strategy for fighting high unemployment. Others, however, fear that new technologies – whether installed or yet to be introduced – will eventually reduce the number of available jobs, thus aggravating unemployment and displacing skilled labour in all sectors of the economy. The diverging expectations about the employment consequences of new technologies mirror the ambiguous character of technological change which both creates jobs and eliminates them. This double-sided nature of new technologies raises two important questions. Does technological change create more jobs than it destroys? Does it create more higher-skilled jobs than it destroys?

It is interesting to note that many of the issues now at the forefront of the debate on technological change and employment were also key issues in earlier discussions. Adam Smith, for example, gave a pessimistic answer to the second question, but an optimistic one to the first. The question of whether and under what conditions technological change leads to persistent unemployment was first raised in 'respectable' literature by Ricardo in the new Chapter 31, 'On Machinery', in the third edition of his *Principles* published in 1821. In this chapter, which according to Sraffa marked 'the most revolutionary change in edition 3' (Ricardo, 1951, p. lvii), Ricardo retracted his previous position that the introduction of machinery benefits all classes in society and instead concluded '[t]hat the opinion entertained by the labouring class, that the employment of machinery is frequently detrimental to their interests, is not founded on prejudice and error, but is conformable to the correct principles of political economy' (Ricardo, 1951, p. 392).

Since Ricardo, we distinguish between the labour displacement effect arising from technological changes and the conditions required to assure the eventual absorption (compensation) of displaced workers. The *compensation theory* asserts that free market mechanisms will re-employ those who have been displaced from their jobs by technological change. The *displacement theory*, on the other hand, asserts that the conditions for compensation are not fulfilled sufficiently, if at all. To be precise, the main issue about which the compensation school and the displacement school differ is not whether technological unemployment, once it occurs, can be absorbed at all in some distant future, but whether the market provides for an *endogenous* mechanism that ensures compensation within the Marshallian short period – as was maintained by Ricardo's contemporary McCulloch – or whether public intervention is necessary to counter destabilizing tendencies of an uncontrolled market. In denying the existence of a self-regulating mechanism that achieves automatic compensation, Ricardo fundamentally questioned whether a free-market system can achieve full employment automatically. Ricardo's analysis of the problem of technological unemployment, from today's point of view, can be regarded as an early and rude type of traverse analysis containing a capital-shortage theory of temporary technological unemployment. Although Ricardo's numerical example abstracts from capital accumulation (i.e. the time paths of employment and output after the introduction of new machinery are unspecified), Ricardo nevertheless correctly emphasized that additional savings and investment are necessary to ensure that displaced workers are re-employed.

The re-employment of displaced workers in the construction of the new machines is often mentioned as the first compensating factor. Against this '*machinery production argument*' Marx raised his 'infallible law' according to which '[t]he new labour spent on the instruments of labour, on the machinery, on the coal, and so on, must necessarily be less than the labour displaced by the use of the machinery; otherwise the product of the machine would be as dear, or dearer, than the product of the manual labour' (Marx, 1954, p. 417). The machinery production argument undoubtedly contains an important element of truth. Even process innovations usually involve the introduction of new capital goods. This implies that a faster speed of diffusion of new technologies presupposes an increased investment demand which may even increase employment in the *short run*. However, a short-run effect (more employment in the industries producing capital goods in the construction phase of new machines) will subsequently be set off against a *long-run* effect (displacement of labour during the utilization phase of new machines). This means that speeding up accumulation may even overcompensate displaced labour in the short run. On the other hand, long-run employment problems will be aggravated if investment demand is only expanded temporarily.

The case for capital shortage found a new protagonist in Marx. But unlike Ricardo and other predecessors, he focused on a shortage of fixed capital, not a deficiency of circulating capital in the form of a wage fund. Overcoming the bottleneck of capital formation is a necessary, but not a sufficient, condition for reabsorbing displaced workers. Neisser threw light on this problem when, in discussing the Marxian analysis of Ricardo's chapter on machinery, he described 'the capitalistic process as a race between displacement of labor through technological progress and reabsorption of labor through accumulation ... whose outcome is impossible to predict ... on purely theoretical grounds' (Neisser, 1942, p. 70). Thus there is a special dialectics at work. An increase in the rate of accumulation (per time unit) might increase the demand for labour, but accompanying changes in technology which would lead to an increase in the amount of capital per worker could neutralize this favourable effect. Neisser's conclusion therefore is clear: no mechanism exists which would secure the full compensation of displaced workers. The outcome of the 'race' is open and it may differ with changing times and between various countries.

Another endogenous compensating factor also operates in a market economy. Technological progress reduces real costs, causing either falling prices or rising profits, thus putting additional real purchasing power in the hands of consumers or in those of the Schumpeterian pioneers. This increases real aggregate demand. Thus displaced workers find new jobs supplying commodities to satisfy the additional aggregate demand. According to the so-called '*classical compensation principle*', in the case of perfect competition, prices fall *uno actu* with cost reductions. This means that lower costs of production are transmitted without delay or curtailment to consumers whose real incomes increase; this in turn stimulates the demand for goods. The price elasticities of consumer demand decide whether an increased demand for labour compensates the initial displacement of workers in the same industry (or industries) where technological progress takes place or in other industries of the economy.

However, introducing more productive technologies does not necessarily increase the total *purchasing* power, only the *productive* power of an economy. If labour displacement occurs, the loss of the purchasing power of those displaced may be compensated by the increase in purchasing power of those still working. But the additional productive capacity may not be absorbed. It was John Stuart Mill who first denied that aggregate purchasing power could be raised in this manner and who instead emphasized that the demand for labour is different from the demand for commodities. What Mill was driving at was the basic idea that production and employment possibilities are limited by the existing stock of real capital. Thus, if capital formation is insufficient, the fall in prices and the increase in real incomes caused by technical progress will be inadequate to ensure the re-employment of all redundant workers. They will assure only that no secondary displacements effects (i.e. no negative employment multipliers) occur. Without additional capital formation overall employment cannot be permanently enlarged.

The extent of compensatory employment also depends on the degree to which substitution between labour and capital is possible in the economy. If proportions are *fixed*, the rate of capital accumulation determines the demand for labour. If *substitution* is possible, the amount of labour employed in equilibrium depends on the ratio between the wage rate and the rate of profit. Contrary to the view of classical economists that compensation depends on accumulating additional fixed capital, neoclassical economists such as J.B. Clark argued that the stock of fixed capital at any moment offers, at least in principle, unlimited employment opportunities. This optimistic conclusion follows from dropping two classical premises, namely the given level of real wages and the fixed coefficients of production. According to the marginal productivity theorem, varying quantities of labour can be combined with any quantity of fixed capital, if only money wages are flexible enough and if real wages thereby adjust to changes in the marginal productivity of labour. In the extreme world of the neoclassical parable, in which the only good 'jelly' is malleable, adjustment is neither costly nor time-consuming, and compensation is automatic.

According to neoclassical theory there is only one reason for persistent unemployment: real wages are too high and too inflexible downwards. This leads to *capital shortage unemployment* in the medium run and *technological* unemployment in the long run. While Marx elaborated Ricardo's arguments pro displacement, Schumpeter concentrated on those pro compensation. Schumpeter (1954) also criticized the classical economists, especially Ricardo, for their inability 'to understand substitution (both of factors and of products) in its full importance' (p. 680). The possibility of substitution between the factors of production affects the extent to which a drop in wages can act as a compensating factor. The diminished demand for labour brought about by mechanization can depress wages. When some capital can be replaced by labour, the displaced workers are re-employed and the impact of new machines lies not in unemployment but in lower wages. This was already the core of Wicksell's basic objection to Ricardo's analysis. Wicksell (1934, pp. 133–44) criticized Ricardo for neglecting wage reductions caused by the diminished demand for labour after the introduction of new machinery. These would lead to the reabsorption of displaced workers. In Ricardo's analysis, a fall in the real wage is considered neither a necessary consequence of, nor an effective remedy for the displacement of workers. Wicksell's argument illustrates the importance of the principle of substitution in connection with a drop in wages. However, Wicksell neither explicitly described the long-run equilibrium level of wages after the introduction of new machinery, nor discussed the general impact of technological change. Instead he considered a special case characterized by a decrease in the marginal productivity of labour.

Within the analysis of growth economics, emphasis in recent years has shifted to problems of structural change and technological unemployment. The analysis of the *traverse*, which is the study of the macroeconomic consequences of technological change and of the necessary conditions for bringing an economy back to an equilibrium growth path, is particularly relevant. Hicks (1973) and Lowe (1976), the two pioneers in traverse analysis, have shown that the decisive problem resulting from technological change is the inappropriateness of the capital stock, since the necessary adjustments are costly and time-consuming. Characteristically, both authors started their investigation from Ricardo's analysis of the machinery problem, but used alternative notions of economic activities, namely *horizontally*-integrated and *vertically*-integrated models of economic structure. Hicks based his traverse analysis on the concept of a neo-Austrian, vertically-integrated production process, in which a stream of labour inputs is transformed into a stream of consumption good outputs. It is a significant property of his model that the intertemporal complementarities in the productive process are put into sharp focus. But the treatment of fixed capital goods is the Achilles heel of the vertical-integration approach, one consequence of it being that in (neo-) Austrian models, the effects of innovations upon industrial structure are not shown. This, on the other hand, is the strength of the horizontal model, as developed by Leontief, Sraffa and von Neumann. However, the horizontal model of the circular flow of mutually dependent economic activities has some difficulties in coping with the fact that even process innovations in most cases involve the introduction of new capital goods. Since both approaches of economic structure – the horizontal and the vertical model – reveal comparative advantages as well as drawbacks, one should follow a complementary perspective to a certain extent.

HARALD HAGEMANN

References

Hicks, J. (1973), *Capital and Time*, Oxford: Clarendon Press.
Lowe, A. (1976), *The Path of Economic Growth*, Cambridge: Cambridge University Press.
Marx, K. (1869) [1954], *Capital, Vol. I*, London: Lawrence & Wishart.

Neisser, H. (1942), '"Permanent" Technological Unemployment', *American Economic Review*, **32**, 50–71.
Ricardo, D. (1951), *On the Principles of Political Economy and Taxation* (1st ed. 1817; 3rd ed. 1821), Vol. I. of *Works and Correspondence of David Ricardo*, edited by P. Sraffa with the collaboration of M. Dobb, Cambridge: Cambridge University Press.
Schumpeter, J.A. (1954), *History of Economic Analysis*, London: Allen & Unwin.
Wicksell, K. (1906) [1934], *Lectures on Political Economy*, Vol. I, London: Routledge & Kegan Paul.

Technology gap

Technology gaps represent the differences in technological advancement between two nations, between rival industries in different countries or between two firms in a given industry. Such gaps imply that technology is not globally uniform and that technological change is not instantaneously diffused across countries. This runs counter to the assumption of the mainstream theory of international trade, for example, and thus calls for an alternative theory of technical change, trade and growth.

In fact, the ample evidence of the existence of such gaps threatens neoclassical economics at an even deeper level. If these gaps are not simply a function of market failure, then technology must be viewed as more than an endowment, and technological choices as determined by more than scarcity. Scarcity, then, does not determine the resource allocation process; nor is Robbins's widely-cited definition of economics (the study of the allocation of scarce resources among competing end uses) any longer a valid guiding principle. Instead, economists must study the structure of production, exchange and accumulation as the interaction of science, politics, markets, culture and uncertainty. It is the learned ability to innovate and to imitate existing products and ways of producing which is the driving force for growth, international competitiveness and industrial policy. Natural endowments – scarcity – take a back seat as an explanation of economic outcomes. It is the incompatability of such a seemingly innocuous and pervasive concept as technology gap with orthodox theory that causes the concept to be so strongly resisted by neoclassical economists.

The rejection of scarcity and of an essential role for endowments also implies that economic policy – the relation between states and markets – takes on a whole new dimension. In a scarcity-driven world, the role of the state is 'to get prices right'; that is, to overcome market failures, either through the internalization of externalities or through the guarantee of an optimal provision of public goods. In a world of endogenous technical change and technology gaps, economic policy includes the effort to promote the innovative process through subsidies, managed trade and workplace democracy.

How is it possible, in an age of the transnational corporation, of bold leaps towards economic integration, of intensely mobile international capital and unprecedentedly rapid information dissemination, for technology to differ significantly across countries? Such gaps may exist for a number of reasons, including the workings of market competition, the structure of the modern corporation, the form of government policy, the particular evolution of nations' institutional structures or, more fundamentally, the nature of innovation, diffusion and technological knowledge. Any discussion of the causes of technology gaps must begin with this last factor.

The conception of technological change which underpins most technology gap theory is in the Schumpeterian tradition. Agents are not assumed *a priori* to share identical knowledge and competence. Technological change is cumulative and path-dependent. It is certainly not random, nor is it predictable, given the inherent uncertainty of the innovation process. Technological change is nation-specific due to differences in national technological activities, which may in turn be partly a function of the intensity of 'stimuli' to innovate in a given nation. These variations may result from differences in demand conditions, relative prices or technology policies (Rosenberg, 1976). Technological change is often firm-specific in that it depends on the ability of a firm to appropriate the profits from innovation. Moreover, technology may often embody 'non-codifiable knowledge' – non-transferable knowledge learned in the process of innovation or production.

While national differences in innovation activity are necessary to explain technology gaps, they are not sufficient. The diffusion of technology also requires time. This would seem obvious given the nature of knowledge described above. But the diffusion process has its own characteristics which further guarantee the likelihood of technology gaps. Diffusion is not simply a question of 'buy-and-use' but, like innovation itself, a 'process of learning, modification of the existing organization of production and, often, even a modification of products' (Dosi *et al.*, 1990, p. 119). In this case a smooth sigmoid diffusion curve, as posited in the mainstream literature, is merely a special case. Moreover, the discontinuity of the diffusion process implies that, even with a steady rate of innovation, technology gaps will persist over time. Disequilibrium will be a more common state than equilibrium.

Before proceeding to a discussion of the implications of technology gaps for growth and trade, it is important to mention how key concepts have been operationalized. Technology gaps are usually measured as differences in productivity between a given nation (sector) and the most advanced or 'frontier' nation (sector) in the world. Innovation activity is proxied either by 'technology input' or 'technology output' measures. The former include expenditures on research and development and on the education and employment of scientists and engineers. The latter are usually captured by patenting activity data in the US or foreign markets.

Recent interest in the question of whether productivity levels across countries have converged over the past 100 years has brought the issue of technology gaps to centre-stage. The convergence debate recalls the Gershenkron hypothesis: that imitation is easier than innovation and thus that 'relative backwardness' has its advantages. Relatively backward nations, assuming they satisfy a threshold level of infrastructure and institutional development, should grow at a more rapid pace than leader countries. Convergence will result. Technology gap models attempt to explain why growth rates differ – why convergence may or may not occur. Fagerberg (1988) distinguishes the technology gap approach from other efforts to explain growth rate differences by its explicit inclusion of diffusion and of innovative performance in the laggard country. The 'distance' between the technological frontier and the laggard country depends on these factors, as well as on innovation in the frontier country. He presents considerable empirical support for a model which includes these specific innovation activity variables. Again, the role of innovative effort (as opposed to nature) is crucial: catch-up requires not only technological imports and investment, but also an increase in national technological activities. Convergence is thus by no means a guaranteed outcome.

Uneven development models based on technology gaps have a long tradition, dating back to Adam Smith and his emphasis on scale economies from the division of labour. The country with the initial technological edge is able to widen that lead by capturing scale economies and further dividing the production process, increasing its scale of operation and thus taking advantage of cumulative cost reductions at higher levels of output. From Marx to Kaldor, such models have sought to explain, not just the lack of convergence among national per capita income levels, but the absolute and relative widening of such standard of living differentials.

Technology gap theories of international trade were developed as a response to the lack of realism of the factor proportions model, which assumes globally uniform and constant returns to scale technology and identical consumer preferences worldwide. Trade is thus due entirely to differences in relative factor endowments. Until very recently Heckscher-Ohlin remained the most widely accepted model of trade among international economists, in spite of the overwhelming empirical evidence against its predictions (the 'Leontief paradox'). Some significant evidence also exists in favour of the Ricardian model of comparative advantage based on productivity differences. A recent input–output study showed that the assumption of identical technology across OECD countries may bias results by over 40 per cent in some cases (Elmslie and Milberg, 1992).

Development of an explicit technology gap model of international trade began with the work of Posner (1961), who saw the rate of international diffusion of technology as central to the explanation of the direction and commodity composition of trade. Vernon (1966) based both a theory of international trade and foreign direct investment on the existence and then disappearance of technology gaps, depending on the degree of maturity (and thus standardization) of the technology. This product life-cycle model of international trade and investment served to refocus attention on technological determinants of trade.

Two recent developments have placed technology gaps and technological differences at the heart of the development of a comprehensive dynamic trade model. Pasinetti (1981) presents a dynamic, disaggregated Ricardian model in which sectoral rates of innovation matter only in relation to a nation's average innovation rate. A policy emphasis on static comparative advantage may thus be inappropriate. Policy should instead focus on sectors with a relatively rapid rate of innovation (compared to the national average and to foreign rivals), whether or not at a given moment in time they are characterized by comparative advantage. Dosi *et al.* (1990) single out technology gaps as the determinants of absolute advantage which in turn dominates comparative advantage in the determination of world market shares. Trade imbalances are not self-correcting and thus changes in national competitiveness depend on the alteration of absolute cost differentials rather than any reallocation of resources due to Ricardian comparative advantage. The model explains the persistence of trade imbalances in many developing countries, as well as the decline of some technology-intensive industries (such as autos, steel and semiconductors) in the US and the UK. Much work remains to be done in this area of absolute-advantage models of trade, in particular generalizing the models to many countries and many commodities. Other factors which need to be introduced more fully include demand, as well as notions of credit and credit constraints to firm innovation activities. This would not only facilitate the analysis of production innovation, but also permit a more satisfying description of the international payments adjustment process.

Still, the rejection of comparative advantage as a determinant of trade is an important manifestation of the abandonment of scarcity as the centre-piece of economic analysis. From a policy perspective, the technology gap trade models (like the technology gap growth models) emphasize the role of government in spurring innovative activity. Countries will not balance trade automatically through a Ricardian resource reallocation. Exchange rate devaluation is also unlikely to be sufficient in a world in which technological sophistication is crucial and depends on innovative activity.

The strength of technology gap theories is precisely that they leave open the explanation of technology differences and their persistence over time.

Such explanations allow for the possibility of endogenous technological change – the social determination of technology and innovation. The most radical feature of the theories of international trade and uneven development which have been motivated by the recognition of the pervasiveness of technology gaps is that they deny scarcity a central role. Technology gaps are instead the outcome of the complex social process of innovation and diffusion.

The ample evidence of the existence and persistence of technology gaps at the national and sectoral levels indicates that the neoclassical theory of technological change is seriously flawed – a special case in which scarcity determines prices and choice of technique, and technology is globally uniform. Once economic analysis is released from the yoke of the scarcity view, a number of possibilities for thinking about the economy and economic policy become evident. I have focused on two of these: the role of innovative activity in the 'catching-up' effort, and the importance of created competitive advantage in the determination of international trade. In each case, equilibrium is an unlikely and unstable outcome. More important, the understanding of innovation and technology gaps as created – not endowed – raises the necessity of state action to alter a nation's technological position. Such 'technology policy' has been accepted practice in countries at all levels of technological development.

WILLIAM S. MILBERG

References

Dosi, G., Pavitt, K. and Soete, L. (1990), *The Economics of Technical Change and International Trade*, New York: New York University Press.

Elmslie, B. and Milberg, W. (1992), 'International Trade and Factor Intensity Uniformity: An Empirical Assessment', *Weltwirtschaftliches Archiv*, **128** (3), 464–86.

Fagerberg, J. (1988), 'A Technology Gap Model of Growth Rate Differences' in G. Dosi *et al.* (eds), *Technical Change and Economic Theory*, London and New York: Pinter Publishers.

Pasinetti, L. (1981), *Structural Change and Economic Growth*, Cambridge: Cambridge University Press.

Posner, M. (1961), 'International Trade and Technical Change', *Oxford Economic Papers*, **13**.

Rosenberg, N. (1976), *Perspectives on Technology*, Cambridge: Cambridge University Press.

Vernon, R. (1966), 'International Trade and International Investment in the Product Life Cycle', *Quarterly Journal of Economics*, **80**.

Theory of the state

The proper role of the state in the economy is probably the longest standing theoretical issue in economics. The conflict between market and state has always been at the heart of the major debates in economic theory. Adam Smith and the classical political economists placed the market-state antagonism at the centre of the stage and developed an impressive theoretical case for the substitution of state regulations and functions by the market. The centrality of this antagonism was challenged by Marx who argued that the fundamental antagonism in capitalism is that between capital and labour. Neoclassical economics turned a blind eye to this fundamental Marxist insight and reasserted the primary position of the market-state antagonism.

The rise of the Soviet state, with its self-proclaimed association with Marxism, confounded the two pairs of antagonisms. The capital-labour antagonism was considered widely as being the same as the market-state antagonism. This was because the Soviet state, which claimed to have abolished the capital-labour antagonism decisively and forever in favour of labour, also resolved the market-state antagonism clearly in favour of the state. An additional contributing factor to this seeming sameness was the secular tendency of the increasing economic importance of the capitalist state, and especially the establishment and wide acceptance of the welfare role of the state after the Second World War. This was seen as a retrogression of capital and an advance of labour in the capital-labour conflict.

Neoclassical economics reacted to these developments by focusing on the only antagonism that it ever recognized – the market-state one – and by elaborating further arguments against state involvement in the economy. It is important briefly to consider these because neoclassical economics is clearly the dominant school of thought in economic theory, with which radical political economy has inevitably had to wrestle.

The traditional neoclassical position is that a possible case for state intervention can be made in the presence of market failure caused by externalities, increasing returns or market imperfections. In addition, distributional inequities resulting from the unconstrained operation of the market may create problems for the social cohesion required by democratic societies and may thus present a further reason for state intervention. Neoclassical economics therefore traditionally accepts that, in the presence of market failure or dangerous distributional inequities, the possibility exists that the state may do better.

Recent developments in neoclassical theory tend to narrow further even this limited scope for state intervention. It is noted that the behaviour of the state and of decision-makers within the state should themselves be the subject of analysis. It cannot be assumed that the state will operate in a disinterested fashion for the promotion of social welfare. On the basis of an analysis relying on the standard neoclassical assumption that decision-makers attempt to maximize their own interests (be they the chances of re-election for politicians or various private advantages for bureaucrats), it is argued that not only is there no presumption that the state will do better than the market in case of market failure but that, in general, it is more likely to do worse.

This aggressive stance towards the state is mirrored in macroeconomic theory where monetarism and the new classical macroeconomics also attempt to limit the scope of state activity by denying any possibility of alleviating unemployment by means of demand management. Finally, the large size of the public sector is argued to be detrimental to the growth prospects of the economy and directly responsible for inflation. These arguments and the attendant hostility to state intervention in the economy have become commonplace not only in academic journals, but also in international organizations and in the press. By the same token, privatization of state activities, which reduces the size of the public sector, is hailed as the modern miracle cure to various economic ills.

Radical political economy (RPE) regards the fundamental antagonism in capitalism to be that between capital and labour. This is its basic Marxist legacy which differentiates its origin and initial inspiration from both classical political economy and neoclassical economics. To be sure, in being drawn into the market-state debate, radical political economy has traditionally leant towards the state (largely in reaction to neoclassical theory), but there is no compelling theoretical reason for this inclination. The market-state antagonism is clearly not identical but subsidiary to the fundamental capital-labour one, and its outcome does not affect the latter in a simple or uni-directional manner. It is evident that an expansion of the state does not necessarily imply a gain for labour; conversely, an advance for the market may not necessarily be prejudicial to the interests of labour. It therefore follows that, since developments in the market-state antagonism do not have a unique and simple sense for the capital-labour issue, their significance in relation to the fundamental antagonism has to be analysed and ascertained on a case-by-case basis.

The second major difference between RPE and neoclassical theory is that the former does not rely solely on the maximizing approach to understand and explain the behaviour of the state. RPE recognized, before neoclassical theory, that the state cannot be assumed to operate disinterestedly; in fact, it always doubted the notion that the state promotes social welfare suspecting, especially in some cruder Marxist versions, that as a rule it instead promotes the interests of capital. But RPE did not seek to understand the behaviour of the state by looking inward and resorting to the usual maximizing methods of economics; on the contrary, it always looked outward to other disciplines, such as history, politics and sociology. It is through contact and interaction with these other disciplines that RPE has tried to gain insights into and understanding of the behaviour of the state. As a result, the theory of the state for RPE is a multi-disciplinary field fertilized by a rich variety of theoretical approaches cultivated in different disciplines. If this is its strength, it follows as a corollary that it lacks a unique theoretical core, allowing opponents to argue that it is more *ad hoc* and less cohesive than neoclassical economics.

A third notable difference is to a large extent due to the above contrast between the multi-disciplinary approach of RPE and the mono-disciplinary emphasis of neoclassical economics. Political science and especially history and political sociology are disciplines that have developed largely positive analyses of the state and have, with the possible exception of politics, virtually no normative dimension. By contrast, in neoclassical economics it is the normative side that is predominant when dealing with the state. This is largely because the only branch of economics in which the state was traditionally recognized as having a valid role to play was normative welfare theory. Being denied a legitimate role by the main body of economic theory, the state was ascribed its 'proper' role in normative fashion by welfare economics. This is possibly the reason that the fiction of the disinterested state promoting social welfare, which was a prescription of welfare theory, was so difficult to shake off in neoclassical economics. In fact, it has only recently overcome this limitation and displayed positive analysis in the work of rational choice theorists, most notably in the area of political business cycles. This work, together with that of Mancur Olson on the rise and decline of nations (which is however informed by other disciplines), makes the difference between RPE's mostly positivist approaches and neoclassicals' traditionally normative outlook one of degree rather than of kind, at least so far as contemporary developments are concerned.

Turning now, inevitably briefly and at a general level, to the kinds of questions that have been addressed by RPE, four general areas of concern may be distinguished.

First, there is the fundamental question concerning the nature of the modern state. The contributions here are mostly by Marxist-inspired writers who examine (1) the relationship between the state and the economy, (2) the relationship between political power and economic power, and (3) the role of different groups and classes in the exercise of both political and economic power. This literature on the whole recognizes that significant shifts in power have occurred over time and that any meaningful analysis of the state must take into account not only conflicting economic interests, but also the specific historical and socio-political context of a particular society. It is also widely accepted that the nature of a modern state extends beyond the elemental function of coercion to reproduction, legitimization and accumulation.

The second area of concern may thus be categorized under the rubric of 'reproduction'. The main issues here relate to the state's expenditure and revenue patterns and the strategic alliances between economic and other interests, both nationally and internationally, that sustain these patterns. Institutional arrangements may be of importance here, with the analytical emphasis on the distributional aspects of state expenditure and taxation.

The third area is associated with the function of 'legitimization'. This covers state actions and policies that support and justify the view of the state as a promoter of the well-being of society as a whole and not the servant of partial interests. Most prominent among these are redistribution policies, especially those contributing to the creation of the welfare state. RPE has been concerned with the explanation of the welfare state's emergence and growth, investigating the class and political interests involved in this evolution. In exploring various facets of the welfare state's significance and functions, it has become apparent that this evolution has aspects that both facilitate and also hinder the smooth functioning of the capitalist system. There is therefore no simple judgment that can be passed on the consonance of the welfare state and its evolution with the needs of capitalist accumulation.

This brings us to the last area of concern which is that of accumulation. The involvement of the state in accumulation and development is old and, in most countries, quite obvious and wide-ranging. There have been many empirical studies documenting this, building into a considerable literature covering both individual countries as well as attempting a comparative approach. The gamut of state policies bearing on accumulation is extensive, though the most noteworthy are the following: investment policy (incentives to private investment, infrastructure and other public investment programmes); labour market, education and training policies; industrial policy, R&D and technology; trade policy and international agreements.

RPE has shown a lively interest in all these areas. However, its most noticeable presence has probably been in the literature on development where the predominance of neoclassical economics is the least assured. This is not only because much of this literature is practical in orientation and has arisen in response to immediate policy concerns, but also because of the historical involvement of the state in development efforts. The need for the state to play an important role in development has been apparent, both in theory and in practice, at least since the writings of F. List and the German industrialization effort in the latter half of the 19th century. After 1945, with the end of the colonial era and a large number of new states facing the daunting task of creating basic economic and social infrastructures (ranging from roads to education to provision of health services), there was a resurgence of interest in development theory which was expected to guide the conscious attempts of states to foster development.

In concluding, it is worth noting that the growth of the transnational firm and the effects of this not only on accumulation but also on the nation-state is another problem area in which RPE has been quite active. This has contributed to a branching off with a significant participation of RPE in the newly-evolved discipline of international political economy, which attempts a new synthesis of politics and economics in the customary domain of international relations.

THANOS SKOURAS

References

Jessop, R. (1977), 'Recent Theories of the State', *Cambridge Journal of Economics*, **1**.
Jessop, R. (1982), *The Capitalist State: Marxist Theories and Methods*, Oxford: Martin Robertson.
Miliband, R. (1969), *The State in Capitalist Society*, London: Weidenfeld and Nicolson.
Offe, C. (1984), *Contradictions of the Welfare State*, London: Macmillan.
Poulantzas, N. (1978), *State, Power and Socialism*, London: New Left Books.

Time

In this overview, alternative conceptualizations of time are presented, and an attempt is made to explain their relevance to economics. It is argued that since economic activity takes place in time, the study of that activity must take account of time. Current concern by economists with the issue of time stems from their reaction to the erosion of the place of time in their study, due to the scientification of economics by over-simplification and mathematics. Thus, in addition to the many other reasons for divisions among economists, dissension has resulted from their different approaches to time, either the denying of a determining role to time or the pursuing of a temporal correspondence between real world events and theoretical constructs. The root of this division is not, however, differing views about the importance of time in economics, but a different understanding of the relationship between economics and conceptualizations of time.

Time can be conceptualized in three ways. Let us call *time 1* the conscious *recognition of* the *sequential order* in which things exist and events occur. This is the awareness of one's existence: *time 1* is the flow of a continuous event series. Let us call *time 2* the individual physical or psychological *experience in relation to* the convention of *chronometric order*. This is an individual's experience measured against the conventions of time : *time 2* is the series of co-valid instances in a recognized order of events demarcated in duration and interval by time-measuring conventions. Let us call *time 3 chronometric convention*. This is the information from the calendar, clock or stopwatch: *time 3* is (co-valid) dates or moments demarcated and ordered by conventional modes of time-telling. Considered to be exogenous to individual psychological or physical perceptions, since its intervals and pace are determined independently of the individual, *time 3* is often referred to as 'objective'.

While each of these conceptualizations relates to experienced time – *chrono-experience* – theoreticians in whose theories time figures have created another conceptualization of time as *t*, the symbolic representation of experienced time – *chrono-evocation*. Since theoreticians have not devised different symbols, each to correspond to one of the three conceptualizations of experienced time, confusion has arisen over what 'kind' of time *t* is meant to evoke.

This does not seem to be problematic in the theories of history and physical science. In history, it is quite obvious that *t*, call it *th*, evokes calendar time (e.g., 1929) and duration as measured by the clock (e.g., 'the king's reign was 50 years'), hence *time 3*. Adding to the scope of *th*, the historian might also consider a theory to include *time 2* (e.g., 'Cabot decided not to return to England *because the voyage seemed too long*') and *time 1* in the recounting of any past series of events. In the physical sciences since the objects of study are a physical matter – without, in principle, a human component – study can be pursued within a framework which conceives time primarily as *time 2*, i.e., as a tool for recording instances and measuring duration. *T* within scientific theory, call it *ts*, evokes beginning and end points, as well as duration, all experienced as in an observation or experiment, but recorded according to the convention of the clock. *Ts* may also tie in *time 3*, by evoking a particular date of an event, or *time 1*, by emphasizing the series of manifestations, but it does so without altering the purpose of *ts* – to evoke experience within measured time.

In the social sciences, however, confusion over just what *t* means seems to be acute. Although their agreed-upon object of study is the human subject, social scientists are divided methodologically, primarily between those who see their research generalizations as deterministic laws, and those who maintain that, while the scholar may observe constants, the complexity of the situation in which those constants appear to hold renders full knowledge of their conditionality impossible and hence also any deterministic conclusions. This division has led to two groups, well represented in economics. The first group emphasizes the collective, reducing the individual to a representative *x* and working mathematically with quantification and aggregation. The second group chooses instead to acknowledge the vagaries of the individual in its attempt to comprehend the dynamics of individual and collective human economic activity.

Questions thus emerge among social scientists as to which conception of time is appropriate to their respective methods. As the name reflects, social sciences are in some way modelled on the physical sciences, an emulation which encompasses their difficulties in approaching time. Like physical scientists, most social scientists have come to conceive it as possible to evoke with their *t* a correlation between a describable or observed event and the beginning/end points and/or duration of that event, as per *time 2*. It must be evident, however, that the time of economics, *te*, does not represent a sequence of successive events, *time 1*. For example, 'expectational' time, when expectations are related to the projected course of events, or 'mechanical' time, when specific events follow automatically one upon another, are not identifiable by conventional time measurement.

Recognition of *time 1* as the time of economics does entail certain constraints. *Time 1* is, from the philosophical perspective, an intuition, endogenous to the mental process, a product thus of individual psychological awareness. It cannot incorporate conventions of time-measurement and is thus subjective. For realist philosophers and indeed for scientists, only *time 2* (as physical experience) and *time 3* (corresponding to conventional time measurement) are conceptualizations available for chrono-evocation. Economists, it seems, have adopted the "realists'" scorn for *time 1* and have tried to compensate for the incapacity of the social sciences to incorporate a chrono-evocation of conventional time in one of two ways, depending on their convictions concerning the principles of economics. If they are persuaded of the permanence of economic laws, they push *te* into the constraints of mathematical symbolism and practical irrelevance; *t* represents only logical temporal possibilities. If they are persuaded of the impermanence of economic generalizations, they search for the closest one-to-one correspondence possible between *te* and the time of experienced economic activity, i.e., the factual possibilities of events occurring. For the first group, *t* attempts to portray the *state of affairs*; for the second, *t* strives to evoke descriptions of *datable or temporal changes and transformations*.

Current confusion concerning the role attributed to time in economics can best be understood in light of the discipline's progressive scientification. The conception of economics as a science with constants and laws analogous to the natural sciences was already within the approach of Physiocrats such as Quesnay. Accompanying this early epistemic conviction concerning the regularity of economic phenomena came a receptiveness to the use of mathematics as a tool for measurement and analysis. Discussion of the theory of value in the ensuing marginalist revolution focused on cost-benefit analysis and comparisons of small increments of gain and loss in production, transaction and exchange, opening the way to the systematic use of calculus. The second generation of marginalists (Wicksteed, Wicksell, Edgeworth and Bowley) rendered more sophisticated the mathematization of the notion of equilibrium; thus by the mid-1930s, the marginalist approach, reincarnated by Hicks and Allen in their general equilibrium model, became accepted. Since the Second World War, this approach has so dominated the discipline that both micro and macroeconomics continue to be grounded in general equilibrium theory, with their subfields existing simply to pursue its applications.

Among the mathematical techniques which scientifized economics has attempted to adopt are numerous reductionist ones. Some economists, even without being fully persuaded by such techniques, have contributed to their strengthening. Marshall, for example, with one foot in marginalism and the other in the classical theories of Ricardo and Mill, vacillated between the contemplation of logical and factual possibilities. Of all his thought, however, it was his 'ceteris paribus' method, reducing varying circumstances, which won the widest acceptance. The concept of homo-economicus has also brought reduction of individuality (Shackle's 'feelings', 'emotion' and 'thought') and abnegated the historical context in which the individual operates. As part of reductionism, subjects – such as individual decisions, actions and behaviour, the dynamics of the market, the notions of expectation and uncertainty, the role of knowledge and the 'animal spirit' (of great pertinence to Keynes, Knight, Hayek, von Mises and others in the 1920s and 1930s) – were slowly transformed. Through the application of the laws of large number, they became symbols of specified states, the ideal representative, the optimum resulting from forces collectively at work, equilibrium as the desirable equitable or ethical position, and the certainty equivalence. Their universality came to be taken for granted.

Division among economists has ensued for, to some, important aspects of economic activity have become a casualty to the absorption of the discipline with mathematization and reduction, hence with the objective and quantitative. Although their objections might point to a general neglect of the subjective and qualitative, in many respects they underline a concern with time. In Robinson's opinion, for example, the dominant economic theories – out of disregard or incapability – did not capture historical events. To Shackle, the theories' preoccupation with equilibrium was vapid, for it left no room for individuals as living human beings. Hayek and von Mises felt that in terms of general equilibrium theories in particular, the description of markets did not resemble actual dynamic markets in which opportunities occur within a sequence of actions and reactions. For Georgescu, the production function of the neoclassical theories did not make sense in the context of the changing state of the market, since factors change during a production process. Keynes insisted that expectations and uncertainty, both indicative of the unknowable future, cannot be treated simply as given data.

Thus it is for the last hundred years that the discipline of economics has become increasingly divided into two methodological approaches. It has been and continues to be dominated by one approach, whose tenants limit economics to the mathematical exploration of economic laws and which continues to refine and make more sophisticated the tools which permit exploration. These economists attempt to devise theories to describe phenomena which appear consistently to occur, and may have to occur, under given circumstances. For them *te* has thus come to be conceived as specifying the point in time (or the duration of time) at which the phenomenon of interest will occur, given the specification of conditions. Although their *te* might thus be seen to represent *time 2* 'mathematically' or 'logically', this can only be achieved by collapsing discrete instants with theoretically different given conditions (*tx*, *ty*, *tz*, etc.) into a single point in space. Since to construct causal or deterministic theories of specific event series is as yet outside the reach of the discipline (for which there is no laboratory or controlled environment for observation and experimentation, and whose studied activities are too complex to reveal unambiguous causal relations), these economists have been able to theorize only about the result of a simultaneous configuration – the state of events *at one point in time* – not about any preceding or consequent situation.

The other methodological approach is pursued by economists who do not consider the foundation of the discipline to rest upon deterministic laws explorable by pure mathematics without great cost or distortion to economics as a study of empirical phenomena. They believe that the principles of economics are either tautological or non-universal, and that their refinement requires both empirical investigation of actual economic activity and recognition of the non-constancy of the necessary conditions for a generality or 'law' to be operative. They believe that although some constants exist, no theory or law (even the acceptable 'laws' of supply and demand or of diminishing marginal utility or productivity) can capture fully either the amalgam of individual circumstances or the changing nature of the social process. Economics, they insist, is about people and the dynamics and problems of their time whose most basic of conditions are very difficult to hold constant. However, their acute concern for the correspondence of actual economic activity with its theoretical description has led them to adopt a *te* representing the chronometric succession of events and to exploit theoretical constructs such as long-run and short-run or Hicks's 'week', and Marshall's short period and long period.

Keynes clearly pointed in the right direction when he asserted that 'it is most certainly true that it is only through change that we recognize the so-called flight of time. ... Our perception of time means, therefore, simply our awareness of change' (Keynes, 1907, pp. 7–8). However, no group of economists today professes that the social sciences in general are disciplines which can deal well only with the conscious recognition of the general sequence of events, *time 1*. Nonetheless, economists (like mathematicians) can neither limit the importance of time entirely as does the one group, nor adhere to a tight chronometric correspondence between economic activity and explanatory theories analogous to *ts*, as does the second group. Indeed, whether it is as the 'time' of mathematics or as the 'time' of the physical sciences, *te* is not acknowledged for what it is – the chrono-evocation of *time 1*. Thus, while it is not the apparent suppression of, nor insistence upon, a temporal dimension which is at issue, economists in general adhere to an erroneous understanding of the social scientific conception of time.

O.F. HAMOUDA AND B.B. PRICE

References

Hamouda, O.F. (1985), 'On the Notion of Short-Run and Long-Run: Marshall, Ricardo and Equilibrium Theories', *British Review of Economic Issues*, **6** (14), 55–82.

Hamouda, O.F. (1990), 'Time, Choice and Dynamics in Economics' in S. Frowen (ed.), *Unknowledge and Choice in Economics*, London: Macmillan.

Hamouda, O.F. and Price, B.B. (1991), *Verification in Economics and History*, London: Routledge.

Keynes, J.M. (1907), 'Time', copy of unpublished manuscript kindly provided by Rod O'Donnell.

Mellor, D.H. (1981), *Real Time*, Cambridge: Cambridge University Press.

Price, B.B. (1991), 'Use of Astronomical Tables by Albertus Magnus', *Journal for the History of Astronomy*, **xxii**, 221–40.

Trade unions

In their classic study of the subject, Beatrice and Sidney Webb (1894) defined a trade union as 'a continuous association of wage earners for the purpose of maintaining or improving the conditions of their working lives' (p. 1). As such it is a term that can also be applied to many staff and professional associations in which the sellers of labour combine in an attempt to regulate the employment relationship. The right of employees thus to organize has been upheld by a number of conventions of the International Labour Organization, most specifically the Right to Organize and Collective Bargaining Convention 98 of 1949. In this and in the relevant legislation of ratifying states (which include all major industrialized countries), emphasis is placed upon the need for trade unions to be financially independent of employers and other non-union organizations.

Since the earliest days of trade unionism, and especially during the present century, numerous and conflicting claims have been made for what the purposes of trade unions might be. As Martin (1989) has observed in his seminal analysis, the issue has exercised the minds of outsiders on a scale and to a degree that prominently marks the trade union out among non-governmental organizations. Syndicalists of various complexions have argued that the true socialism of workers' control could not be achieved through political parties, but only by industrial action through trade unions. Marxist-Leninists were more anxious that trade unions might compromise with capitalism and thereby postpone its overthrow. Marx identified trade unions as having a double aim: first, stopping competition among workers so that, second, they can engage in a general competition with the capitalists. For Lenin it was necessary to protect the working-class movement from the spontaneous striving of trade unionists to 'come under the wing of the bourgeoisie'. For him (and for many who were to implement his prescription), it was necessary to have a separate communist party which could guide trade unions beyond mere reformism to the revolutionary objective of eliminating capitalism.

Revolution has, however, been far from the minds of many who have encouraged trade unionism. There is a colourful collection of what Martin terms 'organicists' who stress the role of unions in upholding the harmony and responsibility that should characterize society, building cooperation rather than focusing conflict. The Christian socialist tradition of Protestant thinking in America and Britain in the 19th century saw trade unions as having a central reforming role in improving the conditions of working-class life. This was to influence the concern of the Fabian Society and of Guild Socialism with worker cooperation. Another tradition that traced itself back to the Middle Ages was that of Social Catholicism which, in a series of papal encyclicals from 1891 to 1981, upheld the view that capital and labour are not naturally hostile and that even if workers have to unite to secure their rights, their union remains a constructive factor of social order and solidarity.

Far less benign have been political philosophies which have seen the role of trade unions as firmly subordinated to the state, and as instruments of the state in pursuit of the goal of maximizing production. Between the wars both Italian Fascism and German National Socialism upheld the virtues of trade unionism so long as it was incorporated within the unity of the state, meanwhile brutally attacking pre-existing trade union traditions on the grounds that their implied role was as a socially divisive 'class weapon'. This authoritarian conception was to survive the Second War in Soviet Communism and to reemerge in Argentine Peronism and subsequently in some newly independent countries such as Mboya's Kenya.

Why has the capture of trade unions been so important in the political struggles of the modern world? Martin (1989) identifies two principal reasons.

> The trade union provides a specifically selective organisational framework for directly communicating with (and possibly influencing or even controlling) the mass of people who comprise the human foundation on which the economic life of modern societies depends. Hence the heavy emphasis commonly placed on an educational function by those who have written about trade union purpose. Secondly, the trade union also provides at least potential access to a peculiar power resource, the strike weapon, which outsiders have been perennially eager either to tap or to curb. The outcome is an institution which is remarkably versatile, as judged by the purposes that have been thrust upon it by its students, its well-wishers, its opponents and, above all, by its would-be manipulators (p. 99).

Insofar as trade unions can be freed of the ideological baggage that has been piled on them, they are most fruitfully conceived in a pluralist framework as pressure groups alongside other pressure groups in a society in which conflicts of interest are endemic, and where success comes not through outright victory but through renegotiable compromise. The Webbs observed how unions pursued their objectives through three distinct sorts of activity. The first was mutual assurance, aiding their members' well-being by acting as friendly societies. The second was political action, aimed at encouraging the state to introduce laws and regulations that would protect the interests of working people. The third was collective bargaining, dealing directly with employers in order to regulate the conduct and terms of work.

It is collective bargaining that has become the dominant function of trade unions in industrialized market economies. Mutual assurance is more a feature of unions in developing countries with limited public services. Political action on behalf of union members tends, in mature democracies, to be absorbed into the objectives of political parties, in an often uneasy alliance with the trade unions themselves. But collective bargaining remains the supreme trade union activity. Although the Webbs conceived of it as an essentially economic activity in which workers substitute a group negotiation for individual bargains, subsequent theorists have broadened the notion to include any procedure in the management of the employment relationship in which a role is provided for trade unions. As Flanders (1975) observed in arguing that the phrase 'joint regulation' would be more appropriate, the conclusion of a collective agreement does not bind anyone to buy or sell any labour; rather it sets out the terms and conditions that will prevail if and when labour is engaged. Trade unions are, in short, engaged in rule-making.

The success of a union in rule-making depends in large part on the pressure it can exert upon its members' employers. The strategy it adopts for this has a major impact upon a trade union's structure. For traditional craft unions and for many professional associations, the main objective was to control labour supply by regulating the definition of occupational competence and by controlling the flow of trainees. Other occupationally-specific unions which could not achieve this sought instead to have sufficiently comprehensive coverage of their occupation to be able to have monopoly power in the labour market. Another strategy was to seek to organize a whole industry in order to cover all employers within a given product market, there being little advantage in extracting a favourable pay settlement from one employer if its unorganized competitors could thereby undercut and out-compete it.

It has, however, been difficult to rely upon any stable bargaining strategy in a world increasingly disorganized by technological change, geographical mobility and international competition. Unions have come to rely more on the sanctions they can mobilise with individual employers and on the goodwill they can command from them. As a result unions have tended to become less occupationally, industrially and geographically specific in their membership, and more dependent upon employers for their bargaining rights.

Success in trade unionism depends upon the ability to mobilize members. This demands the willingness of the membership to incur the individual costs of collective action, often with no direct likelihood of individual gain. Devices such as closed shops, strike pay and disciplinary procedures are inadequate to achieve this. Far more important is the collective commitment that is earned by a broadly egalitarian ethos and a participative system of government. A central issue in the ideology of trade unionism is, consequently, that of the appropriate democratic forms with which to combine membership involvement with organizational effectiveness. Trade union 'rule books' play a critical role in delineating the legitimized procedures for reaching collective decisions.

Collective organization on its own is insufficient to achieve sustained success in collective bargaining. It is also necessary to have a basis of national labour law which provides unions with the security to develop and maintain their organization, and to provide them with rights to engage in collective action without being sued for the consequential costs. Countries differ greatly in the extent to which their labour laws sustain trade union activity. As Clegg (1976) has shown, the origins of these differences usually date back to some period of industrial crisis (such as the American depression) or military defeat (such as the occupation of Germany and Japan after the Second World War) when government intervention in industrial relations was necessary to restore economic activity. Another salient factor has often been whether a country has had a party in power that has been dependent upon trade union support (as in Sweden).

For both governments and employers, a critical question is how far the pursuit by trade unions of their members' interests is inimical to the wider well-being of the economy and society. Trade union economic objectives are, to a considerable extent, conservative: 'united to defend, not combined to injure' was the motto of the British woodworkers' union. Much of their activity is aimed at defending pay differentials, living standards and jobs. Those hostile to trade unions generally focus on the short-term tendency for their actions to force up wage costs and to inhibit managerial discretion to move labour and change production technology.

The long-term picture is very different. Freeman and Medoff (1984) are among those who have demonstrated that employers unchallenged by trade unions (in presence or in prospect) tend to manage labour poorly and to rely upon labour-intensive techniques. They tend to neglect sources of employee discontent, reacting to the slow and expensive signals of labour turnover rather than to the more rapid 'voice' of an articulate representative structure.

It is certainly possible to manage labour humanely and efficiently without trade unions, through intensive use of human resource management techniques. But in large organizations, such techniques tend not to be cheaper than collective bargaining in either wage levels or administrative costs. They also tend to be more fragile when competition sharpens and compulsory job-shedding undermines confidence in the employer's paternalist competence.

When viewed internationally, high levels of trade unionism tend to be associated with above average long-term economic growth, perhaps because they are also often associated with a more corporatist style of economic management which is conducive to high levels of investment and active manpower policies. But it would be wrong to end with an emphasis on the economic role of trade unions. The victorious Allies after the Second World War made sure that they installed robust trade union movements in the defeated countries as a buttress against future totalitarian regimes. The involvement that trade unions offer working men and women in the daily processes of collective bargaining provides a major stimulus to civil rights and the working of democracy in the wider society.

WILLIAM BROWN

References

Clegg, H.A. (1976), *Trade Unionism under Collective Bargaining: A Theory Based on Comparison of Six Countries*, Oxford: Blackwell.

Flanders, A. (1975), *Management and Unions: The Theory and Reform of Industrial Relations*, London: Faber.

Freeman, R.B. and Medoff, J.L. (1984), *What Do Unions Do?*, New York: Basic Books.

Martin, R.M. (1989), *Trade Unionism: Purposes and Forms*, Oxford: Clarendon Press.

Webb, S. and Webb, B. (1894), *History of Trade Unionism*, London: Longmans.

Uncertainty

Uncertainty has been a concept of central significance to some branches of radical political economy, in particular Post Keynesian economics and the middle ground between it and neo-Austrian economics on one side and between it and institutionalist economics on the other. 'Uncertainty' is used in the sense of unquantifiable risk, as distinct from the neoclassical usage which is conflated with quantifiable risk. Its significance is that, where uncertainty is present, behaviour cannot be modelled deterministically.

Within this concept, there is a range of interpretations of both the meaning and scope of uncertainty. As for its meaning, the main differences have been over whether uncertainty represents an absence of knowledge in some absolute sense, or whether it is a relative concept referring to the degree of rational belief or rational doubt (depending on whether the benchmark is certain knowledge or ignorance, respectively). The narrowest scope given to uncertainty is the long-term expectations on which investment decisions are based. Others see it as also explaining the significance of institutions like money and the firm. In its widest application, the prevalence of uncertainty is seen as requiring a distinctive methodology for all economic enquiry (in particular, not relying on any one method).

In what follows, these different conceptions of the meaning and scope of uncertainty will be discussed within three groupings: (1) fundamentalist Keynesians, (2) Post Keynesian monetary theorists and (3) Keynes's *Treatise on Probability*. These groupings are by no means mutually exclusive, but are chosen as a means of presenting the chronological development of views on uncertainty. Finally, a conceptualization of uncertainty as operating at two levels is set out as a means of capturing, within a consistent framework, the different senses of uncertainty extant in the literature.

The term 'fundamentalist Keynesians' was coined by Coddington to refer to those Keynesians who focused on uncertainty, among whom he singled out Joan Robinson, George Shackle and Brian Loasby. All three draw on Keynes's *General Theory* (to which uncertainty is seen as being fundamental) and the 1937 *QJE* article (Keynes, 1973b). All three regard uncertainty as having profound methodological implications which, if taken into account, severely limit the scope of neoclassical economics.

Robinson's views on uncertainty emerged in her analysis of the impossibility for general equilibrium theory to deal with 'the irretrievable past and the unknowable future'. Uncertainty is presented as unknowability, or an absence of knowledge. To the extent that expenditure plans are based on expectations, an absence of knowledge on which to base these expectations must render them, and thus effective demand, volatile. This application of uncertainty to investment plans was absorbed into the neoclassical synthesis;

if the investment decision was formulated under conditions of uncertainty, then it could not be endogenized in a deterministic model.

Shackle focused much more explicitly on uncertainty, contrasting it with probability quantified on the basis of frequency distributions, as has since been developed by Bayesians (see for example Shackle, 1955). For Shackle, uncertainty is a relative concept. He replaced the concept of probability with the subjective concept of 'potential surprise' to capture the fact that, in general, the full array of possible outcomes of an action cannot be known. The degree of potential surprise attached to an hypothesis is thus Shackle's measure of uncertainty, interpreted as the degree of doubt rather than of belief. The subjectivity of potential surprise is important in that decision-makers may ignore evidence which would, objectively, increase the degree of potential surprise, but would impede a decision in favour of action or inaction. Absolute doubt then becomes difficult to conceive of as an objective benchmark. Degree of potential surprise may be ordered, but still does not yield the basis for deterministic prediction of behaviour, given the subjectivity of the concept.

Loasby also attempted to replace the term uncertainty because it was so commonly misinterpreted as risk; his suggested alternative is 'partial ignorance'. As with Shackle, therefore, ignorance is the reference point rather than knowledge; not knowing in general the range of possible outcomes precludes knowledge in any absolute sense. Loasby has carried forward the Shackle analysis of uncertainty in terms of economic behaviour to an analysis of economic theorizing itself, seen as an exercise in reducing partial ignorance. He concludes that organized uncertainty is a condition for progress in a wide range of spheres.

Some Post Keynesian monetary theory, like the neoclassical synthesis, restricts the role of uncertainty to investment decisions. Uncertainty then enters into the monetary process only through the responsiveness of the supply of credit to the demand for credit, which arises in turn from investment plans. This is the view of 'horizontalists' such as Kaldor and Moore. But those who have focused on the role of liquidity preference, and also the endogeneity theorists who focus on the interplay between liquidity preference and endogenous credit creation, extend the role of uncertainty to monetary theory itself. This builds on the monetary theoretic tradition stemming from Keynes and continued by Joan Robinson, Hyman Minsky, Paul Davidson, Victoria Chick and Jan Kregel.

According to Robinson's interpretation of Keynes, uncertainty accounts for the diversity of opinion over asset prices which underpins the speculative demand for money. It is ultimately uncertainty, therefore, which determines the nominal rate of interest. Davidson further puts forward uncertainty as the rationale for money's existence; money is the unit of account for contracts which serve to reduce uncertainty in decision-making. Davidson's analysis of uncertainty itself suggests an absolute absence of knowledge; knowledge in the form of quantified probability is only possible for ergodic systems which rarely pertain in practice.

The significance of uncertainty for monetary theory is also drawn out by some of the 'new fundamentalist' Keynesians, who base their analysis on textual examination of Keynes's (1973a) *Treatise on Probability*. This work has generated a much more careful examination of the meaning of uncertainty and its methodological implications. This in turn is beginning to generate fruitful avenues of theoretical enquiry.

The analysis of uncertainty has in the process taken on a new lease of life; Keynes's work on philosophy is shown to have had profound implications for the method and content of his economic theory. The result has been a more complex understanding of the meaning of uncertainty, opening up new possibilities for its scope. Along with this development has come a renewed interest in Shackle's work in which many of these ideas are already embedded. This work is still active, and actively debated, so that it is impossible to identify a consensus view; the following interpretation should thus be taken as one among many.

In the *Treatise on Probability*, Keynes examined the grounds for rational belief, focusing on those circumstances in which frequency-based probability estimates could not be known. Unfortunately, Keynes did not present an explicit definition of uncertainty. If there is a concensus in the interpretive literature, it appears to be that a proposition is uncertain (in an absolute sense) if the probability relation is unknown or is not comparable to others (in the sense of probability being greater or smaller; see for example Lawson, 1985.) Absolute uncertainty would then arise when evidence which would inform belief is absent, or when the relationship between evidence and the proposition is not known. A known probability, even if less than one, constitutes certainty (with respect to the probability relation, though not the proposition to which it applies). Even knowledge of a convention designed to allow action in spite of uncertainty constitutes knowledge.

A proposition may be based on some knowledge, but may either lack much knowledge of what is relevant to a probability estimation, or simply lack much evidence. Scope therefore arises for considering degrees of uncertainty, both in terms of degrees of relevance and in terms of relative amounts of evidence. These factors were captured by Keynes in his concept of weight. Keynes used weight in two senses: the absolute amount of relevant evidence, and the amount of relevant evidence relative to relevant ignorance. One proposition might therefore be more uncertain than another because it was based on less relevant information, either in an absolute sense or relative to the degree of relevant ignorance, respectively; this proposition would then be said to carry less weight than the other. The second sense of weight is the more general.

But as Runde (1990) has pointed out, new evidence might change the assessment of the extent of evidence which would be relevant to the proposition. Weight might thus decline if new evidence more fully revealed the extent of relevant ignorance. This insight pinpoints the importance of focusing on the process of generating knowledge of what is relevant. It implies that ignorance is no more absolute a benchmark than knowledge, since understanding of ignorance itself requires knowledge.

This line of reasoning suggests that uncertainty may best be understood in terms of first-order and second-order uncertainty. First-order uncertainty is the degree to which relevant evidence (relative to relevant ignorance) is known, given the current state of knowledge. This includes knowledge as to the extent and nature of evidence which would be relevant to the proposition; i.e. knowledge of the logical relations between evidence and proposition. The degree of first-order uncertainty then depends on knowledge of weight, greater weight conveying less uncertainty.

Second-order uncertainty refers to the degree of uncertainty attached to propositions about the nature and extent of evidence which would be relevant; i.e. to the degree of uncertainty attached to assessing weight. (In principle, this classification could proceed to ever-higher orders.) Put another way, second-order uncertainty is uncertainty about uncertainty or, in Shackle's terms, surprise at the degree of potential surprise.

The two orders of uncertainty are conflated in the two polar cases of absolute uncertainty and absolute certainty. In the case of absolute uncertainty, there is either no relevant evidence or no knowledge as to what would be relevant evidence; i.e. no basis for ordering probabilities by means of calculating probability (first-order uncertainty) or of calculating weight (second-order uncertainty). Similarly, certainty requires certainty of both orders: knowledge of relevant evidence and knowledge of precisely what is relevant. But between these extremes there are degrees of uncertainty of both orders.

The potential applications of the recent work on uncertainty are many. For example, conventions can be understood as a substitute for knowledge under conditions of uncertainty of either order. But they are more vulnerable where second-order uncertainty is high. Knowledge of the extent of our ignorance may be forced upon us (positive animal spirits may not survive the shock of lost markets, for example); the bounds of our rationality cannot simply be a matter of choice. But, following Shackle, conventions may deliberately be employed to conceal the extent of relevant ignorance; Keynes's philosophy (and economics) after all justified action on the basis of uncertain knowledge.

The relationship between conventional behaviour and shocks cannot be modelled deterministically. But conventions can provide a stable grounding for analysis as an alternative to deterministic behaviour (as long as their incomplete specification and tendency to evolve are recognized). The new fundamentalist literature has brought uncertainty back to the centre of the methodological debate.

The current state of thinking on uncertainty within radical political economy is itself a matter for some uncertainty. Indeed, to illustrate the point made above, the degree of this uncertainty increases the more one reads different accounts. But recent developments which have further refined the concept of uncertainty, particularly those which interpret it as a relative concept, hold out much promise for further refinements of its application. To lose the benchmark of ignorance makes the concept of uncertainty more complex, yet it increases its power in contributing to an analysis of the economic process.

SHEILA C. DOW

References

Keynes, J.M. (1973a), *The Treatise on Probability*, Collected Writings Vol. VII, London: Macmillan for the Royal Economic Society.

Keynes, J.M. (1973b), 'The General Theory of Employment', in *The General Theory and After: Defence and Development*, Collected Writings Vol. XIV, London: Macmillan for the Royal Economic Society.

Lawson, T. (1985), 'Uncertainty and Economic Analysis', *Economic Journal*, **95**, December, 909–28.

Runde, J. (1990), 'Keynesian Uncertainty and the Weight of Arguments', *Economics and Philosophy*, **6**, October, 275–92.

Shackle, G.L.S. (1955), *Uncertainty in Economics*, Cambridge: Cambridge University Press.

Underconsumption

Underconsumption theories contend that capitalist downturns are caused by the lack of consumer demand. Most underconsumption theories have not been business cycle theories, but rather theories of long-run stagnation which must be carefully distinguished one from the other.

All underconsumptionist long-run stagnation theories include two main components. First, the most important shared belief is that insufficient consumer demand for goods and services is the main cause of depression and unemployment. Second, it is believed that this lack of consumer demand is a problem for the economy at all times, so the usual status of the economy would be stagnation, with only certain exogenous events – such as wars or new inventions – bringing temporary prosperity (see Sherman, 1991, Ch. 9).

There have been many non-socialist underconsumptionist theories, ranging from the earliest beginnings with Lord Lauderdale and the Rev Thomas Malthus in the early 19th century to the later theories of W.T. Foster and W. Catchings in the 1930s. Many of these theories emphasized that industry turns out an increasing flood of commodities, but that some people save part of their income. As a result, consumer demand does not keep up with the flood of commodities; there is a pile-up of unsold goods and production is cut.

Since the problem, according to underconsumptionists, was lack of demand and too much saving, their view ran exactly contrary to the usual classical opinion that more saving is always good for the economy. While most classical economists recommended more saving for economic growth, some underconsumptionists recommended that everyone be forced to respend all of their income rapidly.

Another form of underconsumption theory was popular with liberal reformers such as John Hobson (1922). Hobson stressed that the cause of deficient consumer demand is not a general tendency towards too much saving, but a lack of spending power by the poor. He demonstrated that there was a maldistribution of income, with a few rich people having much, but a large mass of the poor having little. Most wage workers, he said, are poorly paid, so their income and consumption are very limited. On the other hand, the rich have incomes that are far above their consumption needs, so that most of it is saved. There is a lack of consumer demand because those with large incomes have no need to spend much of their income for consumption, while those who are poor have the need, but not the means. Hobson's solution was a more equal distribution of income.

Early socialist writers, such as Sismondi or Rodbertus, argued that the exploitation of workers led to a lack of consumer buying power. They claimed that the worker is not paid his or her full product but is limited to a subsistence wage. Therefore, as production expands, the workers' share in national income must decline. As a result, consumer demand must inevitably decline relative to production. A crisis of overproduction must follow, leading to economic stagnation. Although Marx criticized these simplistic stagnation theories, he presented a sophisticated underconsumptionist theory as his main view of the business cycle. Stagnation theories based on the underconsumptionist hypothesis were amplified by many later Marxists, such as the brilliant Rosa Luxemburg (see the history of underconsumption in Sweezy, 1942).

Modern Marxist underconsumptionist works include Sweezy (1942), Baran and Sweezy (1966) and John B. Foster (1987). Baran and Sweezy argued 'that the normal state of the monopoly capitalist economy is stagnation' (1966, p. 108), but that the system sometimes prevents stagnation by making wasteful expenditures. Some of these expenditures are private waste, such as advertising. Other expenditures are public waste, such as military spending financed by a government deficit. Sometimes the economy revives for a while for one of two main reasons: first, there may be new technological innovations that expand the economy through entrepreneurial greed. Second, the economy may be stimulated by major wars, such as the Second World War, Korea or Vietnam.

There have been many criticisms of the underconsumptionist stagnation view from the political right, left and centre. The basic criticism is that long-run underconsumption theory explains why capitalism declines into stagnation, but has no endogenous explanation of why it should ever recover. Interestingly, Karl Marx stressed that, as opposed to long-run crises of continuous decline or permanent crises in capitalism, a temporary period of 'overabundance of capital, overproduction, crisis, is something different. There are no permanent crises' (Marx, 1952, p. 373).

Another criticism of the underconsumptionist long-run stagnation theory is the argument that lack of consumer demand by itself is not a sufficient condition for a downturn. The demand for producers' goods for investment may always fill any gap between total output and consumer demand.

Although John Maynard Keynes shares the underconsumptionist worries over the lack of demand, his theory is distinguished by a focus on investment. He notes that there will be equilibrium if all of non-consumed income (that is, saving) is equal to investment plans. Only if a theory can show that the total demand by both consumers and investors is insufficient to purchase all of the supply on the market at present prices can it explain a downturn by a demand-oriented theory.

In the Keynesian framework, Paul Samuelson in 1939 stated a cycle theory based on both a limited consumer demand and a limited investment demand (an accelerator principle, which stated that investment was a function of the change in consumer demand). Sweezy (1942) solved the investment problem for underconsumptionists when he also discussed the accelerator principle. Marxist underconsumptionists had long been saying that capitalism cannot build more factories to produce more factories indefinitely. In other words, private investment, it was asserted, cannot grow to fill any gap left by consumption. But why not? In fact, for some time during every expansion, investment always does grow faster than consumption. At first, this faster growth of investment is no problem, but is rather the engine of prosperity because savings are invested to produce output and employment.

Eventually, however, if consumer demand begins to grow more slowly, capitalists will not invest because their expectation is for a lack of demand in the near future when the new goods are produced by the new factories. The accelerator principle thus explains why investment must decline when aggregate demand slows down; it may be emphasized that consumer demand is the largest part of aggregate demand.

The most important criticism of all underconsumptionist theory is the fact that profit expectations are not limited merely by demand, but also by cost considerations. In criticizing early underconsumptionists, Marx pointed out that the problem for capitalists in making profit has two stages. First, the capitalist must create a product with profit embodied in it by keeping costs low enough; these costs include labour, raw materials, and plant and equipment (depreciation). Second, after such a profitable product has been created by workers, it must be sold in order to realize the profit. Underconsumptionists tend to overlook the cost side of the problem.

This issue becomes apparent when some underconsumptionists argue that higher wages will resolve a crisis or prevent a depression. The problem is that higher wages not only create more demand (as both Keynes and Marx emphasized), but also mean higher costs per unit. Therefore, in Marx's terms, higher wages allow more realization of profit, but less production of profit. What each capitalist really wants is lower wages in his or her own plant, but higher wages throughout the rest of the economy.

John Maynard Keynes refers to the underconsumptionists only in passing as part of the dissident underground in the economics profession. Yet he did more to emphasize the importance of the deficiency of effective demand than any other theorist. Although Marx attacked Say's Law before Keynes was born, Keynes destroyed Say's Law in a more rigorous fashion than did Marx, analysing the reasons for the growing gap between consumer demand and national income in an expansion. Keynes's contributions on effective demand, the role of consumption and the importance of income distribution have been expanded and formalized by Post Keynesians.

A consistent formal model of underconsumption, in the Marxist and Post Keynesian traditions, can be stated using just five relationships (see Sherman, 1991, Ch. 9). First, at equilibrium in a closed (purely private), economy, national income must equal aggregate consumer spending plus aggregate investment spending.

$$\text{National income} = \text{Consumption} + \text{Investment}. \qquad (1)$$

Second, national income may be divided in terms of distribution to workers and capitalists.

$$\text{National income} = \text{Property income} + \text{Labour income}. \qquad (2)$$

Third, the basic thrust of an underconsumptionist consumption function is that consumer demand is not only influenced by the amount of national income, but also by its distribution between labour and property owners. Wages workers spend all of their income for consumer goods, but capitalists only a portion of theirs. Therefore:

$$\text{Consumption} = \text{Part of property income} + \text{All of labour income}. \qquad (3)$$

In fact, empirical studies confirm that the marginal propensity to consume out of labour income should be significantly higher than the marginal propensity to consume out of property income (see Sherman, 1991, Ch. 5).

In the Marxist view, the struggle in the production process over distribution of income between capital and labour reflects the exploitation of labour under capitalist relations of production. What is important here, however, is the cyclical movement of the shares of income of capital and labour. The fourth pillar of underconsumption is that the labour share generally falls throughout an expansion and rises throughout a contraction (see Sherman, 1991, Ch. 8). Underconsumptionists explain that capitalist institutions (such as capitalist ownership of the product and fixed-wage contracts) prevent wages from rising as rapidly as profits in a capitalist expansion.

The simplest possible representation of this relationship is to show the labour share as a constant minimum (the long-run subsistence wage?) plus some fixed percentage of national income.

$$\text{Labour income} = \text{Constant} + \text{Percentage of national income.} \qquad (4)$$

As national income rises, labour income rises, but more slowly. As national income falls in a contraction, labour income falls, but again more slowly.

Fifth and last, an underconsumptionist business cycle theory may make use of the simplest version of the accelerator. It says that net investment is a function of the previous change in aggregate demand. Specifically:

$$\text{Investment} = \text{Accelerator times change in national income.} \qquad (5)$$

Given these five relationships (with appropriate time lags), underconsumptionists can tell a consistent story of the entire business cycle (for a formal model along these lines, see Sherman, 1991, Appendix to Ch. 9). To understand the model more fully, its operation may be traced through the phases of the business cycle.

As recovery begins in the first phase of expansion, national income rises which leads to more consumer spending. The increase in output demanded causes more net investment. The new investment means more employment and income (wages and profits), which leads to increased spending on consumption and a further rise in national income. As expansion continues, however, rising output is accompanied by a declining labour share. Reasons include continued unemployment in early expansion, the fact that productivity rises in expansion, that wage bargains are usually fixed for a certain time period, and that capitalists automatically own any increased product due to higher productivity. Consumer demand depends not only on total income, but on how it is divided between labour and property income, because labour has a higher marginal propensity to consume. As the labour share declines, it follows that the overall marginal propensity to consume falls. Consumer demand continues to grow as long as national income is rising, but more and more slowly. The slower growth of aggregate demand causes a decline in investment, leading to declines in income and employment.

As the contraction begins, the decline in net investment leads to a greater decline in national income. Falling national income causes a still further decline in net investment; thus the decline is cumulative. As the decline continues, however, labour income falls more slowly than property income. The consequent rise in the labour share raises the marginal propensity to consume. The higher marginal propensity to consume helps stop the decline in consumption and aggregate demand. Eventually, this leads to improved expectations and a small increase in net investment. This event sets off the recovery and a cumulative expansion begins.

HOWARD J. SHERMAN

References

Baran, P. and Sweezy, P. (1966), *Monopoly Capital*, New York: Monthly Review Press.
Foster, J.B. (1987), 'What is Stagnation?' in R. Cherry *et al.* (eds), *The Imperiled Economy*, Book 1, New York: Monthly Review Press.
Hobson, J. (1922), *The Economics of Unemployment*, London: George Allen and Unwin.
Sherman, H. (1991), *The Business Cycle: Growth and Crisis under Capitalism*, Princeton, New Jersey: Princeton University Press.
Sweezy, P. (1942), *The Theory of Capitalist Development*, New York: Monthly Review Press; reprinted 1970.

Underdevelopment

The wide and persistent economic gap between advanced capitalist countries and the poor countries of the world prompts fundamental questions. Can capitalism succeed in developing the whole world? Are the economic relations between rich and poor countries responsible for the gulf between the promise of economic development and the reality of economic underdevelopment? Will late-arriving countries find it progressively difficult to traverse the road taken by the pioneers?

Drawing inspiration from classical political economy and Keynesian doctrine, development economics emerged in the aftermath of World War II to offer an optimistic vision of development possibilities in post-colonial societies. Its basic message was that capitalist development – aided in important measure by state planning, resource mobilization and industrial protection – could be relied upon to effect technological modernization and rising living standards. At the same time, it asserted that underdeveloped countries required a separate theory of development in view of their dualistic economic structure, late start and vast reserves of underutilized labour power. Though the theory espoused had much in common with classical and Marxian theories of saving and capital accumulation, this claim served to distance the new field from neoclassical orthodoxy.

The case for state-guided development – an industrial 'big push' and balanced growth were favoured policies – rested on a pragmatic recognition of the myopic and timid character of market-directed private investment. This was bolstered by lessons inferred from the experience of Continental countries that followed pioneer England. Gerschenkron (1962) showed how the demonstration effects and tensions set up by uneven development create their own dynamic, reflecting the intensity of the catching-up effort on the part of late industrializers. Alleged obstacles are turned into advantages (German industrial banks and the Soviet state, for example, in the face of capital market deficiencies) and supposedly invariant prerequisites are overcome by effective substitutes (the substitution of scarce capital for the even more scarce skilled labour). The development process is speeded up and the gap is reduced by technological leap-frogging and accelerated accumulation. The lessons of history helped dispel the notion, propagated by Rostow (1960) in his 'non-communist manifesto', of a uniquely ordered path of development through stages, irrespective of an individual country's historical context and institutional arrangements.

Efforts at building a theory for interventionist domestic policy to hasten the process of development were joined by endeavours to rationalize interventions in external trade. Raul Prebisch and Hans Singer formulated the idea that the gains from international trade accrued mostly to rich countries. They argued that primary exporters experience a secular tendency of the prices they receive to decline in relation to the prices (of imported manufactures) that they pay. This tendency results from underemployment in the periphery which holds down wages and from the power of trade unions and manufacturing enterprises in the centre which manage to raise wages and prices as productivity grows. Similarly, Arthur Lewis argued that 'unlimited labour supplies' in subsistence production allow gains from productivity increases in export activities to flow to the consuming countries (in the centre). That a country or region may be impoverished absolutely through a process of unrestrained trade could also be derived from Gunnar Myrdal's thesis of cumulative causation. These ideas were used to argue in favour of industrial promotion and protection and selectively to ignore the international division of labour that orthodox economics assumed was dictated by market prices and efficiency.

Development economics did not inquire into the roots of underdevelopment – why and how the periphery came to specialize in primary exports to the advanced capitalist countries or suffer from mass underemployment and low productivity. Nor did it concern itself with the political-economic ramifications of indigenous class structures and the exercise of state power in newly independent nations. These omissions reflected its primary concern with inventing (and offering) policy solutions to problems of economic growth. In his writings on the colonies, Marx had emphasized the initially destructive but, in the end, constructive (if not liberating) role that the spread of capitalism would play there. Development economics ignored the historical reality of the first of these consequences envisaged by Marx, elaborating instead on the potential prospect of the second.

What the development economists seem to have ignored, however, became central to a theory of underdevelopment fashioned by Baran (1957). Baran sought to connect causally the obviously distorted and stagnant pattern of development in the societies emerging from colonialism with a postulated need of metropolitan capitalist countries to balance the growth of their investable surpluses and the growth of markets and investment opportunities. The link is provided by the economic dominance of the centre over the periphery through trade and investment flows and also by the political configuration that obtains in post-colonial societies. The theory contended that the surplus produced in the periphery is appropriated by an alliance of unproductive domestic elites and foreign capital which, while helping to resolve the contradiction of overproduction in the centre, reproduces a stagnant and highly unequal peripheral economy. Whereas the bulk of the peripheral economy oriented to producing mass consumption goods suffers from want of capital, very little of the surplus generated in the sectors oriented to export production is invested in the domestic economy. Such a regime produces dualism, underemployment, low productivity and export-oriented development.

According to Baran, metropolitan capital plays an important but not exclusive part in blocking progressive capitalism in most peripheral countries. The indigenous bourgeoisie, with its economic bases in comprador, monopolistic and short-term ventures, is too weak to acquire state control and pursue capital accumulation on its own. After colonialism ended, it was confronted not only with the encrusted powers at the top of the social hierarchy (an amalgam of internal feudal and external imperial interests), but also with a threat from below, a revolution of rising hopes for a wider distribution of political power and economic benefits. Rather than seek a progressive alliance with the masses, the bourgeoisie formed a reactionary accommodation with the feudal/imperial interests which, while containing the demands of the masses, rendered capitalist transformation virtually impossible. Getting out of underdevelopment requires expropriation of the assets of both domestic elites and foreign enterprises. The surplus released must then be utilized in a planned and balanced manner to meet the domestic needs of mass consumption, capital goods and infrastructure creation.

Baran's thesis has been extended and generalized by a number of writers including Frank (1967) and Wallerstein (1974) among others. Frank, like Wallerstein, views capitalism as a system of production for exchange and profit. The growth of production for long-distance trade with the capitalist centre is equated with capitalist transformation in the periphery. The global hegemony of the capitalist mode has long been established, so that seemingly 'non-capitalist' relations of production within the periphery are instrumental or functional to capitalist expansion. However, the network of world commerce is also a hierarchy of metropolis, regional satellites, local satellites, etc. in which surplus is extracted upwards and outward. Such development as has taken place in peripheral economies is neither self-generating nor self-sustaining, for it is geared to the needs and dynamic of the centre. Satellite economies experience their greatest economic development when their ties to the metropolis are weakest; for Latin America in this century, the periods of the two Wars and of the great depression have been so identified. The resumption of regular economic relations reorients peripheral industry into channels that produce little development; it can also run up against severe foreign exchange, inflation or debt crises accompanied by political disruptions. These propositions lead to two basic theses: (1) that capitalism has simultaneously generated underdevelopment in some parts of the world and economic development in others, and (2) that autonomous, self-sustained development in the former is impossible within the existing global capitalist framework.

The theory of underdevelopment just outlined is distinguishable from Marxian theory, first, by its emphasis on surplus extraction from the underdeveloped economies through global exchange relations and second, by its placement of international or inter-regional conflict at the centre of the political economy of interests. Accordingly, the chief Marxian criticism of this theory is that it ignores the central importance of class relations and the organization of production within the periphery in setting the path of economic development (Brenner, 1977). By underplaying the growth of wages and technological dynamism in the centre, the theory also greatly exaggerates economic imperatives for the exploitation of the periphery by the centre.

From a historical standpoint, industrial growth in Latin America and elsewhere in the periphery provides a number of examples of unequal relations with the metropolitan countries, leading to aggravated domestic inequalities and socio-political distortions. In an earlier phase, the asymmetry in international relations consisted in colonial plunder and the centre/periphery division of labour, leading to export-led surplus extraction and structural dualism. In recent decades, the asymmetry arises from the forms and rapid pace of technical progress over which the centre enjoys near-monopoly and from the transmission of consumption patterns that are import- and capital-intensive. In consequence, many countries in the periphery are unable to develop competitive advantage fast enough to achieve industrial take-off, but nevertheless have to bear the costs of technological backwash effects and the marginalization of a large part of their populations.

No general theory of underdevelopment can do justice to the convoluted post-war experience of economic development in peripheral countries. While some countries have managed to grow at remarkably high rates, others have achieved very little by way of economic growth. A few countries have been able to exploit their integration into international markets for commodities and capital to their own advantage; many others have had to contend with the debilitating effects of import dependence and export instability. Neither socialist policies nor unfettered capitalism has met with universal economic success (or failure). Very few among the countries of the periphery, including the relatively successful 'newly industrializing countries', pass the test of being 'industrialized' – not only because industrial employment is not expanding as a share of their populations, but also because industry's share in national income has risen to relatively high proportions at much lower levels of industrial labour productivity than was the case in the advanced countries (Sutcliffe, 1984). Such growth has not always been able to overcome serious problems of low life expectancy, poor health, illiteracy or even low private purchasing power which reflect growing inequalities of wealth and political power. Nor has it always brought about political liberation from diverse sources of oppression.

This at least suggests that there is no warrant for general optimism that capitalist industrialization is progressing in a desirable direction in peripheral countries. On the other hand, from another angle, the evidence suggests that the traditional emphases of development economics – capital accumulation, industrialization, mobilization of surplus labour and a modicum of government planning – have proven to be important ingredients in successful economic growth.

Based on this evidence, however, one cannot leap to the conclusion that industrialization within the existing framework, even when fuelled by borrowed capital and technology, is unsustainable or that it produces underdevelopment. Rather, the relevant lesson to be drawn is that success depends not only on the particular phase of global capitalist development in which late industrialization occurs, but also on the particular structures of state, society and economy within which national capitalisms evolve.

J. MOHAN RAO

References

Baran, P. (1957), *The Political Economy of Growth*, New York: Monthly Review Press.

Brenner, R. (1977), 'The Origins of Capitalist Development: A Critique of neo-Smithian Marxism', *New Left Review*, no. 104.
Frank, A.G. (1967), *Capitalism and Underdevelopment in Latin America: Historical Studies of Chile and Brazil*, New York: Monthly Review Press.
Gerschenkron, A. (1962), *Economic Backwardness in Historical Perspective*, Cambridge, MA: Belknap Press.
Rostow, W.W. (1960), *The Stages of Economic Growth: A Non-Communist Manifesto*, Cambridge: Cambridge University Press.
Sutcliffe, R.B. (1984), 'Industry and Underdevelopment Re-examined', *Journal of Development Studies*, **21**, October.
Wallerstein, I. (1974), *The Modern World System*, New York: Academic Press.

Unemployment, The social pathology of

In an introduction to Marxist economics, Catephores (1989) suggests that the key difference between Marxist and orthodox economists lies in the fact that the former highlight the exploitation of labour as the central pivot upon which capitalism turns.

Capitalism consists of a minority wealth-owning class who, personally or through their agents, use a much larger mass of labouring people as an infinitely disposable and renewable resource. It is exploitation in this broader sense which identifies capitalism as an amoral system. To view the system as exploitive at the level of production (as represented by the ratio s/v), while conceptually of considerable analytic value, has little exoteric importance and is virtually irrelevant in experiental terms. Positive rates of surplus value are only one aspect of the exploitation process which is capitalism. Unemployment amongst the mass of people, who usually can only obtain the means of subsistence through the sale of their labour-power, is another.

The aggregate demand for labour, with its concomitant provision of work and wages, varies not only with the cyclical fluctuations which chart the history of capitalism, but also with changes in technology and with changes in the patterns of needs, wants and desires, themselves often not original in Man. These uncoordinated fluctuations have different consequences for each constituent class of the corpus capitalism. In times of recession, for example, the wealth-owning classes, who have paper title to the means of production, may become relatively less wealthy in material terms. The working classes, however, experience the faltering of economic activity and the chaos of markets at an experiental level. People who are unemployed (and almost always their immediate families) are not only impoverished in monetary and material terms, but in psycho-social terms as well. For those who become unemployed, there are often losses which can never be retrieved.

Unemployment is perceived as being created by, and a necessary adjunct of, the capitalist system. Thus Marx (1977) says:

> But if a surplus labouring population is a necessary product of accumulation or the development of wealth on a capitalist basis, this surplus population becomes, conversely, the lever of capitalist accumulation, nay, a condition of existence of the capitalist mode of production. It forms a disposable industrial reserve army, that belongs to capital as absolutely as if the latter had bred it at its own cost. Independently of the limits of the actual increase of population, it creates, for the changing needs of self expansion of capital, a mass of human material always ready for exploitation (p. 592).

And Catephores (1989) points to the commonly-held belief that unemployment may even have a positive value in that it exercises a restraining influence on the wage demands of organized labour: 'Some unemployment is, therefore, one useful way, and, in the last resort, perhaps the only way, of maintaining control over the working classes' (p. 153).

From this perspective unemployment appears as one of the variables within the system to be manipulated for the benefit of the system itself. The human quintessence and the welfare of those who are unemployed do not appear as terms within economic equations. It is this kind of omission together with an apparently dismissive way of regarding people who are unemployed which reveals the pathogenesis of the capitalist system.

One of the dysfunctional aspects of orthodox economics is that there is a failure, perhaps a refusal, to recognize and attach appropriate importance to the significant loss of quality of life experienced by those who become unemployed within market-dominated economies. In the end it is this loss, rather than any reduction in physical or financial asset values, which identifies the real exploitation within the capitalist mode of production.

The very term 'the unemployed' (rather than 'people who are unemployed') dehumanizes the phenomenon of unemployment and reduces people within this category to an abstract quantity. Orthodox economics, clinging pretentiously to the coat-tails of positivism, makes no reference to unemployment as a human condition. As workers are recruited to and discharged from the service of capital, no mention is made, or heed taken, of their needs as human beings. At a normative and unashamedly value-laden level, however, the economic system, whatever its form, should serve the needs of people rather than people serving the needs of the system. Economic systems in themselves have no unilateral importance.

The working classes are aware that the products of their labours yield profits for the owners of the enterprises within which they are employed. For the most part they are untroubled by this and may in fact take some comfort when the firm where they work is successful, in terms of profitability, for this provides some perceived security of employment. Usually, however, working men and women are unaware that their employment yields positive rates of surplus value and that this in turn reveals a process of exploitation at work.

Even if they are aware of this fact, it probably does not figure in any conscious or unconscious calculations of the relative utility and disutility derived from employment and unemployment. Furthermore the fact that they are, almost universally, denied ownership of, or private access to, the means of production is not usually a factor in such subjective calculations either.

Even those who devise arguments to the contrary must be aware that, with very few exceptions, working-class people, however these are defined, prefer employment to unemployment. As Thomas Carlyle stated in *Chartism* (1839): 'A man willing to work, and unable to find work, is perhaps the saddest sight that fortune's inequality exhibits under the sun'. This preference, however, does not arise out of any overweening predisposition towards contemporary work for, as Braverman (1974) pointed out, one view is

> that work has become increasingly subdivided into petty operations that fail to sustain interest or engage the capacities of humans with current levels of education and that the modern trend of work by its 'mindlessness' and 'Bureaucratisation' is 'alienating' ever larger sections of the population (p. 4).

Employment and unemployment incur disutility for many, perhaps most. This preference for employment over unemployment arises from the fact that the former yields relatively less disutility and is usually the only means of securing a means of subsistence above the survival level payments grudgingly metered out by the state.

Being unemployed is an entirely onerous state which inflicts suffering not only on the unemployed and their families, but also on society as a whole. For example, as the level of unemployment rises, the number of suicides increases (Shapiro and Ahlburg, 1983). Moreover, each 1.0 per cent increase in unemployment has been associated with a 1.9 per cent increase in deaths from heart disease, a 5.7 per cent increase in murders, a 3.4 per cent increase in the incidence of mental illness, and an increase of 4.0 per cent in committals to prison (Brenner, 1979).

Unemployment for any significant period results in a loss of self-respect and a deterioration in the value of human capital. There is a very strong tendency for people unemployed for any significant length of time to become demoralized and demotivated; in consequence, the energy devoted to their search for work becomes increasingly depleted. In addition, there is evidence that employers are aware of these effects and actively discriminate against the long-term unemployed in their recruitment programmes. Thus the longer a person is unemployed, the more likely it is that he or she will remain unemployed. Such discrimination invalidates (if such invalidation is needed) the argument that some unemployment exercises a restraining influence on the wage demands of labour, for the long-term unemployed are no longer effectively competing for available employment.

In July 1992 in the UK, the number recorded as unemployed increased by 29,000, pushing the total number registered as unemployed above 2.75 million. While these figures are alarming enough, of even greater significance is the increase in the number of long-term unemployed, i.e. those out of work for more than six months. By May 1992 the figure for this category of unemployed people had risen to 1.439 million, an increase of almost half a million over the previous year.

With few exceptions the working classes are not only denied access to the means of production: for the most part they have also lost the opportunities to provide for themselves using their own labours. Work in employment, as distinct from work in a more creative sense, provides the wherewithal to purchase goods and services in the market which, at the lowest level, satisfy physiological needs. Maslow (1970) identifies a *hierarchy* of needs, with 'physiological needs' forming the lowest echelon. Need satisfaction at this level is fundamental, associated as it is with survival itself – with the necessity for food, for shelter, for warmth and so on. In contradistinction, at the highest echelon are 'self-actualizing needs'. Those who live for at least some of their time at this level fulfil their potential as human beings and as a consequence experience the highest available levels of satisfaction.

Within Maslow's hierarchy, immediately above physiological and survival needs are 'safety needs' which find expression in the need for freedom from fear, the need for law and order, for an absence of chaos and freedom from anxiety. Moving upwards, the next level is concerned with 'social needs' – the need to belong: to the family, to the group, the company, the club, the locality and so on. At the penultimate level, immediately below self-actualizing needs, are 'status or ego needs' where people require some recognition of their worth as human beings. This need can be satisfied in a multiplicity of ways, from being a top brain surgeon or a politician to being recognized as a good father, mother, husband, wife, gardener, angler, musician or whatever.

While economics is often concerned with wants, this theory is concerned with needs in the real sense of the term. Clearly physiological needs have to be satisfied to ensure survival. What is often not recognized is that deprivation of higher-order needs within Maslow's hierarchy also has physiological, behavioural and mental implications which can threaten the integrity of the whole person.

Additionally the psychological theory behind this hierarchy of needs suggests that we all begin at the bottom: it is the physiological, survival needs, followed by the need for safety, which present themselves first of all as a motivating force. Until these needs are satisfied, the higher order needs do not appear on the screen of consciousness. As successively higher needs are met, however, even higher order needs present themselves for the pursuit of satisfying ends. The implicit assumption is that the higher the level of need satisfaction attained, the better the quality and the experience of life itself.

Unemployment, particularly prolonged or quasi-permanent unemployment, condemns people to the lowest levels of the hierarchy where they are perpetually concerned with physiological need satisfaction. Loss of income may engender the loss of home, through the inability to meet mortgage repayments, and the sequestration of other assets to service any other indebtedness incurred previously on the basis that employment is a permanent aspect of life. Ultimately it may mean the break-up of families. In the face of such prospects fear, anxiety and the perception of existing social and economic systems as chaotic become constant companions. Unemployment, at a stroke, can wipe away any possibility of experiencing the satisfaction of higher order needs. The satisfaction of ego/status needs is instantly reduced and unemployed people lose the satisfaction of social needs, as the comradeship of the workplace is no longer available and they become objects of empathy, sympathy and, worse still, pity within the other social groupings of which they are members.

As the experience of unemployment becomes more and more prolonged, the unemployed experience some social disapprobation fostered by the hideous notions that somehow labour prices itself out of the market; or that, at some low wage, work is always available.

The most important aspect of exploitation within the capitalist system is, therefore, to be found in the ways in which labour is first employed and then relegated to unemployment again, or perhaps never employed at all. The contiguous states of employment and unemployment are used to enable the capitalist system, in pursuit of its own aims, to accommodate technological change, to pursue capital accumulation and to adjust to the consequences of uncoordinated, and therefore chaotic, markets. Unemployment cuts across races and sexes. As finance capital becomes more and more internationally mobile, it flits from country to country in search of the highest rate of exploitation, leaving in its wake, without regard, degraded environs and discarded people.

It is this use and abuse of human beings and their relegation to the status of commodities which provide evidence of the truly exploitive nature of capitalism.

TERRY MORETON

References

Braverman, H. (1974), *Labor and Monopoly Capital: The Degradation of Work in the Twentieth Century*, New York: Monthly Review Press.

Brenner, H. (1979), 'Influence of Social Environment on Social Pathology: The Historical Perspective' in J.E. Barrett *et al.* (eds), *Stress and Mental Disorder*, New York.

Catephores, G. (1989), *An Introduction to Marxist Economics*, London: Macmillan Education.

Marx, K. (1977), *Capital*, Vol. 1, London: Lawrence & Wishart, Chapter 25, p. 592.
Maslow, A. (1970), *Motivation and Personality*, New York: Harper & Row.
Shapiro, M. and Ahlburg, D. (1983), 'The Ultimate Cost of Unemployment', *Journal of Post Keynesian Economics*, 276–80.

Unequal exchange

The theory of unequal exchange was originally presented by Emmanuel (1972) as an application of the Marxian transformation problem to the sphere of international trade. The principal contribution of the theory is to identify a mechanism of surplus transfer in trade to explain unequal development. Unequal exchange also provides a foundation for the critique of free trade. Differences in wage levels between advanced capitalist countries (centre) and their poorer trading partners (periphery) may lead to a perverse international division of labour in which the world fails to utilize available resources efficiently.

The first serious neo-Marxian analysis of trade, Emmanuel's *Unequal Exchange*, initiated a lengthy debate among Marxists of various tendencies, neo-Ricardians and neoclassicals. At issue is not only whether trade with extreme capital mobility coupled with extreme labour *im*mobility might produce growing inequality of trading partners over time, but also more fundamental questions. These include the nature and place of the traditional Marxian theory of value versus its Sraffian and neoclassical critics. The political issue of whether workers in advanced countries could be said to be 'exploiting' workers in poorer countries is also at stake.

As originally set forth in Emmanuel (1972), exchange inequality was measured by comparing values with prices, using Marx's own transformation tableau. There is associated with every exchange of commodities not only an equivalent exchange of money, but also an exchange of labour value: that is, the embodied socially necessary labour-time. Consequently, if prices are not proportional to their respective labour values, the implicit exchange of labour-time will be unequal.

Subsequent research has shown that this notion of poor countries yielding up unequal quantities of labour as a subsidy to the consumption of rich countries cannot withstand critical scrutiny. The problem is easily traceable to logical difficulties with the labour theory of value. Neo-Ricardians argue that the labour theory of value is as much a needless detour for the unequal exchange literature as for value theory in general. As long as values are not strictly proportional to prices, various perversities can be shown to exist which vitiate the simplicity of the theory. Gibson (1980) shows that it is possible that a net flow of labour values from periphery to the centre could correspond to a reverse flow of value in price terms. Since prices, not values, determine the control over real resources, it is possible for the periphery to be 'value rich' and 'price poor'. But if it cannot be shown that the centre always benefits through unequal exchange, there can be little gained in the way of a theory of surplus transfer through trade.

Emmanuel (1972) was aware of the logical pitfalls of the labour theory of value which he sought to avoid by distinguishing unequal exchange in the 'broad' and 'strict' senses. The former is associated with sectoral differences in the organic composition of capital and must be netted out from strict unequal exchange. 'It thus becomes clear; notes Emmanuel, 'that the inequality of wages as such, all other things being equal, is alone the cause of inequality of exchange' (1972, p. 61). In the publication of the English language edition, recognizing that the labour theory of value has become a fetter to the clear exposition of his ideas, Emmanuel reformulated the theory in terms of the Sraffian price of production framework (1972, Appendix 5).

The Sraffian approach proved much more fertile; the ground then shifted from simply trying to understand Emmanuel to extensions and refinements of the theory. In the Sraffian vernacular, explicit comparisons can be made with classical, neo-Ricardian and neoclassical trade theory. The neoclassicals are most defensive about the alleged non-optimality of trade (Samuelson 1975 and references cited therein). Evans (1984) correctly points out that Samuelson seems to misinterpret the theory of unequal exchange as support for autarky versus trade.

In fact, unequal exchange is not an argument about trade versus autarky, but about trade at one set of wages (unequal) versus trade at another set of wages (equal). Gibson (1980) proves the 'fundamental theorem' of unequal exchange, showing that higher real wages always improve the terms of trade. The result holds for any number of countries and commodities, so long as each country is specialized in the production of one good and there are no trade pattern reversals. If two countries produce the same good (trade in so-called 'non-specifics') or if a given country produces more than one commodity, the conditions of the theorem are not met and it cannot be concluded that the terms of trade must improve with an increase in real wages.

Restricting the discussion to trade in two specific goods between an aggregate centre and periphery, the unequal exchange equations based on a Sraffian framework are written as follows:

Centre
$$P = (1 + r^c)\, Pa_{11}{}^c + a_{21}{}^c) + w^c 1_1{}^c \quad (1)$$
$$1 = (1 + r^c)(Pa_{12}{}^c + a_{22}{}^c) + w^c 1_2{}^c \quad (2)$$

Periphery
$$P = (1 + r^p)\, (Pa_{11}{}^p + a_{21}{}^p) + w^p 1_1{}^p \quad (3)$$
$$1 = (1 + r^p)\, (Pa_{12}{}^p + a_{22}{}^p) + w^p 1_2{}^p \quad (4)$$

where P is the relative price, r the profit rate, a_{ij} the input-output coefficients describing the use of good i in the production of good j, and l_j the direct labour coefficient for the jth good. Superscripts c and p stand for centre and periphery respectively.

In autarky, the equations of each region are solved for the local rate of profit and the internal terms of trade P, given the technical coefficients and the local wage rate. As trade opens, each country tends to specialize and a new global technique, determined by comparative advantage through the ordinary processes of competition, is established. Let technique A consist of equations (1) and (4) and technique B consist of (2) and (3). It is evident that the trade pattern depends on both the technical production coefficients and the level of wages. Gains from trade insure that the world rate of profit, r, is such that $r > r^c, r^p$. The terms of trade fall between the autarkic price ratios. The fundamental theorem ensures that:

$$dP/dw^p \begin{array}{ll} < 0 & \text{technique } A \\ > 0 & \text{technique } B. \end{array}$$

The substance of the critique of free trade provided by unequal exchange is also easily illustrated. Clearly, if the labour coefficients were to change in equations (1) to (4), the pattern of trade would (or at least could) change. There may be a trade pattern reversal such that the technique shifts from A to B or vice-versa. But with given wages, a change in the wage rate is logically indistinguishable from a change in the labour coefficients. This implies that the pattern of trade depends upon the distribution of income, rendering the idea of a technically efficient allocation of international resources an ephemeral notion at best.

The challenge to the orthodoxy implicit in this argument was taken seriously by Samuelson who wrote several papers on the topic, including a 55-page lead article in the *Journal of International Economics* (Samuelson, 1975). The trade inefficiency Emmanuel identified, called 'deadweight loss' by Samuelson, is equivalent to what Metcalfe, Steedman and Mainwaring referred to as 'neo-Ricardian trade losses' in earlier articles (Steedman, 1979). To circumvent the apparent paradox of free trade leading to perverse patterns of specialization in which the world as a whole is worse off, Samuelson asserts the 'noncomparability of steady states', arguing that the deadweight loss is, in effect, unrecoverable. A transition from an inefficient to an efficient pattern of trade necessarily involves sacrifice of consumption along the traverse between steady states. Samuelson shows that when viewed dynamically, the apparently inefficient system is in fact intertemporally Pareto optimal.

The crux of the issue turns on the role of the rate of profit. If profit is seen as a legitimate social cost to defray 'waiting' or 'abstinence', then Samuelson's argument is irrefutable. But if profit is a deduction from the product of labour with no social rationale, a positive rate of profit can distort the allocation of resources in much the same way as taxes do. This aspect of the debate, more than any other, demonstrates clearly that the critique of free trade which derives from unequal exchange is based fundamentally on a critique of capitalist production.

Certainly the criticism of unequal exchange is not limited to the neoclassicals. The English-language translation of Emmanuel (1969) was published with an appendix by Bettelheim who takes Emmanuel to task for the narrowness of his approach. The technical criticisms offered by Bettelheim are limited to confusions introduced by the labour theory of value. The more profound objection is that Emmanuel produced a theory of unequal development that is simply too mechanistic. In focusing on surplus transfer in trade, Emmanuel disregards more basic methods by which the centre blocks peripheral development, in particular ideological and political domination. For Bettelheim, inequality is prior to exchange and cannot be explained by reference to circulation. The roots of unequal exchange must be analysed in the sphere of production.

Amin (1976) shares the view that low wages are caused by inherently low levels of productivity and that, moreover, most trade does not involve complete specialization. Unequal exchange must be corrected for productivity differentials so that true surplus transfer occurs only when wage differentials exceed productivity differentials. Amin reaches the striking conclusion that, because of unequal exchange, the periphery would be better off under autarky. Evans (1984) points out that Amin's system is somewhat incoherent. As the theory is inconsistent with free international competition, the centre must therefore impose unequal exchange on the periphery. Moreover, Amin's formal presentation is marred by the use of particular examples, so that as a general result it fails to obtain the superiority of autarky versus trade.

For Emmanuel, unequal exchange is ultimately an attempt to explain the mechanisms behind unequal development. Extracted from the confusing and irrelevant environment of the labour theory of value, the proposition is quite straightforward: low wages will bias the long-run terms of trade against the periphery. Surplus that would otherwise have been accumulated for growth and development is extracted by the advanced countries through the mechanism of free trade. Low wages in the periphery are then reproduced by the slow pace of capital accumulation there.

Amin (1976) is correct in pointing out that the simplicity of the result hinges on complete specialization and that this question can only be settled empirically, as noted by Gibson (1980). If most trade is in specifics, Emmanuel is right in arguing that wages determine productivity rather than vice-versa (as, for example, Amin and Bettelheim would have it). Throughout his writing, Emmanuel emphasizes 'the wage' as the independent variable of his account: in making the link between unequal exchange and unequal development, the role of the wage is pivotal.

High wages bring higher levels of development, not only through surplus transfer, but more directly through the effect on the inducement to invest. Higher wages create markets through increasing demand and capacity utilization through an accelerator effect. There are other mechanisms at work as well. High wages induce investment directly as capitalists attempt to substitute relatively cheap capital for expensive labour. High wages also increase the demand for sophisticated consumer goods which require more capital-intensive methods. Labour productivity grows in the process, but it is all linked in Emmanuel's view to the high real wage, a real wage subsidized by poorer trading partners.

Clearly a discussion of the evolution of the world capitalist system calls for a more complete model of trade than that provided by Emmanuel in *Unequal Exchange*. A large literature on such models has emerged which attempts to offer some explanation of how higher wages and prices for peripheral products would feed into a full macro-model of North–South trade. These models have unequal exchange styled effects, but are generally much more complex. Results hinge upon the macroeconomic 'closure' employed for both poles of the system, whether neoclassical, neo-Keynesian or neo-Marxian. It is to be noted that when such models employ supply and demand equations to determine the terms of trade between the North and South, they lose comparability with Emmanuel, who holds that prices are determined by costs – the most important of which is the wage.

BILL GIBSON

References

Amin, S. (1976), *Imperialism and Unequal Development*, New York: Monthly Review Press.

Emmanuel, A. (1972), *Unequal Exchange: A Study of the Imperialism of Trade*, translated by Brian Pearce, New York: Monthly Review Press. Originally published in 1969 as *L'échange inégal*, Paris: Maspero.

Evans, D. (1984), 'A Critical Assessment of Some Neo-Marxian Trade Theories', *Journal of Development Studies*, **20** (2), 202–26.

Gibson, B. (1990), 'Unequal Exchange: Theoretical Issues and Empirical Findings', *Review of Radical Political Economics*, **12** (3), 15–35.

Samuelson, P. (1975), 'Trade Pattern Reversals in Time-Phased Ricardian Systems and Intertemporal Efficiency', *Journal of International Economics*, **5** (4), 309–63.

Steedman, I. (1979), *Fundamental Issues of Trade*, New York: St Martin's Press.

Utility

The term 'utility' has a long history, though its meaning in modern economic theory differs from that implied by earlier usage. Two origins are particularly important. First, there is the work of Bentham and others in the late 18th and early 19th centuries proposing that governments should resolve social choice problems by selecting actions which lead to the 'greatest good of the greatest number'. This view (and variants), known as utilitarianism, is still popular amongst English and American philosophers and can be seen as providing a rationale, and basis, for conventional welfare economics.

Currently, many economists are more likely to associate utility with the theory of risk-taking due to von Neumann and Morgenstern, which in turn can be traced back to Bernoulli's proposed solution to the St Petersburg paradox. By the turn of the 17th century it was customary to value risks (often wagers or insurance options) by their expected value, though in certain circumstances this led to infinite valuations of risky prospects that were not, intuitively, very valuable. Bernoulli showed that if utility were a declining function of money, the paradox could be resolved, though it was not until the work of von Neumann and Morgenstern that the underlying assumptions of utility were made explicit. Further work by Savage (1954) showed how utility could be combined with a subjective interpretation of the probability calculus. Savage's account of subjective expected utility (SEU) has seven to eight axioms (depending on what are counted as different parts of one axiom), but three are taken to be of major significance. These are:

Axiom 1. Completeness: for any pair of options, either you prefer *a* to *b*, or you prefer *b* to *a*, or you are indifferent.
Axiom 2. Transitivity: for any three options, if you prefer *a* to *b* and *b* to *c*, then you prefer *a* to *c*.
Axiom 3. Independence: preferences are linear with respect to probabilities. For example, if in some game the probability of winning the prize is increased from one-third to two-thirds, the game becomes twice as attractive.

If a person's preferences adhere to these three conditions, then it is possible to show that a utility function and probability distribution can be inferred from the person's behaviour. Furthermore, it is possible to allow that decision-makers might want to combine their own personal *prior* probabilities with objective evidence by interpreting Bayes's theorem in a certain way. For this reason SEU is regarded as the basis of the increasingly accepted view of decision-theory known as Bayesianism. Until the 1980s, most economists subscribed to the view that rational behaviour could be described as the maximization of SEU; in fact, the theory continues to be used extensively by economists both in theoretical and empirical work.

Simon's 'theory of satisficing' stresses the importance of cognitive limitations and aspiration levels and provides a critique of the view that economic agents are rational maximizers. This view obtained only limited support in conventional circles, partly because it was believed that satisficing behaviour could be described within the standard mathematical framework of constrained maximization. In addition, it is possible to discern a tendency to defend SEU by reinterpreting its axioms. However an explosion of work in the 1980s suggests that there are grounds for rejecting SEU at every level of interpretation. These grounds are mentioned below though, given the Post Keynesian interest in the analysis of uncertainty, we devote more attention to the problems that arise out of attempts to use subjective probability for such analyses.

Despite Friedman's idiosyncratic suggestion that assumptions should not be tested directly (whether or not this is possible), most researchers accept that mathematical axioms do provide a basis on which the positive status of decision theories can be evaluated. There is an extensive literature related to subjective expected utility which shows that SEU is false in two senses. Not only are its violations numerous, but they are also systematic; for this reason, proponents of SEU have had to emphasize other 'non-scientific' interpretations or justifications. (An excellent review of experiments can be found in Baron, 1988.)

Partly as a response to the growing experimental evidence that intelligent subjects violate SEU, mathematical economists have sought to explore the usefulness of non-expected utility theory. On the one hand, many important results in consumer theory and the theory of general equilibrium can be proved without using the restrictive assumptions of SEU. On the other hand, there are now many theories of preferences and beliefs which employ axioms that are considerably weaker than those of SEU. In short, the theory is not nearly so central to the conduct of mathematical economics as was once supposed; if anything, it is seen as a hindrance to the development of theory.

A common argument for SEU is that it represents an ideal of how rational agents should behave, regardless of how people do behave or how their actions might be described mathematically. Criticisms of this interpretation are perhaps the most important as they tackle SEU's last major line of defence. Normative arguments against SEU address both its conceptualization of uncertainty and its characterization of rational preference.

Economists' views about the proper measurement of uncertainty first came to prominence with the distinction due to Knight (1921) between risk, where objective probabilities exist, and uncertainty, where no such statistics are known. This distinction is rendered otiose by the employment of subjective probabilities in situations of uncertainty – or so it was thought until Ellsberg (1961) showed that sensitivity to uncertainty could indeed lead to behaviour which was incompatible with the probability calculus.

There is no doubt about the correctness of the point Ellsberg makes. However, for some time it was played down, perhaps because the issue arose in a discussion of experimental results which were not attributed with any normative significance. More recently, there has been renewed interest in a variety of non-probabilistic concepts of credence including sub-additive probabilities, probability intervals, no probabilities, potential surprise and weight of evidence.

Though Runde (1990) has shown there to be considerable ambiguity in Keynes's embryonic discussion of weight, the concept raises one issue which probability theory does not. In contrast with probability, which is aleatoric and measures risk, weight is an epistemic concept that measures knowledge. How such a measure is to be operationalized is not yet agreed, though in some situations the weight of a sample might appropriately be given by its size, *n*. To a limited extent, classical procedures for hypothesis testing do this already insofar as they make rejection of an hypothesis depend not just on the mean, but on the sample size as well. (However, there is no reason why a decision-maker should be bound to account for the quantity and quality of his/her information using the arbitrary significance levels that scientific convention favours.) If Keynes's view about the weight of evidence and its relationship to uncertainty is approximately correct and also capable of being linked with a theory of rationality, as I believe it is (see Anand, 1993), then Post Keynesians have a powerful and potentially persuasive critique of conventional theory.

Finally, it should be mentioned that there are methodological reasons for being critical of SEU. First, it is often claimed that the value of axioms like transitivity and independence is that they are *behaviourally testable*. However, it is also possible to discern a tendency to discount experimental results which appear to falsify SEU by reinterpreting observations in such a way that are consistent with it. The question then arises, how far can such immunization be pushed? In fact it is possible to show that any intransitive behaviour can be given a transitive description and vice versa. On the one hand, this implies that the axiom is always defensible against empirical evidence, though the defence is expensive since it robs the axiom of any (falsifiable) behavioural content. Second, it is worth noting that whilst SEU is given a deterministic treatment at the level of theory formation, empirical axiom violations are not regarded as falsifying unless they are *systematic*. If, as seems to be the case, not all choices are made in a purely deterministic way, then tests of any axiom will eventually produce errors. And because most partitions of any error set are unequal in size, there are many possible ways in which the errors could be described as non-random. In short, the practice of testing deterministic assumptions against behaviour which is stochastic is logically bound to lead to violations, it being only a matter of time before they are found.

SEU is important both because it describes the decision-making most often used by economists and because it has played a key role in the mathematization of economic theory. The way in which utility has been ascribed new meaning by mathematical economists is reminiscent of the way in which Christianity assimilated pagan festivals for its own very different purposes. Like Christianity, modern utility theory is a mixed blessing. Mathematical techniques have had their most useful impact, not in formalizing debates, but in promoting new ones. The claim that the axioms of SEU are canons of rationality was a major contribution to a philosophical debate that had virtually stalled. On the other hand, every serious justification for using SEU seems now to be false, unnecessary or untenable. Had the mainstream been clearer about what mathematical formalization can achieve, it might have woken up to this fact a little earlier.

PAUL ANAND

References

Anand, P. (1993), *Foundations of Rational Choice Under Risk*, Oxford: Oxford University Press.

Baron, J. (1988), *Thinking and Deciding*, Cambridge: Cambridge University Press.

Ellsberg, D. (1961), 'Risk, Ambiguity and the Savage Axioms', *Quarterly Journal of Economics*, **75**, 643–69.

Knight, F.H. (1921), *Risk, Uncertainty and Profit*, Boston: Houghton Mifflin.

Runde, J. (1990), 'Keynesian Uncertainty and the Weight of Arguments', *Economics and Philosophy*, **6**, 275–92.

Savage, L.J. (1954), *The Foundations of Statistics*, New York: Dover.

Sen, A.K. (1985), 'Rationality and Uncertainty', *Theory and Decision*, **18**, 109–27.

Value

In economics the concept of 'value' is traditionally traced back either to cost or utility or both. In the course of the development of economic analysis, the term 'value' has gradually disappeared from the vocabulary of economics except as a synonym for 'price'. Differences in the theory of value do have their origin in differences in the theory of income distribution.

In classical political economy, utility was considered essential for a thing to have value, i.e. to be a commodity; yet utility was not seen to regulate its exchange value. The latter rather derived from two sources: scarcity and cost of production. Commodities whose values are determined by their scarcity alone (such as rare paintings), i.e. which cannot be reproduced, were set aside: attention focused instead on those commodities whose amounts can be increased (possibly at rising cost) by the exertion of human industry. These authors adopted a 'long-period' method of analysis: emphasis was on 'natural' or 'normal' prices which expressed the persistent, non-accidental causes at work, whereas 'market' or 'actual' prices were also seen to reflect a number of accidental causes, mostly of a temporary nature, which could not be the object of systematic economic analysis.

William Petty argued that each commodity is ultimately the product of land and labour; therefore 'all things ought to be valued by two natural Denominations, which is Land and Labour'. According to Adam Smith 'labour was the first price – the original purchase-money that was paid for all things'; and David Ricardo contended that 'the value of a commodity, or the quantity of any other commodity for which it will exchange, depends on the relative quantity of labour which is necessary for its production'. Both authors maintained that differences in the quality of labour can be reduced to equivalent differences in quantity by means of the given wage structure. Ricardo also pointed out that 'not only the labour applied immediately to commodities affect their value, but the labour also which is bestowed on the implements, tools, and buildings, with which such labour is assisted'. Hence both direct and indirect labour matters in ascertaining the value of a commodity.

Yet Ricardo did not advocate a pure 'labour theory of value'. He saw that with different proportions of means of production, or 'capital', to (direct) labour in the various industries, and with different durabilities of the fixed capital items, the assumed regulation of exchange value in terms of amounts of labour 'embodied' contradicted the notion of free competition. The latter centres around the concept of a rate of profits that is uniform across sectors. Profits are explained in terms of the surplus product left after making allowance for the requirements of reproduction, including wages. The tendency towards a uniform profit rate is the result of the mobility of capital in search of the most profitable employment. With different proportions and durabilities, relative prices would not only depend on the total amount of labour embodied, but also on the level of the general rate of profits, and would change with that level. Since the price of a commodity equals cost of production plus profit calculated at the going profit rate on the value of the capital advanced, an increase in the profit rate (i.e. a decrease in the real wage rate) tends to increase the (relative) prices of all commodities that are produced with a relatively high proportion of means of production to labour and with capital goods that are relatively long-lived. While Ricardo clearly saw that the 'quantity of labour embodied' principle cannot serve as a 'general rule' of value, he called it 'the nearest approximation to truth' and felt justified to develop most of his analysis in terms of that hypothesis. This included the explanation of the rent of land as a consequence of the high price of corn due to diminishing returns in agriculture.

Karl Marx's analysis of the general rate of profits and 'prices of production' derives from the classical approach. Marx adopted a 'successivist' (as opposed to a 'simultaneous') procedure (Ladislaus von Bortkiewicz): in a first step, he specified the competitive rate of profits as the ratio between the labour value of the economy's surplus product, or 'surplus value', s , and the labour value of total capital advanced, C, consisting of a 'constant capital' (means of production), c, and a 'variable capital' (wage goods), v, so that

$$\text{(value) rate of profits} = \rho = \frac{s}{C} = \frac{s}{c + v}.$$

It is here that in Marx's view the labour theory of value is indispensable, because it allegedly allows the determination of the profit rate independently of, and prior to, the determination of relative prices. In a second step this (value) rate of profits, ρ, is then used to calculate prices, starting from sectoral costs of production, or 'cost prices', measured in terms of labour values. This is the (in)famous problem of the 'transformation' of values in prices of production. This 'transformation' is necessitated by the fact that the surplus value in each sector is 'produced' in proportion to the variable capital employed, but in competitive conditions will be 'appropriated' in proportion to total capital advanced. Hence total surplus value of the economic system has to be redistributed such that a uniform rate of profits across sectors obtains. With p_i as the price of one unit of the i-th commodity and c_i and v_i as the corresponding constant and variable capitals,

$$p_i = (1 + \rho)(c_i + v_i),$$

$i = 1, 2, \ldots, n$, where n is the number of commodities. With the values for c_i, v_i and ρ given, the 'prices of production' seem to be fully determined.

Marx's procedure cannot be sustained. Its main flaw consists in the implicit hypothesis that the value-price 'transformation' affects single commodities only, but does not affect commodity aggregates such as the surplus product or total capital, the ratio of which gives the profit rate. Yet it cannot generally be presumed that the 'price' rate of profits, r, equals the 'value' rate, ρ. Since the profit rate cannot be determined before knowing the prices of commodities, and since the prices cannot be determined before knowing the profit rate, prices and the profit rate have to be determined simultaneously rather than successively.

The classical approach to the theory of value and distribution starts from a given 'system of production' in use, characterized by the following data: (i) the technical conditions of production of the various commodities; (ii) the size and composition of the social product, and (iii) the ruling real wage rate(s). The treatment of wages as an independent variable and of rents and profits as dependent residuals exhibits a fundamental *asymmetry* in classical analysis which is in sharp contrast to neoclassical analysis. Yet the classical economists and Marx were not only concerned with studying the properties of a given 'system of production'. In a second stage of the analysis they investigated which system of production would be chosen by profit-seeking entrepreneurs from a set of available technical alternatives. With free competition the involved choice of technique problem consists of finding, given the real wage rate(s), a *cost-minimizing* system of production (including the utilization of natural resources such as land) in which commodity prices, rent(s) and the rate of profits are non-negative, and no method of production yields extra profits.

Modern formulations of the classical approach were put forward by von Neumann (1937) and by Sraffa (1960). Because of his concern with equiproportionate growth in the production of all commodities, von Neumann set aside the problem of scarce natural resources and assumed constant returns to scale throughout. With wages reckoned among the necessary advances of production, and on the premise that all interest (profits) accruing to the owners of capital will be saved and invested, von Neumann was able to demonstrate the existence of a solution to the choice of technique problem and also (given his assumptions) that the growth and the interest (profit) factor are equal. Von Neumann allowed for universal joint production and pointed out that the joint products method is capable of dealing with fixed capital goods. He imposed the 'rule of free goods' to all products that are in excess supply.

Sraffa's analysis is not limited to the special assumptions just mentioned, but deals with scarce natural resources such as land; however, he sets aside exhaustible resources. His analysis is also more complete in that it deals with several aspects of systems of production not mentioned by von Neumann, including the distinction between basic and non-basic products. Sraffa assumes that the number of independent processes operated in the system is equal to the number of commodities produced. The assumption of 'square systems' is, however, not generally valid in the case of joint production, though it is valid in significant circumstances.

The early marginalists singled out utility as the source of exchange value. They typically started with the case of a pure exchange economy in which utility-maximizing agents trade their initial stocks of goods. Emphasis is on goods that are non-reproducible (in the transaction period), i.e. precisely the kinds of goods that were set aside by the classical authors. The argument centres around the concept of decreasing 'marginal utility' as well as the principle of 'substitution' between consumption goods as relative prices change. This leads to the notion of 'demand function' which gives the equilibrium quantities traded by the consumer as a function of prices. The problem of production and cost was addressed only subsequently. While in the early classical authors we find a backward linkage relating the value of final goods to primary factors, in particular labour, the early marginalist authors were concerned with establishing a forward linkage by means of which factor services could be evaluated, or 'priced', according to the usefulness of final goods (this is the famous problem of 'imputation' of the value of output to the factors of production).

This approach, another variant of 'successivist' reasoning, was eventually replaced by one of simultaneous determination of prices and quantities, including the prices and quantities of 'factor services', i.e. income distribution. Such a simultaneous determination was put forward by Léon Walras, whose ideas filtered into the economics profession only slowly because of his use of symbolic language. It was Alfred Marshall's contribution that paved the way to the rise to predominance of the new doctrine. The principle of substitution was generalized to the sphere of production, with the concept of 'marginal productivity' of factors of production as the mirror-image of that of the marginal utility of goods. To the demand function was added the 'supply function' which gives the profit-maximizing quantities supplied by the producer as a function of prices. The success of Marshall's analysis was largely due to his method of 'partial equilibrium' which, in contradistinction to that of 'general equilibrium', was considered practicably applicable to concrete issues.

The marginalists sought to be able to separate the contribution to the product of each agent of production from that of cooperating agents, and thus solve the problem of distribution in terms of the notion of marginal productivity. The crucial concept in traditional versions of the theory is that of a factor called 'capital', the demand and supply of whose services determines the profit rate in a similar way as the demand and supply of labour is taken to determine the wage rate. In equilibrium the profit rate would be equal to the marginal product of 'capital'. However, in order to be consistent with the concept of a long-period competitive equilibrium, the capital equipment of the economy could not be conceived as a set of given physical amounts of capital goods, but had to be expressed as a *value* magnitude. Otherwise only a short-period equilibrium, characterized by differential rates of return on the supply prices of the various capital goods, could be established. The formidable problem of the marginalist approach consisted of establishing the notion of a market for 'capital', the quantity of which could be expressed independently of the profit rate. If such a market could be conceptualized, profits could be explained analogously to wages and a theoretical edifice could be erected on the universal applicability of the principle of demand and supply. However, as the controversy in the theory of capital in the 1960s and 1970s has shown, this is not possible other than in exceedingly special circumstances.

The data from which the theory typically starts are: (i) initial endowments of the economy with factors of production and goods, and their distribution among agents; (ii) preferences of consumers, and (iii) the set of technical alternatives. On the basis of these givens, the theory tries to find an 'equilibrium' price vector that simultaneously clears all markets. In some representations, demand and supply functions (or correspondences) are constructed for each good and service. The intersection between a demand and the corresponding supply function then gives the equilibrium values of the quantity traded and the price ruling in the respective market. In general equilibrium, the value of excess demand is zero whatever price system is set. This is known as 'Walras's Law'. With 'free disposal' of (joint) products that are in excess supply, prices must be non-negative.

In general equilibrium theory of the Arrow-Debreu variety, the distribution of income is determined on the basis of given *physical* endowments of agents (see Debreu, 1959). This involves the abandonment of the traditional long-period method and its concern with a uniform rate of profits. However, because firms prefer more profits to less, the size and composition of the capital stock will rapidly change. Thus, major factors which general equilibrium theory envisages as determining prices and quantities are themselves subject to quick changes. This makes it difficult to distinguish them from the accidental and temporary factors affecting the economy at any given moment in time. More important, the potentially vast variations in relative prices necessitate the consideration of the influence of future states of the world on the present situation.

This is approached in two alternative ways. Either it is boldly assumed that there is a complete set of future markets, which leads to the concept of 'intertemporal equilibrium', or individual price expectations concerning future deliveries of commodities for which no present markets exist are introduced; this leads to the concept of 'temporary equilibrium'. The basic weakness of the latter concerns the necessarily arbitrary choice of hypotheses about individual price expectations. In addition, the stability properties of this kind of equilibrium are unclear, since small perturbations caused by accidental factors may entail changes in the expectations which define that very equilibrium.

HEINZ D. KURZ

References

Debreu, G. (1959), *Theory of Value: An Axiomatic Analysis of Economic Equilibrium*, New Haven and London: Yale University Press.

Neumann, J. von (1937), 'Über ein ökonomisches Gleichungssystem und eine Verallgemeinerung des Brouwerschen Fixpunktsatzes', *Ergebnisse eines mathematischen Kolloquiums*, **8**. English translation (1945) entitled 'A Model of General Economic Equilibrium', *Review of Economic Studies*, **13**.

Sraffa, P. (1960), *Production of Commodities by Means of Commodities*, Cambridge: Cambridge University Press.

Walsh, V. and Gram, H. (1980), *Classical and Neoclassical Theories of General Equilibrium: Historical Origins and Mathematical Structure*, New York and Oxford: Oxford University Press.

Wage-earner funds

The term 'wage-earner funds' generally refers to intermediate employee-ownership of stock capital in private firms. In the search for a 'third way between big-business capitalism and state-centred socialism', various fund schemes have been discussed throughout Europe (see Meidner, 1981). On a range between 'people's capitalism' and 'fund socialism', the proposals vary significantly in their objectives and constructions. Most of them are primarily concerned with the distribution of incomes and wealth or – more specifically – of share-ownership and economic control. Other schemes are more concerned with growth by way of increased savings and investments, or with stabilization through wage restraints and decreased debt-equity ratios (see Öhman, 1985).

Conservative schemes generally aim at a moderation of wage conflicts and at the propagation of private property through widespread share-ownership. Consequently, such 'people's capitalists' advocate voluntary investment-wage or profit-sharing schemes by which employees acquire individual shares in investment funds. More radical schemes mostly aim at an 'equitable' redistribution of productive property and at economic democracy by way of a trade-union based socialization of investment. Consequently, such 'fund socialists' advocate compulsory profit-sharing and capital-formation schemes, by which wage earners gain collective control over strategic assets in the economy.

Both types of proposals have been discussed in several countries such as West Germany, the Netherlands and Denmark. Yet nowhere has the debate been as radical and real as in Sweden. So far, Sweden is the only country where collective wage-earner funds have been established in a scheme that was meant to serve conflicting purposes of distribution, growth and stabilization. Therefore, the following account of the rationale and dilemmata of wage-earner funds concentrates on the Swedish case.

In 1975, Rudolf Meidner and two other researchers appointed by the Confederation of Swedish Trade Unions, LO, published a proposal for wage-earner funds (*löntagarfonder*) that combined compulsory profit-sharing with collective ownership of stock capital in private firms (see Meidner, 1978 and 1981). In 1976, the LO adopted this scheme with slight modifications, hoping to implement it by means of the unions' close links with the ruling Social Democrats. The initial scheme pursued three goals. The wage-earner funds aimed at:

1. complementing the Solidaristic Wage Policy of the LO by socializing 'excess profits' that resulted from wage restraints;
2. counteracting the concentration of economic power by capitalizing the socialized 'excess profits' in collective investment funds;

3. strengthening the co-determination at the workplace through participation in ownership.

These goals were to be pursued under the restrictions of full employment, price-level stability and sufficient growth rates.

According to the initial LO scheme, 20 per cent of the pre-tax profits of joint-stock companies were to be transferred to a central fund by way of compulsory share issues (non-stock companies were to contribute in cash). The capital itself would remain productive in the original companies, but the property rights to it would be exercised by several bodies representing different collectives of the new employee-owners:

- The board of the central fund would be elected by all trade unions. The fund would administer the incomes from deposited wage-earner shares, investing in more shares of strategic importance and in further education, research and consultation for the benefit of all wage-earners.
- The voting rights of wage-earner shares would be exercised partly by local representatives and partly by branch councils.

Thus the distribution of property rights to the wage-earner funds would be balanced between local, sectoral and general interests of wage earners.

The original fund scheme never materialized, as the Social Democrats were defeated in the 1976 elections to the Swedish parliament. Although the wage-earner fund issue haunted the public debate during several election campaigns after 1976, the radical goals of a redistribution of economic power were toned down in favour of new goals of growth and stabilization in the wake of a deep crisis between 1977 and 1982. Thereafter the funds were to facilitate wage restraints and the formation of risk capital. Stressing these objectives, LO and the Social Democrats endorsed a more decentralized fund scheme that combined compulsory profit-sharing with statutory investment-saving through payroll taxes.

After their re-election in 1982, the Social Democrats introduced collective wage-earner funds in 1984. In the scheme eventually implemented, even the risk-capital motive was toned down in favour of complementary savings for old-age pensions. Thus the newly created wage-earner funds became part of the General Pension Funds system. As such, their impact on savings and investment was marginal. Neither did their statutory risk aversion and their unexpectedly small revenues from payroll and profit taxation allow them to play a distinctive role in the capital market; nor did they cause significant disinvestment or capital flight (as had been 'predicted' by numerous opponents). But while the wage-earner funds never gained much practical importance in the Swedish economy, they remained a hot ideological issue in the political debate. Accordingly, the non-socialist parties announced the abolition of the wage-earner funds when they came back into power in 1991.

Even though the goals of the fund schemes of 1976 and 1984 seem incompatible, the following shows that the same vagueness of elementary definition applied to both the radical and the moderate fund conceptions. The background provided by the Solidaristic Wage Policy certainly was specific, but the conceptual problems of definition apply in general to all collective fund schemes.

Compulsory profit-sharing may be based upon purely political arguments. But usually an economic justification is presented in the form of claims to wage shares that wage earners have been prevented from taking home for reasons either of short-term stabilization or long-term growth. In the Swedish case, both types of arguments were used, with a strong emphasis on distributive equality.

Between the 1950s and the 1980s, the LO pursued a centralized wage policy under the slogan 'equal pay for equal work'. This aimed both at squeezing wage differentials and at keeping wage levels in Swedish industries within the margins of international competitiveness. Sub-marginal firms should not be allowed to compensate for low profitability by lower wages. Instead of tolerating insufficient productivity at the expense of locked-in employees, the unions favoured closures and relocations by means of an active labour-market policy.

This structural rationalization effect of the Solidaristic Wage Policy was limited by the general cost restraints of competitiveness. Therefore, the squeeze of wage differentials had an undesired side-effect: it demanded and produced wage restraints in firms with high profitability, which thereby earned profits in excess of normal returns to capital. Insofar as such 'wage policy rents' added to their capital stocks, the employers gained bargaining power *vis-à-vis* the trade unions.

The LO thus had strong motives for the neutralization of wage-policy rents:

- If they remained as 'excess profits', they would add to the economic power of its adversaries.
- If they dissipated into wage drift, they would jeopardize LO solidarity by increasing wage differentials.
- If they were reduced by centrally negotiated wage increases, cost-push and demand-pull effects could endanger economic stability and growth.

Compulsory profit-sharing seemed to offer a way out of this trilemma. Yet, apart from risks of disinvestment and capital flight, profit-sharing could not escape a basic flaw of the Solidaristic Wage Policy: its lack of precision as to what was to be considered 'equal work'.

For various reasons, the LO had failed to develop an assessment standard of qualifications and working conditions which was independent of market-bound wage determination and yet consistent with the needs of international competitiveness. Without an explicit 'equal work' classification, wage-policy rents could not be properly identified. The seemingly clear-cut economic argument for profit-sharing became a diffuse political argument in terms of defining the mode of 'excess profit' taxation. Those firms that eventually had to share their profits with wage-earner funds were not necessarily those that had profited from the 'equal pay for equal work' policy.

In the Swedish debate, a strict distinction was made between the wage-*structure* arguments for profit-sharing in the early, radical proposals and the wage-*level* arguments in the later, more moderate proposals (see Öhman, 1985, pp. 17ff). While the radical proposals aimed to provide compensations for structural wage restraints, regardless of the wage level, the moderate proposals aimed to trade wage-level restraints for profit-sharing.

Without consistent criteria for 'excess profits', however, the distinction between structural and global arguments was a matter of political emphasis, not of economic substance. Initially, the preservation of union solidarity was the goal, and macroeconomic stability its restriction; later, an equitable distribution of income restraints was made preconditional for macro-stability. The 'cost crisis' in the late 1970s and early 1980s had changed the perspective; however, in view of international competitiveness, wage-*level* restraints were a motive underlying *all* proposals for wage-earner funds.

No matter how well the base of profit-sharing schemes is founded, once they get going they provide a base for capital formation. But while the neutralization of 'excess profits' basically was a negative end, the accumulation of wage-earner capital clearly needed positive objectives.

The main objective of the LO's fund schemes was generally summarized as 'economic democracy': collective ownership of capital should complete the (very limited) co-determination based on labour law. Such socialization of investment conflicted with the 'functional socialism' of the Swedish Social Democrats who had maintained a rather strict separation between a private-company sphere of capital accumulation and a welfare-state sphere of income redistribution. As the private industries were held to be the motor of economic activity, which the welfare state both thrived upon and supported, the Social Democrats had cooperated with 'big business' in the formation of powerful multinational corporations (cf. Israel, 1978; Lundberg, 1985).

Wage-earner funds were to challenge this private concentration of capital and voting power. They threatened to interfere with the functionalistic 'division of labour' between the political ruling party and the economically cooperating, but not essentially co-determining, trade unions. Yet the unions did not make clear how the power of wage-earner funds would be used. Their concept of 'economic democracy' hardly went beyond declarations that wage-earner funds would act 'differently' from other capital owners.

This vagueness had its roots, again, in basic conflicts between goals of distribution and stabilization in trade union policy. Profit-sharing may create a sort of buffer stock. But when it comes to exercising the property rights to such buffer-stock funds, the interdependence of union solidarity and macroeconomic stability tends to develop into a trade-off on a higher level. Either the fund representatives try to influence investment decisions in terms of employment, work environment or other employee interests, or they confirm profit-maximizing investment decisions. Either they support changes in the production process that may reduce profits, thereby risking the obstruction and flight of other capital owners, or they risk the opposition of the affected employees.

The question is whether the 'normal' yield requirements of the stock market would allow for margins that wage-earner funds could exploit for systematic promotion of wage-earner interests. But lack of knowledge about such 'normal yields' in the multinational corporations of a small open economy was and is even deeper than lack of knowledge about 'excess profits'.

Another question is how the funds would decide when local employee interests and central trade union interests conflicted. If the funds have a centralistic bias, the wage earners 'at the base' will hardly win a new perspective of co-determination. If the funds have a local bias, differences between local working conditions (and wages) will grow and impair the internal cohesion of the trade unions.

All in all, the confusion about the contents of 'economic democracy' reduced the Swedish fund plans to an extremely moderate scheme of additional pension funds. This was because the socialization of investment aroused strong opposition from private capital owners and managers while failing to win the support of the large majority of wage earners. There seemed to be a widespread intuition that the trade unions could not overcome their inherent conflicts – between securing employment and real income increases and maintaining their macroeconomic preconditions – simply by assuming dual roles of wage contractors and capital owners.

HANS-MICHAEL TRAUTWEIN

References

Israel, Joakim (1978), 'Swedish Socialism and Big Business', *Acta Sociologica*, **21**, 341–52.

Lundberg, Erik (1985), 'The Rise and the Fall of the Swedish Model', *Journal of Economic Literature*, **23**, 1–36.

Meidner, Rudolf (1978), *Employee Investment Funds: An Approach to Collective Capital Formation*, London: George Allen & Unwin.

Meidner, Rudolf (1981), 'Collective Asset Formation through Wage-Earner Funds', *International Labour Review*, **120**, 303–17.
Öhman, Berndt (1985), 'Collective Workers' Saving and Industrial Democracy', University of Örebro, Department of Government: Research Report 85–1.

Wages, money and real

Wages are payments made to people in exchange for their labour-time. Whilst we will talk of money wages, this should be interpreted to include both monetary and non-monetary payments (e.g. benefits-in-kind) and also the part of wages that may be deferred (e.g. pensions).

In macro-economic analysis, reference is often made to *the* money wage and *the* real wage. The money wage (represented by w below) is taken as representative of the average wages in an economy, although there will always be considerable problems of aggregation. Real wage refers to the ratio of money wage to some appropriate price index.

In neoclassical economics, wages (like any other price) play an allocative role, with relative wages determining the allocation of labour between different activities. In political economy, wages undertake other roles, notably those of distribution and position.

An approach to the determination of real wages and employment found in most economics textbooks is based on the interaction of the demand and supply of labour within an aggregate labour market. This approach can be extended to allow for numerous disaggregated labour markets, permitting the determination of relative wages and the allocation of employment. In the aggregate labour market version, the equilibrium real wage equates the demand and supply of labour, which themselves are functions of the real wage only (though the real wage relevant for demand may differ from that relevant for supply because of, for example, taxation). The adjustment process whereby the rate of change of (expected) real wages depends on the excess demand of labour underlies the Phillips curve and is represented by:

$$\dot{\overline{(w/p)}} = f(ED_L) \tag{1}$$

where w and p are indices of wages and prices respectively and ED_L stands for excess demand for labour; a dot above a variable signifies proportionate rate of change of that variable. From (1), the following can be derived:

$$\dot{w} = g(U) + \dot{p}^e \tag{2}$$

where unemployment U acts as a (negative) proxy for the excess demand for labour and $\dot{p}^e$ is the expected rate of change of prices. This corresponds to the view that whilst real wages are influenced by conditions in the labour market, the adjustment process involves changes in money wages. However, the underlying view is that real wages are settled in the labour market.

Political economists dispute this analysis in numerous ways. First, the demand for labour depends on the level of aggregate demand, and may be little influenced by the real wage. Indeed at the level of the firm, labour costs are generally a small proportion of the total. Second, the supply of labour may be demand-driven in that some people enter or leave the labour force in response to the availability or otherwise of jobs. Further, some would doubt the existence of a labour market in which real wages are determined. Labour, being human, is clearly different from other factors of production and other commodities. There is a difference between labour and labour-power: in other words the productivity of labour depends on work intensity, which itself is influenced by degree of work discipline and management control. Further, the level and structure of wages can be used by employers to stimulate work intensity and productivity.

The post Keynesian approach disputes that the real wage is settled in the labour market; some would go further and question the existence of a labour market in a form anything like that portrayed in neoclassical economics. Keynes argued that '[t]here may exist no expedient by which labour as a whole can reduce its *real* wage to a given figure by making revised *money* bargains with entrepreneurs. ... We shall endeavour to show that primarily it is certain other forces which determine the general level of real wages' (Keynes, 1936, p. 13; emphasis in original). In Keynes's schema, the level of employment is settled by the level of aggregate demand, and the real wage is equal to the resulting marginal product of labour. Whilst that equality appears the same as the neoclassical one, the manner in which the equality is brought about is quite different. Whereas in the neoclassical approach, employment is adjusted to ensure the equality, with both wages and prices being parametric for each firm, for Keynes it was prices which adjusted rapidly. In such an analysis, for a given level of aggregate demand, the level of the money wage is irrelevant. Thus whereas Keynes has often been accused of assuming a fixed money wage, his approach can be seen as involving any level of the money wage. Any effect of the money wage level on employment then arises from its impact on the level of aggregate demand.

In Kalecki's analysis the price/wage relativity is set by the pricing decisions of firms, with the price-cost margin determined by the degree of monopoly (Kalecki, 1971, Ch. 5). Representing the aggregate price decision by:

$$p = (1 + m)\,(wL/Q + g) \qquad (3)$$

the symbols are as above, with the addition that L stands for units of labour employed, Q of output, g the unit (imported) material cost and m the overall mark-up. Then the real wage is given by:

$$(w/p) = [1/(1 + m)] \,.\, (Q/L) - (g/p) \,.\, (Q/L). \qquad (4)$$

Movements in real wages then arise variously from movements in labour productivity, the price-cost margin and the ratio of imported costs to domestic prices. The real wage is strongly influenced by the mark-up, m, which itself is determined by the degree of monopoly. In his original formulation, Kalecki envisaged the degree of monopoly as determined at the level of the industry by factors such as concentration and advertising intensity. He later (1971, Ch. 14) extended this to include the bargaining power of trade unions.

The implicit assumption of both Keynes and Kalecki is that workers accept the real wage set by firms' pricing decisions. Such a view has not gone unchallenged! The classical and Marxian approaches include a subsistence wage linked to the reproduction of labour. This subsistence wage is not the minimum necessary for survival, as it is recognized that the concept of necessity is socially conditioned (Rowthorn, 1980, Chapter 7). The important implication of such a view here is that the mark-up (and the rate of profit, which is usually given more attention in this context) would adjust to conform to this subsistence wage.

It may be accepted that in the short run, firms' pricing decisions set the real wage, but that the setting of money wages makes some (perhaps complete) allowance for subsequent expected price changes. Also, that in the long run, equation (4) or its equivalent is only one equation complemented by another arising from wage setting. Equation (4) can be treated as involving two variables, namely the real wage and the level of employment (with output a function of employment and the mark-up varying with output). The model can be completed by postulating that the level of employment is set by the level of aggregate demand; this is the route taken by Kalecki and Keynes. However, if the aspirations of workers and their ability to achieve those aspirations are positively related to the level of employment, this can be written as:

$$(w/p) = h(L, z) \qquad (5)$$

where z is a vector of other variables (including terms of trade, profitability and bargaining strength). Equations (4) and (5) then provide a model in which the real wage and employment are jointly determined without reference to the level of aggregate demand.

In the Post Keynesian approach, particular emphasis has been placed on the observation that it is money wages that are agreed between employer and employee. This agreement may arise through formal or informal collective bargaining or may be imposed by the employer. The real wage depends on subsequent action by firms over prices.

This approach relies heavily on the notion that money wage determination is seen as the outcome of a bargaining process which is treated as an expression of conflict over relative income shares. The money-wage aspirations of workers find expression both in the conflict between workers and employers and in the struggle of workers to maintain differentials via a desired real wage. The aspirations of workers and their economic and political power are of vital importance to the determination of money wages (Rowthorn, 1980, Ch. 6). One crucial problem with this approach is the determination of the desired real wage. There are a number of ways to tackle this difficulty. One takes the previously achieved peak real wage as the relevant proxy for the desired real wage. Another view puts the emphasis on the costs associated with the pursuit and maintenance of the desired real wage, with these costs being assumed to increase *pari passu* with it. A third view treats the problem as the outcome of a maximization process, where what is maximized is the union's utility function (with the real wage and unemployment being its main variables) subject to the constraints as presented by employers. A predetermined desired real wage has also been utilized, premised on the argument that it is generated by the expectations and aspirations of unions and workers in general, along with a host of other social, political and economic factors.

Whilst this approach relies heavily on the relevant position of the real wage to the desired real wage, there is another important, in fact complementary, constituent element which can be included in this theoretical framework. This is the wage-relativities component which played a key role in the explanation of money-wage stickiness in Keynes's *General Theory* (Hicks, 1974; Wood, 1978). Such a theoretical element can easily be incorporated as a component of the desired real wage. We may think of this link as an attempt by each group of workers to restore their wage differentials relative to other comparable groups. A proposition which is rooted in Keynes (1936, p. 14) is that workers care about both their position in the relative wage structure and the real wage rate. This argument rests on the assumption that workers resist reductions in their wage rates which they perceive as a decrease in their relative wage. The implication of this proposition is that money wage rates are historically given and workers' concern over wage-relativities does not allow wage rates to fall even under conditions of unemployment. This is so since each group of workers expects the average nominal wage of other groups to remain unchanged. Thus workers resist attempts to reduce their demands for wage increases below the expected average rate. We may therefore consider this wage rate as a benchmark below which it is difficult to force wage changes. This is consistent with Wood's (1978) theoretical proposition that there are two types of pressures operating in wage-formation. There are the 'anomic pressures' which are viewed as a result of labour shortages and other competitive influences. More important though, from our point of view, is the second type, the 'normative pressures' which emanate from pay norms and from perceptions of what a 'fair wage' is. This argument provides a general theoretical framework within which Keynes's concern with wage-relativities can be treated as a special case.

A further relevant theoretical element in the money wage determination process is the recognition of the existence of significant hysteresis effects. Wage and profit aspirations of different groups can be expected to depend on past distributional outcomes. It is this feature which may introduce a significant element of inertia into the system. The term hysteresis means 'that which comes after' and postulates that the 'equilibrium' rate of unemployment is a consequence of past actual rates, so that a rise in unemployment may increase its 'equilibrium' rate, if not permanently, then at least for a considerable period. Three main hypotheses have been advanced to explain hysteresis effects. There is the *duration* explanation which draws the distinction between long-term and short-term unemployed. It demonstrates that the long-term unemployed exert little pressure on wages. The second is based on the distinction between insiders (the employed) and outsiders (the unemployed) and is labelled as the *membership* theory. Wage determination in this view is influenced by inside workers rather than by the unemployed. The third hypothesis, the *capacity scrapping* theory, emphasizes the role aggregate demand has on capacity, utilization and thus investment, so that capacity utilization is related to rates of unemployment.

The hysteresis arguments sit comfortably with the theoretical propositions elucidated earlier on wage relativities and desired real wages. In fact, in Arestis and Skott (1993), hysteresis effects are introduced in a model incorporating wage relativities and target real wages to arrive at a general model of money wage determination which performs satisfactorily on both theoretical and empirical grounds. Conflict elements are the backbone of this theoretical framework.

PHILIP ARESTIS AND MALCOLM SAWYER

References

Arestis, P. and Skott, P. (1993), 'Conflict, Wage Relativities and Hysteresis in U.K. Wage Determination', *Journal of Post Keynesian Economics*, **15** (3), Spring, 365–86.

Hicks, J.R. (1974), *The Crisis in Keynesian Economics*, Oxford: Blackwell.

Kalecki, M. (1971), *Selected Essays on the Dynamics of the Capitalist Economy, 1933–70*, Cambridge: Cambridge University Press.

Keynes, J.M. (1936), *The General Theory of Employment, Interest and Money*, London: Macmillan.
Rowthorn, R. (1980), *Capitalism, Conflict and Inflation*, London: Lawrence and Wishart.
Wood, A. (1978), *A Theory of Pay*, Cambridge: Cambridge University Press.

Index

Page references in **bold type** indicate the main text entries.

absolute (intensive) rent 334, 337
accelerator 440, 442
accumulation xii, **1–5**
  development finance 21
  distribution 1, 3–4, 97–101, 185–90
  nature of process 31
  neo-Marxian growth 185–90
  over-accumulation 233
  peripheral 294
  rate 180–82
  regulation theory 85, 328–32, 368
  state role 423
  taxation 401–6
  see also social structure of accumulation
accumulation regimes 85, 330, 331
adaptive expectations hypothesis (AEH) 135, 136
aggregate demand **5–10**, 10–11
  dual labour markets 107–9
  effective demand 117
  employment and wages 474
  neo-Marxian growth 188–9
aggregate supply **10–15**
Aglietta, M. 85, 163–4
agricultural sector 295, 343
allocative efficiency 120
Amsterdam school 329, 331
analytical method 89–91
animal spirits **15–19**, 234
anthropology 34–5
antithesis 86, 88
antitrust **38–43**
arbitrage 381
Arrow–Debreu model 129
Asimakopulos, A. 398–400
aspiration gap 188, 208–9
assembly-line production 121–2, 236–7
  see also Fordism
Austria 354, 355–6
Austrian school 199, 200
autarky 455, 456

balanced growth 83
Balibar, Etienne 273
bank capital *see* finance capital
Bank for International Settlements (BIS) 224
banks **20–24**
  credit creation 115
  financial instability hypothesis 155, 156
  international finance 223–4
  monetary circuits 274–7
  money and credit 279–81
Baran, Paul 289
  dependency 76–7
  monopoly capital 283–6 *passim*
  underdevelopment 84, 445
bargaining position 389–90
  see also collective bargaining; wage bargaining
Bayesianism 113, 458–9
bipolarity 172
bounded rationality 66–7
Braverman, H. 123, 124, 236
Britain *see* United Kingdom
Bruno, M. 50
Burbidge, J. 398–400
business cycles xiii, **24–8**
  equilibrium analysis 128–9
  financial instability hypothesis 153–7
  underconsumption 440–43

Cambridge school 115, 347–8
capacity
  costs of production 54–5
  investment theory 232–3
  utilization 182–4, 254, 391–3
capital
  and capital endowment 251
  fictitious 149–50
  finance **148–53**, 286, 311–12
  industrial 149, 151, 311–2
  international flows 221–2, 223

internationalization 172–3, 202–3, 289
marginal efficiency of 116
merchant (commercial) 311–12
metropolitan 445–6
segmentation 346–7
self-expanding value 242–3
substitution for labour 413–14
taxation 398
see also tax incidence; taxation
trade and prices 226–7
value 466
capital budgeting 378–9
capital credit 150
capital-labour relations 421
labour process debate 236–40
neo-Marxian growth theory 185–9
see also employment relationship; exploitation
capital markets 20
aggregate demand 7–8
contested exchange 304–5
separated from banking 20, 21–2
capital-reversing result 32
capital shortage unemployment 413
capital theory controversies **29–34**
capitalism
dependency theories 75–81
development of 58
dynamics of 201–2
exploitation 138–42
monopoly, 39, 76, **282–6**
regulation theory 329–31
theories of 47
Carabelli, A.M. 18
cartels 151
causality 279
functional 271
central bank 279–81
centralized wage bargaining 50–51
centre-periphery models 63, 384–7
see also peripheral economies
certainty 437
see also uncertainty
champions, national 200–201
Chandler, Alfred 160–61
chaotic dynamical systems 27–8
Chicago school 41
Chick, V. 22
childcare 147
China 299
Christian socialism 430
circuits, monetary **274–8**
circulation
exploitation 140–42
profit rate 326–7
circulation credit 149–50
see also credit
class, social xiii, **34–8**
conflict and SSA 367–70
consumption 43–4, 46
distribution 97–101
distribution of taxes 404
Marxian global political economy 172
Marxist feminism 167–8
power and neo-Marxian growth 185–8
recession and 448
structural change 313
classical economics
competition 38–9
consumption 43–4, 46
distribution 97–8
rent 333–4
surplus approach 389–91
value 462–3, 464
classical statistics 112–13
collective action
social conventions 357–62
see also political action; trade unions
collective bargaining 210, 431–2
see also trade unions; wage bargaining
commercial capital 311–12
commodities 89
taxes on 398
see also tax incidence; taxation
communism 59, 272
compensation principle 280
compensation theory of technological change 411–13
competition **38–43**
accumulation 2
corporations 160–61
discrimination 91–2, 93–6
growth poles 177–8
industrial policy 200–202
labour process debate 239
markets 261, 262
monopoly capitalism 284

perfect 39
profit rate 38–9, 42, 327–8
TNCs 289
computer-based technology 57
concentration 149, 151–2
concertation 353–7
'concrete situations of dependency' 76, 79–80
conflict
approach to inflation 208–9
class 367–70
consensus 49–50
consumption **43–7**
dual consumption function 339–40
female employment and 145–6
international trade 228–9
monetary circuits 276
necessary 35–6
savings 338–41
underconsumption 233, 338–9, **438–43**
consumption goods sector 343–4
content, form and 86–7
contested exchanges 45, 302–5
contingent renewal strategies 302–4
continuous equilibrium analysis 130–31
control
firms and corporations 158–61
unemployment as 449
see also power
conventions
interest rates 219–20
social **357–62**
uncertainty and 437–8
convergence debate 417
cooperation 359–61
core-periphery models 63, 384–7
see also peripheral economies
corporations 39, 40, **158–62**
corporatism **47–52**
neo-corporatism 353–7
costs of production **52–7**
Cowling, Keith 285
credit
international finance 223–4
monetary circuits 275–7
money and 149–50, **278–82**
see also debt
crises **57–62**, 152, 224
SSA 369–70
critical realism 111–12, 267–8
crowding out 321–2
Cuban Revolution 75
cumulative causation **62–5**, 292–3
cycles *see* business cycles

Damania, D. 399–400
Davidson, Paul 222–3
De Janvry, A. 108–9
debt
financial deregulation and 240–41
financial instability hypothesis 156–7
international finance 223–4
monetary circuits 275–7
see also credit
debt crisis 74, 224
debt deflations 153–4
decentralized planning 298–9
decision making **66–70**
monetary circuits 275–6
short period 350–53
utility 458–61
de-industrialization **70–75**
demand xvi
aggregate *see* aggregate demand
effective *see* effective demand
markets and 260
demand function 465
democratic socialism 319, 323
Denmark 357
dependency theory **75–81**, 82, 83–4, 103
deregulation, financial 340–41
de-skilling 103–4
determinism 273
development **81–6**
regulation theory 82, 84–5, 330–31
state role 81, 423, 443–4
underdevelopment *see* underdevelopment
uneven *see* uneven development
see also growth
development economics 443–5
dialectical unity 80–81
dialectics **86–91**
differential (extensive) rent 334–7
diffusion of technology 416–19
directive planning 297–8
directly unproductive profit-seeking activities (DUP) 314
discrimination **91–7**, 450

disequilibrium dynamics 41–2
displacement theory of technological change 411
distribution **97–101**
  and accumulation 1, 3–4, 97–101, 185–90
  aggregate supply 14
  dual labour markets 108–9
inequality 203–7
  neo-Marxian growth theory 185–90
  prices and pricing 309
  social policy 365
  socializaton of investment 375
  surplus approach 389–93
  underconsumption 439, 441–2
  taxation and 400, 402–3, 403–4
  value 464–7
divide and conquer model 92, 96
division of labour **101–5**, 121, 373
doctrine of mathematical expectation (DME) 133, 136
domestic labour 146, 147, 312–13
  debate 167–70
dominant firms 175–9
dual consumption function 339–40
dual labour markets 103, 104, **106–9**, 347
dual-system theories 169
Duhem-Quine thesis 113

Eastern Europe 364
  see also Hungary
ECLA (United Nations Commission for Latin America) structuralist school 76, 78–9, 384–7
eclectic theory 288
ecology 374
econometrics **110–14**
economic democracy 471–2
economies of scale 55–7
effective demand 12, **114–19**
  surplus approach 391–3
efficiency **119–23**
  see also productivity
Eichner, A.S. 307–8
Emmanuel, A. 453–4, 456–7
employee investment funds 377–8, **468–73**
employment
  aggregate supply 12, 14
  contracts **123–7**
  de-industrialization 71, 73
  effective demand 116–17
  female **143–8**
  full 9–10, 182–3, 253–4
  monetary circuits 276
  neo-Marxian growth 187
  wages and 475
  see also unemployment
employment relationship **123–7**
  contested exchange 302–4
  firms and corporations 158–61
  see also capital–labour relations
endogenous cycle theory 25–7
endogenous money 278–82
enterprise, speculation and 381
epistemological hysteresis 196
equilibrium theory/analysis 62, **127–33**
  aggregate demand 6–7
  capital theory controversies 31, 32–3
  inter-temporal 128–9, 251–2, 466–7
  long-run 127–8, 251–3
  partial 465
  shifting 14
  short-run/temporary 129–30, 252–3, 351–3, 467
  static 62
  value 466–7
  Walrasian general equilibrium model 301–4
equity 204, 365, 373
Europe: peripheral Fordism **292–6**
European Community (EC) 239
exclusion 105
  principle of 94–5
expanded reproduction 343–4
expectations 16, **133–8**
expenditure 283
  public *see* public expenditure
  see also consumption
exploitation **138–42**, 325
  social pathology of unemployment 448–52
  underdevelopment 445–7
export sectors 344
extensive (differential) rent 334–7
external disequilibria 385–6

Fabianism 362
factories 159

family wage 168–9
Fascism 430
female employment/unemployment **143–8**
feminism 104, 143–4, 312–13
  Marxist 167–9
  radical 167
Ferge, A. 364–5
fictitious capital 149–50
finance **20–23**
  international **221–6**, 294
finance capital **148–53**, 286, 311–12
financial deregulation 340–41
financial instability hypothesis **153–8**
firms **158–62**
  dominant 175–9
  see also institutions
first-order uncertainty 437
Fitzgibbons, A. 18
flexible specialization 165, 237
folk theorem 360
forces of production 87–8, 270–71
Fordism **162–6**, 292–3, 294
  development and 85
  division of labour 103
  efficiency 121–2
  labour process debate 236–7
  peripheral 85, **292–6**
  post-Fordism **162–6**, 237
form, content and 86–7
France 299–300, 356
Frank, A.G. 75–6, 77, 84, 446
free loanable capital theory 256
full employment 9–10, 182–3, 253–4
functional causality 271
fund socialism 468
  see also wage-earner funds
fundamentalist Keynesians 434–5

game theory 359–60
gender **167–70**
  see also women
general equilibrium theory *see* equilibrium theory
German school of regulation 329, 331–2
Germany 354, 368
global political economy **171–4**
Goodwin, R. 5, 26–7
Gramsci, Antonio 60, 163
Gramscian approach to global political economy 173–4
Greece 295, 296
Green politics 59–60
group utility 69
growth
  balanced 83
  investment and 407
  Keynesian theories **180–85**
  neo-Marxian theories **185–90**
  sectoral balance **342–6**
  steady-state model 129–30
  warranted 3, 180–82, 189
  see also development
growth poles **174–9**
GRREC (Search Group on the Regulation of Capitalist Economies) 329, 331

Harrod, Roy 3, 26, 180–81
Hayek, Friedrich von 266
health status 207
heavy industry model 178–9
hedge financing 156–7
Hegel, G.W.F. 86–91 *passim*
hermeneuticism 266–7, 268
Hilferding, Rudolf 148–53, 282–3
Hobsbawm, E. 59
Hobson, John 439
holistic approaches 86–7
horizontal integration 414
horizontalists 281
human motivation **191–4**
Humean theory of knowledge 264–6
Hungary 364–5
Hymer, S.H. 287–9
hysteresis **195–8**, 477

idealistic socialism 371
imperialism 79–80, 84
imputation problem 465
income distribution *see* distribution
income taxation 398
  see also tax incidence; taxation
increasing returns 62–5
indeterminacy *see* uncertainty
indicative planning 299–300
individualism 122–3
industrial capital 149, 151, 311–12
industrial organization economists 40–42

industrial paradigm 330
industrial policy **199–203**
industrial sector 343
  key industries 176, 177, 178–9
industrialization 70, 447
  see also de-industrialization
inequality **203–8**
inference, statistical 112–13
inflation **208–12**
  endogenous money 281
  financial instability hypothesis 153–4
  social contracts 355–6
  structuralism 387
informal labour market 106–9
information deficiencies 66–7
innovation 408
  long waves 256–7
  technology gap 416–19
  see also technological change
input–output analysis **212–16**
institutionalism xiv
  consumption 45–6
  female employment/unemployment 143, 144
  international finance 224
  power 300
  social policy 363
institutions xiii, xvii
  decision making 69
  efficiency 122–3
  firms and corporations 158–62
  optimum size 56
  realism xvi
  SSA 366–70
  see also capacity; firms
instrumentalism 191–3
intensive (absolute) rent 334, 337
interest organizations
  social contracts 353–7
  social conventions 361
  see also trade unions
interest payments 276–7
interest rate parity theorem 117
interest rates 22–3, **216–21**
  aggregate demand 7–8
  effective demand 117–19
  money and credit 280–81, 282
  natural 33
intermediate output 213
internalization theory 288
international division of labour 103
international finance **221–6**, 294
international Keynesianism 374–5
International Monetary Fund (IMF) 224, 225
international organizations 174, 225, 374
international trade 29, **226–30**
  ECLA 385–7
  global political economy 171–2, 173
  new international trade theory 103
  technology gap 417–18
  underdevelopment 444
  unequal exchange **453–7**
internationalization 79
  capital 172–3, 202–3, 289
  production 285, 289
internationalization-transaction costs theory 287
inter-temporal equilibrium 128–9, 251–2, 466–7
investment **231–5**
  aggregate demand 7–8
  animal spirits 15–19
  development 82–3
  effective demand 116, 118–19
  finance 21–3
  growth and 407
  Keynesian growth theories 180–81, 183–4
  marginal efficiency of (MEI) 307–8
  monetary circuits 276, 277
  pricing/prices and 307–8
  savings 338, 339
  sectoral balance 343–4
  socialization **375–80**
  surplus approach 391–3
  taxation and 404–5
  TNCs 224–5
  uncertainty 16–17, 234–5, 434–5
  underconsumption 440, 441, 442–3
  under-investment 22
investment banking 150–51
investment goods sector 343–4
Ireland 295
irrationality 18
  see also rationality
Italy 354, 356, 357

Japan 300, 368

Jones, D. 237

Kaldor, Nicholas 26
  accumulation 3–4
  cumulative causation 63–4
  Keynesian growth 182–3
  savings 339
Kalecki, Michal 4
  development 82–3
  finance 22–3
  investment 232
  mark-up 210, 283–4, 306–7
  monopoly capitalism 283–4
  pricing 306–7
  profit rate 326–7
  short period 352–3
  taxation 398, 403–6 *passim*
  wages 474–5
Kaleckian approach xiii
  Keynesian growth 183
Keynes, John Maynard
  aggregate demand 6–10
  aggregate supply 10–15
  animal spirits 15–19
  crisis 60
  decision making 68
  econometrics 110
  effective demand 114–19
  expectations 136–7
  finance 21, 154–5
  interest rates 217–20 *passim*
  investment 231–2, 234, 391–2
  liquidity 245, 246–8
  long period 253–4
  short period 352
  socialization of investment 375–9
  speculation 381, 382–3
  transaction costs 126
  uncertainty 436–7
  underconsumption 440, 441
  wages 476–7
  weight 436–7, 460
Keynesian economics xiii
  corporatism 48–9
  fundamentalist 434–5
  growth theory **180–85**
  international 374–5
  new fundamentalist 18–19, 436
  see also Post Keynesian economics
Keynesian welfare state 355
Kondratieff, N.D. 255–6
Korpi, W. 363

labour
  control *see* control
  costs 227
  division of **101–5**, 121, 373
  efficiency *see* productivity
  exploitation *see* exploitation
  input–output analysis 213, 214
  and labour-power 121, 123–5
  low-paid 144
  necessary 394, 395
  productive–unproductive **310–15**, 395
  relationship to capital *see* capital–labour relations; employment relationship
  reserve army 93, 143, 170, 186
  substitution for capital 413–14
  surplus **393–7**
labour laws 432
labour market
  aggregate demand 5–7, 8–10
  corporatism 48–51
  discrimination 91–6
  dual labour markets 103, 104, **106–9**, 347
  female employment and unemployment **143–8**
  power 301–4
  real wages 473–4
  segmented labour market theory 170, **346–9**
labour-power 121, 123–5
labour process debate **236–0**
labour theory of value **240–44**, 462–3
  exploitation 139–42
  productive–unproductive labour 313–14
  unequal exchange 453–4
land *see* rent
Laramie, A.J. 400, 404–5
Latin America 75–81
  see also ECLA
laws of economics 372
Lawson, A. 111–12
LDCs (less developed countries) *see* Third World
Le Bourva, Jacques 278–9
lean production 237–8

legitimation, tax and 401–6
legitimization of state 422–3
Lenin, V.I. 84, 150, 151, 429
Leontief inverse 214
Levine, D.B. 46
liberalism 301
libertarianism 205
liquidity **244–9**
liquidity preference 247–8
  interest rates 217–20, 281
LO (Confederation of Swedish Trade Unions) 468–9, 470–71
loan finance facilities 150
loanable funds theory 217–20
Loasby, Brian 435
long period xiii–xiv, **249–55**
long-period prices xiii, 249–50, 252, 305, 308–10
  see also prices of production
long-run equilibrium analysis 127–8, 251–3
long-term expectations 16
long waves **255–9**
low-paid labour 144
Luxemburg, Rosa 20–21
luxury gods sector 344

machinery production argument 411–12
Mair, D. 399–400, 404–5
Malthus, Thomas 338
managerialism 161
manufacturing 64, 70, 73–4
marginal efficiency of capital 116
marginal efficiency of investment (MEI) 307–8
marginalism 2–3, 390
  long period 250–51
  profit rate 324
  value 465–6
  see also neoclassical economics
Marglin, S.A. 185
mark-up pricing 209–10, 283–6, 306–7
market economies xiv–xv
market failure approach 199–200
market period 249
market-power theory 288
markets **260–63**
  industrial policy 199, 200, 201
  socialism and 373
  and state 261–2, 372–3, 419–21
Marshall, Alfred 249–50, 350–51
Marx, Karl
  accumulation 2
  competition 38–9
  costs of production 52, 53
  crises 440
  dialectics 86–90 *passim*
  division of labour 102–3
  exploitation 138, 139–40, 141–2
  labour theory of value 240–44
  modes of production 269–72
  productive–unproductive labour 310–12, 313
  profit rate 325
  social relations 36
  surplus labour 394–5
  technological unemployment 411–12
  trade unions 429
  unemployment 448–9
  value 463–4
Marxist economics
  competition 39, 40–41
  competition model of discrimination 93–6
  crisis 58–9
  Cuban Revolution 75
  development 82, 83–4
  econometrics 112
  female employment/unemployment 143
  global political economy 172–4
  investment 233–4
  productive–unproductive labour 310–14
  public expenditure 319, 320–21, 323
  social policy 363
  structuralism 384, 387
  TNCs 288–9
  underconsumption 439, 441–3
  see also neo-Marxist economics
Marxist feminism 167–9
Maslow, Abraham 451
mass production 162–3, 165–6, 236–7
  see also Fordism
mathematization of economics 426–7, 461
maximization 67–9
  profits 68–9, 120–23, 158
  utility 44–5, 46–7, 191
mechanization

division of labour 102–3
technological unemployment 410–14
see also technological change
merchant capital 311–12
methodology in economics xv–xvi, **263–9**
metropolitan capital 445–6
migration 62, 107, 292–3
militancy 186–9
minimum wage 389–90
Mitchell, W.C. 24
mixed economies 319
modes of production **269–74**
modes of regulation 330
monetary circuits **274–8**
monetary theories
interest rates 217–20
Post Keynesian and uncertainty 435–6
money
capital theory controversies 33
and credit 149–50, **278–82**
effective demand 115–16, 118–19
financial stability hypothesis 154–5
liquidity 246, 247–8
time xviii
money demand 247–8
money wages xiii, **473–8**
monopolies 178
monopoly capitalism 39, 76, **282–6**
mortality 207
motivation, human **191–4**
multinational corporations *see* transnational corporations
multipolarity 172
mutual assurance 431
Myrdal, Gunnar 61, 62–5, *passim*

nation-states 290–91
National Investment Board (NIB) 377–8
National Socialism 430
naturalism 264–6
necessary consumption 35–6
necessary labour 394, 395
needs 451–2
neoclassical economics 390
competition 39
consumption 44–5, 46–7
development 81
profits 315–16, 317, 318
theory of the state 420–22
wages 473–4
see also marginalism
neo-corporatism 353–7
neo-Marxist economics
development 82, 83–4
growth theory **185–90**
neo-Ricardian economics
competition 39–40
distribution 97–101
international trade 227–9
profits 316, 317, 318
neo-Schumpeterian school 408–9
neo-structuralism 384, 387–8
Netherlands 356–7
Neumann, J. von 464
new classical macroeconomics 130–31
new international trade theory 103
new Keynesian fundamentalism 18–19, 436
New Right 363
non-clearing markets 303–4
non-market sector 345
Nordic school 329, 331
norms, social 359–61
North-South relationship
socialism 373–4
trade models 229–30
Norway 354, 356

occupational structure 73, 313
gender and 144, 147–8
O'Connor, J. 321
OECD (Organization for Economic Cooperation and Development) countries 71, 74
OLI (ownership, location, internalization) framework 288
oligopolies 4–5, 177–8
OPEC (Organization of Petroleum Exporting Countries) 369
optimum size 56
organic crisis 60
organicists 430
organizations *see* institutions
output
costs of production 52–3
de-industrialization 70–73
effective demand 116–17
input–output analysis **212–16**
monetary circuits 276

technlogical change 407
over-accumulation 233
overdraft 279–80
overproduction, crises of 58
ownership oligopolistic/monopolistic advantages 287

Parisian school 329–31
part-time employment 146–7
partial equilibrium 465
partial ignorance 435
Pasinetti, L.L. 98
past events *see* hysteresis
path dependence xviii–xix, 197–8
patriarchy 167
female employment/unemployment 143–4
private and public 169
pension-fund socialism 377–8
see also wage-earner funds
people's capitalism 468
perfect competition 39
peripheral economies
dependency theories 75–81
underdevelopment 443–7
peripheral Fordism 85, **292–6**
Perroux, François 174–9
philosophy of science 264–8
Piore, M. 237
planning **296–300**
political action 431
see also collective action; trade unions
political exchange 353–7
poll tax 399
Ponzi financing 157
Portugal 295
positivism 264–6, 267
post-colonial societies 445
post-Fordism **162–6**, 237
Post Keynesian economics
accumulation 3–4
development 82, 82–3
distribution 97–101
growth theories 181–4
international finance 222–3
money 246
money and credit 278–82
profits 316–17, 318
savings 339–40
uncertainty 435–6
underconsumption 441–3
wages 474, 476
see also Keynesian economics
potential surprise 435
poverty 64, 109
power **300–305**
firms and corporations 158–61
global political economy 171–2
see also capital–labour relations; employment relations; exploitation
prices/pricing **305–10**
effective demand and inter-temporal 117–18
inflation 208–10
input–output analysis 214, 215–16
international trade 226–8
labour theory of value 241–2
liquidity preference 247
long waves 257–8
long-period xiii–xiv, 249–50, 252, 305, 308–10
see also prices of production
mechanism and aggregate demand 9
monopoly capitalism 283–6
natural 38–9
structuralism 82
theory of relative 52, 53, 54
wages and 474–5
see also value
prices of production 305, 308–10, 463–4
privatization 363–4
probability *see* utility
product standardization 261
production xv
costs of **52–7**
crises of overproduction 58
efficiency 119–23
forces of 87–8, 270–71
input–output analysis **212–16**
internationalization of 285, 289
lean 237–8
modes of **269–74**
organization *see* Fordism; labour process debate; peripheral Fordism; Taylorism
prices of 305, 308–10, 463–4
productive labour **310–15**, 395
productivity

accumulation 1
Fordism 121–2
land 335–7
marginal 324
see also efficiency
profit maximization 68–9, 158
efficiency 120–23
profit rate **324–8**
capital theory controversies 29, 32
competition 38–9, 42, 327–8
international trade 227–9
long period 249–51, 252
tendency to fall 334–5
unequal exchange 455–6
value 462–4
profit-sharing 377–8, **468–73**
profits **315–19**
exploitation 139–40
financial instability hypothesis 154–6
investment theory 231–2, 233
labour theory of value 241
underconsumption 440–41
value added 213
property tax 399
protection 171
public choice theory 322
public expenditure **319–23**, 422
reduction in social 363–4
public investment *see* socialization of investment
purchasing power 412–13, 439
putting-out system 159

quasi-planning 300

racial discrimination 91–6
radical feminism 167
radical geographers 329, 332
rate of profit *see* profit rate
rational choice theory 358–61
rational expectations hypothesis (REH) 131–2, 134–6
rationality
animal spirits 18–19
bounded 66–7
motivation 191–4
utility 458–61
real wages **473–8**
realism
critical 111–12, 267–8
expectations 137–8
global political economy 171–2
reciprocal cooperation 359–61
reductionism 426–7
reflux principle 280
regulation, Fordism and 294
regulation school/theory **328–33**
development 82, 84–5, 330–31
Fordism 163–4
institutions and accumulation 368
Reich, M. 92
relations of production 270–71
see also employment relations
removal of conflict theory 287
rent **333–7**
reserve army of labour 93, 143, 170, 186
reswitching result 32
Ricardo, David
accumulation 1–2
international trade 226–7
rent 334–5
socioeconomic classes 97
technological change 410–11
value 462–3
see also neo-Ricardian economics
risk 68, 458, 459
Robinson, Joan
accumulation 3
capital theory controversies 30, 31
competition 40
long period 253
short period 352
uncertainty 434–5
Roemer, J. 140–41, 142
Roos, D. 237
Rowthorn, R. 208–9
Russia *see* Soviet Union

Sabel, C.F. 237
Sachs, J. 50
Sadoulet, E. 108–90
Samuelson, P. 455–6
satisficing 459
savings **338–42**
aggregate demand 7–8
internal and outside 23
underconsumpton 438–9
Say's Law 7, 115, 117, 441
scale economies 55–7

scarcity xvi, 415, 418–19, 462
Schumpeter, Joseph
  accumulation 2–3
  innovation 408
  long waves 256–7
scientific management 103, 121, 163
scientific socialism 371–3
scientification of economics 426–7
second-order uncertainty 437
sectoral balance **342–6**
secular movements, period of 249
segmented labour market (SLM) theory 170, **346–9**
  see also dual labour markets
services 345
  de-industrialization 70, 71, 73
  productive–unproductive labour 313
Shackle, George 137, 435
shifting equilibrium 14
short period 249, 253, **350–53**
short-period pricing 306–8, 309–10
short-run equilibrium 129–30, 252–3, 351–3, 467
short-side power 304, 305
Simon, H.A. 125
Sismondi, J.C.L.S. de 108
Slutsky, E. 25
Smith, Adam 38
  accumulation 1
  division of labour 101–2
Social Catholicism 430
social class *see* class
social contracts 49–50, **353–7**
social conventions **357–62**
social democratic state 319, 323
social norms 359–61
social pathology of unemployment **448–53**
social policy **362–6**
social relations **34–8**
social structure of accumulation (SSA) 331, **336–70**
social welfare *see* welfare
socialism 59, **371–5**
  employment relations 123
  mode of production 269–70, 272
  productive–unproductive labour 313
socialization 193
socialization of investment **375–80**
Solidaristic Wage Policy 468, 470–71
Soviet Union
  planning 296–7
  SSA 370
  state 420
Spain 295, 354
specialization
  flexible 165, 237
  international trade 226, 229–30, 456–7
  see also division of labour
speculation 376, **380–84**
speculative financing 157
Sraffa, Piero 227
  capital theory controversies 30
  competition 39–40
  costs of production 52, 53–4
  input–output analysis 215–16
  prices of production 308–9
  profit rate 324–5
  rent 335–6
  surplus 35
  value 464–5
stabilization 382–3, 387–8
stagnationism 108, 184
  monopoly capitalism 284–6
  underconsumption 438–40
standardizaton of products 261
state
  corporatism 47, 48–9
  interventionist and industrial policy 199–203 *passim*
  and markets 261–2, 372–3, 419–21
  nature of and public expenditure 319–23
  planning **296–300**
  power 301, 305
  role in development 81, 423, 443–4
  role in taxation 401–6
  socialization of investment 375–9
  SSA 367
  theory of **419–24**
  and trade unions 430
static equilibrium theory 62
statistical inference 112–113
  status 105
Ste Croix, G.E.M. de 35–7
steady-state growth model 129–30
Steindl, J. 4, 23, 283, 284
stochastic cycle theory 25–6
stock exchange 151

structural change 408
structural crises 58–9
structural instability 111–12
structural unemployment 385
structuralism 344, **384–9**
  dependency theories 76, 78–9
  development 82, 83
  neo-structuralism 384, 387–8
structuralist macroeconomic theory 384, 388
structure-performance model 262–3
subjective expected utility (SEU) 134, 136–7, **458–61**
subjectivism 266–7
subsistence 43
subsistence wage 389–90, 475
substitution 413–14
substitution principle 465
Sugden, R. 359–60
supply
  aggregate **10–15**
  costs of production 52–4
surplus xv, 240
  class and social relations 34–7
  exploitation 139–40
  monopoly capitalism 283–6
  productive–unproductive labour 310–11
  profit rate 326–7
  and surplus labour 395–6
  underdevelopment 445–6
surplus approach **389–93**
surplus labour **393–7**
Sweden
  concertation 354, 355, 356
  wage-earner funds 378, 468–72
Sweezy, Paul 283–6 *passim*, 289
Switzerland 354, 356–7
synthesis 86, 88

tax incidence **398–401**
taxation **401–6**
Taylor, Lance 388
Taylorism 103, 121, 163
technical division of labour 102–3
technological change 57, 183–4, **405–10**
technological fields 409
technological systems 408–9
technological unemployment **410–15**
technology gaps **415–19**
temporary equilibrium theory 129–30, 252–3, 351–3, 467
terms of trade 173
  deterioration 386
thesis-antithesis-synthesis 86, 88
Third World
  debt crisis 74, 224
  dual labour markets **106–9**
time xviii, **424–9**
  hysteresis 195–8
  see also long period; short period
Titmuss, Richard 362
trade
  cumulative causation 62–3
  influence structures 171
  international *see* international trade
  international finance 223–4
  structure and de-industrialization 72–3
  terms of *see* terms of trade
trade unions 159–60, **429–33**
  corporatism 48–9, 50–51
  open-shop 358
  social contracts 354, 357
  wage-earner funds 468–9, 470–71, 472
transaction costs 126, 287
transaction costs economics (TCE) 158–9
transformation of values 463–4
transnational corporations (TNCs) **286–91**
  control 161
  industrial policy 202–3
  international finance 224–5
  peripheral Fordism 293–4, 295
traverse analysis 414
trusts 151

uncertainty xiii, xvii–xviii, **434–8**
  decision making 16–17, 68–9
  employment contracts 125–7
  expectations *see* expectations
  human motivation 192–3
  interest rates 218
  investment 16–17, 234–5, 434–5,
  utility 459–60
underconsumption 233, 338–9, **438–43**
underdevelopment **443–8**
  dependency 76, 77

imperialism and 84
surplus labour 395–6
under-investment 22
unemployment
aggregate demand 5–6, 8–9
capital shortage unemployment 413
expectations 136
female **143–8**
reserve army of unemployed 93, 143, 170, 186
social pathology of **448–53**
structural 385
technological **410–15**
wage hysteresis effects 477
unequal exchange 64, 173, 227, **453–7**
uneven development 189–90, 417, 444
cumulative causation **62–5**
United Kingdom (UK)
de-industrialization 73–4
female employment/unemployment 145–8
financial deregulation 341
public expenditure 322
social contract 354, 355, 357
social policy 364
unemployment 451
United States (US) 322, 341, 369, 402
universal banking 152–3
unproductive labour **310–15,** 345, 395
user cost 12–13
utilitarianism 204–5, 458
utility **458–61**, 465
group 69
maximization 44–5, 46–7, 191
subjective expected (SEU) 134, 136–7, 458–61
utilization of capacity 182–4, 254, 391–3

value **462–7**
labour theory of *see* labour theory of value
Leontief inverse 214
surplus labour 396–7
women's contribution 168
value added
de-industrialization 70–72
input–out analysis 213, 214–15

Veblen, Thorstein 45–6, 327–8
Verdoorn's Law 64
vertical integration 214–15, 414
verticalists 280

wage bargaining 50–51, 210, 476
see also collective bargaining
wage discrimination 94–6
wage-earner funds 377–8, **468–73**
wages xiii, **473–8**
family 168–9
gender differences 144
for housework 168–9
inflation 208–9, 210–11
minimum 389–90
neo-Marxian growth theories 185–6, 187–9
subsistence 389–90, 475
underconsumption and 442
unequal exchange 454, 456–7
Walrasian model 301–4
Walras's Law 466
warranted growth 3, 180–82, 189
weak equity axiom 207
wealth
distribution *see* distribution
power and 171–2, 304–5
weight 436–7, 460
welfare
policies **362–6**
public expenditure 320–21
social contracts 355–6
state role 422
Wicksell, K. 413–14
Womack, J. 237
women 366
employment/unemployment **143–8**
see also gender
Wood, A. 233–4
work effort 186
see also productivity
work organization *see* Fordism; labour process debate; peripheral Fordism; post-Fordism; Taylorism
World Bank 225

Young, Allyn 63